Linux System Administration Black Book

Dee-Ann LeBlanc

CORIOLIS

President and CEO
Keith Weiskamp

Publisher
Steve Sayre

Acquisitions Editor
Charlotte Carpentier

Marketing Specialist
Tracy Schofield

Project Editor
Toni Zuccarini Ackley

Technical Reviewer
David Williams

Production Coordinator
Meg E. Turecek

Cover Designer
Jody Winkler

Layout Designer
April Nielsen

CD-ROM Developer
Michelle McConnell

Linux System Administration Black Book

The Coriolis Group, LLC
14455 N. Hayden Road
Suite 220
Scottsdale, Arizona 85260

(480) 483-0192
FAX (480) 483-0193
www.coriolis.com

Library of Congress Cataloging-in-Publication Data
LeBlanc, Dee-Ann
Linux system administration black book / by Dee-Ann LeBlanc
p. cm.
ISBN 1-57610-419-2
1. Linux. 2. Operating systems (Computers). I. Title.
QA76.76.O63 L4325 2000
004.4'69–dc21 00-043141
CIP

Printed in the United States of America
10 9 8 7 6 5 4 3 2 1

CORIOLIS™

The Coriolis Group, LLC • 14455 North Hayden Road, Suite 220 • Scottsdale, Arizona 85260

Dear Reader:

Coriolis Technology Press was founded to create a very elite group of books: the ones you keep closest to your machine. Sure, everyone would like to have the Library of Congress at arm's reach, but in the real world, you have to choose the books you rely on every day *very* carefully.

To win a place for our books on that coveted shelf beside your PC, we guarantee several important qualities in every book we publish. These qualities are:

- *Technical accuracy*—It's no good if it doesn't work. Every Coriolis Technology Press book is reviewed by technical experts in the topic field, and is sent through several editing and proofreading passes in order to create the piece of work you now hold in your hands.
- *Innovative editorial design*—We've put years of research and refinement into the ways we present information in our books. Our books' editorial approach is uniquely designed to reflect the way people learn new technologies and search for solutions to technology problems.
- *Practical focus*—We put only pertinent information into our books and avoid any fluff. Every fact included between these two covers must serve the mission of the book as a whole.
- *Accessibility*—The information in a book is worthless unless you can find it quickly when you need it. We put a lot of effort into our indexes, and heavily cross-reference our chapters, to make it easy for you to move right to the information you need.

Here at The Coriolis Group we have been publishing and packaging books, technical journals, and training materials since 1989. We're programmers and authors ourselves, and we take an ongoing active role in defining what we publish and how we publish it. We have put a lot of thought into our books; please write to us at **ctp@coriolis.com** and let us know what you think. We hope that you're happy with the book in your hands, and that in the future, when you reach for software development and networking information, you'll turn to one of our books first.

Keith Weiskamp
President and CEO

Jeff Duntemann
VP and Editorial Director

I dedicate this book to my friend Andrew,
who helps me stay sane during crunch times.

About The Author

Dee-Ann LeBlanc is a computer book author, course developer, and technical trainer specializing in Linux. She has done several books on the subject, including *Linux Install and Configuration Little Black Book* and *General Linux I Exam Prep* for The Coriolis Group, and writes a monthly column on integrating Linux with other operating systems for *Linux AppDev*. Dee-Ann is both a Red Hat Certified Engineer and a SAIR/GNU Linux Certified Professional who teaches Linux, Unix, and other courses for two different online schools, presents the occasional seminar at computer conferences, and develops courses for a number of online venues.

In her copious spare time, Dee-Ann works on a medieval fantasy novel, is walked by her dog Zorro, and squeezes in a few minutes to spend time with her husband Rob and see the beautiful scenery in BC, Canada.

Acknowledgments

I would first like to acknowledge all of the staff at The Coriolis Group who worked so hard to make this project a success: Toni Zuccarini Ackley, William McManus, David Williams, Meg Turecek, Michelle McConnell, and Jody Winkler. I would also like to thank the students who keep me on my toes and are constantly giving me great ideas for things to include, and the readers who contact me to let me know what they liked and didn't like about my various books, and what they would like to see included in later projects.

Contents At A Glance

Chapter 1	Red Hat Linux	1
Chapter 2	User Management	21
Chapter 3	File System Management	59
Chapter 4	Package Management	101
Chapter 5	Kernel Management	125
Chapter 6	GUI Management	151
Chapter 7	Networking	171
Chapter 8	Printing	217
Chapter 9	System Security Basics	239
Chapter 10	KickStart For Repeat Installations	293
Chapter 11	DNS With BIND	315
Chapter 12	Internet Email: **sendmail** + IDA	351
Chapter 13	The Apache Web Server	407
Chapter 14	The Squid Internet Object Cache	453
Chapter 15	FTP And Telnet	475
Chapter 16	NIS And NIS+	491
Chapter 17	NFS	501
Chapter 18	Samba	511
Chapter 19	Text Processing Tools	561
Chapter 20	Shell Scripting	597
Chapter 21	Perl Scripting	627
Chapter 22	Linux C Programming	643
Chapter 23	Additional System Administration Tools	659
Appendix	GNU General Public License	687

Table Of Contents

Introduction .... **xxv**

Chapter 1
Red Hat Linux **1**

In Depth

Installation Tips 2
Other Distributions 6

Immediate Solutions

Getting New Versions Of Red Hat Linux 8
Updating Your System Through Red Hat 8
Navigating GNOME 9
  Configuring The GUI 10
  Opening Programs 11
  Opening Linuxconf 12
  Accessing Help 13
  Getting A Command Prompt 14
Navigating KDE 15
  Configuring The GUI 15
  Opening Programs 17
  Accessing Help 19
  Getting A Command Prompt 19

Chapter 2
User Management **21**

In Depth

Types Of User Accounts 23
Analysis Of The **useradd** Process 25
Analysis Of The **userdel** Process 28
Clever Uses For Groups 29

Immediate Solutions

Creating Shell Accounts 31
  Creating Shell Accounts From The Command Line 31
  Creating Shell Accounts In GNOME 31
  Creating Shell Accounts In KDE 35

Creating Restricted Access Accounts 37
Creating Restricted Access Accounts At The Command Line 37
Creating Restricted Access Accounts In GNOME 38
Creating Restricted Access Accounts In KDE 40
Creating Software Accounts 42
Changing Account Creation Defaults 42
Changing Default Home Directory Contents 42
Changing User Defaults At The Command Line 44
Changing User Defaults In GNOME 44
Changing User Defaults In KDE 44
Renaming Users 46
Renaming Users At The Command Line 46
Renaming Users In GNOME 46
Renaming Users In KDE 48
Disabling Users 49
Disabling Users At The Command Line 49
Disabling Users In GNOME 49
Disabling Users In KDE 50
Removing Users 50
Removing Users At The Command Line 50
Removing Users In GNOME 50
Removing Users In KDE 52
Installing Software For Users To Run 53
Creating Groups 53
Creating Groups On The Command Line 53
Creating Groups In GNOME 53
Creating Groups In KDE 54
Adding Users To Groups 55
Adding Users To Groups On The Command Line 55
Adding Users To Groups In GNOME 55
Adding Users To Groups In KDE 56
Forwarding User Mail 57
Forwarding User Mail On The Command Line 57
Forwarding User Mail In GNOME 57
Forwarding User Mail In KDE 58

Chapter 3
File System Management.. 59

In Depth

Hard Drive Overview 61
Behind The Scenes 61
Making Sense Of The Linux File System 64

Protecting Your Data 68
Limiting User Storage Space 75

Immediate Solutions

Creating Linux File Systems 76
Listing ext2 File System Settings 77
Changing Permissions 77
  Changing Permissions Explicitly 77
  Changing Permissions Relatively 77
  Setting Special Bits 78
Setting The Umask 79
Changing Ownerships 79
Changing Groups 79
Checking For File System Errors 79
Backing Up And Restoring File System Structure 80
  Backing Up File System Structure 80
  Restoring File System Structure 80
Backing Up File Systems 81
Restoring File Systems From Backup 83
Moving File System Portions Onto Partitions 83
Adding And Removing Media To The File System 84
  Adding Temporary Media 84
  Removing Temporary Media 85
  Adding Permanent Media 86
  Removing Permanent Media 88
Seeing What Is Currently Mounted 89
Navigating The File System In GNOME 89
  Opening GNU Midnight Commander At The Command Line 89
  Opening GNU Midnight Commander Within A GNOME Session 90
  Navigating Directories In GNU Midnight Commander 90
  Browsing And Opening Files In GNU Midnight Commander 90
Navigating The File System In KDE 94
  Opening KFM At The Command Line 94
  Browsing In KFM 95
Setting Up Disk Quotas 95
  Preparing The Machine 95
  Setting The Quotas 96
Shutting Down And Rebooting 97
Making A Custom Boot Disk 98
Making A Rescue Disk 98

Chapter 4
Package Management 101

In Depth

Types Of Tools 102
Choosing What To Download 104
Package Management Principles 105

Immediate Solutions

Creating **gzip**ed Files 108
Opening **gzip**ed Files 108
Creating Z **compressed** Files 108
Opening Z **compressed** Files 109
Creating **tar** Files 109
Examining The Contents Of **tar** Files 110
Opening **tar** Files 110
Opening Or Creating Tarballs 110
Installing A Binary 111
Creating RPMs 111
Installing RPMs 114
Viewing The Contents Of An RPM File 115
Listing Which RPMs Are Installed 115
Removing An RPM 115
Verifying An RPM File 115
Checking A PGP-Signed RPM 116
Using GNOME's RPM Tool 116
  Opening GNOME RPM 116
  Installing RPMs With GNOME RPM 117
  Removing RPMs With GNOME RPM 119
Using KDE's RPM Tool 120
  Opening Kpackage 120
  Installing RPMs With Kpackage 120
  Removing RPMs With Kpackage 121

Chapter 5
Kernel Management 125

In Depth

The Linux Kernel 126
Kernel Documentation 130

Immediate Solutions

Getting The Kernel's Version And Other System Information 135
Obtaining The Latest Kernel Source 135
Installing A New Kernel 136
Configuring The Kernel With **config** 137

Configuring The Kernel With **menuconfig** 141
Configuring The Kernel With **xconfig** 143
Listing Loaded Modules 145
Inserting Modules Manually 145
Removing Modules Manually 146
Getting System Information 147
Setting Module Parameters 148
Building An Alias Statement 148
Building An Option Statement 149
Updating LILO 149

Chapter 6
GUI Management 151

In Depth
Linux GUI Components 152
The Files 155

Immediate Solutions
Installing The X Server In Red Hat 158
Installing GNOME Or KDE In Red Hat 159
Installing GNOME 160
Installing KDE 160
Finding GUI Components Online 162
Adding A Window Manager 162
Adding A Window Manager In GNOME 162
Adding A Window Manager At The Command Line For GNOME 163
Adding A Window Manager At The Command Line For KDE 164
Adding A Theme 164
Adding A Theme In GNOME 165
Adding A Theme In KDE 165
Adding A Theme Everyone Can Use 166
Changing Desktop Environments 167
Restarting The X Server 167
Restarting When You Started With **startx** 168
Restarting When You Started X By Default 168
Changing The Default Run Level 168

Chapter 7
Networking 171

In Depth
Introduction To Linux Networking 173
Routers 179
The Partial Address Class 180
The Centrally Managed Network 180

Immediate Solutions

Configuring Networking 186
Getting A Set Of IP Addresses 187
Registering A Domain Name 187
Checking Whether A Domain Name Is Already Taken 189
  Using Linux To Check Whether A Core Domain Is Taken 189
  Using A Web Browser Under Any OS To See Whether A Domain Is Taken 189
Determining The Values For Subnetting A Class C Network 189
Applying Subnet Values To A Network 191
Expressing Address Ranges 192
Manually Configuring Basic Static Networking For A LAN 192
Configuring Basic Networking With Linuxconf For A LAN 193
Adding A Virtual Site 196
Assigning More Than One IP Address To An Interface At The Command Line 197
Assigning More Than One IP Address To An Interface In Linuxconf 197
Configuring A Second Network Interface At The Command Line 198
Configuring A Second Network Interface In Linuxconf 199
Setting Up Routing At The Command Line 200
Setting Up Routing Using Linuxconf 201
  Configuring Basic Routing 201
  Configuring Routing Among Your Networks 202
  Configuring Routing To Remote Hosts 203
  Configuring Routing For Concurrent Networks 203
Configuring The Routing Daemon In Linuxconf 204
Setting Up IP Masquerading 205
Setting Up Dial-Out Connections 206
  Configuring Linuxconf To Connect 206
  Configuring Minicom To Connect 209
  Configuring **kppp** To Connect 210
Setting Up A DHCP Server 213
Configuring The **pump** Client 214
Administering Machines Remotely 216

Chapter 8
Printing 217

In Depth

Introduction To Printing Under Linux 218
Linux Printing Issues 223
Introduction To GhostScript 223
Nonsoftware Technical Problems 224

Immediate Solutions

Setting Up A Local Printer In The Control Panel 225
Setting Up A Local Printer At The Command Line 228
Setting Up A Network Printer In The Control Panel 231
Setting Up A Network Printer At The Command Line 233
 Setting Up A Machine To Host A Network Printer 233
 Setting Up Remote Printers To Print Over A Network 234
Setting Up Popular Print Filters 235
Testing The Printer 236
Printing A File 236
Viewing A Print Queue 237
Canceling A Print Job 237
Checking A Printer's Status 238
Disabling And Enabling A Print Queue 238

Chapter 9
System Security Basics 239

In Depth

Leaving The Door Wide Open 240
Online Security Resources 245
Available Tools 247
Attacks And Intrusions 254
Firewalls And You 256

Immediate Solutions

Activating And Deactivating The Shadow Suite 264
Shutting Off Unnecessary Daemons And Background Processes 264
Shutting Off Unnecessary Non-Daemon Network Services 267
Restricting Network Access With **tcp_wrappers** 267
Obtaining And Installing ssh 269
Setting Up ssh On A Server 270
Setting Up ssh On A Client 276
Removing Unnecessary Packages 279
Creating And Using A Named Pipe 280
Logging 280
Installing **swatch** 281
Analyzing Logs 281
Preparing For A Breach 282
Recovering From A Breach 282
Becoming The Superuser 283
Installing The Crack Password Checker 283
Securing Passwords With Crack 284

Setting Password Rules 285
Fighting Denial-Of-Service Attacks 285
Getting And Installing PGP 285
Setting Up An IP Firewall 287
Setting Up A Proxy Firewall 289
Refusing Login Access To All But Root 290

Chapter 10
KickStart For Repeat Installations 293

In Depth

Introduction To KickStart 294
The Structure Of A KickStart Script 295
The Test-Edit Cycle 304

Immediate Solutions

Installing The First Machine 306
Building The Initial KickStart File 307
Scripting Tips For KickStart 308
Making A KickStart Boot Disk 308
Booting Directly To KickStart 309
Setting Up An NFS Installation Export 310
Adding KickStart Data To Your DHCP Server 311
Installing With KickStart 311
Upgrading With KickStart 312
Cloning Machine Configurations 313

Chapter 11
DNS With BIND 315

In Depth

The Domain Name System 316
Name Service Under Linux 317
Introduction To /etc/named.conf 319
The Zone Files 328
Name Service–Related Programs 333

Immediate Solutions

Installing The Name Server 336
Configuring The Master Name Server 336
Configuring The Slave Name Server 338
Configuring A Forwarding-Only Server 340
Creating The Initial Cache 342
Creating The Reverse Local Zone File 343
Creating Your Domain Zone 344

Creating Your Reverse Domain Zone 346
Creating Encrypted Keys 347
Installing And Running **dnswalk** 348

Chapter 12
Internet Email: sendmail + IDA 351

In Depth
How Email Gets To Its Destination 352
Introduction To **sendmail** 357
Mailing Lists 369

Immediate Solutions
Installing All Of The Pieces 370
Configuring Your **sendmail** Server At The Command Line 370
Building sendmail.cf At The Command Line 372
Tweaking Your /etc/sendmail.cf 372
Adding Additional Mail Server Hostnames 372
Centralizing Your Outgoing Mail Addresses 373
Adding Configuration File Version Information 373
Setting Your Log Level 374
Reducing Server Load 375
Configuring Your **sendmail** Server In Linuxconf 376
Basic **sendmail** Configuration In Linuxconf 376
Configuring Mail Routing In Linuxconf 380
Configuring Email Masquerading In Linuxconf 383
Configuring Email-To-Fax Service In Linuxconf 384
Configuring Virtual Email Service In Linuxconf 389
Configuring Your Anti-Spam Settings Under Linuxconf 391
Setting Up Mail Aliases By Hand 393
Protecting Yourself From Spam 394
Building A CW File 397
Building A Mailer Table 397
Building A Virtual Addressing Table 398
Building An Access Database 398
Removing Mail From The Queue Under Linuxconf 399
Configuring **procmail** 400

Chapter 13
The Apache Web Server 407

In Depth
Introduction To Apache 408
The Configuration File 410
Other Linux Web Servers 437

Immediate Solutions
Installing Apache 439
Configuring Apache 439
Configuring Apache Access 440
Configuring **httpd** 443
Setting Up Virtual Web Service 446
Configuring What Web Browsers See 448
Customizing Your Logs 451
Setting Up .htaccess 452

Chapter 14
The Squid Internet Object Cache 453

In Depth
Introduction To Web Caching 454
An Introduction To The Squid 454

Immediate Solutions
Installing The Squid 458
Configuring The Squid 458
Setting Up Parent And Sibling Caches 466
Setting Up Web Server Acceleration 469
Setting Up Multicasting 470
Configuring A Client To Utilize Caching 470

Chapter 15
FTP And Telnet 475

In Depth
FTP Issues 476
Telnet Issues 482

Immediate Solutions
Securing FTP 483
Installing Anonymous FTP 487
Securing Telnet 488
Creating A **shutdown** Message 488

Chapter 16
NIS And NIS+ 491

In Depth
Introduction To NIS And NIS+ 492
Using An NIS System 494

Immediate Solutions
Installing The NIS Server 496
Installing The NIS Client 496

Setting Up An NIS Server 497
Setting Up An NIS Client 499

Chapter 17
NFS 501

In Depth
Introduction To NFS 502
The NFS Configuration File 502

Immediate Solutions
Setting Up NFS Exports 505
Mounting Remote File Systems With NFS 505
Making And Mounting A Central /usr Directory 506
Creating The /usr Export 506
Mounting The /usr Export 508
Setting Up An NFS Installation Server 509

Chapter 18
Samba 511

In Depth
Introduction To Samba 512
The Samba Configuration File 513

Immediate Solutions
Installing Samba 527
Configuring Samba 527
Offering Linux Partitions 537
Building A File Share Statement 541
Mounting Windows Shares Under Linux 546
Offering Windows Shares 546
Offering Linux Printers 550
Building A Print Share Statement 551
Utilizing Windows Printers Under Linux 554
Implementing Encrypted Passwords Over Samba 555
Creating A User Map 556
Creating A Host Map 557
Creating Login Scripts 558

Chapter 19
Text Processing Tools 561

In Depth
The **vi** Editor 562
Pattern Matching 568
The **sed** Editor 570
Additional Tools 574

Immediate Solutions

Maneuvering In **vi** 578
Filtering Text In **vi** 579
Copying And Pasting Text In **vi** 581
Indenting Text In **vi** 581
Using Regular Expressions 583
Running **sed** With Multiple Commands 584
Building A **sed** Script File 586
Running **sed** With External File Scripts 588
Using The **cut** Command 588
Using The **join** Command 589
Checking Spelling With **ispell** 590
Building **ispell** Dictionaries 592
Reducing **ispell** Dictionary Sizes 594
Using The **tr** Command 595

Chapter 20
Shell Scripting 597

In Depth

The Shell 598
Bash Shell Scripting 599

Immediate Solutions

Changing The Active Shell 609
Installing The Public Domain Korn Shell 609
Changing Your Bash Login Prompt 610
Writing Your Own Package Update Script 611
Writing Your Own User Creation Script 615
Writing A Script To Find A File In Your RPMs 620
Writing A Script To Monitor System Load 623

Chapter 21
Perl Scripting 627

In Depth

Introduction To Perl 628
Perl Programming 628

Immediate Solutions

Installing Perl 636
Getting And Installing A Perl Library Module 636
Running A Perl Program 638
Writing A CGI Script With Perl 639
Processing A Web Form 639

Chapter 22
Linux C Programming 643

In Depth

Linux C Components 644

Immediate Solutions

Installing The C Compiler 647
Compiling C Code With **gcc** 647
Debugging Code With **gdb** 653
Finding Resource-Hogging Sections With **gprof** 656
Installing The Build Manager 658

Chapter 23
Additional System Administration Tools 659

In Depth

The Automounter 660
Timed Processes 661
Search Tools 662

Immediate Solutions

Installing The **automount** Daemon's Controller 666
Configuring The Automounter 666
Configuring A Base Mount Point 667
Configuring Who Can Use **at** 668
Creating An **at** Job 669
Listing Existing **at** Jobs 671
Deleting Existing **at** Jobs 672
Changing The **batch** Load Average 672
Altering System **cron** Jobs 672
Manipulating User **cron** Jobs 674
Using **find** 676
Changing The **locate** Database Update Time 684
Using **locate** To Find Files 684
Using **which** To Find Programs 685
Using **grep** To Find What You Need 685

Appendix
GNU General Public License 687

Index 695

Introduction

Thanks for buying *Linux System Administration Black Book*. If you are looking for resources on system administration then you probably have read all about the wonders of the Linux operating system. Its multi-user, multitasking nature makes it a natural for sharing a single machine amongst multiple people and providing Internet services. However, this robust, powerful operating system comes with a price. Linux is not the easiest system to figure out, along with the rest of its Unix family members.

It can take years to get proficient at using Linux on a day-to-day basis. There are so many things you can do with the operating system and so many ways to accomplish most tasks that there always seems to be something to learn. If you are used to working on Linux as an end user, Linux system administration in some ways requires a whole new set of skills. I hope you find that *Linux System Administration Black Book* fills in the gaps.

Is This Book For You?

Linux System Administration Black Book was written with the intermediate or advanced user in mind. It is expected that you have some knowledge of using Linux at the command line and in the GNOME or KDE desktop environments already. However, I have tried to provide detailed instructions so that if you do not have experience in an area you will not be lost.

Among the topics that are covered are:

- User account management
- Setting up for automated installs
- Configuring and managing domain name service
- Setting up an NFS installation server
- Building useful shell scripts
- Understanding file system permission intricacies
- Rolling your own RPMs
- Fine-tuning the kernel

- Understanding and setting up X
- Implementing user file system usage limits
- Centralizing user accounts
- Using DHCP to automatically assign network information at boot time
- Installing popular print filters
- Installing the secure shell
- Setting up and managing email with **sendmail**
- Setting up and managing an Apache Web server
- Understanding and implementing a caching server
- Securing and fine-tuning FTP and Telnet
- Integrating multiple operating systems with Samba
- Shell and Perl scripting
- C programming tools available in Linux

How To Use This Book

Linux System Administration Black Book is written to be both a learning tool and a resource. Although you do not need to read the book all the way through, there are sections that contain information that will help you understand later chapters. I will give you a brief walkthrough here to help guide you to the chapters that are the most useful to you.

Chapter 1 contains a refresher on Linux, a list of popular distributions, information about Red Hat Linux in particular, and a discussion of installation issues. If you are unfamiliar with installing Red Hat or navigating the two desktop environments that come with it—GNOME and KDE—then take a look at this chapter.

Chapters 2 through 5 address some important setup and management issues. If you intend to have a lot of users on your system, do not skip Chapter 2. When it comes to Chapters 3 and 4, I highly recommend that you read or at least review them before proceeding through the rest of the book. Working with the file system and various package types will haunt you throughout your system administration tasks. If you do not thoroughly read Chapter 5 initially, be sure to go over it at some point. System administrators should understand what the kernel is, what it does, and how to work with it.

Chapter 6 addresses the Linux GUI. Although a user does not need to understand the nuances involved with the GUI, a system administrator does. However, you need not work with this chapter until you feel the need.

Chapter 7 is important to anyone who intends to network their Linux box. Choose for yourself what topics in this chapter apply, but at the very least make sure that you understand TCP/IP and the basics of how it works, and how to assign IP information to an interface under Linux.

Chapter 8 covers printing. You only need to look through this chapter if you have a printer to set up on a Linux box.

Chapter 9 is quite important. If you intend to have a Linux box connected to the Internet, then read this chapter. Although you do not have to implement everything in here, you at least need to know what is available and why you might want to use it. This allows you to make an educated choice about your level of security concerns.

Chapter 10 covers installation automation. Red Hat Linux comes with a tool called KickStart. If you need to set up a large number of identical or nearly identical machines—both in hardware and in purpose—then read this chapter thoroughly.

Chapters 11 through 15 each discuss a different networking service in detail. I recommend reading the In Depth portions of each and determining whether the tools covered there are of any use to you. Chapter 12 (**sendmail**) and Chapter 13 (Apache) I expect to be popular.

Chapters 16 through 18 deal with systems integration of various sorts. If you have a large network of Linux machines that you want to set up central services on, investigate Chapters 16 (NIS) and 17 (NFS). If you need to integrate your Linux network with other operating systems, especially Windows operating systems, read Chapter 18 thoroughly.

Chapters 19 and 23 cover a number of tools that you will find useful as a system administrator. I recommend reviewing this information at some point when you want to learn how to get more mileage out of the command line.

Chapters 20 through 22 cover various programming tools available in Linux. Definitely review Chapter 20. If you need to write CGI scripts, investigate Chapter 21 and invest in a good book on Perl and CGI, such as The Coriolis Group's *Perl Black Book*. Chapter 22 is useful if you find yourself needing to compile a lot of C source on your system.

The *Black Book* Philosophy

Written by experienced professionals, Coriolis *Black Books* provide immediate solutions to global programming and administrative challenges, helping you complete specific tasks—especially critical ones that are not well documented in other books. The *Black Book*'s unique two-part chapter format—thorough technical overviews followed by practical immediate solutions—is structured to help you use your knowledge, solve problems, and quickly master complex technical issues to become an expert. By breaking down complex topics into easily manageable components, this format helps you quickly find what you're looking for, with the instructions and code you need to make it happen.

Contact Information

I welcome your feedback on this book. You can either email The Coriolis Group at **ctp@coriolis.com** or email me directly at **dee@renaissoft.com**. Errata, updates, Linux resource listings, and more are available at **www.Dee-AnnLeBlanc.com**.

Chapter 1

Red Hat Linux

If you need an immediate solution to:	*See page:*
Getting New Versions Of Red Hat Linux	8
Updating Your System Through Red Hat	8
Navigating GNOME	9
Configuring The GUI	10
Opening Programs	11
Opening Linuxconf	12
Accessing Help	13
Getting A Command Prompt	14
Navigating KDE	15
Configuring The GUI	15
Opening Programs	17
Accessing Help	19
Getting A Command Prompt	19

In Depth

Red Hat Linux 6.2 is a robust and popular distribution. Its installation tools make the task of installing Linux far easier than it was just a few years ago. This chapter covers some of the larger issues of installing Red Hat, allowing you to focus on the details rather than getting stuck on the bigger decisions. It also gives an overview of how to keep your installation up-to-date with the latest releases and how to navigate through the two graphical user interfaces (GUIs) that come by default with the distribution.

Installation Tips

There are a number of issues to keep in mind when going through the Red Hat installation process. Most of these issues surround decisions involving the volume of software to install or the look and feel of the final product.

Installation Issues

There are a number of items you need to keep in mind as a system administrator when it comes to system installation. These concerns boil down to the purpose the machine is meant to serve. A machine meant to be a workstation for an end user's word processing has vastly different needs than a server meant to handle a bunch of Web sites and nothing else.

Choosing Partitions

You can choose to partition your system in a number of ways. For a basic end-user system, I would usually just create a 16MB or so /boot partition, a 120MB or so swap partition, and give the rest to a root (/) partition. Another commonly chosen item is a /home partition, which allows you to reinstall the system later without having to wipe out everything saved in the user's home directory.

On the other end of the spectrum are servers, whether dedicated or otherwise. It is certainly possible to go overboard with creating partitions, but there are times when it makes sense to segregate certain parts of the file system onto their own partitions. Table 1.1 lists those partitions you might want to create, a minimum recommended size for the partition, and the reasons to create each. Use this information as well as your own knowledge to determine your own partitioning scheme.

Table 1.1 File system sections to place on their own partitions.

Mount Point	Minimum Size	Reason To Create
/boot	16MB	The boot partition is crucial to getting a Red Hat Linux system up and running—not all versions of Linux keep the kernel in /boot. One way to help avoid problems is to create a separate boot partition so that if another part of the file system fails, the boot process is not disturbed.
/home	400MB	The size of this partition varies greatly with the number of users you intend to host on the machine and what type of file system space you expect them to need. As stated in the text, at times you may choose to fully reinstall a machine, which involves wiping everything from the file system. If the home directories are on a separate partition you can choose not to delete it during the install process.
/tmp	200MB	The size of this partition varies greatly with the number of users you intend to host on the machine and what processes utilizing temporary space will be run there. The tmp directory is one of the most heavily utilized parts of the file system. As such, it has a high chance of suffering from wear and tear. Another consideration is that some savvy users will use the tmp directory to briefly store large files and have been known to overrun it. In either case, if you have it off by itself instead of in the root partition, the only portion of your file system that can be damaged is the /tmp partition.
/usr	300MB	For many systems this minimum size will not be large enough. It is best used on a workstation, not a server, which might need 800MB or more. One especially interesting aspect is that you can mount a usr partition off of a central server instead of keeping one locally. This situation allows you to centrally manage what software is available to the user population rather than having to update packages on each and every machine.
/var	300MB	This portion of the file system contains information that changes on a regular basis, such as log files (/var/log), mail spools, print spools, and more. Along with the tmp directory, var is one of the most highly utilized portions of the file system and therefore is prone to wear and tear more quickly than other sections. Another issue is that sometimes spool files or log files can grow out of control due to program or system problems. Either way, having var off on its own partition limits the amount of damage that can happen to the rest of the file system if something goes wrong.

Choosing Packages

Which packages you install also highly depends on what the machine is meant to do. An end-user GUI workstation will need many bells and whistles and GUI programs, whereas a print server at the very most would want a basic GUI with few extras. You may not even want to waste CPU speed by running a GUI on a server machine.

On a machine where every bit of space counts, or security concerns cause you to only want to install things you know you will use, be sure to choose the Custom install class, and the Select Individual Packages option in the Package Group Selection dialog box. This action gives you the opportunity to go through what will be installed one by one and add or remove items.

Installation Classes

Red Hat offers a number of installation classes that help reduce roadblocks for system administrators new to installing Linux or, specifically, Red Hat Linux. In general, many system administrators would benefit most from using the Custom installation class. For a test installation, however, using one of the other classes does speed up the process.

Server Class

The Server installation class assumes that the machine Red Hat is being installed on is meant to be some form of server, so all of its hard drive space is fair game because servers do not tend to be dual boot machines. After all, a server's purpose is to wait and listen for client requests, whether for mail or news or Web or another purpose. These services would not always be available if the machine had to be also used as, say, a Windows 98 workstation. This class assumes that many of the fun tools and features that a user might want on a workstation will not be desired because servers are not usually used as workstations. Doing word processing or Web surfing on a server slows it down by using up vital resources.

According to Red Hat, the Server class uses a minimum of 1.7GB of space to create the partitions listed in Table 1.2.

Table 1.2 Red Hat Server class partition structure and sizes.

Mount Point	Size	Growth
/	256MB	None
/boot	16MB	None
/home	512MB	If space is available
/usr	512MB	If space is available
/var	256MB	None
swap	64MB	None

WARNING! The Server installation class deletes everything on the system and replaces it. If you are setting up a dual boot machine, choose the Workstation or Custom class.

Workstation Class With GNOME Or KDE

The Workstation installation class assumes that the machine Red Hat is being installed on is meant to be a user workstation. Although the entire hard drive is not taken over by the installation, all Linux partitions are assumed to be meant for Red Hat and will be reformatted and installed over. This class assumes that many of the server tools are not necessary on the machine because workstations are typically used by end users, not to run services.

NOTE: *There is a bug in Red Hat 6.2 that installs and launches GNOME even if you use the KDE Workstation install. Do a Custom installation if you want to use KDE.*

According to Red Hat, the Workstation class uses a minimum of 850MB of space to create the partitions listed in Table 1.3.

WARNING! The Workstation installation class deletes all Linux partitions on the system and replaces them. If you already have another Linux distribution installed, choose the Custom class.

Custom Class

The Custom installation class is the most versatile class, and it is recommended for those who are familiar with the installation process. You have a fine level of control over exactly what packages go on the system, which services start at boot time, and more. Although any of this information can be changed after installation, fine-tuning it at the beginning is preferable.

The Custom class allows complete freedom of installation. There are no preset partitions, partition sizes, or packages that will be placed during a Custom install. Use the Workstation and Server classes to help you determine how much room you should have available for this installation class.

NOTE: *Many people like to choose Custom just so they can see exactly what is being installed. This information is also available in the Reference Guide that comes with all versions of the purchased Red Hat 6.2, or online at* ***www.redhat.com/support/manuals/RHL-6.2-Manual/ref-guide/****.*

Table 1.3 Red Hat Workstation class partition structure and sizes (with either GNOME or KDE).

Mount Point	Size	Growth
/	770MB	If space is available
/boot	16MB	None
swap	64MB	None

Upgrade Option

The Upgrade option is not actually an installation class. It is an option that allows you to upgrade a current installation instead of installing a new version of the operating system and its associated packages. However, this option is not always the smoothest way to update a system. Sometimes it is better to use the RPMs (Red Hat Package Manager formatted files, as discussed in Chapter 4) provided by Red Hat and upgrade the system manually.

GNOME Vs. KDE

Red Hat 6.2 and later versions offer the option of installing either the GNOME (GNU Network Object Model Environment) or KDE (K Desktop Environment) GUI early on in the installation process if you use a Workstation class. If you use the Custom class, choosing which GUI involves looking at the list of overall packages available for installation. GNOME is the GUI selected by default. If you want to use KDE, deselect GNOME and select KDE. You also have the option of installing both GUIs.

Both desktop environments are open source and freely available for use. They both come with suites of applications designed to automate everyday end-user and system-administration tasks. There is a slight difference in how the organizations behind these two environments deal with software developers, so be sure to read their Web sites thoroughly if you intend to develop tools or applications for GNOME (**www.gnome.org**) or KDE (**www.kde.org**).

Choosing which GUI to use often involves several questions:

- Which look and feel most appeals to you?
- Which desktop environment's philosophy do you prefer?
- Are specific tools you want or need available in only one of the environments?

For more information about Linux and GUIs, see Chapter 6.

Other Distributions

There are many Linux distributions available in addition to Red Hat. This book focuses on Red Hat-specific items, but most of the content will work with any Linux flavor. Only small adjustments in file locations or tools may be necessary. In fact, a number of distributions are built on top of Red Hat. A list of some of these is outlined in Table 1.4.

Red Hat is, of course, not the only Linux distribution out there. There are new Linux distributions being introduced on a regular basis all over the world. Table 1.5 lists a number of the available distributions and where you can find out more about them.

Table 1.4 Popular Linux distributions based on Red Hat Linux.

Name	Home Page	Architectures
DLD	**www.delix.de**	Intel x86 and compatible
LinuxPPC	**www.linuxppc.org**	PPC (Power PC) machines (see Web site for full listing)
Mandrake	**www.linux-mandrake.com**	Intel x86 and compatible

Table 1.5 Other popular Linux distributions.

Name	Home Page	Architectures
Caldera	**www.caldera.com**	Intel x86 and compatible
Debian	**www.debian.org**	DEC Alpha, Intel x86 and compatible, Motorola 680x0, SPARC
LinuxPPC	**www.linuxppc.org**	PPC (Power PC) machines (see Web site for full listing)
Mandrake	**www.linux-mandrake.com**	Intel x86 and compatible
Slackware	**www.slackware.com**	Intel x86 and compatible
SuSE	**www.suse.com**	Intel x86 and compatible, DEC Alpha
TurboLinux	**www.turbolinux.com**	Intel x86 and compatible

Immediate Solutions

Getting New Versions Of Red Hat Linux

You can always find out what the latest and greatest of Red Hat's releases are by going to **www.redhat.com**. The boxed set is available for purchase through them as well as in stores that carry computer software. You can also download the contents of the installation CD and/or source CD from **ftp://ftp.redhat.com** if you have a sufficiently large bandwidth to make it worthwhile. For inexpensive Red Hat CDs that come with user manuals in digital form (without technical support), visit:

- **www.cheapbytes.com**
- **www.linuxmall.com**

Updating Your System Through Red Hat

Red Hat continuously makes updates available for its distribution. Some of these updates come from teams working on packages not written by Red Hat. Once the patches or new programs arrive at Red Hat, the programming team tests them and compiles RPMs that will add the new functionalities smoothly to the user's systems. Important updates include security fixes as holes are discovered. Keeping abreast of security issues is covered in detail in Chapter 9.

One way to keep up to date with Red Hat updates is to join the Red Hat Announce mailing list. To join this list, do the following:

1. Open a blank email.
2. Address it to **redhat-announce-list-request@redhat.com**.
3. Put the word "subscribe" in the subject line.
4. Leave the body blank.
5. Send the email.
6. Respond to the email as required, confirming that you want the subscription.

It is not necessary, however, to join the mailing list. All updates are posted to the FTP server (**ftp://ftp.redhat.com**) and its mirrors. The directory name is based on the version number and architecture. For example, if the version is Red Hat

Linux 6.2 and the architecture is Intel x86 and equivalent, the directory is /pub/redhat/updates/6.2/i386. In Chapter 20, you will learn how to write a shell script that automatically checks for and fetches new updates, and notifies you that they have arrived.

TIP: *Updates are also made available at the home sites for most of the tools you use in Linux, such as GNOME. Utilizing these requires you to be a little more careful of dependencies and other such issues, but many system administrators like to use items directly from the source when they want to keep up with the latest versions.*

Navigating GNOME

If you chose the GNOME GUI during the installation process, once you log in you are faced with a screen containing a number of windows that open automatically. Clear these windows out of the way for now by either clicking on OK in the dialog boxes, or by clicking on File|Close or File|Exit.

Once the initial items are cleared off the screen, GNOME initially looks like what is shown in Figure 1.1.

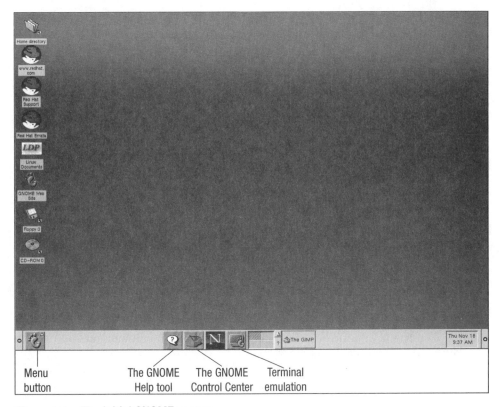

Figure 1.1 The initial GNOME screen.

Configuring The GUI

To configure the GNOME GUI, do the following:

1. Boot the machine.
2. Log into the account containing the GUI settings you want to configure.
3. If the Linux box does not automatically go into the GUI, type “startx” to start it.
4. Look at the taskbar on the bottom of the screen and locate the toolbox icon shown in Figure 1.1.
5. Click on the toolbox icon to open the Control Center, as shown in Figure 1.2.
6. Click on the menu item corresponding to the aspect you want to configure. For example, to configure the environment’s background, click on the Background option under the Desktop menu (see Figure 1.3).
7. Choose the settings as you see fit.
8. The set of buttons (Try, Revert, OK, Cancel, and Help) at the bottom of the screen in Figure 1.3 are at the bottom of every Control Center option. When you have selected the new settings that you want to use, click on the Try button.

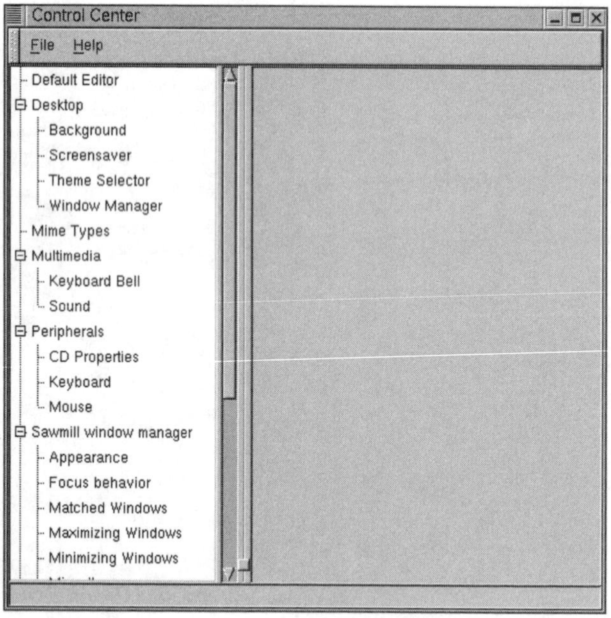

Figure 1.2 The GNOME Control Center.

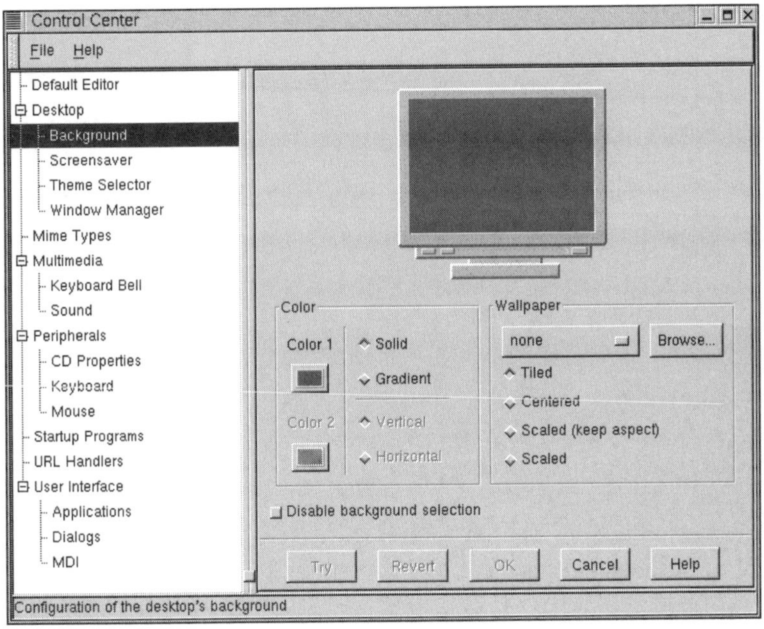

Figure 1.3 The GNOME Control Center Background configuration option.

9. If the settings are acceptable, click on OK to close the dialog box or proceed to the next Control Center option. Otherwise, click on Revert to return to the previous settings.

Related solutions:	Found on page:
Finding GUI Components Online	162
Adding A Window Manager	162
Adding A Theme	164
Changing Desktop Environments	167

Opening Programs

To open the file system navigator used in the GNOME GUI, do the following:

1. Boot the machine.
2. Log into the account containing the GUI settings you want to configure.
3. If the Linux box does not automatically go into the GUI, type "startx" to start it.
4. Look at the taskbar on the bottom of the screen and locate the footprint icon shown earlier in Figure 1.1.
5. Click on the footprint icon to pull up the GNOME menu shown in Figure 1.4.

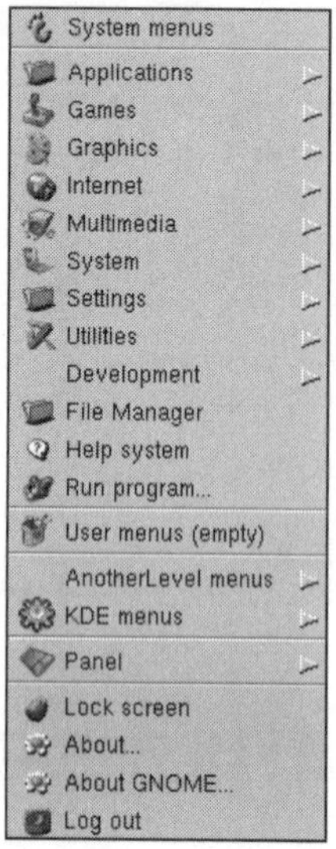

Figure 1.4 The GNOME main menu.

6. Move the mouse pointer over each of the options in the menu. If there is a submenu, move the mouse over to it. Continue doing so until you locate the item you want to open.
7. Click on the item you want to open.

Related solution:	Found on page:
Navigating The File System In GNOME	89

Opening Linuxconf

To find the GNOME GUI tool you can use to configure user accounts and other aspects of the Linux box, do the following:

1. Boot the machine.
2. Log into the account containing the GUI settings you want to configure.
3. If the Linux box does not automatically go into the GUI, type "startx" to start it.
4. Look at the taskbar on the bottom of the screen and locate the footprint icon shown earlier in Figure 1.1.
5. Click on the footprint icon to pull up the GNOME menu shown earlier in Figure 1.4.
6. Click on the System Menus option to pull up the System menu shown in Figure 1.5.

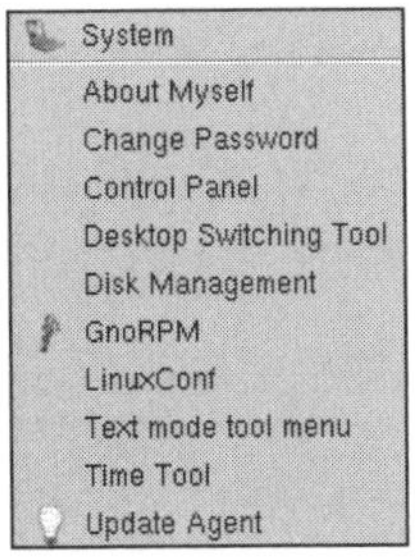

Figure 1.5 The GNOME System menu.

7. Click on the LinuxConf System menu option. At first, the Linuxconf Welcome dialog box opens. Read the information in this dialog box.
8. Click on the Quit button when finished reading the information. The Linuxconf tool itself now opens, as shown in Figure 1.6.

NOTE: *Sometimes it takes a while for anything to happen after clicking on the Quit button. If after a minute or so nothing has happened, click on it again. Otherwise, just be patient and wait for the machine to catch up.*

Accessing Help

To access GNOME GUI Help, do the following:

1. Boot the machine.
2. Log into the account containing the GUI settings you want to configure.

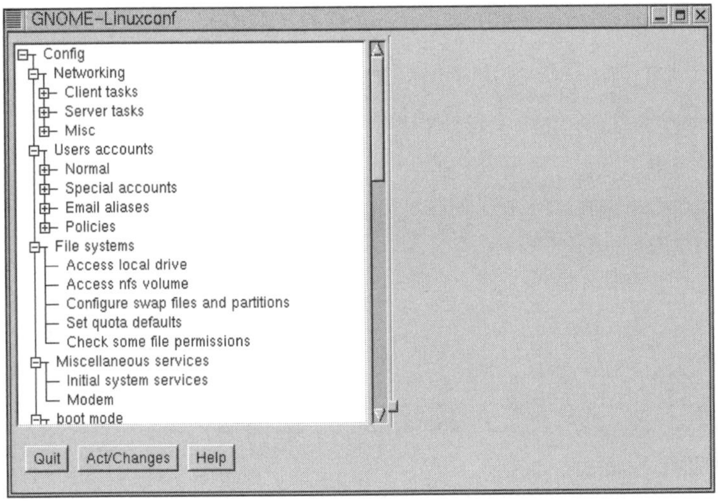

Figure 1.6 The GNOME Linuxconf system configuration tool.

3. If the Linux box does not automatically go into the GUI, type "startx" to start it.
4. Look at the taskbar on the bottom of the screen and locate the GNOME Help tool icon shown earlier in Figure 1.1.
5. Click on the Help tool icon to open the GNOME Help Browser shown in Figure 1.7.

Getting A Command Prompt

To get to a command prompt within the GNOME GUI, do the following:

1. Boot the machine.
2. Log into the account containing the GUI settings you want to configure.
3. If the Linux box does not automatically go into the GUI, type "startx" to start it.

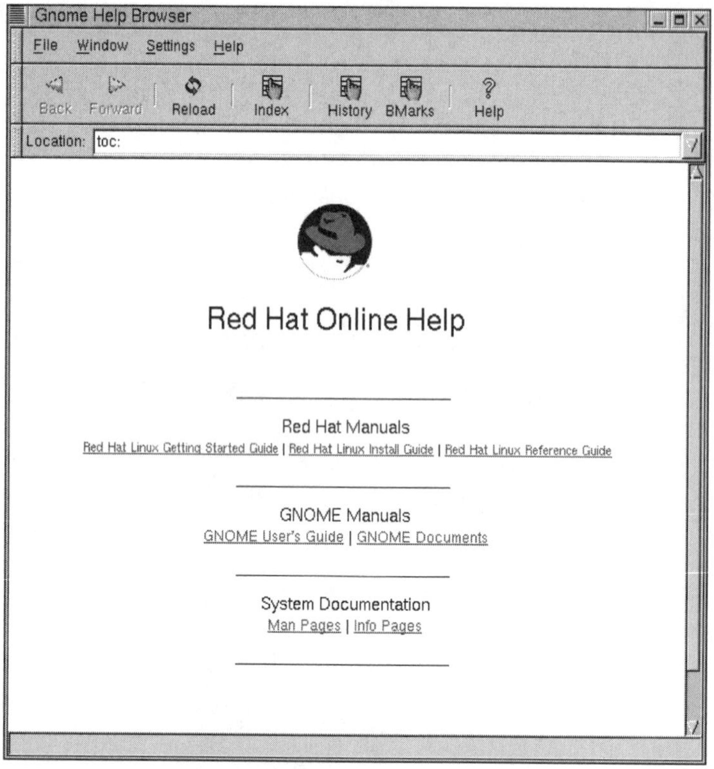

Figure 1.7 The GNOME Help Browser.

4. Look at the taskbar on the bottom of the screen and locate the Terminal emulation program icon shown earlier in Figure 1.1.
5. Click on the Terminal emulation icon to open a Terminal window, as shown in Figure 1.8.

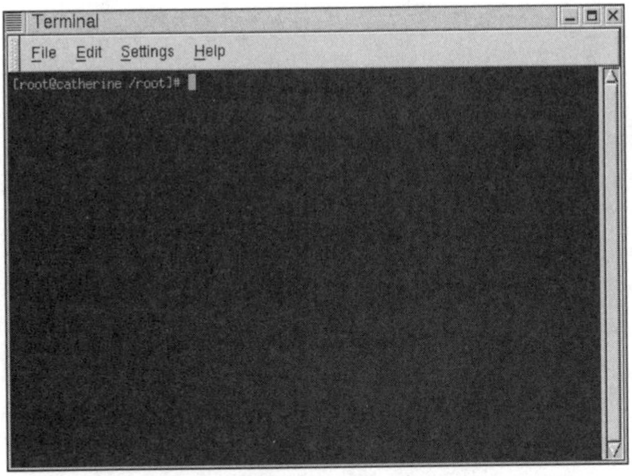

Figure 1.8 The initial GNOME Terminal window.

Navigating KDE

If you chose the KDE GUI during the installation process, once you log in you are faced with a clean slate with a bunch of icons at the bottom of the screen, as shown in Figure 1.9.

NOTE: *The KDE choices in a user session are different from those in a superuser session, because they will not have system controls available.*

Configuring The GUI

To configure the KDE GUI, do the following:

1. Boot the machine.
2. Log into the account containing the GUI settings you want to configure.
3. If the Linux box does not automatically go into the GUI, type "startx" to start it.
4. Examine the taskbar at the bottom of the screen and locate the KDE Control Center icon, as shown in Figure 1.9.

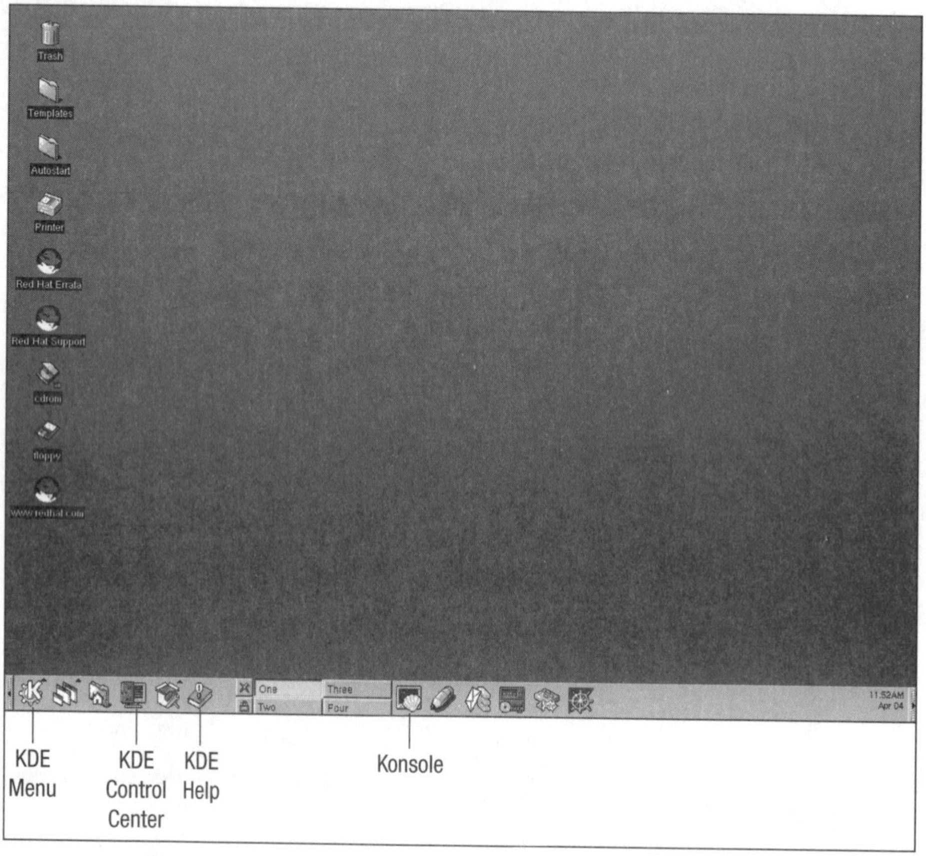

Figure 1.9 The initial KDE screen for the superuser account.

5. Click on the KDE Control Center icon to open the KDE Control Center shown in Figure 1.10.
6. Click on the plus (+) sign next to the menu group(s) you want to expand.
7. Click on the menu item for the KDE aspect you want to configure. For example, see the Login Manager under the Applications menu, shown in Figure 1.11.
8. Configure the aspect to your specifications.
9. The buttons along the bottom of the KDE Control Center are almost always the same, with only slight variations between menu items. Click on the Apply button to put the changes into effect immediately, or at the end of the configuration session click on OK to make all changes.
10. Click on File|Exit to close the KDE Control Center.

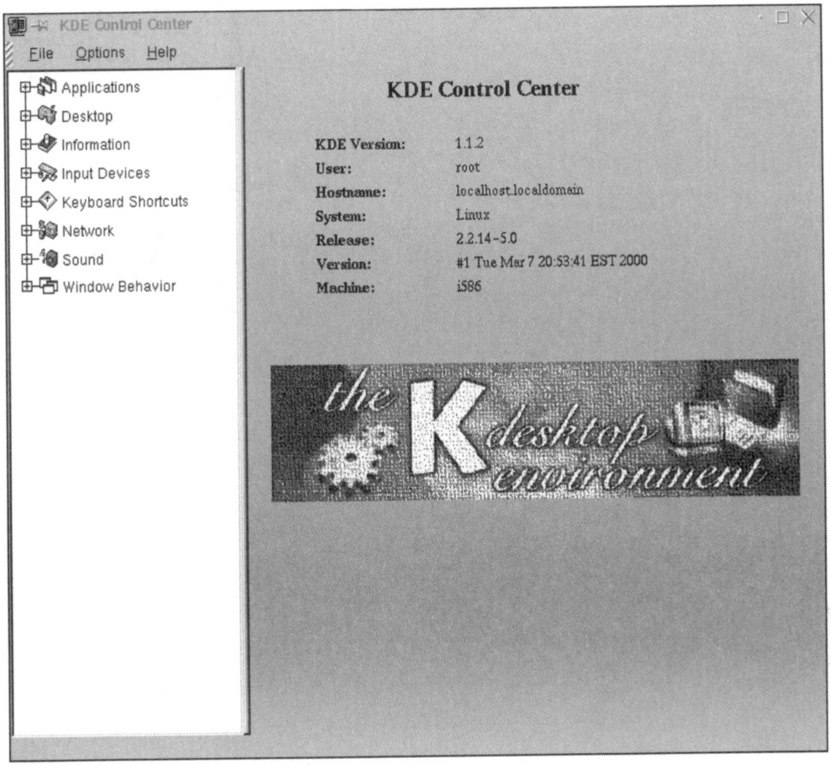

Figure 1.10 The KDE Control Center.

Related solutions:	Found on page:
Finding GUI Components Online	162
Adding A Window Manager	162
Adding A Theme	164
Changing Desktop Environments	167

Opening Programs

To open the file system navigator used in the KDE GUI, do the following:

1. Boot the machine.
2. Log into the account containing the GUI settings you want to configure.
3. If the Linux box does not automatically go into the GUI, type "startx" to start it.
4. Look at the taskbar on the bottom of the screen and locate the K icon, shown earlier in Figure 1.9.
5. Click on the K icon to pull up the KDE main menu, shown in Figure 1.12.

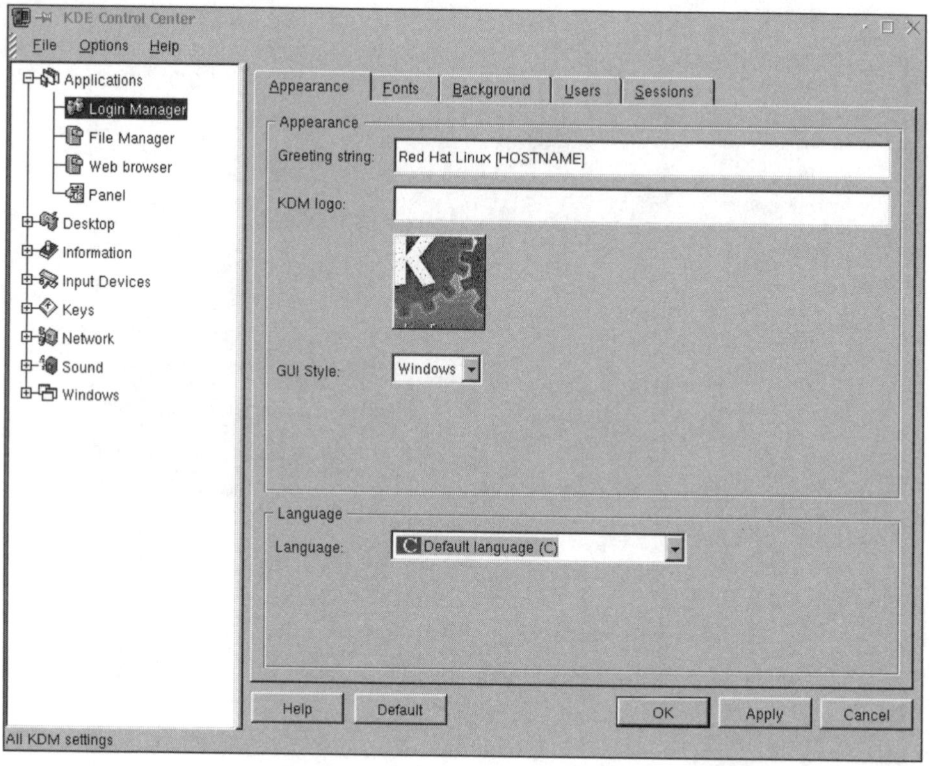

Figure 1.11 The KDE Control Center with the Applications menu's Login Manager open.

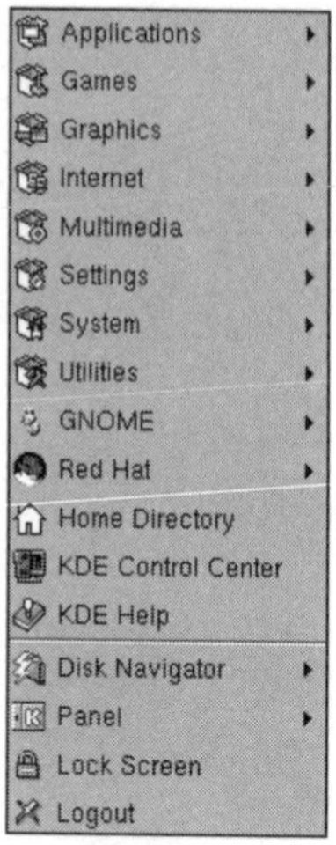

Figure 1.12 The KDE main menu.

6. Move the mouse pointer over each of the options in the menu. If there is a submenu, then move the mouse over to it. Continue doing so until you locate the item you want to open.
7. Click on the item you want to open.

Related solution:	Found on page:
Navigating The File System In KDE	94

Accessing Help

To access KDE GUI Help, do the following:

1. Boot the machine.
2. Log into the account containing the GUI settings you want to configure.
3. If the Linux box does not automatically go into the GUI, type "startx" to start it.
4. Examine the taskbar at the bottom of the screen and locate the KDE Help icon, shown earlier in Figure 1.9.
5. Click on the KDE Help icon to open the KDE Help browser, shown in Figure 1.13.

Getting A Command Prompt

To get to a command prompt within the KDE GUI, do the following:

1. Boot the machine.
2. Log into the account containing the GUI settings you want to configure.
3. If the Linux box does not automatically go into the GUI, type "startx" to start it.
4. Click the Konsole icon, shown earlier in Figure 1.9, to open a Konsole session, which is shown in Figure 1.14.

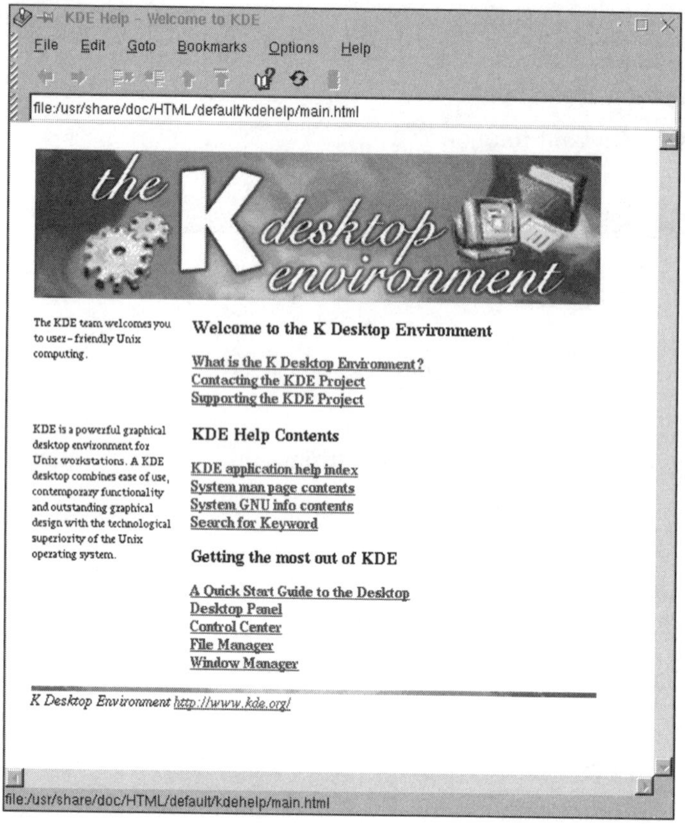

Figure 1.13 The KDE Help browser.

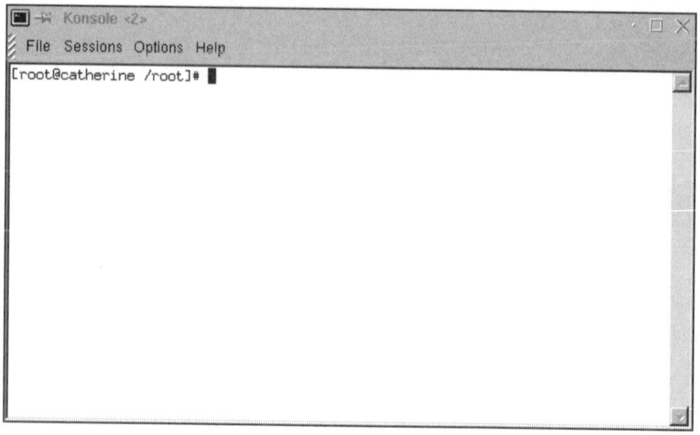

Figure 1.14 The Konsole terminal emulator in KDE.

Chapter 2

User Management

If you need an immediate solution to:	*See page:*
Creating Shell Accounts	31
Creating Shell Accounts From The Command Line	31
Creating Shell Accounts In GNOME	31
Creating Shell Accounts In KDE	35
Creating Restricted Access Accounts	37
Creating Restricted Access Accounts At The Command Line	37
Creating Restricted Access Accounts In GNOME	38
Creating Restricted Access Accounts In KDE	40
Creating Software Accounts	42
Changing Account Creation Defaults	42
Changing Default Home Directory Contents	42
Changing User Defaults At The Command Line	44
Changing User Defaults In GNOME	44
Changing User Defaults In KDE	44
Renaming Users	46
Renaming Users At The Command Line	46
Renaming Users In GNOME	46
Renaming Users In KDE	48
Disabling Users	49
Disabling Users At The Command Line	49
Disabling Users In GNOME	49
Disabling Users In KDE	50

(continued)

If you need an immediate solution to:	*See page:*
Removing Users	50
Removing Users At The Command Line	50
Removing Users In GNOME	50
Removing Users In KDE	52
Installing Software For Users To Run	53
Creating Groups	53
Creating Groups On The Command Line	53
Creating Groups In GNOME	53
Creating Groups In KDE	54
Adding Users To Groups	55
Adding Users To Groups On The Command Line	55
Adding Users To Groups In GNOME	55
Adding Users To Groups In KDE	56
Forwarding User Mail	57
Forwarding User Mail On The Command Line	57
Forwarding User Mail In GNOME	57
Forwarding User Mail in KDE	58

In Depth

As a system administrator, how much time you spend managing users depends on many factors, including the total number of users and how often you have to add or delete accounts. Not all of these users are even people. Some are programs or daemons—programs that run unattended to handle specific requests. This chapter covers user accounts and user management in depth, including the subtleties that, in the end, make for a more secure system.

Types Of User Accounts

At first, many people think that there is simply one type of user account in Linux. This assumption is not only incorrect but leads to security holes that easily could be avoided. There are essentially three types of accounts used in Linux. The first is the *full user account*, or *shell account*, the type of login account most people think of with Linux or Unix. The second is a *restricted access account*, where the user only has access to specific services on the machine.

Another form of account is not for human users but for daemons and other programs that need to run as themselves. Running such programs under the root account is dangerous, because it gives them too high a level of access. It is better to give these programs their own account where they have exactly as much access and control as they need. Then, if those processes are compromised or something goes wrong, they can only cause trouble in their own areas.

Shell Accounts

A full user account is the most general of Linux accounts. It offers shell login access as well as use of everything else a user has permission to run or open. This type of account is created with quick commands, like **useradd**. Unfortunately, shell access is in some ways a serious security hole. If someone has access to the command line—which is what the shell offers—it saves them a step for breaking into the system. With shell access, people can view the contents of the /etc/passwd file, compile programs explicitly for your machine's configuration, run them for malicious purposes, and explore the file system looking for weaknesses in the permission and ownership structure. Even if the person who owns the account has no hostile intentions, having a bad password can lead to that account being compromised. If a user only needs access to, say, POP email, it is an unnecessary risk to create a shell login.

TIP: *Only give people full user accounts if they actually need shell access.*

Restricted Access Accounts

Rather than creating full accounts for users who only need access to specific features, give them non-shell accounts. Some popular services that do not require access to the shell are:

- POP email
- Usenet news
- SLIP or PPP dial-in access

These accounts can be changed into shell accounts at any time if necessary. The advantage of only allowing access to specific services should be clear by now. If users only have access to check their POP email, they cannot get to a command line in order to wreak havoc with the system. Also, if someone breaks into the account—which is more likely to be the case, because users as a general rule are more interested in getting their own things done than causing problems—that person really has not gained much of a foothold. However, it does give the intruder access to the service provided by the restricted account. It is no fun having people mess around with your POP mail, for example, especially if there is critical information they can get from it.

Strong passwords are just as important with restricted accounts as they are with shell accounts. However, with a restricted account the damage of a break-in may be felt more by the user than the provider. Note the word "may." If someone manages to crack a PPP account's password, then the provider's resources are taken up with that intruder's traffic and use of a dial-in.

Programs And Daemons

Some programs and daemons actually need their own user IDs. A program or daemon runs as the user that it is owned by, so if the item runs as root it has all of the privileges that root does. This makes it just as dangerous as a person running as root. A buggy program or daemon can accidentally damage a file system if its permissions are too broad. It is also wise not to give programs read, write, or execute access to areas they do not need to see. This issue is not a worry unless someone breaks in and changes them, or through bad system administration practice you get in the habit of making "quick fixes" to things by loosening permission structures.

People routinely find holes in, for example, the **sendmail** daemon. Older versions of it without the proper security patches have a bug that people can exploit to run programs or access data. Each program or daemon should be segregated as much as possible, to the point where it can do its job but nothing else. This concern is also why there is such a large emphasis in Chapter 9 on watching for and applying security patches that are provided whenever new weaknesses are discovered.

Analysis Of The useradd Process

When you add a user from the command line, you generally use the **useradd** program to do so unless you have written a custom account creation script. It is important to understand what this program actually does when it comes time to customize how new user accounts are created.

Add The User To /etc/passwd

All user accounts must be entered into the file /etc/passwd. This is the central file containing basic user authentication information, such as the login name, user ID code, and password, as well as any other items that define who is using the account. A line in /etc/passwd breaks down into the following:

```
loginname:password:UID:GID:FullName:homedir:shell
```

For example, the user "dog" added as user 520 and group 520 has an entry that probably looks like this:

```
dog:$1$mItsHPvG$4Ph:Canis Lupus Familiarus:/home/dog:/bin/bash
```

Password Entry

The password looks like gibberish in the example—and on your system. This fact is due to the password being stored in an encrypted format. Unfortunately, this encryption is not too hard to break with the proper tools. The /etc/passwd file must be available for all programs to access; therefore, it is world-readable. If you are using shadow passwords (more about this topic in Chapter 9), the password will just be an "x".

Related solutions:	Found on page:
Activating And Deactivating The Shadow Suite	264
Setting Password Rules	285

User And Group IDs

The UID and GID are often transparent and are assigned automatically in sequence by the account creation program. So, the user added after "dog" would have a

UID and GID of 521. This practice of having identical user and group names and numbers (user "dog," group "dog," UID 520, GID 520) is specific to Red Hat-based distributions. Most Linux distributions assign all users to the "user" group instead.

TIP: *UID and GID numbers for user accounts start at 500 in Red Hat, and they are incremented from there—with an upper limit somewhere around 65,000.*

Home Directory

The home directory entry's value depends on what type of user and account you are adding. A shell account user's home is /home/*loginname* unless you change the new user defaults. When dealing with a program or daemon, the home directory is where that program or daemon is stored—for example, the shutdown program is stored in the /sbin directory, so that is its home directory.

Shell Entry

The shell is the environment a user works within, and it is what provides the command line interface—more on Linux shells in Chapter 23. There are a variety of shells available, each of which has its own special language and command. The default shell in Linux is typically /bin/bash. When dealing with a restricted access account, however, the shell should be set to /bin/false. This practice prevents the user from actually logging into a command prompt because /bin/false is not a shell at all. It is a program that very briefly runs and then ends, never giving access to a shell. Its entire purpose is not to provide a command prompt to restricted access accounts.

A shell setting for a program is the full path to the program itself—for example, the shutdown program's shell listing would be /sbin/shutdown.

Add The User To /etc/group

The Red Hat Linux distribution is different from many in that it creates a special group for each user during the **useradd** process. This new group has the same name and ID as the user itself. A line in /etc/group breaks down into the following:

```
groupname:grouppassword:GID:loginname(s)
```

For example, in Red Hat the user "dog" would appear in /etc/group as:

```
dog:at3B3ad.2bWEK2de:520:
```

NOTE: *The terms "special" and "private" are both used to refer to Red Hat's distinctive policy of creating individual groups for each user.*

Password Entry

Not all groups require password entries. A password is for those who might try to use the **chgrp** command to change to a different group than they are by default. Any group that people should not be able to change into without authentication should have a password set. As with the /etc/passwd file, the password listed in /etc/group is encrypted. And if you are using the shadow suite, this password will only be an "x" and the real password is stored in /etc/gshadow. See Chapter 20 for more information on the shadow suite.

Related solution:	Found on page:
Activating And Deactivating The Shadow Suite	264

UID List

Notice that the UID portion of the sample /etc/group listing is blank. Users that are explicitly assigned to a group in /etc/passwd do not need to be assigned in /etc/group as well. However, /etc/passwd only allows you to assign only one group to a user. If you want to add a user to any additional groups you must do so in /etc/group.

To add more than one user to a group, use the format "user1,user2,user3" and so on.

Create The User's Home Directory

The **useradd** program also creates a home directory for the user. By default, this home directory is created as /home/*loginname*. Once this directory is created, the proper permissions and ownerships are set for it. The permissions on a shell user's home directory are rwx------, so that only the user who owns the directory can access it—rwx------ only gives access to the owner of the directory, no one else aside from root can get in (permissions are discussed in detail in Chapter 3). The user and group ownerships in Red Hat Linux's default **useradd** setup are both set to the same thing—the identical user and group names. For example, when doing a listing of the user dog's home directory, the list might look like what is shown in Figure 2.1.

Set Up The User's Default Files

Finally, the **useradd** program goes to a skeleton user directory stored in the directory /etc/skel. Within this directory are the login settings and scripts that need to go into a new user's directory. All files are as generic as possible, using environment variables like $HOME for a home directory instead of an absolute path. (Environment variables and shell scripting are covered in Chapter 20—these files will make more sense then.) Everything within the skeleton directory goes into every new shell account home directory.

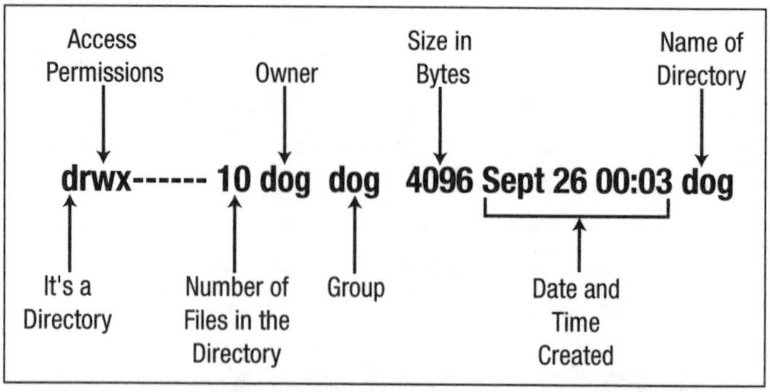

Figure 2.1 A long form listing of the user dog's home directory from within the home hierarchy.

Analysis Of The userdel Process

When you delete a user account by using the command line program **userdel**, it is important to understand what this program does and does not do. It takes care of most of the user removal process for you but not all of it. If you want to completely remove a user account from the system, you will have to do some extra work.

Remove The User Entry From Files

First, the **userdel** program removes the user account from the user management files. This action prevents the user from being able to log in, and it prevents anyone from being able to change to the user's personal group. To accomplish this task, the **userdel** program opens the /etc/passwd file and removes the user's entry there, then the /etc/shadow file, if it exists, is opened and the entry is removed from there as well (more on the shadow suite in Chapter 9). The account removal tool then does the same in /etc/group, removing the user's personal group and also removing the account from any other groups. If you are using shadow groups, the program also goes into /etc/gshadow (see Chapter 9 for more on shadow groups).

Remove The Files

Once the user entries are removed from the user management files, **userdel** turns to the account's home directory and deletes it. However, this is all it deletes. The user may have programs or files installed elsewhere. Items may exist in the /tmp directory, /usr/sbin, or other locations the user might have had access to, such as /var/spool/mail where mail spools are kept (more on email in Chapter 12). See the section "Removing Users" in the Immediate Solutions section for instructions on how to make sure that legacy files are not left behind.

Clever Uses For Groups

Many people seem to forget completely that groups exist. This fact is a shame. There are facets to using groups that can make your life as a system administrator easier and your file system more secure.

Group Storage

A good use for user groups is to create them for project teams. Each member of these teams tends to need access to the same set of materials, such as project guidelines, data, and documents. Creating either a separate partition or a section in the main file system for team files to reside on reduces the need for excessive use of symbolic links between user directories.

Furthermore, with tools like Network File System (NFS) and Samba at your fingertips, group file storage areas can be made network accessible.

Related solutions:	Found on page:
Setting Up NFS Exports	505
Mounting Remote File Systems With NFS	505
Building A File Share Statement	541
Mounting Windows Shares Under Linux	546

Group Access

Sometimes the need to utilize groups creatively is more one of access to scattered programs or special areas of the regular file system than just grouping users. For example, the accounting department may need access to specific programs on its company's main server. Levels of administrative access can also be made using this function. For example, you can make an access level called "webmaster" below root that has access to the FTP areas or HTML storage areas. To give this access, you would go to each of the hierarchies that this group should have access to and see what groups they are assigned. Then, in /etc/group you need to do two things: First, create the webmaster group and place the users who need this access under that group. You can then add webmaster to the groups that already have access to the locations.

Group Isolation

As a reverse of the other methods of using groups, you can also utilize groups to keep specific people out. Sometimes there are programs or files that most people on the system should have access to but perhaps interns or those who have not reached a certain security or trust clearance should not be able to see. A way to accomplish this is to create a group that holds the people that should not have access to those files—say, for example, "untrusted." Then, create a directory whose group ownership is that group. Set the permissions so that the owner and the world have access but the group itself does not. These permissions might look like rwx---rwx.

Immediate Solutions

Creating Shell Accounts

There are various tools available that allow you to create shell accounts quickly. In fact, there is one tool for each interface: a command line program, a GNU Network Object Model Environment (GNOME) tool, and a K Desktop Environment (KDE) tool.

Creating Shell Accounts From The Command Line

Do the following to create a new shell account from the command line:

1. Log in as root.
2. Type "useradd *loginname*". For example, to add the dog account, type "useradd dog".

NOTE: *In Red Hat, you can use* ***adduser*** *instead of* ***useradd****. This is not true in all Linux distributions.*

3. Before a user can log in, you have to assign a password. To do this, type "passwd *loginname*".
4. At the prompt, enter the user's initial password. This is a temporary password that you will give to the user, preferably over the phone. The user will be required to change it after the first login. Notice that you cannot see the password as you type. You can't even see the number of letters you typed.
5. You are now prompted to retype the password to ensure there were no typos. Enter the password again. This entire password addition process might look like:

```
[root@den /root]# passwd dog
Changing password for user dog
New UNIX password:
Retype new UNIX password:
passwd: all authentication tokens updated successfully
```

Creating Shell Accounts In GNOME

Do the following to create a new shell account within GNOME:

1. If GNOME is not already started, start it by typing either "startx" or "init 5" at the command line.

2. Log in as root.
3. Click on the GNOME footprint icon to open the main menu.
4. Click on the System menu.
5. Click on the Linuxconf item on the System menu. The Linuxconf tool opens.
6. Find the Users Accounts option in the list on the left side of the screen.
7. Click on Users Accounts|Normal|User Accounts to pull up the Users Accounts tab shown in Figure 2.2.
8. Click on the Add button to open the User Account Creation tab shown in Figure 2.3.
9. The only field that you must fill in is the first, Login Name. Fill in the user's account name here. If you want to leave everything else to their defaults, skip to Step 16.
10. If you want to, add a full name or nickname for the user account in the Full Name field.
11. If you want to assign the account to a primary group that is not the default user group—identical to the user's login name—then enter the group's name in the Group text box. There is also a drop-down list box available for you to click on and choose from if you want to use an existing group.

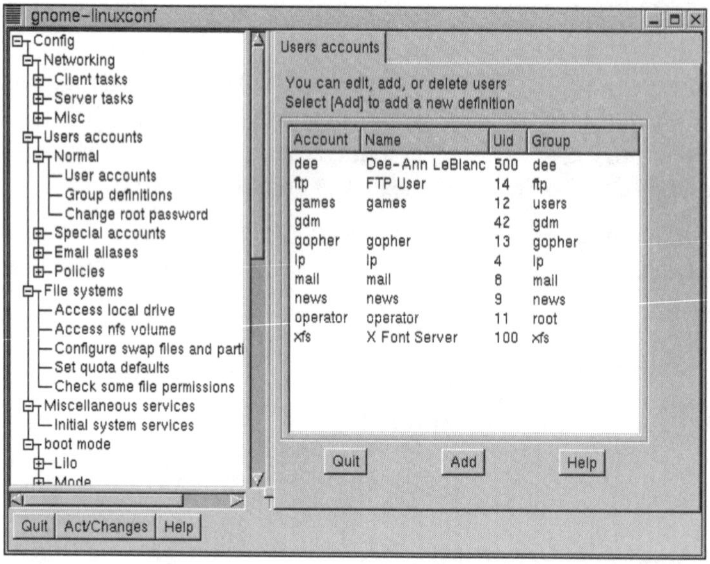

Figure 2.2 The GNOME Linuxconf Users Accounts configuration tab.

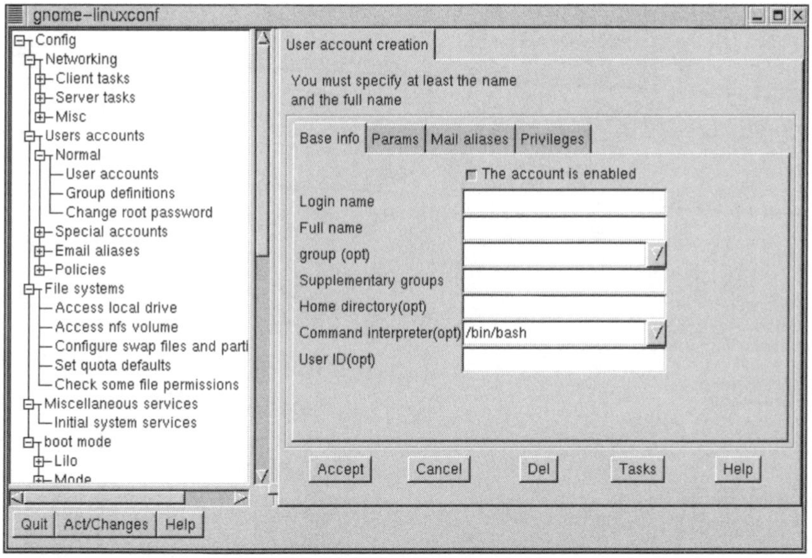

Figure 2.3 The GNOME Linuxconf User Account Creation tab.

12. If you want the user to belong to other groups as well, as listed in /etc/group, enter these group names in the Supplementary Groups field.
13. If you want to use a home directory that is not /home/*loginname*, then enter the path to the directory in the Home Directory field.
14. If you do not want the account to use the default (bash) shell, then enter the path to the shell in the Command Interpreter field.
15. If you want to use a specific UID instead of the next one in line, then type that number into the User ID field.
16. Click on the Accept button to pull up the Changing Password tab shown in Figure 2.4.
17. Type the user's default password into the New UNIX Password field.
18. Click on the Accept button to test the password for its security soundness.
19. If the password is detected to be a security risk, you will get the Error tab shown in Figure 2.5. If not, skip to Step 21.
20. Click on the Ok button to close the Error tab and open the Changing Password tab. Type the password again in the Retype New UNIX Password field. However, I recommend that you choose a more secure password.

TIP: *Remember: Passwords are a system's first line of defense.*

---

21. Click on the Accept button to complete the account addition process.

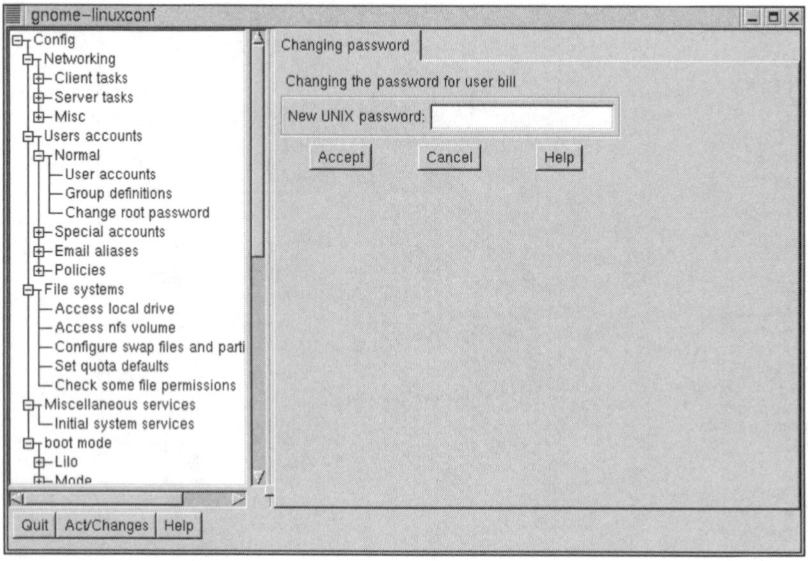

Figure 2.4 The GNOME Linuxconf Changing Password tab.

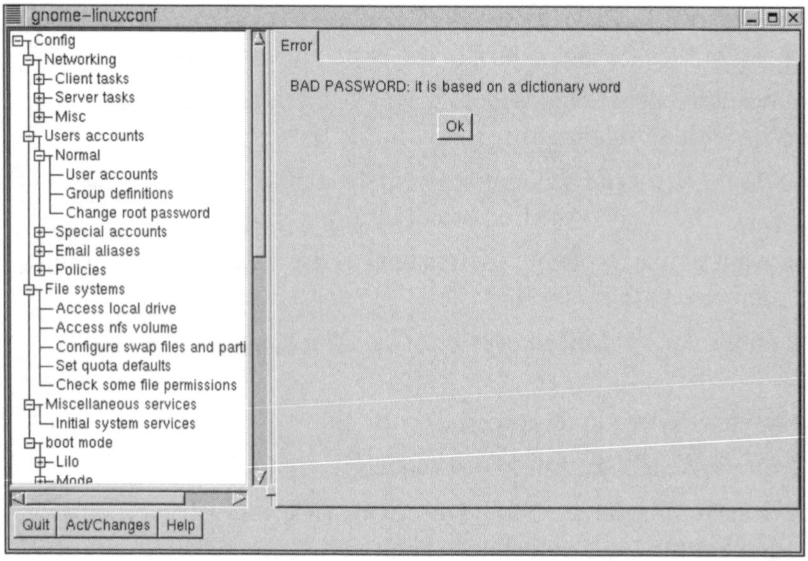

Figure 2.5 The GNOME Linuxconf Error tab.

Related solution:	*Found on page:*
Setting Password Rules	285

Creating Shell Accounts In KDE

To create a full shell account in KDE, do the following:

1. If KDE is not already started, start it by typing either "startx" or "init 5" at the command line.
2. Log in as root.
3. Click on the KDE menu icon.
4. Click on Utilities|Konsole to open a terminal.
5. Type "kuser &" and press Enter to open the KDE User Manager shown in Figure 2.6.
6. Click on User|Add to open the Enter Username dialog box, as shown in Figure 2.7.
7. Type in the username for the new account.
8. Click on OK to pull up the User Properties dialog box, shown in Figure 2.8.
9. Fill in the fields of information you want to assign to the user.
10. Choose a shell in the Login Shell drop-down list box. The standard Linux shell is /bin/bash.

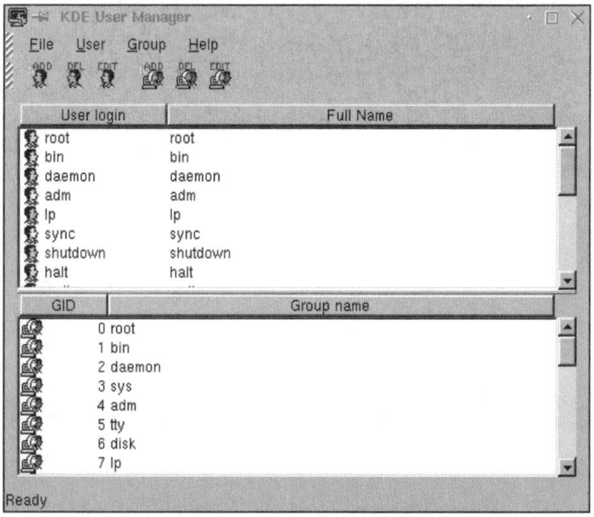

Figure 2.6 The KDE User Manager dialog box.

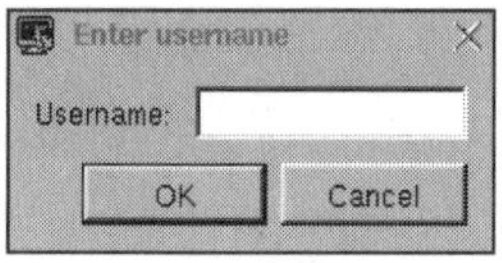

Figure 2.7 The KDE User Manager Enter Username dialog box.

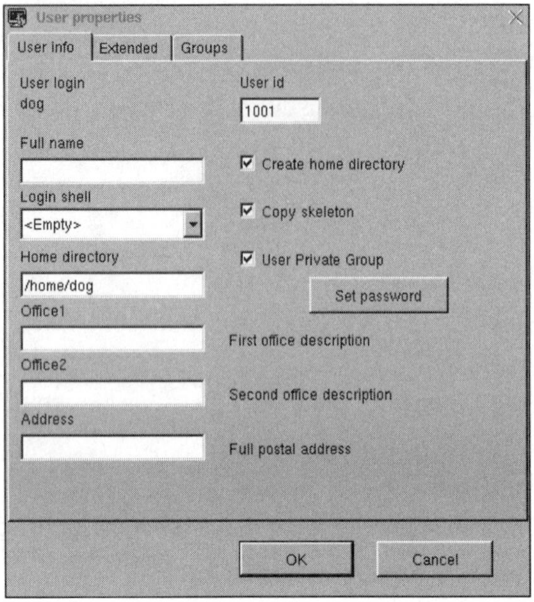

Figure 2.8 The KDE User Manager User Properties dialog box for the user "dog".

11. Keep the defaults of having the Create Home Directory and Copy Skeleton items checked, as well as the User Private Group, unless you want this particular user only to be added to the users group in /etc/group.
12. Click on the Set Password button to open the Enter Password dialog box.
13. Click on OK to accept the password.
14. Click on OK to close the User Properties dialog box.
15. Click on File|Quit to bring up the Data Was Modified dialog box shown in Figure 2.9.
16. Click on the Save button to save the changes and close the User Manager.

Related solution:	*Found on page:*
Getting A Command Prompt	19

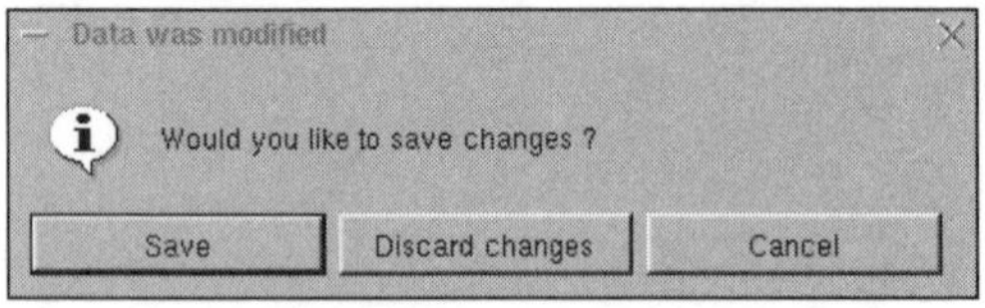

Figure 2.9 The KDE User Manager Data Was Modified dialog box.

Creating Restricted Access Accounts

Creating a restricted access account can be trickier than adding a standard, full user shell account. Some tools are provided in the GUI, but making the account from the command line is a fairly quick procedure.

Creating Restricted Access Accounts At The Command Line

To add a restricted access account at the command line, do the following:

1. Log in as root.
2. Type "vi /etc/passwd" to open the account management file.
3. Type "G" to go to the end of the file.
4. Type "o" to open a new line below the cursor, and go into Insert mode.
5. Create an entry for the user. Because restricted access tends to mean "no shell access," be sure to assign the /bin/false shell. Also, do not assign a home directory to the user. If the last user in the file is UID and GID 560, then the entry might look like this:

```
cat::561:561:House Kitty:/dev/null:/bin/false
```

TIP: *The location /dev/null in Unix and Linux stands for "throw it away."*

6. Press the Esc key and then type ":wq" to save and exit the file.
7. Type "vi /etc/shadow/" to edit the shadow password file if you are using the shadow suite—the file will not exist if you do not have the suite activated. You need to add an entry there, too, because the shadow suite directs programs that need to authenticate users to the shadow file. For more on this file, see Chapter 9.

NOTE: *You only need to edit /etc/shadow if you have the shadow suite enabled. The file will not exist if the suite is not in use. In all sections previous to this under the Immediate Solutions, the programs that handled your user creation work also handled /etc/shadow for you, so this aspect was handled transparently.*

8. Type "G" to go to the end of the file.
9. Type "o" to open a new line below the cursor, and go into Insert mode.
10. Add a line in the format "*loginname*::::::::". For example, for the cat user mentioned earlier, it would be "cat::::::::".

NOTE: *There are eight colons (:), one for each /etc/shadow field, as explained in Chapter 9.*

11. Press the Esc key and then type ":wq!" to save and exit the file. The exclamation point (!) is necessary to override the read-only setting for /etc/shadow.
12. Add the user's password by typing "passwd *loginname*".
13. Enter the user's default password. Make it a secure one or one that has been chosen already. The user can't get to a shell prompt to change it.
14. Enter it again to check for typos.
15. If you want to be doubly sure, type "tail /etc/passwd" to confirm that there is now an "x" in the password field of the user's entry. Then type "tail /etc/shadow" to see that all of the fields for the user are now filled in.

TIP: *The **useradd** command also has flags that you can use to create some types of restricted access accounts. Typing "useradd* loginname *-N -g popusers -s /bin/false" will create a POP-only account with no home directory.*

Creating Restricted Access Accounts In GNOME

To create a restricted access account in GNOME, do the following:

1. If GNOME is not already started, start it by typing either "startx" or "init 5" at the command line.
2. Log in as root.
3. Click on the GNOME footprint icon to open the main menu.
4. Click on the System menu.
5. Click on the Linuxconf item on the System menu. The Linuxconf tool opens.
6. Find the Users Accounts option in the list on the left side of the screen.
7. Click on the plus next to the Special Accounts submenu if necessary to expand it.
8. Click on one of the menu items listed in Table 2.1.

Table 2.1 Choices in the Linuxconf Special Accounts submenu.

Option	Purpose
POP	The account needs access to POP email, but not a shell.
PPP	The account needs dial-in access to use PPP through the server, but no shell.
SLIP	The account needs dial-in access to use SLIP through the server, but no shell.
UUCP	The account needs dial-in access to use UUCP through the server, but no shell.
Virtual POP	The account needs access to POP email for a virtual domain, but not a shell.

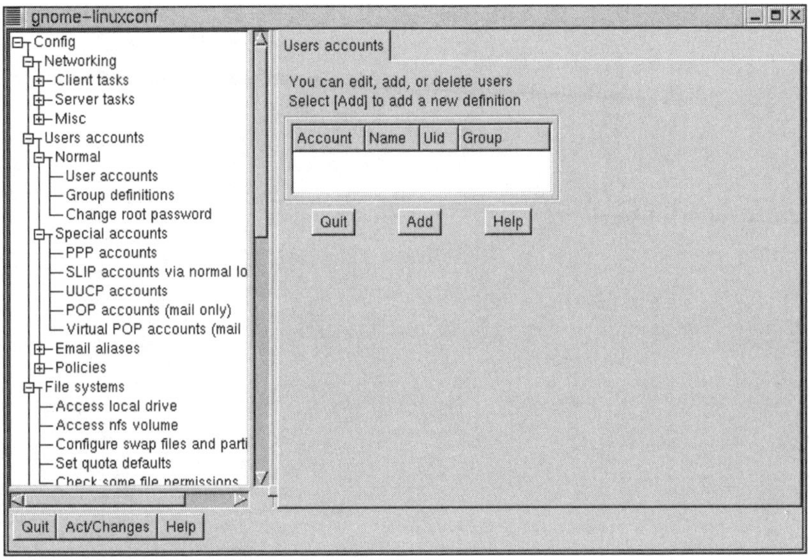

Figure 2.10 The GNOME Linuxconf Users Accounts tab for the Special Accounts submenu.

9. Regardless of which option you choose, you get the Users Accounts tab shown in Figure 2.10.

NOTE: *If you choose the Virtual POP option and there is no virtual domain, you will get an error.*

---

10. Click on the Add button to pull up the User Account Creation tab shown in Figure 2.11—or a similar one; this is specifically the POP tab. Notice that this tab is different than the one shown in Figure 2.3. It is specialized for restricted access accounts.
11. Fill in the Login Name field.
12. Fill in any other fields you have specific reason to.
13. Click on the Accept button to pull up the Changing Password tab shown earlier in Figure 2.4.
14. Enter the user's password. Remember that the user cannot log into the shell to change it, so it is best to use the password the user requested or one that you assign. Be sure to give the user the password in a secure fashion, perhaps by phone or snail mail.

NOTE: *Although POP clients often have an option to change their passwords, some of these restricted access accounts are SLIP and PPP dial-ins. It is not easy to change these passwords.*

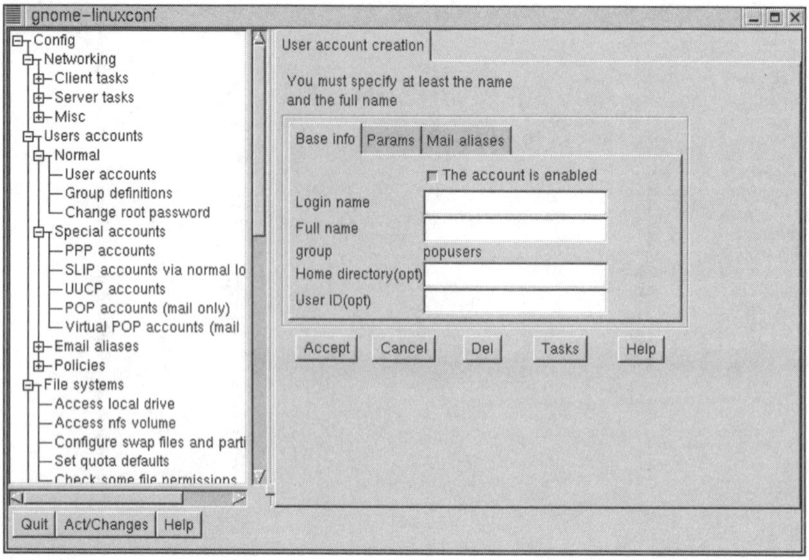

Figure 2.11 The GNOME Linuxconf User Account Creation tab for POP-only accounts.

15. If the password is detected to be a security risk, you will get the Error tab shown earlier in Figure 2.5. If not, skip to Step 17.
16. Click on the Ok button to close the Error tab and open the Changing Password tab. Type the password again in the Retype New UNIX Password field. However, I recommend that you choose a more secure password for this account.
17. Click on the Accept button to complete the account addition process.

Related solution:	*Found on page:*
Setting Up Dial-Out Connections	206

Creating Restricted Access Accounts In KDE

The process used to create a restricted access account in KDE is almost identical to the one used for creating a shell account. To accomplish this task, do the following:

1. If KDE is not already started, start it by typing either "startx" or "init 5" at the command line.
2. Log in as root.
3. Click on the KDE menu icon.
4. Click on Utilities|Konsole to open a terminal.
5. Type "kuser &" and press Enter to open the KDE User Manager shown earlier in Figure 2.6.

6. Click on User|Add to open the Enter Username dialog box shown earlier in Figure 2.7.
7. Type in the username for the new account.
8. Click on OK to pull up the User Properties dialog box, shown earlier in Figure 2.8.
9. Fill in the Full Name field if you would like to.
10. Leave the Login Shell drop-down list box as <Empty>.
11. Deselect the Create Home Directory checkbox.
12. Click on the Groups tab to open the screen shown in Figure 2.12.
13. Scroll through the Groups Not Belonged To list box and click on the group corresponding to the type of restricted access account you want to create. Commonly chosen options are popusers, pppusers, and slipusers.
14. Click on the User Info tab to return to the previous screen.
15. Click on the Set Password button to open the Enter Password dialog box.
16. Click on OK to accept the password.
17. Click on OK to close the User Properties dialog box.
18. Click on File|Quit to bring up the Data Was Modified dialog box shown earlier in Figure 2.9.
19. Click on the Save button to save the changes and close the User Manager.

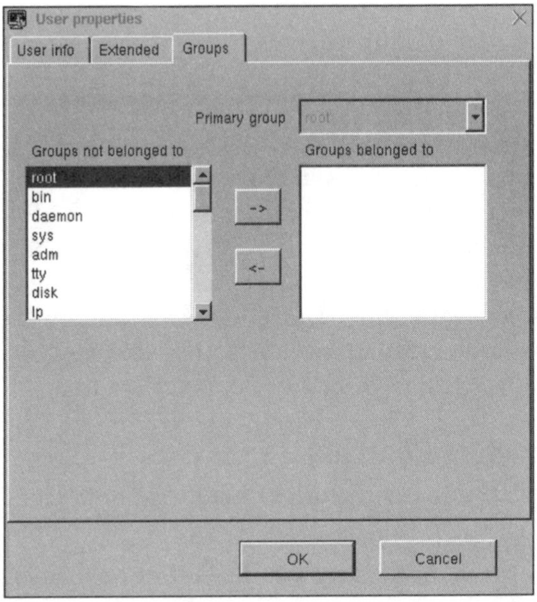

Figure 2.12 The KDE User Manager User Properties dialog box, Groups tab.

Creating Software Accounts

Creating an account for a daemon or program to run under as its own user is effectively the same as creating any other account. Rather than including step-by-step instructions here, consider these bulleted points and follow the instructions in the appropriate "Creating Shell Accounts" section:

- Look in the existing user list and see if the program belongs in an existing software user, for example, in the "games" user.
- If the program does not belong in an existing software user, give the new account a meaningful name so you will understand what it's for.
- Be sure to give the account a low UID to ensure that it resides with the other software accounts.
- Depending on your personal preferences for group assignments, most programs get their own groups and then may be added to others. The primary reason for giving a package its own group is that if security is compromised, it does not have additional access to other items.
- A program does not get a user shell, and it does not need a login environment. Instead, enter the full path to the program in the shell field.

NOTE: *You may not have to create a new user account for the new software. If the program came as an RPM (Red Hat Package Manager package) or some other package with an installation feature, the installer may have created the account for you.*

Changing Account Creation Defaults

It is possible to change the defaults for new accounts. These defaults only affect users added after changes have been made. Each interface has its own tools for making these changes. How you change user defaults, however, depends on what aspect you want to change. If you want to change various aspects of the account itself, then see the appropriate "Changing User Defaults" sections. However, if you want to change the files that are placed in the user's home directory by default, then see the "Changing Default Home Directory Contents" section.

Changing Default Home Directory Contents

To change the contents of the initial home directories created for new accounts, do the following:

1. Get to a command prompt as root, either through the GUI or on a virtual terminal.

2. Change to the /etc/skel directory.
3. Type "ls -la" to list all files, including hidden files. What files are listed depends on what items you chose during the installation process, including which desktop environment you went with.
4. Type "more filename" to view the contents of each file. The purpose of each file you are likely to find is shown in Table 2.2.
5. Type "vi filename" to edit any one of the files.
6. Alter the contents to your satisfaction. Be sure that anything you change is something you want to affect every new user added after these changes are made.
7. Type ":wq" to save and exit the file.

Related solutions:	*Found on page:*
Maneuvering In **vi**	578
Filtering Text In **vi**	579

Table 2.2 Files in the skeleton user directory.

File	Purpose
Desktop	This directory contains the skeleton of what will eventually be the individual user's desktop—workspace—configuration information during a GUI session.
.bash_logout	This file executes commands when you log out. By default, it clears the screen so that the login prompt will be the only thing waiting for the next login session.
.bash_profile	Every user login looks to the /etc/profile file for which environment variables to set and programs to run during the login process. After this, the login process looks to this user-configured file within the user's home directory, which can include additional items and even reverse or change what was done in the /etc/profile file. Items set within this file can change items that were already set in /etc/profile.
.bashrc	Every user login looks to the file /etc/bashrc for which functions and aliases to set during that login. After this, the login process looks to this user-configured file within the user's home directory, which can include additional functions and aliases and can override /etc/bashrc files. Items set within this file can change items that were already set in /etc/bashrc.
.kde	This directory contains the skeleton of what will eventually contain the individual user's KDE configuration information.
.kderc	This file is present only if a GUI was installed. It is specifically a KDE configuration file for the user.
.screenrc	This file contains customization information for the Screen window manager.

Changing User Defaults At The Command Line

If you want to change the account creation defaults at the command line, do the following:

1. Log in as root.
2. Type "useradd -D" to display the current defaults.
3. Determine what defaults you want to change. The options available are listed in Table 2.3.
4. Build the statement by beginning it with **useradd -D**, and then add each item to be changed. For example:

```
useradd -D -g users -s /bin/ksh
```

5. Verify that the defaults are now correct by typing "useradd -D" again.

Changing User Defaults In GNOME

There is no specific way to change user defaults in GNOME. Instead, open a terminal window and change them at the command line.

Related solution:	Found on page:
Getting A Command Prompt	14

Changing User Defaults In KDE

To change user defaults in KDE, do the following:

1. If KDE is not already started, start it by typing either "startx" or "init 5" at the command line.

Table 2.3 Options for changing account creation defaults with useradd.

Flag	Purpose	Valid Entries
b	Change the default home directory.	Path to the new home hierarchy; current value /home.
e	Change the default date to expire the account.	Date in the format mm/dd/yy.
f	Change the default wait after a password expires. If this wait time is exceeded without the password being updated, disable the account.	Number of days to wait. Enter "0" if the account should expire immediately. To not use this feature at all, enter " -1" (default).
g	Change the default group that new users are assigned to.	Existing group name or GID.
s	Change the default shell that new users are assigned to.	Path to the already installed shell.

2. Log in as root.
3. Click on the KDE menu icon.
4. Click on Utilities|Konsole to open a terminal.
5. Type "kuser &" and press Enter to open the KDE User Manager shown earlier in Figure 2.6.
6. Click on File|Preferences to pull up the Edit Defaults dialog box shown in Figure 2.13.
7. If you want to change the default shell, choose it from the Shell drop-down list box.
8. If you want to change where new home directories go, change the entry in the Base Of Home Directories text box. The directory listed in this box will be the top home directory, within which all user home directories will be created.
9. If you do not want user home directories to be automatically created, deselect the Create Home Dir checkbox. You might want to do this if you almost always create non-shell accounts.
10. If for some reason you do want a home directory created but do not want the items from the skeleton directory put into it, be sure the Copy Skeleton To Home Dir checkbox is deselected.
11. If you don't want to use Red Hat's default, which creates a new group for every user, be sure to deselect the User Private Group checkbox.
12. When you are finished making your changes, click on the OK button.

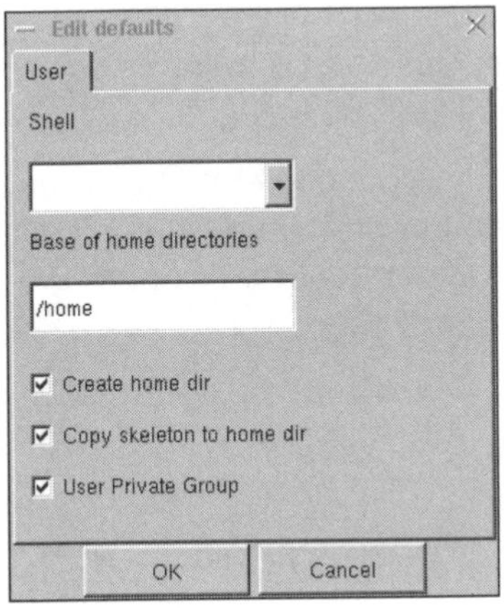

Figure 2.13 The KDE User Manager Edit Defaults dialog box.

Renaming Users

Renaming a user account may involve changing the user's name in /etc/passwd, /etc/shadow, and /etc/group. In addition, the home directory must be moved with the renamed account (unless you have reason to leave it where it is).

Renaming Users At The Command Line

To rename a user's account at the command line, do the following:

1. Log in as root.
2. Type "usermod -d /home/*newname* -m -l *newname oldname*".

Renaming Users In GNOME

To rename a user's account in GNOME, do the following:

1. If GNOME is not already started, start it by typing either "startx" or "init 5" at the command line.
2. Log in as root.
3. Click on the GNOME footprint icon to open the main menu.
4. Click on System|Linuxconf. The Linuxconf tool opens.
5. Find the Users Accounts option in the list on the left side of the screen.
6. Click on the Normal option under the Users Accounts menu.

NOTE: *Follow Steps 7 through 12 only if you are using the Red Hat default of assigning a special group to every new user or if you want to change the group name while you're changing the rest.*

7. Click on the Group Definitions option under the Normal menu to pull up the User Groups tab shown in Figure 2.14.
8. Click on the special group assigned to the account you want to rename. For example, if I wanted to change the "dog" account to "canid," I would click on the dog group in the listing. Clicking on one of the groups opens the Group Specification tab.
9. Select the contents of the Group Name text box within the Group Specification tab.
10. Type the new name of the group.
11. Click on the Accept button. This action returns you to the User Groups tab shown in Figure 2.14.
12. Click on the Quit button to close the User Groups tab.
13. Click on the User Accounts option under the Normal menu to pull up the Users Accounts tab shown earlier in Figure 2.2.

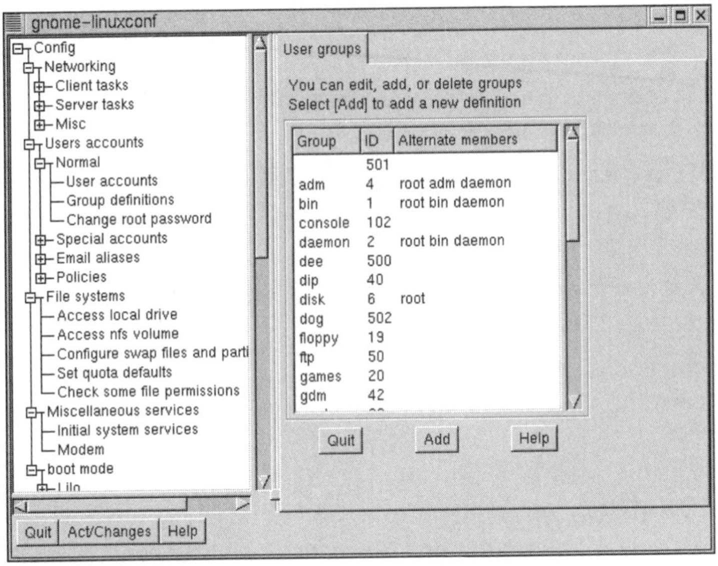

Figure 2.14 The GNOME Linuxconf User Groups tab.

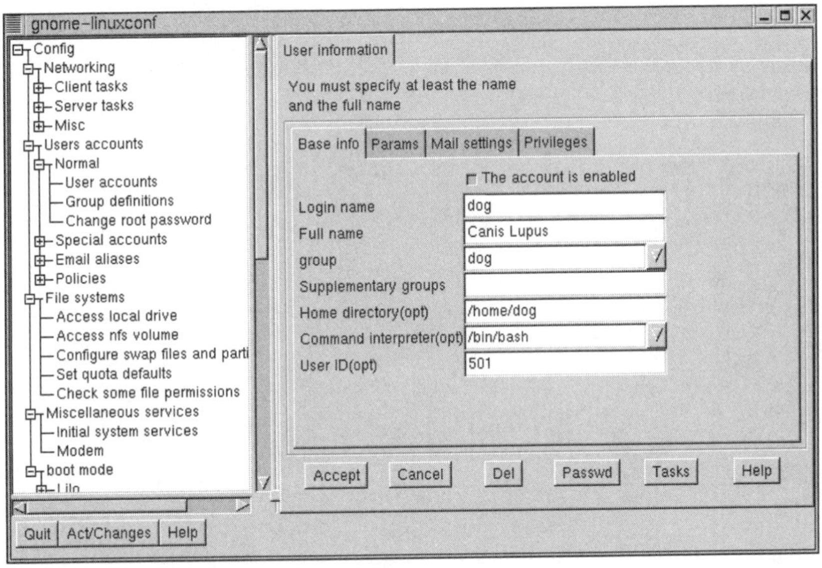

Figure 2.15 The GNOME Linuxconf User Information tab showing the "dog" user.

14. Single-click on the item you want to change within the Account list. This action pulls up the User Information tab shown in Figure 2.15.
15. Select the text in the Login Name text box.
16. Replace the current login name with the one you want to use.

NOTE: *You can change any of the other items within the text boxes at this point as well.*

17. Replace the current Group entry with the username or another default group you want to change the account to.
18. You may need to replace the account's home directory to match its new username. For example, if you changed "dog" to "canid" then you would change "/home/dog" to "/home/canid".
19. Click on the Accept button. This action may open the User Home Directory tab shown in Figure 2.16.
20. If the dialog box shown in Figure 2.16 opens, click on the Yes button to create the new home directory. This action returns you to the Users Accounts tab.

Renaming Users In KDE

KDE does not provide a GUI-based method for renaming a user account. You will need to follow the instructions in the section "Renaming Users At The Command Line" for how to proceed.

Related solution:	Found on page:
Getting A Command Prompt	19

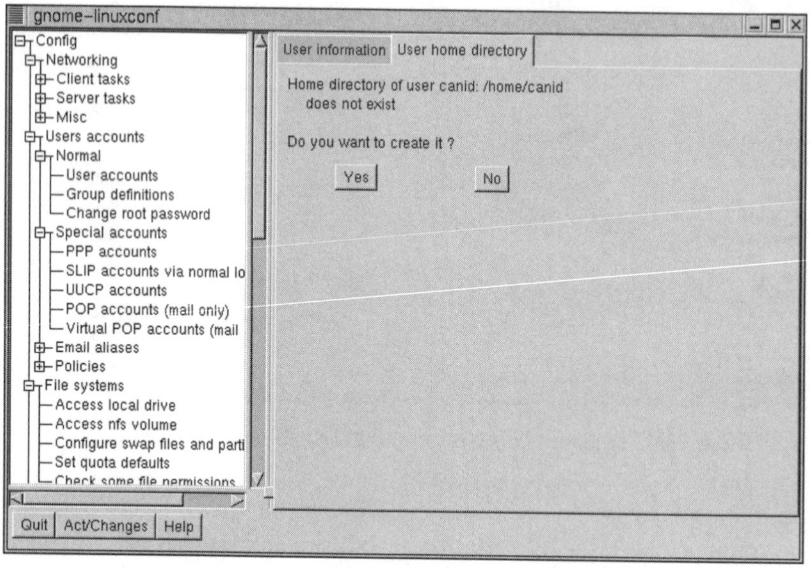

Figure 2.16 The GNOME Linuxconf User Home Directory tab showing the "dog" user renamed as "canid".

Disabling Users

Disabling users involves removing their access to the system without actually removing their accounts. This measure is generally used to ensure that accounts are not broken into undetected when the users should not be accessing them—say, while they are on vacation or when they are behind on payments.

Disabling Users At The Command Line

To disable a user's account at the command line, do the following:

1. Log in as root.
2. Type "vi /etc/passwd"—or "vi /etc/shadow" if you are using shadow passwords—to open the user management file.

TIP: *If all the entries in /etc/passwd have an "x" for the password entry (second item), you need to look at /etc/shadow.*

3. Locate the entry for the account you want to disable.
4. Change the second field in the entry to an asterisk (*). Although adding almost any single character to this field prevents anyone from logging into the account, the asterisk has a special meaning to the system. It renders the password for the account into a nonsensical string of characters.
5. Type ":wq" to save and exit the file.

Disabling Users In GNOME

To disable a user's account in GNOME, do the following:

1. If GNOME is not already started, start it by typing either "startx" or "init 5" at the command line.
2. Log in as root.
3. Click on the GNOME footprint icon to open the main menu.
4. Click on System|Linuxconf. The Linuxconf tool opens.
5. Find the Users Accounts option in the list on the left side of the screen.
6. Click on Users Accounts|Normal|User Accounts to pull up the Users Accounts tab shown earlier in Figure 2.2.
7. Single-click on the item you want to change within the Account list. This action pulls up the User Information tab shown earlier in Figure 2.15.
8. Click on the The Account Is Enabled checkbox to select it.
9. Click on the Accept button to activate the change and return to the Users Accounts tab.

Disabling Users In KDE

KDE does not provide a GUI-based method for disabling a user account. You will need to follow the instructions in the section "Disabling Users At The Command Line" for how to proceed.

Related solution:	Found on page:
Getting A Command Prompt	19

Removing Users

Fully removing a user involves not only deleting his or her account and removing the home directory, but also hunting down any files owned by that user that might lie outside the home directory.

Removing Users At The Command Line

To remove a user from the command line, do the following:

1. Log in as root.
2. Type "find / * -user *username* > ~/userfiles" to find all of the files belonging to the user you are about to delete and save the list to the file "userfiles" in your root home directory.
3. Type "userdel -r *user*" to delete the user's account from the /etc/passwd, /etc/group, and /etc/shadow files where applicable, along with the user's home directory.

TIP: *If you don't want to delete the home directory just yet, do not include the* ***-r*** *flag.*

4. Examine the ~/userfiles file and determine which of the programs and files there can be safely deleted and which might be shared with other users. Delete each file and directory that can safely go with the **rm** and **rmdir** commands.

TIP: *If you think something might be shared but are not sure, try renaming it and see if anyone notices its absence. This is somewhat of a brute force method, but it works.*

Removing Users In GNOME

To remove a user in GNOME, do the following:

1. If GNOME is not already started, start it by typing either "startx" or "init 5" at the command line.

2. Log in as root.
3. Click on the GNOME footprint icon to open the main menu.
4. Click on System|Linuxconf. The Linuxconf tool opens.
5. Find the Users Accounts option in the list on the left side of the screen.
6. Click on Users Accounts|Normal|User Accounts to pull up the Users Accounts tab shown earlier in Figure 2.2.
7. Single-click on the item you want to change within the Account list. This action pulls up the User Information tab shown earlier in Figure 2.15.
8. Click on the Delete button to pull up the Deleting Account *user* tab, a version of which is shown in Figure 2.17.
9. Choose one of the options offered:
    - Click on the Archive The Account's Data option if you want the contents of the home directory to be saved. Selecting this option tells Linux to look and see if the directory /home/oldaccounts exists. If it does not, then the directory is created. A compressed package containing the contents of the user's home directory is then saved to this location. This option is a safe choice if you are unsure whether users are utilizing anything within the home directory and you want to be able to restore it if it is missed.
    - Click on the Delete The Account's Data option if you want the contents of the home directory to be removed. Choose this option if no users are

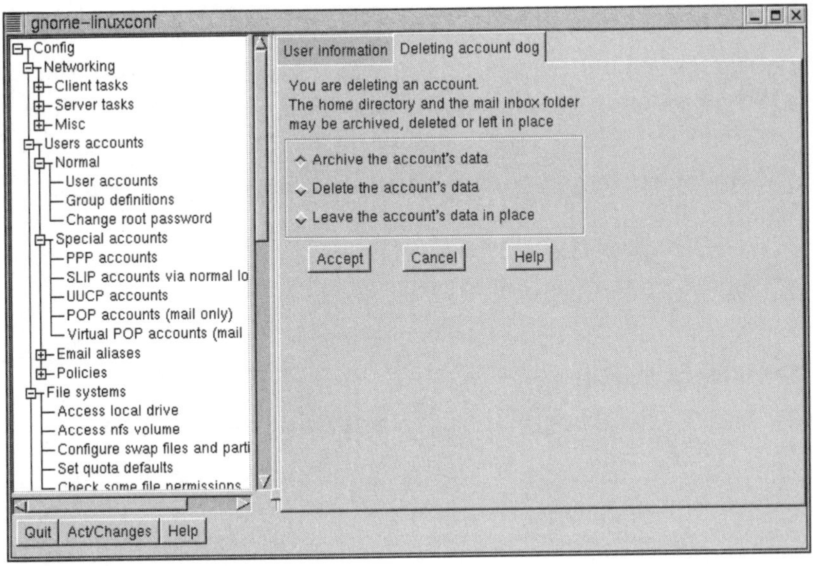

Figure 2.17 The GNOME Linuxconf Deleting Account *user* tab, specifically for the user "dog".

utilizing anything in this directory or if you do not want people to continue using the program that is being shared.

- Click on the Leave The Account's Data In Place option if you want the contents of the home directory not to be touched. Choose this option if you know that people are utilizing some of the data or programs in this user's home directory. You can then remove all other data from the home directory by hand if you want to.

10. Click on the Accept button to activate the change and return to the Users accounts tab.

Removing Users In KDE

To remove a user in KDE, do the following:

1. If KDE is not already started, start it by typing either "startx" or "init 5" at the command line.
2. Log in as root.
3. Click on the KDE menu icon.
4. Click on Utilities|Konsole to open a terminal.
5. Type "kuser &" and press Enter to open the KDE User Manager shown earlier in Figure 2.6.
6. Click on the account that you want to remove within the listing.
7. Choose Delete in the User menu to pull up the Warning dialog box shown in Figure 2.18, to confirm that you do indeed want to delete the user's account.
8. Click on the Delete button to continue with the account removal, and pull up the Warning dialog box, shown in Figure 2.19, to confirm whether you want to delete the private user group for the user's account if it exists.
9. Click on the Delete button to complete the private group removal.

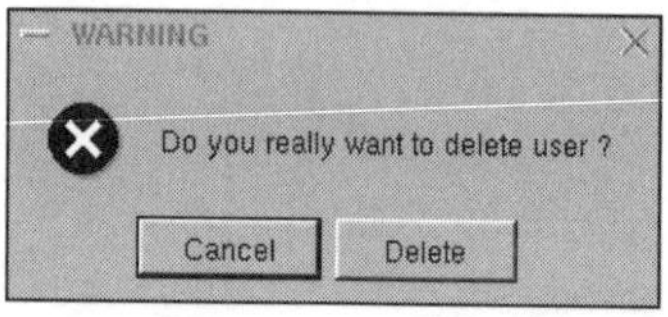

Figure 2.18 The KDE User Manager Warning before deleting user dialog box.

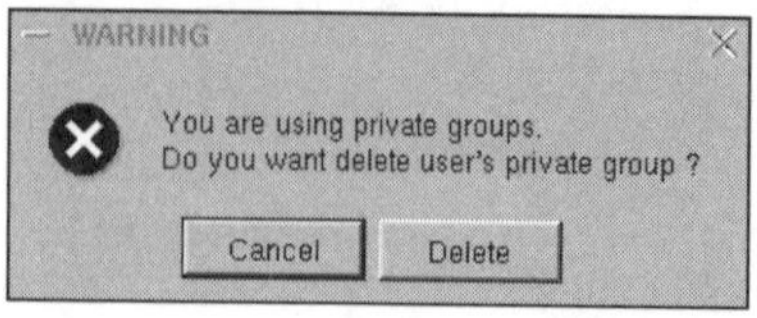

Figure 2.19 The KDE User Manager Warning dialog box for deleting private groups.

Installing Software For Users To Run

There are a number of things to keep in mind when you are preparing to install software for your users, or even for your own use with a non-superuser account:

- A user has to have permissions to run the program. Therefore, do not place it in a location that is accessible to root only.
- Do not loosen the permissions on a current directory to allow user access to the programs contained therein. This action is counterproductive for security purposes.
- If the application allows users to write data, be sure to configure it carefully so that it is secure.
- If the application uses some kind of hierarchy of user types, be sure to set this properly.
- Install the man pages—online manuals—for the package.

Creating Groups

It is useful at times to create a new group to place users in rather than using one that already exists. This group information goes into the file /etc/group, but none of the methods discussed in this section requires you to edit that file directly.

Creating Groups On The Command Line

To create a new group at the command line, do the following:

1. Log in as root.
2. Type "groupadd *groupname*" to create the new group.

Creating Groups In GNOME

To create a new group in GNOME, do the following:

1. If GNOME is not already started, start it by typing either "startx" or "init 5" at the command line.
2. Log in as root.
3. Click on the GNOME footprint icon to open the main menu.
4. Click on System|Linuxconf. The Linuxconf tool opens.
5. Find the Users Accounts option in the list on the left side of the screen.
6. Click on Users Accounts|Normal|Group Definitions to pull up the User Groups tab shown earlier in Figure 2.14.

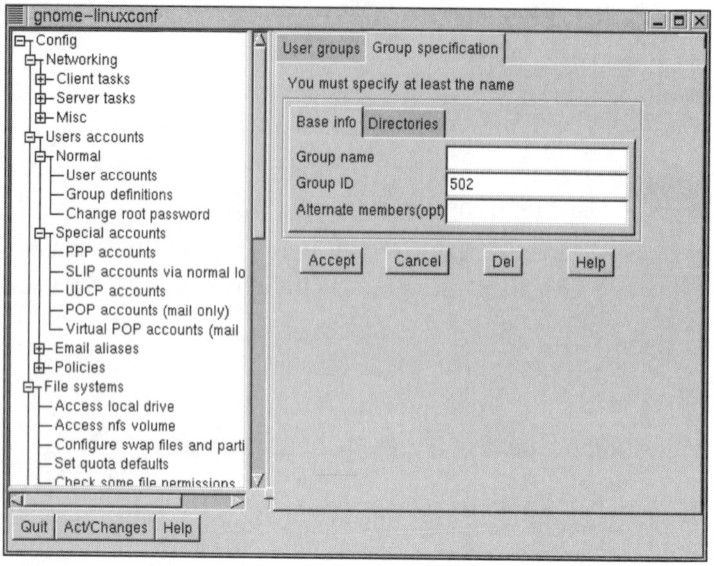

Figure 2.20 The GNOME Linuxconf Group Specification tab.

7. Click on the Add button to pull up the Group Specification tab shown in Figure 2.20.
8. Type the name for the new group in the Group Name text box.
9. If you want to, change the default GID setting in the Group ID text box.
10. Click on the Accept button to return to the User Groups tab.

Creating Groups In KDE

To create a new group in KDE, do the following:

1. If KDE is not already started, start it by typing either "startx" or "init 5" at the command line.
2. Log in as root.
3. Click on the KDE menu icon.
4. Click on Utilities|Konsole to open a terminal.
5. Type "kuser &" and press Enter to open the KDE User Manager shown earlier in Figure 2.6.
6. Click on Group Add to pull up the Add Group dialog box shown in Figure 2.21.
7. Type the name of the new group in the Group Name text box.

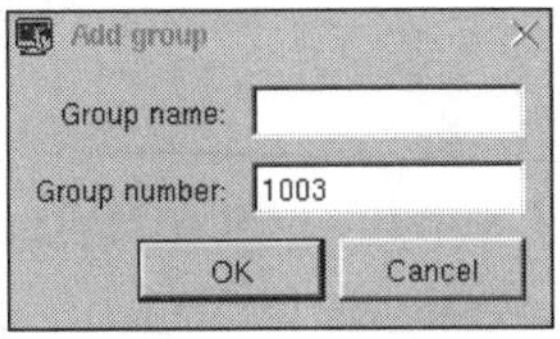

Figure 2.21 The KDE User Manager Add Group dialog box.

8. If you want to change the default new GID, type the new GID in the Group Number text box.

NOTE: *Notice that the KDE User Manager uses a different default GID to start with than the GNOME Linuxconf.*

---

9. Click on OK to return to the main User Manager screen.

Adding Users To Groups

When you create a user account, that user is automatically added either to his or her own private group or to the "users" group, depending on how you have your defaults configured. However, a user can belong to more than one group at a time. The primary group—the one listed in /etc/passwd—is the one the user operates under and whose name is assigned to the group ownership of any file or directory created with that account. Any secondary groups, however, allow the user to access extra areas that members of those groups can reach.

Adding Users To Groups On The Command Line

To add a user to an existing group at the command line, do the following:

1. Log in as root.
2. Type "usermod -G *newgroup user*".

NOTE: *The newgroup must already exist.*

Adding Users To Groups In GNOME

To add a user to an existing group within GNOME, do the following:

1. If GNOME is not already started, start it by typing either "startx" or "init 5" at the command line.
2. Log in as root.

3. Click on the GNOME footprint icon to open the main menu.
4. Click on System|Linuxconf. The Linuxconf tool opens.
5. Find the Users Accounts option in the list on the left side of the screen.
6. Click on Users Accounts|Normal|User Accounts to pull up the Users Accounts tab shown earlier in Figure 2.2.
7. Single-click on the item you want to change within the Account list. This action pulls up the User Information tab shown earlier in Figure 2.15.
8. Type the name of an existing group you want to add the user to in the Supplementary Groups text box. If you want to enter more than one additional group, place a space between the terms.
9. Click on the Accept button to return to the User Accounts tab.

Adding Users To Groups In KDE

To add a user to an existing group within KDE, do the following:

1. If KDE is not already started, start it by typing either "startx" or "init 5" at the command line.
2. Log in as root.
3. Click on the KDE menu icon.
4. Click on Utilities|Konsole to open a terminal.
5. Type "kuser &" and press Enter to open the KDE User Manager shown earlier in Figure 2.6.
6. Click on User|Edit to pull up the User Properties dialog box shown earlier in Figure 2.8.
7. Click on the Groups tab (see Figure 2.12 earlier in the chapter).
8. To add the user to a secondary group, first click on the group's name in the Groups Not Belonged To list box.
9. Now click on the arrow button pointing to the right to add the selected group to the Groups Belonged To list box.
10. If you want to add the user to any more groups, return to Step 7. Otherwise, continue with Step 11.
11. Click on the OK button to return to the KDE User Manager main screen.

Forwarding User Mail

This section is not as out of place as it may seem at first. Automatically forwarding mail from one account to another is something that can be set within the mail server, but this task must be accomplished by the system or mail administrator creating mail aliases. A faster method involves the creation of a special forwarding file.

Related solution:	Found on page:
Setting Up Mail Aliases By Hand	393

Forwarding User Mail On The Command Line

To set a user's account to forward mail elsewhere at the command line, do the following:

1. Log in either as root or as the user whose account you want to forward.
2. Type "vi .forward" to create the file ~/.forward, and open it for editing.

NOTE: *The tilde (~) refers to the home directory for the login session. For example, if you are logged in as root—the root home directory is /root in Red Hat, not in the home hierarchy——~/.forward would be /root/forward. However, if you are logged in as mary, ~/.forward would be /home/mary/.forward.*

3. Type "i" to enter Insert mode.
4. Type the email address the mail should be forwarded to.
5. Press the Esc key and then type ":wq" to close and save the file. All mail arriving at this account will be forwarded to the address you put in the .forward file.

Forwarding User Mail In GNOME

To set a user's account to forward mail elsewhere in GNOME, do the following:

1. If GNOME is not already started, start it by typing either "startx" or "init 5" at the command line.
2. Log in as root.
3. Click on the GNOME footprint icon to open the main menu.
4. Click on System|Linuxconf item. The Linuxconf tool opens.
5. Find the Users Accounts option in the list on the left side of the screen.
6. Click on Users Accounts|Normal|User Accounts to pull up the Users Accounts tab shown earlier in Figure 2.2.

7. Single-click on the item you want to change within the Account list. This action pulls up the User Information tab shown earlier in Figure 2.15.
8. Click on the Mail Settings tab, shown in Figure 2.22.
9. Type the email address you want to forward all mail to in the Redirect Messages To text box.
10. Click on the Accept button to return to the Users Accounts tab.

Forwarding User Mail In KDE

KDE does not provide a GUI-based method for forwarding a user's mail. You will need to follow the instructions in the section "Forwarding User Mail On The Command Line" for how to proceed.

Related solution:	Found on page:
Getting A Command Prompt	19

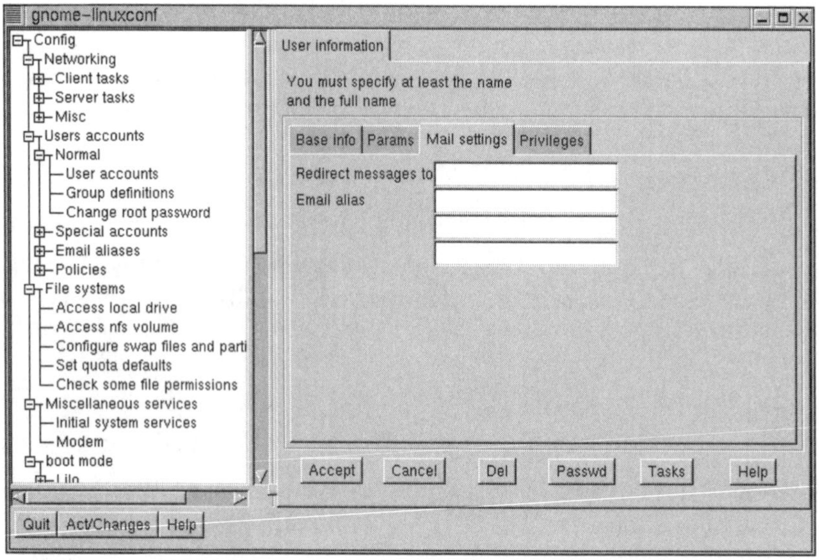

Figure 2.22 The GNOME Linuxconf User Information Mail Settings tab.

Chapter 3

File System Management

If you need an immediate solution to:	See page:
Creating Linux File Systems	76
Listing ext2 File System Settings	77
Changing Permissions	77
Changing Permissions Explicitly	77
Changing Permissions Relatively	77
Setting Special Bits	78
Setting The Umask	79
Changing Ownerships	79
Changing Groups	79
Checking For File System Errors	79
Backing Up And Restoring File System Structure	80
Backing Up File System Structure	80
Restoring File System Structure	80
Backing Up File Systems	81
Restoring File Systems From Backup	83
Moving File System Portions Onto Partitions	83
Adding And Removing Media To The File System	84
Adding Temporary Media	84
Removing Temporary Media	85
Adding Permanent Media	86
Removing Permanent Media	88
Seeing What Is Currently Mounted	89

(continued)

If you need an immediate solution to:	See page:
Navigating The File System In GNOME	89
Opening GNU Midnight Commander At The Command Line	89
Opening GNU Midnight Commander Within A GNOME Session	90
Navigating Directories In GNU Midnight Commander	90
Browsing And Opening Files In GNU Midnight Commander	90
Navigating The File System In KDE	94
Opening KFM At The Command Line	94
Browsing In KFM	95
Setting Up Disk Quotas	95
Preparing The Machine	95
Setting The Quotas	96
Shutting Down And Rebooting	97
Making A Custom Boot Disk	98
Making A Rescue Disk	98

In Depth

The file system is a combination of the partitions and directories that make up your Linux system, plus or minus any devices you add and remove along the way. It is important to keep the file system healthy and organized or you end up spending more time searching for files and programs than actually administering the system. When the file system does eventually fail—which will happen on a machine that is used over a long period of time—how you have managed this system and prepared for this problem determines how traumatic the experience is.

Hard Drive Overview

First, it is important to understand the overall structure and terminology used in this chapter, although you should already understand the basics of breaking down drives for installation and moving around a file system. As with other operating systems, the Linux kernel plus the files associated with it are stored on a hard drive, which is a physical unit. Within each hard drive are partitions, which function somewhat as virtual hard drives. Then, inside each partition, you build a file system.

Behind The Scenes

Linux uses the *second extended (ext2) file system*, which was created specially for use with this operating system. This file system is not relegated to hard drives, but is placed on any media that you use to store Linux data. Understanding how the file system is broken down is helpful when you are trying to figure out file system manipulation commands.

Data Storage Layout In ext2

Data within the ext2 file system is stored in a series of identically sized data blocks, as shown in Figure 3.1. These blocks are generally 1,024 bytes, though you can set them to be a different size while making a file system. Whether a file is 10 bytes or 1,020 bytes, it takes up one data block, which cannot be used to store anything else. Those files larger than 1,024 bytes, whether they are 1,025 or 2,026 bytes, take up two data blocks. Due to the nature of file systems with files continuously being added and deleted, these blocks may or may not be physically next to one another.

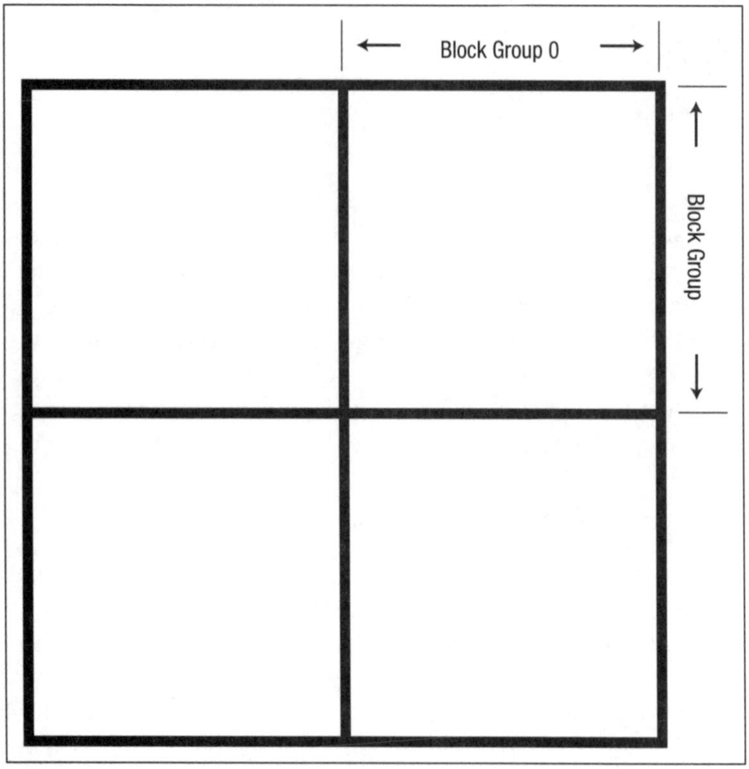

Figure 3.1 A device with an unmapped ext2 file system.

Individual data blocks are organized into block groups within the file system. File system integrity is a primary reason for using groups of blocks instead of just one large set of blocks. If all the data blocks exist in a mass, then damage in one critical area harms everything. Block groups not only break the data blocks into neighborhoods, they also provide for information resiliency and redundancy.

Mapping The ext2 File System

Linux must be able to sort out which data blocks contain which files or file segments. If data continues onto another block, there is also the issue of how many there are in total, and in what order the data blocks should be read. All this information is contained within a file system object called an *inode*, which stores the following facts about a file or object:

- The type of object defined by the inode. Object types are: devices (block or character), directories, pipes, files, or symbolic links.
- The item's permissions.
- The owner and group for the item.

- How large the item is, listed in bytes.
- When the item was created.
- When the item was last changed.
- Pointers to where the item is physically located on the device. If this item is a file that takes up more than one data block, then the location of all the blocks and the order in which they should be accessed is listed.

An inode is named with a number that is unique within the partition or device it resides on. There is no requirement that particular inodes must go into particular block groups. However, block groups always contain the same blocks, even if the information within them changes. Figure 3.2 shows an example of how an inode might relate to a file system.

For mapping purposes, only block group 0's information is important. This factor exists because every block group has a copy of every other block group's information.

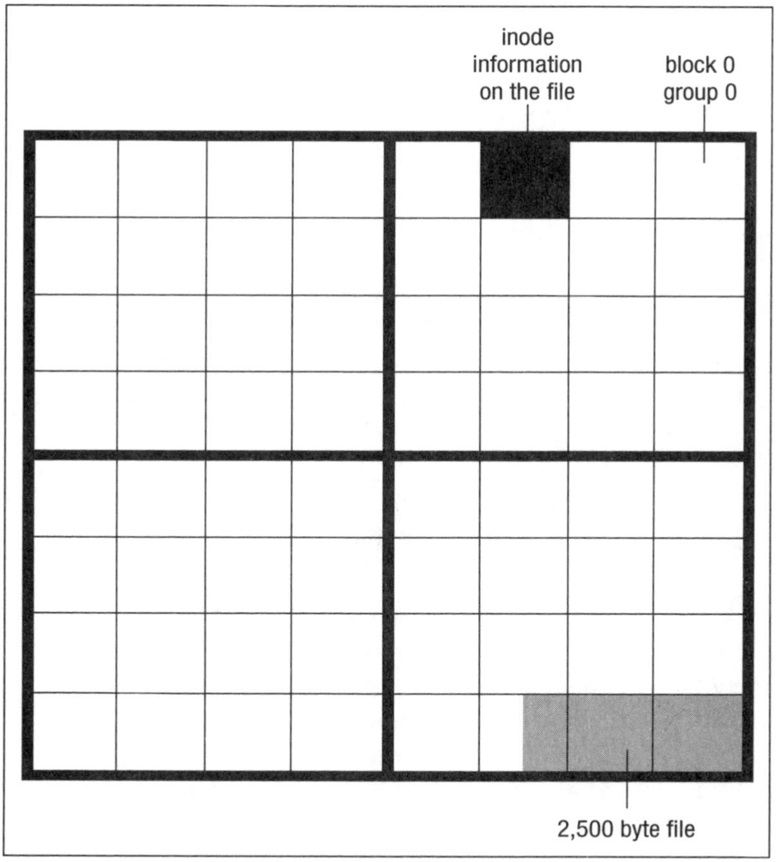

Figure 3.2 Using inodes to map data information to data within block groups.

As long as block group 0 is not damaged, all is fine. If it is damaged, the file system repair programs can glean the data from the other block groups.

The Superblock

A special block contains information about the overall file system, rather than its components. This segment is called the *superblock* and is available for you to look at with the **dumpe2fs** command. Some of the data contained within the superblock includes:

- How many total inodes and blocks are on the file system.
- How many blocks are not in use.
- How many inodes are not in use.
- How large an individual data block is. This value is typically 1,024 bytes.
- How many blocks make up a block group.
- How many times the file system has been mounted.
- How many times the file system can be mounted before a file system check is forced.
- Which block group this copy of the superblock is stored in.

Every block group contains a copy of the superblock for redundancy purposes. As with block group data, the copy of the superblock in block group 0 is the only one that is used in a healthy file system.

Making Sense Of The Linux File System

As a system administrator, it is important to understand the file system at a far deeper level than the average user needs to. Users only really need to know some of the basics, such as how to add to their own home directories, and often they do not entirely understand the intricacies of permissions. If a system administrator does not understand such things, the entire machine may either have compromised security or be hampered in its day-to-day functioning.

The File System Hierarchy Standard

There seems to be an unending march of new flavors of Unix. Not only do new Linux distributions come out on a regular basis, but there is also FreeBSD and a number of commercial Unix variants. Companies that want to put out software that works on Unix and its cousins have found it increasingly difficult to develop code that easily installs across Unix flavors and even across Linux variants.

The first response to this issue resulted in the Linux File System Standard (FSSTND), completed in 1994. This standard lays out the directories that should exist in a Linux file system and how they should be utilized. The goal was to make it possible for developers to write for Linux in general without having to worry about which distribution the software would go onto, and hence strengthen the Linux operating system as a market force. In some ways this goal was reached, as there is general agreement over where many types of files should go. In other ways, however, it was not. For example, almost all distributions have different ways of managing their boot time networking information. As long as the differences remain minimal and can be dealt with by reading environment variables or looking in known locations, then the spirit of the goal is still intact.

TIP: *For more on the FSSTND, see* ***www.pathname.com/fhs/1.2/fsstnd-toc.html****.*

A natural outgrowth of the FSSTND was to look at making it easier for developers to target their applications to more than one flavor of Unix at a time. From this desire grew the File System Hierarchy Standard (FHS). This standard aims to serve more than the Linux community. All of Unix is encompassed within it, as far as where particular types of data and binaries should reside on any Unix file system. Table 3.1 explains where you should find particular types of files according to the FHS.

Table 3.1 Unix file system layout according to the FHS.

Location	Contains
bin	Binaries that are necessary for the basic running of the system, as well as system rescue
boot	Unchanging files required to boot the machine before the kernel takes over
dev	Device driver files
etc	Configuration files, plus files that only apply to the host in question
home	User home directories
lib	Libraries, shared libraries, and kernel modules
mnt	Mount point for those file system devices you only mount temporarily
opt	Add-on packages that are otherwise not necessary for the system to function
root	The superuser's home directory
sbin	Binaries used for system administration purposes
tmp	Space for programs that need to create temporary files
usr	A read-only hierarchy containing files that can be shared among machines, except for the X subdirectories contained within
var	Data files that regularly change. This portion of the file system is important to back up regularly, because it sees a lot of use and is subject to wear and tear.

TIP: *For more on the FHS, see* ***www.pathname.com/fhs****.*

Demystifying Permissions

File permissions are of utmost importance for a system administrator. If they are incorrectly set, they can wreak havoc with your system. Even worse, a tendency to be lax with permissions on a system that is accessible from the Internet or has a lot of users is dangerous on the security front.

What Permissions Are

Permissions control who has read, write, and execution access on file system items (files, directories, and more). This control is broken down into different segments of the user population in order to offer a more refined approach to who can get to what.

How Permissions Are Broken Down

File system permissions are broken down into three sets of three. In order, these sets refer to the owner's permissions, the group's permissions, and everyone else's permissions. Each set of three is structured identically, though the contents may differ. The individual parts are bits, and so are either on or off. The first bit determines whether the person can read the file or look in the directory, the second identifies whether the person can write to the file or directory, and the third specifies whether the person can execute the item. When a bit is on, it is represented by its appropriate letter:

- r for read
- w for write
- x for executable

When it is off, it is a dash. So for a binary where the owner has full access, everyone in the group has read and execution access, and all other users have only read access, the permissions would be rwxr-xr--.

Permissions By Numbers

It can be cumbersome to have to type out all nine characters of a permission set when you want to make changes quickly. There is another way of writing permissions that involves calculating the bit value of each triad.

Once again, break down the permissions into three sets of three, and consider the sets individually. Having one of the permission bits on adds to the value of the set:

- Read permission adds four
- Write permission adds two
- Execution permission adds one

In this example, rwxr-xr--, consider each of the sets separately. The first set, rwx, is 4 + 2 + 1, or 7. The second set is 4 + 0 + 1, or 5. The third is 4 + 0 + 0, or 4. So the numeric permissions break down into 754.

The Mask Vs. The Umask

The *mask* of a file system item is the same as its permission. The two terms are equivalent. Another useful item is the *umask*. This term refers to the bits that are not turned on in the mask or permission sets.

The umask is an incredibly useful tool for a system administrator. Many users do not understand permissions, and so never alter them when creating files and directories within their home directory. When users do this with weak default permissions, the act can cause security problems. Therefore, changing the default creation mask by setting the default umask to a stronger setting can save many headaches.

The umask for the rwxr-xr-- is ----w--wx. This format is unwieldy because it gets hard to keep track of dashes, so the umask is more often discussed in numeric terms. In fact, the format is not entirely correct. Technically it is, but due to security reasons you cannot make an item executable by default. Therefore, there will never be an odd number in a umask setting. So, instead, the umask for the example is ----w--w-, or 022.

SUID And SGID

The terms SUID (set user ID) and SGID (set group ID) are tossed around a lot in Linux manuals without ever really discussing what they are used for. These terms are used when an executable must be able to run "as" a particular user or group member, rather than just a process belonging to that user or group. When you hear or read something telling you to "run the program as root," this is what the speaker is referring to.

The Sticky Bit

Another odd phrase you might come across is "turn on the sticky bit." This permission bit is an extra piece of protection for some directories. Its primary use is for directories or hierarchies where everyone needs to have access to the contents, but no one should be able to touch anyone else's files. (Some examples where this is useful are the /tmp or /var/spool/mail directories.) If the sticky bit is used, then no user can delete, move, or rename a file unless he or she is the file's owner in the file listing; he or she is the directory's owner; or he or she is the root or has used **su** to become the superuser from another login.

Creatively Using Partitions

As the system or LAN you administer becomes larger and more complex, there may come a time when you need to consider breaking down the file system. There are a number of reasons why this issue may arise. It is your own unique circumstances that determine where additional partitions would really help your system or LAN.

Many Shell Accounts

In networks where there are a large number of accounts, it can be useful to break down the home portion of the file system further. For example, at an ISP you might have a partition mounted as /home/users where all paid user shell accounts are added, and another partition mounted as /home/staff where all staff member shell accounts are added. Keeping these items on separate partitions not only allows you to refine access permissions to these areas, but also lets you easily use separate quotas for users and administrative staff.

Shared Departmental Data

In environments where there is a lot of work done in teams, it is useful to create individual areas where each team can easily access its collective data without making it open to the general public. One way to accomplish this task is to give each department its own partition for shared data. This partition would be accessible by all department members, a feature that can be implemented using secondary groups.

Lots Of Small Files

A finite number of inodes is available for each partition. Perhaps you have many small files, such as data or temporary files from a software package. For example, let's say that one day you look at the partition's remaining inodes and find that you have very few left, and yet you have a lot of free space. You may need to give this batch of small files its own partition so it cannot hamper the rest of the file system's workings.

NOTE: *Although many people used to the MS-DOS or Windows world might consider defragmenting partitions under such circumstances, there are no defragmenting tools for Linux. There are no such tools because disk fragmentation does not cause appreciable problems in the ext2 file system.*

Protecting Your Data

It happens to everyone eventually. You go to boot the computer or access a file and discover that the file system is damaged. Sometimes you get lucky and it's only the /tmp directory that is bad. At other times, vital areas are corrupted. The deciding factor in whether this problem is a minor annoyance or a catastrophe is whether you have recent and reliable data backups.

Introduction To Backup Schemes

There are a variety of backup schemes you can use. A backup scheme is a reference to your backup approach. There are a number of issues that affect how you determine what your backup scheme will ultimately be.

Portion Of File System

Take a look at how easy each portion of the file system is to re-create. Be careful how you determine whether something is simple or not—what may seem simple now may not seem so easy five months later when you need to fix things after a crash.

It is possible to back up the entire file system if you have media large enough to hold it, or if you can span it among multiple media. However, as you will learn in the two sections on incremental backups in this chapter's Immediate Solutions section, it is not necessary to back up the entire file system every time. Items that administrators commonly back up most frequently are:

- The /home hierarchy
- Hierarchies that contain file server data, such as FTP or Web server file storage areas
- Any special directories containing program data
- Log files with data you cannot afford to lose, such as Web access data
- The /etc hierarchy, if you have configured many services lately

Frequency

The frequency with which you make backups depends on your particular situation. You do not need to back up all items at the same frequency. Instead, you can have a separate backup set up for each important portion of the file system.

The main indicator of how often you need to back up a file system segment is how often the data changes, and how much of a problem it would be to lose data that is not yet backed up if a crash happens. If a month will not make much of a difference due to part of the hierarchy being fairly static, and the information there is not difficult to re-create, then that portion would not need to be backed up often. However, for data that can change at any moment and frequently—such as home directories and mail spools—a daily backup is highly recommended.

Redundancy

If you keep one set of backup media and write over the media each time you back up, you miss out on the issue of redundancy. Perhaps an intruder crept in and you were unaware of him or her for a week. Those daily backups may contain corrupted files, and you have no way of checking them against anything older. This is only one reason to consider keeping redundant backups around. Other problems can occur because of program errors, user errors, or other situations that do not require malicious intent.

Incremental Backup Scheme

Often, the goal of a backup is to be able to replace the entire system with a trusted copy if necessary. This goal brings up the issue of how much of the system to back up at a time. Technically speaking, it would be good to do a nightly full backup. Unfortunately, this task is not realistic.

Instead of doing a full backup every 24 hours, many people use a scheme of incremental backups. The aim of this scheme is to keep a copy of the file system as up to date as possible without doing daily full backups.

One incremental plan some might adopt is as follows:

1. Do daily backups together on a single storage media. A specialized shell script (see Chapter 20 for details on shell scripting) combined with automated reminders to be sure the media is in place and the script itself automated to run in early morning hours might back up:
   - Home directories
   - Web sites
   - Mail spool
   - Log files
2. Once a week back up items that change regularly, but not daily. Again you would use a separate storage media for this purpose, perhaps labeled "weekly" to distinguish it from the others. This backup would be larger, taking more time than a daily backup. On it you might have:
   - The entire daily backup scheme
   - The /etc hierarchy
   - The /opt hierarchy, if you install application packages there
   - The /usr/src hierarchy, if you work with source code regularly
3. Once a month, or once every two weeks, depending on how often your overall system changes, you could do a full file system backup. Be sure to label this media so you do not overwrite it with one of the more frequent backups.

NOTE: *This last step actually provides a very small amount of redundancy.*

Incremental Backup With Redundancy

If you have the time and inclination, it is wise to build some form of redundancy into your backup scheme. As discussed in the section "Introduction To Backup Schemes," there are many reasons to have redundant backups—everything from not catching an error that perpetuates for several days or weeks to an intruder who makes fundamental changes that have to be reversed.

When you begin adding redundancy to a backup scheme, the first thing you might notice is that many more backup media are required. This fact occurs because you will be keeping more copies of previous backups instead of overwriting the backups each time.

Another difference is in the form of reminders. A redundant backup scheme, by its very nature, is more complex to keep track of. It is important to put together a reminder setup, so that you remember which tapes to put in on which days.

One method you might use for implementing an incremental, redundant backup scheme is called the Tower of Hanoi:

- *Day 1*—Use a new reusable media to make a backup. Mark it "1".
- *Day 2*—Use a new reusable media to make a backup. Mark it "2".
- *Day 3*—Use the "1" media to make your backup.
- *Day 4*—Use a new reusable media to make a backup. Mark it "3".
- *Day 5*—Use the "1" media to make your backup.
- *Day 6*—Use the "2" media to make your backup.
- *Day 7*—Use the "1" media to make your backup.
- *Day 8*—Use a new reusable media to make a backup. Mark it "4".
- *Day 9*—Use the "1" media to make your backup.
- *Day 10*—Use the "2" media to make your backup.
- *Day 11*—Use the "1" media to make your backup.
- *Day 12*—Use the "3" media to make your backup.
- *Day 13*—Use the "1" media to make your backup.
- *Day 14*—Use the "2" media to make your backup.
- *Day 15*—Use the "1" media to make your backup.
- *Day 16*—Use a new reusable media to make a backup. Mark it "5".
- *Day 17*—Return to Day 1.

You are probably wondering where the incremental component comes into the picture. None of the backup media (1 through 5) needs to be a full file system backup. When you write the cron jobs and shell scripts to help with this scheme, choose which media number reflects which parts of the file system. Also, be sure to occasionally pull a media that contains a full file system out of the loop and replace it with another, labeling it with the date it was made. This adds archiving capabilities.

Backup Hardware

The backup media you have available to you tends to determine how much data you back up at once. If the media does not hold a lot of information or is slow, then you might tend to keep backups short and sweet. However, if the media is fast, or it holds a lot of data, then you will probably be freer with how much information you choose to put on it.

High-Density 3.5 Inch Floppy Disks

Because modern Linux systems can easily approach 800MB or larger, few people would want to do a full system backup on high-density floppy disks with their storage capacity of 1.44MB. However, floppies are still good for smaller backups, even if these cover more than one disk. The **tar** utility can span the backup across floppies (see Chapter 4 for more information on using **tar**).

LS-120 Floppies

Many people have begun to migrate to LS-120 floppies. Part of the reason is that the drive is backward-compatible—it reads and writes high-density disks as well as LS-120s. The primary reason, though, is that an LS-120 floppy can hold 120MB of data. At this storage capacity you still need to use multiple disks for a full backup, but the LS-120 is quite handy for partial backups.

Zip Disks

Another popular item used for data storage and backups is the Zip disk. This diskette format requires its own hardware and is not compatible with others, and it comes in both 100MB and 250MB storage ranges. Be sure to get a Zip drive that supports 250MB storage if you have a large volume of data you need to back up.

CD Writers

At one point, the CD writer was too expensive for any but large businesses. Today, the price has come down dramatically. The question you have to ask yourself, however, is whether you want to use a media that cannot be reused. A single CD can hold 650MB of information. This option is perfect for data you want to keep in perpetuity, for example, documents or graphics. As a valid backup option, however, it needs to be paired with some form of rewriteable media unless you have a limitless source of writeable CDs—and limitless storage space.

DVD Writers

DVD writers are fairly new on the market as data storage solutions go, but they are following the same trend that the CD writers did. Once again, a standard writeable DVD can only be written to once. The DVD writer is another option that is good for data you want to keep permanently, or at least for a significantly long time. A single DVD can hold up to around 17GB of data; often, an entire Linux file system can be backed up in that amount of space. This media could be a good choice for full file system backups that you want to keep for redundancy's sake.

CD And DVD Rewriters

There is another class of writeable CD and DVD drives and media called *rewriteable*. These are special CDs and DVDs that can be written to more than once, and they require drives that can properly manipulate them. The rewriteable drives and media are more expensive than the writeable versions, but many feel the reusability makes up for the expense. This factor is especially relevant while discussing data backups, as these CDs and DVDs are useful for temporary storage.

A rewriteable CD or DVD holds the same amount of data as the writeable version. However, rewriteable drives and media both cost significantly more than their single-write counterparts.

Tapes

An amazingly wide range of tape backup solutions is available. Which option you choose depends primarily on how much data you have to back up and how large your budget is to procure the hardware, and perhaps the software, necessary to accomplish the task. The larger your budget, the faster the unit and the larger its storage capacity, up to 40GB or more.

Removable Rack Hard Drives

One backup option gaining notoriety is the removable rack hard drive. This solution requires that you purchase a docking bay, which is placed within the hard drive bay in the computer. Along with the docking bay, you also need to get a number of removable chassis, which hold the hard drives. All that is necessary to swap drives, then, is to remove one chassis and pop in another. Using this solution is an excellent way to make a full backup of a system that can easily be popped in to replace a failed file system.

TIP: *It is highly recommended to get more than one chassis from the beginning. This action prevents you from having to swap hard drives out of the units, which can cause data corruptions if the drive gets bumped around a lot, and it also avoids the problem of needing new chassis later and not being able to get ones that exactly fit the docking bay.*

RAID Backup

RAID (Redundant Array of Inexpensive Disks, or sometimes Independent for the "I") is a backup and redundancy solution used by many ISPs and businesses to protect against data loss and downtime. Both hardware and software versions are available with the Linux operating system, though the implementation sometimes requires recompiling the kernel (see Chapter 5 for more information on the kernel).

There are six initial types of RAID setups, as well as others currently in use. Table 3.2 outlines the initial types and their defining features.

NOTE: *RAID solutions can also be implemented without having multiple drives by utilizing software RAID.*

Table 3.2 RAID types and features.

Raid Level	Alias	Description And Discussion
RAID 0	None	A series of physical drives that are treated as one large drive. Data is spread across all drives. Not for backup use. No redundancy or error protection is built in.
RAID 1	Disk mirroring	Two disk drives that contain identical data, but the system only sees them as one drive. If the first mirrored drive crashes, the second one takes over. However, you are not protected from data corruption with this model without other backup policies in place.
RAID 2	None	A series of physical drives that are treated as one large drive. Data is spread across all drives, which includes error correction information in special data segments. Obsolete because modern drives automatically save the same correction information.
RAID 3	None	A series of physical drives that are treated as one large drive. One of these drives exclusively stores parity information. Excellent choice for error recovery concerns. However, due to the nature of RAID 3, it is not a good choice for systems with many users.
RAID 4	None	A series of physical drives that are treated as one large drive. One of these drives exclusively stores parity information. Slightly different from RAID 3 in that a piece of data is more likely to be all on one drive. Excellent choice for error recovery on multiuser systems.
RAID 5	None	A series of physical drives that are treated as one large drive. Parity information is spread across each drive. Excellent choice for error recovery on multiuser systems. Has faster write access than RAID 4.

Limiting User Storage Space

When you have a lot of users, the problem of disk space inevitably crops up. Some of this issue can be dealt with by placing the /home hierarchy (or /home/users) on its own partition. However, doing this does not prevent specific users from overrunning the available space with stored files. The quota tool allows you to manage specifically how much access users have to disk space.

Quota Creation Process

There are some things you need to do to set up Linux and the file system before you can enable quotas. This process is fairly quick; it is made easier by the fact that modern Linux kernels incorporate quota support by default, which was not always the case. Preparing to use quotas mostly involves telling the file system where to utilize quotas and what types of quotas to look for. Once you complete this process, you need to create the quotas themselves. See the section "Setting Up Disk Quotas" in the Immediate Solutions section for more details on both tasks.

Quota Options

When you are creating a quota for a user or group, there are three options to keep in mind:

- *Soft limit*—Defines how much drive space users can take up. Users surpassing this limit receive warnings that they are over their quota.
- *Hard limit*—Specifies a file system full error when users try to put a file in their home directory that goes over this value.
- *Grace period*—Defines how long users have to bring their file system usage below the soft quota mark. An account that remains over the soft quota past the grace period is automatically disabled. Used with soft limits.

Soft and hard limits work well together. A good combination would be to create a soft limit to warn a user that he or she should start clearing out file space, and then a hard limit that the user cannot go over in order to protect your file system.

Immediate Solutions

Creating Linux File Systems

In some operating systems, you "format" a device to prepare it to hold files. In Linux, and Unix in general, you "make a file system." To make a file system, do the following:

1. Choose what device you want to make the file system on.
2. Determine the distinction for that device. The third partition on the first IDE drive would be /dev/hda3, or perhaps you want to use the floppy drive, which is /dev/fd0.
3. Choose what file system options you want to use. If you are just formatting a floppy disk, you probably want the defaults. However, some people have preferences when it comes to formatting partitions. A list of commonly used options is shown in Table 3.3.

Table 3.3 Common mke2fs file system creation options.

Flag	Purpose	Value
-b	Specifies how large the blocks that make up the file system should be.	Size of blocks in bytes
-c	Checks each block individually to make sure it is not damaged.	None
-i	Specifies how many bytes are managed by each inode. Determines the overall count of inodes on the file system.	Number of bytes managed
-N	Specifies how many inodes should exist on the file system.	Number of inodes
-m	Reserves a certain portion of the file system for the superuser.	Percent of file system to reserve; default is 5 percent
-q	Runs without sending output to STDIN (Standard Input).	None
-v	Produces verbose output.	None
-F	Runs even if the device is not a block special device, or if it is mounted or otherwise in use.	None

(continued)

*Table 3.3 Common **mke2fs** file system creation options* **(continued).**

Flag	Purpose	Value
-L	Assigns a name to the file system.	Label for file system
-R	Sets the number of blocks contained within the RAID stripes being created. (Used only for RAID file systems.)	Number of blocks
-S	Writes superblock and group information, does not write over inodes. A good option for attempted file system recovery.	None

4. Make sure the device is within the machine, whether it means the floppy is in the drive or the new hard drive is installed.
5. Build the command. In general, it looks like **mke2fs*flags device***. An example might be **mke2fs -v /dev/fd0**.

Listing ext2 File System Settings

To take a look at what settings you are currently using with your ext2 file system, use the **dumpe2fs** command in the format **dumpe2fs *device***. This command can give a large amount of information, so often it is good to pipe it through the **more** command, such as **dumpe2fs /dev/hda1|more**.

Changing Permissions

To change the permissions for a file system item, use **chmod *value item***. How to construct the value is somewhat of a complex process. There are two different methods available for changing permissions: explicit and relative.

Changing Permissions Explicitly

You can change permissions explicitly using either their numeric or direct representations. See the section "Demystifying Permissions" in the In Depth section for an explanation on how both forms of permissions work, keeping in mind that the direct version is that which you see in a file listing. An example of setting new numeric permissions is **chmod 644*file***.

Changing Permissions Relatively

Another method available for changing permissions with **chmod** is by breaking them down into which segment you want to change and what change you want to make. Using the relative method involves pulling together three different sets of operators, as outlined in Tables 3.4, 3.5, and 3.6.

When combining the three components, they go in the order "triad action result." So, for example, to allow a file's owner to execute a file you would use **chmod u+x *file***. Likewise, to remove write permission from both the group and outside users, you would use **chmod go-w *file***.

Setting Special Bits

There is also a special way to SUID, SGID, and set the sticky bit. You can accomplish this through either the explicit or relative method:

- If you are setting permissions explicitly, put the designation for the special bit in the beginning, so there are four instead of three numbers. Table 3.7 outlines which number designates which special bit. An example of this process is using **chmod 1644 *file*** to set permissions to trw-r--r--.
- If you are setting permissions relatively, there are special characters that refer to setting IDs and the sticky bit. These characters are outlined in Table 3.7. An example of this process is using **chmod g+s *file*** to add the SGID bit.

Table 3.4 The chmod command's triad specification characters.

Character	Meaning
u	The operation is for the user triad.
g	The operation is for the group triad.
o	The operation is for the other users triad.
a	The operation is for all three triads.

Table 3.5 The chmod command's action specification characters.

Character	Meaning
+	Add the permission specified to the specified triad.
-	Remove the permission specified to the specified triad.
=	Change the triad specified to exactly what permission is given.

Table 3.6 The chmod command's result characters.

Character	Meaning
r	The read permission.
w	The write permission.
x	The executable permission.

Table 3.7 Characters used to set special bits.

Type	Number	Character
Sticky	1	t
SGID	2	g+s
SUID	4	u+s

Setting The Umask

To set a new umask for a file system item, you would use the format **umask *value item***. For example, **umask 026 file**.

Changing Ownerships

To change the user who owns an item in the file system, use **chown *user item***. The ***user*** portion of the command can be either the login name or the UID.

TIP: *You can change the owner and group at the same time by typing "chown user.group item".*

Changing Groups

To change the group that owns an item in the file system, use **chgrp *group item***. The ***group*** portion of the command can either be the group name or the GID.

TIP: *You can also use the **chown** command to change the group assignment.*

Checking For File System Errors

To check for errors on the file system, use the **fsck** command in the format **fsck *flags path***. The available flags are shown in Table 3.8.

This command is commonly used in the format **fsck -r /**, which begins at the root directory and moves through the file system. If you want to ensure that all Linux partitions defined in /etc/fstab have been checked, you would use **fsck -t ext2 -A**.

Table 3.8 Popular flags used with the fsck command.

Flag	Purpose
-r	Checks with the person running the command before making repairs, instead of making them automatically.
-t	Signals that the person running the command will specify the only file system type to check.
-A	Checks every file system defined in /etc/fstab. Best used in conjunction with **-t** to ensure that only ext2 file systems are checked.
-V	Runs in verbose mode.

Backing Up And Restoring File System Structure

Sometimes it is worthwhile to back up the structure of your file system separate from the file system itself. This information is immensely useful to have if you accidentally alter permissions or ownerships in important sections of the file system, or a misguided program does it for you. Trying to backtrack and fix things without a roadmap is not pleasant.

Backing Up File System Structure

Make a backup of the file system structure in the following manner:

1. Because you want to include the entire file system, type "cd /" to go to the root of your file system.
2. Type "ls -lR > listing" to save the file system structure to the file "listing".
3. If desirable, compress the listing by typing "gzip listing", which gives you a file called listing.gz.

TIP: *This method is also how the large Linux FTP sites are able to offer a file containing the listing of their directories. They just begin the command from the top of the FTP file system, not from the machine's file system.*

Related solutions:	Found on page:
Creating **gzip**ed Files	108
Creating Z **compress**ed Files	108
Opening Or Creating Tarballs	110

Restoring File System Structure

Restoring the structure of your file system after a "glitch" is not as easy as just typing a single command. However, there is a straightforward process to follow:

1. Locate the file containing your file system listing, for example, /listing.gz.

2. Unzip the file if necessary by typing "gunzip listing.gz", which produces the file /listing.
3. There are a number of ways to approach this issue from here; I will illustrate one of them. Type "less listing" to display the beginning of the file. The reason I chose the **less** program instead of **more** is that **less** highlights search terms when they are found.
4. Choose a logical starting point within the file system. (You should know where the glitch hit. If not, you still must have a reason for starting this process.)
5. Determine a distinctive chunk of text to search for, so that you do not have to page through the listing.
6. Type "/*text*", where *text* is the search term, and press Enter.
7. If the term does not match what you were looking for, type a slash (/) and press Enter once again. Continue this until you find the correct entry.
8. In another terminal or terminal window, type "ls -l *entry*" to list the full information for the item you are trying to fix.
9. Compare the information between the listing file and the current entry listing. Use the **chmod**, **chown**, and **chgrp** commands, respectively, to fix any problems.
10. Return to Step 4 for the next item you need to fix.

NOTE: *How useful the backup file system listing is depends on how recent it is. Be sure to back up often.*

Related solutions:	Found on page:
Creating **gzip**ed Files	108
Creating Z **compress**ed Files	108
Opening Or Creating Tarballs	110

Backing Up File Systems

One of the most important things any system administrator can do is set up some form of backup routine. Only if there are absolutely no files on a machine that you might want to keep should you ignore this issue. Although the specifics differ here and there, there is a general process to follow when creating a backup routine:

1. Determine what type of information you want to back up, and create a backup scheme, as discussed in "Protecting Your Data" in the In Depth section.

2. Determine which media you want to use to store the particular backup segment in question, with the help of "Backup Hardware" in the In Depth section.
3. Which media you choose determines what software you need in order to create the backups. A map of which media requires which software is given in Table 3.9.
4. Load the kernel module or install the driver that you need for the media.
5. Install the software if necessary.
6. If you are using special software, read the documentation and learn how to use it. Otherwise, read the **tar** man page and see Chapter 4 for various tips on how to use the **tar** package.
7. Build your archive onto the media.
8. Verify that the archive worked. You know a backup worked if you are able to pull any files back off of the media. See the section "Restoring File Systems From Backup" for how to accomplish this task.

Table 3.9 Drivers and outside software necessary for various backup media.

Media	Driver	Software
CD writer or CD rewriter	cdrecord or cdrdao	There are a number of programs out there that you can use to write the data to the CD. See the CD writer HOWTO at **www.linuxdoc.org/HOWTO/CD-Writing-HOWTO-1.html** for more information.
DVD writer or DVD rewriter	Universal Disk Format (UDF) file system driver, hardware driver	Program that can write to both ISO9660 and UDF. This technology is not quite ready for production use as yet. Watch your favorite Linux news sites for more information.
Floppy disk	No special drivers	No special software is necessary.
LS-120	pf driver	No special software is necessary.
RAID	Kernel patch	Raidtools software.
Removable rack hard drive	No special drivers, but special equipment needed to swap things out	No special software is necessary.
Tape drive	ftape driver, which is already installed in most distributions	No special software is necessary, but sometimes it is worthwhile to have.
Zip disk	ppa driver (kernel module)	No special software is necessary.

9. Clearly label the backup media.
10. Store the backup media in a safe place.

Related solution:	Found on page:
Creating **tar** Files	109

Restoring File Systems From Backup

Restoring a file system, or part of a file system, is a process that depends somewhat on what software you are using. What follows is the general process for restoring files from backup:

1. Locate the media containing the data you need to restore.
2. Mount the media onto the file system.
3. Determine how much of the information on the media you want to restore.
4. Determine how much of the information your software (**tar** or another package) forces you to restore. You may not be able to work one file or directory at a time.
5. Use the **tar** application, as discussed in Chapter 4, or the software package you used to create the backup in order to extract the needed files.
6. Test the file system to ensure that the restoration succeeded.
7. Unmount the media.
8. Return the media to proper storage.

Related solution:	Found on page:
Opening **tar** Files	110

Moving File System Portions Onto Partitions

System needs tend to change over time. You may find after a while that you want to move a file system hierarchy onto its own partition instead of leaving it on root or on another partition. To accomplish this task, do the following:

1. Install the new hard drive if necessary.
2. Create the new partition using a tool such as **fdisk**.
3. Rename the current version of the hierarchy using the **mv** command. For example, **mv /home /old-home**.

4. Create a new directory with the original name using the **mkdir** command. For example, **mkdir /home**.
5. Mount the partition onto the now empty mount point, which is the new directory you just made.
6. Use the **cd** command to change into the moved version of the hierarchy. For example, **cd /old-home**.
7. Use the **cp** tool in the form **cp -rp . *newdir*** to recursively copy the files—along with their owner, group, permission, and timestamp settings—from the current location to the new partition. For example, **cp -rp . /home**.
8. Use the **cd** command to change to the new partition. Take a few moments to ensure that everything copied over properly. Try running programs and editing files and generally putting the partition through its paces.
9. Once you're sure that the transfer went well, delete the old version with the **rm** command in the format **rm -r *olddir***. For example, **rm -r /old-home**.

WARNING!* *Double-, triple-, and quadruple-check that you have typed this command properly before you press Enter. The last thing anyone needs is to delete the wrong portion of the file system!

10. See the section "Adding Permanent Media" on how to add this partition to /etc/fstab.

Adding And Removing Media To The File System

There are two different approaches to adding and removing media, depending on its purpose. Temporary media, such as floppy disks and CD-ROMs, are often added and removed in short periods of time. However, if you are adding new partitions that you want to permanently make part of the file system, then you will use a different approach.

Adding Temporary Media

To add media temporarily to the file system, do the following:

1. Physically add the media to the file system. This act may involve putting a floppy disk in a drive, a Zip disk in a Zip drive, or a CD-ROM in the CD-ROM bay.
2. Determine which device driver pertains to the media. Table 3.10 lays out the paths for commonly used drivers.
3. Determine which file system is used on this device. Table 3.11 lays out the file system formats commonly used with temporary media in Linux.

Table 3.10 File system temporary media device drivers.

Device	Driver
First floppy disk	/dev/fd0
Second floppy disk	/dev/fd1
CD-ROM	/dev/cdrom

Table 3.11 File system formats on temporary media.

Format	Used For	Devices Found On
ext2	Linux	Floppy disks, hard disks, Zip disks, tapes
iso9660	Specialized for CD-ROM	CD-ROMs
msdos	MS-DOS, Windows 3.x, Windows 9x, Windows 2000	Floppy disks, hard disks, Zip disks, tapes; if used with Windows 9x or 2000, typically only on floppies
vfat	Windows 95, Windows 98, Windows 2000	Floppy disks, hard disks, Zip disks, tapes

4. Determine where you want to mount this media. Typically, it is added to the file system within the /mnt hierarchy. Red Hat already has /mnt/floppy and /mnt/cdrom created by default. If you want to put the item somewhere else, you need to make sure its mount point already exists.
5. Build the statement in the following format: **mount -t*fstype device mountpoint***. For example, to mount a floppy formatted with MS-DOS onto /mnt/floppy, you would type "mount -t msdos /dev/fd0 /mnt/floppy". However, if you want to add a device that is in ext2 format, you can leave out the **-t*fstype*** component.

TIP: *Red Hat and some other distributions provide a further shortcut. To mount a CD-ROM, simply type "mount /mnt/cdrom" and the rest is taken care of automatically. The same goes for a Linux-formatted floppy disk. However, a disk formatted with MS-DOS must be mounted using the full command listed in the example unless you create your own shortcut. See the section "Adding Permanent Media" for information on how to do this.*

Removing Temporary Media

There is much less thought necessary to remove temporary media from the file system, compared to what you have to figure out when you add them. To accomplish this task, do the following:

1. Determine either the mount point or the device driver for the item you wish to remove.

***WARNING!* It is important not to physically remove any temporary media from your PC until after the media has been properly unmounted. Not all information is written to disk right away—some is held in memory until the next time it is necessary to write to it. Part of the process of unmounting a device is making sure those last pieces of information are included.**

2. Type "umount *mountpoint*" or "umount *device*". For example, **umount /dev/fd0** and **umount /mnt/floppy** both unmount a disk from the first floppy drive.
3. Physically remove the media.

Adding Permanent Media

On a day-to-day basis you likely will not be pulling hard drives in and out of a machine—unless you use removable rack drives—but there are times when you may need to add one. When this occurs, do the following:

1. Make a note of what kind of device this is. For example, is it a SCSI or IDE hard drive?
2. Physically add the media to the system.
3. Make a note of where the media is in the system. Is it the third SCSI drive, for example, or is it the second IDE drive?
4. Log in as root.
5. Type "cp /etc/fstab /etc/fstab.backup" to create a backup of the master file system controller.
6. Type "vi /etc/fstab" to open the master file system controller for editing.
7. Type "G" to go to the end of the file.
8. Type "o" to open a new line at the end.
9. A line in /etc/fstab is presented in the following manner:

   ```
   device  mountpoint  type  options  dump  order
   ```

   Determine which device the new portion of the file system resides on. For example, if you just added a new drive to the SCSI chain and it's the third hard drive on the chain, then it is /dev/sdc. However, that is not specific enough. Once you have partitioned and made a file system on the device, you will know which partition you want to mount. For example, to mount the second partition on the third SCSI drive, the device would be /dev/sdc2.
10. The mount point for a permanent segment of the file system does not tend to be within the /mnt hierarchy. Instead, the device fits seamlessly into the file system. For example, if you created a /boot partition during the installation process, that partition looks like a directory to anyone who does a file

system listing. The mount point for a permanently mounted item still has to exist on the root file system before you will be able to mount the device. For example, the /boot directory had to exist on the root file system before the /boot partition could be inserted at that location.

11. Determine the type of file system you are mounting. Usually, this file system type is ext2 for a permanently mounted device. The options listed in Table 3.11 earlier in the chapter are all available to you, and more.

TIP: *Type "man mount" for a full listing of file system types and mount options.*

12. Choose the options you want the file system segment to be mounted with. Table 3.12 outlines a number of commonly used options. It is often a good idea to consider the "defaults" choice first. If you want to use more than one option, separate them with a comma and no spaces.

Table 3.12 Mount options often used in /etc/fstab.

Option	Purpose
async	Does all input and output to this segment of the file system independently of each another.
auto	Mounts this portion of the file system automatically at boot time.
defaults	Includes the following options: async, auto, dev, exec, nouser, rw, and suid.
dev	Utilizes both character and block special devices on this portion of the file system.
exec	Contains all the binaries on this portion of the file system to be executed.
noauto	Does not allow this portion of the file system to be mounted automatically.
nodev	Ignores both character and block special devices on this part of the file system.
noexec	Does not allow the binaries on this part of the file system to be executed.
nosuid	Does not accept SUID or SGID bits.
nouser	Excludes nonroot users from mounting this portion of the file system.
ro	Mounts the file system as a read-only device.
rw	Mounts the file system as a read-write device.
suid	Accepts SUID and SGID bits.
sync	Does all input and output to this segment of the file system as an orderly stream of data.
user	Allows nonroot users to mount the device onto the file system. Useful for floppy and CD-ROM devices if you want to allow users access to them. Includes the following options: nodev, noexec, and nosuid.

13. The *dump* item can only be three different things: a blank entry, a zero (0), or a one (1). If you leave the last two fields (*dump* and *order*) empty, the /etc/fstab entry is considered not to be a permanent part of the file system, so in this case you must fill in these last two. If you want to ensure that the **dump** utility backs up this segment of the file system, then enter a 1. If not, enter a 0. If you do not intend to use the **dump** utility, you can use either a 0 or 1.
14. The last entry in an /etc/fstab file system definition is the order the item should be mounted at boot time. The root file system is always mounted first, and so has a 1 beside it. After this, number the choices sequentially in the order you want them mounted. Anything with a 0 beside it denotes a device that is not automatically mounted. You can also leave this field blank if the device is not automatically mounted.
15. Fill in the entire /etc/fstab entry. For example, if you want to add the second SCSI drive in the chain's first and only partition to the file system as /Projects, with the default settings for a permanent item and **dump** turned on and also ensure that it is the third device mounted at boot time, enter the line:

```
/dev/sdb1  /Projects  ext2  defaults  1  3
```

16. Press the Esc key, then type "ZZ" to exit and save the file.

NOTE: *To actually test the new /etc/fstab file, you will have to reboot the machine. See the section "Shutting Down And Rebooting" later in the chapter for more information.*

Removing Permanent Media

When you need to remove a hard drive or other permanent media from your system, do the following:

1. Log in as root.
2. Type "vi /etc/fstab" to open the file system controller.
3. Use the arrow keys to move to the line that defines the media's device, mount point, and the rest.

TIP: *The section "Adding Permanent Media" covers how to read /etc/fstab and create an entry.*

4. Type "dd" to delete the entire line.
5. Type "ZZ" to save and exit the file.

TIP: *Double-check that you have a boot disk for the machine, as well as a rescue disk, just in case something goes wrong when you are trying to bring it back up. See the sections "Making A Custom Boot Disk" and "Making A Rescue Disk" later in this chapter.*

---

6. Shut down the machine. See the section "Shutting Down And Rebooting" later in this chapter for assistance.
7. Remove the media from the machine.
8. Turn on the machine and boot it.

Seeing What Is Currently Mounted

Use the **df** command with no flags to get a list of what devices are mounted—temporarily or permanently—onto the file system. This is also a good method of quickly seeing how much of these file systems are already in use and how much room there is left.

Navigating The File System In GNOME

GNU Midnight Commander is a fully functional desktop navigation tool provided with the GNU Network Object Model Environment (GNOME) desktop environment. Because there are many different things you can do with this tool, its use is broken down into categories.

Opening GNU Midnight Commander At The Command Line

To open the GNU Midnight Commander when you are working in command line mode, do the following:

1. Enter the GUI by typing either "startx" from any account or "init 5" from root.
2. Log into GNOME with the account you want to navigate within.

NOTE: *If your session is set to start K Desktop Environment (KDE) and not GNOME, then you will need to either go to the KDE navigation section or change which desktop environment you are using.*

---

3. Close the Help browser, but leave the GNU Midnight Commander open. An example of what this window might look like is shown in Figure 3.3.

Related solution:	Found on page:
Changing Desktop Environments	167

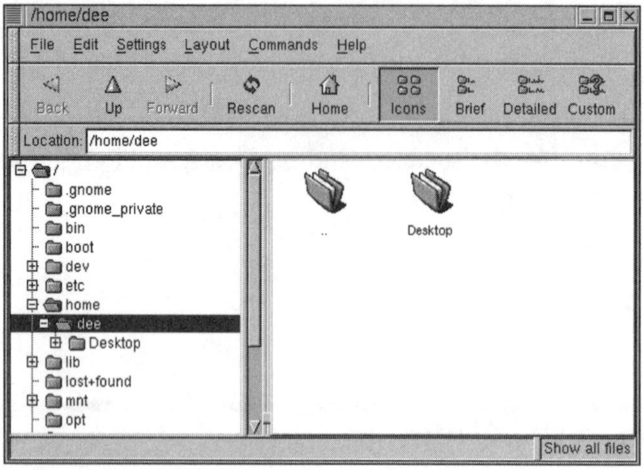

Figure 3.3 The GNU Midnight Commander for the "dee" user account.

Opening GNU Midnight Commander Within A GNOME Session

If you are already in the GNOME GUI, do the following to open GNU Midnight Commander:

1. Click on the footprint icon to open the GNOME menu.
2. Click on the File Manager menu option. The GNU Midnight Commander opens as shown in Figure 3.3.

Navigating Directories In GNU Midnight Commander

GNU Midnight Commander functions much as other file managers you might be familiar with. Navigation is primarily done on the left side of the screen. Each of the folders listed there refers to a directory. To navigate, use one or a combination of the following actions:

- A plus sign (+) next to a folder on the left means that you can open it and see what is inside. Click on the plus to see what subfolders there might be.
- Click on a folder on the left to see its actual contents, which show on the right.
- A minus sign (-) next to a folder on the left means that you have it expanded. If you want to close that folder, click on the minus sign.

Browsing And Opening Files In GNU Midnight Commander

As stated before, GNU Midnight Commander functions much as other file managers you might be familiar with. File browsing and opening is primarily done on the right side of the screen. To browse and open files, do the following:

1. Open GNU Midnight Commander and navigate to the directory whose files you want to view.
2. Choose which style you want to use to browse. The styles available are shown in Figure 3.4.

   The options, from left to right, are:

   - *The Icons style*—This is chosen by clicking on the Icons button shown in Figure 3.4. When you select this form of browsing, all files are represented by icons related to their file type and directories are shown as folders, as displayed in Figure 3.5.
   - *The Brief style*—This is chosen by clicking on the Brief button shown in Figure 3.4. When you select this form of browsing, directories have folder icons beside their names and files are listed by file name, as displayed in Figure 3.6.
   - *The Detailed style*—This is chosen by clicking on the Detailed button shown in Figure 3.4. When you select this form of browsing, directories have folder icons beside their names and files are listed by file name. The size of the item and the last time it was modified are also included. This format is shown in Figure 3.7.

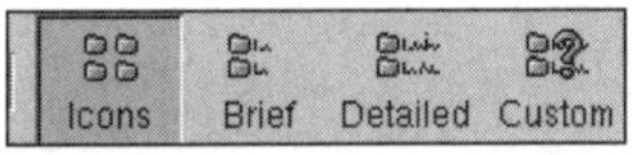

Figure 3.4 GNU Midnight Commander's file browsing styles.

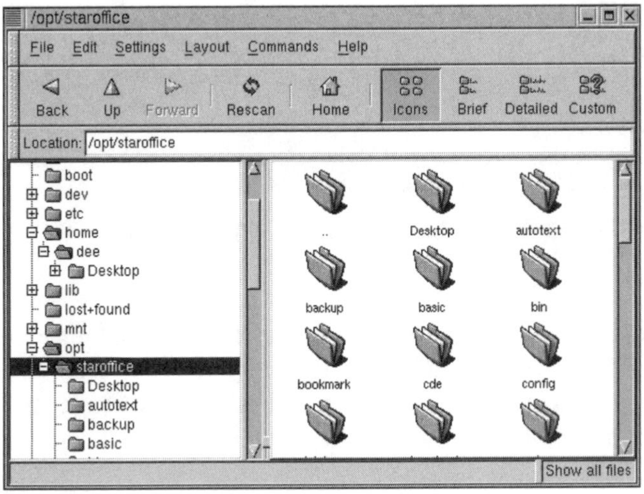

Figure 3.5 GNU Midnight Commander's Icons style, showing the /opt/staroffice directory.

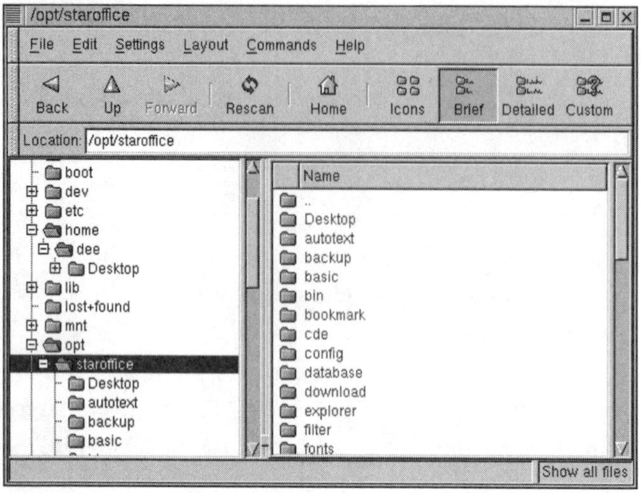

Figure 3.6 GNU Midnight Commander's Brief style, showing the /opt/staroffice directory.

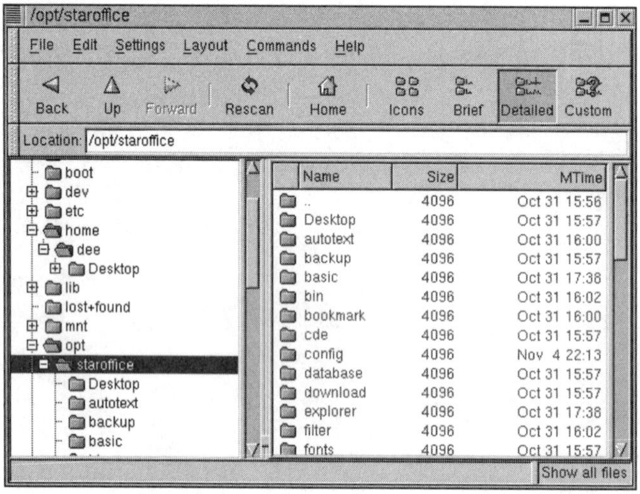

Figure 3.7 GNU Midnight Commander's Detailed style, showing the /opt/staroffice directory.

- *The Custom style*—This is chosen by clicking on the Custom button shown in Figure 3.4. This style can be modified at your leisure. By default, this option shows directories with folder icons beside their names and files listed by file name. The item's size and permissions are also included, as shown in Figure 3.8.

3. Double-click on a file or directory to open it. If Midnight Commander is not sure of what program to use to open the file, it will give you the gmc dialog box shown in Figure 3.9.

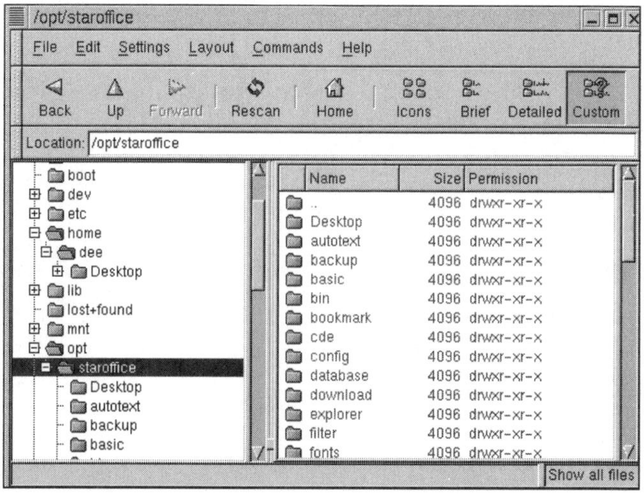

Figure 3.8 GNU Midnight Commander's Custom style, showing the /opt/staroffice directory.

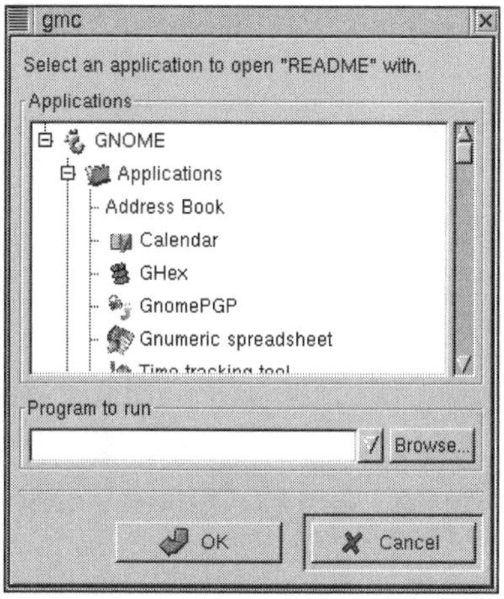

Figure 3.9 GNU Midnight Commander's gmc display program dialog box.

4. Click on the program you want to use out of the Applications listing, or click on the Browse button to select the program by navigating through the file system.
5. Click on the OK button once you have selected the program to utilize. The program then opens to the file you wanted to work with.

Navigating The File System In KDE

KDE File Manager (KFM) is a fully functional desktop navigation tool provided with the KDE desktop environment. Because there are many different things you can do with this tool, its use is broken down into categories.

Opening KFM At The Command Line

To open the KDE File Manager from the command line, do the following:

1. Enter the GUI by typing either "startx" from any account or "init 5" from root.
2. Log into KDE with the account you want to navigate within.

NOTE: *If your session is set to start GNOME and not KDE, you will need to either go to the GNOME navigation section or change which desktop environment you are using.*

3. Click on the Personal Directories icon shown in Figure 3.10. This action opens the KDE File Manager, as shown in Figure 3.11.

Figure 3.10 The KDE Personal Directories icon.

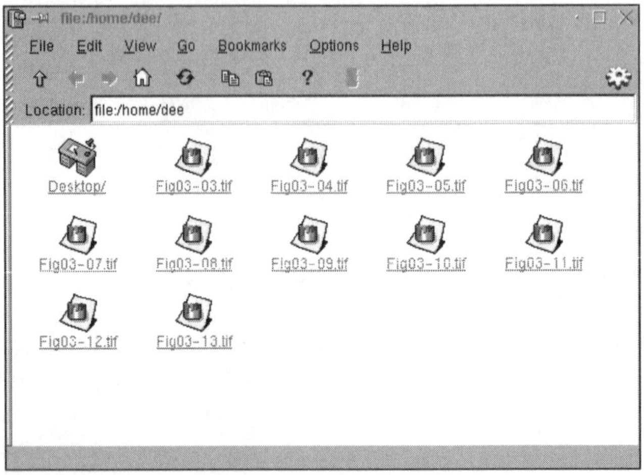

Figure 3.11 The KDE File Manager for the "dee" user account.

Related solution:	***Found on page:***
Changing Desktop Environments	167

Browsing In KFM

The KFM is simple to browse and works much like a Web browser. To move through the directory structure, do one of the following:

- Click on the item you want to open, whether it is a folder (directory) or an icon referring to a file.
- Utilize the Location text box and type "file:*path*" for where you want to go. For example, "file:/usr/sbin".
- Click on the up arrow to move up in the directory tree.

TIP: *Click on the Home icon to return quickly to your home directory.*

Setting Up Disk Quotas

There are two different stages to setting up usage quotas. In the first stage, you configure the machine itself to look for the quotas. In the second stage, you assign the quotas.

Preparing The Machine

To set up your machine to look for quota information, do the following:

1. Log in as root.
2. Use the **cd** command to go to the base directory for the partition you want to enforce quotas over. You must create quotas on a partition-by-partition basis; you cannot apply them only to particular directories.
3. Use the **touch** command to create the files "quota.user" and "quota.group".
4. Open the file /etc/fstab to edit. If you are unused to working with this file or with your favorite editor, be sure to make a backup of it first.
5. Locate the line that defines the partition to which you want to add quotas.
6. Move the cursor to the mount options column (column 4).
7. If you're using **vi**, press "i" to enter Insert mode.
8. Add the text ",usrquota" to the end of the current options to add user quotas. If you want to assign quotas by group, add the text ",grpquota". You also can add both. An example of what the resulting file might look like is:

```
/dev/hda3  /tmp  ext2  defaults,usrquota,grpquota  1  3
```

NOTE: *If you are not sure if you want one of the options, go ahead and add it now.*

9. Save and exit the file.
10. Reboot the machine.

Setting The Quotas

To set user and/or group quotas, do the following:

1. Log in as root.
2. Choose which type of quota you want to assign, user or group. For a user quota, type "edquota -u *user*", or for a group quota, type "edquota -g *group*".

TIP: *This is where it is helpful if you have all of your users in a "users" group, in case you want to give all the users the same quota assignment.*

This command opens a file containing text similar to the following:

```
Quotas for user sally:
/dev/hdb3: blocks in use: 153, limits (soft = 0, hard = 0)
inodes in use: 95, limits (soft = 0, hard = 0)
```

3. Fill in the soft and hard limits you want to use for the user, either as inodes (bottom line) or blocks (middle line), or both if you want to limit both the total space used and the total number of inodes used. See "Limiting User Storage Space" in the In Depth section if you are unsure of what the terms mean. The editor used for this command is **vi**, so you need to enter Insert mode by pressing "i" before you can change values.
4. Press the Esc key when you are finished.
5. Type "ZZ" or ":wq" to save and exit the file.
6. Type "edquota -t" to set the grace period. You cannot set this period individually; you have to set it for the entire file system. This command opens a file containing text similar to the following:

```
Time units may be: days, hours, minutes, or seconds
Grace period before enforcing soft limits for users:
/dev/hdb3: block grace period: 0 days, file grace period: 0 days
```

7. Notice that there are two different grace periods available. These two periods correspond to the two different types of quotas available. If you set only a block or inode quota, set the respective grace period. If you set both quotas, be sure to set both grace periods. The editor used for this command is **vi**, so you need to enter Insert mode by pressing "i" before you can change values.

8. Press the Esc key when you are finished.
9. Type "ZZ" or ":wq" to save and exit the file.
10. Type "quotaon" to turn on quotas to start working at this moment. This command is later executed during the boot scripts.

Shutting Down And Rebooting

It is imperative that you properly shut down or reboot a Linux machine. Do not just shut off the power or press the Reset switch! A proper shutdown or reboot makes sure that all information held in RAM is properly written to disk, and in general it ensures that everything is neat and tidy.

Typically, the **shutdown** command is used to manage both shutting down and rebooting, though alternative choices are listed in Table 3.13. This command is versatile, offering not only choices involving whether the machine should prepare to be powered off or just reboot itself, but also when this should happen and what message users should be warned with. A selection of **shutdown** options is listed in Table 3.14.

Table 3.13 Alternative commands used to shut down and reboot Linux machines.

Command	Result	Equivalent To
halt	Shuts down the machine.	**shutdown -h now**
init 0	Shuts down the machine.	**shutdown -h now**
init 6	Reboots the machine.	**shutdown -r now**
reboot	Reboots the machine.	**shutdown -r now**

Table 3.14 Flags available for the shutdown command.

Flag	Purpose	Arguments	Example
None	Warning to give to users so they have time to stop and save their work.	Warning in quotes	**shutdown -ht 300 "System going down for maintenance. Back up in 3 hours."**
-c	Cancels a shutdown or reboot queued up to go.	None	**shutdown -c**
-f	Marks the file system to not be checked during the next boot.	None	**shutdown -rf now**
-h	Shuts down the machine.	None	**shutdown -h now**

(continued)

Table 3.14 Flags available for the shutdown command (continued).

Flag	Purpose	Arguments	Example
-r	Reboots the system.	None	**shutdown -r now**
-t	The time to wait before the command should go into effect.	Seconds to wait, using the word **now** signifies that the event should happen immediately (the flag is not necessary with **now**)	**shutdown -ht 30**

Making A Custom Boot Disk

The boot disk you got with the distribution materials is not sufficient if the machine is already installed and not booting properly. You need to have a custom boot disk on hand that has the information necessary for your configuration. To make this disk, do the following as root:

1. Type "uname -r" to get the exact version of the kernel you are using.
2. Put a floppy in the floppy drive—it must be a floppy disk, you cannot use another type of media to make a boot disk.
3. Type "mkbootdisk --version *version*", where *version* is the result of the command in Step 1. Press Enter.
4. Be sure the floppy is in the drive, and then follow the instructions on the screen. Once the program is finished writing to the floppy, it is safe to remove it from the drive.
5. Clearly label the floppy as a boot disk for the particular machine in question and put it in a place you can find it easily if needed.

NOTE: *This process works on most current Linux distributions.*

Making A Rescue Disk

Red Hat offers a special rescue disk to make system recovery easier, in conjunction with the custom boot disk. Do the following as root to create a rescue disk:

1. Place a floppy in the floppy drive.
2. Mount the Red Hat distribution CD, or copy the rescue.img file onto the file system from its FTP site.

3. Type "dd if=/mnt/cdrom/images/rescue.img of=/dev/fd0 bs=1440k".
4. When the image is finished writing, clearly label the disk as a rescue disk and put it with the boot disk(s). Rescue disks are not individual to particular machines, so you don't need a specific one for each machine.

Chapter 4

Package Management

If you need an immediate solution to:	*See page:*
Creating **gzip**ed Files	108
Opening **gzip**ed Files	108
Creating Z **compress**ed Files	108
Opening Z **compress**ed Files	109
Creating **tar** Files	109
Examining The Contents Of **tar** Files	110
Opening **tar** Files	110
Opening Or Creating Tarballs	110
Installing A Binary	111
Creating RPMs	111
Installing RPMs	114
Viewing The Contents Of An RPM File	115
Listing Which RPMs Are Installed	115
Removing An RPM	115
Verifying An RPM File	115
Checking A PGP-Signed RPM	116
Using GNOME's RPM Tool	116
Opening GNOME RPM	116
Installing RPMs With GNOME RPM	117
Removing RPMs With GNOME RPM	119
Using KDE's RPM Tool	120
Opening Kpackage	120
Installing RPMs With Kpackage	120
Removing RPMs With Kpackage	121

In Depth

There are a variety of tools available in the area of package management. These tools are needed on a regular basis, especially when you get into installing new software, backing up file systems, and updating your Linux installation. In this chapter, you will learn how to recognize package types on sight, when to use the various types available, and how to manipulate them.

Types Of Tools

The tools used in package management can be classed roughly into two categories: compression tools and packaging tools. Each of the available items has its own features, weaknesses, and capabilities. Become familiar with them so that you know which tool to choose when it comes time to use these programs to prepare files or packages to share with other people or to store for archival.

Compression Tools

There are essentially two different file compression tools commonly used in Linux: **gzip** and **compress**. The **gzip** command is a GNU compression utility that creates files with the .gz extension. Most compressed files in the Linux world were created with this tool. The **compress** program, on the other hand, makes files with the .Z extension.

These two programs use different compression algorithms. The **compress** tool is not used as heavily today as **gzip**, simply because **gzip** is a newer program with more efficient compression methods. However, you will still run across .Z files, because **compress** is a utility found across all flavors of Unix.

Packaging Tools

On the other end of the scale are the packaging tools. These items may or may not include a compression aspect, but their primary purpose is to bundle files such that they can be installed on the recipient's machine in the right place, with the right permissions, and potentially include other considerations depending on the program you choose. A number of distributions now make their own package management tools to try to make life a little easier for the average Linux administrator.

The tar Tool

The **tar** (tape archive) packaging tool is used across all Unix platforms. This is a powerful utility that deserves in-depth study if you are going to use it in a serious manner, such as preparing packages for other people to unpack and use or utilizing it for your own backup needs. You can recognize a **tar** package by the .tar extension.

Its primary function is the bundling of files. You can use **tar** to store a group of files or even several hierarchies of directories without losing their permissions or file system structure. This feature is immensely useful for packaging source code or programs that others will download and utilize.

The RPM Tool

The RPM (Red Hat Package Manager) tool is used primarily in Red Hat and related distributions, but can be installed on a wider basis and in fact has been ported to other flavors of Unix. RPM is not so much a storage format as it is a centralized package management system. It maintains a database of what RPMs you have installed already and checks this database when you wish to add a new package to ensure that other items it needs are already there. You can recognize an RPM package by the .rpm extension; however, if it is an RPM containing source code only, then it might have the extension .src.rpm or .srpm.

One of the greatest advantages of the RPM tool for those who are not programmers by nature is that the format negates the need for compilation and also removes your need to deal with source code or raw binaries. An RPM software installation is usually far less frustrating than compiling source or trying to determine if you have everything you need for your new binary to work. Even better, it places all of the files that come with the program, such as libraries and configuration files, exactly where they need to be, as opposed to the **tar** tool, which tends to unpack things into a single place.

NOTE: *Typically, programs themselves come in RPM format and source code comes in a tar archive.*

Other Custom Tools

The Debian distribution (**www.debian.org**) has its own package management tool, called **dpkg**, and Stampede (**www.stampede.org**) has its **slp** tool. When you see a .deb extension, this is for Debian's **dpkg**. The .slp extension is for Stampede.

TIP: *There are programs out there, such as alien, that can convert between the various package management formats.*

The Linux Software Map

The Linux Software Map (LSM) extension .lsm stands off on its own because it is not actually the product of any special tool. Instead, this extension represents a text file following a template provided by the LSM. This template details a set of information about the package, such as the site where new versions can be found and a description of what it is used for.

The actual Linux Software Map is located at **www.execpc.com/lsm**. Essentially, the LSM is a database of all the software available for Linux. This tool is only as good as the number of programmers who register with it, so if you end up developing programs for Linux, be sure to list them with the LSM.

Choosing What To Download

Not all programs offer a variety of package choices, but many do. There are pros and cons for each option. Some of these considerations are important under particular situations, whereas others are something you need to consider every time you go to download something.

Choosing Source, Binary, Or RPM

There are times when you have a choice of what type of format you want to download a program in. Perhaps there is an RPM available on the Red Hat site, but it is not entirely up-to-date. Or perhaps there is no RPM available at all, but you want or need to use the package, and both source code and binary versions are available.

Choosing between these three options—source, binary, or RPM—is sometimes quite straightforward. If an RPM is available and you do not need to make any alterations to the source code, then by all means use the RPM, because Red Hat is an RPM-based distribution. Using an RPM is a good way to ensure that the package is properly entered into the RPM package database so its interactions with other packages can be tracked.

NOTE: *If you are using another distribution that is not based on RPMs, this format should not be your first choice.*

If there is no RPM available but there is a binary available, then many people will try the binary before trying to compile the source. This fact is especially true for those who are not comfortable with programming and compilers.

There are a few reasons to choose source over the other options:

- You need to make alterations to the code.
- You need to at least look over the code, to see if alterations are necessary. If you do not need to make any changes, you may decide to actually install an RPM or binary instead.

- There are no other package versions available, for whatever reason.
- The types of packages available do not fit with your package management scheme or are not in formats you are comfortable with.
- You need to see the code so you can properly interface your own application with it.

NOTE: *See Chapter 22 for information on compiling C code in Linux.*

Choosing A Download Site

Something important to consider is where to download your software from. If you download from random sites, you cannot be sure what you are getting. Even if the package is a legitimate item offered in other places, it could have been tampered with. Even an RPM can be disassembled, altered, and then reassembled.

Good types of sites to consider when you want to download programs or scripts are:

- Clearinghouse sites for packages that have a testing policy to ensure that the programs have not been altered.
- The home site for the package.
- The Web site **www.redhat.com** if you are using the Red Hat distribution; otherwise, the home site for your specific distribution.

Some excellent clearinghouses for programs and scripts that Linux users and system administrators might like are:

- **www.slashdot.org**
- **www.freshmeat.net**
- **www.linux.org/apps/lsm.html**
- **http://linux.tucows.com**
- **ftp://sunsite.unc.edu/pub/Linux/**

Package Management Principles

There are a number of worthwhile principles to keep in mind when dealing with packages. Some of these principles involve where you store things and others involve the details of such storage. These issues may not seem to matter much now, but when you have been running a machine for a while, where and how you organize things can make all the difference in the world. Especially when you're looking for that program you wrote a year ago to keep track of sports stats.

Location, Location, Location

It is important to have a consistent policy for where you store the packages you download. Not only do you need to have a standard for where you put the packages, you also need to consider where you will unpack the source code you acquire and where you should put the binaries you get.

Much of this issue is dealt with by studying the File System Hierarchy Standard (FHS), which was discussed in Chapter 3. Generally, you might choose to create a Downloads directory in your home directory, which is where you would put things downloaded from the Internet until you are ready to deal with them.

Once it is time to deal with the files, location becomes essential. The sections devoted to opening the various file types go into these considerations in detail.

Naming

What you name a package when creating it is important if you intend to keep it around for a while. Keep the following points in mind when choosing a package name:

- If the item is time-sensitive, include a date reference. The timestamp may not always be useful if you move the file around.
- Make the name a reflection of what the package does. Cute or "cool" names do not stand the test of time if you cannot remember why you chose them for that item.
- If the package is one in a series of versions that you are building or keeping, be sure to include a version reference in the name.

Dependencies

Although modern package management tools such as RPM warn you if you have to install or upgrade other packages to install the new one properly, older tools do not. It is important to understand what may be involved when you want to install a new program. Knowing in advance can save you a lot of time and effort tracking down dependent packages and deciding that perhaps this new software is not worth installing after all once your machine is half updated and half not.

There are a number of items that you need to watch for when deciding whether to install a new package. One of the first things to look at is the lowest kernel version that this software works with. If you require a kernel upgrade—or need to find out how to see what version of the kernel you have—see Chapter 5 for information on how to proceed with this task and what is involved. The plus to upgrading the kernel is that you may have to upgrade other packages in the process that will make the rest of your system up-to-date for the new software.

If your kernel is fairly up-to-date, you likely will not need to upgrade it. This is especially true if the software package is not particularly new. However, even if the kernel is all right you may need newer versions of other programs it uses—or compilers, or libraries, or any number of other issues. Whenever you download a program, or before you download it, be sure to read the attached README file. It should contain such information.

Immediate Solutions

Creating **gzip**ed Files

To **gzip** a file, use the format **gzip** ***flags file(s)***. The available flags are listed in Table 4.1.

__NOTE:__ Unless you use the ***-c*** *flag, the original file will be deleted and replaced with the* ***gzip*** *version. Use the format* ***gzip -c file > file.gz*** *to keep from replacing the original.*

Table 4.1 Commonly used flags for the gzip command.

Flag	Purpose
--best	Uses the most thorough compression setting. This option also is the slowest form of compression.
-c	Sends the output to STDOUT instead of replacing the input file with the zipped version. Useful in conjunction with a redirection to a separate file.
--fast	Uses the fastest compression setting. This option also gives the least compression.
-r	Includes all files inside the directory listed as the argument.
-v	Lists the names of the files and how much they were compressed.

Opening **gzip**ed Files

To uncompress a **gzip**ed file, use the format **gunzip** ***file***. The contents of the **gzip**ed file will be placed in the same directory as the original.

Once you **gunzip** the file, the .gz file no longer exists. If you want to keep a copy, be sure to back it up before uncompressing it.

Creating Z **compress**ed Files

To create a Z **compress**ed file, use the format **compress** ***flags file***. Table 4.2 lists the flags available for use.

Table 4.2 Commonly used flags for the compress command.

Flag	Purpose
-c	Sends the output to STDOUT instead of replacing the input file with the compressed version. Useful in conjunction with a redirection to a separate file.
-r	Includes all files inside the directory listed as the argument.
-v	Lists the names of the files and how much they were compressed.

*TIP: The **zcat** command does the same thing as **compress -c**.*

Opening Z **compress**ed Files

To uncompress a Z **compress**ed file, use the format **uncompress *file***.

*TIP: The **gunzip** command will also uncompress a Z **compress**ed file.*

Creating **tar** Files

To create a **tar** archive, do the following:

1. Determine the range and location of the items you want to archive.
2. The format used with the **tar** command to create an archive is, at its most basic level, **tar -cf *name*.tar *original***. The **c** flag tells **tar** that you are creating an archive, and the **f** flag tells **tar** that you will specify what file to place the archive into. Now, you need to decide which other flags you need to use. The potential flags are outlined in Table 4.3.
3. Once you have chosen the flags, fill out the command by listing which files should be included in the archive. You can list them by directories, files, or a combination thereof. For example, if you wanted to create an archive in the file /root/archives/March_work-files.tar that contained the contents of /root/bin and /etc and the file /root/notes, you would use the following:

```
tar -cvf /root/archives/March_work-files.tar /root/bin /etc /root/notes
```

Table 4.3 Flags used with tar to create archives.

Flag	Purpose
--exclude=file	Does not include a specific file. Useful when you are archiving directories.
<Tab-c	Creates an archive.
-f	Saves the archive to the file stated in the command.
-M	Breaks the **tar** archive into multiple volumes. Used to store the archive on multiple media.
-P	Uses absolute paths instead of relative. Not recommended unless you have a very specific reason.
-v	Prints file names during the archiving process.
-z	**gzip**s the files before placing them in the archive.

Examining The Contents Of **tar** Files

To view the contents of a **tar** archive without unpacking it, use the format **tar -tf *name*.tar**.

Opening **tar** Files

To unpackage a **tar** file, use the format **tar -xvf *name*.tar**. Although the **v** is not an essential flag, it is useful for keeping track of progress.

Opening Or Creating Tarballs

A *tarball* is a packaging combination commonly used in the Linux and Unix worlds. You can recognize one of these files by either a .tar.gz extension, or a .tgz extension. Either way, there are two steps to creating or opening one of these files. To open one of these files, follow the instructions in the section "Opening **gzip**ed Files" and then "Opening **tar** Files". To create a tarball, first create the **tar** archive as discussed in "Creating **tar** Files," and then **gzip** the archive as discussed in "Creating **gzip**ed Files."

TIP: *You can also create a tarball by using the* ***-z*** *flag when you create a* ***tar*** *archive; for example,* ***tar -zcvf homearchive.tar /home****. To fully open a tarball, try* ***tar -zxvf homearchive.tar****.*

Installing A Binary

There are some considerations to keep in mind while installing binary files:

- I cannot stress enough the value of reading the README and other files that come with the binary.
- Find out what kernel version is required by the binary.
- Find out what other programs are required by the binary.
- If there are any man pages, be sure to install them in an appropriate place. To find out what the appropriate place is, look at the file name. There should be a number on the end. Then, go to the directory /usr/man. Put the new man page in the directory that matches the extension number.
- Place any non-man documentation in /usr/doc, in a directory containing the name of the program and its version.

Creating RPMs

Making your own RPM is a complex process. As a system administrator, however, there will be times when you want to slightly modify the source for particular packages for your own use and then build an RPM that you can install on your other systems. To build a simple RPM on your own that is based on the source available to you from the Red Hat source RPM (SRPM), do the following:

1. Either find the SRPM on the source CD you got from Red Hat or on an FTP site that contains the Red Hat distribution—if you are dealing with an open source package.

NOTE: *SRPMs end with the extension .src.rpm, but otherwise the file should be named exactly the same as the actual package file. For example, samba-2.0.5a-12.i386.rpm has its source code in samba-2.0.5a-12.i386.src.rpm on the source CD that came with Red Hat 6.1.*

2. Install the source RPM just like you would a program RPM. (See the following section for information on how to install RPMs.)
3. Use the **cd** command to change to the directory /usr/src/redhat/SOURCES. The contents of the SRPM were placed here.
4. There are probably multiple files in the SOURCES directory. The source code for the package is likely in the tarball that matches the package name. Use **tar -zxvf *package*.tar.gz** to unpack and uncompress the source into a local hierarchy.

5. Edit the source code to suit your needs. If you need assistance, see the chapter appropriate for the type of code you are dealing with—Chapter 20 for shell scripting, Chapter 21 for Perl scripting, or Chapter 22 for C programming.

TIP: *It is recommended that you make a copy of any file you are going to change before you change it. Doing this allows you to make the RPM out of the original source plus your own patches, which is considered a clean method of doing things.*

---

6. Back up to the SOURCES directory with the **cd** command.
7. Make your patch file using the **diff** command in the format **diff -c *directory/originalfile directory/changedfile* > *mychanges*.patch**.
8. Remove the unpackaged version of the source with the **rm** command in the format **rm -rf *directory***.
9. Type "cd ../SPECS" to change to the SPECS directory. There should be a *package*.spec file there.
10. Use **vi *package*.spec** to open the spec file for editing.
11. Look for a series of lines that begin with "Source" at the beginning of the document. Move the cursor to the last Source line.
12. Look for the patches section next, if there is one. If there is, move the cursor to the last of the Patch lines. If not, put it beneath the Sources section with a blank line between what you're about to add and the Sources section.
13. Type "o" to open a new line for editing beneath the setup line.
14. Add something similar to the following line, where the name of the patch file is the actual name of the file you created:

    ```
    Patch0: mychanges.patch
    ```

    If patch items already exist, be sure to change the number to the next available patch number.
15. Press the Esc key to return to command mode.
16. Type "/^%setup" and press Enter. This action moves you down through the file to a list of lines that begin with a percent sign and then "setup".

NOTE: *The caret (^) in the previous entry ensures that the search only looks at the beginning of the line.*

---

17. If there are no %patch lines, then put the cursor on the %setup line. Otherwise, place the cursor on the last %patch line.
18. Type “o” to open a new line for editing.
19. Add a line similar to the following, where the patch number matches what you added in Step 14:

```
%patch0 -p1
```

20. Press the Esc key to return to command mode.
21. Type “1G” to go to the beginning of the file.
22. Type “/changelog” to locate the log of changes that have been made to this file.
23. Move the cursor onto the first asterisk (*) directly below the changelog line.
24. Type “O” to move this line down and put an empty one in its place, then enter Insert mode.
25. Type the first line of the new changelog in the following format:

```
* Day Month date year Firstname Lastname <email>
```

These items break down as follows:

- *Day*—The first three letters of the day of the week
- *Month*—The first three letters of the name of the month
- *date*—The calendar date corresponding to the day
- *year*—The four digits representing the year
- *Firstname*—Your first name
- *Lastname*—Your last name
- *email*—Your email address

For example:

```
* Wed Oct 11 2000 Alice Bates <alice@animals.org>
```

26. Type the second and any additional lines in the format:

```
- notes
- more notes
```

You can have one or more lines of changelog notes. List all of the changes you made in this file. The lines must begin with the dash, but there does not have to be a space after it. For example, both of the following are correct:

```
- Added a patch and changed this file to use that patch
-when building the new RPM.
```

27. Type "1G" to jump to the top of the file.
28. Move the cursor down to the line that begins with "Release".
29. Place the cursor on top of the number at the end of the line.
30. Use the "x" key as many times as you need to delete the number.
31. Type "i" to enter Insert mode.
32. Type the next integer after the one that was there. For example, if it says "Release: 15", type "16".
33. Press the Esc key.
34. Type "ZZ" to save and exit the file.
35. Use the format **rpm -bp *package-yourversion*.spec** to prepare the files necessary to build your RPM.
36. Use the format **rpm -bb *package*.spec** to build your binary RPM.

Installing RPMs

To install an RPM file, generally you use the format **rpm -ivh *fullpackagename*. rpm**. The available installation-related flags are listed in Table 4.4.

Table 4.4 Commonly used installation-related flags for the RPM tool.

Flag	Purpose
-F	Replaces the package with the new version if it is already installed; otherwise, it does not install it.
-h	Prints hash marks (#) to show installation progress.
-i	Installs the package if it is not already installed.
--oldpackage	Is used in conjunction with the **-U** or **-F** flag. Replaces the existing package with the one you are trying to install even if the one you are installing is older than the previous one.
-U	Installs the package if it is not installed. If it is installed, replaces it with the new version.
-V	Displays information while going through the installation process.

TIP: *You can install more than one RPM at a time by listing them all on the command line at once in the format* **rpm -ivh file1.rpm file2.rpm file3.rpm**.

Viewing The Contents Of An RPM File

There are two different formats used for determining what files are in an RPM, depending on whether the RPM is installed already:

- If the RPM is already installed, use the format **rpm -ql *packagename*** without the extension or full file name.
- If the RPM is not installed, use the format **rpm -qlp *packagename*.rpm** with the full path (if not in the current directory), file name, and extension.

TIP: *Want to see if a particular item is installed from an RPM but you don't know which package to look for? Use the command combination* **rpm -ql * | grep item**.

Listing Which RPMs Are Installed

If you want to get a list of which RPMs are already installed, use **rpm -qa**. It is recommended to use **rpm -qa|more** because usually the list is quite long.

Removing An RPM

To remove an RPM package from your system, use the format **rpm -e *packagename***.

NOTE: *Do not use the .rpm extension here or the package's full file name. The package name is sufficient.*

Verifying An RPM File

The RPM tool offers a useful feature that allows you to check that the version of a package you have installed is the same that you installed originally. This technique is useful to ensure that intruders have not changed anything and also in case you fear you have deleted vital files. To verify the RPMs on your system, use the format **rpm -Va *options***. The options available are shown in Table 4.5.

Table 4.5 Commonly used RPM verification options.

Option	Purpose
--nofiles	Does not warn about missing files.
--nomd5	Does not warn about MD5 checksum errors.
--nopgp	Does not warn about PGP signature problems.

The output is a set of eight characters. If all is clear, then the character is a period. Otherwise, it is a letter. The characters from left to right are:

- *5*—The MD5 checksum is incorrect.
- *S*—The file sizes are incorrect.
- *L*—The symlinks are incorrect.
- *T*—The last modification date for the file is incorrect.
- *D*—The device is incorrect.
- *U*—The user setting is incorrect.
- *G*—The group setting is incorrect.
- *M*—The permissions are incorrect.

Checking A PGP-Signed RPM

If you have an RPM with a PGP (Pretty Good Privacy) signature attached, use **rpm -checksig*filename*** to check the signature.

Related solution:	Found on page:
Getting And Installing PGP	285

Using GNOME's RPM Tool

The GNU Network Object Model Environment (GNOME) desktop environment offers the GNOME RPM tool for those who prefer to use a GUI program to handle their packages. This section is divided into various tasks you might want to do with the program.

Opening GNOME RPM

To open GNOME RPM from within GNOME, do the following:

1. Click on the footprint icon to open the menu.

2. Click on the System menu.
3. Click on GnoRPM to open the program, which is shown in Figure 4.1.

Related solution:	Found on page:
Navigating GNOME	9

Installing RPMs With GNOME RPM

To install an RPM with the GNOME RPM tool, do the following:

1. Click on the Install button shown in Figure 4.1. The Install dialog box, displayed in Figure 4.2 opens.

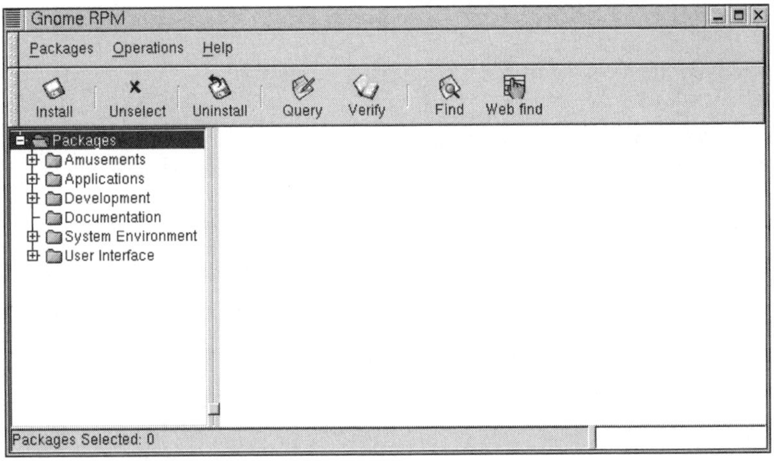

Figure 4.1 The GNOME RPM tool.

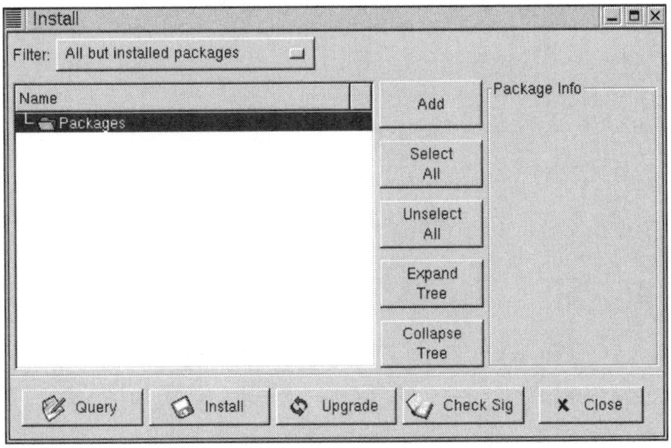

Figure 4.2 The GNOME RPM Install dialog box.

TIP: *If you want to upgrade the package instead of just installing it, click on the Upgrade button.*

2. Click on the Add button to open the Add Packages dialog box shown in Figure 4.3.
3. Use the file browser to locate the package you want to install.

NOTE: *If the package you want to install is on removable media such as a CD-ROM, you need to mount that media first.*

4. Click on the package to select it. There is a small box next to each package. If there is a check in the box, the package is marked to be installed. If the box is not checked, you need to mark it for that package to be installed. Click on the Select All button to mark all of the packages at once.
5. Return to Step 3 if you want to add another package.

WARNING! Do not ignore RPM dependency warnings. Even if you do manage to get the software installed, it will probably not run properly because it does not have everything it needs.

6. Make a note of which items the packages you wanted to install depend on.
7. Click on No to close the Dependency Problems dialog box and postpone the install. An Information dialog box opens, as shown in Figure 4.4.
8. Click on OK to close the Information dialog box.
9. Follow Steps 1 through 4 to add the package(s) necessary to satisfy the dependency requirements.

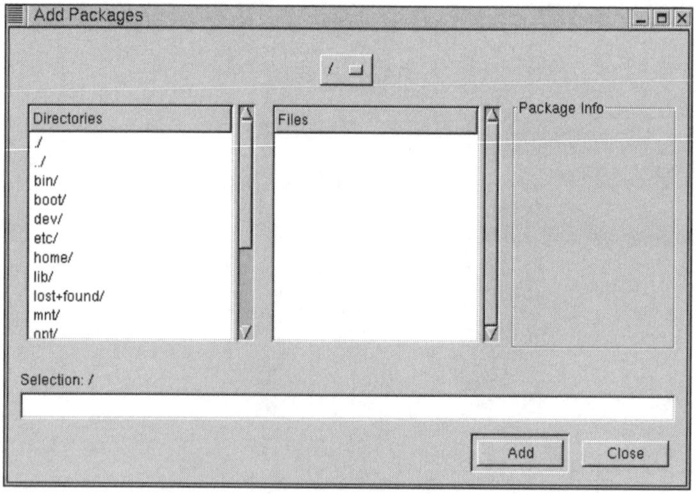

Figure 4.3 The GNOME RPM Add Packages dialog box.

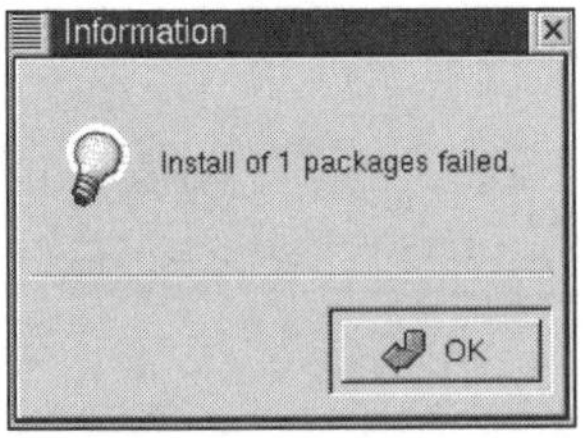

Figure 4.4 The GNOME RPM Information dialog box.

10. Click on the Install button to begin the installation process. A dialog box opens to show you the progress of the installs.
11. Once the installs are complete, click on the Close button to close the Install dialog box.
12. Click on Packages|Quit to close GNOME RPM.

Removing RPMs With GNOME RPM

To remove an RPM from your system with the GNOME RPM tool, do the following:

1. Browse in the left-hand side of the main GNOME RPM dialog box until you locate the package you want to remove.
2. Click on the package to select it.
3. Click on the Uninstall button (shown earlier in the chapter in Figure 4.1) to open the Continue Removal dialog box shown in Figure 4.5.
4. To continue to remove the package, click on the Yes button. The package is now uninstalled.

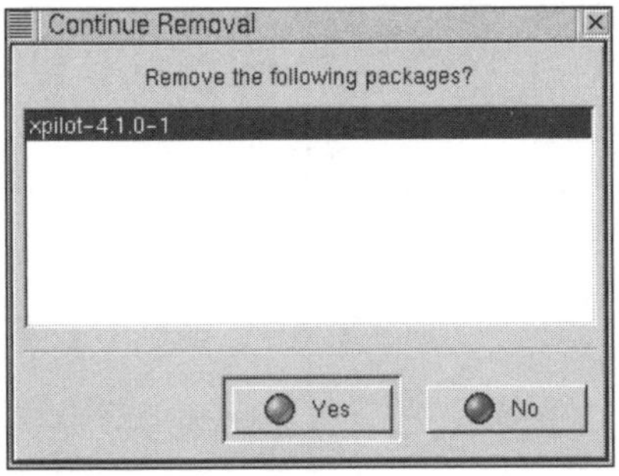

Figure 4.5 The GNOME RPM Continue Removal dialog box.

Using KDE's RPM Tool

The KDE desktop environment offers the Kpackage tool for those who prefer to use a GUI program to handle their packages. This section is divided into various tasks you might want to do with the program.

Opening Kpackage

To open Kpackage from within KDE, do the following:

1. Click on the K button to open the menu.
2. Click on the Utilities menu.
3. Click on Kpackage in the Utilities menu to open the Kpackage utility, as shown in Figure 4.6.

Related solution:	Found on page:
Navigating KDE	15

Installing RPMs With Kpackage

To install an RPM using the Kpackage tool, do the following:

1. Click on the Open Package button to open the Select Document To Open dialog box shown in Figure 4.7.
2. Browse to locate the package you want to install.

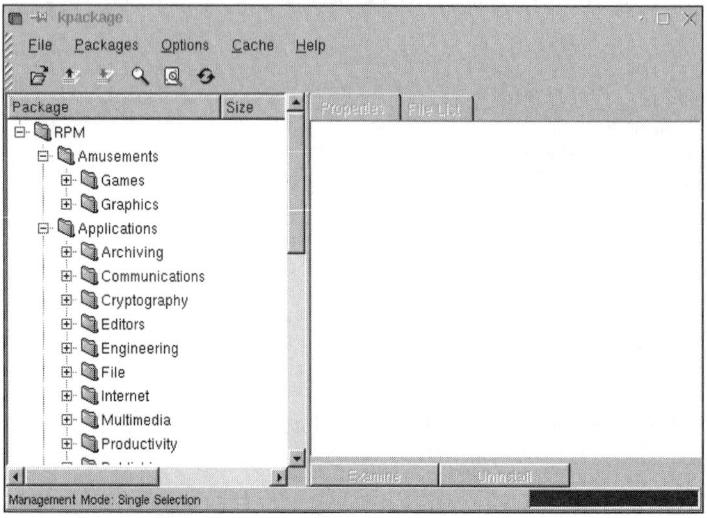

Figure 4.6 The KDE Kpackage RPM manager.

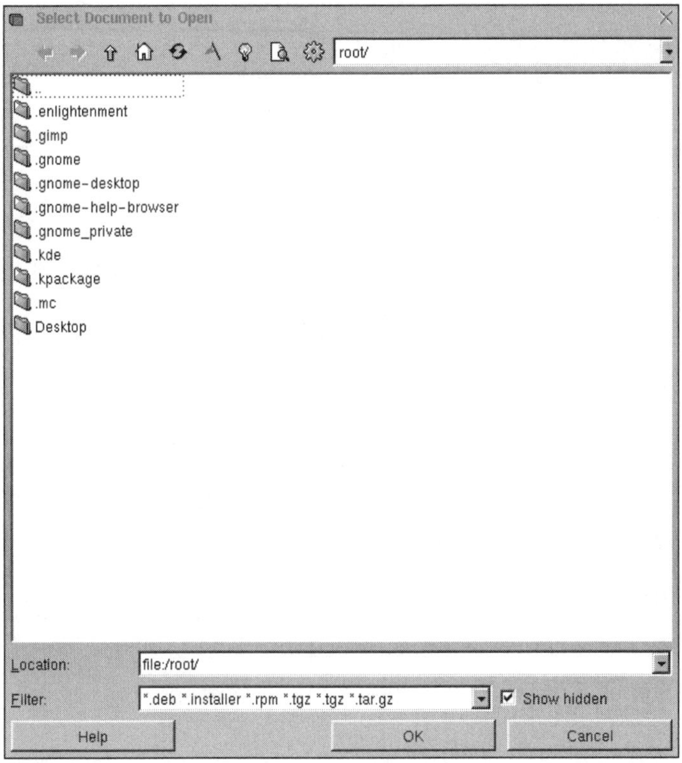

Figure 4.7 The KDE Kpackage Select Document To Open dialog box.

NOTE: *If the package you want to install is on removable media, such as a CD-ROM, you need to mount that media first.*

---

3. Click on the item you want to install so that it is selected.
4. Click on the OK button to get the package information and installation options, as shown in Figure 4.8.
5. Read the package information in the Properties tab.
6. Click on the File List tab to see what files are installed with the package.
7. Click on the Install button to install the RPM.
8. Once finished, you can either return to Step 2 to install another package, or click on File|Quit to close Kpackage.

Removing RPMs With Kpackage

To remove an RPM using the Kpackage tool, do the following:

1. Browse the left side of the screen to locate the package you want to remove.

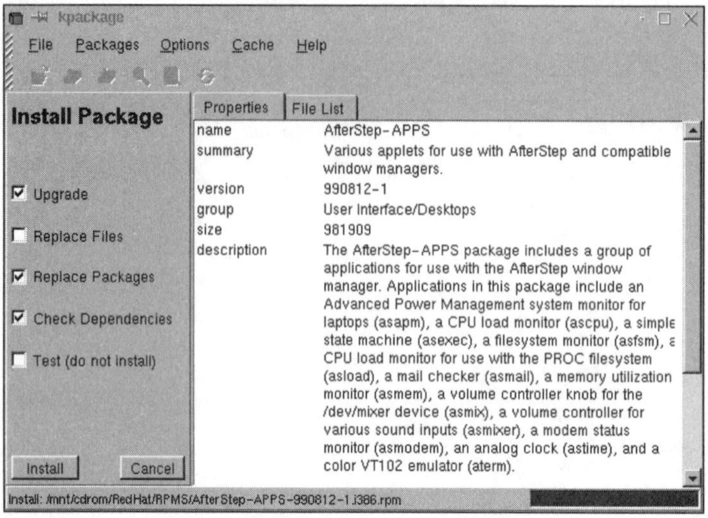

Figure 4.8 The KDE Kpackage Install Package dialog box.

2. Click on the package to select it. This action pulls up the information about the package and its files, as shown in Figure 4.9.
3. Click on the Uninstall button. The Uninstall dialog box appears, as shown in Figure 4.10.
4. Click on the Uninstall button to remove the RPM from your system.

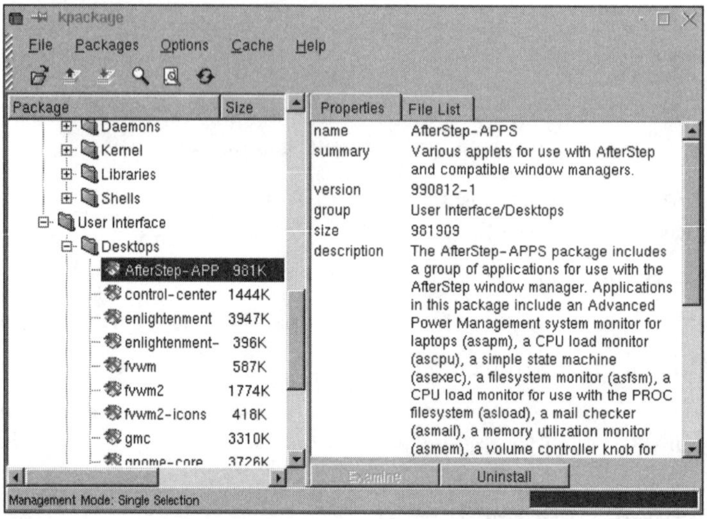

Figure 4.9 The KDE Kpackage's Uninstallation information.

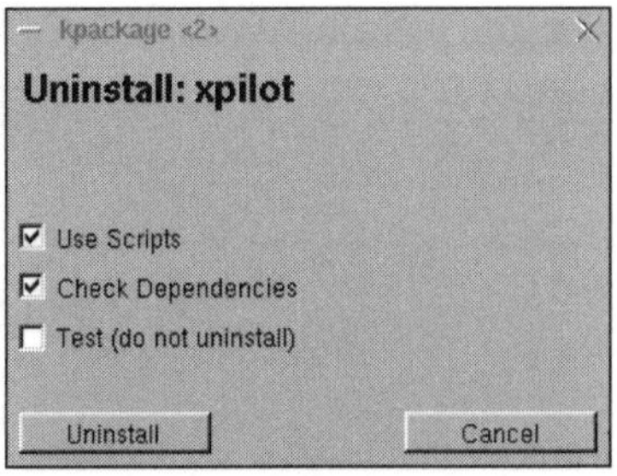

Figure 4.10 The KDE Kpackage's Uninstall dialog box.

Chapter 5

Kernel Management

If you need an immediate solution to:	*See page:*
Getting The Kernel's Version And Other System Information	135
Obtaining The Latest Kernel Source	135
Installing A New Kernel	136
Configuring The Kernel With **config**	137
Configuring The Kernel With **menuconfig**	141
Configuring The Kernel With **xconfig**	143
Listing Loaded Modules	145
Inserting Modules Manually	145
Removing Modules Manually	146
Getting System Information	147
Setting Module Parameters	148
Building An Alias Statement	148
Building An Option Statement	149
Updating LILO	149

In Depth

Although an end user rarely needs to concern herself with the kernel, most system administrators do. Whether you are an ardent believer in optimizing the kernel to improve system performance or simply are forced to upgrade it to use a new software package or hardware device, it is something you will eventually have to deal with. Fortunately, if you understand the processes behind it, kernel management is not that daunting of a subject.

The Linux Kernel

The *kernel* is Linux itself. Everything around it is just bells and whistles, trappings to make it attractive to us. Keeping the kernel healthy keeps the entire system stable, or at least more stable than it would be otherwise. There are a number of issues to consider in the area of kernel management. Some of these warrant immediate concern, whereas others are considerations for the long term and your own system administration policies.

Kernel Parts

The *kernel* essentially has two main components—although a kernel programmer would say this is an oversimplification. The first component is the compiled portion, which is constantly held in memory. This part only should consist of those items that are necessary on a nearly constant basis. The rest should go in the kernel's second component: kernel modules.

Items that are used intermittently—some device drivers, for instance—are placed in kernel modules. These pieces can be loaded and unloaded on the fly, ensuring that the kernel itself is not taking up a large part of your RAM and yet you still have full system functionality.

Modules that are used very rarely can actually be loaded by hand when you need them and then removed when you are finished.

When To Customize

There are two schools of thought about the kernel. Some feel that the default kernel installed by most distributions is acceptable in and of itself. Others swear that performance is vastly improved by compiling a customized version of the kernel that removes pieces you do not need and modularizes as much as possible.

Particular situations sometimes present themselves that make building a custom kernel desirable, or even necessary. These situations include:

- You install a program that requires a kernel feature that you do not have activated.
- You add a new device that you use almost continuously and don't want to have to load the module by hand.
- You buy a new device that is not available in the current kernel.
- Your current kernel is quite old and you know that not far in the future you need features that are not available in it, so you want to install the latest version to catch up with the times.

When To Upgrade

New versions of the kernel seem to come out almost daily. However, I strongly recommend that you resist the temptation to upgrade every time a new version is available. Not only would that be a full-time job, it can also make your system unstable. It is better to pick and choose when to upgrade according to your system's needs and the time you have available to deal with potential problems.

Typically, the choice to upgrade is foisted upon you when you need to add new software or devices that require a newer version of the kernel.

Choosing A New Kernel

There are a number of things to keep in mind when choosing a new kernel:

- If you need support for new devices, does the new version support it?
- Does the new version support all your old devices? Sometimes a new version breaks a few items that are fixed in the next.
- Is the kernel stable?
- If the new device is supported only by an experimental kernel, is it worth the stability risk?

As you can see, there is a lot that you need to understand about a new kernel. One of the most important items is whether you are dealing with an experimental or production kernel. This issue is fairly clear-cut once you understand the difference between the two kernel streams.

Kernel preparation works in two different development paths. The *experimental kernel* is just what it sounds like—code that is currently under development. New device drivers and new features are tested here first. When enough new items are added, the solid experimental kernel becomes a *production kernel*, and a new experimental kernel process begins. The production kernel is the one that most system administrators use on their machines.

This method of managing kernel development can make selecting a kernel a confusing process. The important information to understand is how each kernel version is named, so you can choose the most appropriate options at a glance.

A kernel's name ends with a string of numbers in the format X.Y.Z. Each number is incremented as new features and bug fixes are added. X is the slowest to change; it could be years before there are kernels that begin with 3, for example. Deciding to change a major version number is a subjective act. Moving from a 2-based kernel to 3 would represent some kind of monumental advance. For example, when the version numbers jumped from 1 to 2, the following new items were added:

- Support for four new hardware architecture platforms (including Apple PowerPC and Atari)
- Additional IDE device drivers, better IDE error handling, autodetection of some IDE characteristics, and the ability to handle more controllers
- Additional SCSI device drivers
- Greatly expanded Ethernet card list
- The modern modular structure
- Advanced Power Management (APM) for devices such as laptop computers
- IP tunneling, masquerading, and additional routing capabilities
- ISDN support
- The VFAT and SMB file system support, among others
- File system quota support

Essentially, Linus Torvalds determines it is time to change the X kernel number when he feels that we are dealing with a brand-new starting point for kernel development.

The Y component changes on a semiregular basis, perhaps every six months or so. This is the crucial digit when determining whether the kernel is production or experimental. Experimental kernels have an odd-numbered Y component; for example, 2.3.12, 3.7.16, and 4.19.92. Production kernels, on the other hand, have an even-numbered Y component, such as 2.2.12, 3.8.16, or 4.20.92. The method for advancing this component is explained earlier in this section.

Perhaps the easiest to explain is the Z changes. Any time a change is made to the kernel code, the Z component advances. This method is used among most software developers. It is a way of knowing exactly what source code you are looking at. In fact, you may even see kernel versions in the format X.Y.Z-A. When you see this, you are looking at a version that was altered specifically for your Linux distribution.

For those who are more visually oriented, Figure 5.1 shows the full kernel development path and how the branches work out.

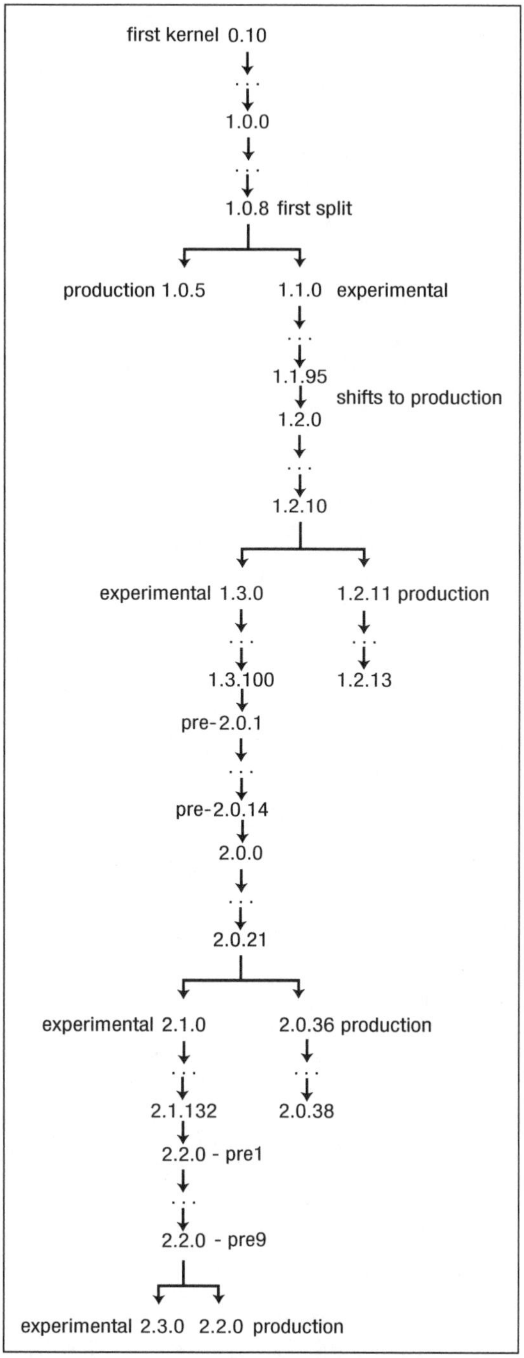

Figure 5.1 The kernel development stream.

Kernel Documentation

The kernel source code comes with a set of documentation by default. Many of these files are useful for tracking down information about particular kernel modules or driver settings. What follows is a tour of the documentation directories so you know what is available and where to find it. To start looking for any kernel documentation file—if you already have the source code installed—go to /usr/src/linux/Documentation.

General Kernel Files

Some of the documentation files are somewhat general. For example, the 00-INDEX file contains a list with one-line descriptions of all of the documentation files. This is useful if you download a version newer than the one that comes with Red Hat 6.2, because there may be subtle changes from what you see here. Another file is probably daunting for many, but some may be brave enough to tackle it. It is BUG-HUNTING, and contains instructions for how to track down and report a bug in the kernel. The oops-tracing.txt file contains additional information about this issue.

NOTE: *If you are interested in delving farther into kernel matters, a good place to start is "The Linux Kernel," which is available at* ***http://metalab.unc.edu/Linux/LDP/tlk/tlk.html****, thanks to the Linux Documentation Project.*

If you intend to write any code for the kernel, whether it is a bug fix or a patch to add a particular feature, be sure to read the CodingStyle file. This document is essentially a style guide for formatting kernel code. If you feel that this is infringing on your creativity, try to imagine what the kernel code would look like if the hundreds of people who have contributed code to the Linux kernel each used their own style conventions. Another important file in this regard is magic-number.txt, which lists the data structure magic numbers already in use.

For those who are interested in how the kernel handles input/output (I/O) mapping, take a look at the files IO-mapping.txt and ioctl-number.txt. If you like to run a wide range of binary file types and want to be able to do so from the command line, read the file binfmt_misc.txt. For Java-specific issues, read java.txt. You can also find out how the kernel deals with errors by reading the file exception.txt, and how it handles dependencies during configuration in smartconfig.txt.

The kernel-parameters.txt file contains the parameters accepted by the kernel at boot time. Also, there is a document that explains the workings of the program that manages kernel modules. This file is kmod.txt. Another deals with background information about the Linux kernel's ability to dynamically load and unload modules: modules.txt. To see how the kernel handles file locking, read the file locks.txt, and the related background information file mandatory.txt. Memory issues are covered in memory.txt.

Pointers to a wide range of kernel documentation are available in the file kernel-docs.txt.

Architecture-Specific Files

There are some files among the kernel documentation that specifically deal with one form of hardware architecture or another. These files are:

- *ARM-README*—Notes from the ARM code development team regarding specific issues ARM users need to consider.
- *IO-APIC.txt*—Useful for those who have Intel or Intel architecture-based SMP-capable motherboards. Not all motherboards are completely IO-APIC compliant. This file discusses how to tell if your motherboard is compliant, and how to deal with problems.
- *arm*—This subdirectory contains additional files relating to the ARM version of Linux.
- *i386*—This subdirectory contains additional files relating to the i386 (Intel) version of Linux.
- *m68k*—This subdirectory contains additional files relating to the Macintosh 68k version of Linux.
- *mca.txt*—Discussion of i386 Microchannel architecture handling under Linux.
- *mtrr.txt*—Discussion of Memory Type Range Control on Intel Pentium Pro and Pentium II systems.
- *powerpc*—This subdirectory contains additional files relating to the Macintosh PowerPC version of Linux.
- *sgi-visws.txt*—Discussion of Linux handling of SGI Visual Workstations.

Hardware-Specific Files

There is a small difference between architecture-specific and hardware-specific files: Architecture refers to the overall type of system design; hardware is more a device label than a design label. The files among the kernel sources that are related to specific devices are:

- *README.DAC960*—Information specific to the Mylex DAC960/DAC1100 PCI RAID Controller.
- *cdrom*—This subdirectory contains information files on a number of CD-ROM models and manufacturers.
- *computone.txt*—Information specific to the Computone Intelliport II/Plus Multiport serial driver.

- *cpqarray.txt*—Information specific to Compaq's SMART2 Intelligent Disk Array controllers.
- *digiboard.txt*—Information specific to the Digiboard PC/Xi, PC/Xe, and PC/Xeve multi-modem hardware.
- *digiepca.txt*—More information pertaining to Digiboard technology.
- *fb*—This subdirectory contains information files on frame buffer drivers and devices. Frame buffering is related to how your machine handles graphics.
- *filesystems*—This subdirectory contains information files on the various file system types that Linux understands.
- *ftape.txt*—Discussion regarding the ftape tape driver.
- *hayes-esp.txt*—Information specific to Hayes ESP (Enhanced Serial Port) modems.
- *ide.txt*—Information regarding the Linux kernel's handling of IDE devices.
- *isdn*—This subdirectory contains information about the kernel's ISDN handling and the various drivers available, including information about PPP over ISDN.
- *joystick-api.txt*—Information on writing code that utilizes Linux's joystick capabilities.
- *joystick-parport.txt*—Information on Linux and parallel port joysticks.
- *joystick.txt*—Information on Linux joystick drivers.
- *md.txt*—Discussion of Linux Multi Disk device handling.
- *mkdev.ida*—This is actually a shell script that helps you to set up device information for SMART RAID IDA controllers.
- *networking*—This subdirectory contains information on the various network card device drivers available in Linux.
- *paride.txt*—Discussion of Linux and IDE parallel port devices.
- *parport.txt*—Discussion of Linux parallel port support and modules.
- *pci.txt*—Discussion of what to avoid when writing PCI drivers.
- *pcwd-watchdog.txt*—Discussion of how Linux handles the ISA Berkshire PC Watchdog card.
- *ramdisk.txt*—This file is not really hardware-specific, but it does involve a driver: the RAMdisk driver used in Linux.
- *riscom8.txt*—Notes about the RISCom/8 multiport serial driver.
- *rtc.txt*—Discussion about the realtime clock driver used in Linux to go along with the PC and Alpha architectures.

- *scsi-generic.txt*—Discussion about the Linux drivers used to handle SCSI devices that are not disks, tapes, or CD-ROMs.
- *scsi.txt*—Brief discussion about SCSI support under Linux.
- *serial-console.txt*—Breaking up console output to various devices.
- *smp.tex*, *smp.txt*—Discussion of how to set up multiprocessor handling during kernel configuration.
- *sound*—This subdirectory contains information on each of the sound drivers available in Linux.
- *specialix.txt*—Coverage of the Specialix I08+ multiport serial driver.
- *stallion.txt*—Coverage of the Stallion multiport serial driver.
- *sx.txt*—Coverage of the Specialix SX/SI multiport serial driver.
- *video4linux*—This subdirectory contains information and Application Program Interfaces (APIs) regarding video drivers for Linux.
- *watchdog.txt*—Discussion of Watchdog timer interface drivers under Linux.

Extra-Useful Files

I thought I would put one group of files together in this section. These are the files that anyone who is getting ready to upgrade their kernel should read or at least look through before doing so. These files are:

- *Changes*—This file contains a list of kernel resource Web sites. However, that is not what makes this file something to put under this section. The wonderful thing about the Changes file is that it includes a list of what version you need of all of the software that the kernel or building the kernel requires, and how to determine what version you have now. Further, it contains notes about what capabilities were updated in this particular kernel release.
- *Configure.help*—This file contains a list of every single kernel feature and driver that you can turn on or off during the kernel configuration process, along with a paragraph or more discussing what this feature does and who may or may not want to use it. If you are not sure whether you want to implement something, this is the place to look for further information.
- *devices.tex*, *devices.txt*—Both of these items are the same file. One is in TEX format, which is a markup language for laying out documents. The other is an ASCII text file. The devices file contains a list of all of the device numbers and files handled by the kernel.
- *initrd.txt*—There is often confusion about the boot RAM disk you can create when compiling a new kernel. This file addresses what type of uses this RAM disk has and how to put them into practice.

- *kbuild*—This subdirectory contains files dealing with the kernel build process. Recommended reading.
- *proc.txt*—This file contains a discussion of the /proc section of the file system and what it contains.
- *sysctl*—This subdirectory contains files dealing with making changes to the /proc/sys/ files. If you think you might want to mess with these files, or want at least to understand what you might be able to do with them, read the file stored here.
- *sysrq.txt*—Many people do not know that they can turn on a set of key bindings that allows them to send commands directly to the kernel. Of course, you may not want to turn this on if others have access to the machine. Learn about the magic key bindings and why or why not to use them in this file.

Miscellaneous Widgets

Some items defy easy categorization. Those files are listed here:

- *VGA-softcursor.txt*—How to alter your cursor in command line mode.
- *logo.gif*—The unofficial Linux logo.
- *logo.txt*—Explanation of logo.gif.
- *nbd.txt*—Discussion of the experimental network block device drivers.
- *nfsroot.txt*—How to mount the root file system through an NFS mount on a diskless system. See Chapter 17 for information on NFS.
- *spinlocks.txt*—Discussion of making spinlocks efficient in both multi- and uniprocessor machines.
- *svga.txt*—Discussion of kernel-level video mode selection on 80x86 machines.
- *unicode.txt*—Discussion of how the kernel uses Unicode to refer to characters.
- *xterm-linux.xpm*—X pixel map of a penguin.

Immediate Solutions

Getting The Kernel's Version And Other System Information

The **uname** command allows you to get system information by choosing the appropriate flags. The flags available with **uname** are listed in Table 5.1.

Table 5.1 Flags available with the uname command.

Flag	Purpose
-a	Gives the information for all of the flags at once.
-m	Lists what architecture this machine is.
-n	Lists the machine's host name.
-p	Gives the machine's processor type.
-r	Gives the kernel version.
-s	Lists what operating system you are using.
-v	States when this operating system was installed.

Obtaining The Latest Kernel Source

It is important to get your kernel source from a trustworthy site. Some of the best places to get source from are:

- **www.kernelnotes.org**
- **www.kernel.org**

TIP: *If you want to know which version of the kernel you are currently running, type **uname -r**.*

Installing A New Kernel

Installing a new kernel, whether it is an upgrade or a newly compiled version of the one you already have, is a complex, but not intensely difficult, process. To add a new kernel, do the following:

1. Acquire the kernel source, either from one of the sites listed in the section "Obtaining The Latest Kernel Source" or from the distribution CD. For Red Hat 6.2, the Red Hat Package Manager (RPM) is kernel-source-2.2.14-50.i386.rpm.
2. Install the source. If you are not using an RPM, unpack the tarball in /usr/src.
3. There are certain packages you need to make sure are also installed. Here's a list of them with Red Hat 6.2 version numbers included for the full file name:
   - *kernel-headers-2.2.14-50.i386.rpm*—Contains the header files for the kernel source
   - *cpp-1.1.2-30.i386.rpm*—The C preprocessor package used for compilation
   - *egcs-1.1.2-30.i386.rpm*—The C compiler
   - *glibc-devel-2.1.3-15.i386.rpm*—The C development library set
   - *make-3.77-6.i386.rpm*—The build manager you will utilize to compile the source
   - *ncurses-5.0-11.i386.rpm*—Necessary to control the cursor if you choose the **menuconfig** option to configure the kernel parameters
   - *ncurses-devel-5.0-11.i386.rpm*—Necessary to control the cursor if you choose the **menuconfig** option to configure the kernel parameters
4. Change to the /usr/src/linux-*version* directory for the package. For Red Hat 6.2, this is /usr/src/linux-2.2.14.
5. Type "make oldconfig" to build a configuration file based on your current kernel settings. This is a good starting point if you do not want to risk forgetting to include things you have added already.
6. Choose which kernel configuration tool you want to use. See the following sections for your options: "Configuring The Kernel With **config**," "Configuring The Kernel With **menuconfig**," and "Configuring The Kernel With **xconfig**."
7. Once you have chosen a kernel configuration tool, follow the instructions in the section that covers it as listed in Step 6, then go to Step 8.

8. Type "make dep" to build a list of source dependencies. See Chapter 22 for more on working with C source code.

NOTE: *Keep in mind that although each of these* ***make*** *steps is short to read, they can take several minutes or longer, depending on your CPU's speed.*

---

9. Type "make clean" to clean out the temporary files used up to this point.
10. Type "make bzImage" to compile the base kernel.
11. Type "make modules" to compile the modules that the kernel will load on the fly.
12. The compiler places the kernel source in the directory /usr/src/linux/arch/i386/boot/bzImage. Copy this file into the /boot directory.
13. Rename /boot/bzImage to /boot/vmlinuz-*version* with the **mv** command, where *version* is the new kernel version you are in the process of installing.
14. Copy the file /boot/System.map to /boot/System.map-old.
15. Copy the file /usr/src/linux/System.map to the /boot directory.
16. Type "make modules_install" to install the modules to /lib/modules/*version*.
17. Although not necessary, it is a good policy to create a special boot version of the kernel containing modules that are needed by boot time hardware—for example, if your primary hard drive is SCSI. To do so, use **mkinitrd /boot/initrd-*version* *version***.
18. Proceed to the section "Updating LILO" at the end of the chapter. You will not be able to boot with the new kernel until you tell LILO where to find it.

Related solutions:	Found on page:
Opening Or Creating Tarballs	110
Installing RPMs	114

Configuring The Kernel With config

The **config** kernel configuration tool is entirely text-based with no bells and whistles. It takes some time to work through the entire configuration process, as **config** obtains the new kernel configuration by asking questions one at a time. Although an end user probably shouldn't use this option, it is useful for system administrators to try it a few times just to get a feeling for how many choices they can make if they want to. Rather than provide a sample run-through, which is a lengthy process, I note here items that you should pay particular attention to. They are given in the order that you might encounter them, with the default being the leading choice, which is a capital letter or capitalized word:

1. To start this configuration tool, type "make config". Compiling code scrolls by, and then the following question appears:

```
* Code maturity level options
*
Prompt for development and/or incomplete code/drivers
(CONFIG_EXPERIMENTAL) [Y/n/?]
```

NOTE: *The lines that begin with asterisks are headers shown by the* ***config*** *program to label what the questions pertain to. Also, the answer options often change order. They are arranged in the order from most likely to be chosen to least likely to be chosen.*

2. For an important production server, I recommend choosing "n". You are better off using trusted, solid code for such a machine. So, type "n" and press Enter. If you want to answer "Y," you just press Enter, as the capital "Y" denotes the default. Next, you see the following:

```
*
* Processor type and features
*
Processor family (386, 486/Cx486, 586/K5/5x86/6x86,
Pentium/K6/TSC, PPro/6x86MX) [386]
```

3. The valid answers are each of the individual entries, but for those that are separated by slashes you only need to type one of the parts between the slashes. For example, if the machine has a Pentium processor, you type "Pentium" and press Enter. If you have a 386 processor, you just press Enter because this item is noted as the default. Next, you see the following:

```
Maximum Physical Memory (1GB, 2GB) [1GB]
```

4. As you can see, there are only two options available here. If for some reason this machine has between 1GB and 2GB RAM in it, type "2GB" and press Enter. Otherwise, accept the default by pressing Enter. Next you see:

```
Math emulation (CONFIG_MATH_EMULATION) [Y/n/?]
```

NOTE: *Not all of the configuration tool's output is shown here. There are often statements in between those listed that refer to code definitions related to your settings.*

5. If you have a 486DX or faster processor, then type "n" and press Enter, because math emulation is built into processors of those speeds. Otherwise, press Enter to accept the default. Next appears:

```
MTRR (Memory Type Range Register) support (CONFIG_MTRR)
[Y/n/?]
```

TIP: *When you're unsure of what to answer, you can choose the question mark. This reply gives you a description of the kernel option you are considering, so you can make a more educated choice.*

6. This option is primarily of use to Intel P6 machines as well as others classed along the Pentium 6 line. Type "n" and then press Enter if you do not have such a machine, or just press Enter if you do. The next item is:

```
Symmetric multi-processing support (CONFIG_SMP) [N/y/?]
```

7. If you have multiple processors on the motherboard, then type "y" and press Enter. Otherwise, you do not need this option, so press Enter to accept the default. Next is:

```
*
* Loadable module support
*
Enable loadable module support (CONFIG_MODULES) [Y/n/?]
```

8. There are few situations where you do not want this option. Without it, you have to compile everything directly into the kernel. Press Enter to accept the default.

Now is where I begin only covering specific items of interest. Remember that you can read Help information at any time to learn about each item. It is quite an educational experience to read all of the Help information. The ones I will mention are where you may want to change the defaults to your benefit.

TIP: *All of the Help information for the kernel configuration options is also available in the Documentation subdirectory of /usr/src/linux in the file Configure.help.*

9. If you are installing Linux on a laptop with Advanced Power Management features, the following is a highly useful feature. Otherwise, you don't need it:

```
Advanced Power Management BIOS support (CONFIG_APM) [Y/n/?]
```

NOTE: *Notice that there are a lot of items that refer to specific brands of hardware or fixes for them.*

10. There are a number of options that refer to Integrated Development Environment (IDE) support. If there are no IDE devices on your system, you may not need this support. Read the Help information to see exactly what the item does before shutting it off.
11. It is useful to have the following items turned on or at least modular if you intend to use RAID (discussed in Chapter 3):

```
Multiple devices driver support (CONFIG_BLK_DEV_MD) [Y/n/?]
Autodetect RAID partitions (CONFIG_AUTODETECT_RAID) [Y/n/?]
Linear (append) mode (CONFIG_MD_LINEAR) [M/n/y/?]
RAID-0 (striping) mode (CONFIG_MD_STRIPED) [M/n/y/?]
RAID-1 (mirroring) mode (CONFIG_MD_MIRRORING) [M/n/y/?]
RAID-4/RAID-5 mode (CONFIG_MD_RAID5) [M/n/y/?]
Mylex DAC960/DAC1100 PCI RAID Controller support
(CONFIG_BLK_DEV_DAC960) [M/n/y/?]
```

12. Useful features for machines that will act as packet-filtering firewalls are:

```
Network firewalls (CONFIG_FIREWALL) [Y/n/?]
Unix domain sockets (CONFIG_UNIX) [Y/m/n/?]
IP: policy routing (CONFIG_IP_MULTIPLE_TABLES) [N/y/?]
(NEW)
IP: firewalling (CONFIG_IP_FIREWALL) [Y/n/?]
IP: firewall packet netlink device
(CONFIG_IP_FIREWALL_NETLINK) [Y/n/?]
IP: use FWMARK value as routing key
(CONFIG_IP_ROUTE_FWMARK) [N/y/?] (NEW)
```

NOTE: *Sometimes routing and filtering items overlap. Read the Help information.*

13. A machine you plan to use as a router should have the following items turned on:

```
IP: advanced router (CONFIG_IP_ADVANCED_ROUTER) [N/y/?]
IP: equal cost multipath (CONFIG_IPROUTE_MULTIPATH)
[N/y/?] (NEW)
IP: use TOS value as routing key (CONFIG_IP_ROUTE_TOS)
[N/y/?] (NEW)
IP: verbose route monitoring (CONFIG_IP_ROUTE_VERBOSE)
[N/y/?] (NEW)
IP: large routing tables (CONFIG_IP_ROUTE_LARGE_TABLES)
[N/y/?] (NEW)
IP: fast network address translation
(CONFIG_IP_ROUTE_NAT) [N/y/?] (NEW)
IP: optimize as router not host (CONFIG_IP_ROUTER) [N/y/?]
```

14. Useful features for a proxy firewall are:

```
IP: transparent proxy support
(CONFIG_IP_TRANSPARENT_PROXY) [Y/n/?]
IP: masquerading (CONFIG_IP_MASQUERADE) [Y/n/?]
IP: ICMP masquerading (CONFIG_IP_MASQUERADE_ICMP) [Y/n/?]
```

15. If you want to do virtual hosting and assign multiple IP addresses to the same interface, include:

```
IP: aliasing support (CONFIG_IP_ALIAS) [Y/n/?]
```

16. The following helps protect from denial-of-service attacks:

```
SYN flood protection (CONFIG_SYN_COOKIES) [N/y/?]
```


Related solutions:	Found on page:
Adding A Virtual Site	196
Fighting Denial-Of-Service Attacks	285
Setting Up An IP Firewall	287
Setting Up A Proxy Firewall	289

Configuring The Kernel With **menuconfig**

The **menuconfig** kernel configuration tool is a nongraphical, menu-driven program that allows you to move back and forth through various types of kernel options and change things until you are happy with the final result. To utilize this tool, do the following:

1. Type "make menuconfig" to run the tool. Some compiler code scrolls by, and then the tool opens in the virtual terminal, as shown in Figure 5.2.

NOTE: *This item needs the two ncurses packages to be installed. If you have not installed those packages,* ***menuconfig*** *will not build properly.*

2. If you are new to kernel configuration, it is a good idea to go through the menus one by one and change items as you see fit. I will walk you through an example to show you how to navigate with this tool. To select the Processor Type And Features menu, use the down arrow to move down to the menu.

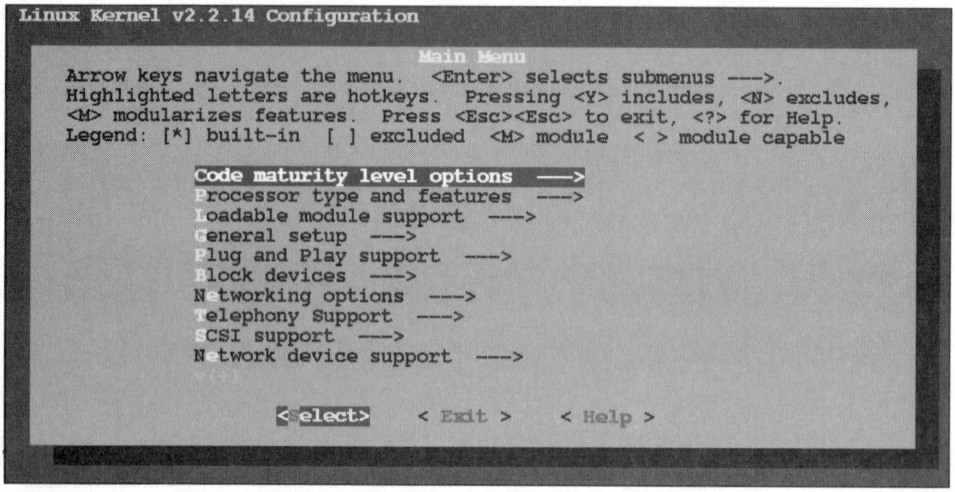

Figure 5.2 The **menuconfig** kernel configuration tool.

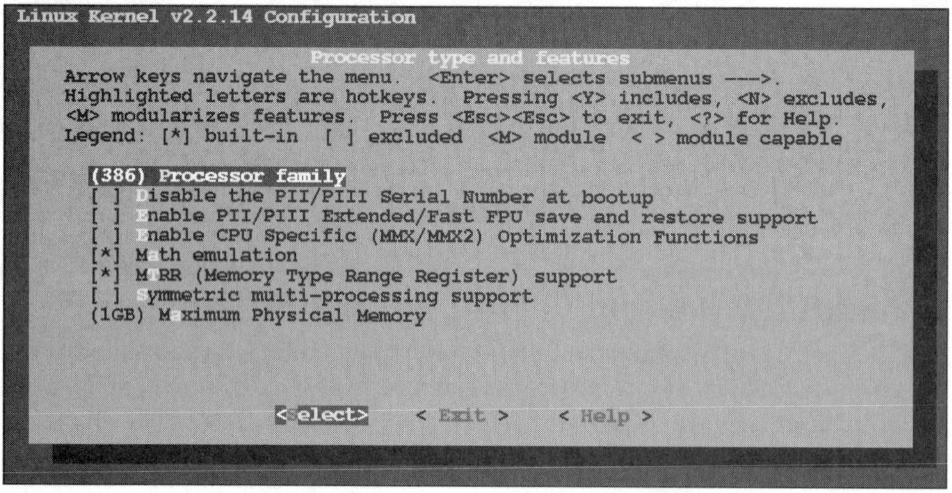

Figure 5.3 The **menuconfig** Processor Type And Features dialog box.

3. To open the menu, press Enter. This brings up the Processor Type And Features dialog box shown in Figure 5.3. Notice that some of the items are kernel options and some are submenus.
4. Press Enter to go into the Processor Family submenu.
5. Use the up and down arrows to move to your CPU speed.
6. Press the spacebar to select the option and automatically move back to the previous menu, Processor Type And Features.

7. Use the up and down arrows to move to the Math Emulation item.
8. If the box is selected—meaning it has an asterisk in it—use the spacebar to deselect it if the machine is a 486DX or faster.
9. Use the up and down arrows to go to the MTRR (Memory Type Range Register) Support option.
10. Type a question mark to pull up the Help information. A dialog box opens containing an entry explaining what this kernel option is for. This information is gleaned from the file Configure.help mentioned in the In Depth section "Kernel Documentation."
11. Read the entry. Use the arrow keys to scroll the text.
12. Press Enter when finished reading.
13. Use the right and left arrow keys to move through the lower menus, to the Exit option.
14. Press Enter to back up to the main **menuconfig** menu.
15. Use the right and left arrow keys to choose the Exit option.
16. Press Enter to exit the tool.
17. If you want to save the configuration, move your cursor to Yes. If not, select No.
18. Press Enter to finish.

Configuring The Kernel With **xconfig**

The **xconfig** kernel configuration tool is a GUI-based program that allows you to use your mouse to move through the various groups of kernel options. To use this tool, do the following:

1. Enter the GUI, if necessary, by typing "startx".
2. Open a Terminal window.
3. Type "/usr/src/linux/make xconfig".
4. Compilation information will scroll past, and then the **xconfig** tool opens, as shown in Figure 5.4.
5. If you are new to kernel configuration, it is a good idea to go through the options one by one and change items as you see fit. I will walk you through an example to show you how to navigate with this tool. Click on the Old CD-ROM Drivers (Not SCSI, Not IDE) option to open the Old CD-ROM Drivers (Not SCSI, Not IDE) dialog box, shown in Figure 5.5.

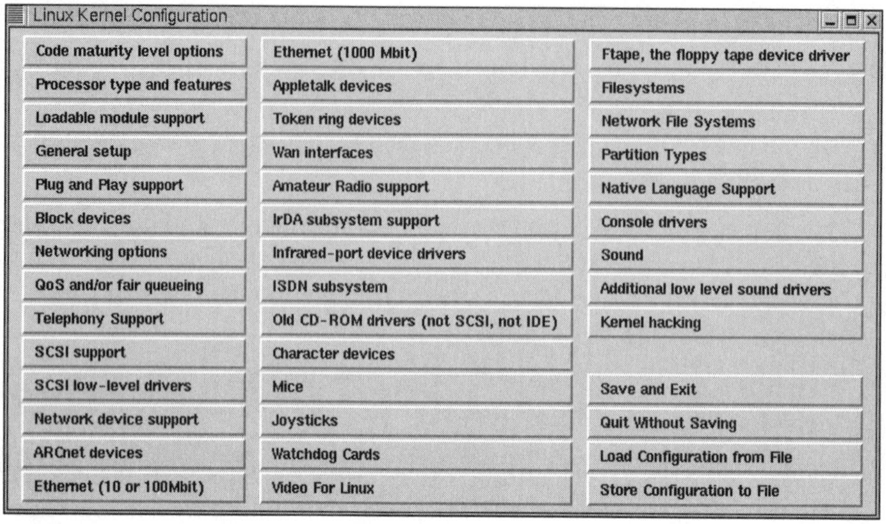

Figure 5.4 The **xconfig** kernel configuration tool.

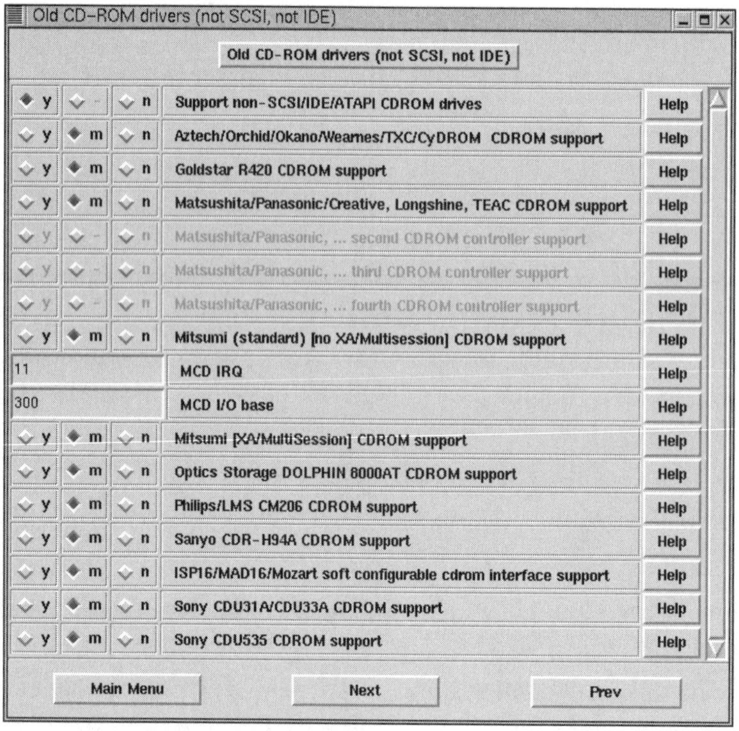

Figure 5.5 The **xconfig** Old CD-ROM Drivers (Not SCSI, Not IDE) dialog box.

6. It is useful to learn how to read these dialog boxes. If the first line mentions whether or not to support a feature, consider this first before fussing with anything below it. The reason I selected this dialog box as an example is that unless you have a CD-ROM drive that is old enough to not be SCSI, IDE, or anything related to these, you do not need it. Click on the "n" next to Support Non-SCSI/IDE/ATAPI CDROM Drives to deactivate this option. Notice that all the other options in the dialog box are no longer available.
7. Click on the Main Menu button to close the dialog box.
8. Click on the Native Language Support button to open the Native Language Support dialog box.
9. Click on "n" for each language you do not need support for.
10. When finished, click on the Main Menu button.
11. When you are finished with the configuration, click on the Save And Exit button to save the changes. A dialog box opens.
12. Read the contents of the dialog box, which explains that you have just completed configuring your kernel and what the next command in the kernel compilation process is. Then click on OK.

Related solution:	Found on page:
Getting A Command Prompt	14

Listing Loaded Modules

To see what kernel modules you currently have loaded, use the **lsmod** command or use **more /proc/modules**.

Inserting Modules Manually

To insert a kernel module, do the following:

1. Use the **cd** command to change to the /lib/modules directory.
2. View the directory's contents with the **ls** command. If you have never added a new kernel before, there should be just one subdirectory. This subdirectory is named for the kernel version it serves.
3. Change to the appropriate kernel version's directory.

Table 5.2 Module types within each /lib/modules/version subdirectory.

Directory	Contents
block	Drivers for block devices (other than CD-ROM and SCSI, which have their own section), which are random access media where you can look at any portion of it at any time rather than being forced into a sequence. A quick way to tell if you are dealing with a block device is if the data volume is discussed in bytes.
cdrom	Drivers for a variety of popular CD-ROM drives.
fs	Modules for supported file system types.
ipv4	Modules for IP version 4 services, such as IP masquerading.
misc	Miscellaneous modules that do not belong specifically in any of the other subdirectories.
modules.dep	File containing a list of which modules are dependent on which other modules. This file is generated by the **depmod** command.
net	Networking device driver modules, such as Ethernet drivers.
pcmcia	PCMCIA device drivers.
scsi	SCSI device drivers.
video	Monitor and video card drivers.

4. Locate the module you want to insert. There are a number of subdirectories present in this location. Table 5.2 lists descriptions of what each subdirectory contains.
5. Change to the appropriate subdirectory.
6. Type "insmod *module*", where *module* is the name of the module you want to load.

Removing Modules Manually

To remove a loaded kernel module, do the following:

1. See the section "Listing Loaded Modules" for how to get a list of what modules are currently in action.
2. Determine which module you want to load.
3. Type "rmmod *module*" to unload the module. If there are active modules that depend on the one you are trying to remove, you will get a dependency error.

4. If you got a dependency error, determine whether the dependent module is one that you need. You may need to keep it, which means that you should keep the initial module you wanted to unload. However, you may not need the dependent one either.
5. To remove the initial module plus its dependent modules, type "rmmod -r *module*".

Getting System Information

There is an unusual directory hierarchy that is not actually stored on the hard drive. The /proc directory and its contents are created in RAM by the Linux kernel to store up-to-date information on the system. To get information about your Linux box, its processes, and more, go to this hierarchy. Table 5.3 outlines what you will find in each /proc subdirectory.

TIP: *If you need more in depth information, type "man proc".*

Table 5.3 The type of information within each /proc subdirectory or file.

Directory	Contents
number	Each directory with a number for a name corresponds to a process that is currently running. Within it are the details on how the process was invoked and what its current status is.
cpuinfo	File containing CPU and system architecture information.
devices	File containing a list of device groups and their assigned numbers.
dma	List of Industry Standard Architecture (ISA) direct memory access (DMA) channels that are in use and by what item.
filesystems	List of the file system types the kernel is compiled to understand.
interrupts	Number of interrupts available on each interrupt request (IRQ) setting, including which device is using which IRQ.
ioports	Hexadecimal port addresses in use by various input/output (I/O) devices.
kcore	Binary file containing the information stored in RAM.
kmsg	Binary file containing kernel messages, accessible with the **dmesg** command.
ksyms	Information created and used by the kernel for managing modules.
loadavg	Average of the load the server is under, taken by seeing how many jobs were running at 1 minute, 5 minutes, and 15 minutes ago.

(continued)

Table 5.3 The type of information within each /proc subdirectory or file (continued).

Directory	Contents
meminfo	Amount of free and used RAM, swap space, and more.
modules	Full text listing of the modules loaded by the kernel.
net	Directory containing a group of files that hold information about various aspects of the machine's networking setup. This information is typically easier to follow using the **netstat** and **ifconfig** tools, rather than looking at the raw files.
pci	All PCI devices found at boot time and the configurations assigned to them.
scsi	Directory containing information about the SCSI devices on the machine, as well as more detailed data on the individual devices.
stat	Detailed statistics on what the kernel and system have been doing.
sys	Directory containing information related to kernel variables.
uptime	How many seconds the system has been up without being rebooted, and how long it has spent idle.
version	Current kernel version.

Setting Module Parameters

To change the kernel's module parameters, you edit the file /etc/conf.modules. There are two different types of statements you can build here: *aliases* and *options*. You may want to consider building an alias in /etc/conf.modules if a driver has a name you find difficult to remember, or if you have multiple devices that all essentially use the same driver. Aliases are popular for setting device names to generic device types. On the other hand, you may have the need to add an option to the file. Options are useful if you need to pass parameters to the kernel at boot time for any of the device drivers.

Building An Alias Statement

To build an alias to place in /etc/conf.modules, do the following once you have the file open to edit:

1. Add a new line on which to add the statement. In vi, you type "o" to add and open a new line directly below the cursor.
2. This line is built in the format **alias *alias module***. Choose what you want the alias to be. The choice is mostly dependant on the purpose for the alias: Is it meant to simplify an overly complex module, or is it to allow you to break out a number of different items and point them to the same module? For an example, I do not want to have to remember which specific Ethernet card I have, so my alias is "eth0".

3. The module component is the module the alias should point to. If my second Ethernet card uses the tulip device driver, my full statement looks like:

```
alias eth1 tulip
```

4. Save and exit the file. If you are using vi, press Esc and then type "ZZ".

Building An Option Statement

To build an option to place in /etc/conf.modules, do the following once you have the file open to edit:

1. Add a new line on which to add the statement. In vi, you type "o" to add and open a new line directly below the cursor.
2. This line is built in the format **option *module options***. The module can be either a real module name or an alias that you set within this same file. If Linux is having a hard time finding my second Ethernet card—which is ISA, and Linux cannot autodetect ISA devices—at boot time I need to help it out with some options. So, the module entry for this example is "tulip".
3. Next, you have to add the options themselves. In the case of an Ethernet card, if the kernel cannot find it then I need to explicitly feed it the proper I/O address. In the case of this card, the address is 0x340, so my line will be:

```
option tulip 0x340
```

4. Save and exit the file. If you are using vi, press Esc and then type "ZZ".

Updating LILO

Once you have made a new kernel with a new version, you need to tell Linux Loader (LILO)—the default boot manager used with Linux—where it can find the image file so that the machine can boot with the fresh kernel. To accomplish this task, do the following:

1. Open the file /etc/lilo.conf with the vi editor or your favorite text editor.
2. Look for the section that defines the current kernel boot parameters. It should look something like:

```
image=/boot/vmlinuz-2.2.14-5.0
      label=linux
      initrd=/boot/initrd-2.2.14-5.0.img
      read-only
      root=/dev/hda1
```

3. Place the cursor on the **image** line.
4. Copy the entire section into the editor's buffer. In vi, for a five-line section like the previous example you would type "5yy".
5. Move the cursor onto a blank line above the image line, then type "p" to paste the text. Now you have two identical image definitions.
6. Change the version numbers in the top instance to match the new kernel version, and change the label so you can tell the difference between the two. For example, you might end up with:

```
image=/boot/vmlinuz-2.2.25
      label=linux-new
      initrd=/boot/initrd-2.2.25.img
      read-only
      root=/dev/hda1

image=/boot/vmlinuz-2.2.14-5.0
      label=linux
      initrd=/boot/initrd-2.2.14-5.0.img
      read-only
      root=/dev/hda1
```

TIP: *The reason you are putting the new kernel first is that the first image is booted by default.*

7. Save and exit the file. Type "ZZ" to do this in vi.
8. Type "/sbin/lilo -v" to run LILO in verbose mode. This action ensures that all necessary files are placed properly for boot purposes.
9. When you reboot, press the Tab key to see the label choices. Boot with the new kernel. If everything goes smoothly, come back and remove the old kernel from the listing, and remove it from the /boot directory as well. Be sure to run LILO again to put the changes into effect.

Chapter 6

GUI Management

If you need an immediate solution to:	*See page:*
Installing The X Server In Red Hat	158
Installing GNOME Or KDE In Red Hat	159
Installing GNOME	160
Installing KDE	160
Finding GUI Components Online	162
Adding A Window Manager	162
Adding A Window Manager In GNOME	162
Adding A Window Manager At The Command Line For GNOME	163
Adding A Window Manager At The Command Line For KDE	164
Adding A Theme	164
Adding A Theme In GNOME	165
Adding A Theme In KDE	165
Adding A Theme Everyone Can Use	166
Changing Desktop Environments	167
Restarting The X Server	167
Restarting When You Started With **startx**	168
Restarting When You Started X By Default	168
Changing The Default Run Level	168

In Depth

The importance of GUI management depends on what type of machine you are dealing with. Some server machines really do not need a GUI component, and some machines are even done a disservice because the GUI usurps resources that could otherwise be put to better use. However, on end-user machines, or those requiring multimedia components for development purposes, you need to be able to add and remove components as well as configure them. For example, some users may prefer a different GUI from the one installed by default.

Linux GUI Components

The GUI used in Linux is a client/server system, which you would think refers to a server managing the basics behind the scenes and a client handling the details for the user. However, the reverse is actually true. The Linux GUI server tends to reside on the end-user machine and the clients may or may not be stored locally. The server for the Linux GUI is *XFree86*, also called the *X Window System* or just *X*. This server is based on the commercial X11 server that is the original X Window System. X is used across most Unix flavors, and it is even available on some non-Unix platforms.

The X Server

Red Hat gives you the opportunity to install XFree86 during the installation process. If you do not install it then, that is fine because you can add it at any time. There are a number of components to the X server. The server itself has a specific job to do. As with most servers, the X server's job is to run things behind the scenes. The X server may be on the same machine the end user is working on, or it may be on a network machine. Its job is mostly to draw things. The server draws all of the graphics you see on the GUI desktop that do not directly involve an application you are running.

NOTE: *The "86" in XFree86 has nothing to do with versions. According to the XFree86 Project (**www.xfree86.org**), the term actually refers to the x86 processor, or Intel architecture.*

Window Managers

One item installed on the client side is the *window manager*. This tool manages window movement, iconification, and resizing, but not the actual drawing and look of the windows. A window manager is not the actual X client, however. Instead, it is an intermediate program, taking window movement instructions from the server and translating them into actual motion.

As the system administrator, you are not saddled with the task of fully customizing every user's environment. However, because you know what your user base will be, you may want to set a default working environment that makes sense to the users. Choosing a window manager—whether you stick with the defaults or use something new—is part of this task. The default window manager provided with the GNU Network Object Model Environment (GNOME) in Red Hat is Enlightenment (**www.enlightenment.org**). The K Desktop Environment (KDE) uses its own window manager by default. Other popular choices are:

- AfterStep (**www.afterstep.org**)
- Blackbox (**http://portal.alug.org/blackbox/**)
- IceWM (**http://icewm.cjb.net**)
- Sawmill (**www.dcs.warwick.ac.uk/~john/sw/sawmill/**)
- Window Maker (**www.windowmaker.org**)

Some of these items actually come on the Red Hat CD-ROM—AfterStep and Window Maker to be specific. Installing the included window managers requires the following RPMs, listed in the order you need to install them:

- AfterStep—AfterStep-1.8.0-1.i386.rpm
- Window Maker—libPropList-0.9.1-1.i386.rpm, WindowMaker-0.61.1-2i386.rpm, and wmakerconf-2.1-1.i386.rpm
- Sawmill—(If you are running GNOME) Sawmill-gnome-0.24-3.i386.rpm, sawmill-0.24-3.i386.rpm

Display Managers

The other side of the X client coin is the *display manager*. This tool manages the look and feel of your desktop. The feel includes such issues as user logins, because people can log in and out of their sessions without ever leaving the GUI. You generally do not run out and replace your display managers as often as you might your window managers. Three display managers are common, and they each come with Red Hat Linux:

- *gdm*—GNOME's display manager.
- *kdm*—KDE's display manager.
- *xdm*—The X display manager.

A quick glance at the next section tells you that all three of these belong to larger packages. The xdm segment is the most generic. It belongs to the overall X Window System.

Desktop Environments

Notice that so far that the GNOME (**www.gnome.org**) and KDE (**www.kde.org**) packages themselves have not been listed—just their components. This is due to the fact that GNOME and KDE are not X client pieces. Instead, these two items are desktop environments, providing a fully integrated set of window and display managers, plus their own themes, tools, icons, and more. You can configure them further as well, once you have installed them.

You are not required to use the window managers that come with these desktop environments. Feel free to change them as you wish, though some may work better than others. If there is a specific look and feel you want to create for your users, be sure to experiment and confirm that the configuration you choose works for their day-to-day needs before setting it up for your user base.

When it comes to choosing between GNOME and KDE, much of the decision comes down to user preference. The interfaces are slightly different. There are tools available in each that are not natively available in the other, though Red Hat includes menus in both cases that let you cross over and use the other tools if you have both environments installed. Other reasons people choose one over the other involve the environment's level of maturity. KDE is older, so there has been more time to work the bugs out. However, GNOME is not far behind.

The GUI And System Performance

One trade-off you have to consider when deciding if you want to install a GUI on a system, and if so which one, is system performance. Few would argue that running anything graphical on a system slows it down slightly. There are many calculations involved in displaying graphics. However, there is debate over whether running a GUI on a server machine is a strict no-no.

Part of the reason for the disagreement is that this issue has to be broken down into components. Server machines have a special set of needs that have to be addressed. Not only that, but what those needs are depends on what service the machine provides. Some services are more processor-intensive than others—especially under heavy load. The best way to determine how the system is doing with and without a GUI is to build a shell script that monitors the system load. Chapter 20 contains an example of generating such a script. If the load is consistently above 1.00 then you may have a problem. The further above 1.00 it gets, the worse your problem.

There are a few things you can do if the load average is too high:

- Make sure you are not running a screensaver. No server machine should have a screensaver going, especially fancy ones that require a lot of math. This just takes up CPU time.
- Shut off the GUI when you are not actively using the machine. If you use the box rarely, this can be enough to make a significant performance difference.
- Shut off fancy GUI features, such as animation and sounds.
- Change to less processor-intensive GUI components. For example, consider the following window managers, all available at **www.themes.org**: BlackBox, FLWM, IceWM, Window Maker, and wm2.
- Add additional RAM to the machine.
- Remove the GUI completely, because the machine just cannot handle it while also handling its services.

The Files

There are a number of files used by the X Window System, GNOME, and KDE. Trying to figure out how and when these files are used, and which they should turn to when changing systemwide or personal GUI configurations, leads many users into immense frustration and hours of Web searching. Although I have tried to address as many specific needs as I can think of in the Immediate Solutions portion of this chapter, this section includes listings of the configuration files used by X, GNOME, and KDE.

The X Window System Files

There is some variation between distributions when it comes to where to find some X files. However, which files are used for what is fairly standardized across distributions. The confusing part to the X files is that which files you alter depends on how you enter the GUI. In this section, I refer to booting into the GUI, and starting it by hand. Booting refers to having your system set to enter the GUI by default. Starting it by hand means the system boots to the command line and you use the **startx** command to enter X.

Some files are important regardless of how you enter the GUI:

- */etc/X11/XF86Config*—The primary X configuration file for your machine's hardware.
- */usr/X11R6/lib/X11/fonts/*—Directory containing a series of subdirectories that hold all of the X fonts.
- */usr/X11R6/lib/X11/app-defaults/*—Directory containing configuration files for the various applications available in X, and what states they will open into.

Other files are used specifically by the two different methods of starting the X Window System. If you boot directly into the GUI, then the following files are important:

- */etc/X11/xdm/Xsession*—The master script that launches the window manager you set your system to use by default. You can also set X to open specific terminal windows (called xterms) in this file. Once it has executed its own content, Xsession typically calls other X configuration scripts, including the individual user's own .Xsession, discussed next.
- *~/.Xsession*—A user's personalized version of the Xsession file. Here you can add information for booting your own window manager preferences. This information is generally in the form of an **if** statement because this file is a shell script. Shell scripting is discussed in more detail in Chapter 20. This file is also an opportune place to automatically launch xterms for your own use.
- */etc/sysconfig/desktop*—If your system boots into GNOME by default, then this file may not exist. It is used to set the desktop that you want to use. Your choices—by default—are: GNOME (no need to set this, it is assumed if the file does not exist), KDE, or AnotherLevel. If the file contains only the text KDE or the text AnotherLevel then if the system boots into the GUI, all users by default will get KDE or AnotherLevel.

TIP: *Remember, case is important in Unix variants. Type "KDE" or "AnotherLevel", not "kde" or "anotherlevel".*

- *~/.wm_style*—Each user can set an alternate window manager by placing its name in this file in their home directory. By default, the choices are: AfterStep, Window Maker, Fwm95, or Lesstif.
- */etc/X11/xdm/Xresources*—Master file used to set parameters for the various X applications available.
- *~/.Xresources*—Each user can set their own parameters for X applications here.

If you boot onto the command line and only start X when you want to use the GUI, then the following files apply:

- *xinitrc*—Master file used to set the system resources for the GUI.
- *~/.xinitrc*—Individual user's resource setting script.

Regardless of how you enter the GUI, the following two files might be of interest:

- *Xclients*—Master script used to start the desktop environment and window manager set in the other files.
- *~/.Xclients*—The user's file that starts the desktop environment and window managers. One way to tell the system to use something different than the default is to execute the startup scripts in here.

The GNOME And KDE Files

Another thing many administrators lose sleep over is trying to find the files for both the GNOME and KDE environments. The most important files are the programs that start the environments. These are /usr/bin/gnome-session for GNOME, and /usr/bin/startkde for KDE. You would put the full path for these commands in a file such as ~/.Xclients to start the appropriate environment.

Other than this, the files for these desktops tend to be spread out. Typing "locate gnome | more" or "locate kde | more" gives you a feeling for just how far. Notice that in some cases, depending on which desktop is assigned to a particular user, there might be a ~/.kde or ~/.gnome directory where you can find even more configuration files. In most of these cases, these files are created and maintained by the environments themselves. However, a knowledgeable user can tweak them.

Immediate Solutions

Installing The X Server In Red Hat

Installing the X server is a multistep process in Red Hat. You have to determine which X server is appropriate for your video equipment and more. To install the full GUI if you did not do so during the initial installation process, do the following:

1. Log in as root.
2. Insert the first Red Hat CD-ROM into the CD-ROM drive.
3. Mount the CD-ROM with a statement such as the shortcut **mount /mnt/cdrom**, which is available in Red Hat.
4. Type "cd /mnt/cdrom/RedHat/RPMS" to change to the Red Hat Package Manager (RPM) directory.

TIP: *One feature of the bash shell that can save you much typing from here on is the Tab key. There is a technique called Tab completion that allows you to type a partial file name and, when you have typed enough to make it distinct from the others in the directory or path you are referring to, you can press Tab and the rest of the name automatically appears on the command line.*

5. Type the following to install the X server components you need:

   rpm -ivh XFree86-libs-3.3.6-20.i386.rpm XFree86-xfs-3.3.6-20.i386.rpm XFree86-3.3.6-20.i386.rpm

NOTE: *It is important to use this exact order. The packages are listed in order of dependency, so that those packages requiring other packages are listed after the items they need.*

6. Type "rpm -ivh gtk+-1.2.5-2.i386.rpm Xconfigurator-4.2.8-2.i386.rpm" to install the Red Hat tool that will help you configure your X server.
7. Type "Xconfigurator" to run the configuration tool. This instance is just a test, a quick cheat if you will. You are using it to see which specific X server you need to install. This choice will be revealed to you once you choose your video card.

***WARNING!* Be sure to choose the right video card entry, or if yours is not listed choose to enter a custom value. You can damage your equipment by being sloppy with video configuration.**

8. When Xconfigurator exits with an error and lists which X server is not installed, note which server this is. You will find this server among the XFree86 files. For example, if the program exits complaining about XF86_SVGA, it wants the server XFree86-SVGA-3.3.6-20.i386.rpm.
9. Install the server. For example, **rpm -ivh XFree86-SVGA-3.3.6-20.i386.rpm**.
10. Run Xconfigurator again. This time, it should go through the entire configuration process.

TIP: *It is a good idea to test the X server at this point in the Xconfigurator program. Otherwise, the X server may not be properly configured.*

---

11. Once the program exits, your X server is installed and running. However, you still need to install GNOME or KDE—see the following section "Installing GNOME Or KDE In Red Hat."

Related solution:	Found on page:
Adding And Removing Media To The File System	84

Installing GNOME Or KDE In Red Hat

To install either the GNOME or KDE desktop environment in Red Hat Linux, begin with the following:

1. Log in as root.
2. Insert the first Red Hat CD-ROM into the CD-ROM drive.
3. Mount the CD-ROM with a statement such as the shortcut **mount /mnt/cdrom**, which is available in Red Hat.
4. Use **cd /mnt/cdrom/RedHat/RPMS** to change to the RPM directory.
5. Make sure you have already installed the X server, as discussed in the section "Installing The X Server In Red Hat."
6. Proceed to the appropriate subsection to complete the installation.

Installing GNOME

To install the GNOME desktop environment, do the following:

1. Type the following to install the pile of graphics and sound libraries necessary to run the Enlightenment window manager:

   rpm -ivh libtiff-3.5.4-5.i386.rpm libpng-1.0.5-3.i386.rpm libjpeg-6b-10.i386.rpm libungif-4.1.0-4.i386.rpm freetype-1.3.1-5.i386.rpm audiofile-0.1.9-3.i386.rpm esound-0.2.17-2.i386.rpm libgr-2.0.13-23.i386.rpm libgr-progs-2.0.13-23.i386.rpm imlib-1.9.7-3.i386.rpm fnlib-0.4-10.i386.rpm

TIP: *One feature of the bash shell that can save you much typing from here on is the Tab key. There is a technique called Tab completion that allows you to type a partial file name and, when you have typed enough to make it distinct from the others in the directory or path you are referring to, you can press Tab and the rest of the name automatically appears on the command line.*

2. Type "rpm -ivh enlightenment-0.15.5-48.i386.rpm" to install the Enlightenment window manager.
3. Type the following to install the many graphics and sound libraries necessary for the GNOME desktop environment:

   rpm -ivh xpm-3.4k-2.i386.rpm ORBit-0.5.0-3.i386.rpm gnome-audio-1.0.0-8.noarch.rpm gnome-libs-1.0.55-12.i386.rpm libgtop-1.0.6-1.i386.rpm libghttp-1.0.4-1.i386.rpm libxml-1.8.6-2.i386.rpm libglade-0.11-1.i386.rpm xloadimage-4.1-13.i386.rpm xscreensaver-3.23-2.i386.rpm control-center-1.0.51-3.i386.rpm magicdev-0.2.7-1.i386.rpm
4. Type "rpm -ivh gnome-core-1.0.55-12.i386.rpm" to install GNOME itself.
5. Often from here you would create your own X initialization files, but Red Hat provides a package to start this process for you. Use "rpm ivh xinitrc-2.9-1.i386.rpm" to install it.
6. There are a number of other GNOME packages you may want to install as well. These items are listed in Table 6.1.

Installing KDE

To install the KDE desktop environment, do the following:

1. Type the following to install the many graphics and sound libraries necessary for KDE:

   rpm -ivh libungif-4.1.0-4.i386.rpm libjpeg-6b-10.i386.rpm libpng-1.0.5-3.i386.rpm qt-2.1.0-4.i386.rpm qt1x-1.45-3.i386.rpm kdesupport-1.1.2-12.i386.rpm compat-libs-5.2-2.i386.rpm xpm-3.4k-2.i386.rpm kdelibs-1.1.2-15.i386.rpm libtiff-3.5.4-5.i386.rpm

Table 6.1 GNOME packages to add to the base GNOME configuration.

Package	Purpose
enlightenment-conf-0.15-9.i386.rpm	The configuration component for the Enlightenment window manager
gnome-games-1.0.51-4.i386.rpm	A set of games
gnome-linuxconf-0.25-2.i386.rpm	The GNOME Linux configuration tool; highly recommended
gnome-media-1.0.51-2.i386.rpm	A set of multimedia tools
gnome-objc-1.0.2-6.i386.rpm	Objective C GNOME libraries; highly recommended
gnome-pim-1.0.5-1.i386.rpm	The GNOME Personal Information Manager; contains a calendar, to do list, and contact list management software
gnome-users-guide-1.0.72-1.noarch.rpm	A reference for users trying to find their way through GNOME
gnome-utils-1.0.50-4.i386.rpm	A variety of utilities for GNOME, such as a calculator

TIP: *One feature of the bash shell that can save you much typing from here on is the Tab key. There is a technique called Tab completion that allows you to type a partial file name and, when you have typed enough to make it distinct from the others in the directory or path you are referring to, you can press Tab and the rest of the name automatically appears on the command line.*

2. Type “rpm -ivh kdebase-1.1.2-33.i386.rpm” to install KDE itself.
3. Often from here you would create your own X initialization files, but Red Hat provides a package to start this process for you. Type “rpm -ivh xinitrc-2.9-1.noarch.i386.rpm” to install it.
4. There are a number of other KDE packages you may want to install as well. These items are listed in Table 6.2.

Table 6.2 KDE packages to add to the base KDE configuration.

Package	Purpose
kdeadmin-1.1.2-6.i386.rpm	KDE system administration tools
kdebase-lowcolor-icons-1.1.2-33.i386.rpm	KDE icons that work best with an 8-bit video card
kdegames-1.1.2-3.i386.rpm	A set of games
kdegraphics-1.1.2-3.i386.rpm	A set of graphics tools
kdemultimedia-1.1.2-7.i386.rpm	A set of multimedia tools
kdenetwork-1.1.2-13.i386.rpm	A set of networking tools; recommended
kdetoys-1.1.2-3.i386.rpm	A set of amusements for KDE that do not quite qualify as games
kdeutils-1.1.2-4.i386.rpm	A variety of utilities for KDE, such as a calculator

Finding GUI Components Online

If you want to locate additional window managers, display managers, or themes—unified looks created by various people—you can do so online. To locate them, do one or more of the following:

- Go directly to the GNOME (**www.gnome.org**) or KDE (**www.kde.org**) Web site.
- Go directly to the sites listed in the In Depth section "Window Managers."
- Go to **www.themes.org** to peruse a long list of available options, including various graphically unified themes that you can apply to GNOME or KDE.

Once you find an item you would like to try, download it to your system and save it in a separate directory from the main GUI tools. Put it where you can easily tell what items you can erase at a later date without worry, such as in a subdirectory in your home directory.

Some new GUI elements are actually included on the Red Hat CD-ROM. In these cases, you can install the RPMs and not worry about where the files are placed, because you can uninstall the RPMs later.

Adding A Window Manager

When you want to add a new window manager and try it out, you need to find a way to tell the GUI where to find it and what it is. GNOME and KDE each offer tools that allow you to do this quickly and easily. You can change such settings directly at the command line as well.

Adding A Window Manager In GNOME

If you want to try a new window manager in GNOME and have already downloaded it, do the following:

1. Click on the Toolbox icon to open the GNOME Control Center.
2. Click on the Window Manager under the Desktop tree to open the Window Manager dialog box, shown in Figure 6.1.
3. Click on the Add button to open the Add New Window Manager dialog box.
4. In the Name field, type in the window manager's name. This item exists only for your reference, so give it the name of the file or something else that reminds you of it.

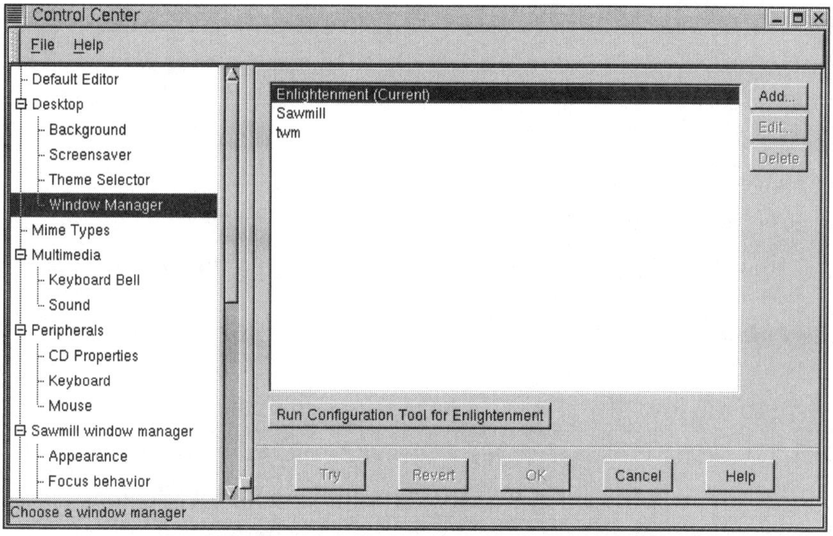

Figure 6.1 The GNOME Control Center Window Manager.

5. In the Command text box, enter the actual command that has to be run in order to run this window manager. This command is often the lowercased name of the program itself. You can find what you need to type here by looking in the window manager's documentation.
6. In the Configuration Command text box, enter the command that has to be run in order to open the window manager's configuration tool if there is one. Once again, if one is available the command you need to type will be included in the documentation.
7. Click on OK. Now the new item is included among the window managers listed in the Control Center Window Manager.

Adding A Window Manager At The Command Line For GNOME

If you want to try a new window manager for GNOME with your personal account and have already downloaded it, do the following:

1. Log into the account you want to change the window manager for.
2. Type "vi ~/.xinitrc" to open or create the local X configuration file.
3. Type "i" to enter vi's insert mode.
4. Type the path for the window manager here. For Enlightenment, this would be "/usr/bin/enlightenment".
5. Press the Esc key.
6. Type "ZZ" to save and exit.

Adding A Window Manager At The Command Line For KDE

If you want to try a new window manager in KDE and have already downloaded it, you actually have to add it at the command line and not within any of the KDE tools:

1. Log in as root.
2. Type "vi /usr/bin/startkde" to open the KDE start script.
3. Type "/kwm" and press Enter to run a search for the line that says only:

```
sleep2;exec kwm
```

4. Cursor to the text "kwm" and type "xxx" to delete the three letters.
5. Type "i" to enter vi's insert mode where the text "kwm" once was.
6. Type the name of the window manager as required by its documentation. This is just the one-word command, not the full path.
7. Press the Esc key.
8. Type ":w /usr/local/kde/bin/start*newname*" to save this new version of the KDE start script and press Enter.
9. Type ":q" to exit the file.
10. Now, if you want to use this window manager in a different account other than the superuser account, log out and then log into that account.
11. Type "vi ~/.xinitrc" to open your local X configuration file.
12. Type "i" to enter vi's insert mode.
13. Type "/usr/local/kde/bin/start*newname*" so the new startup script gets run. Any other user can do this as well.
14. Press the Esc key.
15. Type "ZZ" to save and exit.

Adding A Theme

There are a number of custom themes available on the Internet. These themes allow you to set the look and feel of your desktop all around a particular subject, color, or shape. If you have already downloaded a theme you want to install, follow the appropriate instructions here to get it working.

Adding A Theme In GNOME

If you want to try a new GNOME theme and have already downloaded it, do the following:

1. Click on the Toolbox icon to open the GNOME Control Center.
2. Click on the Theme Selector under the Desktop tree to open the Theme Selector dialog box, shown in Figure 6.2.
3. Click on the Install New Theme button to open the Select A Theme To Install dialog box.
4. Browse to the location where you placed your new theme.
5. Click on the new theme to select it.
6. Click on OK. Your new theme is now included in the Available Themes list box.

Adding A Theme In KDE

If you want to try a new KDE theme and have already downloaded it, do the following:

1. Click on the KDE Control Center icon to open the KDE Control Center.
2. Click on the plus next to the Desktop menu to expand it.
3. Click on the Theme Manager under the Desktop menu to open the Theme Manager dialog box, shown in Figure 6.3.

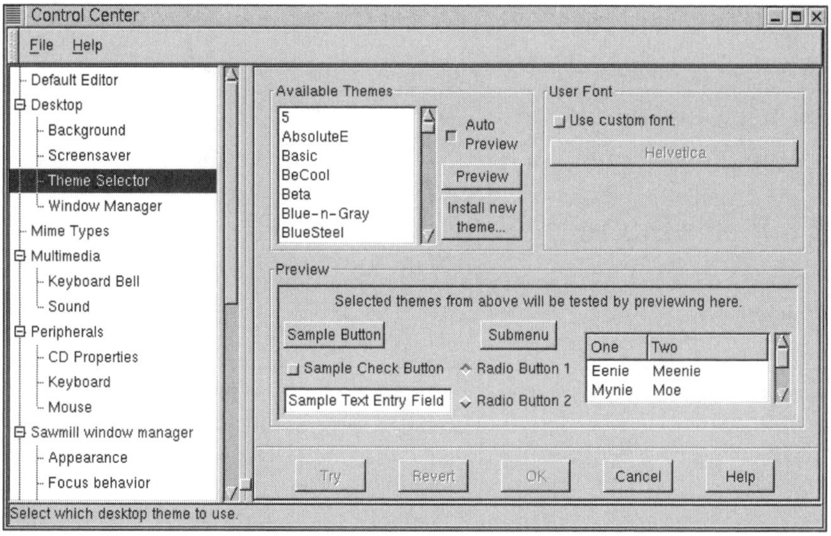

Figure 6.2 The GNOME Control Center Theme Selector.

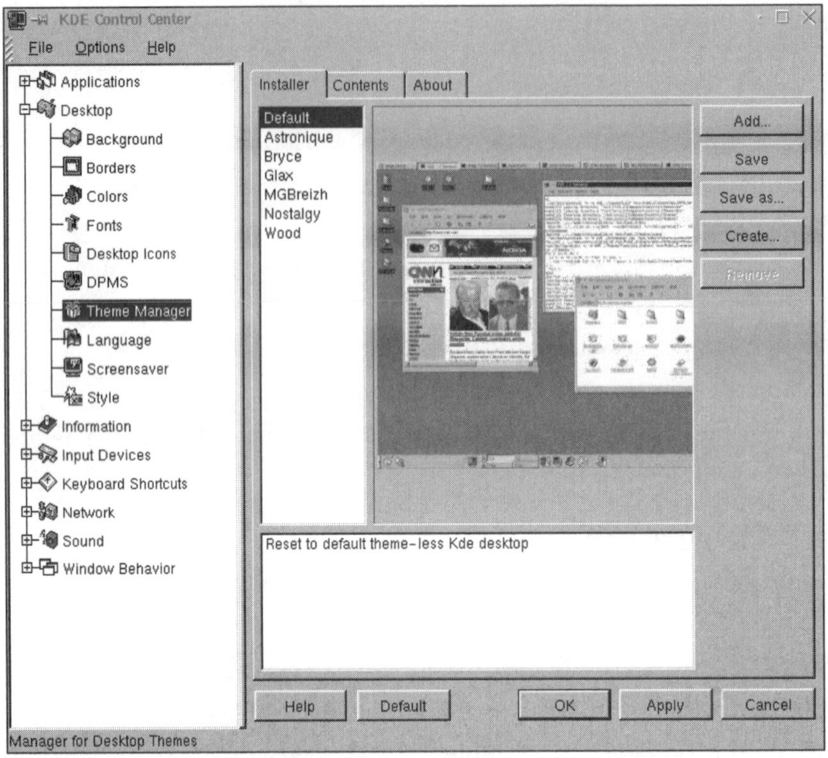

Figure 6.3 The KDE Control Center Theme Manager.

4. Click on the Add button to open the Add Theme dialog box.
5. Browse to the location where you placed your new theme.
6. Click on the new theme to select it.
7. Click on OK. Your new theme is now included in the Installer list box.

Adding A Theme Everyone Can Use

To add a theme as the superuser so that all users can use it, do the following:

1. Log in or **su** to root.

NOTE: *The **su** command stands for superuser. The system administrator, the owner of the root account, is the superuser. This is the person with the highest user privileges on the system. When you type "su" by itself, the system assumes you are trying to gain root access—and you cannot get in without the root password. If you type "su user", then it assumes you want to gain access to that user's account. However, using the **su** command is not the same as logging in. You do not get that user's environment variable or shell settings.*

2. Themes tend to be formulated for specific environments. Change to the /usr/share/apps/kthememgr/Themes directory to add a theme for KDE or the /usr/share/themes directory to add a theme for GNOME.
3. It is a good idea to keep any additional themes in a separate directory in case you decide to (or need to) delete them at a later date. Use the **mkdir** command to add a subdirectory for the new themes, or make a backup snapshot of the current listing with something similar to **ls -la > themedir** so you know what was there originally.
4. Place the new theme in the new or current theme directory.
5. Check the permissions on the directory and the theme and make sure they are the same as those of the parent directory (in case of the new theme directory), and that the new theme's permissions are the same as the other themes' permissions.

Changing Desktop Environments

If you already are set to use GNOME and want to change to KDE, or vice versa, then do the following:

1. Boot the machine.
2. Log into the account whose GUI settings you want to configure.
3. If the Linux box does not automatically go into the GUI, then type "startx" to start it.
4. Open a Terminal window, as discussed in either the GNOME or KDE "Getting A Command Prompt" section in Chapter 1.
5. Type "switchdesk" at the command prompt to open the Desktop Switcher dialog box.
6. Click on the desktop environment you want to change to.
7. Click on OK to accept the change.
8. Click on OK in the informational dialog box that opens.

Restarting The X Server

How you restart your X server depends on how you started it in the first place. You may have your system booting directly into the GUI, or you may have users starting their X clients manually at the command line when they want to use them.

Restarting When You Started With **startx**

If you launch the GUI by typing "startx", there is no single command that will stop the server. However, there is a fairly quick procedure that allows you to stop the X session and restart it:

1. Click on the Footprint icon in GNOME or the K icon in KDE to open the program menu.
2. Click on the Logout or Log Out menu option.
3. Choose the Logout or Log Out option in the dialog box.
4. Click on OK. The X session closes.
5. Type "startx" to start your new session.

Restarting When You Started X By Default

If your settings launch the machine into the GUI by default, you can restart X by doing the following:

1. Log in as root.
2. Type "init 3" to close the GUI and return to the command prompt.
3. Press Enter once the process daemon stops and process start statements stop scrolling down the screen.
4. Log into the same account you were using before if you got the login prompt.
5. Type "init 5" to pull X and the GUI back up.

NOTE: *If you are not doing this as root, then* ***init 3*** *will not work for you. Instead, press Ctrl+Alt+F4. This will take you out of the GUI and into a command prompt login screen. You can then log in as root and type "init 3" there. Once the system finishes changing to runlevel 3, type "init 5" to return to the GUI and log into the user account you were configuring before this started.*

Changing The Default Run Level

If your system normally boots into the GUI or to the command line and you want to reverse this, do the following:

1. Log in as root.
2. Type "vi /etc/inittab" to open the system initialization file that handles what type of login environment the system boots into.
3. Look for a line similar to:

```
id:3:initdefault:
```

4. The number is the important item. Use the arrow keys to move the cursor on top of it.
5. Type "r" to begin a character replacement.
6. Type "3" to change your system so it boots to the command line, or "5" to change it so it boots into the GUI.

TIP: *If you are not using Red Hat Linux, look above this line and there should be a key to the available run levels in your distribution. Type the appropriate number or letter here instead.*

---

7. Press the Esc key, and then type "ZZ" to save and close the file. The next time you reboot, the changes go into effect.

Chapter 7

Networking

If you need an immediate solution to:	See page:
Configuring Networking	186
Getting A Set Of IP Addresses	187
Registering A Domain Name	187
Checking Whether A Domain Name Is Already Taken	189
Using Linux To Check Whether A Core Domain Is Taken	189
Using A Web Browser Under Any OS To Check Whether A Domain Is Taken	189
Determining The Values For Subnetting A Class C Network	189
Applying Subnet Values To A Network	191
Expressing Address Ranges	192
Manually Configuring Basic Static Networking For A LAN	192
Configuring Basic Networking With Linuxconf For A LAN	193
Adding A Virtual Site	196
Assigning More Than One IP Address To An Interface At The Command Line	197
Assigning More Than One IP Address To An Interface In Linuxconf	197
Configuring A Second Network Interface At The Command Line	198
Configuring A Second Network Interface In Linuxconf	199
Setting Up Routing At The Command Line	200
Setting Up Routing Using Linuxconf	201
Configuring Basic Routing	201
Configuring Routing Among Your Networks	202
Configuring Routing To Remote Hosts	203
Configuring Routing For Concurrent Networks	203
Configuring The Routing Daemon In Linuxconf	204
Setting Up IP Masquerading	205

(continued)

If you need an immediate solution to:	See page:
Setting Up Dial-Out Connections	206
Configuring Linuxconf To Connect	206
Configuring Minicom To Connect	209
Configuring **kppp** To Connect	210
Setting Up A DHCP Server	213
Configuring The **pump** Client	214
Administering Machines Remotely	216

In Depth

One thing most Linux system administrators become intimately familiar with is networking. You have many options available regarding how you organize and implement your network. The key is knowing what these options are, what situations they are right for, and how to implement them. This chapter covers the basics of getting your network set up and running.

Introduction To Linux Networking

One of Linux's strengths is as a network server. Linux networking natively speaks the same language as the Internet, which makes providing Internet services and interfacing a Linux local area network (LAN) fairly painless, because no translation machines are needed in the middle. Before you begin configuring Linux networking, you need to understand a bit about the Transmission Control Protocol/ Internet Protocol (TCP/IP), which is the language computers use to talk across the Internet. TCP/IP is actually a suite of protocols that all work together to create smooth communication across the Internet and TCP/IP networks. Each of these protocols has a very specific job to do.

TCP/IP Addressing

When you have a bunch of machines all talking to one another on a network or set of networks, the network protocols need a way to determine which machine the message came from and which machine the message is going to. TCP/IP uses IP addressing to serve this purpose.

You have likely seen an IP address before. It comes in the format ###.###.###.###, where each set of three digits can be anywhere from 0 (000) to 255. These addresses are broken down into network and host components. The size of each of these components is variable, within the constraints of the addressing format. TCP/IP is able to tell what the network portion is by the first triad (set of three numbers). The range of numbers possible in the first triad is divided into classes. These classes are listed in Table 7.1.

After TCP/IP determines which address class the IP address lies within, it knows which portion of the address to use toward the network and which to use toward the host, as shown in Figure 7.1.

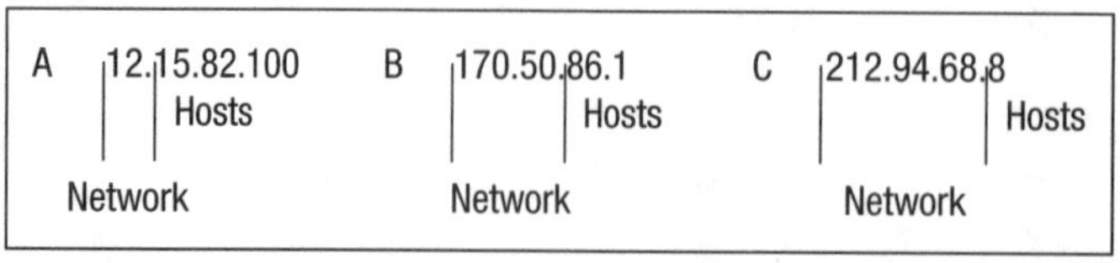

Figure 7.1 Which portion of the three primary IP classes refers to the network, and which to the host.

Table 7.1 IP address classes.

Class	Range
A	0.0.0.0 through 127.255.255.255
B	128.0.0.0 through 191.255.255.255
C	192.0.0.0 through 223.255.255.255
D	224.0.0.0 through 239.255.255.255
E	240.0.0.0 through 247.255.255.255

Because only class C addresses and smaller are given out today as a general rule, the examples throughout this book fall within class C parameters.

There is also a special address shared by every machine using TCP/IP. This address is 127.0.0.1, and is called the *loopback* address. The IP address 127.0.0.1 always refers to the machine you are on. If you want to refer to it by name instead, use "localhost".

The Protocols

As I mentioned earlier, TCP/IP is a collection of protocols that together moves traffic along the Internet and related networks. As a method of grouping protocols into like types, a series of layers each refers to a specific level of functionality within the TCP/IP collection. The layers are, from bottom to top, commonly called the Local Networking layer, the Internet layer, the Transport layer, and the Application layer—the names can vary slightly from person to person, but understanding what each layer does helps with the confusion.

The Local Networking Layer

At the very bottom of the TCP/IP layers is the Local Networking layer, which is where everything starts. It refers to the protocols that carry information across your LAN and everyone else's LAN (or whatever solution they have). This layer even includes the protocols that run your modem. The items that reside in this TCP/IP layer are networking device drivers, such as Ethernet card drivers and modem drivers.

The Local Networking layer takes over when traffic enters the LAN itself, and gives control over when traffic leaves it.

The Internet Layer

The Internet layer is where the IP of TCP/IP resides. This layer is responsible for telling data where to go to get from one network to another across the Internet, or across whatever network it resides within. IP understands Internet addressing, breaks down data for travel across the Internet, reassembles data when it reaches its destination host or network, making sure it gets to the proper subnetwork if necessary.

IP packets are called *datagrams*. Each datagram has a header associated with it that contains the following information:

- *The version of the Internet Protocol that produced the packet*—This is version 4 until the move is finally made to IPv6.
- *How large the header is*—This header is made up of four-byte chunks called *words*. The header length is given as the number of chunks, so when multiplied by four it gives the appropriate header length.
- *Type of service*—This field is not currently used, but was included in case a method of prioritizing packets was put into place. However, some operating systems and protocols do use it for their own purposes. Typically, it has the value 0.
- *Length*—How many bytes long this datagram is.
- *Identification*—An identifying number that allows the recipient to locate where this datagram belongs in the sequence of packets sent. Essential for putting the data back together properly.
- *Flags*—One or more settings that determine what can and cannot be done with this datagram. There are currently three possible choices. The first means there are no flags. The second states that this datagram cannot be *fragmented*, or broken into pieces. The third specifies that it has been broken into pieces, and this is not the last piece.
- *Which fragment*—A measure of where in the full datagram this fragment goes, if the packet was fragmented.
- *Time to live*—How many seconds this datagram may exist on the Internet. If it still is trying to get where it is going when this time runs out, the datagram is deleted.
- *Protocol*—Specifically which protocol this packet's data belongs to. The full list is available at **www.faqs.org/rfcs/rfc762.html**, in the section "Assigned Internet Protocol Numbers".

- *Header verification*—A number based on the header's contents, computed when it is first built and each time it is changed. Recipient machines make the same computation and ensure that their number matches the original. If the numbers are not the same, the header was damaged, and a new copy of the datagram is requested from the source.
- *Source IP address*—The IP address the datagram came from.
- *Destination IP address*—The IP address the datagram is headed to.
- *Options*—Various options that can be attached to the header. Mostly unused except when a TCP/IP connection is being established.
- *Zeros*—The last part of an IP header is a sequence of zeros that ensure that the full header size is a factor of 32.

TIP: *Go to* ***www.faqs.org/rfcs/rfc760.html*** *to read the official specification for how an IP datagram is put together.*

The Transport Layer

The Transport layer actually moves the data across the Internet. Two primary protocols are used for this purpose: TCP and the User Datagram Protocol (UDP)—not to be confused with the term *datagram* discussed in the previous section. TCP handles services that require a steady connection with error checking and recovery. Its data is sent in streams, where each part is sequentially numbered and re-sent if not received at the other end. A value called the *Maximum Transmission Unit (MTU)* is set for each network, declaring the maximum packet size this network handles. When a packet's size exceeds the MTU, TCP breaks it into *fragments*, which are pieces of a packet. Each fragment has its own header information, which contains everything needed to piece the packet together again. If only Humpty Dumpty had been so organized.

UDP, on the other hand, does no error checking and does not even truly connect with the receiving machine. It still has its uses, however, for both very small amounts of data and very large. In something like streaming audio or video, it is not imperative that every single byte reach its source, and waiting to resend can warp the results worse than losing bits and pieces. UDP is also useful on LANs that have nearly ideal throughput. In fact, UDP is faster than TCP in these circumstances because there is no error checking overhead.

The Application Layer

The top of the TCP/IP layer grouping is the Application layer, which is where the various programs that utilize the Internet reside: Web browsers using the Hypertext Transfer Protocol (HTTP), File Transfer Protocol (FTP) clients getting files from servers, email programs sending mail over the Simple Mail Transfer Protocol (SMTP), and more. Each of these protocols has its own way of doing things, but at some point, each passes and receives data from the Internet layer. Table 7.2

Table 7.2 Application-layer protocols and their associated Internet-layer protocol.

Application-Layer Protocol	Internet-Layer Protocol
DNS	UDP
FTP	TCP
HTTP	TCP and UDP
NFS	UDP
POP3	TCP
SMTP	TCP
Telnet	TCP

lays out a list of the more popular Application-layer protocols and whether they use TCP or UDP.

NOTE: *For a full list of which Application-layer and Internet-layer protocols are used for which Internet services, see the file /etc/services.*

There is talk of migrating NFS to TCP. Although this is not an immediate issue, it does show that the Internet-layer protocol used to transport information is not set in stone.

Network Address Components

A LAN or other type of network has a number of special addresses that must be assigned for everything to work properly. Some of these addresses are chosen for you, but you must know about them so that you do not try to assign them to a workstation. Other addresses you can choose for yourself, but you will find that you are guided by tradition or necessity.

Netmask Address

The first special address that you are likely to encounter is the *netmask*. By default, the netmasks in Table 7.3 are used for the main addressing classes.

As long as you are talking about an entire class address (regardless of which class) these netmasks stay the way they are. However, when you get into

Table 7.3 Standard netmasks.

Class	Netmask
A	255.0.0.0
B	255.255.0.0
C	255.255.255.0

subnetting—subdividing your network into a group of smaller networks—or only have part of a set of addresses from within a broken up C class, then you have to adjust the netmask to reflect that fact. See the section "Applying Subnet Values To A Network" for more information.

Network Address

The *network address* is the other half of the equation that tells TCP/IP how large your network is, along with the netmask. These two numbers added together in binary format must equal zero. How to accomplish this is covered in the section "Applying Subnet Values To A Network." Typically, if you have a class C network, then your network address ends in .0. For example, the network address for the machine 192.168.15.12 on a class C LAN is 192.168.15.0.

Gateway Address

Another item you need to know is the *gateway address*. This one is actually pretty straightforward. A gateway is the interface that traffic needs to travel through to reach another network, whether it is another part of the LAN or the Internet. So, for example, if you have a simple LAN with one machine with one Ethernet card managing its Internet connection, then that Ethernet card's IP address is the gateway address.

Broadcast Address

The *broadcast address* typically is the last available address in your IP address block. A broadcast address is used to send data simultaneously to all machines on the network. You can then configure the machines individually regarding whether or not each should listen for broadcast information.

Virtual Machines

Virtual hosting, sites with different names all sharing the same hardware, is an issue that is becoming more and more common on the Internet. This service is not difficult to accomplish, but there is no centralized way of setting it up, aside from adding the virtual site's information to the host database. See the section "Adding A Virtual Site" for more information.

After you have the basic site information in place, configuring virtual network services is a matter of properly setting up the service in question. The specific details for each service are covered where the service itself is covered. For example, to set up virtual email services, see Chapter 12, which covers email.

Expanding Your Address Base

As the IP addressing crunch gets worse and worse, it gets harder to convince providers to assign more than the standard number of IP addresses that they have set internally. Although subnetting is one option of increasing your address

Table 7.4 TCP/IP addresses reserved for isolated networks.

Class	Address Range
A	10.0.0.0 through 10.255.255.255
B	172.16.0.0 through 172.31.255.255
C	192.168.0.0 through 192.168.255.255

base, if you give at least one of the subnets a set of internal-only addresses, as shown in Table 7.4, another option is called *IP masquerading*. When you use this technique, you can set up one machine as the masquerading server and let it tell the rest of the world that it is the one sending all the commands. It then passes data through in both directions so that the machines behind it can pretend they are also connected to the world.

See "Setting Up IP Masquerading," in the Immediate Solutions section, for details on how to set up this service. Actually, two different reasons exist to use masquerading: the reason just described, and another that is related to security (covered in more detail in Chapter 9).

Routers

When you have more than one network speaking TCP/IP, you need at least one machine whose job it is to manage what traffic goes to which network. In a single network, this machine is the *gateway*, the computer that passes traffic to and from the outside world. However, you may have more than one network. You may have your LAN or other network type divided into subnetworks, commonly called *subnets*. Each of these subnets is a separate network with its own IP address pool. The problem presented by this configuration, however, is that traffic is coming in from and going out to the entire network through one gateway.

Without any kind of central management, the data does not know which subnetwork to go to. The machine that provides this traffic control function is called a *router*. Often, a router is not dedicated only to that task—it may also serve as a gateway or other type of server. Linux machines make excellent routers, though you can also buy single-purpose boxes to take care of this need.

There are a number of issues that routers handle. Most of these items deal with converting addressing information from one format to another. One of these is the Address Resolution Protocol (ARP). This tool's function is quite specific: It matches IP addresses to hardware addresses. In the case of Ethernet network addressing, hardware is known by Media Access Control (MAC) addresses, which are the alphanumeric codes assigned to Ethernet cards. Every Ethernet card has a unique MAC.

The Partial Address Class

Today it is difficult to get an entire class C address unless you have a demonstrable need for one. You are most likely to be handed a group of addresses from within a class C that belongs to your upstream provider. This situation leads to the nightmare of trying to figure out netmasks and other items for just part of a class C.

Newer routing protocols were required to simplify this process. These protocols see Internet addressing in a whole new light. They throw the whole concept of address classes out the window and instead use *classless routing*. This type of data routing sends both the IP address and the mask that shows where its network bits end and where its host bits begin, instead of assuming that all machines beginning with specific ranges of numbers have their network and host bits in the same exact spots.

Classless routing allows for some interesting tricks. You can use it to divide a network into subnets of different sizes instead of having to have them all the same size. It also lets people create sub-subnets, sub-sub-subnets, and even deeper subnets if they need to. Although the details of this type of networking are beyond the scope of this book, you can learn more about it in *IP Fundamentals*, by Thomas A. Maufer.

The Centrally Managed Network

The larger your network gets, the more onerous it becomes to add each new machine. Adding a new machine to a network requires editing every /etc/hosts file, adding user accounts and passwords on the new machine, having users change their passwords, and more. Fortunately, various tools are available to make your life easier as a system administrator.

IP Addresses On Demand

Maintaining lists of addressing information on large networks on every machine is time-consuming and fraught with problems. This issue is especially troublesome if the network has to be reconfigured, if machines have to be moved around regularly, or if the network has more machines than available addresses due to growth after initial address allocation. With the Dynamic Host Configuration Protocol (DHCP) service, you can either hand out random IP addresses to machines as they boot or assign them permanent IP addresses. Additionally, you can give out netmasks, assign names, and specify the addresses of the name servers that the machines should use. The **pump** program handles both DHCP and the older Bootstrap Protocol (BOOTP) service in Red Hat Linux.

TIP: *DHCP is especially useful for situations where you do not have enough IP addresses to go around and not everyone needs to be connected at the same time.*

Red Hat 6.2 comes with the Internet Software Consortium's (ISC) DHCP/BOOTP server. Version 2 is capable of testing whether IP addresses are already in use before handing them out. If you want to get the source code for this server for any reason, go to **www.isc.org/products/DHCP/**.

The configuration file for the ISC DHCP/BOOTP server is /etc/dhcpd.conf. This file contains a series of parameters, options, and declarations that, together, make up the assignment rules and behavior for the server. These items deal with the *lease* handed out by the DHCP server. Think of DHCP as a car leasing company. You request a car, and the leasing company leases it to you for a set period of time. DHCP works in a similar manner. A client requests address assignments and the server leases it the IP addressing information it needs to become part of the network.

Parameter statements are compact and straightforward. Many of them are listed in Table 7.5. You use a parameter in the following format:

```
parameter values;
```

Options are also one-line items. A list of commonly used options is available in Table 7.6. You use an option entry in the format:

```
option option value;
```

Table 7.5 Some of the parameters available in /etc/dhcpd.conf.

Parameter	Purpose	Value
authoritative	Default. Means that the server has the last word on what IP addresses are valid for a client. If a client asks for an IP address that the server believes is inappropriate, the server makes it request a new one.	None.
default-lease-time	How long a lease is assigned to a client if it does not request a certain amount of time.	Number of seconds to keep the lease.
filename	A boot file needed by the client. Often used in conjunction with the KickStart tool, covered in Chapter 10.	Path to the file in the format required by the client operating system.
fixed-address	Assigns one or more specific IP addresses to a client. Used only in a host declaration.	IP address or comma-separated list.

(continued)

***Table 7.5 Some of the parameters available in /etc/dhcpd.conf* (continued).**

Parameter	Purpose	Value
get-lease-hostnames	Looks up the hostname assigned to the IP address when it is given to a machine, and assigns it as the hostname option.	**on** or **off**. **off** by default.
max-lease-time	The maximum amount of time the server is willing to allow a client to have a lease.	Length in seconds.
next-server	If the server containing the boot file is not the same as the DHCP server, this parameter explicitly declares where to look.	The boot file server's IP address.
not authoritative	The server does not necessarily know more than the client about what IP information is valid for it. A client's IP request is assumed to be correct.	None.
server-name	Tells the client the DHCP server's name.	Name of server in quotes.
use-host-decl-names	Tells the DHCP server to always assign the name used for the host declaration as the machine's hostname.	**on** or **off**.
use-lease-addr-for-default-route	Useful for Windows 95 machines only. Do not use for Linux boxes.	**on** or **off**.

Table 7.6 Most of the options available in /etc/dhcpd.conf.

Option	Purpose	Value
all-subnets-local	The client should assume all subnets in the same network use the same MTU size.	**1** for yes, **0** for no.
arp-cache-timeout	How long data remains in the ARP cache before it is deleted.	Time in seconds.
bootfile-name	Boot file the client should use. This is the same as the **filename** parameter, but required by some clients.	Full path to the file.
broadcast-address	The subnet broadcast address for this client.	Broadcast IP address.
default-ip-ttl	The time-to-live value the client should assign to all IP packets.	
default-tcp-ttl	The default time-to-live for TCP packets sent from the client.	A positive integer greater than 1.
dhcp-client-identifier	Assigns a unique identifier to the DHCP client.	An identification string in quotes.

(continued)

***Table 7.6 Most of the options available in /etc/dhcpd.conf* (continued).**

Option	Purpose	Value
domain-name	The domain and extension this client belongs to for purposes of name lookups.	Domain and extension in quotes.
domain-name-servers	A list of domain name servers these clients should use.	A comma-separated list of IP addresses.
host-name	Specifies the client's hostname.	Hostname in quotes.
interface-mtu	Specifies the MTU this client should use.	Positive integer, 68 or above.
ip-forwarding	Allows you to declare whether you plan to use **ipchains** to set up IP forwarding on the client.	**0** for no, **1** for yes.
irc-server	IRC servers available to the client.	Comma-separated list of IP addresses.
merit-dump	Specifies where the core file should go in the event of a crash. Useful for automated core cleanup.	Path including file name.
nis-domain	The NIS domain the client belongs to.	Name of domain in quotes.
nis-servers	The NIS servers this client has access to.	A comma-separated list of IP addresses.
nisplus-domain	The NIS+ or NYS domain the client belongs to.	Name of domain in quotes.
nisplus-servers	The NIS+ or NYS servers this client has access to.	A comma-separated list of IP addresses.
nntp-server	The NNTP servers this client has access to.	A comma-separated list of IP addresses.
ntp-servers	The NTP servers this client has access to.	A comma-separated list of IP addresses.
pop-server	The POP servers this client has access to.	A comma-separated list of IP addresses.
routers	The routers this client has access to.	A comma-separated list of IP addresses.
smtp-server	The SMTP servers this client has access to.	A comma-separated list of IP addresses.
static-routes	A list of routes to add to the routing cache.	A comma-separated list of pairs—first the destination network and second the router used to reach it.

(continued)

***Table 7.6 Most of the options available in /etc/dhcpd.conf* (continued).**

Option	Purpose	Value
subnet-mask	The client's subnet mask.	IP address.
tcp-keepalive-interval	How often to send messages that keep a TCP connection alive.	Number of seconds to wait before sending. **0** means not to do this by default.
time-servers	The time servers this client has access to.	A comma-separated list of IP addresses.
www-server	The Web servers this client has access to.	A comma-separated list of IP addresses.

When it comes to declarations, these look a little odd when given in a general format:

```
declaration {
  parameter1
  parameter2
  ...
  parametern
  declaration1
  declaration2
  ...
  declarationn
}
```

As you can see, often you end up with declarations inside other declarations when building your dhcpd.conf file. The declarations available are listed in Table 7.7.

Table 7.7 Declarations available in /etc/dhcpd.conf.

Declaration	Purpose	Subdeclaration Issues
group	Used to apply identical parameters to a series of declarations.	Cannot include range.
host	Used to apply parameters to a specific host, denoted by its MAC.	None.
range	Defines the range of addresses in the subnet in question.	No subdeclarations allowed.
shared-network	Specifies which subnets share the same networking cables.	Must declare subnets inside this statement.
subnet	Identification information and settings for a particular subnet.	None.

Centralized Account Management

Sometimes, the most frustrating part of managing a large network is trying to make sure all the machines have the right user account information. You may not necessarily want all users to have accounts on all machines, but if you need any sort of crossover and have a lot of users coming and going, it can be quite frustrating and time-consuming to keep up with accounts. Many administrators utilize the NIS or NIS+ package to centralize account management. These packages are covered in Chapter 16.

Immediate Solutions

Configuring Networking

To configure your networking, follow this general order of events:

1. Where you start depends on what type of connection you are setting up:
    - If you are setting up a modem connection, see "Setting Up Dial-Out Connections", later in this chapter.
    - To set up the basic networking information for an internal LAN connection, go to either "Manually Configuring Basic Static Networking For A LAN" or "Configuring Basic Networking With Linuxconf For A LAN."

NOTE: *If you need to set up a LAN and a modem connection that connects that LAN to the outside world, start by configuring the LAN internals and configure the PPP connection last.*

2. Test the connections. Try talking to the outside world. If you just set up a LAN, make sure the machines can talk both inside and outside the network.
3. Shore up your security—as discussed in Chapter 9—before you continue. Or, at least do some of the initial work in this area, for now.
4. Set up your domain name resolution, as discussed in Chapter 11.
5. Set up the other Internet and network services, such as email, Web, and so on.
6. Finish shoring up your security.

Related solutions:	Found on page:
Shutting Off Unnecessary Daemons And Background Processes	264
Shutting Off Unnecessary Non-Daemon Network Services	267
Restricting Network Access With **tcp_wrappers**	267
Removing Unnecessary Packages	279
Analyzing Logs	281
Preparing For A Breach	282
Securing Passwords With Crack	284

(continued)

Related solutions:	Found on page:
Setting Password Rules	285
Setting Up An IP Firewall	287
Setting Up A Proxy Firewall	289
Configuring The Master Name Server	336

Getting A Set Of IP Addresses

If you intend to use more than just an internal LAN with network numbers reserved for internal use (see Table 7.4 earlier in the chapter for a list of these numbers), then you need to register for a set of IP numbers for your network. To get these numbers, do the following:

1. Determine both your current number of hosts and what you may add to the LAN in the next few years. It is good to keep a margin for error here, but do not go overboard. The Internet has an addressing shortage, so the current IP assignment mantra is to take just what you need.
2. Today, IP addresses are typically assigned by Internet Service Providers (ISPs) out of their own designated address blocks. Talk with your upstream service representative to find out what range(s) they can offer.

Registering A Domain Name

After you have the IP addresses for your network, if you want to use your network on the Internet, you need to register a domain name. To find an available name and register it, do the following:

1. Make a list of the types of names that are appropriate for your domain. Just focus on the name portion for now, not the extension. After you have a list of at least five possibilities, move on to Step 2.
2. Determine the set of extensions that suits your site. Two different groups are available. One of these groups is based on the country you are located in. A full set of the available country extensions is available at **http://metalab.unc.edu/pub/docs/rfc/rfc1394.txt**. The other available group is a set of core extensions, as shown in Table 7.8.
3. Now comes the potentially frustrating part. Many domain names are already taken. See the next section, "Checking Whether A Domain Name Is

Table 7.8 The core domain extensions.

Extension	Used For
.com	Commercial sites
.edu	Educational sites
.gov	U.S. government sites
.mil	U.S. military sites
.net	Large networks that do not necessarily belong in the other areas
.org	Organizations, commercial and noncommercial

Already Taken," to go through the various domain name and extension combinations available to you. The end decision depends on a couple of factors:

- *Which extension is the most appropriate for your site?* Carefully read the purpose for each of the main extensions. Although the system does offer some flexibility, you need to ensure that the full name for the site gives the right impression. This issue includes whether the site is considered for local or international purposes, and whether it fits within the rules set for some of the more limited extensions. Money is also a factor. Some extensions cost more than others.
- *What name variations on your list are available under the extension you chose?* In the worst-case scenario, every item on your list is already taken. You need to make another list if this happens. Use more variations or even consider a new base name. A thesaurus comes in handy for choosing synonyms.

4. Determine where you want to register your domain name. No longer do you have to use the central registration agency, InterNIC, which is now called Network Solutions (**www.networksolutions.com**). Other companies also handle domain registration. A listing of these companies is available at **www.icann.org/registrars/accredited-list.html**.
5. Register the domain as instructed by the registry you chose.
6. Wait for the appropriate number of hours while your name information propagates across the root servers. Each registry's instructions tell you how long to wait. During this time, you can configure your name information according to the instructions in Chapter 11.

Related solutions:	Found on page:
Configuring The Master Name Server	336
Configuring The Slave Name Server	338

Checking Whether A Domain Name Is Already Taken

Many domain names are already registered or in use. It is not sufficient to just look and see if there is a Web site at that domain. There may be no Web site at that domain—after all, not everyone uses the Web—or a domain name speculator who has no plans to use the real estate may own the name. Such people buy domain names just to resell them at a higher price. This frustrating fact plagues many people who are trying to find a useful, available name.

Using Linux To Check Whether A Core Domain Is Taken

In Linux, to see whether a core domain is taken—essentially .com, .edu, or .net—type “whois *domain.extension*”.

NOTE: *Install the* ***fwhois*** *RPM if the command does not exist on your machine.*

Related solution:	***Found on page:***
Installing RPMs	114

Using A Web Browser Under Any OS To See Whether A Domain Is Taken

If you want to see whether a domain name is already taken, but you are not yet using Linux or currently are not sitting in front of a Linux machine, go to **www.networksolutions.com/cgi-bin/whois/whois** and do a search from there. Notice that the bottom of the page offers pointers to other search services.

Determining The Values For Subnetting A Class C Network

Subnetting a network can be a quick and easy task, or it can be a time-consuming job with a lot of frustration. Which of these options it turns out to be—or whether it is something in between—depends on what range of addresses you have available and how many subnets of what sizes you need to make. To break up your available addresses into subnets, do the following:

1. If you have a class C network, break it into subnets by choosing the proper netmask. First, decide roughly how many machines you want on each subnet.
2. After you know how many machines you want per subnet, look to Table 7.9 for a list of how many hosts you get for each subnet.

Table 7.9 Approximate hosts per subnet, according to the number of subnets in a class C network.

Number Of Subnets	Hosts Per Subnet
2	127
4	63
8	32
16	15

NOTE: *This table provides approximate values, because you lose at least two addresses to networking issues.*

3. Determine the netmask to use for your subnetted network. See Table 7.10 for the netmasks to use depending on how you have divided an entire class C address pool.
4. Determine the IP address ranges for each subnetted segment. Use the value determined in Table 7.9 to build these ranges. The number in the Hosts Per Subnet column is your boundary line. For example, if you are creating four subnets, then you have a value of 63 hosts per subnet. This gives you the following range set:
   - .0 through .63
   - .64 through .127
   - .128 through .191
   - .192 through .255
5. Remove the subnet network address from availability for each subnet. Table 7.11 shows the class C subnet network addresses for subnets broken into 2, 4, 8, and 16 pieces.
6. Remove the subnet broadcast address from availability for each subnet. Table 7.12 shows the class C subnet broadcast addresses for subnets broken into 2, 4, 8, and 16 pieces. You might be starting to see a pattern now.

Table 7.10 Commonly used netmasks for breaking up class C networks.

Number Of Subnets	Class C Netmask
2	255.255.255.128
4	255.255.255.192
8	255.255.255.224
16	255.255.255.240

Table 7.11 Commonly used subnet network address endings for class C networks.

Number Of Subnets	Subnet Network Address Endings
2	.0, .128
4	.0, .64, .128, .192
8	.0, .32, .64, .96, .128, .160, .192, .224
16	.0, .16, .32, .48, .64, .80, .96, .112, .128, .144, .160, .176, .192, .208, .224, .240

Table 7.12 Commonly used subnet broadcast address endings for class C networks.

Number Of Subnets	Subnet Broadcast Address Endings
2	.127, .255
4	.63, .127, .191, .255
8	.31, .63, .95, .127, .159, .191, .223, .255
16	.15, .31, .47, .63, .79, .95, .111, .127, .143, .161, .175, .191, .207, .223, .239, .255

Applying Subnet Values To A Network

Although this chapter is not meant to teach all of the basics of networking, you should keep in mind the following points when you are putting a subnet into place:

- Machines that straddle two networks must each be set up as routers so the kernel knows where to send data destined for the various networks.
- Machines that straddle two networks need a different interface for each network. So, for example, if the machine is a router between two different Ethernet-joined subnets, then it must have two Ethernet cards, one for each network cable.
- The first and last subnets cannot be used for hosts. The first subnet is reserved for subnet identification, and the last is reserved for whole-network broadcast.
- The first and last addresses within a subnet cannot be used for hosts. The first is the network address for the subnet, and the last is the broadcast address.

Expressing Address Ranges

To express a range of IP addresses that are not divided by network numbers, do the following:

1. Determine the contiguous range of addresses you want to refer to. For example, 192.168.40.0 to 192.168.40.20.
2. Determine the IP address class this range belongs to. For the example, 192 is a class C address.
3. Determine the netmask for the address class. A netmask for a class C address is 255.255.255.0. This base netmask refers to the entire network. In this case, the final 0 means that any number from 0 through 255 is included.
4. The format to express this address range is *address/mask*, where the address is the start of the range and the mask is a netmask reflecting how large the range is. Therefore, the first part of the expression is 192.168.40.0. To calculate the second part, start with 255.255.255.255. Now, remove 20 from the last portion of the netmask, making it 255.255.255.235. Your pair is now 192.168.40.0/255.255.255.235.

Manually Configuring Basic Static Networking For A LAN

To set up basic TCP/IP networking, do the following:

NOTE: *If you are setting up a dial-up connection, see "Setting Up Dial-Out Connections," later in this chapter, instead of following LAN and other Ethernet networking sections.*

1. Log in at the command line as root.

NOTE: *You can do this either in command-line mode or in a terminal window within the GUI.*

2. Type "vi /etc/hosts" to open the file that contains your host-to-IP address mapping information.
3. By default, the first line in this file looks similar to the following:

```
127.0.0.1     localhost
```

   It is important to leave this line intact. The localhost definition allows you to loop back to your own machine, meaning that you can connect back to it without utilizing a networking interface.

4. If you configured the basic networking information during your Red Hat installation, then another line may appear after the localhost line. This line is in the format:

```
IPAddress     FullDomain     HostNameORNickname
```

   For example, the line might look like the following:

```
192.168.12.5    cheetah.animals.org    cheetah
```

5. From this point, the rest of the information contained within this file consists of lines that define the other hosts on your network. Each time you add a new host, you need to—or should—add an /etc/hosts entry to each of the machines.
6. After you finish filling out the /etc/hosts file, press the Esc key and then type "ZZ" to close the file.
7. Red Hat Linux specifically uses the file /etc/sysconfig/network to store key networking information accessed at boot time. Type "vi /etc/sysconfig/network" to open this file.
8. Either look for the line beginning with the variable HOSTNAME or create one. This line must be in the format HOSTNAME=*name*, where *name* is only the host's name, not the full domain name. For example:

```
HOSTNAME=cheetah
```

9. After you finish filling out the /etc/sysconfig/network file, press the Esc key and then type "ZZ" to close the file.
10. Determine the netmask you need to use for the machine.
11. Type "ifconfig eth0 *IPaddress* netmask *netmask*" to assign the IP address to that particular Ethernet card.

Configuring Basic Networking With Linuxconf For A LAN

To configure networking for your LAN within Linuxconf, do the following:

1. Open the Linuxconf configuration tool.
2. Select Config|Networking|Client Tasks|Basic Host Information from the menu to open the This Host Basic Configuration dialog box, shown in Figure 7.2.

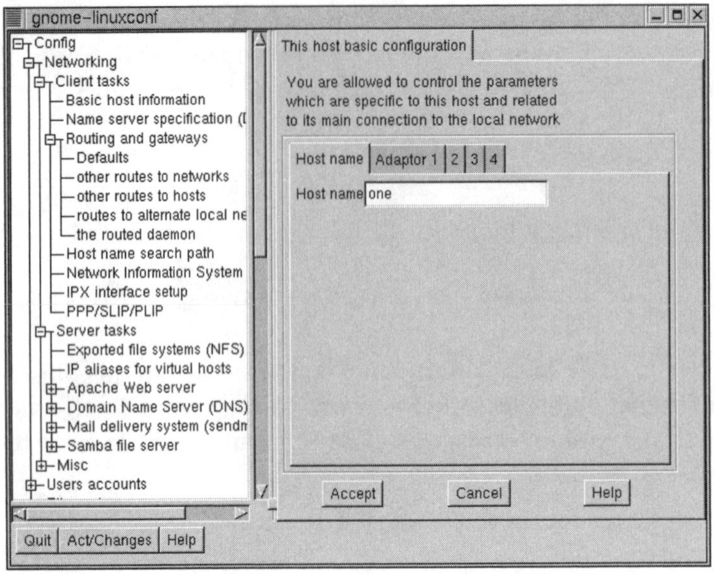

Figure 7.2 The This Host Basic Configuration dialog box, Host Name tab, within Linuxconf.

3. Type the machine's name—just the hostname, not the whole domain name—in the Host Name text box.

NOTE: *If you configured this information or any other information during the installation process, some of these items will already be filled in.*

4. Click the Adaptor 1 tab, shown in Figure 7.3, to configure your networking interface; for example, your Ethernet card.
5. Make sure that the Enabled checkbox is selected. Doing this activates the interface, meaning that Linux now looks for the Ethernet card (for example) and expects you to provide configuration information for it.
6. Addressing information can be assigned to a machine via any one of the following three methods:
   - Manually, where you fill in the information yourself
   - DHCP, which is a client/server offering that sets up networking on the fly
   - BOOTP, which is an older client/server offering that has since been replaced by DHCP

   If you are not sure which method you want to use for now, select Manual. Otherwise, click either Dhcp or Bootp where appropriate.

TIP: *If you want to use* ***pump****, choose Dhcp.*

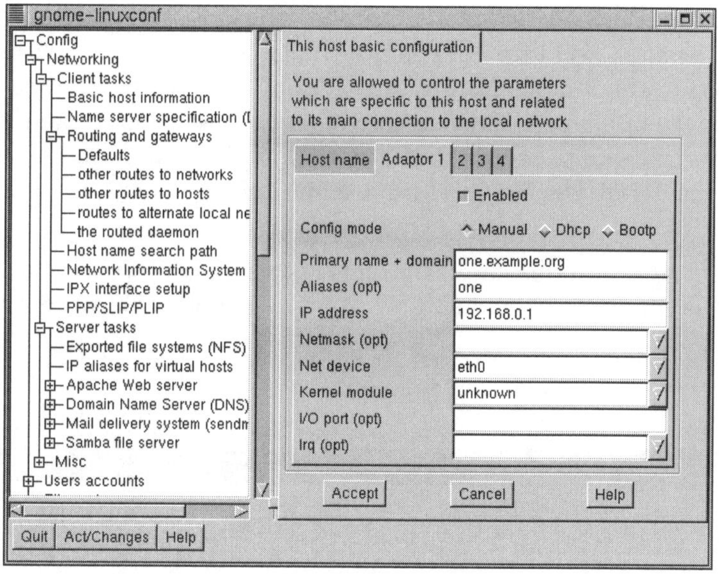

Figure 7.3 The Adaptor 1 tab within Linuxconf.

7. If you selected Dhcp or Bootp, skip to Step 14. Otherwise, it is time to fill in your networking information. Type the fully qualified hostname—which means you need to include the domain name—into the Primary Name + Domain text box. For example, "cheetah.animals.org".
8. If you want to create any aliases for this machine, add the hostnames in the Aliases (opt) text box separated by spaces. Typically, you would add the hostname to this list so that it is not always necessary to type the fully qualified domain name (FQDN).
9. Enter the machine's IP address in the IP Address text box.
10. Enter the machine's netmask value in the Netmask (Opt) text box, or click the drop-down list box and choose the appropriate netmask value from there.
11. Enter "eth0" or select this value from the drop-down list box next to the Net Device text box.
12. In the Kernel Module drop-down list box, tell Linux what type of Ethernet driver it needs to use. This information should be available in the card's manual. If not, you can often locate the information on the manufacturer's Web site.

TIP: *If you still cannot find the driver information you need, check out the Linux Ethernet HOWTO at* ***www.linuxdoc.org/HOWTO/Ethernet-HOWTO.html****.*

13. Linux can automatically detect the I/O port used by most PCI cards. However, if it cannot find yours or you have an older ISA Ethernet card, you may need to enter an I/O port in the I/O Port (Opt) text box. Each card has a range of I/O ports it is capable of using, and the card's manual or manufacturer's Web page lists this information. These port addresses are in the form 0x###, where # is a hexadecimal item. A common example is 0×300.
14. If IRQ conflicts exist for this card—or if it is not working properly and you have tried everything else—manually select an IRQ in the Irq (Opt) drop-down list box.
15. Click the Accept button to close the dialog box.

Related solution:	Found on page:
Opening Linuxconf	12

Adding A Virtual Site

When you want to host a virtual domain, two major steps are required to set it up. The first major step, making sure that the network knows where to find this machine, is described in this section. The second major step is covered under the specific network service you want to set up. To accomplish the first major step of setting up a virtual site:

7. Networking

1. Choose an IP address for the virtual site. In the case of many services, you can just assign internal use IP addresses, as shown earlier in Table 7.4. Pretend that an entire network is on that machine.
2. Type "vi /etc/hosts" to open the host management file on the machine containing the interface.
3. Place the cursor on the line defining your localhost entry. It should be one of the first lines in the file.
4. Type "o" to create a new line after this entry.
5. Add a name definition here. For example, if you are creating the virtual host hyacinth.flowers.org using the virtual class C network 192.168.3.0, and you decide to give this machine the host IP 192.168.3.10, the entry might look like this:

```
192.168.3.10        hyacinth.flowers.org
```

6. Press the Esc key and then type "ZZ" to close the file and save the changes.

7. Now you need to assign the IP address to an interface. To accomplish this, use IP aliasing. Type "ifconfig *interface:virtualnumber virtualIP*". For example, if hyacinth is the first virtual machine you are adding, type "ifconfig eth0:0 192.168.3.10".

Assigning More Than One IP Address To An Interface At The Command Line

It is possible to use a technique called *IP aliasing* to assign multiple IP addresses to the same interface. Follow the instructions in "Adding A Virtual Site," earlier in the chapter, to accomplish this task. However, if you do not want to assign name information, you do not need to add any /etc/hosts entries.

Assigning More Than One IP Address To An Interface In Linuxconf

It is possible to use a technique called *IP aliasing* to assign multiple IP addresses to the same interface. To accomplish this, do the following:

1. Open the Linuxconf configuration tool.
2. Select Config|Networking|Server Tasks from the menu.
3. Click IP Aliases For Virtual Hosts to open the Edit IP Aliases Configurations dialog box.
4. Click the "lo" (loopback) device to open the IP Aliases For Device Lo dialog box, shown in Figure 7.4.
5. For each IP address or group of IP addresses that you want to assign to this interface, fill in the following parameters:
   - The IP alias or range, as described in the dialog box
   - The netmask for this IP address or range, if necessary
6. When you are finished making these assignments, click Accept to close the IP Aliases For Device Lo dialog box.
7. Click Quit to close the Edit IP Aliases Configurations dialog box.

Related solution:	Found on page:
Opening Linuxconf	12

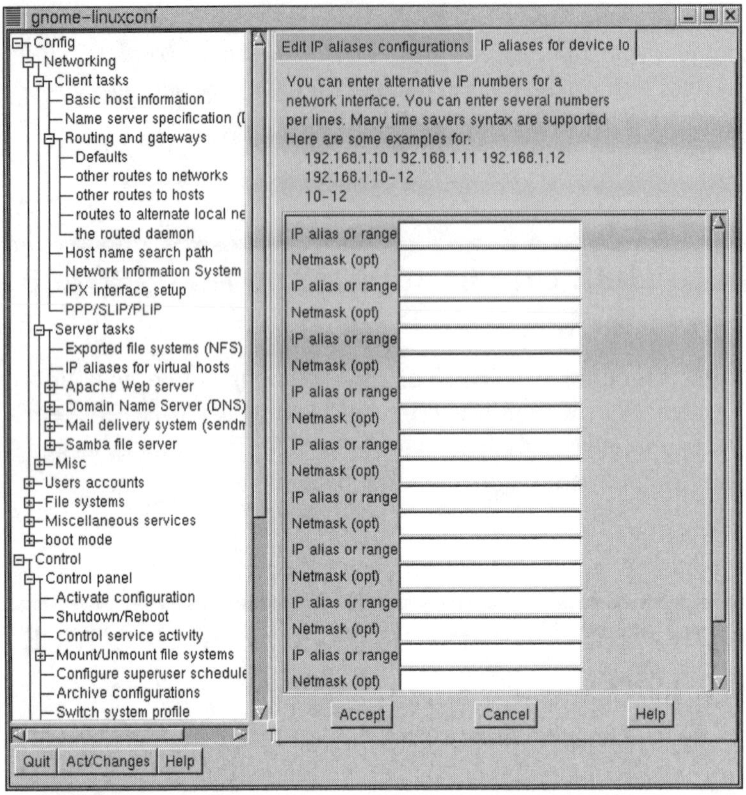

Figure 7.4 The Linuxconf tool open to the IP Aliases For Device Lo dialog box.

Configuring A Second Network Interface At The Command Line

To set up Linux to utilize two different network interfaces—for example, two Ethernet cards—while at the command line, do the following:

1. The second Ethernet card is typically called eth1. Type "ifconfig eth1 *IPaddress* netmask *netmask*" to assign the appropriate IP address to this card.
2. Type "vi /etc/hosts" to open the host configuration file.
3. Move the cursor to where you want to add the host definition.
4. Press "o" to open a blank line beneath the current line, and enter Insert mode.
5. Enter the host definition. For example:

```
192.168.10.41        cat.animals.org      cat
```

6. Press the Esc key and then type “ZZ” to save and close the file.
7. To learn how to add routing for this interface, see the upcoming sections “Setting Up Routing At The Command Line” and “Setting Up Routing Using Linuxconf.”

Configuring A Second Network Interface In Linuxconf

To set up Linux to utilize the second of two different network interfaces—for example, two Ethernet cards—in Linuxconf, do the following:

1. Open the Linuxconf configuration tool.
2. Select Config|Networking|Client Tasks|Basic Host Information from the menu to open the This Host Basic Configuration dialog box, shown earlier in Figure 7.2.
3. Click the 2 tab to configure your second networking interface; for example, your second Ethernet card. This action opens a tab similar to that shown earlier in Figure 7.3.
4. Ensure that the Enabled checkbox is selected. Doing this activates the interface, meaning that Linux now looks for the Ethernet card (for example) and expects you to provide configuration information for it.
5. Addressing information can be assigned to a machine by using any one of the following three methods:
   - Manually, where you fill in the information yourself
   - DHCP, which is a client/server offering that sets up networking on the fly
   - BOOTP, which is an older client/server offering that has since been replaced by DHCP

   If you are not sure which method you want to use for now, select Manual. Otherwise, click either Dhcp or Bootp where appropriate.

TIP: *If you want to use **pump**, choose Dhcp.*

---

6. If you answered Dhcp or Bootp, skip to Step 13. Otherwise, it is time to fill in your networking information. Type the fully qualified hostname—which means you need to include the domain name—into the Primary Name + Domain text box. For example, “gazelle.animals.org”.
7. If you want to create any aliases for this machine, add the hostnames in the Aliases (Opt) text box separated by spaces. Typically, you add the hostname to this list so that you don’t always need to type the FQDN.
8. Enter the machine’s IP address in the IP Address text box.

9. Enter the machine's netmask value in the Netmask (Opt) text box, or click the drop-down list box and choose the appropriate netmask value from there.
10. Enter "eth1" or select this value from the drop-down list box next to the Net Device text box.
11. In the Kernel Module drop-down list box, tell Linux what type of Ethernet driver it needs to use. This information should be available in the card's manual. If not, then often you can locate the information on the manufacturer's Web site.

TIP: *If you still cannot find the driver information you need, check out the Linux Ethernet HOWTO at* ***www.linuxdoc.org/HOWTO/Ethernet-HOWTO.html****.*

---

12. Linux can automatically detect the I/O port used by most PCI cards. However, if it cannot find yours or you have an older ISA Ethernet card, you may need to enter an I/O port in the I/O Port (Opt) text box. Each card has a range of I/O ports it is capable of using, and the card's manual or manufacturer's Web page lists this information. These port addresses are in the form 0x###, where # is a hexadecimal item. A common example is 0x330.
13. If IRQ conflicts exist for this card—or if it is not working properly and you have tried everything else—manually select an IRQ in the Irq (Opt) drop-down list box.
14. Click the Accept button to close the dialog box.

Related solution:	Found on page:
Opening Linuxconf	12

Setting Up Routing At The Command Line

To set up routing in Linux, do the following:

1. Log in as root.
2. Type "route add -net *networkIP* netmask *netmask* dev *device*" to create a route on this machine.

Setting Up Routing Using Linuxconf

Setting up routing entails many subtleties, depending on where the machine in question is situated in the network hierarchy. This section is divided into subsections reflecting the different aspects of routing that Linuxconf is able to configure.

Configuring Basic Routing

To set up your basic routing information on any machine, do the following from Linuxconf's Routing And Gateways section:

1. Open the Linuxconf configuration tool.
2. Select Config|Networking|Routing And Gateways to expand the menu.
3. Click Set Defaults to open the Defaults dialog box, shown in Figure 7.5.
4. In the Default Gateway text box, enter the IP address of the interface that this machine talks to in order to reach the outside world.

NOTE: *You may not want the machine to try talking directly to the Internet. If it is in a subnet and has to pass through a different gateway before the data can reach the Internet or any other network, then enter the IP address for this interface instead.*

---

5. If the machine you are configuring needs to act as a packet router for machines behind it, then click on the Enable Routing checkbox.
6. Click the Accept button to save the changes.

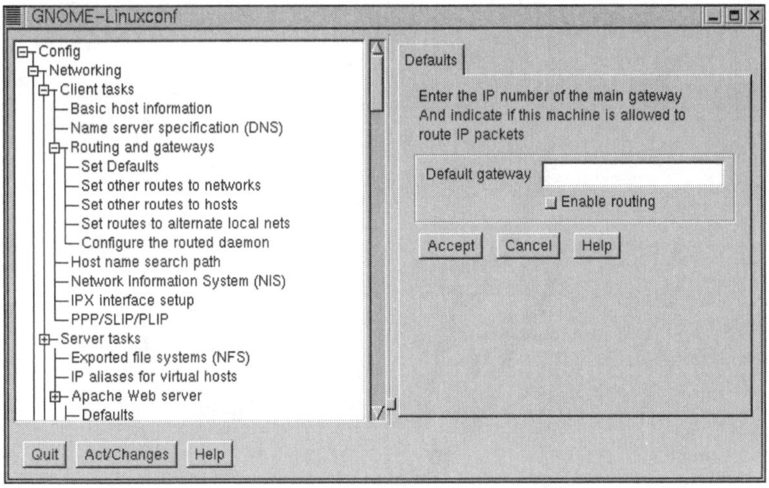

Figure 7.5 The Linuxconf Defaults routing configuration dialog box.

7. Networking

Configuring Routing Among Your Networks

If you have subnets set up so that you have multiple networks, then your machines have to know how to communicate across the networks. For each machine that needs to understand multiple networks, do the following:

1. Open the Linuxconf configuration tool.
2. Select Config|Networking|Routing And Gateways to expand the menu.
3. Click Set Other Routes To Networks to open the Route To Other Networks dialog box.
4. Click the Add button to open the Route Specification dialog box, shown in Figure 7.6.
5. In the Gateway text box, enter the IP address of the gateway for the route you are defining. Although you could enter the name of the machine instead, this requires a lookup and slows down the system—and lookups fail when there are DNS problems.
6. In the Destination text box, enter the address for the network this gateway leads to. If you are just trying to connect to the Internet, you do not need to fill in this section at all, but if you are trying to talk to another subnet, you need to enter that subnet's network address here.
7. Enter your netmask in the Netmask (Opt) text box.
8. Click Accept to close the Route Specification dialog box. The route you just added appears in the Route To Other Networks list box.
9. Return to Step 4 to add another network, or click Quit to close the Route To Other Networks dialog box.

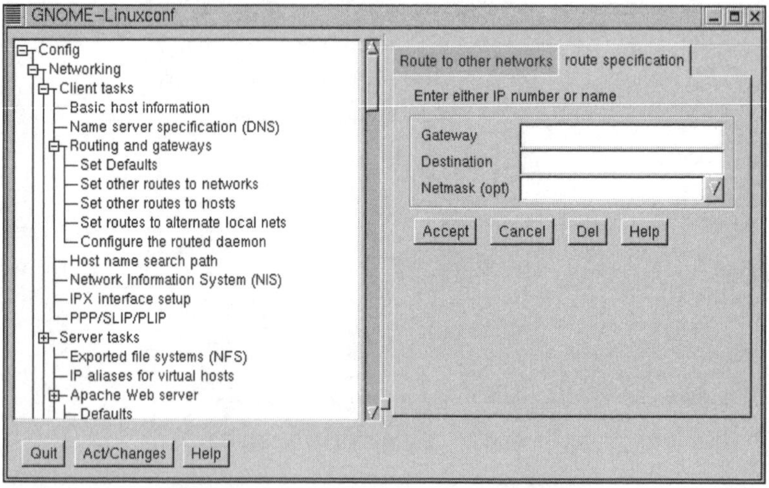

Figure 7.6 The Linuxconf Route Specification dialog box.

Related solution:	Found on page:
Opening Linuxconf	12

Configuring Routing To Remote Hosts

If you have a wide area network (WAN) in which a single or a collection of remote hosts has to be reached through a specific interface that is not obvious by network numbering or settings, do the following to set up the routing information for data to go to this device:

1. Open the Linuxconf configuration tool.
2. Select Config|Networking|Routing And Gateways to expand the menu.
3. Click Set Other Routes To Hosts to open the Route To Other Hosts dialog box.
4. Click the Add button to open the Route Specification dialog box, shown previously in Figure 7.6.
5. In the Gateway text box, enter the IP address for the interface that data must travel through in order to get to the remote host.
6. In the Destination text box, enter the IP address for the remote host.
7. Click Accept to close the Route Specification dialog box. The new host route now appears in the listing.
8. If you have any more remote hosts to add, return to Step 4. Otherwise, click Quit to close the Route To Other Hosts dialog box.

Configuring Routing For Concurrent Networks

If you have more than one LAN or other network on location, and each of these networks is talking over the same set of cabling, then you need to set additional routing information. To set this information, do the following:

1. Open the Linuxconf configuration tool.
2. Select Config|Networking|Routing And Gateways to expand the menu.
3. Click Set Routes To Alternate Local Net to open the Route To Alternate Local Networks dialog box.
4. Click Add to open the Route Specification dialog box, which is similar to that shown previously in Figure 7.6.
5. In the Interface text box, enter the interface that your data has to travel through for the network you are defining. You can use names, IP addresses, or devices. The drop-down list box on the right contains a device listing you can use.

6. In the Destination text box, enter the network address for the network you are sending to with this definition.
7. Enter the netmask for this network in the Netmask text box, or choose it from the drop-down list box.
8. Click Accept to close the Route Specification dialog box. The new network route now appears in the listing.
9. If you have any more networks to add, return to Step 4. Otherwise, click Quit to close the Route To Alternate Local Networks dialog box.

Configuring The Routing Daemon In Linuxconf

To use Linuxconf to configure your routing daemon, phone, do the following:

1. Open the Linuxconf configuration tool.
2. Select Config|Networking|Routing And Gateways to expand the menu.
2. Click Configure The Routed Daemon to open the Routed Daemon Configuration dialog box, shown in Figure 7.7.
3. If more than one Ethernet card is in the machine, deactivate the Does Not Export Any Routes (Silent) checkbox.
4. Click Accept to close the dialog box.

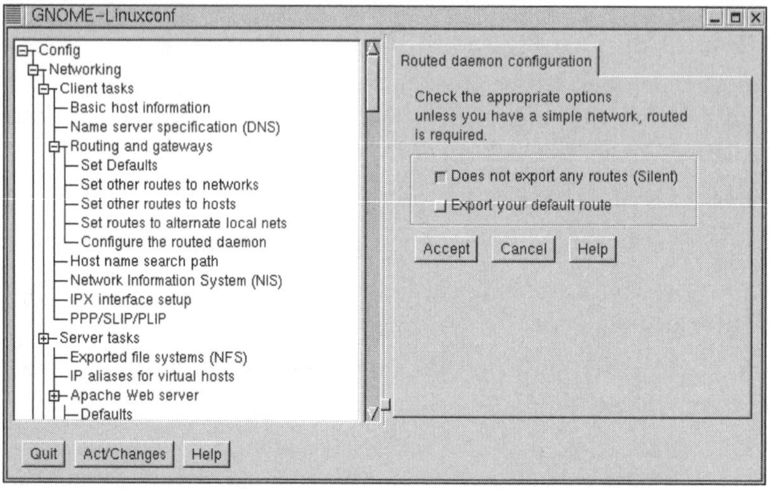

Figure 7.7 The Linuxconf Routed Daemon Configuration dialog box.

Setting Up IP Masquerading

To set up IP masquerading, do the following:

1. Log in to the command line or a terminal window as root on the machine that is fronting for the masquerade.
2. Referring to Table 7.4, choose which addressing class of internal-only IP addresses you want to use for the machines that are masquerading. Typically, people choose class C.
3. Type "vi /etc/rc.d/rc.masq" to open the brand-new file you will use to store your masquerading settings.
4. Enter the following command to build a current list of all kernel module dependencies:

```
/sbin/depmod -a
```

5. Now you need to decide what services you want users behind the masquerading server to be able to use. These services and their modules are listed in Table 7.13.
6. For each service you want to include, enter a line in the format "/sbin/modprobe *module*".
7. Enter the following line to set your default forwarding policy to refuse data, which is just a good security measure:

```
/sbin/ipchains -P forward DENY
```

8. Enter a line similar to the following to forward only the information for the class C local-only IP address you chose:

```
/sbin/ipchains -A forward -s privateIPclassC/24 -j MASQ
```

9. Press the Esc key and then type "ZZ" to save and close the file.
10. Type "chmod 700 /etc/rc.d/rc.masq" to change the permissions for this file.
11. Type "vi /etc/sysconfig/network" to open the network boot initialization file.

Table 7.13 Modules needed to masquerade specific services.

Service	Module
FTP	ip_masq_ftp
IRC	ip_masq_irc
RealAudio	ip_masq_raudio

12. Type "/FORWARD_IPV4" and press Enter to search for this variable.
13. Use the arrow keys to move to the word "false".
14. Press the "x" key once per character until the word is fully deleted.
15. Press "i" to enter Insert mode.
16. Type "true".
17. Press the Esc key and then type "ZZ" to save and close the file.
18. Type "vi /etc/rc.d/rc.local" to open the final boot initialization file.
19. Type "G" to go to the end of the file.
20. Type "o" to open a new line below the cursor's location.
21. Type "/etc/rc.d/rc.masq" to tell the machine to load your masquerading settings at boot time.

Setting Up Dial-Out Connections

How you set up your system to dial out depends on what program you are using to make your connection. Choose the appropriate section to set up your machine to make its PPP (Point-to-Point Protocol), SLIP (Serial Line Internet Protocol), or PLIP (Parallel Line Internet Protocol) connection to your ISP or another outside location. You can use:

- Linuxconf in either GNOME or KDE
- Minicom in GNOME, KDE, or at the command line
- kppp in either GNOME or KDE

Configuring Linuxconf To Connect

To set up your dial-out PPP connection in Linuxconf, do the following:

1. Log in to the GUI as root.
2. Open Linuxconf.
3. Select Config|Networking Branch|Client Tasks from the menu tree.
4. Click PPP/SLIP/PLIP to open the PPP/Slip/Plip Configurations dialog box.
5. Click the Add button to open the Type Of Interface dialog box.
6. The default option is PPP. If you are setting up a SLIP or PLIP connection instead, click the appropriate radio button.
7. Click Accept to open the PPP Interface ppp0 dialog box, shown in Figure 7.8—assuming that you set up a PPP connection.

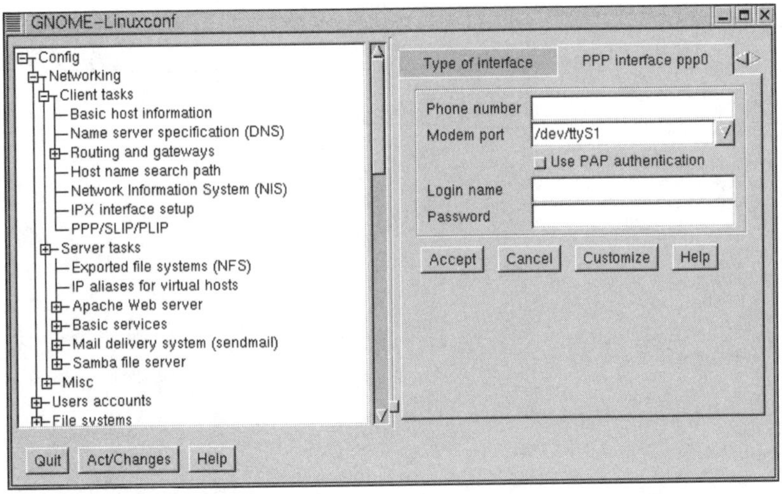

Figure 7.8 The Linuxconf PPP Interface ppp0 dialog box.

8. Enter the phone number your modem needs to dial in the Phone Number text box.
9. Select or enter your modem's location in the Modem Port dialog box. If you know that your modem's device driver is already linked to the location /dev/modem, then leave it at the default. Otherwise, if your modem is the first serial port—in what corresponds to COM1 in Windows—then choose /dev/ttyS0. If it is in the second serial port, or COM2, then choose /dev/ttyS1.
10. If the ISP requires the Password Authentication Protocol (PAP), then make sure the Use PAP Authentication checkbox is selected.
11. Enter your user ID and password in the Login Name and Password text boxes.
12. Click the Customize button to open the second PPP Interface ppp0 dialog box, shown in Figure 7.9.
13. If you have this computer's modem directly linked to another, then deselect the Use Hardware Flow Control And Modem Lines option.
14. If you know for a fact that you need it, select the Escape Control Characters option.
15. If for some reason you do not want the connection to close if common errors occur, deselect the Abort Connection On Well-Known Errors option.
16. If you want non-superuser accounts to be able to initiate this connection or break it, then select Allow Any User (De)Activate The Interface.
17. If your modem is slower than 28.8Kbps, change the value in the Line Speed drop-down list box.

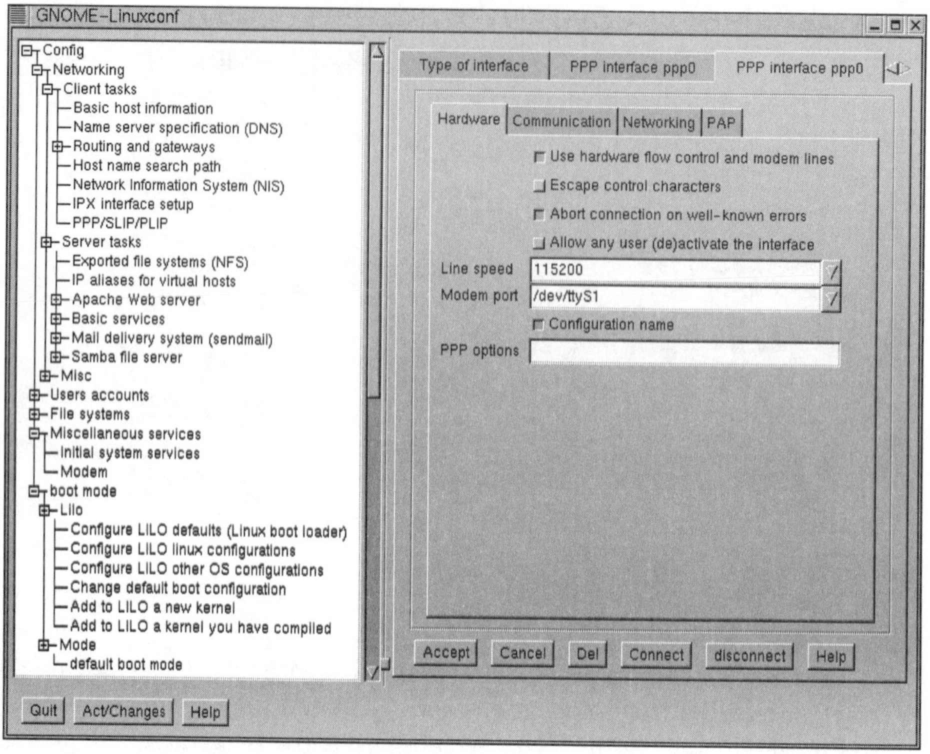

Figure 7.9 The second Linuxconf PPP Interface ppp0 dialog box, with the Hardware tab displayed.

18. Click the Communication tab to open the PPP Interface ppp0 Communication section.
19. You have a few options for what to do in the Chat section:
    - Try what is already there by default to see if it works.
    - If the ISP told you what to use for your chat script, enter that in the Expect and Send boxes.
    - Determine what the server requires manually, perhaps by following the instructions in the following section with minicom.
20. If you have to use PAP authentication, click the PAP tab and fill in the Username and Secret text boxes.
21. Click the Accept button to save these changes and close the PPP Interface ppp0 dialog box.
22. Click the Quit button to close the PPP/Slip/Plip Configurations dialog box.

Configuring Minicom To Connect

To set up your dial-out PPP connection, do the following:

1. Open an X terminal window as root, or log in to terminal mode—runlevel three, where the system boots to a login prompt instead of to the GUI—as root.
2. Type "rpm -q minicom" to see if the minicom package is installed. If not, install it from the Red Hat CD-ROM.
3. Type "minicom -s" to start the program in Setup mode. A small text menu appears in the middle of the terminal.
4. Press "A" to jump the cursor to the Serial Device item. If your modem is on what would be COM1 in Windows, then type "/dev/ttyS0". If it is on COM2, then type "/dev/ttyS1". Then, press Enter.
5. Press "E" to open the Comm Parameters dialog box.
6. Press "I" to change the connection speed to the maximum, unless your modem is slower than 28.8Kbps.
7. Choose the appropriate Data/Parity/Space values.
8. Press Enter to close the dialog box.
9. Press Enter to return to the configuration menu.
10. Select Exit to go directly to the minicom screen.
11. Press the key combination Ctrl+A, and then press "D" to open the Dialing Directory.
12. Move the cursor along the bottom menu to the Edit option, and then press Enter to open the Edit dialog box.
13. Press "A" to jump to the Name line.
14. Enter a descriptive name for this dial-in account, and then press Enter.
15. Press "B" to jump to the Number line.
16. Enter the phone number your modem needs to dial, and then press Enter.
17. Press "F" to go to the Username line.
18. Enter your login name, and then press Enter.
19. Press "G" to go to the Password line.
20. Enter your password, and then press Enter.
21. Change any other values you know you need to change for your ISP.
22. Press Enter to close the dialog box.
23. Press the Esc key to close the dialing directory.

24. Press the key combination Ctrl+A, and then press "X" to exit minicom.
25. Select Yes in the confirmation dialog box, and then press Enter.

Related solutions:	Found on page:
Adding And Removing Media To The File System	84
Installing RPMs	114

Configuring **kppp** To Connect

If you are using KDE, you have the option of using its **kppp** tool to make your Internet connection. After you are in KDE as root, do the following:

1. Click the K icon to open the main menu.
2. Click Internet|kppp to open the **kppp** tool. If this is the first time you have opened this program, you get a Recent Changes In kppp dialog box. Read its contents, follow any instructions if necessary, and then click OK to continue.

NOTE: *If you did not install the ppp daemon (**pppd**) for some reason, **kppp** tells you in a dialog box. You will need to install the daemon before you can make your connection.*

3. Click Setup to open the kppp Configuration dialog box, shown in Figure 7.10.
4. Click the New button to open the New Account dialog box, shown in Figure 7.11.

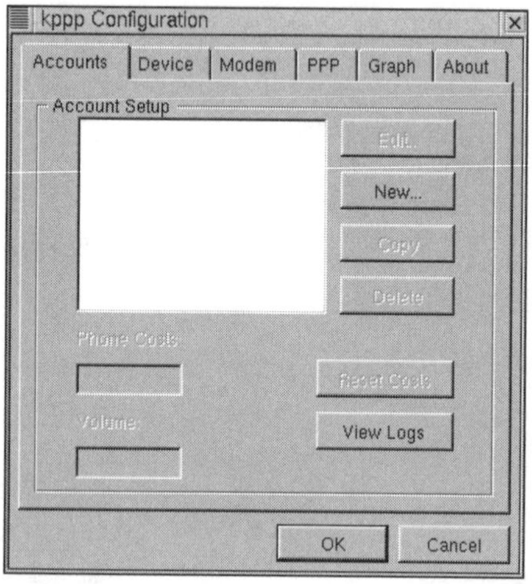

Figure 7.10 The kppp Configuration dialog box, with the Accounts tab displayed.

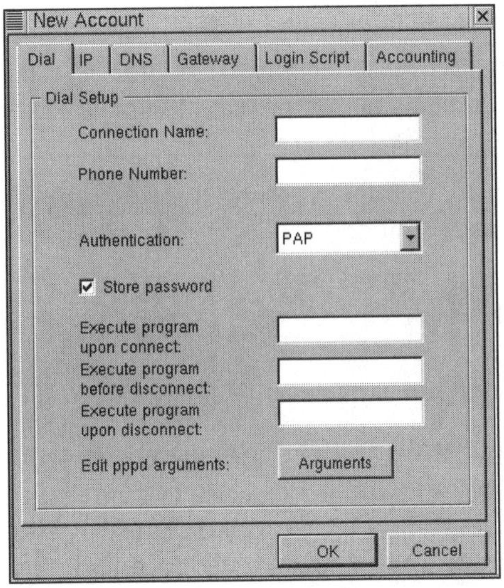

Figure 7.11 The kppp New Account dialog box, with the Dial tab displayed.

5. Enter a descriptive name in the Connection Name text box. This is what will be displayed in the connection dialog boxes later.
6. In the Phone Number text box, enter the phone number your modem needs to call.
7. In the Authentication drop-down list box, select the type of login procedure your ISP requires. If you have not been told to use anything like PAP, choose Script-Based.
8. If you do not want **kppp** to remember the connection password, deselect the Store Password checkbox.
9. You can tie making the connection, or disconnecting, to running particular programs. If you need to do this, fill in the appropriate text box with the full path and arguments needed to call the program.
10. If you need to use any specific arguments with the PPP daemon **pppd**, click the Arguments button. This opens the Customize pppd Arguments dialog box. For a list of available arguments, type "man pppd".
11. Click the IP tab.
12. If your ISP assigned you permanent IP information, click the Static IP Address radio button. Fill in the IP Address and Subnet Mask text boxes.
13. If you intend to use the GUI on this machine, be sure you don't activate the Auto-configure Hostname From This IP option. You would have to loosen your machine's security to make this work properly in the GUI.
14. Click the DNS tab.

15. Enter your domain name or the ISP's domain name—whichever is appropriate—in the Domain Name text box.
16. Enter the IP address for the domain name server provided by your ISP in the DNS IP Address text box.
17. Click the Add button to add this entry to the DNS Address List. Return to Step 16 if you have more DNS servers to add.
18. If you need to disable your local name servers while you are connected to your ISP, then check the Disable Existing DNS Servers During Connection checkbox.
19. Click the Gateway tab.
20. If for some reason you do not want traffic destined for machines outside of your local machine or LAN to go through this PPP connection, click the Static Gateway radio button and fill in the Gateway IP Address with the address for the interface that traffic should go through normally to get outside.

NOTE: *If you don't want to set a default gateway on this machine, deselect the Assign The Default Route To This Gateway checkbox.*

---

21. Click the Login Script tab, which is where you automate the actual login process.
22. Your ISP may have told you exactly what you need in your login script. If not, you may need to use minicom to connect first by hand and then build a login script from that experience. The process used to build a login script begins with entering a string of text that **kppp** will see when it is time to input its first piece of information. For example, if the first prompt is Login:, you might type "ogin:" in the text box, because you do not need to use the entire word.
23. Click the Add button. The word "Expect" now appears on the left of the lower portion of the dialog box, and the term "ogin:" appears on the right.
24. Select Send in the drop-down list box.
25. In the text box, enter the data that the script needs to respond to the prompt with. In the case of the Login: prompt, you need to send your username. If your account was "moose," then you would type "moose" in the text box.
26. Click the Add button. Now, the "Send" term and "moose" appear below.
27. Continue the process from Steps 22 through 26 until you have entered all the steps needed in the login script.
28. Click OK to close the New Account dialog box.

29. Click OK to close the kppp Configuration dialog box.
30. Click Quit to close **kppp**.

Setting Up A DHCP Server

To set up a DHCP server to hand out addressing information to machines on your network at boot time, do the following:

1. Log in as root.
2. Type "man dhcpd" to quickly check and see whether the DHCP server is already installed. If it is, skip to Step 6.
3. Type "df" to see if the Red Hat CD-ROM is already part of your file system. If the CD-ROM is not already mounted, place it in the drive and type "mount /mnt/cdrom" to mount it.
4. Type "cd /mnt/cdrom/RedHat/RPMS" to change to the Red Hat packages directory.
5. Type "rpm -ivh dhcp-", press the Tab key to complete the package name, then press Enter. This installs the DHCP RPM for you.
6. Type "vi dhcpd.conf" to open the DHCP server's configuration file for editing.
7. First, you need to enter your global rules. This section might look like the following for the network 192.168.14.0, with an ISP that has a secondary name server at 192.168.87.9:

```
max-lease-time 43200;
default-lease-time 14400;
option all-subnets-local 1;
option domain-name-servers 192.168.14.1, 192.168.87.9;
```

8. Now comes the interesting part. I am going to assume that you have a single network you need to service. To avoid making this example too simple, I also will assume this network is broken into eight subnets, two of which are handed their network information by DHCP and share the same Ethernet cabling. The rest of your DHCP configuration file might look like the following:

```
shared-network ADMIN {
  subnet 192.168.14.96 netmask 255.255.255.224 {
    range 192.168.14.97 192.168.14.127;
  }
```

```
    subnet 192.168.14.160 netmask 255.255.255.224 {
      range 192.168.14.161 192.168.14.191;
    }
  }
```

NOTE: *Notice that without the indentation, this file would be very difficult to follow. Neatness often counts when coding.*

9. Press the Esc key, then type "ZZ" to save and close the file.
10. Type "/etc/rc.d/init.d/dhcpd restart" to restart your DHCP daemon with its new configuration.

Configuring The pump Client

To set up the **pump** client for DHCP or BOOTP service, do the following:

1. Log in as root.
2. Type "vi /etc/pump.conf" to open the **pump** configuration file.
3. Build the configuration file. The options available are shown in Table 7.14.

Table 7.14 Options for the /etc/pump.conf file.

Option	Purpose	Arguments	Example
device	Allows you to set device-specific parameters rather than global parameters. The device is typically a networking interface.	Any other parameter.	**device eth0 { timeout 10 }**
domainsearch	Use the following domain name lookup order.	The domains to search by default.	**domainsearch "blue.colors.org carrot.veggies.org colors.org veggies.org"**
nodns	When you are setting up a particular device statement, you can use this option to tell it not to include this particular device in the nameservice lookup files.	None.	**device ppp0 { nodns }**

(continued)

7. Networking

Table 7.14 Options for the /etc/pump.conf file (continued).

Option	Purpose	Arguments	Example
retries	How many times to try again if any stage of the DHCP setup process fails.	A nonzero integer.	**retry 5**
timeout	Wait the declared number of seconds before giving up on the DHCP setup process.	A nonzero count of seconds.	**timeout 30**

A sample configuration file on a machine with only one interface might contain:

```
retries 5
timeout 15
domainsearch "home.net kitchen.home.net"
```

4. After you finish creating the file, press the Esc key, and then type "ZZ" to close and save the file.
5. Make sure that the **pump** client is called at boot time. A good place to put this statement is /etc/rc.d/rc.local, which is one of the files called by Red Hat Linux during the boot process. Type "vi /etc/rc.d/rc.local" to open this file for editing.

NOTE: *Other distributions each have their own specific collection of files used at boot time. If you are using another Linux distribution, read the manuals to determine which file is most appropriate to add this information to.*

6. Type "G" to jump to the end of the file.
7. Type "o" to open a blank line after all other lines.
8. Type "/sbin/pump -i *interface* -l *hoursleased*". The two variables are as follows:
   - ***interface***—The networking interface that **pump** uses to contact the DHCP server, and to which pump is trying to assign addressing information—for example, eth0.
   - ***hoursleased***—How long this interface gets to keep its addressing information—for example, 100. When the time runs out, **pump** contacts the DHCP server again for an update. The value you choose for this assignment depends on how often you expect to move machines. Remember that if addressing information is assigned and you move the machine in the middle of its lease, that IP address is essentially unavailable until its lease times out.
9. After you enter this information, press the Esc key, and then type "ZZ" to close and save the file.

Administering Machines Remotely

To administer your machines remotely, you have a few options:

- Use the **telnet** program to log in to a user account on the machine you need to work with, and then use the **su** program to gain superuser status if you know the root password for that machine.
- Use the **vnc** program—available from **www.uk.research.att.com/vnc/**—to connect remotely to Linux, Macintosh, Unix, or Windows machines. This tool allows you to work at a remote machine that also has **vnc** installed as though you were sitting at its console.

Related solutions:	*Found on page:*
Becoming The Superuser	283
Securing Telnet	488

Chapter 8

Printing

If you need an immediate solution to:	*See page:*
Setting Up A Local Printer In The Control Panel	225
Setting Up A Local Printer At The Command Line	228
Setting Up A Network Printer In The Control Panel	231
Setting Up A Network Printer At The Command Line	233
Setting Up A Machine To Host A Network Printer	233
Setting Up Remote Printers To Print Over A Network	234
Setting Up Popular Print Filters	235
Testing The Printer	236
Printing A File	236
Viewing A Print Queue	237
Canceling A Print Job	237
Checking A Printer's Status	238
Disabling And Enabling A Print Queue	238

In Depth

Traditionally, printing has been a hassle to set up under Linux. Basic text printing is not the problem. The problem is figuring out how to handle the myriad file formats out there. Fortunately, Linux administrators today have a good selection of tools to work with when they want to set up printing. After you have printing set up, though, the job is not over. You still need to understand how to use it at a user level and at an administrative level.

Introduction To Printing Under Linux

Understanding how to work with the Linux print system means knowing all of the bits and pieces and how they interrelate. When setting up printing, you first have to deal with the printer's configuration file, /etc/printcap, which I talk about in the next section. After that, I'll discuss the family of commands that together form the printing and print management section of Linux. Finally, I will take you on a walk through the life of a simple print job.

The /etc/printcap File

The printer configuration file is made up of a series of print definitions. Understanding how these definitions are laid out is part of the key to setting up a thorough, precise printer control file. The general format for a print definition is:

```
shortname|longname:\
  :statement1:\
  :statement2:\
  ...
  :statementn:
```


You have a lot of leeway in naming your printer. In general, the default printer statement begins with "lp" for the short name entry, which stands for "line printer." This is a holdover convention from when most Unix printers were line printers, and is useful as a naming scheme because users always at least know one printer's name. If you already have a default printer definition, then make this short entry another two-letter item.

The long name should be descriptive, something a user might remember if they cannot remember the short abbreviation. For example, if the printer's short name was "ij" then its long name might be "inkjet". Keep in mind that you can have a number of names assigned to the printer if you want. If you want to have ij, inkjet, ink, and jet all assigned to the same printer, you could begin with:

```
ij|ink|jet|inkjet:\
```

The important thing is that all of the names are on the same line of code.

From here, you build the printer definition. Which definition items you decide to use depends on the context. Various contexts are covered in the Immediate Solutions section of this chapter. The more interesting items that are not the core options covered in the solutions are listed here in Table 8.1.

The Printer Command Family

There are a number of commands you have to deal with when managing your printer(s) under Linux. It can get confusing trying to keep them straight, so I laid

Table 8.1 Non-core but interesting printer configuration options.

Option	Purpose	Values	Example
af	Name of the file to use for print accounting	Path to file	**af=/var/accounting/print**
ff	String that users can include in text files to cause a form feed	Combination of letters in single quotes	**ff='\ff'**
hl	Prints the header page last	None	**hl**
if	Explicitly names the input filter to use for this printer	Path to filter	**if=/etc/filter**
pc	Price per foot of paper or per page	Positive integer in hundredths of cents	**pc=300**
pl	Page length	Positive integer, number of lines	**pl=70**
pw	Page width	Positive integer, characters	**pw=125**
rg	Only members of the listed group may use this printer	Group name	**rg=admin**
rs	The only people who can print to this printer over the network are those who also have accounts on this machine under the same name	None	**rs**
sb	Keeps the new print job banner to just one line of information	None	**sb**
sf	Ignores form feeds	None	**sf**

Table 8.2 Print-related commands in Linux.

Command	Purpose
lpc	Printer control program
lpd	Print daemon
lpq	Print spool control program
lpr	The print spooler
lprm	Print job removal
pac	Generates print accounting reports

them out for you here in Table 8.2. Each has a specific function in the grander scheme of print job and printer management.

The Printer Control Program

You use the **lpc** command in the format:

```
lpc command value
```

The available commands are listed in Table 8.3.

Table 8.3 Available commands for lpc.

Command	Purpose	Values
?	Prints help information about a command.	**lpc** command
abort	Kills the active print daemon that manages this printer's spool, then disables printing to this printer.	Either **all** for every printer, or the printer name for the specific printer
clean	Removes any unprintable files from the printer's queue. Good for cleaning out temporary information.	Either **all** for every printer, or the printer name for the specific printer
disable	Turns the printer's queue off so it will not pull any more jobs from the spool.	Either **all** for every printer, or the printer name for the specific printer
down	Turns the printer's queue off and does not allow new jobs to be spooled.	Either **all** for every printer, or the printer name for the specific printer; plus a brief message explaining why the printer is down
enable	Turns the printer's queue on so new jobs can be spooled.	Either **all** for every printer, or the printer name for the specific printer
help	Prints help information about a command.	**lpc** command

(continued)

Table 8.3 Available commands for lpc **(continued).**

Command	Purpose	Values
restart	Shuts down the current **lpd** session and opens a new one.	Either **all** for every printer, or the printer name for the specific printer
start	Turns printing on for the printer and starts a print daemon for its spool.	Either **all** for every printer, or the printer name for the specific printer
status	Gives the current status of the spooling daemon and queue.	Either **all** for every printer, or the printer name for the specific printer
stop	Shuts off the spooling daemon when it has no more jobs to handle and then disables printing.	Either **all** for every printer, or the printer name for the specific printer
topq	Moves the specified jobs to the top of the queue.	The printer name, the job number, then the user
up	Turns on the printer's queue and allow jobs to be spooled.	Either **all** for every printer, or the printer name for the specific printer

The Print Daemon

You use **lpd** in the format:

```
lpd flag port
```

Believe it or not, there is only one flag available for **lpd**. It is not included by default because you may not want to use the flag at all. This flag is **-l**, which logs valid network jobs as they arrive to be spooled. If you want, you can also have **lpd** listen on a nonstandard port for network print jobs.

The Print Spool Controller

You use **lpq** in the format:

```
lpq flag job user
```

There are two flags available with this command:

- **-l**—Prints a single line of information about each job.
- **-P*printer***—Specifies exactly which printer you are interested in.

There can be more than one print job listed, separated by spaces.

The Print Job Remover

You use the **lprm** command in the format:

```
lprm flag jobs user
```

Once again, there are only two available flags for this command:

- **-** —(Yes, a dash.) Removes all jobs from this user.
- **-P*printer***—Specifies exactly which printer you are interested in.

The Report Generator

You use the **pac** command in the format:

```
pac flags name
```

The flags available for **pac** are listed in Table 8.4. You only include the ***name*** value if you want to generate a report for just one user.

The output from this command goes into /var/account/.

The Linux Printing Process

In a Unix system or Unix variant such as Linux, a file goes through a particular process when you try to print it. Understanding this process helps you both configure and administer it. What follows is an example of what happens to a file when you print it under Linux.

Suppose that you have the file ~/picture.jpg. You know that an inkjet printer named ij is installed on the network, so you type "lpr -Pij ~/picture.jpg" to print the file, having read "Printing A File" in the Immediate Solutions section of this chapter. The image file is now sent to the spool defined in /etc/printcap—the print services configuration file. In this case, because the printer is not local to the machine, its spool is on the NFS mount /share (see Chapter 17 for more information on NFS) in the directory /share/printers/spool/ij.

Whenever a file arrives in the print queue, the system notifies the print daemon, **lpd**, which spawns off a child **lpd** to handle the queue if it was inactive when this job arrived. Because the image file was sent directly into a queue that is also

Table 8.4 Flags available for the pac command.

Flag	Purpose
-P*printer*	The specific printer you want to generate a report for.
-c	Sorts the output by cost instead of alphabetically by name.
-m	Groups all charges together for a user, regardless of what host they printed from.
-p*price*	Cost of a page in dollars. Overrides the value in /etc/printcap.
-r	Sorts in reverse order.
-s	Includes a summary of the account information.

NFS-mounted on the print server, and because this machine points within its own printcap file to the same print spool file, **lpd** waits for data to arrive in /share/printers/spool/ij. When your print job enters the spool, it either waits its turn in the queue, if other jobs are already printing and waiting, or gets sent to the printer directly, if nothing else is waiting.

However, ~/picture.jpg is not a raw ASCII text file. It is an image file—a JPEG (Joint Photographic Experts Group format) file, to be precise. Fortunately, you had the foresight to realize that people were pretty likely to print more than just raw text to a color printer. With the APSFilter program installed—as discussed in "Setting Up Popular Print Filters," in the Immediate Solutions section—your machine knows how to print a JPEG file. The image is converted and sent as a PostScript file to the printer.

Linux Printing Issues

With Linux, as with any other operating system, you need to consider the following items when setting up your printers and when printing:

- You cannot pass print jobs between Linux and another operating system without special tools. After your printers are set up and running, see Chapter 18 for information on how to share print jobs between Linux and other operating systems.
- Printing to a local printer and printing to a network printer are two entirely separate configuration issues. You need to configure network printers specially.
- Printing anything other than raw ASCII text files requires special filters to process the data and convert it into PostScript format. PostScript is a print-formatting language first developed by Adobe. It is more of a programming language than a markup language—more like C than HTML. If your printer is not PostScript-capable, you may be relegated to using only ASCII text documents.
- If you do not have print filters installed to do the conversion for you, there is a program called GhostScript that can handle this.

Introduction To GhostScript

When the Unix community needed a program that could handle PostScript format files, the GNU (Gnu's Not Unix, at **www.gnu.org**) folks, along with Aladdin Enterprises (**www.aladdin.com**), stepped in and gave us GhostScript, which actually is a suite of tools.

The GhostScript program, **gs**, is a PostScript and PDF (Adobe's Portable Document Format) interpreter. You can use this tool to view or print the contents of a

PostScript file. Fortunately, today's print filters make printing PostScript files far less complicated than this process used to be, so you probably do not need to learn the **gs** syntax for this issue. Because both GhostScript and PostScript are graphically oriented, you need to view GhostScript output in the GUI. The nightmare you then have to face is the frightening number of options for **gs**.

Fortunately, two other programs are available—**gv** and **ghostview**—that give a prettier face to the GhostScript viewer. Both of these programs are GUI interfaces that are much friendlier to use than the main **gs** program.

The home page for GhostScript is located at **www.ghostscript.com**. Perusing this site is highly recommended if you intend to use GhostScript for serious purposes, because three versions of this software are available. Each version has different licensing restrictions. Documentation for GhostScript and its related tools is also available at this site, as are the tools themselves.

Nonsoftware Technical Problems

One large issue that comes up again and again is troubleshooting printing under any operating system. The advice offered in this section applies to any operating system, not just Linux. If you are having trouble with your printer, try the following:

- Make sure the printer cable is firmly connected at both ends: cable to printer, and cable to computer.
- Make sure the printer is plugged in.
- Make sure the printer is turned on.
- Make sure the printer is in the ready state, if it has an offline state.
- If this is a network printer, and you are having problems printing from the network, see whether it prints locally. If it does, then check network connectivity for this machine.

Immediate Solutions

Setting Up A Local Printer In The Control Panel

To set up a printer that is directly connected to the machine you are on, do the following:

1. Log into the GUI as root.
2. Click the GNOME footprint icon to open the main menu. If you are using KDE, then instead click the K icon, and then click the Red Hat menu.
3. Click System to open the System menu.
4. Click Control Panel to open Red Hat's Control Panel, shown in Figure 8.1.

NOTE: *Most Linux distributions have their own special tools for setting up printing. However, the command-line method works for all distributions.*

---

5. Click the Printer Configuration icon to open the Red Hat Linux Print System Manager, shown in Figure 8.2.

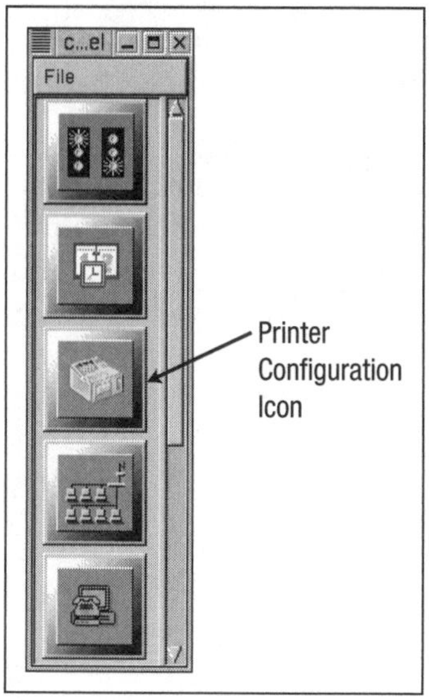

Figure 8.1 Red Hat's Control Panel.

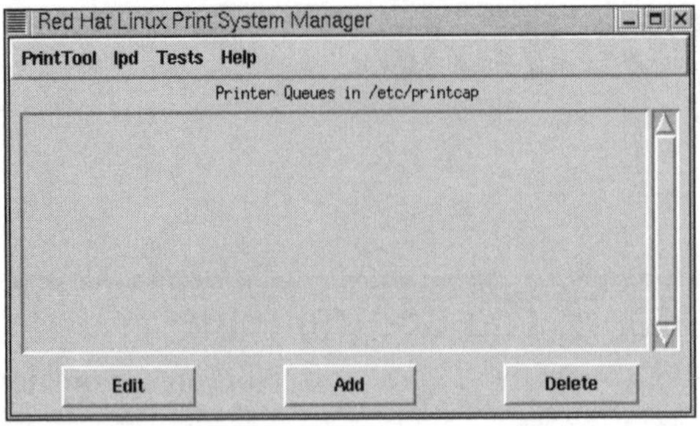

Figure 8.2 The Red Hat Linux Print System Manager.

6. Click the Add button to open the Add A Printer Entry dialog box.
7. Click the Local Printer radio button.
8. Click OK to close the Add A Printer Entry dialog box and autodetect any printers you have connected to any parallel ports. Do not panic if nothing is found.
9. Read any intermediate dialog boxes that appear, and then click OK to open the Edit Local Printer Entry dialog box, shown in Figure 8.3.
10. Enter a brief, meaningful printer name in the Names text box. Typically, the primary printer on a Linux or Unix system is named "lp" by default, to make life easier for users.
11. Alter the Spool Directory to reflect where this printer's spool files should go. If you are setting up the default printer (lp), then leave the default spool directory as is.
12. If you want to limit how large a print job can be, enter the size (in K) in the File Limit text box. The default entry is 0, which means there is no limit on print job size. This is fine for most people, but if you are running a large network, you may want to make some kind of limit. You never know what some people might print by accident.

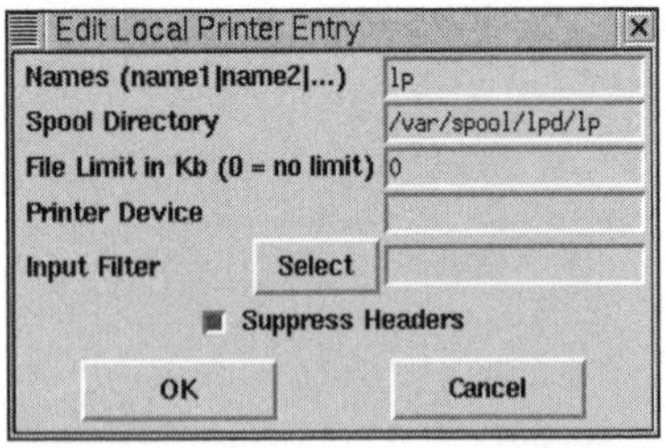

Figure 8.3 Red Hat's Edit Local Printer Entry dialog box.

NOTE: *A knowledgeable user can get around this restriction if they need to. Using* ***lpr*** *with the* ***-s*** *flag creates a symbolic link to line up the file for printing instead of copying it to the print queue, thus avoiding the size restriction. If this occurs, you have no control over pausing or removing the print job. It has to be allowed to finish printing out.*

13. If you want to point to a specific printer device driver, then enter this location in the Printer Device text box.
14. It is highly recommended, at this point, that you click the Select button to open the Configure Filter dialog box, shown in Figure 8.4. This segment of the Print System Manager is one of the primary reasons many people use this tool to set up their printers.
15. Click the type of printer you have in the Printer Type list box. If you cannot find exactly the right one, you may need to go to the manufacturer's Web site to try to find out what type is comparable. Otherwise, choose Text-Only for a printer that can only handle text files, or choose PostScript for a printer that can handle PostScript files.
16. If choices are listed under the Resolution section, select the default print resolution you want to use on this printer.
17. If choices are listed under the Paper Size section, select the paper size you intend to use.
18. If choices are listed under the Color Depth/Uniprint Mode section, choose the appropriate one.

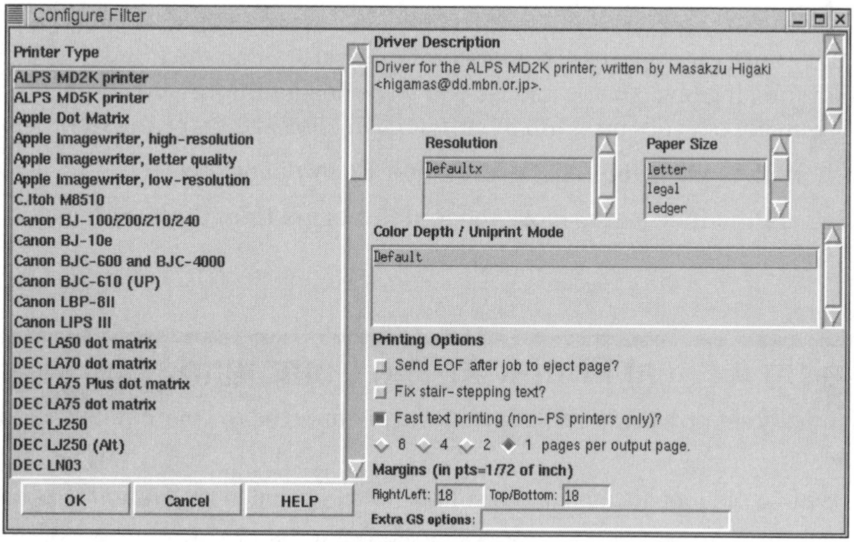

Figure 8.4 Red Hat's Configure Filter dialog box.

8. Printing

19. If you want to ensure that multiple files are never printed to the same page, you may want to select the checkbox next to Send EOF After Job To Eject Page? in the Printing Options area. If you select this checkbox and then tend to get a blank page at the end of every print job, return to this dialog box and deselect the checkbox. The blank page is a sign that the printer does not need this extra command.
20. With raw text files, sometimes a problem called "stair stepping" occurs with the alignment of text on each new line, whereby each line is indented a little further than the previous one. If this happens to you, select the Fix Stair-Stepping Text? option.
21. If you are using a printer that cannot handle PostScript, but for any reason you did not configure as text-only, then be sure the Fast Text Printing (Non-PS Printers Only)? option is selected. This option ensures that your text is sent directly to the printer instead of through a print filter.
22. By default, your printer is configured to print one page of printer output per piece of paper. However, you can have it send multiple pages of data to go onto one piece of paper. If you want to do this:
    - Make sure the Fast Text Printing (Non-PS Printers Only)? option is not selected.
    - Click the 2, 4, or 8 radio button to specify how many pages of printer output should go onto a piece of paper.
23. Change the margin settings if you feel the need.
24. Click OK to close the dialog box.
25. Make sure the Suppress Headers option is selected in the Edit Local Printer Entry dialog box (that is, unless you want header information at the beginning of every print job identifying which user printed the file).
26. Click OK to close the Edit Local Printer Entry dialog box.
27. Select PrintTool|Quit to close the Red Hat Linux Print System Manager.

Setting Up A Local Printer At The Command Line

To manually set up a printer that is currently connected to your computer, do the following:

1. Log into the root account at the command line, or open an X terminal as root.
2. Type "vi /etc/printcap" to open the printer configuration file. Note the very large warning at the beginning stating that you should not edit this file by hand. It is your decision whether to continue or use the Control Panel method instead.

3. Type "G" to go to the bottom of the empty file.
4. Type "o" to open a new line underneath the current one.
5. An /etc/printcap entry is a multiline statement defining this printer and its attributes. Start with a line that assigns a name to the printer, in the format ***shortname|longname*:**. The colon and backslash combination at the end declares that this statement is not yet complete.

   For example, the default name for the primary printer is lp (line printer) by Unix tradition. If this is your primary printer, you might enter the following:

```
lp|default printer:\
```

TIP: *In fact, you can have more than two names and nicknames assigned in this line. If you want to call the default printer "lp" and also refer to it as "lj" because it is a laserjet printer, then you can use the line* ***lp|lj|default printer:****.*

6. The next line is typically a pointer to the printer driver you want to use for your particular printer, in the format **:lp=/dev/*device*:**. This driver may be linked to point to a generic location, such as /dev/lp0, or may be more specific. The colon at the beginning of the line declares that this is a continuation of the same statement, and the colon and backslash at the end state that the definition continues to the next line.

   For example, your default printer might use the driver declaration:

```
:lp=/dev/lp0:\
```

NOTE: *You do not have to put every new definition on a new line; you can just separate them all with colons on a line. However, it is easier to glance through them if you use one definition per line.*

7. Another necessary line is the spool directory definition. The machine needs to know what directory to store files in while they wait to be printed. This line is entered in the format **:sd=/var/spool/lpd/*name*:**. Typically, ***name*** is the same as the device name, just to help keep things straight. So, for this example, you would enter the following:

```
:sd=/var/spool/lpd/lp0:\
```

8. For the sake of making sure your print services are logged properly, add a line that sets the log file to use. This line is used in the format **:lf=/var/log/*name*:**. Once again, the ***name*** typically used here is the device name. So, you might use the following entry:

```
:lf=/var/log/lp0:\
```

9. As with many devices, you need to use a lock file so that the print daemon is not trying to send multiple files to the printer while the printer is busy. Add this line in the format **:lo=/var/spool/lpd/*name*/lock/*name*.lock:**. In this case, you might use the following:

```
:lo=/var/spool/lpd/lp0/lock/lp0.lock:\
```

10. This is it for the lines you must add for a local printer. Additional statements and arguments are laid out in Table 8.5. Be sure to end the last line in this print definition without the ":\" component.

NOTE: *You would use the **pl** or **pw** commands only if you were using something other than 8.5-by-11-inch standard letter-size paper.*

11. Press the Esc key and then type "ZZ" to save and close the file.
12. If you intend to print more than ASCII text, go to the section "Setting Up Popular Print Filters," later in the chapter.
13. Now you need to create the directories and files you are using. In the case of this example, these are as follows:
    - */var/spool/lpd/lp0*—The print spool
    - */var/log/lp0*—The error log file
    - */var/spool/lpd/lp0/lock/lp0.lock*—The lock file

NOTE: *From here forward, change the directory and file names to match what you used.*

14. Type "ls /var/spool/lpd" to see whether this directory exists. If you get an error, continue with Step 15. If you don't, skip to Step 18.

Table 8.5 Useful /etc/printcap statements for setting up a local printer.

Type	Purpose	Example
mx#	Limits how large a print job can be, in K. A 0 means unlimited. The default is 1000, or 1MB.	**mx#2000**
pl	Specifies how long (vertically) the page is, in lines. The default is 66.	**pl=80**
pw	Specifies how wide (horizontally) the page is, in characters. The default is 132.	**pw=150**
sh	Does not print headers at the beginning of every print job containing data about who printed the file.	**sh**

15. Type “mkdir /var/spool/lpd” to create the directory that contains all the local spool directories.
16. Type “chown root.daemon /var/spool/lpd” to change the directory’s ownership.
17. Type “chmod 775 /var/spool/lpd” to change the directory’s permissions.
18. Type “mkdir /var/spool/lpd/lp0” to create the spool directory for this printer.
19. Type “chown root.daemon /var/spool/lpd/lp0” to change the spool directory’s ownership.
20. Type “chmod 775 /var/spool/lpd/lp0” to change the spool directory’s permissions.
21. Type “touch /var/log/lp0 /var/spool/lpd/lp0/lock/lp0.lock” to create the log file and the lock file.
22. Type “chown root.daemon /var/log/lp0 /var/spool/lpd/lp0/lock/lp0.lock” to change the ownership of the log and lock files.
23. Type “chmod 664 /var/log/lp0 /var/spool/lpd/lp0/lock/lp0.lock” to change the permissions of the log and lock files.

Setting Up A Network Printer In The Control Panel

To configure a machine to send print jobs to a printer connected to another machine on your network, do the following:

1. Log into the GUI as root.
2. Click the GNOME footprint icon to open the main menu. If you are using KDE, then instead click the K icon, and then click the Red Hat menu.
3. Click System to open the System menu.
4. Click Control Panel to open Red Hat’s Control Panel, shown earlier in Figure 8.1.
5. Click the Printer Configuration icon to open the Red Hat Linux Print System Manager, shown earlier in Figure 8.2.
6. Click the Add button to open the Add A Printer Entry dialog box.
7. Click the Remote Unix (lpd) Queue radio button.

NOTE: *Although setting up Samba/SMB printing is also a type of network printing, see Chapter 18 for a thorough discussion of SMB and Samba and why you might or might not want to use it before exploring this option. You do not need SMB unless you are trying to share printers across multiple operating systems.*

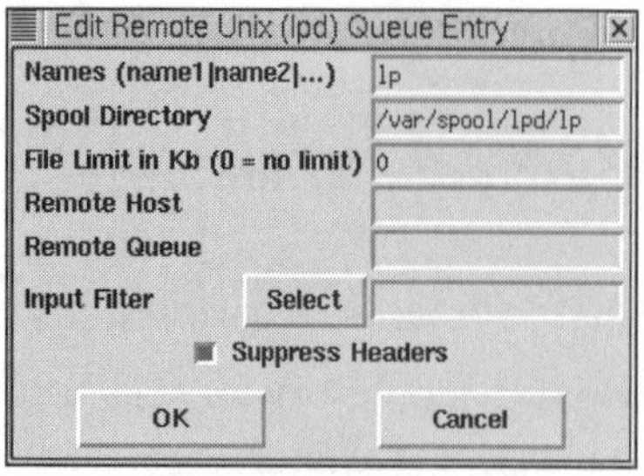

Figure 8.5 Red Hat's Edit Remote Unix (lpd) Queue Entry dialog box.

8. Click OK to open the Edit Remote Unix (lpd) Queue Entry dialog box, shown in Figure 8.5.
9. Enter a short, simple name you want to use for this printer. Typically, the default printer on a network is simply called lp. If a local printer already is configured as lp, then set a different name for this one.
10. Edit the Spool Directory entry to match the printer name. This means that you need to edit the last portion of the entry. Keep in mind that this directory is the spool that exists locally, on this machine.
11. If you want to limit the size of the print jobs that people can submit to this printer, enter the maximum value (in K) they are allowed to send in the File Limit text box.
12. Enter the IP address of the machine that hosts the network printer in the Remote Host text box.
13. Enter the path to the printer's spool directory on the machine it's connected to in the Remote Queue text box.
14. Click Select to configure information for the specific printer in question. This opens the Configure Filter dialog box, shown previously in Figure 8.4.
15. Click the name of your printer—or one reasonably close, or one of the generics—in the Printer Type list box.
16. Select the default print resolution.
17. Select the paper size you intend to use.
18. Choose the appropriate color depth.
19. If you want to ensure that multiple files are never printed to the same page, select Send EOF After Job To Eject Page? under Printing Options. If you select this option and then tend to get a blank page at the end of every print job, return to this option and turn it off.
20. With raw text files, sometimes a problem called "stair stepping" occurs with the alignment of text on each new line, whereby each line is indented

a little further than the previous one. If this happens for you, select the Fix Stair-Stepping Text? option.

21. If you are using a printer that cannot handle PostScript, but for any reason you did not configure as text-only, then be sure the Fast Text Printing (Non-PS Printers Only)? option is selected.
22. By default, your printer is configured to print one page of printer output per piece of paper. However, you can have it send multiple pages of data to go onto one piece of paper. If you want to do this:
    - Make sure the Fast Text Printing (Non-PS Printers Only)? option is not selected.
    - Click the 2, 4, or 8 radio button to specify how many pages of printer output should go onto a piece of paper.
23. Change the margin settings, if you feel the need.
24. Click OK to close the dialog box.
25. Select the Suppress Headers option, if it is not already selected.

NOTE: *If you have a network where a lot of different people are printing documents, you may in fact want to make sure this option is not selected.*

26. Click OK to close the Edit Local Printer Entry dialog box.
27. Select PrintTool|Quit to close the Red Hat Linux Print System Manager.

Related solutions:	Found on page:
Offering Linux Printers	550
Utilizing Windows Printers Under Linux	554

Setting Up A Network Printer At The Command Line

Setting up network printing involves two different issues. You have to set up remote machines to send jobs to the machine with the printer, and you have to set up the machine with the printer to receive and accept the remote files.

Setting Up A Machine To Host A Network Printer

To set up a local printer that also needs to be able to host network print jobs, do the following:

1. Follow the complete instructions in the section "Setting Up A Local Printer At The Command Line" earlier in the chapter, and then return here.

2. Type "vi /etc/hosts.lpd" to open the file that allows you to configure where people can send in print jobs from. Chances are good that this file is empty, or nearly so.
3. Type "i" to enter Insert mode.
4. Enter lines appropriate for your needs. All hosts that people are allowed to print from should be represented. Your options are given in Table 8.6.

   For example, to allow anyone on the domain animals.org to print to this machine, except for the user "guest" on any machine, include the following lines:

```
.animals.org
-.animals.org   guest
```

5. Press the Esc key and then type "ZZ" to save and close the file.

Setting Up Remote Printers To Print Over A Network

To set up a network printer at the command line by hand, do the following:

1. Read the section "Setting Up A Local Printer At The Command Line" earlier in the chapter, and then return here. Better yet, you should already have set up the remote Linux printer on the machine it is connected to.
2. Type "vi /etc/printcap" to open the file for editing.
3. Type "G" to go to the end of the file, because you may as well add the new definition there.
4. Type "o" to open an empty line below the cursor's location and enter Insert mode.
5. Begin your print definition with a name assignation, as was done in the local printer scenario. For example, you might use the following:

```
la|otter|laser on otter:\
```


Table 8.6 Options available in /etc/hosts.lpd for specifying which machines may print.

Option	Result
.domain.extension	Allows all hosts on the domain.
host.domain.extension	Allows a specific host on a domain.
host.domain.extension user	Allows a specific user on a specific host on a domain.
-option	Refuses any of the preceding.

6. In this case, you are not printing to a local device. Therefore, your device assignment line is as follows:

```
:lp=:\
```

7. The printer may not be on this machine, but you still need to tell /etc/printcap where to spool files that are waiting for printing. Typically, you would use a location that is available to both this machine and the remote one. Perhaps an NFS share mounted at /shares/print, using a line such as this:

```
:sd=/shares/print/otter:\
```

8. For a printer that is not on this machine, you need to use some additional /etc/printcap setting options. The first of these options defines which machine the printer is connected to. You set this line in the format **:rm=*host*:**. For example:

```
:rm=otter:\
```

9. Next, you need to specify to which local printer on the remote host the print jobs for this definition go. Here, you use the local name for the remote printer, as follows: **:rp=*localname*:**. For example, if this printer is lp on otter and this is the last line in the print definition, you would use:

```
:rp=lp
```

10. Any print filtering is done at the remote end. Press the Esc key and then type "ZZ" to save and exit this file.

Related solution:	Found on page:
Mounting Remote File Systems With NFS	505

Setting Up Popular Print Filters

Two popular print filters available on the Internet are **apsfilter** and **magicfilter**. To utilize these items, do the following:

1. Download one or the other of the two scripts from **http://metalab.unc.edu/pub/Linux/system/printing/**.

2. Unpack the tarballs into your preferred source directory—/usr/src by default.
3. Change into the new directory created for the filter source.
4. Do the following to start the automated setup and installation process:
   - Type "./SETUP" for **apsfilter**. This program walks you through the entire filter setup process.
   - Type "./configure" for **magicfilter**. Now, you need to compile the code. Type the following sequence of commands: "make" and then "make install".

NOTE: *Both of these programs alter your /etc/printcap file. Take a look to see what it did.*

Related solution:	Found on page:
Opening Or Creating Tarballs	110

Testing The Printer

To test your printer, which means printing raw text while skipping the print daemon, do the following:

1. Choose a short file that is raw ASCII text, rather than an image or word processing document.
2. Determine the device corresponding to the printer you want to test—it should be a local printer; do not do this test over a network.
3. Type "cat *file* > /dev/*device*". For example, "cat /root/test.txt > /dev/lp0". If the printer is hooked up properly, the file prints out. If the job does not print, check the items listed in the section "Nonsoftware Technical Problems" in the In Depth section.

Printing A File

To print a file through the print daemon, do the following:

1. Determine which file you want to print.
2. Determine which printer—by one of the name listings in /etc/passwd—you want to print to.

NOTE: *Here is where the beauty of the printing setup comes in. You do not need to know whether the printer is local; you just need the printer's name.*

---

3. Use the **lpr** command in one of the following two formats:
   - **lpr *file*** if you are printing to the default printer, lp. For example, **lpr ~/text**.
   - ***lpr* -P*printername file*** if you are printing to a nondefault printer. For example, **lpr -Pij ~/text**.

Viewing A Print Queue

To view the contents of a queue, do the following:

1. Determine which printer's queue you want to look at.
2. Determine which user's files you want to single out, if any.
3. Use the **lpq** command in one of the following formats:
   - **lpq** to see the full contents of the default (lp) print queue.
   - **lpq -P*printername*** to view the contents of a specific printer's queue. For example, **lpq -Pij**.
   - **lpq *user*** to view a specific user's print jobs for the default printer. For example, **lpq paul**.
   - **lpq -P*printername user*** to view all jobs queued for this user on the specific printer listed. For example, **lpq -Pij paul**.

TIP: *If **lpq** reports that no print daemon is running, type either "lpc restart all" to restart **lpd** for everything, or "lpc restart printername" to restart it for that one printer.*

Canceling A Print Job

To cancel a print job that is queued up, do the following:

1. Use the **lpq** command as discussed in the preceding section, "Viewing A Print Queue," to find the print job for the specific user who initiated it. Make a note of the job number.
2. Use the **lprm** command in one of the following formats:
   - If you want to remove all print jobs from all queues that were sent by a specific user, type "lprm -*user*" as root. As you can see, it is dangerous to use this command as root if you are not careful.

- To remove a specific job number from a specific printer, type "lprm -P*printername job*". For example, "lprm -Pij 103".

Checking A Printer's Status

To check on a print queue and a daemon's status, do the following:

1. Log in as root to the machine the printer is connected to.
2. Type "lpc status *printername*" to check the status. For example, "lpc status ij".

Disabling And Enabling A Print Queue

To disable a print queue so that you can take the printer down for maintenance, and then bring it back up, do the following:

1. Log in as root.
2. Type "lpc disable *printername*" to close the print queue so that it will not accept new jobs.

NOTE: *You can also type "lpc down printername message" if you are not sure how long this maintenance will take. For example, to take the printer ij down until you can replace a part, you might type "lpc down ij Waiting for a new part, use lj instead." Then, to bring the queue back up when the time comes, type "lpc up printername".*

3. Do the maintenance you need to get done.
4. Type "lpc enable *printername*" to open the queue again for business.

Chapter 9

System Security Basics

If you need an immediate solution to:	*See page:*
Activating And Deactivating The Shadow Suite	264
Shutting Off Unnecessary Daemons And Background Processes	264
Shutting Off Unnecessary Non-Daemon Network Services	267
Restricting Network Access With **tcp_wrappers**	267
Obtaining And Installing ssh	269
Setting Up ssh On A Server	270
Setting Up ssh On A Client	276
Removing Unnecessary Packages	279
Creating And Using A Named Pipe	280
Logging	280
Installing **swatch**	281
Analyzing Logs	281
Preparing For A Breach	282
Recovering From A Breach	282
Becoming The Superuser	283
Installing The Crack Password Checker	283
Securing Passwords With Crack	284
Setting Password Rules	285
Fighting Denial-Of-Service Attacks	285
Getting And Installing PGP	285
Setting Up An IP Firewall	287
Setting Up A Proxy Firewall	289
Refusing Login Access To All But Root	290

In Depth

System security is important for a number of reasons. The overall issue is keeping unwanted intruders out of your machines. People try to break in for many reasons: curiosity, status, revenge, profit, or even boredom. Although the reasoning determines what they do once they get in there, the central issue remains the same. Most system administrators are not running a theme park. They do not want uninvited guests wandering through their systems. This chapter not only teaches you how to initially secure your system but also provides strategies for keeping it secure over time.

Leaving The Door Wide Open

Dealing with system security includes two phases. The first phase involves the tweaks you make directly after installing the system, which is the focus of this section. The second phase is more of an ongoing process. For pointers on how to handle the second phase, see "Online Security Resources," later in the In Depth section.

Leaving The Login Door Open

One basic way that many administrators and users weaken system security is through poorly chosen passwords. The password is your first line of defense against system break-ins. Even the least knowledgeable of potential intruders knows that if they just try long enough they have a chance at guessing someone's password. Programs are available that are written just for this purpose. See the section "Securing Passwords With Crack" for instructions on how to utilize one of these programs for your own purposes.

New Password Considerations

The following are guidelines to consider when choosing a password:

- *Do not use dictionary words.* These are easily tested against master word files using a variety of password cracking programs.
- *Use combinations of lower- and uppercase letters, numbers, and allowed symbols.* Many people automatically use lowercase letters for typing ease, or just capitalize the first letter. This is too predictable. The more you mix things up in your password, the more secure it is. That is, unless you make it some kind of recognizable pattern, such as AbCd123. All keyboard symbols are allowed in a password under Linux.

- *Do not use personal information.* We have all seen it in the movies. Someone is able to hack into a system because they did some research and tried all of the account owner's personal information as password variants. While some of the movie versions are a bit farfetched, it is dangerous to use birthdays or pet names or other well-known information as a password. This especially applies to people who know significant information about you who might want to mess with your account in anger or as a practical joke. Or, they may just tell the wrong person.

NOTE: *Although Linux does not offer a password hint feature as part of the login process, there are many computer services and products that do these days. You need to be really careful with these hints! If you use obvious personal information for a password, then it makes life really easy for the people that know you and want to break in.*

- *Do not write your password down on a piece of paper and "hide" it in your desk drawer.* A caveat to this rule used by some people is to bury the password in an address or some other fake information. This practice still is risky if not done very carefully.
- *Use acronyms.* One good method of making effective passwords is to think of a long sentence, and use one letter from each word as the password. However, make sure that the resulting password does not run afoul of the other concerns listed here.

Shadow Passwords

Another issue is how the passwords are stored. The file /etc/passwd must be readable by all users for your system to function properly. This issue is unavoidable. Unfortunately, this means that if someone breaks into any account on your system, they can grab a copy of /etc/passwd. After someone has a copy of the master user and password file, they have a list of every existing account and the access to decrypt every password.

There is a solution to this issue that is so widely used that it is implemented by default in most Linux distributions, including Red Hat: the shadow password suite. Most other packages available in Linux today work properly with shadow passwords. The programs that do not support the shadow suite are specifically mentioned where they are covered throughout the book. This situation is much improved from even a few years ago, when choosing whether or not to use shadow was a serious decision.

When you convert your system to using shadow passwords (see "Activating And Deactivating The Shadow Suite," in the Immediate Solutions section, for instructions on how to do this), a version of /etc/passwd is placed in a new file: /etc/shadow. Every password field in /etc/passwd is changed to an "x" and the passwords are instead stored in /etc/shadow. A line in the shadow password file is added in the format:

```
user:pass:lastchg:allowchg:expire:expirew:disable:dcount:reserved
```

These fields translate to the following:

- ***user***—The login name for the user being defined.
- ***pass***—The user's encrypted password.
- ***lastchg***—The number of days since January 1, 1970, that this password was last changed.
- ***allowchg***—The number of days that must pass from the last change before the user's password can be changed again.
- ***expire***—The number of days that the user can use the same password. This count begins when the password is changed.
- ***expirew***—The number of days before the user has to change his or her password that a warning begins to appear. This value is counted backward from the ***expire*** date.
- ***disable***—How many days to wait after the password expires before you disable the account automatically. This value is useful for those accounts that are rarely used, because the users are not likely to notice any problems if intruders break in.
- ***dcount***—How many days since January 1, 1970, that this account was disabled.
- ***reserved***—Used by programs.

Although the password portion of shadow is what you see discussed the most, you can also convert to using shadow groups. Many people do not feel the need to go this far, but if you have any groups with password access required, you may want to implement this feature as well. The /etc/groups password information is placed in /etc/gshadow in this case.

See "Activating And Deactivating The Shadow Suite," in the Immediate Solutions section, for more information.

Special Login Options

Savvy (or sometimes just lazy) users often use a program called **rlogin** to streamline the remote login process for their other Linux or Unix accounts. In many ways, this program is just a version of **telnet** with the login process automated. It is this automation that people—both legitimate users and intruders—like.

You set up for **rlogin** by creating the file ~/.rhosts in the account you want to have remote access to. This file contains the names of computers that you intend to remotely access this account from. Then, from one of those remote computers, you just type something similar to "rlogin -l *account hostname*" and you are able to remotely log in without needing to enter a password.

Perhaps you already see the security problem here. If someone breaks into an account that has **rlogin** permissions on other machines, then they have effectively broken into your accounts on all of the other machines, as well. Sure, they have to figure out what hosts and what accounts—or do they? Typically, people have the same username on various machines on the network. Also, if you have **rlogin** in one direction, you probably have it set up in both directions. It does not take too long to figure out.

Now, suppose that the intruder just got access to three of your machines using **rlogin**. As can any other user, they can grab a copy of your /etc/passwd file. Do you have the shadow suite on all the machines? Did you set up your security properly on all the machines? As you can see, this one program can lead to a domino effect in your network after someone manages to break into an account. Some system administrators forbid the use of **rlogin** altogether, which you can do by deleting, renaming, or moving the **rlogin** program.

Leaving The Network Door Open

Several security holes are created right out of the box with almost all Linux distributions. This is especially true when you take the easy way out and use the general installation choices, or do not take the time during the installation phase to carefully select what should be included and what should be left out. You can end up leaving your system's door wide open in the process, by offering services and packages that you do not need. Most people, whether they are knowledgeable intruders or just following instructions, can break into a site that the system administrator did not take the time to secure.

Most Linux distributions, including Red Hat, turn on a number of daemons by default. An inexperienced system administrator simply leaves these in place. However, every unneeded networking service—which is what many daemons handle—provides a potential way to break in for an intruder. Because this isn't a perfect world, people are constantly testing, and trying to poke holes in, network services in hopes of finding a new way in. They also keep notes on what holes exist to exploit them later. See "Shutting Off Unnecessary Daemons And Background Processes," in the Immediate Solutions section, for information on how to reduce this risk.

When it comes to closing down unnecessary network services, one daemon requires special attention: the superdaemon, **inetd**. Whereas some network services run their own daemons, others really do not need to do so, which is where the superdaemon comes in. It manages connections for the services that do not require their own daemons. See "Shutting Off Unnecessary Non-Daemon Network Services," in the Immediate Solutions section, for instructions on how to remove the services that you do not need from the superdaemon's control.

Another concern is the file /etc/issue.net. Whenever someone tries to **telnet** into your system from outside, this file displays—by default—information about your system. It essentially contains the **telnet** welcome message. However, if you leave system information in the /etc/issue.net file, any potential intruder will immediately go to his or her handy information database or chart and look up standard weaknesses in, say, Red Hat Linux 6.2. If you have not plugged all the known holes, then intruders may very likely get in.

The way to solve this problem is simple—remove system information from this file. Make the welcome message more generic.

TIP: *Do the same with /etc/issue, because its contents are often copied to /etc/issue.net at boot time.*

Leaving The Process Door Open

Another method of making things too easy for intruders involves sloppy use of permissions and other such process and file system issues. Chapter 3 deals with the file system issues of permissions and ownership. It is worth some experimentation to figure out the subtleties of the permission structure. Remember that weak or thoughtless permissions are one of the fastest ways people get into file system areas they should not be in.

One major concern among security pundits, as discussed somewhat in Chapter 3, is the issue of SUID (set user ID). Some programmers and administrators, for convenience, like to set processes to run SUID root, which means that the process starts and then runs as though it is the root user. This practice has several concerns:

- If something is wrong in the script or program running as root, it has the permission level to do some serious system damage. In fact, you cannot set a script to run as root in the bash shell. It will not work.
- If you have a policy of using SUID and SGID (set group ID), it is easier to miss programs planted by intruders.

NOTE: *Internal security concerns do not apply so much to single-user machines if they are not steadily connected to the Internet. However, any connected machine stands the risk of being attacked.*

Online Security Resources

Security specifics change quickly. Although you can learn many things from books on the topic—a source I highly recommend—you also need to utilize the Internet to keep up to date on the latest information regarding security. Keep in mind that people who want to break into your system are using this resource, if not already one step ahead. You cannot afford to be more than one step behind.

Distribution Fixes

After you install a distribution, the first thing you should do is grab all the security fixes that have been released since that distribution shipped. For Red Hat 6.1, these fixes are available at **www.redhat.com/updates.html**. Fixes for bugs in Red Hat 6.2 are listed at **www.redhat.com/support/errata/rh62-errata-bugfixes.html**, and security fixes are at **www.redhat.com/rh62-errata-security.html**. The first thing you might notice on this Web page is an explanation of the number of days of priority FTP access available, upon registration, to those who bought particular levels of 6.2:

- *Red Hat Linux 6.2 Standard*—30 days of access to the priority FTP server once you register your product.
- *Red Hat Linux 6.2 Deluxe*—90 days of priority FTP access once you register.
- *Red Hat Linux 6.2 Professional*—180 days of priority FTP access once you register.

Registering also activates the Update Agent, which you can use to automatically fetch and apply fixes. See "The Red Hat Update Agent" later in the In Depth section for a discussion of the pros and cons of using this feature.

TIP: *To register, go to* ***www.redhat.com/now****.*

Although all of these registration features are useful, they are not necessary. You can do anything you need without them, except use the Update Agent. However, people were using shell scripts to do the same function before the Agent was available, and so can you. See Chapter 20 for more information on writing shell scripts.

Notification Lists

Over time, various security holes and other bugs are discovered throughout the collective tools in any Linux distribution—or any operating system, for that matter. Distribution-level lists, general Linux lists, as well as product-specific lists of such holes and bugs are available. You can even go higher and find general lists on Internet security and computer security. At the very least, subscribe to the distribution alert list, which allows you to receive immediate notification when security fixes are available. The Red Hat Watch list is a good place to start. To subscribe to this list or see recent postings, go to **www.redhat.com/mailing-lists/redhat-watch-list/**.

TIP: *If you want a more general list that keeps you notified of all package updates posted to the Red Hat site, including the security updates, go to* ***www.redhat.com/mailing-lists/redhat-announce-list/*** *instead. Instructions for joining this list are included in Chapter 1.*

For a more general Linux security discussion list, go to **www.redhat.com/mailing-lists/linux-security/**. Keep in mind that discussion lists can get busy. Be sure to keep the introductory posting that the mailing list software sends you, so you know how to change the list to digest mode, if necessary.

Security Web Sites

All system administrators should visit certain security Web sites regularly. Yes, this is a lot of reading, but if you are serious about your system security—which you should be—you need to visit these sites. Take the time in the beginning to go through these sites seriously, and then slowly build a list of bookmarks for the exact sections you want to check regularly. This type of system works well until the sites reorganize. Fortunately, this does not happen often, because it causes too many problems with so many people linking to them.

The general security Web sites are as follows:

- **www.cert.org**—CERT is a veteran Internet security group, founded in 1988 by DARPA (Defense Advanced Research Projects Agency). Its initial function was Internet security emergency response. Today, it applies that wealth of knowledge to researching the latest in Internet security needs and helping grow the ranks of Internet security specialists and emergency response teams.
- **www.ciac.org**—CIAC (Computer Incident Advisory Capability) is only one year younger than CERT, established in 1989 by the Department of Energy to handle Internet security issues and education. Today, it still works with the DOE, but also provides education and a technology watch to the Internet community.
- **www.rootshell.org**—A security news and documentation site. Typically, Rootshell lists news items involving sites that were cracked, and information about how it was done so that you can better secure your own systems. There is also a collection of articles relating to security issues.
- **www.sans.org**—SANS (System Administration, Networking, and Security) is a security news-dissemination and education organization. It produces a series of online digests, physical books and papers, and security education conferences.

A few of these sites also offer newsletters and mailing lists that are well worth checking out.

Available Tools

Many tools are available to help you beef up your site's security. Some of these tools are already on the Red Hat or other distribution CD-ROMs. Some are installed automatically but not fully implemented. Others you merely need to download before you can use them. All in all, you are not alone, because many resources are available to help you.

Pluggable Authentication Modules

Most people never deal with Pluggable Authentication Modules (PAMs). You see the term during the Red Hat installation process in the authentication section, but it is never really explained. PAM is a system through which user authentication is left to the operating system, not to individual programs. A program simply needs to properly call the PAMs to include login or password prompts for security purposes.

Because the documentation for this package is much larger than the average man page, some of the reference material is in the directory /usr/doc/pam-0.72 (give or take a change in version number), which includes several subdirectories containing the documentation in a variety of formats. Anything from text to HTML to PostScript (ps) format is available.

The Red Hat Update Agent

If you purchased Red Hat Linux 6.1 or later, you are entitled to technical support and priority FTP access as outlined at **www.redhat.com/now**. Part of this support scheme involves a program called the *Red Hat Update Agent*, a tool that automates much of the process of grabbing program updates. This feature is mentioned in this chapter because it is an excellent way to stay on top of the latest security bug fixes, if you have access to it.

One concern among many administrators is allowing such a tool to just grab and install things at its own whim. The point of security is to be aware of everything that is happening on your system, not to let something else handle it all. Fortunately, Red Hat considered this when it wrote this tool and thus gives you the option of downloading the updates but not installing them automatically.

For Red Hat's coverage of setting up and using this tool, go to **www.redhat.com/support/manuals/RHL-6.2-Manual/ref-guide/ch-up2date.html**.

The Secure Shell

A variety of *shells*—command-line working environments, discussed further in Chapter 20—are available in Linux. Each has its advantages and disadvantages. However, one stands out in the realm of security: ssh, the secure shell. Because this shell involves encryption, U.S.-based distributions cannot include it because of the encryption export munitions rules. See "Obtaining And Installing ssh," in the Immediate Solutions section, for information on where to download this shell and how to install it.

This shell is considered secure—or at least more secure than others—because it uses a public and private key code to determine who can and cannot access it from outside. The same type of public and private key scheme is used by the popular Pretty Good Privacy (PGP) tool. In the ssh key system, each server machine and any potential host machines have their own public and private keys. The server machine is also considered a host, so it actually has two sets of keys. Communication between the two boxes is accomplished by using a combination of the sender's private key and the receiver's public key to encrypt the data. Other forms of authentication may be required, as well, because ssh is used by individual users, not just between machines.

Such an encryption scheme requires trustworthy keys. How solid an ssh key is depends on how many bits you use to generate it. Three sets of keys are involved in ssh, and each one is created at a different bit level. The strongest key is the one that identifies the machine, or host. It is generated with 1,024 bits, which is pretty much the standard for strong encryption these days. The second-strongest key is the one generated by the ssh server, sshd. This daemon creates a 768-bit key when it starts and then changes it regularly.

Really, shh uses two and a half keys. The last "key" is actually a 256-bit random number generated by the client. This number is encrypted, used as a key throughout the client/server connection, and then discarded when the connection closes.

The primary reason why a setup like this is used is that it is useful for when you want to remotely log in to another machine. If you regularly use **telnet** or **rlogin** to access accounts on other machines—especially if you use either of them over the Internet—then you should seriously consider implementing this shell. All communications between the two machines get encrypted, so it saves you from having your login or other information sniffed by nosy people. You can also use ssh for fancier purposes, such as a wrapping around other processes.

NOTE: *Two versions of ssh exist, which is the source of some confusion. The first version, discussed in this chapter, is called ssh. Its sequel is ssh2. However, the license for using ssh2 is more limited. If your needs fall under ssh2's licensing, then by all means use the new version. For more on the issue, see "Obtaining And Installing ssh," in the Immediate Solutions section.*

Kerberos Authentication

One type of authentication that comes up time and time again is Kerberos, usually in the context of network security, such as when establishing a dial-in connection. Kerberos is specifically a network authentication tool. Like ssh and PGP, Kerberos uses public and private keys. The public keys in this case are generated on demand for a specific connection, and then discarded. They are called *tickets*.

Kerberos has multiple versions, which confuses the issue a bit. Kerberos v5, produced in 1995, is the version used by programs such as ssh and is the successor to Kerberos v4. If you do any research, it is important to look for MIT's Kerberos v5; otherwise, you may get data on other versions.

Kerberos is a client/server application. There are two different Kerberos servers: Key Distribution Center (KDC) and Distributed Computing Environment (DCE). The term *KDC* refers to two different servers: the Authentication Server (AS) and the Ticket Granting Server (TGS). Often, these two servers share a single machine, and only root has access to it—otherwise, anyone could potentially tamper with the keys it stores.

When a user needs to use Kerberos authentication, their client requests a Ticket Granting Ticket (TGT) from the AS. The client keeps its TGT for as long as it is valid—often around eight hours. Whenever it needs to do Kerberos authentication it uses the TGT to go directly to the TGS. No intermediary is needed until the TGT expires.

TIP: *An excellent guide to the basics of Kerberos is located at* ***www.isi.edu/gost/brian/security/kerberos.html****.*

Logging

One important tool available to you is the collective set of logs generated by your daemons and other system processes. These logs are generated in two different ways. The main logging tool on a Linux system is the syslog daemon, **syslogd**. It centrally manages logging for your main system services. Additional programs, such as Web servers, also come with their own logging facilities.

The syslog daemon's configuration file is /etc/syslog.conf. Entries in this file are in two columns: what to log, and where to log it.

What To Log

You use the first column in the format:

```
what.priority
```

The ***what*** portion of the syslog.conf entry specifies the process type the rule applies to. Your options are listed in Table 9.1.

Table 9.1 Process types available in /etc/syslog.conf.

Type	Will Log
*	All possible process types
auth	Authorization-related messages
auth-priv	Private authorization-related messages
cron	Messages from the **cron** and **at** daemons
daemon	Messages from system daemons that are not expressly listed in this file
kern	Kernel messages
local0 – **local7**	Messages sent to a specific virtual terminal
lpr	Print daemon messages
mail	Mail server messages, regardless of which server you are using
news	News server messages
syslog	Messages from **syslogd**
user	General messages

After you specify which item you want to log, you need to determine how much information from this item you want to record. Remember that the room on your hard drives isn't unlimited. It may take some time before you find the right balance for your needs. Table 9.2 lists the levels of logging available to you. Keep in mind that unless you explicitly tell **syslogd** not to, it will log all information that is considered more critical than the level you chose. So, choosing **debug**, for example, logs everything.

Table 9.2 Levels of information to log, listed in order of most critical to least critical.

Level	Will Log
none	Nothing from this type of item
emerg	Messages that may be involved with a malfunction or crash
alert	Messages requiring you to look into something
crit	Messages involving critical issues
err	Error messages
warning	Messages containing warnings
notice	Messages containing notices given by the program
info	Messages containing general information
debug	Debugging messages
*	All levels for this type of item

The basic layout of one type and one priority level can be expanded somewhat. If you want to log a number of items at the same priority level to the same place, you can use the following format to assign this:

```
what1,what2,what3.priority
```

You can also group multiple rules together to go to the same location, using the following format:

```
what1.priority1;what2.priority2
```

An additional feature is included in the **syslogd** used by Red Hat and many other distributions that allows you to tell the logging daemon to log only the priority level you listed, rather than that level and everything more critical. You accomplish this by putting an equal sign (=) in front of the priority, such as this:

```
what.=priority
```

TIP: *Type "man syslog.conf" to see whether your version includes this feature, if you are using a different distribution than Red Hat.*

You can also specifically tell the logging daemon to not include a particular priority, by putting an exclamation point (**!**) in front of it. This feature is useful in a statement such as the following:

```
what1.priority1;what1.!priority2
```

Where To Log

After you set what information is logged from what particular services, you need to tell the logging daemon where to put that information. This brings us to the second column in the /etc/syslog.conf file: the result column. Often, what you see in this column is the path to the file that the log information goes to. After information is logged, the file is then synchronized. If a lot of information is pouring into the log file, the constant syncing can affect program or systemwide performance. If you want to turn this feature off for this particular file, add a minus sign (-) in front of the path, such as this:

```
-/var/log/errorlog
```

NOTE: *Information is not always immediately saved to the hard drive. Syncing moves the data from the buffers onto the drive.*

You do not always have to send log data to a file. The specific version of **syslogd** used by Red Hat Linux and many other distributions also offers the possibility to send the data to a *named pipe*. If you are familiar with working at the command line, then you have probably used a general pipe at some point. You might have typed something like "ps aux | grep mail" to see whether the **sendmail** daemon was running, for example. A named pipe is slightly different. See "Creating And Using A Named Pipe," in the Immediate Solutions section, for information on how to set one up. To signify that you are pointing the log output to a named pipe, place a pipe symbol at the beginning of the path statement, such as:

```
|/var/log/logpipe
```

You can also send the log information to a variety of other places, as described here:

- To send it to a virtual console, use the path to its device designation, such as:

  ```
  /dev/tty3
  ```

- You can centralize your logging on one machine on the network by running **syslogd** on both the remote machine and the log server. Then, when you set up the log file, place the destination segment in the format:

  ```
  @host
  ```

  Where the information eventually ends up depends on where that service's information goes in the log server's /etc/syslog.conf.

- To send information to a user who is logged in, make the destination one or a series of login names, such as:

  ```
  user1,user2
  ```

- To send information to everyone who is currently logged in, which may be necessary with emerg-level messages, put an asterisk (*) in the destination field. For example:

  ```
  *
  ```

Log Monitoring With swatch

Many system administrators spend a lot of time setting up log files, and then only occasionally look through them to see whether something is wrong. This is not a secure policy. In this world of computer automation, you need an automated watchdog looking over your log files—enter the **swatch**, or System Watcher, tool.

The **swatch** Perl program (more on Perl in Chapter 21) has a simple function: It watches the files you tell it to watch on a continuous basis. When it comes across strings you consider to be suspicious, it does what you have instructed it to do. This tool obviously has a wider range of applications than just monitoring log files. However, it certainly is perfect for this security task.

Each line in /etc/swatchrc, the **swatch** configuration file, is built in the following format:

```
pattern     action     time
```

The key here, then, is to build your patterns such that they are effective. This strategy involves understanding the *metacharacters*—characters that refer to other characters—available to you. Table 9.3 lists the metacharacters available to you in **swatch**. It often takes some experimentation to be fully comfortable with some of these expression-building tools. Try experimenting before you let them do your security work for you.

Table 9.3 Metacharacters available in swatch, and in Perl in general.

Character	Purpose	Example	Example Matches	Does Not Match
*	Matches any number of characters of any type	**c*t**	cat, cart, carrot	canter
^	Matches characters at the beginning of a line	**^Quick**	Quick Brown Fox	The Quick Brown Fox
.	Matches any single character	**c.t**	cat, cot	cart
\	Treats the following character as a regular character, not a metacharacter	**c\.t**	c.t	cat
$	Matches characters at the end of a line	**$laugh**	You make me laugh	Don't laugh at me
[ ]	Matches one of the contained items	**c[a,u]b**	cab, cub	caub
I	Matches one or the other of the patterns	**c[a,u]b I m*t**	cab, cub, mutt, met	cub mutt
+	Matches one or more of the patterns	**c[a,u]b + m*t**	cab, cub, mutt, met, cub mutt	cart
?	Matches none or one of this pattern	**c?.t**	cat	cart
( )	Groups together patterns	**c(alu + o)t**	cat, cut, cot	caught

After you build the pattern, you need to assign the action, which can be any one of the items outlined in Table 9.4. When an action has a value associated with it, you use the format ***action=value***.

Finally, you can specify how often the pattern has to match before it becomes a concern. This is optional; you do not have to include it in any /etc/swatchrc rule. If you do, however, use one of the formats listed in Table 9.5.

Attacks And Intrusions

The number of ways for people to attack your network or machines, or just sneak their way in, is ever growing. The only way to keep up on these techniques is to read the security sites previously listed in "Online Security Resources." However,

Table 9.4 Actions available in the swatch tool.

Action	Result	Values	Default
bell	Sounds a speaker bell and echos the contents of the line that matches the pattern	A nonzero positive integer, reflecting the number of bells	1
echo	Echos the line that matches the pattern	Formatting for the line, out of the following options: **blink**, **bold**, **inverse**, **normal**, or **underscore**	Normal
exec	Commands to execute if pattern matches	Path to command	None
ignore	Ignores the line that matches this pattern	None	None
mail	Sends mail if the pattern matches	*address1:address2...*	User running the program
pipe	Sends the matched line through a pipe to a command	Path to command	None
write	Echos the matched pattern to the listed users with the **write** command	*login1:login2...*	None

Table 9.5 Time intervals between matches in /etc/swatchrc.

Format	Units
##	Seconds
##:##	Minutes:seconds
##:##:##	Hours:minutes:seconds

some attack techniques are common, and some classes of attacks follow the same pattern even when the details change. This section reviews these common techniques and patterns.

Network Attacks

One group of methods that makes a system administrator's life frustrating is the *network attack*. This type of attack can involve either modem-related issues or Ethernet-related issues—networking in general. How these two items get abused overlaps greatly. The most common type of network attack is *denial of service*, which has had a lot of time in the press lately because it has been used to disrupt major Internet services.

A denial-of-service attack can come in many forms. In general, it is a series of requests for service that come in rapid succession, overloading the system and blocking off the opportunity for real users to access the service. If you have a small amount of bandwidth—such as a 56.6Kbps modem connection to the outside world—then this type of attack can effectively cut off all traffic for your network.

You do not have to have a large, internationally known site to fall prey to denial of service or any other type of attack. Many people discover the annoyance of not being able to use their connection properly just from having had arguments with others in chat rooms or newsgroups. See "Fighting Denial-Of-Service Attacks," in the Immediate Solutions section, for information on how to prepare for and handle them when they happen. It is imperative that you prepare ahead of time. Unless you have a secondary account you can use to download tools, you may have no way to get them during an attack.

Machine Attacks

Another common type of attack is one directed at a specific machine. A potential intruder first might try to **telnet** in and see whether the machine offers any information about what operating system and version number you are using. The earlier section "Leaving The Network Door Open" addresses how to ensure that your machines do not make things this easy.

After the intruder has the information about the operating system, or has decided they can't get it, they start testing ports. Which services listen on specific ports is standard across the Internet. If the unwanted guest knows what operating system and version you have, they know exactly what version of software you are using, if you have not bothered to use any security patches. They will test those known weaknesses first. If they do not know which operating system you have, it just takes them longer, because they have to work through a list of unknown weaknesses for the services available on a number of operating systems.

Unless you have done your homework, the intruder will find a way in. Even if you have done your homework, they still might be successful. "Preparing For A Breach," in the Immediate Solutions section, explains what you should always have readily available for when you suspect you might have a break-in.

Account Attacks

In a way, account attacks are the most insidious, because if the account breached is not used very often and you are not carefully monitoring user activities, they can go unnoticed for some time. I cannot stress how important it is to have a strong password policy and enforce it regularly. See the sections involving passwords in the Immediate Solutions section to learn more about the options available to you and how to use them.

Account attacks typically take the form of someone repeatedly trying passwords until they get in. They may be guessing them by hand, or running a utility that does the guessing for them. In fact, they may run the same Crack program covered in this chapter. In the Immediate Solutions section, "Analyzing Logs" explains one good way to watch for this type of activity.

Firewalls And You

Many folks in the computer field think of firewalls immediately when they hear the word *security*. Whether a firewall is right for you depends on how much access you need to the outside world, and how much access you want people from the outside world to have to your system. Typically, when you build your firewall rules, you begin by denying all access, and then punch holes with specific rules allowing specific things. If you punch enough holes that your firewall looks like Swiss cheese, you have made it essentially useless. Firewalls are primarily useful for network segments or subnets that hold mission-critical data that should not be accessible to the outside world and so is worth restricting.

More than one type of firewall is available. On Linux, you typically implement either an IP filtering firewall or a proxying firewall. Which of these you choose depends on what you want people to be able to see in your network, and what amount of information you want to block. You also have the option of implementing a basic amount of IP filtering that is not a firewall at all.

What distinguishes a firewall from another form of security program is placement. A firewall lives on a single machine that is the only form of contact between the network segment it protects and the outside world, as represented in Figure 9.1. Because this scheme requires two entirely separate IP addresses and a significant amount of traffic, you need to have two Ethernet cards in the firewall machine; one to handle traffic to and from the outside world, and another to handle traffic to and from the internal network.

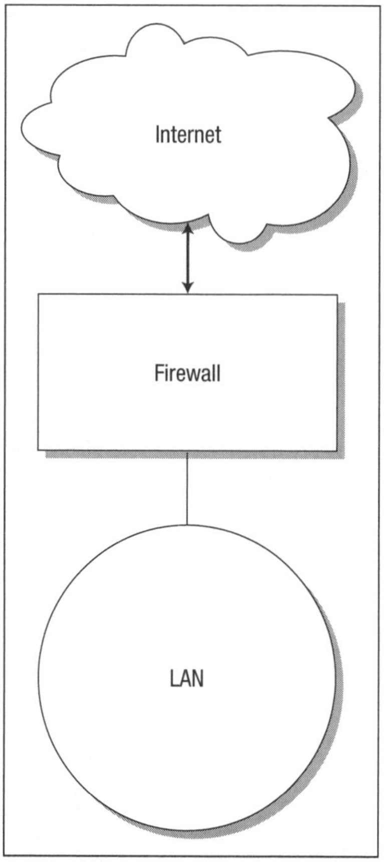

Figure 9.1 A firewall protecting a subnet on an otherwise open network.

Non-Firewall IP Filters

The pseudo-firewall uses a feature called **tcp_wrappers**. This tool is not a firewall, because you use it on individual machines rather than on a main machine that protects the network. Those who cannot use a firewall—either because a firewall would be too restrictive or because it would cause too much difficulty with applications or services users require—can use **tcp_wrappers** to better secure specific machines.

__NOTE:__ The __tcp_wrappers__ tool is by definition limited. Remember that if you need tighter security for just one or two machines, you can still use a firewall for just those machines if necessary. You do not have to put an entire network behind a firewall. Also, keep in mind that the best protection from intrusion is to not network a machine at all.

It is important to understand the layout of the files used with **tcp_wrappers**. These files—/etc/hosts.allow and /etc/hosts.deny—contain a series of access rules that are read in order until a match is found. You add one rule per line, unless you add the backslash (\) character at the end of the line to tell the system the rule extends down to the next line. Comments, as usual, are lines that begin with a hash mark (#).

A line in either of these files is written in the following format:

```
daemons : clients : command
```

The ***command*** item is optional. Building these two or three pieces requires some serious thought. In the Immediate Solutions section, "Restricting Network Access With **tcp_wrappers**" explains how to put everything together.

NOTE: *If you use **tcp_wrappers**, you need to set it up individually on every machine you want to use it for.*

One of the tools available to you when building your statements is the wildcard. Table 9.6 lists the wildcards available to you when setting up **tcp_wrappers**.

If you want to make a rule with an exception, use the **EXCEPT** operator.

TIP: *Finding the man page relating to this tool's accept and deny files is not simple. Type "man 5 hosts_access" to read the entire set of rules for these files.*

Filtering Firewalls

A *filtering firewall* examines all the traffic coming in and out of your site and checks it against the rules you set within it. Any traffic that does not conform to the rules, whether incoming or outgoing, is blocked. Only traffic that matches the

Table 9.6 Wildcards in /etc/hosts.allow and /etc/hosts.deny.

Wildcard	Purpose For Host	Purpose For User
ALL	Matches everything; the same as how an asterisk (*) is normally used	Same as host
KNOWN	Matches if both the machine's name and IP address are known; fails if DNS is not available for any reason	Matches if the user is known
LOCAL	Matches all hosts local to this machine	None
PARANOID	Matches any host whose name does not match its registered IP address	None
UNKNOWN	Matches any host whose name or address is not available	Matches any unknown user

rules passes through. It is imperative not to make your rules too lax. If you find that you must poke too many holes, consider other forms of security instead.

The IP filtering firewall used under Linux uses a feature called **ipchains**. This function is actually already in use on your system. By default, however, it just lets everything through. It becomes a firewall tool when you tighten its rules and place the machine between a portion of the network and the outside world.

By default, the following are the three chains:

- *Input chain*—Analyzes all traffic coming into the interface from the outside
- *Output chain*—Examines all data before it is sent out of the machine
- *Forward chain*—Used for packets that need to be redirected to somewhere other than where they want to go

Although you can create your own chains, it is not necessary when setting up a basic firewall.

Chain rules are complex, but in general, you use **ipchains** in the following format:

```
ipchains flag chain statement action
```

The type of statement you use depends on the flag involved. Available flags are listed in Table 9.7.

Table 9.7 Flags used with ipchains.

Flag	Purpose
-A	Adds a rule to the end of the chain
-C	Checks the specified packet against the chain to see whether it gets through
-D	Removes a specific rule from the chain
-F	Deletes every rule from the chain
-h	Displays help information
-I	Adds a rule to a specific location in the chain
-L	Lists all the rules in the chain
-M	Specifies that you want to work with masquerading information
-N	Creates a new chain
-P	Sets the default policy for what the chain does with data
-S	Alters masquerading timeout values
-R	Replaces a specific rule in the chain
-X	Deletes the user-created chain specified
-Z	Empties the chain counters

Our focus here is on the **-A** flag, which adds a rule to a chain. The statements that coincide with this flag reflect the variety of traffic that passes through a network in an average day, or even in an hour. As such, the statements are not something that can be summarized in a simple table.

Testing A Packet's Destination

One key item of interest for traffic coming into—and going out of, to a lesser degree—your network is where it is ultimately headed. The most complex version of a destination statement you can have is this:

```
-d ! address/mask ! port1:port2
```

The optional items are the exclamation points, the mask, and the second part of the port. This statement breaks down into the following segments:

- **!**—The exclamation points translate to the word "not." If you use one in the first position, you are saying that packets that match this rule cannot be from the following address. Using one in the second position means packets matching the rule cannot be from the following port.
- ***address***—The IP address this rule refers to, or the network address if used in conjunction with a mask value.
- ***mask***—A netmask that explains what portion of the network listed applies to the rule. See Chapter 7 for information on how to calculate this value.
- ***port1***—The specific destination port number at the specified address(es) that this rule applies to.
- ***port2***—Used if you want to express a range of ports rather than a single port. If you use this item, you need to adjust the first port as well. The range does not include the numbers listed, so if you list 4:9, this refers to 5 through 8.

Testing The Interface

Another item worth testing is the interface this packet came in from or is going out to. An interface test is done in the format:

```
-i ! interface
```

In this case, only the exclamation point is optional. The ***interface*** variable is the Ethernet card the rule refers to.

Testing The Protocol

Often, you need or want to know what service people are trying to access in your network. This means watching both the protocol they are using and the port. Testing packet protocols is done in the following format:

```
-p ! protocol
```

As usual, the exclamation point is optional and signals that the rule matches only if the following protocol is not associated with the packet in question. Typically, the protocol entry would be icmp (**ping** packets), udp, or tcp. These entries must be in lowercase, as listed.

TIP: *For a full listing of the protocols accepted by your network's services, type "more /etc/protocols".*

Testing A Packet's Origination Point

Although we often focus on where the packet is going, sometimes we need to be concerned with where it came from in the first place. You make this test in the following format:

```
-s ! address/mask ! port1:port2
```

This format should be familiar. See the prior section "Testing A Packet's Destination" for an explanation of what each piece of this statement stands for. Keep in mind that you are not testing where it is going, however. You are testing where it originated.

Testing For TCP Session Initiation

When a client tries to initiate a connection with a TCP server, it sends a SYN packet. Blocking these packets in the input chain is one way of allowing your users to initiate TCP sessions with servers inside and outside of your network while not allowing outsiders to make TCP connections with machines inside your network. To test for SYN packets, use this format:

```
! -y
```

You need to use this feature in conjunction with the **-p** flag with the TCP protocol set. As usual, the exclamation point is optional.

Setting The Packet's Fate

Not all **ipchains** statements involve testing data. One allows you to list what happens to the packet if it matches the test criterion. You add this statement in the following format:

```
-j option
```

Table 9.8 outlines the available fates for a packet that matches an **ipchains** rule.

See "Setting Up An IP Firewall" in the Immediate Solutions section for information on implementing **ipchains**.

Table 9.8 Matched packet options in ipchains.

Option	Result
ACCEPT	Lets the packet pass through to its destination.
DENY	Refuses to pass the packet; does not notify the sender of the refusal.
MASQ	Converts packets on their way out so that they look like they are coming from the firewall, and converts packets on the way in so that they are headed for the proper machine. Only valid for forward or custom chains, not for input or output.
REDIRECT	Reroutes the packet to a local IP address and port. Only valid for the input or custom chains.
REJECT	Refuses to pass the packet, and sends an ICMP packet letting the sender know the data was refused.
RETURN	Jumps to the next chain to examine its rules, or defaults to the chain's policy action.

Proxying Firewalls

A *proxying firewall* hides the structure of the network behind it. All traffic going from internal machines to the outside world looks as though it comes from the proxy itself. This means that any service that your users want to access has to have a client on the end-user machine, and a proxy server on the firewall to send out the request and pass along the results.

When writing this book, I considered two proxying firewalls that are freely available under Linux:

- *SOCKS*—Available at **www.socks.nec.com**
- *Firewall Tool Kit (FWTK)*—Available at **www.tis.com/research/software**

FWTK is the firewall covered under "Setting Up A Proxy Firewall," toward the end of the Immediate Solutions section. A third popular choice is Gauntlet Firewall, available at **www.pgp.com/asp_set/products/tns/gauntlet.asp**.

One of the major configuration files you have to deal with when setting up FWTK is /usr/local/etc/netperm-table. It contains a series of one-line pairs in the following general format:

```
application: rule value
```

You can specify multiple applications in one of two formats. Use this one to specifically list the applications:

```
application1, application2, ...:
```

Use the following to specify that all applications fit the bill:

```
*:
```

The same application can appear in multiple rules, so do not feel like you have to squeeze everything in together. If more than one rule exists for the same type of result, then the proxied program uses the first rule it comes across. Be sure to go over the file periodically as you add more to it, to ensure that you don't accidentally have items ignoring their own rules.

Standalone Firewalls

Firewalls are not always in the type of format where you install software on a box that also may be acting as a router and more. Several specialized firewalls are available that do not actually share equipment with any of your production machines. Some of these firewalls are "black boxes" that you buy preinstalled and plug in between your network or protected area and the outside world. Others are programs that you put on a box by themselves.

Some of the possible solutions in this area are the following:

- *Phoenix Adaptive Firewall*—Available at **www.progressive-systems.com/products/**
- *Sinus Firewall*—Available at **www.sinusfirewall.org**
- *FirePlug EDGE Project*—Available at **http://edge.fireplug.net**

Immediate Solutions

Activating And Deactivating The Shadow Suite

The shadow suite has two major components: passwords and groups. Although shadow passwords are generally active by default on a Red Hat installation, if you have them deactivated, you can turn them on with the command **pwconv**. To remove them, use the command **pwunconv**.

Shadow groups are typically not already active. To turn them on, use the command **grpconv**. To remove the group shadow feature, use **grpunconv**.

Shutting Off Unnecessary Daemons And Background Processes

To stop unnecessary daemons and other processes from starting automatically in Red Hat Linux, do the following:

1. Log in as root.
2. Type "ps aux | more" to show the list of all running processes without the beginning scrolling off the top of the screen.
3. Look through the processes. Some of these are things you need, and some are started from the assumption that you might need them.

TIP: *Utilize the **man** system if you cannot tell whether you want a particular item. Type "man process" to learn what it does.*

4. Type "cd /etc/rc.d" to change to the parent directory that contains all the runlevel boot directories. Red Hat's runlevels are laid out in Table 9.9.
5. Type "cd rc#.d", where # stands for the runlevel whose boot information you want to edit.
6. Type "ls S*" and press Enter. Everything you see here is a daemon that starts when you enter this runlevel. The number after each *S* corresponds to when the daemon starts. The lower the number, the sooner it starts.

Table 9.9 Red Hat Linux runlevels.

Runlevel	Description
0	Shuts the system down
1	Single-user mode
2	Multiuser mode but no NFS capability
3	Full multiuser mode; standard runlevel for booting to the command line
5	Full multiuser mode with GUI; standard runlevel for booting into the GUI
6	Reboots the machine

7. If you are concerned about making mistakes at this point, type "ls -la S* > /root/runlisting". This command saves the long version file listing to the file /root/runlisting so that you can return to what you had before if necessary.
8. Delete the files that correspond to services you do not want to use. The items in this directory are not the real daemons. They are all soft links to the real daemons. So, as long as you backed up the file listing, you can restore items later if necessary.
9. Now that you have removed unneeded daemons, you can begin removing other programs that start at boot time. If it helps you to gather your thoughts, type "shutdown -r now" to reboot the machine immediately, and look again at what processes are running after you are back up.
10. In Red Hat Linux, type "vi /etc/rc.d/rc.local" to open the file where you are most likely to find non-daemon programs that start at boot time. By default, this file contains the following:

```
#!/bin/sh
#
# This script will be executed *after* all the other init scripts.
# You can put your own initialization stuff in here if you don't
# want to do the full Sys V style init stuff.

if [ -f /etc/redhat-release ]; then
    R=$(cat /etc/redhat-release)

    arch=$(uname -m)
    a="a"
    case "_$arch" in
        _a*) a="an";;
        _i*) a="an";;
    esac
```

```
        NUMPROC=`grep -cl "^cpu[0-9]+" /proc/stat`
        if [ "$NUMPROC" -gt "1" ]; then
            SMP="$NUMPROC-processor "
            if [ "$NUMPROC" = "8" -o "$NUMPROC" = "11" ]; then
                a="an"
        else
            a="a"
            fi
        fi

        # This will overwrite /etc/issue at every boot.  So, make any
           changes
        # you want to make to /etc/issue here or you will lose them when
        # you reboot.
        echo "" > /etc/issue
        echo "$R" >> /etc/issue
        echo "Kernel $(uname -r) on $a $SMP$(uname -m)" >> /etc/issue

        cp -f /etc/issue /etc/issue.net
        echo >> /etc/issue
    fi
```

11. In the default version of this shell script (for more on shell scripting, see Chapter 20), no new programs are started. Look through to see whether you or any installation routines have added anything. If so, comment them out by putting a hash mark (#) at the beginning of the line.
12. Press the Esc key, and then type "ZZ" to save and exit the file. The new changes will show at boot time.
13. Reboot the system when it is convenient, so you can make sure it boots smoothly.

NOTE: *Each Linux distribution handles boot information a bit differently, especially both runlevels and system initialization files. You may have to follow a different procedure if you are using another distribution. To determine a distribution's runlevels, type "more /etc/inittab". A runlevel key should be located near the beginning of the file.*

Related solutions:	Found on page:
Shutting Down And Rebooting	97
Writing Your Own Package Update Script	611
Writing Your Own User Creation Script	615

Shutting Off Unnecessary Non-Daemon Network Services

To stop network services that do not require daemons, do the following:

1. Log in as root.
2. Type "vi /etc/inetd.conf" to open the superdaemon's configuration file.
3. Use the arrow and Page Up and Page Down keys to move through the file. Any line that starts with a hash mark is commented out, and thus not in use. Carefully consider each uncommented line and decide whether you are using that service.

TIP: *Utilize the **man** system if you cannot tell whether you want a particular item. Type "man process" to learn what it does.*

---

4. If you decide you do not need the service (common examples are **finger** and **talk**), place the cursor on the beginning of its line.
5. Type "i" to enter Insert mode.
6. Type a hash mark (#) to comment out the line.
7. Press the Esc key to return to Command mode.
8. After you finish editing this file, type "ZZ" to save and close it.
9. Type "/etc/rc.d/init.d/inet restart" to stop the superdaemon and start it with its new configuration.

NOTE: *This process works the same regardless of which distribution you are using. The primary difference here might be what is on or off by default, or what is included in the listing. Also, the way you restart inetd may be different in another distribution. A basic method that works on any distribution is to type "ps aux | grep inetd" to get the Process ID (PID) that inetd is running under, and then type "kill -HUP PID" to restart the service.*

Restricting Network Access With **tcp_wrappers**

To restrict network access on a specific machine without using a full-blown firewall, do the following:

1. Log in as root.
2. Type "vi /etc/hosts.deny" to open the file that allows you to block who has access to the network.
3. This file already has some descriptive content. Type "G" to move the cursor to the last line.

4. Type "o" to create a new line beneath the current position, and then enter Insert mode.
5. Add the following line to tell the machine to make sure that incoming traffic's claimed address matches its real address:

```
ALL: PARANOID
```

6. What you add from here depends on what you want to block. At the bare minimum, you need to add the following if you want to allow the sendmail server to move mail through this system:

```
ALL EXCEPT sendmail: ALL
```

7. Remember that **tcp_wrappers** looks in /etc/hosts.allow to see what is explicitly allowed as well. Anything that does not match in /etc/hosts.allow but is not email will be blocked by this setup. If you need to open anything else explicitly, add additional **EXCEPT** portions to this statement. Remember that you need to use the actual daemon's name in the daemon portion. Many of these names are listed if you type "ls /usr/sbin/in*". For example, you might use the following if you have a Web server on a specific machine:

```
ALL EXCEPT sendmail EXCEPT httpd: ALL
```

NOTE: *Don't knock too many holes in this file! This is security, remember: deny, and then explicitly allow.*

8. When you are finished, press the Esc key, and then type "ZZ" to save and close the file.
9. Type "vi /etc/hosts.allow" to open the file that lets you state what kinds of connections should definitely be let through.
10. It is more important for this file to understand how to refer to individual machines or groups of machines than it is for the deny file to understand. Whenever you punch holes, try to make them as small as possible so that you do not accidentally allow intruders' packets as well. Instead of the standard asterisk used in so many files as wildcards, you can use the following characters together as a wildcard: back quote, period, backslash, and front quote. The following are the formats available:
    - '*.domain.extension*\', as in '.animals.org\'
    - '*ip1.ip2.*\', as in '192.168.170.\'
    - '*ip1.ip2.ip3.ip4/nm1.nm2.nm3.nm4*\', as in '192.168.170.9/255.255.255.90\'

Add rules that let the traffic into the machine that it needs. For example, if you need to be able to **telnet** from your machine in another part of the office to this one, add a line such as this:

```
in.telnetd : 192.168.170.12
```

11. When you are finished, press the Esc key, and then type "ZZ" to save and close the file.

NOTE: *Do not open too many holes right away. Sometimes, instead of poking your security full of holes, it is better to see what you explicitly need to add.*

Obtaining And Installing ssh

To get and then install the secure shell software—which must be done on both client and server machines—do the following:

1. Go to the URL **www.ssh.org/download.html**.
2. Read this Web page. Two different versions of ssh are available, ssh and ssh2. These instructions are for ssh, because it has the less-restrictive version license.
3. Click the appropriate mirror site's URL to enter that site's FTP folder.
4. Click the newest version of ssh available. At the time of this writing, the version to download was ssh-1.2.27.tar.gz. Do not be fooled by newer-looking versions that start with ssh-2. These files are ssh2.

TIP: *You can also use FTP to go directly to one of the mirror sites after you get the URL address from the main ssh Web page.*

5. Close the Web browser or FTP connection.
6. Move the file to your preferred source location (for example, **mv ssh-1.2.27.tar.gz /usr/src**).
7. **gunzip** the file (for example, **gunzip ssh-1.2.27.tar.gz**).
8. Unpack the file with **tar** (for example, **tar -xvf ssh-1.2.27.tar**).
9. Change into the source directory with the **cd** command (for example, **cd ssh-1.2.27**).

TIP: *If the newest series 1 version is higher than 1.2.27, see the INSTALL file to make sure that the installation instructions have not changed.*

10. Type "./configure" to run the ssh configuration script. You must type the command with ./ in front of it unless you type the entire path, such as "/usr/src/ssh-1.2.27/configure". You would have to have this directory in your path statement to be able to directly type "configure".
11. Type "make" to start the ssh compilation process. Depending on your machine's speed and RAM, this compile may take a minute or several minutes.
12. Type "make install" to run the installation portion of the ssh Makefile. This process places the ssh binaries where they need to be on your system. For more on **make** and Makefiles, see Chapter 22. The installation may take several minutes or longer, because code keys need to be generated.
13. Type "make clean" to tidy up your file system by removing the intermediate files created during the compile process.

Related solutions:	Found on page:
Opening **gzip**ed Files	108
Opening **tar** Files	110
Compiling C Code With **gcc**	647

Setting Up ssh On A Server

To set up the secure shell on the machine you want to provide ssh secured access to, do the following:

1. Log in as root.
2. Type "vi /etc/sshd_config" to open the ssh server configuration file.
3. Many options are available for /etc/sshd_config. Table 9.10 breaks them down into categories to make them more manageable. Be sure to consider each option carefully, starting with the definitions that state who you allow to access this machine through ssh. Choose the options that apply to your needs.

TIP: *When typing all of these keywords, you do not need to be careful about the case. This is a rare instance in Linux where case does not matter.*

4. Now, choose the options that apply to the level of authentication you want to require. Table 9.11 lists what these options are and how to use them.

Table 9.10 Options for determining whom you allow to have ssh access.

Option	Purpose	Values
AllowGroups	Specifies exactly which groups are allowed to log in. This item refers to primary groups only. It does not look at secondary groups.	***group1 group2 group3...***
AllowHosts	Specifies exactly which hosts users can log in from.	***host1 host2...***
AllowSHosts	Double-checks any remote login attempts against the following host pattern.	***host1 host2...***
AllowUsers	Double-checks any remote login attempts against the following two types of user patterns, which can be mixed or used singly.	***user user@host...***
DenyGroups	Refuses to allow the specified groups to log in. This item refers to primary groups only. It does not look at secondary groups.	***group1 group2 group3...***
DenyHosts	Refuses to allow anyone from the specified hosts to log in.	***host1 host2...***
DenySHosts	Refuses to allow anyone from the specified hosts to log in, even if they are listed in the appropriate login files created when setting up the client (~/.rhosts or ~/.shosts).	***host1 host2...***
DenyUsers	Refuses to allow anyone to log in if they match the following two types of user patterns, which can be mixed or used singly.	***user user@host...***
PermitRootLogin	Allows root to log in to this machine. It is always a security hole to allow remote access by root.	**yes** (root can log in regardless of method), **no** (root cannot log in regardless of method), or **nopwd** (root can log in but not with just a password authentication), with a default of **yes**.

Table 9.11 What a remote machine or user needs to be able to gain ssh access.

Option	Purpose	Values
AccountExpireWarningDays	Specifies when to start printing messages warning that the account is about to expire.	A positive integer; the default is 14 days. 0 shuts off this feature.
ForcedEmptyPasswdChange	Forces a user to enter a password if either they left it blank or this is their first login. This is not a secure default.	Either **yes** or **no**; the default is **no**.
ForcedPasswdChange	Forces the user to change their password if it is expired.	Either **yes** or **no**; the default is **yes**.
IgnoreRhosts	Does not accept entries in ~/.rhosts or ~/.shosts as valid for authentication.	Either **yes** or **no**; the default is **no**.
IgnoreRootRhosts	Does not accept entries in ~/.rhosts or ~/.shosts as valid for authentication for a remote root login.	Either **yes** or **no**; the default is whatever you have **IgnoreRhosts** set to.
KerberosAuthentication	Specifies that Kerberos v5 authentication is accepted.	Either **yes** or **no**; the default is **yes**.
KerberosOrLocalPasswd	Specifies whether a failed Kerberos authentication defaults to a regular password check.	Either **yes** or **no**; the default is **no**. It is not a good idea to change this default, because if Kerberos authentication fails, it means that the user may be an intruder.
KerberosTgtPassing	Specifies whether a Kerberos TGT can be passed to the ssh server.	Either **yes** or **no**; the default is **yes**.
PasswordAuthentication	Allows password authentication.	Either **yes** or **no**; the default is **yes**.
PasswordExpireWarningDays	Specifies when to start printing messages warning that the password is about to expire.	A positive integer; the default is 14 days. A 0 shuts off this feature.
PermitEmptyPasswords	Specifies whether the server allows login to accounts with empty passwords.	Either **yes** or **no**; the default is **yes**. It is often a good idea to change this value to **no**.

(continued)

***Table 9.11 What a remote machine or user needs to be able to gain ssh access* (continued).**

Option	Purpose	Values
RhostsAuthentication	Allows standard **rlogin**.	Either **yes** or **no**; the default is **no**. It should be left this way; otherwise, there is no point in installing the secure shell!
RhostsRSAAuthentication	Allows **rlogin** in conjunction with RSA authentication, using the keys generated at the client and server ends.	Either **yes** or **no**; the default is **yes**.
RSAAuthentication	Considers RSA authentication sufficient.	Either **yes** or **no**; the default is **yes**.
TISAuthentication	Allows authentication through the Gauntlet **authsrv** program.	Either **yes** or **no**.

5. Another group of options determines various aspects of the ssh server's behavior. Choose the ones you want to use from Table 9.12.
6. Finally, determine whether you want to specify any files for the ssh server, using the options listed in Table 9.13.

Table 9.12 How ssh interacts and behaves.

Option	Purpose	Values
CheckMail	Determines whether ssh should tell you that you have new mail when you are remotely connected to the machine that receives it.	Either **yes** or **no**; the default is **yes**.
FacistLogging	Logs all ssh-connected happenings verbosely. The problem with this option is that it violates user privacy; thus, you should not activate it unless you are investigating suspicious activity or are in a corporate environment that has a clear policy regarding such logging.	Either **yes** or **no**; the default is **no**.

(continued)

***Table 9.12 How ssh interacts and behaves* (continued).**

Option	Purpose	Values
IdleTimeout	Specifies how long to wait before breaking an idle connection.	A positive integer followed by **s** for seconds, **m** for minutes, **h** for hours, **d** for days, or **w** for weeks; the default is seconds.
KeepAlive	Tells the server to send messages to the client to ensure that the connection is still open and valid. It closes the connection if it cannot reach the client.	Either **yes** or **no** in both server and client configuration files; the default is **yes**.
KeyRegenerationInterval	Allows the server to automatically generate a new security key on a regular basis. This prevents keeping one in place long enough for someone to manage to decrypt it.	A positive integer; the default is every 3,600 seconds. Use 0 to shut off this feature.
ListenAddress	Identifies the interface that sshd is listening on.	IP address of interface
LoginGraceTime	Specifies how long the server waits before hanging up on a user who has not fully logged in for any reason.	A positive integer in seconds; the default is 600. Use 0 to shut off this feature.
Port	Sets a specific port for sshd to listen on.	Unique port not assigned to another process; the default is 22.
PrintMotd	Specifies whether to print the contents of /etc/motd when a connection is made, which the system would do during a **telnet** session or local login.	Either **yes** or **no**; the default is **yes**.
QuietMode	Specifies to use minimal logging. Only log fatal errors.	Either **yes** or **no**; the default is **no** because no logging means no security analysis.
ServerKeyBits	Specifies the number of bits used to generate the server security keys.	512, 768, and 1,024 are the most common options; the default is 768.

(continued)

Table 9.12 How ssh interacts and behaves **(continued).**

Option	Purpose	Values
SilentDeny	Specifies whether sshd tells the user or the log files that a connection is denied, or if it just silently refuses.	Either **yes** or **no**.
StrictModes	Checks home directory and ~/.rhosts to make sure they have secure permissions.	Either **yes** or **no**; the default is **yes**.
SyslogFacility	Sets the type of program syslog sees sshd as.	**AUTH**, **DAEMON**, **USER**, **LOCAL0**, **LOCAL1**, **LOCAL2**, **LOCAL3**, **LOCAL4**, **LOCAL5**, **LOCAL6**, or **LOCAL7**; the default is **DAEMON**.

Table 9.13 File specification options for ssh servers.

Option	Purpose	Values
HostKey	Sets the file that contains the machine's security key.	Path to file; the default is /etc/ssh_host_key.
RandomSeed	Sets the file that contains the seed used for sshd's random number generation. This file is updated regularly.	Path to file; the default is /etc/ssh_random_seed.
XauthLocation	Sets the path for the **xauth** program.	Path to file.

7. You are ready to assemble your options into the ssh server configuration file. A line in /etc/sshd_config uses the following straightforward format:

```
option = value
```

   List the combined options you want to use first, to make sure that they will work properly together.

TIP: *Typing "man sshd" opens the extensive man page for the ssh server.*

---

8. Work out the values for each option you decide to keep. Be as precise as possible.
9. Press the Esc key, and then type "ZZ" to close and save the file.
10. Edit any files that are needed by any of the options you chose.

11. Type "vi /etc/rd.d/rc.local" to open the last initialization file run at boot time.
12. Type "G" to go to the end of the file.
13. Type "o" to open an empty line below your current location and enter Insert mode.
14. Type "/usr/local/sbin/sshd" to tell the system to start this program at boot time.
15. Press the Esc key, and then type "ZZ" to close and save the file.
16. Go to the following section, "Setting Up ssh On A Client," and do your client setups. Then, return here.
17. Type "/usr/local/bin/make-ssh-known-hosts *domain.extension*" to run the Perl program that builds the /etc/ssh_known_hosts file. This file contains a listing of the machines on your network and all of their keys.

TIP: *You need to rerun this program occasionally to adjust for changes in the hosts listing and in the client keys. This is a good job for* ***cron****.*

Related solution:	Found on page:
Manipulating User **cron** Jobs	674

Setting Up ssh On A Client

To set up the secure shell client on a machine that you want to be able to access ssh-secured machines from, do the following:

1. Log in as root.
2. Type "vi /etc/ssh_config" to open the ssh client configuration file.
3. You need to set up your rules from most specific to least specific. Therefore, you should begin with the sections that refer to the specific hosts you intend to access. To build a rule for a specific host or set of hosts, you use the **host** keyword. Hosts are specified with the following:
   - Exact hostname
   - An asterisk to signify multiple unknown characters or all hosts
   - A question mark to signify an unknown character

   Think of a specific host you want to create connection rules for, and then type "i" to enter Insert mode.

4. Enter a line in the following format:

```
host = pattern
```

5. After you enter this line, everything beneath it applies only to this machine or group of machines. The options you may want to set are shown in Table 9.14.

TIP: *Type "man ssh" to get the full list of options.*

Enter the appropriate options in the format *option* = *value*.

Table 9.14 Common options used in /etc/ssh_config.

Option	Purpose	Values
Compression	Specifies whether to compress the data traveling along the ssh connection.	Either **yes** or **no**.
CompressionLevel	Specifies how tightly to compress the data. Type "man gzip" to review the available levels.	An integer from 1 to 9; 1 is fastest, with the least compression, and 9 is the tightest compression, but slower to implement because of the processing time. The default is 6.
ConnectionAttempts	Specifies how many times to try to make a connection before giving up.	Positive nonzero integer.
GlobalKnownHostsFile	Points to a different keyring file than /etc/ssh/_known_hosts.	Path to file.
KeepAlive	Tells the client to send messages to the server to ensure that the connection is still open and valid. It closes the connection if it cannot reach the server.	Either **yes** or **no** in both server and client configuration files; the default is **yes**.
KerberosAuthentication	Use Kerberos v5 authentication for this host.	Either **yes** or **no**.
KerberosTgtPassing	Specifies whether a Kerberos TGT can be passed to the ssh server.	Either **yes** or **no**; the default is **yes**.

(continued)

***Table 9.14 Common options used in /etc/ssh_config* (continued).**

Option	Purpose	Values
NumberOfPasswordPrompts	Specifies how many login attempts the user gets before ssh disconnects.	An integer between 1 and 5, inclusive; the default is 1.
PasswordAuthentication	Allows password authentication.	Either **yes** or **no**; the default is **yes**.
PasswordPromptHost	Determines whether the remote hostname appears at the password prompt.	Either **yes** or **no**.
PasswordPromptLogin	Determines whether to include the remote user ID in the password prompt.	Either **yes** or **no**.
Port	Sets a specific port for ssh to send a connection request to.	Unique port not assigned to another process. The default is 22.
RhostsAuthentication	Allows standard **rlogin**.	Either **yes** or **no**; the default is **no**. It should be left this way.
RhostsRSAAuthentication	Allows **rlogin** in conjunction with RSA authentication, using the keys generated at the client and server ends.	Either **yes** or **no**; the default is **yes**.
RSAAuthentication	Considers RSA authentication sufficient.	Either **yes** or **no**; the default is **yes**.
StrictHostKeyChecking	Prevents ssh from automatically adding host keys to ~/.ssh/known_hosts, and prevents connections to machines whose keys have changed.	Choose among **yes**, **no**, or **ask**.
TISAuthentication	Allows authentication through the Gauntlet **authsrv** program.	Either **yes** or **no**.
User	Declares the username to use when logging in to the host.	Username.
UserKnownHostsFile	Points to an alternative to the user-specific known hosts file instead of ~/.ssh/known_hosts.	Path to file.
XauthLocation	Sets the path for the **xauth** program.	Path to file.

6. When you finish entering the information for this specific host, create a new host statement. If this statement refers to another specific host, return to Step 3 to build it. Otherwise, use the following line to start adding global parameters:

```
host = *
```

7. Enter the appropriate global options in the format *option = value.*
8. When you are finished, press the Esc key, and then type "ZZ" to save and close the file.

Removing Unnecessary Packages

To find and get rid of packages you do not need on a Red Hat Linux system, do the following:

1. Utilize the RPM tool by typing "rpm -qa|more" to list every RPM that you have installed.
2. Either make a list of the packages you want to remove or remove them in another virtual terminal. The command to remove an RPM is **rpm -e *package***.
3. After you are satisfied that you have removed all the RPMs you do not use, it is time to start the hunt for other programs. The type of items you are looking for are things that were not installed as RPMs. A good place to start is /usr/src—or your preferred location for downloaded programs—to see what packages you compiled and installed.
4. If you find source packages you want to remove, you will need to track down their files and delete them. Examine the Makefile (more on Makefiles in Chapter 22) for an "uninstall" make target.
5. If no removal target exists, examine the Makefile to find the "install" target, and use this to track down the individual files.
6. After you remove the RPMs and compiled programs, you are left with the binaries and scripts you either downloaded or wrote yourself. These are the trickiest items to find and remove, and after doing so one or two times, you will probably want to keep an administrator's notebook in which you jot down what you installed or changed and where.

Creating And Using A Named Pipe

To create a named pipe, use the **mkfifo** command, using the format **mkfifo *lpath/file***. After you create the file, you can use it at will. To use it at the command line, use redirection—the < and > symbols. However, named pipes are typically used by programs to share information.

Logging

To properly set up logging on your system, do the following:

1. Log in as root.
2. Type "vi /etc/syslog.conf" to open the configuration file for the daemon that handles system logging.
3. In Red Hat Linux 6.1, this file, by default, contains the following code—minus some comments:

```
#kern.*                             /dev/console
*.info;mail.none;authpriv.none      /var/log/messages
authpriv.*                          /var/log/secure
mail.*                              /var/log/maillog
*.emerg                             *
uucp,news.crit                      /var/log/spooler
local7.*                            /var/log/boot.log
```

4. Refer to "Logging" in the In Depth portion of this chapter to adjust what you would like to have logged and where. If you have a network, you may want to seriously consider setting up a log server, to make your life a little easier.
5. Press the Esc key, and then type "ZZ" to save and close the file.
6. Type "/etc/rc.d/init.d/syslog restart" to restart the syslog daemon so that it loads the new configuration.
7. Type "ls /var/log/btmp".
8. If the file does not exist, type "touch /var/log/btmp". You want this file to be there, because when this file exists, your system logs all failed login attempts.

TIP: *If /var/log/btmp exists, use the **lastb** command to see the list of failed attempts.*

Installing **swatch**

To install the **swatch** log-analysis tool, do the following:

1. Log in as root.
2. Type "man swatch" to see whether the **swatch** (Simple Watcher) program is already installed. If it is, skip to the section "Analyzing Logs."
3. Place the first Red Hat CD-ROM in the CD-ROM drive.

NOTE: *Not all distributions come with **swatch**. You can FTP this tool from **ftp.stanford.edu/general/security-tools/swatch**.*

---

4. Type "mount /mnt/cdrom" to mount the distribution CD-ROM.
5. Type "cd /mnt/cdrom/RedHat/RPMS" to change to the directory that contains the RPMs that come with Red Hat.
6. Type "rpm -ivh swatch" and press the Tab key to let the bash shell complete the file name for you.
7. Type "umount /mnt/cdrom" to unmount the CD-ROM. You can now remove it from the drive.

Analyzing Logs

To watch your log files for signs of trouble, do the following:

1. Follow the instructions in the preceding section, "Installing **swatch**," to see whether the tool is installed, and if it is not, follow the instructions to install it.
2. Log in as root. You need root's privileges and file access to monitor all the log files.
3. Type "vi /etc/swatchrc" to create the **swatch** configuration file.
4. Type "i" to enter Insert mode.
5. Determine the text you need to watch out for in each of the log files. Unfortunately, no cookie-cutter approach is available for this yet. You have to build your rules based on experience.
6. After you know what to watch for, use the format and values discussed in the In Depth section "Log Monitoring With **swatch**" to build your rules.
7. When you are finished, press the Esc key, and then type "ZZ" to save and exit the file.

8. Type "vi /etc/rc.d/rc.local" to open the last system initialization file.
9. Type "G" to go to the end of the file.
10. Type "o" to open a new line for editing below the cursor.
11. Type "/usr/bin/swatch -c /etc/swatchrc".
12. Press the Esc key, and then type "ZZ" to save and exit the file. The **swatch** tool will run automatically when you next boot.

Preparing For A Breach

To put together your emergency fix kit, do the following:

- Keep a copy of the distribution CD-ROM set available.
- Make regular backups of your file system structure and use a shell script run by **cron** to watch for changes in size in vital programs such as **ls**, **ps**, **top**, and **find**.
- Make regular, redundant backups of your file system.
- Make floppies with pristine copies of vital system programs that you did not install with RPM from the installation media.

Related solutions:	Found on page:
Backing Up File System Structure	80
Backing Up File Systems	81
Altering System **cron** Jobs	672

Recovering From A Breach

To fix things after you discover you had a breach, do the following:

1. Get your emergency fix kit. You did make one, didn't you?
2. Type "rpm -Va" to verify all the RPMs installed on your system.
3. Replace any RPMs that have been corrupted.
4. Make a backup of your current file system.
5. Use the **diff** tool to compare crucial program sizes and creation dates for items that were not installed with RPM, and see which have been tampered with.
6. Replace any changed programs with your pristine versions.

Related solution:	Found on page:
Verifying An RPM File	115

Becoming The Superuser

Time and time again, you are told that it is bad to do anything as root that you do not have to. The superuser account simply has too much power attached to it. It is far too easy to mess things up while using it. One method many administrators use to combat this issue is typing "su" whenever they want to do something as the superuser. This method allows them, after they enter the root password, to do things with root privileges without actually being logged in as root.

The drawback of using **su** is that it does not provide a full login shell. If you **su** to the superuser, you do not have the superuser's path statement or anything else that would be executed at login time. This is the reason that you are instructed to log in to the root account in many of the solutions in this book.

After you are done with the superuser account, type "exit" to return to the account you logged in to.

TIP: *You can use **su** to become any user. If you are logged in as root, simply type "su user". From any other account, you need the user's password. As usual, you will not have a full login shell for that user, so you will not have their path statement.*

Installing The Crack Password Checker

To be able to test user password viability, do the following on each machine:

1. Log in as root.
2. Use a Web browser to go to **http://rpmfind.net/linux/RPM/contrib/libc5/i386/crack-4.1f-1.i386.html**.
3. Click the header "crack-4.1f-1 RPM for i386" to start the download process. The file downloads as a bunch of what looks like junk in a Web page.
4. Click File|Save As to open the Save As dialog box.
5. Make sure the Format For Saved Document dropdown list box says Source.
6. Browse to find the location you want to save this file to, or type the path in the Selection text box.
7. Click OK to save the Web page's contents.

8. Change to a command prompt.
9. Use the **cd** command to change to where you saved the file. For example, **cd /usr/src/RPMS**.
10. Type "rpm -ivh crack" and press the Tab key to complete the file name, then press Enter to install the RPM.

Related solutions:	Found on page:
Installing RPMs	114
Installing RPMs With GNOME RPM	117
Installing RPMs With Kpackage	120

Securing Passwords With Crack

After you install Crack, as discussed in the preceding section, you can move on to using this tool. To test user password viability, do the following on each machine:

1. Log in as root.
2. Type "/root/crack-4.1f/Scripts/shdmrg > /root/temppass" to temporarily merge your /etc/shadow and /etc/passwd files together for Crack to check the passwords.
3. Choose the options you want to run Crack with from Table 9.15.
4. Type "Crack *options* /root/temppass" to run the utility. Keep in mind that it's processor-intensive, so it is best to use this program when user load is low.

TIP: *After you are sure this process works properly for your needs, build a shell script to do it regularly without your intervention.*

Table 9.15 Crack program options.

Option	Purpose
-debug	Prints verbose messages while going through the Crack script.
-f	Runs Crack in the foreground rather than the background.
-m	Sends email to any users whose passwords Crack guesses. This email contains whatever is in the file /root/crack-4.1f/Scripts/nastygram.
-n#	Uses the **nice** utility to slow down Crack so that it does not load down the processor.

Related solution:	Found on page:
Changing Your Bash Login Prompt	610

Setting Password Rules

To set password maintenance rules so that your users have to use some secure procedures, you have the following options available to you:

- For current users, type "vi /etc/shadow" to open the shadow password file, as discussed in the In Depth section "Shadow Passwords." Then, edit the individual fields for the users you want to limit.
- Use the **useradd** command's ability to change default account settings. This allows you to change two of the options for all accounts added in the future. Type "useradd -De *date*" to set when an account is due to be disabled. This is useful for when users notify you they are going on vacation. You can also type "useradd -Df" to set how many days can pass after a password expires before the account is disabled.

TIP: *If you want to change settings for one specific account, use the* ***usermod*** *command in the same format as the* ***useradd*** *command.*

Fighting Denial-Of-Service Attacks

One of the most frustrating things that can happen to any system administrator is the denial-of-service attack. The best way to protect yourself from it is to keep up to date on the latest security issues and keep your system up to date. Because new attacks are continuously being developed, this is the only way to deal with such issues.

Fortunately, Linux is already secured by default from some of the older attacks. Your only recourse at times will be to contact your service provider and have them help with blocking the offending packets.

Getting And Installing PGP

The Pretty Good Privacy (PGP) package once could not be included in any U.S.-based Linux distributions because of encryption export laws—someone from outside the U.S. or Canada could have bought the distribution. Even now, with the laws just freshly relaxed, encryption is only slowly finding its way into the mainstream as companies test the new rules. Fortunately, you can download PGP from the Internet rather than wait for it to be packaged directly in a distribution. To download and then install PGP, do the following:

1. Use a Web browser to go to **http://web.mit.edu/network/pgp-form.html**.

2. Read the instructions on the page if you are a U.S. or Canadian citizen. If not, you need to find another place to download PGP from, due to U.S. encryption laws.
3. Fill out the form and click the Submit button. This takes you to the freeware version's download page.
4. Scroll down until you see something similar to "Linux Red Hat 5.0+ (Package)." This is the RPM version of PGP.
5. Download this version and place it wherever you prefer to put your RPM files. Many people keep a ~/Downloads directory for such use.
6. This file comes with a long name; for example: PGPcmdln_6.5.2_Lnx_FW.rpm.tar.gz. Notice that this file is actually packaged and compressed. First, you need to **gunzip** and **untar** the file. Two text files come with the RPM itself.
7. Type "rpm -ivh PGPcmdfw_6.5.2_Linux.i386.rpm" to install the PGP package. Adjust this if what you have has a different file name.
8. No PGP installation is complete if you do not have your own key generated. Type "pgp -kg" to start this process.
9. Choose which type of encryption algorithm you want to use. If you have no preference, press Enter to go with the default.
10. Press Enter again to choose the default task and generate a new PGP signature key.
11. If for some reason you want smaller than a 1,024-bit key, enter the number of bits you want used now. Otherwise, type "1" and then press Enter.

WARNING! The fewer bits used to generate the key, the less secure it is.

12. Every key needs a user ID. Either enter your full name with your email address in brackets, or some other name you want to be known by with an email address in brackets, and then press Enter. For example, you might use:

```
Jane Q. Public <jane@qpublic.org>
```

13. If you want your key to expire after a certain time period, then enter the number of days for which it should be valid, and then press Enter. Otherwise, just press Enter to accept the default of Forever.
14. You have now reached the most important part of generating a key. A key is, in some ways, only as good as the pass phrase (password) you choose. In this case, you can actually use entire sentences with spaces and punctuation. I highly recommend you do this! Type your phrase and then press

Enter. This is what you will have to type whenever you want to encode or decode something, so do not forget it.

15. Type the same phrase again and press Enter.
16. When asked whether you also need an encryption key, answer Yes, because you just installed PGP.
17. Choose how many bits you want this key generated for. Selecting 1024 is still safe these days.
18. If you want the encryption key to expire after a certain time period, then type the number of days for which it should be valid, and then press Enter. Otherwise, press Enter to have it last Forever.
19. Now you move on to the key-generation process. PGP uses you to generate some necessary random numbers. Type on the keyboard until it beeps and tells you "Enough, thank you."
20. PGP generates your signing key. This may take just a moment or several minutes, depending on your computer's speed.
21. Press Enter to set this key as your default PGP signature key. PGP now generates your encryption key. If you chose a larger bit size for this key, then the generation process takes longer.
22. After the keys are generated, PGP exits.

Related solutions:	Found on page:
Opening **gzip**ed Files	108
Opening **tar** Files	110

Setting Up An IP Firewall

To set up a firewall that just does IP filtering, do the following:

1. Log in as root.
2. Type "ipchains -L" to see what rules and policies are already in place, if any. You should get the following unless you already have some rules set:

```
Chain input (policy ACCEPT):
Chain forward (policy ACCEPT):
Chain output (policy ACCEPT):
```

TIP: *If traffic exists between your network and the outside at this moment, then continuing from here without knowing exactly what rules you want to enact could be a pain to your users. Run through this section with a paper and pen or in a text file, working out exactly what you want to use, and then come back and type it all in.*

3. Type "ipchains -P input DENY" to set an overall policy for the input chain that refuses any incoming IP traffic that does not match an individual rule.
4. Now you must seriously think about what kind of traffic you want to allow to pass through your firewall to your network. Your rules will be read in the order you add them. Although you can insert items in between existing rules, start by jotting things down on paper and trying to imagine how they might flow. The rules most likely to match incoming data should be first, going down to the more specific and focused. In other words, try to go from generic to specific.
5. After you know what you want to add, it is time to add them. This is where your syntax becomes important! For the purpose of setting up an IP firewall, your rule creation statements will start with either **ipchains -A input** or **ipchains -A output**, depending on whether you are trying to regulate the traffic coming into or out of your network.
6. Creating the rule statement itself requires precision. The In Depth section "Filtering Firewalls" covers the individual rule pieces. Piece rule statements together to make the most precise rules you can.
7. Determine the ultimate destination for packets that match your rules, and assign the appropriate final option as described earlier in Table 9.8. To illustrate all of this with an example, suppose that I want to monitor incoming packets—which means starting with **ipchains -A input**—to prevent them from accessing any of my internal Web servers, which are meant for intranet use only. Traffic from the Internet arrives through the primary interface on the firewall machine, which is eth0, and traffic to the hidden network goes through the secondary interface, eth1. Looking in /etc/services, I refresh my memory and see that HTTP traffic travels through both TCP and UDP to port 80 by default. The machines I want to keep hidden are all on the private network 192.168.60.0, so the statement I end up with is the following:

```
ipchains -A input -i eth0 -d 192.168.60/255.255.255.0 80 -j REJECT
```

8. Continue adding your rules until you have the ones you feel you need in place.
9. Now, you need to ensure that these chains are not lost when you reboot the machine. Linux does not automatically save them. Type "ipchains-save > /root/firewall_chains" to run the script that saves your chains, and send the data to /root/firewall_chains. Choose another location if you wish.

NOTE: *You need to do Step 9 every time you make a change to your* ***ipchains*** *rules.*

10. Type "vi /etc/rc.d/rc.local" to open the last system initialization file.
11. Type "G" to jump to the end of this file.
12. Type "o" to open a new line at the end of this file.
13. Type "ipchains-restore < /root/firewall_chains" to run the script that pulls the data out of /root/firewall_chains and rebuilds the firewall automatically.
14. Press the Esc key, and then type "ZZ" to save and close the file.

Setting Up A Proxy Firewall

To set up a proxying firewall, do the following:

1. Log in as root.
2. Read the FWTK license at **www.tis.com/research/software/fwtk_readme.html**.
3. Follow the instructions on how to agree to the license, if you are willing to agree to it. If not, you may need to choose another tool.
4. You should get a response email telling you where to FTP to get the toolkit. You must use an FTP tool—a Web browser will not work.
5. Download the file equivalent to fwtk2.1.tar.Z. Also, get the doc-only version, because that is the only way you will have any documentation if you need it. No documentation is included in the main package.
6. Unpack and uncompress the file in /usr/src (or your preferred location for source code).
7. Type "cd fwtk" to change into the new directory.
8. Type "mv Makefile.config Makefile.config.original" to rename the original Makefile configuration file.
9. Type "cp Makefile.config.linux Makefile.config" to use the Linux-specific Makefile configuration file as your starting point.
10. Type "vi Makefile.config" to open this configuration file for editing.
11. Cursor down to the line similar to:

```
CC=cc
```

12. Type "i" to enter Insert mode.
13. Change the line to read:

```
CC=gcc
```

14. Press the Esc key, and then type "ZZ" to save and close the file.
15. Type "ls /usr/X11". If you get a message similar to "File Not Found," then type "ln -s /usr/X11R6 /usr/X11" to create a symbolic link so that the compiler can find the libraries it needs.
16. Type "make" to build the firewall toolkit. This may take a few minutes, depending on your computer's speed.
17. Type "make install" to put the program files in place.
18. Type "vi /usr/local/etc/netperm-table" to open the **netacl** daemon's configuration file. This file fortunately contains default values for you to work with.
19. Read through this file carefully, and make edits where it seems appropriate.
20. When finished, press the Esc key, and then type "ZZ" to save and close the file.
21. Type "vi /etc/rc.d/rc.local" to open the last system initialization file to be run at boot time.
22. Type "G" to go to the end of the file.
23. Type "o" to open a new line for editing at the end of the file.
24. For each service you decided to proxy, you need to run **netacl** on its default port. Type a series of lines in the following format for each service:

```
/usr/local/etc/netacl -daemon port service service
```

25. After you are finished, press the Esc key and then type "ZZ" to save and close the file.
26. Reboot the machine and make sure the server works as you expect.

Related solutions:	Found on page:
Opening Z **compress**ed Files	109
Opening **tar** Files	110

Refusing Login Access To All But Root

A cool administration trick is available for when you want to prevent users from logging in to a machine. You could have a number of reasons for doing this. Perhaps you are doing some maintenance and need to take the machine down soon, so you do not want to let people log in and get started on something. Or, maybe this box has had a problem with user security, so you want to make sure that no one can log in until after you figure out what the issue is. To keep nonroot users from logging in, do the following:

1. Log in as root.
2. Type "vi /etc/nologin".
3. Type "i" to enter **vi** insert mode.
4. Type the message that you want your users to see when they try to log in and are refused.
5. Press the Esc key, and then type "ZZ" to save and close the file.

TIP: *Eventually, you will probably want to let the users back in. When the time comes, delete the file by typing "rm /etc/nologin". Access is restricted only as long as the file exists.*

Chapter 10

KickStart For Repeat Installations

If you need an immediate solution to:	*See page:*
Installing The First Machine	306
Building The Initial KickStart File	307
Scripting Tips For KickStart	308
Making A KickStart Boot Disk	308
Booting Directly To KickStart	309
Setting Up An NFS Installation Export	310
Adding KickStart Data To Your DHCP Server	311
Installing With KickStart	311
Upgrading With KickStart	312
Cloning Machine Configurations	313

In Depth

When you have a large network of machines that all have the same basic purpose, such as providing workspace in an end-user environment, doing the same installation repeatedly quickly gets tedious. Red Hat provides the KickStart tool to help you avoid this headache. Using KickStart, you simply have to set up one machine the way you want it, fiddle with a few details, and then let KickStart do the installation on your other machines. Too bad this tool can't switch disks for you, too. The good news, though, is that if you have a full-featured network—the meaning of which is covered throughout this chapter—you can even minimize this minor issue.

Introduction To KickStart

KickStart is a tool that automates the installation of identical or nearly identical Red Hat Linux boxes. The word "identical" refers not only to the software setup or end purpose but also to the hardware. If you have a large group of vastly different machines, then you may not be able to use this tool. But, before you give up completely, read through the rest of this chapter to see whether any of the options available will allow you to work through the hardware differences with little difficulty.

Although this chapter focuses primarily on using KickStart for mass installations, it has many different uses, such as the following:

- If you repeatedly need to return the same machine to its original state, but that state is not one of the simple install class defaults, making a KickStart installation setup enables you to accomplish the task without fussing with package selection every time.
- You can make your own set of "install classes" to clone machines using KickStart. If you buy all the same hardware, set up one machine to precisely as it should be for your new class, following the instructions in the section "The Test-Edit Cycle." If you want to create more than one new class, do the same to other machines until all your classes are created. You should keep these classes on file for when you need them (be sure to make backups).
- An even more complex option involves setting up duplicates of machines that have been active for some time. By using KickStart's post-installation instructions and a Network File System (NFS) install, you can include all the packages needed to get a machine ready for use. Here, your shell scripting skills and capabilities limit you—see Chapter 20 for more information on shell scripting.

NOTE: *This chapter is very Red Hat specific. Some Red Hat derivative distributions, such as Mandrake, may include KickStart; you will have to check the specific distribution. Other distributions may develop their own installation automation tools over time.*

Despite all the warnings about KickStart requiring identical hardware setups to be used effectively, you actually have a slight amount of leeway. Red Hat 6.1 and later versions can autodetect certain items during installation, and you can explicitly tell KickStart not to set up other items during the install. Some of the hardware items that KickStart doesn't require to be identical are monitors, video cards, many IDE hard drives, and many PCI cards.

The Structure Of A KickStart Script

The KickStart script, ks.cfg, is broken into three sections: system information, packages, and post-installation instructions. Each of these sections serves a specific function and phase of the data required for a full installation. Together, the script sections relieve you from having to intervene with the installation process after you get it started. You can even choose to be prompted only on specific parts of the install.

No markers begin the first section, system information. The other two sections begin with a percent sign (%). The only time this sign appears in the KickStart configuration file is in the following two lines:

```
%packages
%post
```

These lines are typically separated by many lines of code.

System Information

Items in the system information section must appear in the proper order. This order is the same in the KickStart file as it is when you do an install by hand. Therefore, if you are used to doing Red Hat installs, this file's contents should look familiar.

Language Settings

First, you need to tell Red Hat what language you want to use. You do this in the format **lang *code***, where ***code*** is the International Organization for Standardization (ISO) language code. For example, if you want to do an English installation, it should be as follows:

```
lang en
```

The other languages available are Czech (cs), French (fr), German (de), Hungarian (hu), Icelandic (is), Indonesian (in), Norwegian (no), Polish (pl), Romanian (ro), Russian (ru), Slovak (sk), Spanish (es), and Ukrainian (uk)—two-letter language codes from ISO standard 639.

Network Settings

Next, you specify the network configuration method to use. You have two options: Dynamic Host Configuration Protocol (see Chapter 7 for more on DHCP) and static. If you have a DHCP server set up to assign addressing information to machines that need it, the line should be as follows:

```
network --bootproto dhcp
```

For static networking, you need to give all the basic interface identification information, in the format:

```
network --bootproto static --ip IPaddress --netmask netmask
--gateway gateway --nameserver nameserver
```

NOTE: *The preceding information must all be on one line. Do not use the above text exactly as you see it. The text had to be separated for book formatting reasons.*

Install Method

Now, you specify what method to use for the installation. This is another easy one. You can choose either CD-ROM or NFS. For a CD-ROM install, you just need the following:

```
cdrom
```

For NFS, however, you need to use this format:

```
nfs --server host --dir /path
```

See Chapter 17 for details on how to set up an NFS installation server and how to determine the ***path*** portion of this line.

Devices Present

The next portion of the system information section is slightly more freeform. It is where you specify the devices within your system. A device line begins with the word "device". The following three choices are also useful in helping you determine what you need to define in this section:

- **cdrom**—Older CD-ROM drives that are neither SCSI nor IDE
- **ethernet**—Non-PCI Ethernet cards
- **scsi**—SCSI cards

With the device-type portion in place, the statement is now, for example, **device scsi**. After this, you need to include the actual device name or kernel module it requires; sometimes these are one and the same. Unfortunately, you cannot get this name from /usr/src/linux/Documentation/devices.txt, because it has to be the specific hardware device name. Instead, look to the hardware compatibility document for either Linux in general (available at the Linux Documentation Project) or for your distribution. For Red Hat Linux 6.1, go to **www.redhat.com/support/hardware/intel/62/rh6.2-hcl-i.ld.html**. The statement might now be as follows:

```
device scsi aic7xxx
```

If you need to assign any boot options to this device, add the **--opts** flag, follow it with the options, and then put the following values within quotes. When specifying more than one of the same kind of device when the devices do not share the same kernel module—for example, two Ethernet cards from different manufacturers—add **--continue** at the end of the statement so that the system knows more than one device exists and does not skip any other declarations of the same type.

NOTE: *You can have as many device statements as you need.*

Keyboard Type

Next comes the keyboard configuration. For a U.S. keyboard, this line is as follows:

```
keyboard us
```

If you are using a different type of keyboard, Red Hat recommends getting its type from the **kbdconfig** program in /usr/sbin/.

Device Probing

At this point, the configuration program probes for the devices present on your system. If you want to disable this feature and specify all of them manually, be sure to include the following line:

```
--noprobe
```

Partition Settings

Now, we get down to the business of disk partitioning. If KickStart is handling partitioning from scratch for you, be sure the following line exists before any partitioning starts:

```
zerombr yes
```

This will wipe all information from your current partition table. Another way to accomplish this is with:

```
clearpart --all
```

If you already have the drives partitioned, then do not use either of the previous two lines of code. Use the following if you do not want all partitions wiped:

```
zerombr no
```

After this, if you only want to remove all Linux native and swap partitions, include the following:

```
clearpart --linux
```

At this time, you cannot remove any other partition types using this method. After the old partitions you no longer want to keep are removed, it is time to create new ones. KickStart uses the **part** command to accomplish this, in this format:

```
part mountpoint --size MB
```

Two optional flags are available as well:

- **--grow**—Add if you want the partition to be "growable"—that is, have its size extended if room is left after all the partitions are assigned.
- **--maxsize MB**—If you list this partition as "growable," you can add this flag after, to limit how large the partition can get.

So, to create a 16MB boot partition, you might use:

```
part /boot --size 16
```

For a /home partition that must be at least 200MB, you might use:

```
part /home --size 200 --grow
```

NOTE: *Partitions are created in the order they appear in the KickStart file.*

Action Type

The next piece of a KickStart file tells the installation program whether you want to install or upgrade. Assuming that you are using this tool to do a raw install, you need to use:

```
install
```

On a large network, which may include centralized home directories and user programs, it may be most useful to do a clean install on many of the machines rather than an upgrade. See the Immediate Solutions section “Upgrading With KickStart” to learn ways to make the most out of using this tool for upgrading existing Red Hat installations.

System Configuration

Now, it is time to move on to the various configuration statements. Each of these statements involves a step of the setup process done during a normal install. The first of these configuration statements is for the mouse:

```
mouse type
```

Available types are listed in Table 10.1.

Table 10.1 Mouse types available in KickStart.

Type	Used For
none	No mouse on the system
alpsps/2	ALPS GlidePoint PS/2 mouse
ascii	Serial ASCII MieMouse
asciips/2	PS/2 ASCII MieMouse
atibm	ATI bus (PS/2) mouse
generic	Generic two-button serial mouse
generic3	Generic three-button serial mouse
genericps/2	Generic two-button PS/2 mouse
generic3ps/2	Generic three-button PS/2 mouse
geniusnm	Serial Genius Netmouse
geniusnmps/2	PS/2 Genius Netmouse
geniusnsps/2	PS/2 Genius Netmouse Pro
thinking	Serial Kensington Thinking Mouse
thinkingps/2	PS/2 Kensington Thinking Mouse
logitech	Serial C7 Logitech mouse
logitechcc	Serial CC Logitech mouse
logibm	Logitech bus (PS/2) mouse
logimman	Serial Logitech MouseMan/FirstMouse
logimmanps/2	PS/2 Logitech MouseMan/FirstMouse
logimman+	Serial Logitech MouseMan+/FirstMouse+

(continued)

Table 10.1 Mouse types available in KickStart **(continued).**

Type	Used For
logimman+ps/2	PS/2 Logitech MouseMan+/FirstMouse+
microsoft	Microsoft-compatible serial mouse
msnew	Microsoft serial mouse Revision 2.1A or higher
msintelli	Serial Microsoft IntelliMouse
msintellips/2	PS/2 Microsoft IntelliMouse
msbm	Microsoft bus (PS/2) mouse
mousesystems	Serial Mouse Systems mouse
mmseries	Serial MM Series mouse
mmhittab	Serial MM HitTablet mouse

After the mouse identification comes the time zone, which is set with the **timezone** item. Many options are available, depending on what country you are in and whether the country is large enough to span multiple time zones. Some commonly used zones are shown in Figure 10.1—for the rest, run the **timeconfig** command to find your time zone. Along with the time zones, you can tell your system to use Greenwich Mean Time (GMT) by adding the **--utc** flag. In my KickStart file, this line might look like this:

```
timezone --utc Canada/Pacific
```

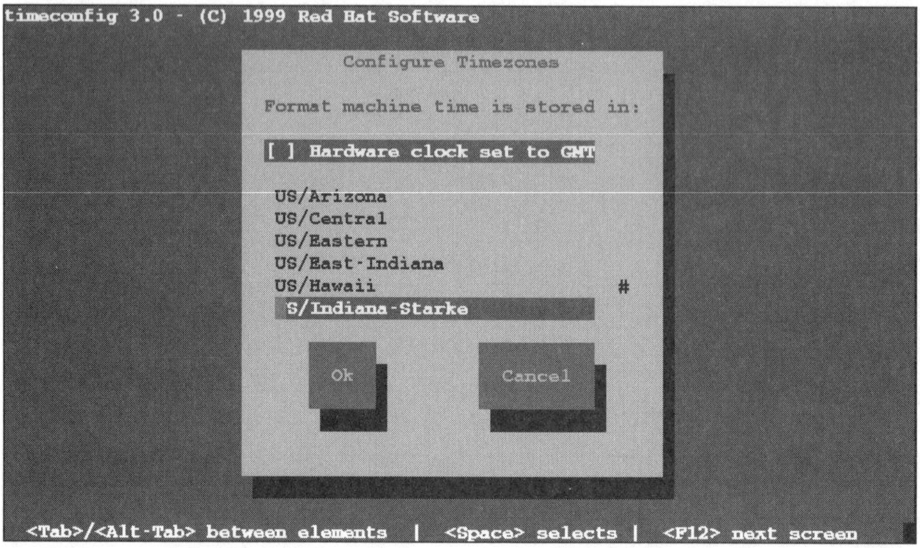

Figure 10.1 Some commonly used time zones as shown in **timeconfig**.

Setting up video information is more complicated; how much so depends on how well your hardware is autoprobed. Regardless, this setup simply depends on knowing your hardware and doing your research. The X configuration line begins with **xconfig**. Although you could just leave it as is, you will end up with an autoprobed video card (hopefully) and a generic 640x480 video mode. Options available to go with the **xconfig** item are the following:

- **--card**—Information identifying your video card. You only need this or the **--server** option, not both.
- **--hsync**—Your monitor's horizontal sync rate. This and **--vsync** are needed only if the monitor type is not available in the list. Numbers should be in either a comma-separated list or a range with a dash.
- **--monitor**—Information identifying your video display. If you have this information, you do not need **--vsync** or **--hsync**.
- **--server**—Instructions on which X server to install. You only need this or the **--card** option, not both.
- **--vsync**—Your monitor's vertical sync rate. This and **--hsync** are needed only if the monitor type is not available in the list. Numbers should be in either a comma-separated list or a range with a dash.

Too many monitors and video cards exist to try to list them all here. Type the following to get a list of all of your options saved into the file /root/xhardware:

```
Xconfigurator --help 2> /root/xhardware
```

NOTE: *You need to include **2>** because just **Xconfigurator --help** sends information to STDERR, not STDOUT, and therefore a standard redirection of **>** will not work.*

All the values associated with these options need to be listed in quotes. In the simplest case, in which the monitor type is known and the video card probes properly, you might use the following:

```
xconfig --monitor "mag DX700T"
```

Now, you need to set the root password. Although both encrypted and unencrypted options are available, you are best off sending encrypted versions if you are installing over a network. If you are just installing locally using a floppy and a CD-ROM, then encryption is not necessary. The statement for setting this password is **rootpw**, which can be used in either of two ways. For unencrypted passwords, type the following:

```
rootpw password
```

If you want to have the password encrypted, first you need to set this password for an account on another machine. Then, open /etc/shadow or /etc/passwd and copy the encrypted version of the password, as follows:

```
rootpw --iscrypted encryptedpassword
```

Following the same theme, the next item involves how the machine handles authentication. The basic statement that handles authentication is **auth**. Three major options are available with this statement: NIS (see Chapter 16), shadow passwords, and MD5 passwords (refer to Chapter 9). If you want to use shadow passwords—which is highly recommended, unless you are using a specific tool that does not understand them—include the flag **--useshadow**. To include MD5—also recommended—use the flag **--enablemd5**.

If you want to use NIS to centralize your users for network management purposes, first add the flag **--enablenis**. Then, you need to include the flag **--nisdomain *domain***, where ***domain*** is the name assigned to your NIS domain. You also need **--nisserver *server***, where ***server*** is the hostname for your NIS server.

If you are not using NIS but are using shadow and MD5, then your line might look like this:

```
auth --useshadow --enablemd5
```

However, if you are using NIS, you might have:

```
auth --enablemd5 --enablenis --nisdomain hidden.dom --nisserver
192.168.0.14
```

NOTE: *As usual, the code above needs to all be on the same line. It has to be broken up in this case for printing reasons.*

Last, but certainly not least, is the LILO configuration section. This line begins with **lilo** and, in fact, can just be left with that one word if you don't need any of the options. The LILO installation flag is **—location**, which refers to where LILO is installed. Available options are the following:

- **mbr**—The default location
- **partition**—Specifically, the root partition
- **none**—Do not install LILO

For this line, you might just have **lilo**, or you might have

```
lilo --location none
```

TIP: *For a graphical walkthrough of creating this file, check out **www.fezbox.com**.*

Packages

This section is filled with all the RPMs that need to be installed on the new machine. No paths are necessary. All the packages are assumed to be in the same location. On the CD-ROM, this location is /mnt/cdrom/RedHat/RPMS. The NIS setup will be discussed in detail in Chapter 16.

Here is a small snippet of the beginning of what might be in your packages section:

```
%packages
filesystem
basesystem
ldconfig
glibc
mktemp
termcap
bash
ncurses
sed
gawk
```

Take a look now in the /mnt/cdrom/RedHat/RPMS directory. All of these names are the beginning of an RPM. In fact, type "rpm -qi sed" and you get information about this package. After an RPM is installed, the version and other extended file name information do not matter. The same goes for the packages listed here.

TIP: *If you are doing an NIS installation, you can add any RPM you want to the packages directory, and list it here to be installed automatically. Combine this option with making your own RPMs (refer to Chapter 4), and the KickStart tool looks much more powerful.*

Post-Installation Instructions

The post-installation section is the final section of the KickStart file. Typically, this section is blank from the beginning, and you can choose whether to fill it in. Many people have no need to fill in this section if they just want to clone the initial installation. However, if you want to continue the setup after this point, the **%post** section allows you to do so.

To get the most out of the post-installation possibilities, spend some time getting familiar with shell scripting (covered in detail in Chapter 20). Depending on your skill level, you can do many things with this section that will help you to avoid having to duplicate configuration steps as you complete the installs on all of your machines.

The Test-Edit Cycle

You will hear much about the Test-Edit-Compile cycle later in this book, when we get to shell scripting and Perl and C programming. This cycle applies to any instance in which you want to ensure that the file you prepared instructs the computer to do exactly what you want it to do. Remember the old phrase "garbage in, garbage out"? Sometimes, our imprecise human nature confuses computers terribly.

A KickStart install automation file has only two steps: test and edit. You don't need to compile anything here. Adding the word "Cycle" to the title indicates that this procedure is not something you do just once. You have to repeat this set of processes until you finally get the result you are looking for. Sometimes this process ends quickly, but other times it is frustrating and tedious. However, if you want your machines installed properly so that you do not have to go back and fix all of them, then follow this process faithfully.

In the case of preparing an automated installation, the various pieces of this cycle are covered in different sections of the Immediate Solutions section. Start with the section "Installing The First Machine." After all, your KickStart results rely on how that first machine is handled.

After the first machine is up and running, do not proceed to what you might usually do—in other words, do not start setting things up! Treat bulk installs such as this as a multiphase process. The Test-Edit cycle is just one phase in the beginning of the process. In fact, it is a phase you have not even entered yet. Next, you need to look at the section "Building The Initial KickStart File," which provides the instructions for making the file that automates the rest of the installs. After you prepare this file, you are ready to start the cycle.

As the cycle's name suggests, the first thing you might do is test your current KickStart script. However, the first time, you are recommended to go straight to the Edit phase. Sometimes, the file is not generated exactly right and needs a bit of tweaking. The earlier section "The Structure Of A KickStart Script" should be of great help when you're reviewing your new script. Make sure that everything is correct, and then return to the beginning of the cycle, back to Test.

Choose one of the machines that you intend to set up as a clone of the first machine, and then turn to the Immediate Solutions section "Installing With KickStart" for instructions on how to do a KickStart installation. After you complete the installation, examine the system to see whether it meets your specifications.

Now return to the Edit part of the cycle. Adjust the KickStart file to accommodate any errors in the test installation. Then, return to Test and do the install all over again, either on the same machine you tested it on before or on another machine. Continue this process until the machine installs exactly as it is supposed to.

After the machine tests fine for the install, it is time to work on your configuration. See the Immediate Solutions section "Cloning Machine Configuration" for instructions on how to accomplish this. It often helps to write code in small chunks, test it, and then try again. So, set up one section of your **%post** scripting, and then test it in an automatic installation. Make sure that it works the way you want it to. Add the next section, and then test it. Continue going through the Test-Edit cycle until you have a process that works perfectly. Then, and only then, try putting this process into mass production to see how it works.

Immediate Solutions

Installing The First Machine

To install the initial machine in a way that makes your KickStart build process easiest, do the following:

- If at all possible, do a network installation using NFS as the file server. Those who are not using NFS may want to have multiple copies of the Red Hat installation CD-ROM available, because otherwise you'll be able to do only one install at a time.
- Choose a Custom-class installation, which ensures that you will have the least amount of tweaking to do later.
- If you intend to use DHCP to provide network information to these machines, set up the DHCP server before you install the prototype.
- Go through the trouble of choosing Select Individual Packages when it is time to choose package groups. Doing this allows you to micromanage exactly what programs are placed on the machine. You will not have to go back afterward and remove the items that will not be used during a security sweep later.

TIP: *Don't worry about accidentally deleting packages that are necessary to satisfy installation dependencies. The installer double-checks this before proceeding and allows you to turn on the option to install the missing dependencies.*

- If you want to offer multiple video modes to your users, customize the X configuration during the install.

Now, continue to the section "Cloning Machine Configurations."

NOTE: *If you intend to use the **%post** section to add configuration items to the KickStart file, you should still follow this procedure.*

Related solutions:	Found on page:
Setting Up A DHCP Server	213
Setting Up NFS Exports	505

Building The Initial KickStart File

To build the initial KickStart file, do the following:

1. Log in to the newly installed machine as root.
2. Place the Red Hat CD-ROM in the drive, if it is not already there.

TIP: *Use the* ***df*** *command to see whether the CD-ROM is already mounted.*

3. Type "mount /mnt/cdrom" to add the CD-ROM to your file system.
4. Type "cd /mnt/cdrom/RedHat/RPMS" to change to the directory with the RPM packages.
5. Type "rpm -ivh mkkick" and press the Tab key to finish the rest of the file name, and then press Enter to install the KickStart file builder.
6. Type "mkkickstart *flags* > /*path*/ks.cfg" to create the KickStart install script. The available flags are shown in Table 10.2.

Related solutions:	*Found on page:*
Setting Up A DHCP Server	213
Setting Up NFS Exports	505

Table 10.2 Flags used when running mkkickstart.

Flag	Purpose	Values
--dhcp	Uses DHCP to configure networking for this machine at boot time.	None
--nfs	Installs over an NFS mount.	*host:path*
--nonet	Does not clone the networking configuration. Using this flag is a good idea for machines you are preparing for different networking environments, or that have different networking hardware.	None
--nox	Does not clone the X configuration. Using this flag is a good idea for machines that will not have a GUI or those that have different video hardware.	None
--version	Displays the version of **mkkickstart** you have.	None

Scripting Tips For KickStart

When putting together a script to handle post-installation information in KickStart, keep the following items in mind:

- Use the **echo** command to print out explanations of each step. This lets you see at a glance where the installation is and relieves you from having to go back through and do this later if you need to debug the post-installation section.
- If you have particularly complex routines to execute, have the KickStart script call other scripts. Just remember to include these scripts on the boot disk—if they will fit—or in the same network directory as the KickStart script.
- Remember that if you are having a hard time debugging a complex script, you can comment out sections by starting each line with a hash mark (#) to isolate pieces of code.

Making A KickStart Boot Disk

To make a Red Hat boot disk that also contains a KickStart installation automation file, do the following:

1. Log in as root.
2. Use the **df** command to see whether the Red Hat CD-ROM is mounted. If not, place it in the drive and type "mount /mnt/cdrom" to add it to the file system.
3. Place the floppy disk that you intend to use as the boot disk for your automated install into the floppy drive.

WARNING!* *All data on this disk will be erased.

4. Type "dd if=/mnt/cdrom/images/boot.img of=/dev/fd0" to create a new Red Hat boot install disk. Use bootnet.img if you are doing an NFS install.

NOTE: *Do not use the* ***mkbootdisk*** *command. This command creates a customized boot disk for the machine in question. You need a boot disk that handles the installation process.*

5. After the drive light goes off, the copying is done. Now, type "mount -t vfat /dev/fd0 /mnt/floppy" to add this disk to your file system.

NOTE: *The installation disk is in MS-DOS format, not ext2.*

6. Type "mcopy" to see whether this tool is installed on your file system. If it is not, you need to mount the CD-ROM, change into the RPMS directory, and type "rpm -ivh mtools*" to install the package that contains this command.
7. Type "mcopy /root/ks.cfg /mnt/floppy".

TIP: *If you want to always use KickStart with this boot disk, see the following section, "Booting Directly To KickStart," for instructions.*

8. Type "umount /mnt/floppy" to properly write any remaining data to the disk. After the light turns off, you can remove the disk from the drive.

Booting Directly To KickStart

To alter your Red Hat installation boot disk so that it starts up your KickStart file automatically, do the following:

1. Log in as root.
2. Type "vi /root/syslinux.cfg" to create the file that will make your automatic boot possible.
3. Enter the following code to automatically go into a CD-ROM KickStart install:

```
default ks
prompt 0
label ks
  kernel vmlinuz
  append ks=floppy initrd=initrd.img
```

NOTE: *If you are doing an NFS install, the last line should have just **ks**, not **ks=floppy**.*

4. Press the Esc key, and then type "ZZ" to save and exit the file.
5. Type "mount -t vfat /dev/fd0 /mnt/floppy" to add this disk to your file system.
6. Type "cd /mnt/floppy" to change to the base floppy directory.
7. Type "cp /root/syslinux.cfg /mnt/floppy".
8. When asked whether you want to replace the original file, press Enter. You can re-create another copy of this disk any time, if necessary.
9. Make sure all data is properly written before you remove the disk, by typing "umount /mnt/floppy" and waiting until the drive light turns off.

Setting Up An NFS Installation Export

To set up an NFS export specifically for containing the data needed for an automated KickStart installation, do the following:

1. If necessary, install an additional hard drive in this machine to contain all the data from the Red Hat Linux CD-ROM plus any additional packages you might want installed by default.
2. Log in as root on the machine that you chose to serve files for automated installs.
3. Create the directory that you want to put the files in, by using the **mkdir** command. This directory is either exactly where you will make the installation section, or a mount point for adding the drive or partition that will hold this material. For the sake of an example, I will create the mount point "/network/kickstart".
4. If necessary, set up the partition or drive to mount at boot time, by editing the /etc/fstab file. It must be mounted one way or another before you continue.
5. Insert the Red Hat Linux CD-ROM into the CD-ROM drive.
6. Type "mount /mnt/cdrom" to add it onto your file system.
7. Change to the installation server's mount point. For example, type "cd /network/kickstart".
8. Copy the entire contents of the CD-ROM into this directory, if you want. What you really need is everything in the RedHat directory and below.
9. Copy the ks.cfg file into the base of your NFS export directory. For the example, I would type "cp /root/ks.cfg /network/kickstart".
10. Now that you have all the parts in place, you need to set up the export. Chapter 17 covers NFS in detail. Here, I will just give you an example of how the code might be configured in /etc/exports:

```
/network/kickstart    *.animals.org(ro,root_squash)
```

NOTE: *The key things to notice here are that you want the installation server accessible only to your internal machines; write capabilities aren't needed for those who use this export; and special privileges definitely aren't needed.*

Related solutions:	Found on page:
Creating Linux File Systems	76
Adding Permanent Media	86
Setting Up NFS Exports	505

Adding KickStart Data To Your DHCP Server

To add sections to your DHCP server configuration so that it can feed boot file information to your clone machines, do the following:

1. Log in on the DHCP server machine as root.
2. Type "vi /etc/dhcpd.conf" to open the DHCP server's configuration file.
3. In the appropriate section for this machine, find where you want to add your code.
4. Type "o" to open a new line beneath the cursor's location.
5. Look on the NFS server that houses the installation export and find the directory that contains the KickStart file(s).
6. Add the line:

```
filename "/path_to_export";
```

7. Now, add the line:

```
next-server NFSinstallserver;
```

NOTE: *In the preceding line, you need either the IP address for the NFS installation server or the full host.domain.extension for the machine.*

8. Press the Esc key, and then type "ZZ" to save and close the file.
9. Type "/etc/init.d/rc.d/dhcpd restart" to restart your DHCP server with the new configuration information.

Related solutions:	Found on page:
Setting Up A DHCP Server	213
Setting Up NFS Exports	505

Installing With KickStart

To install a machine using a KickStart script, do the following:

1. If you are running a network installation, be sure to have your NFS installation server set up as detailed in Chapter 16, and also have the new machine properly plugged in to the network.

2. If you are running a network install and want to have the KickStart file on the network as well, you need to use a DHCP server to pass the information. See the preceding section, "Adding KickStart Data To Your DHCP Server," for details.
3. Regardless of whether you are doing a CD-ROM or NFS install, you begin by placing your prepared Red Hat boot disk in the floppy drive and turning the machine on. See the earlier section "Making A KickStart Boot Disk" to make this disk, if you have not already made it.
4. When you get the installation boot prompt, use whichever of the following applies:
   - **linux ks=floppy** if the KickStart file is on the boot disk
   - **linux ks** if you are doing an NFS install and do not want to have KickStart on the boot disk
5. After you press Enter, simply sit back and watch for the following:
   - Unexpected prompts for information that was not included in the KickStart file
   - A failed installation with an error message
   - Any other unexpected behavior

   Have something else around to do, because the installation might take a while. After it gets to the point of putting in packages, you should be able to turn your attention to other things.
6. Examine the product of the automated installation and see whether it is what you expected and/or wanted. Continue the Test-Edit cycle if desired or needed.

Related solutions:	Found on page:
Setting Up A DHCP Server	213
Setting Up NFS Exports	505

Upgrading With KickStart

To upgrade a machine that has already been set up and configured using KickStart, you need to do the following things differently from a normal install:

- Instead of having a line saying **install** in the KickStart file, replace it with **upgrade**.

- You do not need to set everything up. All the items before the **upgrade** line should be filled in, but you can accomplish this easily enough by generating a KickStart file for this setup.
- The only packages that need to be listed are the ones you want to have replaced with newer versions. If you want everything upgraded, you should be able to just leave the automatically generated package list in place and let KickStart grab the new versions from the CD-ROM or the network. Some of the package names may have changed, however. You can quickly determine whether changes have occurred by comparing the list generated by KickStart on this machine to either the /mnt/cdrom/RedHat/RPMS directory with the new CD-ROM or the list of packages in the *Reference Guide* (either the hardcopy or online version).

Cloning Machine Configurations

To clone machine configurations so that KickStart reproduces the setup on demand, do the following:

1. Sit down at the original machine you used to build the KickStart installation. Open a copy of the KickStart setup file in one of the virtual terminals—if you followed the examples, type "vi /root/ks.cfg".
2. Think through what you need to configure. Performing tasks such as the following is fairly basic and usually has to be done on all machines:
   - Assigning IP addresses
   - Assigning hostnames
   - Setting up special network information
   - Creating user accounts
   - Mounting drives with centrally controlled applications, home directories, and more
   - Plugging standard security holes
3. Decide which of these items will be handled by some form of remote services, such as DHCP, NFS, NIS, or any of the other network centralization tools.
4. One by one, set up everything that needs to be done. Do not use any fancy tools that cannot be run from the command line. As you configure each item, mirror how to do it in the KickStart **%post** section.
5. After you finish, test the new KickStart file on either the same machine you originally tested it on—wiping the current setup and starting over—or another one.

6. Examine the product of the automated installation and see whether it is what you expected. Continue the Test-Edit cycle if desired or needed.

Related solutions:	Found on page:
Creating Shell Accounts From The Command Line	31
Setting Up A DHCP Server	213
Shutting Off Unnecessary Daemons And Background Processes	264
Shutting Off Unnecessary Non-Daemon Network Services	267
Logging	280
Setting Up NFS Exports	505

Chapter 11

DNS With BIND

If you need an immediate solution to:	*See page:*
Installing The Name Server	336
Configuring The Master Name Server	336
Configuring The Slave Name Server	338
Configuring A Forwarding-Only Server	340
Creating The Initial Cache	342
Creating The Reverse Local Zone File	343
Creating Your Domain Zone	344
Creating Your Reverse Domain Zone	346
Creating Encrypted Keys	347
Installing And Running **dnswalk**	348

In Depth

Computers and the Internet may speak happily in strings of numbers, but people do not. The founders of the Internet fortunately took this issue into account. Thanks to the Domain Name System (DNS), people simply have to remember the name of the network they want to interact with and the specific machine on that network. The Domain Name System then takes charge, converting the name to IP information, and then often converting it back to a name when it reaches its destination.

The Domain Name System

The system that provides domain service is a widespread network of computers set up in a hierarchical fashion. Each computer in this network has a specialty and knows one particular group of names. This fact prevents any one machine from getting overloaded with additions and changes as more and more sites flood onto the Internet.

At the top level of this hierarchy are the root servers, depicted in Figure 11.1. One root server—and a backup—exists for every domain extension on the Internet. An overview of the available extensions was given in Chapter 7, in the context of obtaining your own domain name, so Figure 11.1 simply is intended to refresh your memory. (If you need to, quickly review Chapter 7 before reading further in this chapter.) Most of these root servers are maintained by separate organizations, each of which is responsible for its own extension.

NOTE: *A domain extension is also called a zone.*

Each root server maintains a list of the domains under its extension. Each domain is mapped in the zone server's files to a single contact IP address, typically that machine's gateway to the world. It also contains the IP address of that domain's primary and secondary name servers.

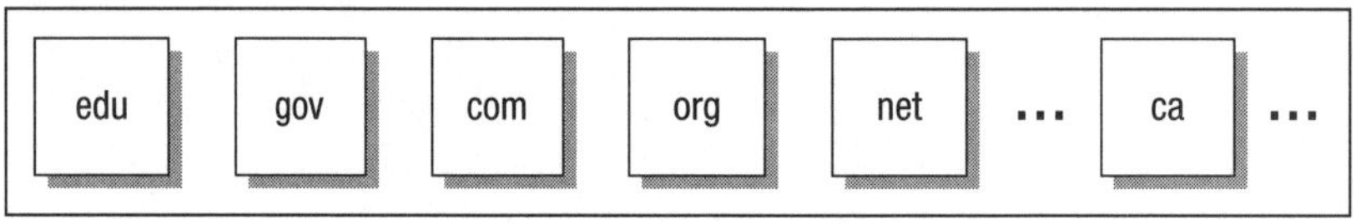

Figure 11.1 The DNS root servers.

A non-root name server contains information about all the machines and domains under its umbrella. Not every domain has its own name server. Even before it became common to host many domains on the same hardware, domains were not required to have their own name servers. However, every domain must have available at least two name servers that carry the data mapping all of their hosts to IP addresses, their primary mail servers, and more. The location of these name servers does not matter; what matters is that their administrators agree to keep the information in their name servers and keep it updated.

Generally speaking, the best arrangement is to have one name server at your own site and another off site, perhaps on your service provider's equipment. This is a common and highly recommended setup, because if you have both name servers on your own equipment and something goes wrong, you end up with no backup that works. Every piece of traffic trying to come to your site will get lost, except in cases where the data is still in someone's cache.

Figure 11.2 represents the potential journey of a name service request.

Name Service Under Linux

Regardless of the operating system, more than one program handles the tasks collectively called *name service*. These various tasks typically fall to the name server itself, the resolver, and the tools that get information about sites. Linux is no different. The Linux operating system almost always uses **named** as the name server. However, this **named** program is not always the same thing. Generally, the **named** program used under Linux is part of the Berkeley Internet Name Domain (BIND) suite of DNS tools.

NOTE: *BIND is the suite used under Red Hat Linux and many other distributions, so that is what I cover here. Other name service tools are available for Linux.*

Multiple types of name servers are available in Linux—and in most other operating systems:

- *Master name server*—The server that you set up by hand and feed all the information about your domain into.
- *Slave name server*—Your secondary server, the one that provides backup for the first. Regardless of whether you have it on Linux or another operating system, it has to be set up such that it downloads a copy of the master's records whenever a change is made.
- *Caching-only name servers*—Record the results of DNS lookups and keep them, relying on the master name server for anything they do not know. You typically install a caching-only name server on machines that are not already providing primary or secondary name service.

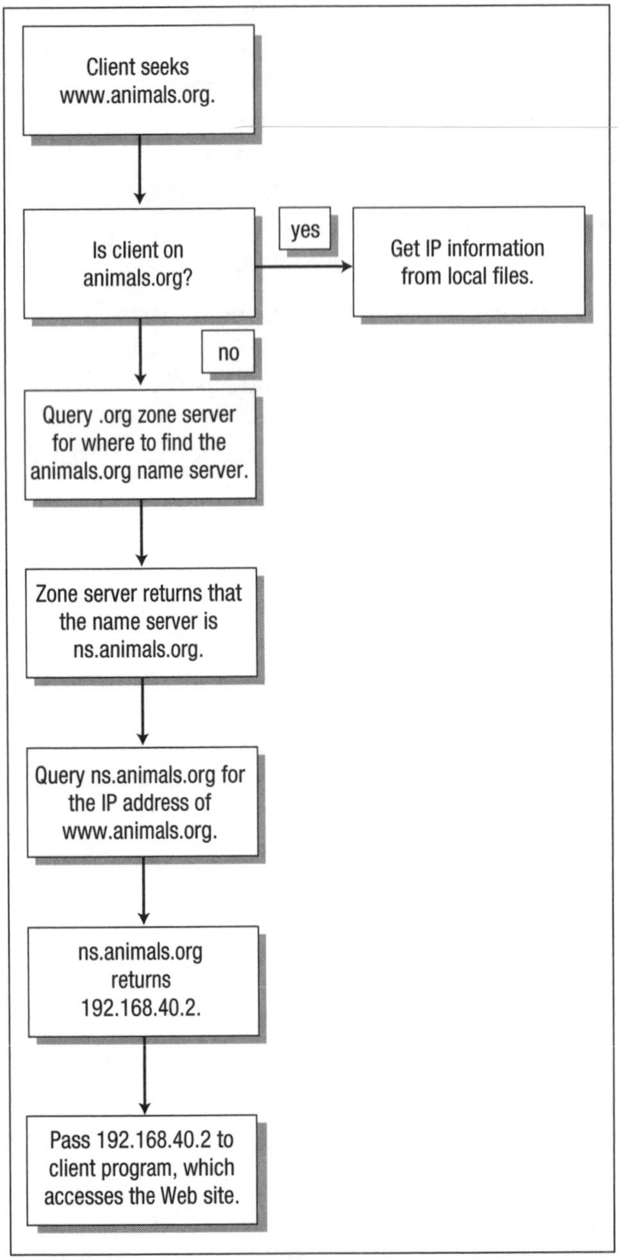

Figure 11.2 An example name service request from and to a Linux machine.

Another piece of the name service puzzle is the resolver. This program is what actually does the dirty work of the lookups shown in Figure 11.2. The end user does not use the resolver directly. Instead, network applications send their name resolution requests to it. This setup allows the applications to do what they do best, while resolution is handled the same regardless of what program you are using.

Finally, the tools are programs such as **dig**, **dnswalk**, **host**, and **nslookup**, which are all important items in your name service arsenal.

Introduction To /etc/named.conf

The file /etc/named.conf is the primary configuration file for the BIND version of **named**. This file is broken into a few sections, and it is important to understand how to put it together properly if you want a working name service. The first section is where you define any options you want to use. Some of the options available are shown in Table 11.1. The "Options And Zone?" column in this table refers to whether the option can be used in both the **options** statement at the beginning of the file and in individual **zone** statements. If it cannot, you can use it only globally in options or locally in one or more zones.

Table 11.1 Options available in /etc/named.conf.

Option	Purpose	Value	Options And Zone?
allow-transfer	Specifies which hosts may receive zone transfers.	Comma-separated list of IP addresses for hosts, surrounded with curly brackets ({ }).	Yes
allow-update	Specifies which hosts may submit DNS updates.	A list of IP addresses for the hosts allowed; the default is none.	No
also-notify	Specifies non-name server IP addresses you want zone change notifications sent to; used in conjunction with the **notify** option.	Semicolon-separated list of IP addresses.	No
blackhole	Specifies comma-separated list of IP addresses for hosts that the name server will not respond to or utilize for queries.	List of IP addresses for hosts, surrounded with curly brackets ({ }).	No
cleaning-interval	Specifies how long to wait between cleaning expired records out of the cache.	Number of minutes to wait; the default is 60 minutes. 0 means never.	No

(continued)

Table 11.1 Options available in /etc/named.conf **(continued).**

Option	Purpose	Value	Options And Zone?
coresize	Specifies the maximum size that a core dump file can be.	A number in the format **#k**, **#M**, or **#G**, depending on how large you want the file to be.	No
datasize	Specifies the maximum amount of memory the server is allowed to use.	A number in the format **#k, #M**, or **#G**, depending on how large you want the file to be.	No
dialup	Synchronizes local zone maintenance according to the **heartbeat-interval** setting. Used for dial-on-demand systems.	**yes** or **no**; the default is **no**.	Yes
directory	Specifies the directory containing the configuration files used by the server.	Full path to directory.	No
forward	Directs all name service queries to another server. Must be used in conjunction with the **forwarders** option.	**only** or **first**. If **only**, then this server answers no queries itself. If **first**, it answers queries if the specified server cannot.	Yes
forwarders	Specifies which machines host the name servers to forward queries to.	Semicolon-separated list of IP addresses.	Yes
heartbeat-interval	Specifies how long zones marked as **dialup** should wait before performing zone maintenance items, which requires a network connection.	Number of minutes to wait; the default is 60 minutes. If 0, no zone maintenance will occur.	No
max-ncache-ttl	Specifies how long failed name request information is stored in the server cache.	Number of seconds, not to exceed seven days; the default is three hours.	No
max-transfer-time-in	Specifies the maximum length of time the server will wait for a zone transfer to complete before it closes it.	Time in minutes; the default is three hours.	No

(continued)

Table 11.1 Options available in /etc/named.conf (continued).

Option	Purpose	Value	Options And Zone?
notify	Informs servers when changes are made to a zone.	**yes** or **no**.	Yes
statistics-interval	Specifies how often to log name server statistics to /etc/named.stats.	Number of minutes between logging; the default is once an hour. 0 turns this off.	No

Option statements are entered in the following format:

```
options {
        option1 value1;
        option2 value2;
        ...
        optionn valuen;
};
```

NOTE: *For the full options list, type "man named.conf".*

The second section is where you define your zones. These are local zones, not root server–type zones, and so refer to the domains you provide name service for. Every site has at least four zones. The first is your caching name service. Every machine should have this zone, because it immensely speeds up name lookups over time. Second is the localhost zone, which (as you know by now) is self-referential. Third is the zone file for the domain itself. Fourth is the reverse zone.

Different zone statement formats are used, based on which name service you are configuring. For a master name server, a zone statement is in the following format:

```
zone domain {
  type master;
  file path_to_file;
  zone_option1;
  zone_option2;
  ...
  zone_optionn;
};
```

The local options allowed in a master name server's zone statements are as follows: **allow-query**, **allow-transfer**, **allow-update**, **also-notify**, **dialup**, and **notify**. Along with your master name server, you also need to have a slave name server somewhere. This is your backup server in case something goes wrong with the master. The following is the zone format for a slave name server:

```
zone domain {
  type slave;
  masters {MasterIP1}
  zone_option1;
  zone_option2;
  ...
  zone_optionn;
};
```

A slave server can use these options: **allow-query**, **allow-transfer**, **allow-update**, **also-notify**, **max-transfer-time-in**, and **notify**.

The third type of zone is for forwarding-only name servers. These types of servers pass on all name service requests to the master or the slave. They do not handle any requests themselves, except for keeping their own name resolution cache. The following is the format for a zone statement in these servers:

```
zone domain {
  type forward only;
  zone_option1;
  ...
  zone_optionn;
};
```

Because this type of server is simply set up, it only takes the options **forward** and **forwarders**.

Caching-only name service is the last form, which has the simplest zone statement of all:

```
zone "." {
  type hint;
  file path_to_cache;
};
```

When you create zones for a domain, you typically need to make two. The first zone is the forward zone, which you write in the familiar domain style of *domain.extension*. The second format tends to confuse people. The reverse zone involves writing the IP address in a format that is easier to manipulate by computers. Typically, an IP address is written from least to most specific. For example, 192.168.15.1 refers to the network 192.168.15, with the host 1.

When you define the reverse zone in your /etc/named.conf file, however, you use the following format instead: ***host.backwards-network*.in-addr.arpa**. So, for the preceding example, the reverse zone would be **1.15.168.192.in-addr.arpa**.

Other types of statements are available besides option and zone. These types are laid out in Table 11.2. Each of these statements has its own syntax and items it might include.

If you need to specify a list of IP addresses in one of the other definitions, but it is a long list and you do not like the cluttered look it creates, you can use an **acl** statement to build an alias that points to that list. This statement is used in the following format:

```
acl alias {
  addresses
};
```

The ***addresses*** portion of the statement can consist of either a variable or a semicolon-separated list of IP addresses. Available variables are:

- **any**—All hosts
- **localhost**—Only the name server itself
- **localnets**—Only the network the name server is on
- **none**—No hosts

The following syntaxes are available to you to specify IP addresses or groups of IP addresses:

- A full IP address; for example, 192.168.0.5.
- An IP range; for example, specifying a subnet with 192.168.0.32/27.

Table 11.2 Additional statement types available in /etc/named.conf.

Type	Purpose
acl	Defines a list of IP addresses.
controls	Defines a series of channels that the **ndc** program can use to communicate with the name server.
include	Tells the name server to load the listed file at its position when reading /etc/named.conf.
key	Defines information on the keys used for authentication and authorization.
logging	Defines what the name server logs and where it logs it. Can only appear once in /etc/named.conf.
server	Sets configuration options for remote servers.

- A specific key's ID, if you want to match by key instead of by address. See the discussion of the **key** statement for more on this item.
- Another alias.

TIP: *To specify "but not this item," put an exclamation point in front of it.*

If you determine that you need to be able to use the **ndc** program to send commands to your name server, you need to create a channel for **ndc** to use. This channel is a named pipe—see Chapter 9 for a discussion of what a named pipe is. You create this item with a **controls** statement, which is used in the following manner:

```
controls {
  IPidentifier;
  localidentifier;
};
```

The ***IPidentifier*** section is used to allow **ndc** to send instructions via TCP/IP. This is necessary for remote control of **named**, but many administrators feel that this is safer to do across a secure Telnet connection, using the ***localidentifier*** instead. An ***IPidentifier*** has zero or more of the following lines:

```
inet 127.0.0.1
port port
allow {alias1; alias2; ...};
```

The ***localidentifier***, on the other hand, uses the following:

```
unix path
perm mode
owner UID
group GID;
```

An **include** statement in /etc/named.conf is not as flexible as many would like it to be. You cannot use it inside any other statement. It has to stand on its own. However, if you want to have some particular section of /etc/named.conf outside of the main file—perhaps an **acl** statement where you define all of your aliases, or a **key** statement with its information stored in a separate file with strong permissions so it cannot be read by anyone—you can do so in the following format:

```
include path_to_file;
```

Before you can use a key anywhere as an authentication mechanism, you first must define it and give it a key ID. To do this, you make a **key** statement in the following manner:

```
key keyID {
  algorithm algoID;
  secret codestring;
};
```

The available ***algoIDs*** are Digital Signature Algorithm/Digital Signature Standard (DSA/DSS), Hash Method Authentication Code-Message Digest 5 (HMAC-MD5), and RSA (the first letters of the three inventors' last names). The DSA/DSS algorithm was released in 1994 as the digital authentication standard used by the U.S. government. It is fast at creating new signatures but slow at verifying them, which makes it not always the best choice in a client/server environment. Its cousin, RSA, is just the opposite. It generates signatures slowly, but verifies them quickly. This is one reason RSA is typically chosen over DSA/DSS.

NOTE: *For more on DSA/DSS and RSA, go to **www.rsa.com**. HMAC is discussed in context in a variety of Requests For Discussion (RFCs) available at **www.faqs.org/rfc**.*

See the Immediate Solutions section "Creating Encrypted Keys" for assistance in implementing this feature.

Although it is possible to control some aspects of logging with **syslogd**, it is wise to take advantage of server-specific configuration when you can. You can do this with **named** by using the **logging** statement. This particular statement is complex, with many optional pieces to it, so it is broken down some here. It starts, predictably, with the following:

```
logging {
```

The first potential section of a **logging** statement defines one or more channels through which information is passed to a specific place. If you choose to include a **channel** statement, it begins with:

```
channel name {
```

Next, you build one of the following three items: **file**, **syslog**, or **null**. A **file** statement declares a specific file that this channel points to, such as

```
file "path";
```

On the other hand, perhaps you want to have **syslogd** handle the logging. You can do this with the following:

```
syslog who;
severity level;
```

TIP: *Review Chapter 9's discussion of logging to refresh your memory of which entities* ***syslogd*** *knows and what the severity levels are.*

Or, maybe you want to send particular types of data into the great /dev/null void (anything sent here gets discarded). You can do so with the following:

```
null;
```

You can also choose what gets printed. Three items are available for this:

```
print-category value;
print-severity value;
print-time value;
```

In all three cases, the value is either **yes** or **no**. None of these three is necessary. Choose as many or as few as you need. Finally, the **channel** part of the **logging** statement is done, so close it, if you used it, with the following:

```
};
```

The other subsection available in a **logging** statement is **category**, with which you can lump a number of different channels together and specify categories of information that need to be logged. The available categories are listed in Table 11.3.

Table 11.3 Categories available in /etc/named.conf.

Category	Logs
cname	Messages that list what points to a CNAME value.
config	Messages pertaining to the configuration file.
db	Database operations.
default	What you get if you do not specify categories. Many consider this setting to be sufficient, because it logs **syslog** and **debug** messages.
eventlib	Messages that pertain to timed events, user-action–initiated events, events opened by other programs, and more.
insist	Messages pertaining to internal consistency checks.
lame-servers	Messages pointing out that a server **named** dealt with was not fully compliant with the latest protocols.
load	Messages pertaining to zone data loading.
maintenance	Messages pertaining to maintenance routines.
ncache	Messages regarding failed lookup caching.

(continued)

***Table 11.3 Categories available in /etc/named.conf* (continued).**

Category	Logs
notify	Messages pertaining to the NOTIFY protocol, which is used to send explanations as to why connections failed.
os	Messages regarding problems with the operating system itself.
packet	Complete dumps of the packets sent and received. This has to point to a file.
panic	Server panic messages.
parser	Problems reading /etc/named.conf.
queries	Messages with summaries of the name service queries received.
response-checks	Query response error messages.
security	Authentication requests, both those that succeeded and those that failed.
statistics	Name service usage statistics.
xfer-in	Incoming zone transfer information.
xfer-out	Outgoing zone transfer information.
update	Information regarding dynamic zone updates.

A **category** statement looks like this:

```
category catname {
  channelname;
  cat1;
  cat2;
  ...
  catn;
};
```

Now, finally, you can close your **logging** statement:

```
};
```

The last statement type available in /etc/named.conf is the **server** statement, which is where you tell **named** about servers it accepts and sends zone files to. This statement is used in the following format:

```
server serverIP {
  settings;
};
```

Four settings are available. You can use none of them or any combination of them. The first is the **bogus** setting. This prevents your name server from believing anything the specified name server tells it. You use this item in one of the two following configurations:

```
bogus yes;
bogus no;
```

Next, you can secure your zone files somewhat by using a **keys** setting. You already have to have set up a **key** statement elsewhere. After you have, use the following to implement key-based authentication:

```
keys {
  keyID1
  keyID2
  ...
  keyIDn
  };
};
```

The Zone Files

A DNS zone file is where you specifically lay out which IP addresses map to which hosts, and other useful information such as the primary mail servers for your domain. Each entry in this file is called a *resource record.* What types of records, and how many, depend on which zone file you are setting up. This information is given in the context of the tasks in the Immediate Solutions section. This section covers the theory underlying how the file is laid out. One interesting thing to note is that zone files are the same regardless of the operating system you are using. They have to be, because you never know what operating system the organization providing your backup DNS runs its name service under.

A zone file begins with the Start of Authority (SOA) record, which is what you use to lay out overall information about the zone before you get into the details. This statement is laid out in the following manner:

```
@     IN     SOA     domain.extension.    admin.domain.ext.    (
                     serial_number
                     refresh
                     retry
                     expire
                     minimum )
```

The parts that you do not change are:

- **@**—The zone's name. The **@** is a self-referential wildcard—meaning that it stands for the default domain name.

- **IN**—The protocol group that this domain name belongs to. **IN** stands for the Internet protocol group, or the Internet class of naming.
- **SOA**—The type of resource record this section of the file represents. **SOA** stands for the Start of Authority resource record.

After this is the section that you need to customize:

- ***domain.extension.***—This zone represents the zone administrator's email address.

NOTE: *Notice the dot at the end of the extension—this dot must be here. The same goes for the next entry.*

- ***admin.domain.ext.***—This is the same thing as ***admin@domain.ext***. In this case, the ***admin*** item does not refer to a hostname.
- ***serial_number***—This entry must change every time you update the zone file. This is what allows your slave servers and other servers that grab copies of the zone to know that a change has been made. The serial number must be in a format that you can increment, and that computers can tell you have incremented. You and the computer both must be able to tell where in the sequence of zone changes this file lies. Some administrators accomplish this by using a date format such as YearMMDD#, which might look like 200010152. The extra number on the end allows for multiple changes on the same day. Other administrators, however, just start at 1 and keep adding. Both methods are legitimate. If you choose any type of complicated scheme, make sure to document it with a comment at the end of the line. For example, if you use YearMMDD#, you might have this comment at the end:

```
200010152 ; YearMMDD#
```

NOTE: *The semicolon, regardless of where it appears in the file, ensures that everything after it is ignored by* ***named*** *when it parses the zone file.*

- ***refresh***—This expresses how long a slave name server should wait between checks with the master server to see whether this file has changed. You have to enter this in seconds, but this does not mean that the interval has to be short. It depends on how often you tend to change the host information for this zone, and how long you can risk waiting for the zone information to propagate. For a three-hour wait between check-ins, you might use:

```
10800 ; 3 hours
```

- ***retry***—This signifies how long the slave name servers should wait to recheck if they try to check for a change and cannot reach the master server. Don't make this time frame too long, because the main down time for the master would be while you are restarting it to load new zone data. Once again, you have to enter this value in seconds. For a five-minute wait to try again, you might use:

```
300 ; 5 minutes
```

- ***expire***—This variable tells any slave name servers how long to trust downloaded zone information before grabbing a new copy. The slave server needs to get a new version of the zone file at this point even if the serial number has not changed. Once every two months is often sufficient for this, but it still has to be entered in seconds. Assuming a 30-day month, the line might be:

```
5184000 ; 60 days
```

- ***minimum***—This expresses the minimum amount of time a caching name server should store any record gleaned from this zone file. After this time span passes, the record is deleted according to the server's own settings. Typically, people use a value of one day, or:

```
86400 ; 1 day
```

After the SOA resource record, the remaining file is populated with other types of resource records. The types available are listed in Table 11.4. Each record type has its own format.

An **A** record has the full format:

```
host     ttl     class     A     IPaddress
```

Table 11.4 Resource record types in zone files.

Type	Purpose
A	Specifies the IP address assigned to a host.
CNAME	Assigns a nickname (canonical name) to a host.
HINFO	Indicates the type of hardware this host is running on.
MX	Specifies where mail should be delivered to for this domain.
NS	Specifies the machine that provides name service for the domain.
PTR	Maps names to IP addresses.
SOA	Specifies the initial settings defining this zone.
WKS	Indicates which well-known services are available at which addresses.

Typically, the ***ttl*** and ***class*** portions are not used. However, you need to understand the full statement so that you can make your own decisions:

- ***host***—The name of the machine you are defining. Often, this is just the hostname.
- ***ttl***—The time to live value for this resource record—how long any resolver should keep this record in its cache before flushing it and asking for a new version.
- ***class***—This value is always **IN** when you are setting up name service for TCP/IP purposes. Because it defaults to the last class used, and **IN** is the class in the SOA, you do not need to include this item.
- ***IPaddress***—The IP address matching this host entry.

NOTE: *All terms used to define these records mean the same from type to type unless otherwise specified.*

Next is the **CNAME** record. You assign a canonical name, or nickname, to a host in this format:

```
nickname      ttl      class      CNAME      host
```

The ***nickname*** is the alternate name you want to assign to this machine, whereas the ***host*** is the name of the machine you want to assign the **CNAME** to.

After this comes the **HINFO** record. Whether you choose to include information about the host's hardware or not is up to you. Some consider it a security risk, whereas others use it to keep track of large networks of different kinds of hardware. An alternative to this use is to use commented lines—beginning with semicolons—to denote different segments of the network. A **HINFO** record is used in this format:

```
host      ttl      class      HINFO      hardware      software
```

The ***hardware*** and ***software*** entries are strings of data. If these strings contain no spaces, then you do not need to put them in quotes. Otherwise, they need to be in double quotes.

A commonly used record type is the **MX** record, or mail exchange record. You enter this in the following format:

```
host      ttl      class      MX      preference      mserver
```

Often, however, you only see the **MX**, ***preference***, and ***host*** portions of this statement. The ***host*** part of the record refers to the machine whose preferences you are setting, as usual. If this line comes after an **A** record, DNS assumes that it refers to the same machine as listed in the above host statement. The ***preference*** setting is used to set which mail host you prefer incoming mail to go to, because often multiple mail servers are available. This setting does not matter if just one mail host exists, but if there are multiple mail hosts, the lower the number, the higher the preference. Finally, ***mserver*** tells the system which mail server you want the mail to go to.

An **NS** record is used in this format:

```
domain    ttl    class    NS    nserver
```

You need to have one **NS** record here for every DNS server for this domain. The ***domain*** entry refers to the *domain.extension*—or zone—that this resource record defines, and the ***nserver*** item is the name of the machine providing name service.

The **CNAME** record is not the only resource record you can use to point multiple machines' names to one machine. In some situations, a **PTR** (pointer) record is more appropriate. This record typically is used in a reverse domain file, whereas **CNAME** is used in the domain files. A **PTR** record is used in the following format:

```
reverseIP.IN-ADDR.ARPA    ttl    class    PTR    name
```

When filling in this record, you would use the reverse IP for the machine you are creating the alias for, and the actual machine in question as the ***name*** entry.

Finally, the **WKS**, or Well Known Services, resource record is used in the following format:

```
host   ttl   class   WKS   address   protocol   services
```

These records are useful for creating aliases for the machines that provide various network services. This way, if you happen to change which machine hosts the service, you can quickly change the zone file and a few host files and be done with the issue as far as the rest of the Internet is concerned—after the new information propagates. The entries in this record are as follows:

- ***host***—As usual, the machine you are actually referring to.
- ***ttl***—The time to live value. If you anticipate needing to move this host, you may want to set its ***ttl*** shorter than you might for others.
- ***class***—This entry is still always **IN** if you decide to include it.
- ***address***—The IP address for the machine you are actually referring to.

- ***protocol***—The IP-level protocol used by the service you are directing to this alias.
- ***services***—The network services you are directing to this alias.

Name Service–Related Programs

Many programs for working with various aspects of DNS are available to system administrators and other knowledgeable users. Some of these programs you may use only once in a blue moon, and others you may never use at all. The key is to know that these programs are available, and what they are used for, just in case you happen to need them.

Getting Information From Name Servers

As you have already seen, the **dig** (domain information groper) tool is useful, at the very least, for building your initial cache file. Typically, you use it in the following format:

```
dig @server domain query-type in
```

The ***server*** component tells **dig** what name server to query—if you leave it empty, it assumes you are testing your own server. Use either the name format ***host.domain.extension*** or the machine's IP address with this command. For the domain entry, give the ***domain.extension*** whose information you want. This may be simply the same domain that the host is on, or the server may have zone records for a number of different domains.

At the end of this command string are the two query items. The first refers to the query type, which is one of the options listed in Table 11.5. Typically, a ***class*** entry appears, but as with many DNS-related items, the only class that makes sense in our case is **in**, for Internet.

Table 11.5 Query types allowed with the dig command.

Type	Purpose
a	Asks for the network address. This is the default.
any	Asks for all available information about the domain.
mx	Asks for which mail exchangers the domain uses.
ns	Asks which name servers the domain uses.
soa	Asks for a copy of the domain's SOA record.
hinfo	Asks for the host information available in the zone files.
axfr	Requests a zone transfer.

TIP: *This command actually has much more to it. Type "man dig" to investigate further.*

Debugging Your Setup

A domain administrator can get highly frustrated trying to figure out why a huge set of zone files detailing an entire class C network, including subnetworks, special services, and more, is not resolving properly. Enter the **dnswalk** tool. This program is a zone debugger, available at **www.visi.com/~barr/dnswalk/**. These zones have to be loaded into the name server before this tool can go through them, so it is not helpful if you cannot get the server to load the files. See the Immediate Solutions section "Installing And Running **dnswalk**" if you want to give this tool a try.

Getting Information About Hosts

Sometimes, you need to get information about a particular machine on another domain, or maybe you want to test and make sure that some of the special service machines on your domain are showing up properly. The tool that helps you on this front is the **host** command. You use this command in the following format:

```
host flags machine
```

NOTE: *A similar command called* ***nslookup*** *does essentially the same thing.*

Available ***flags*** for the **host** command are given in Table 11.6. The ***machine*** entry can be either the hostname for a local machine or the full ***host.domain.extension*** value. That is, unless you use the **-l** flag, in which case you can just use ***domain.extension***.

TIP: *For additional information on the types available with the* ***-t*** *flag, see the* ***named*** *man page.*

Table 11.6 Flags available with the host command.

Flag	Purpose	Values
-a	Gives all available information about the host specified.	None
-d	Debugging mode. Shows all network transactions.	None
-l	Gives information for the entire domain. Essentially does a full zone transfer.	None
-r	Asks your own name server only; does not send the request out to others.	None

(continued)

Table 11.6 Flags available with the ***host*** *command* **(continued).**

Flag	Purpose	Values
-t	Specifies the type of information you are looking for.	One or more of **a**, **ns**, **md**, **mf**, **cname**, **soa**, **mb**, **mg**, **mr**, **null**, **wks**, **ptr**, **hinfo**, **minfo**, **mx**, **uinfo**, **uid**, **gid**, and **unspec**. You can also use **any**, to specify all of them
-v	Prints out the data literally as it would appear in a zone file.	None
-w	Does not time out after one minute. Waits until the answer arrives.	None

The Name Server Control Program

Throughout this chapter I refer to the **ndc**, or name daemon control, program. This tool enables you to interface with **named** to do a variety of tasks. It has two different modes. One is a command-line mode, in which you type everything you want to do and then press Enter. The other is a prompt mode, in which you type series of commands until you are finished. This discussion focuses on the prompt mode. To enter it, type "ndc".

The available commands in prompt mode are listed in Table 11.7. Some of these are primarily useful when you are trying to understand what is wrong with your name service setup.

Table 11.7 Commands available in ***ndc*** *prompt mode.*

Command	Purpose
/debug	Turns on or off **named**'s **debugging** output.
/exit	Closes **ndc**.
/h	Prints out current help information.
/quiet	Turns on or off **named**'s prompts and result text.
/silent	Turns on or off **named**'s nonfatal error announcements
/trace	Turns on or off **named**'s system and protocol tracing information.

Immediate Solutions

Installing The Name Server

To check whether the name server is already installed, and install it if necessary, do the following:

1. Log in as root on the machine you want to use as the master name server.
2. Type "rpm -q bind" to see whether you already have the name server installed. If so, you are finished.
3. If it is not installed, insert the Red Hat CD-ROM into the CD-ROM drive.
4. Type "mount /mnt/cdrom" to mount the CD-ROM onto your file system.
5. Type "cd /mnt/cdrom/RedHat/RPMS" to change to the packages directory.
6. Type "rpm -ivh bind-8" and press Tab to complete the file name, and then press Enter to install the name server package.

Configuring The Master Name Server

To configure your name server after it is installed, do the following:

1. Log in as root on the machine you intend to use as your master name server.
2. Type "vi /etc/named.conf" to open the primary name server configuration file.
3. Because you typically create the file when you first open it, there really is no end to jump to because it is empty. Type "i" to enter Insert mode.
4. Determine which global options you want to set. These options were listed earlier, in Table 11.1. The following is an example of a filled-in **options** statement:

```
options {
  directory "/etc/named/";
  coresize 10M;
  max-transfer-time-in 60;
};
```

5. Unless you have a specific reason not to, it is a good idea to set up caching for the master name server, because this speeds up name-lookup times. Here's an example of a filled-in caching server statement:

```
zone "." {
  type hint;
  file "Master.cache";
};
```

NOTE: *This file is stored in /etc/named, because that is what I set as the directory in Step 4.*

6. Create your reverse local zone. As described in the In Depth section "Introduction To /etc/named.conf," this zone's address is in reverse IP format. The reverse local zone statement for the network 192.168.90.0 might be as follows:

```
zone "0.0.127.in-addr.arpa" {
  type master;
  file "reverse.local";
};
```

NOTE: *Your reverse local zone will always have this name, regardless of your network address.*

7. Create your domain zone. For the domain animals.org, you might use the following:

```
zone "animals.org" {
  type master;
  file "animals.org";
  notify yes;
};
```

NOTE: *When used in a zone, options do not have to be braced within an **options** statement.*

8. Create the reverse domain zone. This zone covers the entire network, so no host numbers are needed. Using the data already given in this example, the reverse domain zone might be as follows:

```
zone "90.168.192.in-addr.arpa" {
  type master;
  file "90.168.192";
  notify yes;
};
```

9. Decide whether you want to add any other statements. For example, you might decide to include:

```
logging {
  channel {
    file "/var/log/named.log";
    severity notice;
  };
  category lame-servers {
    null;
  };
};
```

10. Press the Esc key, and then type "ZZ" to save and close the file.
11. Proceed to the section "Creating The Initial Cache," and then return to Step 12.
12. Proceed to the section "Creating The Reverse Local Zone File," and then return to Step 13.
13. Proceed to the section "Creating Your Domain Zone," and then return to Step 14.
14. Proceed to the section "Creating Your Reverse Domain Zone," and then return to Step 15.
15. Type "/etc/rc.d/init.d/named restart" to restart the name server with its new configuration.

Configuring The Slave Name Server

To configure your name server after it is installed, do the following:

1. Log in as root on the machine you intend to use as your slave name server.
2. Type "vi /etc/named.conf" to open the primary name server configuration file.
3. Because you typically create the file when you first open it, there really is no end to jump to because it is empty. Type "i" to enter Insert mode.
4. Determine which global options you want to set. These options were listed earlier, in Table 11.1. This section might be nearly identical to your master name server's, or quite different. It depends on the machine the server is installed on and what you need it to do in comparison with the master.

The following is an example of a filled-in **options** statement on a slave name server:

```
options {
  directory "/etc/named/";
  coresize 5M;
  max-transfer-time-in 90;
  max-ncache-ttl 21600;
};
```


5. To keep server load down all around, it is a good idea to create a cache on your slave name server. Rather than downloading the master server's cache, let it keep its own:

```
zone "." {
  type hint;
  file "Slave.cache";
};
```

6. Decide which zones this slave server provides backup DNS for. If you have only one slave server, it is a good idea to use it to provide backup service for all of your zones. Working under this assumption, the next zone then is the reverse local zone. The slave server's entry for this, with the master server at 192.168.90.9, might look like this:

```
zone "0.0.127.in-addr.arpa" {
  type slave;
  masters {
    192.168.90.9
  };
  file "reverse.local";
};
```

7. Create the domain zone, which might be similar to the following:

```
zone "animals.org" {
  type slave;
  masters {
    192.168.90.9
  };
  file "animals.org";
};
```

8. Create the reverse domain zone. Its slave server entry follows the same pattern as the others:

```
zone "90.168.192.in-addr.arpa" {
  type slave;
  masters {
    192.168.90.9
  };
  file "90.168.192";
};
```

9. What other statements you use in this file depends on how seriously you want to take the slave server. Remember that it is your backup for when the master server goes down, so it must reliable. At least a certain amount of logging is in order. The slave **logging** statement might be as follows:

```
logging {
  channel {
    file "/var/log/named.log";
    severity warning;
  };
  category lame-servers {
    null;
  };
};
```

10. Press the Esc key, and then type "ZZ" to save and close the file.
11. Proceed to the section "Creating The Initial Cache," and then return to Step 12.
12. Type "/etc/rc.d/init.d/named restart" to stop the name server and restart it with its new configuration.

Configuring A Forwarding-Only Server

To configure a forwarding-only name server after it is installed, do the following:

1. Log in as root on the client machine.
2. Type "vi /etc/named.conf" to open the primary name server configuration file.
3. Because you typically create the file when you first open it, there really is no end to jump to because it is empty. Type "i" to enter Insert mode.

4. The **options** statement in this case should tell the forwarding name server where to forward its requests. This is done in this format:

```
options {
  forwarders 192.168.90.9;
};
```


5. A client machine should maintain its own cache unless it does not have the spare hard drive space to so do. Add the caching statement with the following:

```
zone "." {
  type hint;
  file "My.cache";
};
```

6. For all other zones, you use the forwarding statement format. So, the next three statements might look like this:

```
zone "0.0.127.in-addr.arpa" {
  type forward only;
};
zone "animals.org" {
  type forward only;
};
zone "90.168.192.in-addr.arpa" {
  type forward only;
};
```

7. Determine what other types of statements you might want to include. Some people will try to attack a machine through the name service port, so it is a good idea to do some form of logging:

```
logging {
  channel {
    file "/var/log/named.log";
    severity warning;
  };
  category lame-servers {
    null;
  };
};
```

8. Press the Esc key, and then type "ZZ" to save and close the file.
9. Proceed to the section "Creating The Initial Cache," and then return to Step 10.
10. Type "/etc/rc.d/init.d/named restart" to stop the name server and restart it with its new configuration.

Creating The Initial Cache

To build the cache file your name server starts with, do the following:

1. Log in as root on the machine that needs the cache.
2. Type "more /etc/named.conf" if you need to refresh your memory regarding which file you told the name server its cache is in, and which directory its files go to. The values from the earlier section "Configuring The Master Name Server" are used here, so the cache file is /etc/named/Master.cache.
3. Use the following command format to build your cache file:

   ```
   dig @rs.internic.net . ns > cache_path
   ```

   For example:

   ```
   dig @rs.internic.net . ns > /etc/named/Master.cache
   ```

4. Type "/etc/rc.d/init.d/named restart" to restart the name server with the new cache file.

NOTE: *You need to regenerate this file on occasion. This is a good use for* ***cron*** *and shell scripting.*

Related solutions:	Found on page:
Altering System **cron** Jobs	672
Manipulating User **cron** Jobs	674

Creating The Reverse Local Zone File

When you need to build the reverse local zone file, do the following:

1. Log in as root on the machine you need to create the zone file for.
2. Type "more /etc/named.conf" if you need to refresh your memory regarding which file you told the name server its reverse local zone is in and which directory its files go to. I will use the values from the section "Configuring The Master Name Server," so the reverse local zone file is /etc/named/reverse.local.
3. Use the **vi** command to create the new file. For example, **vi /etc/named/reverse.local**.
4. Build your Start of Authority record, as explained in the In Depth section "The Zone Files." Pulling the data together from that section's example results in the following:

```
@     IN     SOA     animals.org.   nsadmin.animals.org.   (
                 200010152 ; YearMMDD#
                 10800 ; 3 hours
                 300 ; 5 minutes
                 5184000 ; 60 days
                 86400 ; 1 day )
```

5. Add a record specifying that name service for the domain resides within the domain itself, with the following line:

```
NS     host.domain.extension.
```

6. Add name service for the name server itself, with the following line:

```
1          PTR    localhost.
```

7. Press the Esc key, and then type "ZZ" to save and close the file.
8. Type "/etc/rc.d/init.d/named restart" to restart the name server with the new zone file.

Creating Your Domain Zone

To create your domain zone file, do the following:

1. Log in as root on the machine you need to create the zone file for.
2. Type "more /etc/named.conf" if you need to refresh your memory of these items:
   - Which file you told the name server its domain zone is in
   - Which directory this name server's files go in
   - Which file you created your reverse local zone in

   I will use the values from the section "Configuring The Master Name Server," so the reverse local zone file is /etc/named/reverse.local and the domain zone file is /etc/named/animals.org.
3. Type "cp /etc/named/reverse.local /etc/named/animals.org" to copy your Start of Authority section over.
4. Type "vi /etc/named/animals.org" to open the domain zone file for editing.

NOTE: *If you want to use different SOA values for this zone, feel free to edit them. The SOA value provided here is a shortcut.*

5. Move the cursor, using the arrow keys, to the line containing the PTR record.
6. Type "dd" to delete this line.
7. Move the cursor to the line containing the NS record.
8. Type "o" to open a new line for editing beneath the cursor position.
9. Add a line for your secondary name server. The general format for the records is given in the In Depth section "The Zone Files," so I am going to use examples in this section rather than generalities. If your slave name server is located on 192.168.12.5 on the machine ns.myisp.net, then this entry might be as follows:

```
NS      ns.myisp.net.
```

10. Add a line or series of lines for the main SMTP server(s) on your site. If your primary SMTP server is 192.168.90.10 with the name smtp.animals.org, then this line might look like this:

```
MX      1      smtp.animals.org.
```

11. You now need to name the individual machines. Start with the following:

```
localhost                   A     127.0.0.1
```

12. How you order things from here is up to you. I am going to suggest a way that helps you read things at a glance as your zone file grows. Many system administrators use this layout today. Start with the machines with a single purpose, such as the following section:

```
smtp                        A     192.168.90.10
www                         A     192.168.90.15
ns                          A     192.168.90.1
```

13. If some of these machines have aliases that point to them, then you can create the CNAMEs here. You need to create the initial entry before you can point a CNAME to it, so if you have not already done this, wait until later in the file. Here are some sample CNAME definitions:

```
pop                         A     smtp.animals.org.
mail                        A     smtp.animals.org.
```

14. You now need to define all the hosts on your network. You should do this in pairs of lines, such as the following:

```
hostname                    A     IPaddress
                            MX    5                 smtp.animals.org.
```

Type in your first pair, and then the A record for the next pair. You might have something similar to the following:

```
husky                       A     192.168.90.40
                            MX    5                 smtp.animals.org.
collie                      A     192.168.90.41
```

Leave an open blank line beneath the last **A** record.

15. Press the Esc key to enter Command mode.
16. Move the cursor up to the MX record.
17. Type "Y" to copy the current line into your buffer.
18. Move the cursor down to the blank line.
19. Type "p" to paste the contents of the buffer into the blank line.

20. Type "o" to open a new line beneath the current line—the new MX record—and enter Insert mode.
21. Enter your next host line and a blank line beneath it.
22. The MX record is already in the buffer now. Press the Esc key, cursor down to the empty line, and type "p" to paste its contents.
23. Type "o" to open a new line beneath the current one and enter Insert mode.
24. Repeat Steps 21 through 23 until you have added all of your hosts.
25. Add any remaining CNAMEs.
26. Press the Esc key to return to Command mode, and then type "ZZ" to save and exit the file.
27. Type "/etc/rc.d/init.d/named restart" to restart the name server with the new zone file.

Creating Your Reverse Domain Zone

To create your reverse domain zone file, do the following:

1. Log in as root on the machine you need to create the zone file for.
2. Type "more /etc/named.conf" if you need to refresh your memory of these items:
   - Which file you told the name server its reverse domain zone is in
   - Which directory this name server's files go in
   - Which file you created your reverse local zone in

   I will use the values from the section "Configuring The Master Name Server," so the reverse local zone file is /etc/named/reverse.local and the domain zone file is /etc/named/90.168.192.
3. Type "cp /etc/named/reverse.local /etc/named/90.168.192" to copy your SOA section over.
4. Type "vi /etc/named/90.168.192" to open the reverse domain zone file for editing.

NOTE: *If you want to use different SOA values for this zone, feel free to edit them. The value provided here is a shortcut.*

5. Move the cursor, using the arrow keys, to the line containing the PTR record.
6. Type "dd" to delete this line.
7. Move the cursor to the line containing the NS record.
8. Type "o" to open a new line for editing beneath the cursor position.
9. Add a line for your secondary name server, just as you did when creating the domain zone file. If your slave name server is located on 192.168.12.5 on the machine ns.myisp.net, then this entry might be as follows:

```
NS     ns.myisp.net.
```

10. From here on, all the resource records are PTRs. The format for this type of record is discussed in the In Depth section "The Zone Files." Some people like to separate these into groups for easier reading, especially mirroring these groups after the domain zone file. A sample of what you might have here follows:

```
1                              PTR    ns.animals.org.
10                             PTR    smtp.animals.org.
15                             PTR    www.animals.org.
;
40                             PTR    husky.animals.org.
41                             PTR    collie.animals.org.
```

    Notice that in this context, you only use the host number to identify the machine in the PTR record. You do not need the entire reverse IP address.
11. Press the Esc key to return to Command mode, and then type "ZZ" to save and close the file.
12. Type "/etc/rc.d/init.d/named restart" to restart the name server with the new zone file.

Creating Encrypted Keys

To create an encrypted key necessary for authentication, do the following:

1. Log in as root on the name server you need the key for.
2. Type "dnskeygen *flags*" to generate the key. The flags and any values they might have are explained in Table 11.8.

Table 11.8 The flags available with dnskeygen.

Flag	Purpose	Value
-a	Indicates this key is invalid for authentication.	None
-c	Indicates this key is invalid for the purposes of encryption.	None
-D	Generates a DSA/DSS key.	Size of the key, among the following bit sizes: 512, 576, 640, 704, 768, 832, 896, 960, and 1,024
-h	Uses this key for hosts or services.	None.
-H	Generates an HMAC-MD5 key.	Size of the key, either 128 or 504 bits
-R	Generates an RSA key.	Size of the key, either 512 or 4,096 bits
-F	Uses a large base number when generating an RSA key. This means the encryption will be more secure, but the key will take longer to generate.	None
-n	Sets the key's name, or **keyID**.	Full domain name for the zone, or name of key (**keyID**)
-s	Generates a stronger key, sacrificing speed.	A positive integer; the higher the number, the stronger the key
-u	Uses this key for user processes.	None
-z	Uses this key for zone validation.	None

You have to use some of the flags, and they have to be in the right order. The order is given if you type "dnskeygen". For example, I might type the following:

```
dnskeygen -R 4096 -z -n animals.org
```

TIP: *The private key is stored in the file Kname_alg_size.private, and the public key is in Kname_alg_size.key. The authors of* ***dnskeygen*** *were kind enough to have the public key saved in the appropriate zone file format so that you can copy it into a file, if necessary, or include it with an* ***include*** *statement.*

Installing And Running **dnswalk**

To get and install the **dnswalk** tool, do the following:

1. Log in as root on the machine you want to test your name server from. It should be a machine that has the authority to talk to the name server. If you are unsure, use the name server machine itself.

2. Type "mkdir /usr/src/dnswalk" to make a directory to download this file into.
3. Go to **www.visi.com/~barr/dnswalk/** and download the current version of **dnswalk** into /usr/src/dnswalk. This version is currently 2.0.2.
4. Type "gunzip dnswalk" and press Tab to expand the file name, and then press Enter to uncompress the file.
5. Type "tar -xvf dnswalk" and press Tab to expand the file name, and then press Enter to unpack the file. It does not create a subdirectory for itself.
6. Go to **www.fuhr.org/~mfuhr/perldns/** and download the current version of Net::DNS, which is a Perl DNS module, into /usr/src/dnswalk. This version is currently 0.12.
7. Type "gunzip Net" and press Tab to expand the file name, and then press Enter to uncompress the file.
8. Type "tar -xvf Net" and press Tab to expand the file name, and then press Enter to uncompress the file.
9. Type "cd Net-DNS-0.12" to change into the new directory.
10. Type "perl Makefile.PL" to run the Perl program that builds your Makefile.
11. Type "make" to run the process that creates all the files you need.
12. Type "make test" to run a preinstallation test.
13. Type "make install" to install Net::DNS.
14. Type "cd .." to change back into the **dnswalk** directory.
15. Now, whenever you want to run **dnswalk**, type "perl dnswalk *domain.extension.*". Notice the period after the extension. It must be there!

NOTE: *After you know it works, feel free to move the* ***dnswalk*** *tar file into a location such as /root/scripts or /root/perl and unpack it into a* ***dnswalk*** *directory there. This program does not need to be kept in /usr/src.*

Chapter 12

Internet Email: sendmail + IDA

If you need an immediate solution to:	*See page:*
Installing All Of The Pieces	370
Configuring Your **sendmail** Server At The Command Line	370
Building sendmail.cf At The Command Line	372
Tweaking Your /etc/sendmail.cf	372
Adding Additional Mail Server Hostnames	372
Centralizing Your Outgoing Mail Addresses	373
Adding Configuration File Version Information	373
Setting Your Log Level	374
Reducing Server Load	375
Configuring Your **sendmail** Server In Linuxconf	376
Basic **sendmail** Configuration In Linuxconf	376
Configuring Mail Routing In Linuxconf	380
Configuring Email Masquerading In Linuxconf	383
Configuring Email-To-Fax Service In Linuxconf	384
Configuring Virtual Email Service In Linuxconf	389
Configuring Your Anti-Spam Settings Under Linuxconf	391
Setting Up Mail Aliases By Hand	393
Protecting Yourself From Spam	394
Building A CW File	397
Building A Mailer Table	397
Building A Virtual Addressing Table	398
Building An Access Database	398
Removing Mail From The Queue Under Linuxconf	399
Configuring **procmail**	400

In Depth

Email is possibly the most popular service on the Internet. It is also one of the most abused. It is important to understand how to set up a mail server so that it closely matches your needs but does not sit wide open for those people who might exploit it to bounce mass mailings off of. Setting up and running an email server has many other subtleties, so make sure to take the time to become thoroughly familiar with its inner workings.

How Email Gets To Its Destination

The life of a piece of email begins when a user opens a new mail document in his or her mail client. This client, regardless of which it is, immediately asks for two pieces of information: the recipient's email address, which is typically in the form *user@domain.extension* on the Internet, and the subject, which is as irrelevant to the email delivery process as is the mail's content. However, some email clients will not even allow you to send an email message without some kind of subject in place.

How Email Travels

After the user finishes writing an email, he or she clicks or presses whatever is necessary to send it off into the digital world. The client hands the mail off to the local Mail Transfer Agent (MTA). If the mail is destined for another user on this same machine, the local mail handler (**procmail**, in this case, but often **/bin/mail**) takes care of it. However, if the mail is meant for another machine—whether on your network or elsewhere on the Internet—the mail is passed on to a **sendmail** server. This server first determines whether the piece of email is meant for someone locally, in which case it delivers it.

If the mail is meant for someone on the Internet, **sendmail** uses your resolver to contact the zone server for the destination's domain extension. That zone server tells your system who runs name service for the particular domain. The resolver then contacts the local name server for its MX record to find out which machine at that domain is the primary mail server. The **sendmail** server then sends the piece of email, using the Simple Mail Transfer Protocol (SMTP), to the mail server listed in the MX record.

The recipient's mail server receives the mail through SMTP and analyzes the header information through its own rules. If all is well, the mail is delivered to the recipient through whatever tools are used by the recipient's network and operating system combination.

How Email Headers Are Put Together

The header attached to a piece of email is important at many steps. As a mail administrator, you can minutely control how this header is put together, if you want to. Many people do not see the need. The important thing, however, is to be able to read a mail header and use this knowledge to diagnose problems or track down offenders. Mail servers do this on a narrower basis, using the rules you place in their configuration files to analyze header information and make decisions about acceptance, rejection, and delivery.

A sample mail header might look as follows:

```
Return-Path: <msmith@spices.com>
Received: from thyme.spices.com (192.168.33.130 [192.168.33.130]) by
davinci.inventors.com with SMTP (Microsoft Exchange Internet Mail Service
Version 5.5.2650.21)
   id 1F5AK1W9; Wed, 8 Mar 2000 18:57:11 -0800
Received: from cinnamon ([192.168.1.30])
   by thyme.spices.com (8.9.1/8.9.0) with ESMTP id SAA02477
   for <dsmith@inventors.com>; Wed, 8 Mar 2000 18:53:19 -0800 (PST)
Message-Id: <4.2.2.20000308184720.02166ef0@thyme.spices.com>
X-Sender: msmith@thyme.spices.com
X-Mailer: QUALCOMM Windows Eudora Pro Version 4.2.2
Date: Wed, 08 Mar 2000 18:47:34 -0800
To: "Diane Smith" <dsmith@inventors.com>
From: Mary Smith <msmith@spices.com>
Subject: Movies
In-Reply-To: <NDBBLMLPKLJPNFAHBBIDEEKJCHAA.dsmith@inventors.com>
Mime-Version: 1.0
Content-Type: text/plain; charset="us-ascii"; format=flowed
```

The following discussion walks you through this header information, beginning with the first line:

```
Return-Path: <msmith@spices.com>
```

The Return-Path header is one of the Trace Information header types listed in Table 12.1. This header provides information to the recipient's email client that ensures that when the recipient replies to the mail, the email address that comes up is properly formatted.

Table 12.1 The full list of Trace Information header types.

Header	Purpose
DL-Expansion-History:	Provides data regarding the expansion of MTS distribution lists. This header is only used when you are dealing with having SMTP talk to an X.400 protocol.
Path: (Usenet news header)	Specifies which news servers the post passed through.
Received: (SMTP mail header)	Specifies which mail servers the mail passed through.
Return-Path:	Specifies where a direct response to this email should go.

Following the first line is a collection of Received headers, which are also part of the Trace Information header type:

```
Received: from thyme.spices.com (192.168.33.130 [192.168.33.130]) by
davinci.inventors.com with SMTP (Microsoft Exchange Internet Mail Service
Version 5.5.2650.21)
   id 1F5AK1W9; Wed, 8 Mar 2000 18:57:11 -0800
Received: from cinnamon ([192.168.1.30])
   by thyme.spices.com (8.9.1/8.9.0) with ESMTP id SAA02477
   for <dsmith@inventors.com>; Wed, 8 Mar 2000 18:53:19 -0800 (PST)
```

Every piece of email has one or more Received headers, each of which is a record of a mail server this email passed through, and when. You read these headers from bottom to top. In this case, the mail originated at the machine cinnamon on the network spices.com. This machine passed the mail to its mail server, thyme, using the Extended Simple Mail Transfer Protocol (ESMTP). The thyme.spices.com resolver looked at both the destination address and the MX record for the destination domain. It found in that MX record that the email server to contact was davinci.inventors.com, and so used SMTP to deliver the mail to the recipient's mail server, which then delivered it to the recipient.

After this is the Message-Id header, which is one of the Message Identification And Referral header fields. A list of these fields is provided in Table 12.2.

Next in the message header is the unique identification value assigned to this particular piece of email:

```
Message-Id: <4.2.2.20000308184720.02166ef0@thyme.spices.com>
```

Following this unique ID value comes this line:

```
X-Sender: msmith@thyme.spices.com
```

Table 12.2 The full list of standard Message Identification And Referral header fields.

Header	Purpose
Content-Base:	Identifies a URL with the directory in which you can find the Web page for a piece of HTML email.
Content-Id:	Specifies a special identifier to uniquely label MIME message content for high-level user agents.
Content-Location:	Identifies the exact URL where you can find the Web page for a piece of HTML email.
In-Reply-To:	Usually includes the Message-Id value from the email this mail contains a response to.
Message-Id:	Identifies the unique ID value generated for this message.
References:	Specifies the Message IDs that this email refers to.

Often, this means that this user uses both Post Office Protocol (POP) and SMTP mail servers and has his or her primary email address set as the POP address. However, you have to use SMTP to send email—you cannot use POP. Therefore, the X-Sender header item was added to tell the recipient's mail client which account to send to when sending responses. X-Sender is part of the Sender And Recipient Indication mail header options, shown in Table 12.3.

After this line comes another Sender And Recipient Indication item:

```
X-Mailer: QUALCOMM Windows Eudora Pro Version 4.2.2
```

Then comes this line:

```
Date: Wed, 08 Nov 2000 18:47:34 -0800
```

Table 12.3 The full list of standard Sender And Recipient Indication header fields.

Header	Purpose
bcc:	Identifies recipients not listed for others to see.
cc:	Identifies secondary recipients copied on the mail.
From:	Identifies the account the email came from.
Sender:	Identifies the account the email came from. Often not used.
To:	Identifies the intended recipients.
X-Mailer:	Includes information about the mail client used by the sender.
X-Sender:	Specifies an email address you can use to reply to if the From: address is not able to accept replies.

The Date header is part of a small group that refers to date and time information. It is the only header item in its group that is standard for email use. This header specifies either when the mail was written or when the mail was passed to the sender's mail server, depending on how this server is set up.

After the Date header is a pair already covered in the Sender And Recipient Indication headers in Table 12.3:

```
To: "Diane Smith" <dsmith@inventors.com>
From: Mary Smith <msmith@spices.com>
```

The following is a miscellaneous header type:

```
Subject: Movies
```

It is listed with its cousins in Table 12.4.

Another item already mentioned is the In-Reply-To header, which tells you which email this particular mail was written in response to:

```
In-Reply-To: <NDBBLMLPKLJPNFAHBBIDEEKJCHAA.dsmith@inventors.com>
```

After this is another header that is the only one in its class that is standard for email use:

```
Mime-Version: 1.0
```

This header contains information about which MIME standard the message was formatted to adhere to. Finally, the following line ends the mail header:

```
Content-Type: text/plain; charset="us-ascii"; format=flowed
```

Content-Type is one of two headers used in email among the Encoding Information type of headers:

Table 12.4 Miscellaneous mail header fields.

Header	Purpose
Comments:	Includes meta-information about the mail message. Should be enclosed in parentheses.
Content-Description:	Often contains labels for attached files.
Keywords:	Includes comma-separated terms or phrases used for database searches.
Subject:	Specifies the email's topic.

- *Content-Transfer-Encoding:*—The coding method used in a MIME message
- *Content-Type:*—The format used to view this mail's content

How Mail Queues Are Put Together

When one of your users sends a piece of email that has to pass through **sendmail**, that mail at some point has to spend time in the mail queue. How long it spends there depends on how large your mail volume is at the moment, how fast your machine is, how much RAM it has, how fast your connection is, how large the mail is, and how much bandwidth is available for sending mail over the connection at this moment.

You can find your mail queues in /var/spool/mail. Any user that has mail in their inbox has a file in this directory. This file is a text file containing all mail the user has in their inbox in the order it arrived. The fact that your queue is a text file is what makes mail insecure. Any curious system administrator could waltz through anyone's mail queue on their site, as could anyone who gained root access on the system.

Introduction To sendmail

Just as email is one of the most popular services on the Internet, **sendmail** is one of the most popular servers on the Internet. It is a powerful tool that lets you finely configure many aspects of your site's mail handling. Unfortunately, this means that **sendmail** traditionally has been a daunting server to configure. IDA's additions to this server have greatly reduced this concern. You now configure **sendmail** by using macros, which enables you to just give the key information. The macro processor, **m4**, does the rest when it builds your full configuration file for you.

The MC File

Configuring **sendmail** + IDA begins with the macro configuration file, which ends in the extension .mc. You can make this file from scratch, or use the example files often provided along with the **sendmail** code. This is the first file you edit when you begin to set up your email server. The Red Hat macro configuration file is relatively short, so I will walk you through it.

TIP: *Go to **www.sendmail.org** if you want to download a fresh version of this code.*

The first line in the macro configuration file is almost always the following:

```
divert(-1)
```

This line should appear before any large comment section that you do not want to include in the final **sendmail** configuration file. Typically, it is used only at the beginning of the MC file. Its presence there ensures that the instructions included for the user are not transferred to the resulting file during the macro conversion process.

Next is the section that you do not want to have sent to the new file: the instructions. Each line may begin with either of two things: a hash mark (**#**) or a delete through newline (**dnl**). The **dnl** format is shown in the following code section. The **dnl** codes tell the macro processor to ignore everything from its location to the end of the line.

NOTE: *Because **dnl** codes are used here instead of hash marks, you could actually skip the **divert** statements altogether.*

```
dnl This is the macro config file used to generate the /etc/sendmail.cf
dnl file. If you modify the file you will have to regenerate the
dnl /etc/sendmail.cf by running this macro config through the m4
dnl preprocessor:
dnl
dnl         m4 /etc/sendmail.mc > /etc/sendmail.cf
dnl
dnl You will need to have the sendmail-cf package installed for this to
dnl work.
divert(0)
```

After you get past the instructions, the first line tends to be an **include** statement. Notice that the first quote is a backward quote, whereas the ending one is an apostrophe. All string data must be surrounded by this configuration of quotes. Next is an **include** statement, which tells the macro processor to open the specified file and insert its contents in place of the statement. In this case, the **include** is as follows:

```
include('../m4/cf.m4')
```

The file you include here is the following:

```
divert(-1)
#
# Copyright (c) 1998 Sendmail, Inc.  All rights reserved.
# Copyright (c) 1983, 1995 Eric P. Allman.  All rights reserved.
# Copyright (c) 1988, 1993
# The Regents of the University of California.  All rights reserved.
#
```

```
# By using this file, you agree to the terms and conditions set
# forth in the LICENSE file which can be found at the top level of
# the sendmail distribution.
#
#  This file is included so that multiple includes of cf.m4 will work
#
# figure out where the CF files live
ifdef('_CF_DIR_', '',
   'ifelse(__file__, '__file__',
      'define('_CF_DIR_', '../')',
      'define('_CF_DIR_',
         substr(__file__, 0, eval(len(__file__) - 8)))')')

divert(0)dnl
```

The macro processor transfers nothing above this point in the included file. However, the processor does not ignore the text. A section of code above the closing **divert** section is designed to make sure that the macro processor knows where the files are located that are needed during the conversion process. This section does get processed. It just does not send any output to the resulting file.

After the **divert** statements is programming code—note that this code is directly in the MC file, instead of being added with an **include** statement. However, the code does have an **include** statement in it. It is important to look at the contents of included files if you want to fully understand what is happening, because they may have a large amount of additional code in them. The rest of the code from the included file is as follows:

```
ifdef('OSTYPE', 'dnl',
'include(_CF_DIR_''m4/cfhead.m4)dnl
VERSIONID('@(#)cf.m4   8.29 (Berkeley) 5/19/1998')')
```

This code looks rather odd at first. It is reorganized here so that it makes more sense at a glance:

```
ifdef('OSTYPE',
      'dnl',
      'include(_CF_DIR_''m4/cfhead.m4)dnl
      VERSIONID('@(#)cf.m4     8.29 (Berkeley) 5/19/1998')
')
```

The **ifdef** (if defined) statement in the first line is more straightforward than the one listed earlier. This statement looks to see whether the OSTYPE macro is defined. If it is defined, then the macro processor exits the **ifdef** statement. However, if it is not defined, the macro processor includes the file listed and sets the VERSIONID value as instructed.

Returning to the redhat.mc file, the next line is the following:

```
define('confDEF_USER_ID',"8:12")
```

A **define** statement creates a new macro or assigns a value to an existing macro. The first item is the name of the macro, which is confDEF_USER_ID in this instance. Second is what this macro expands to, if you want to set that value immediately. In this case, the macro expands to 8:12. Two back quotes and two apostrophes are included because the colon is a metacharacter. The double quotes allow it to be taken literally rather than be specially interpreted.

Next is the following line:

```
OSTYPE('linux')
```

You want this line to appear like this regardless of which Linux distribution you use. After this line is the following:

```
undefine('UUCP_RELAY')
undefine('BITNET_RELAY')
```

An **undefine** statement is used to remove existing macros from the final product. Many macros are available in **m4**, but the ones discussed here are those that are specific to configuring **sendmail**. The **m4** macro processor itself is a very useful tool. To learn more about it, go to **www.gnu.org/manual/m4-1.4/m4.html**.

The two macros removed at this stage are UUCP_RELAY and BITNET_RELAY. These were both at one point fairly standard, but today are not often used. Unless you are using Unix-to-Unix Copy (UUCP) to deliver mail and use intermittently connected machines, you need nothing UUCP-related. And, unless you have a specific need to send email to BITNET (Because It's Time Network)—a network originally created to connect universities together, which uses a different addressing structure than the Internet—removing this macro isn't harmful, either.

NOTE: *For more information on the various relay macros, go to* ***www.sendmail.org/m4/domains.html****.*

After this section comes a series of macro definitions, such as these:

```
define('confAUTO_REBUILD')
define('confTO_CONNECT', '1m')
define('confTRY_NULL_MX_LIST',true)
define('confDONT_PROBE_INTERFACES',true)
define('PROCMAIL_MAILER_PATH','/usr/bin/procmail')
```

In this case, you create the macro confAUTO_REBUILD with no values, and then assign:

- confTO_CONNECT to **1m**
- confTRY_NULL_MX_LIST to **true**
- confDONT_PROBE_INTERFACES to **true**
- PROCMAIL_MAILER_PATH to **/usr/bin/procmail**

Table 12.5 explains the meaning of each of these macros. Unfortunately, there are too many macros for me to list in this chapter. I will provide pointers for specific macro groups where I can. For instance:

- For a full list of the configuration (conf) macros, see **www.sendmail.org/m4/tweakingoptions.html**.
- For mailer-related macros, see **www.sendmail.org/m4/ostype.html**.

After the definition statements is a group of feature statements:

```
FEATURE('smrsh','/usr/sbin/smrsh')
FEATURE(mailertable)
FEATURE('virtusertable','hash -o /etc/mail/virtusertable')
FEATURE(redirect)
FEATURE(always_add_domain)
FEATURE(use_cw_file)
FEATURE(local_procmail)
```

Table 12.5 Macros defined in the redhat.mc file.

Macro	Purpose	Values
confAUTO_REBUILD	Automatically rebuilds the mail alias files.	**true** or **false**; the default is **false**.
confDONT_PROBE_INTERFACES	Does not add local interfaces (Ethernet cards) to a special list of equivalent addresses.	**true** or **false**; the default is **false**.
PROCMAIL_MAILER_PATH	The path to the **procmail** mail handler program.	Full path to program.
confTO_CONNECT	Shortens how long **sendmail** will wait before ending a connection attempt with a timeout.	Number of minutes to wait, in the format of **#m**; 0 is the default, which means do not change the current value.
confTRY_NULL_MX_LIST	When dealing with a host with this server as the preferred mail server in the domain's MX records, tries to connect directly to that host to pass along email.	None.

FEATURE is a macro that enables you to request that specific **sendmail** features be activated, and set values for them if necessary. Table 12.6 explains the features in the preceding list. You can get a full list of **sendmail** features at **www.sendmail.org/m4/features.html**.

Table 12.6 Features defined in the redhat.mc file.

Feature	Purpose	Values
accept_unresolvable_domains	Tells **sendmail** to accept incoming mail from hosts that cannot be located through the DNS system.	None.
access_db	Includes a database for explicitly accepting and denying email based on the sender's domain name.	The command **hash -o** with the path to the database file; the default is **hash -o /etc/mail/access**.
always_add_domain	Always attaches the *domain.extension* to the sender address, even if the mail is going between people who both have accounts on the same machine.	None.
blacklist_recipients	Must be used in conjunction with the access_db feature. Includes user-specific information in the access database so you can block mail to certain local recipients.	None.
local_procmail	Uses **procmail** as the mail handler for email going between people on the same machine. Redundant if the PROCMAIL_MAILER_PATH **define** statement is used.	None of its own.
mailertable	Includes a database used for defining mail routing for specific domains.	The command **hash -o** with the path to the database file; the default is **hash -o /etc/mailertable**.
redirect	Refuses email addressed to *user*.REDIRECT, which is a method of mail forwarding, but also can be abused.	None.

(continued)

***Table 12.6 Features defined in the redhat.mc file* (continued).**

Feature	Purpose	Values
relay_based_on_MX	Allows relaying from this site if your mail server is listed as the MX record in the remote site's zone files.	None.
smrsh	Has **sendmail** run in the Sendmail Restricted Shell (smrsh) instead of the bash shell.	Path to smrsh; the default is /usr/libexec/smrsh.
use_cw_file	Reads in the contents of sendmail.cw.	None; can set path for sendmail.cw with the confCW_FILE macro.
virtusertable	Reads in a file containing mappings for virtual email addressing.	The command **hash -o** with the path to the virtual addressing table; the default is **hash -o /etc/virtusertable**.

NOTE: *The **hash** command is used to tell the shell to memorize the path to a particular file.*

After this code is a set of mailer macros:

```
MAILER(procmail)
MAILER(smtp)
```

These macros define which type of mail-moving utilities and protocols you intend to use. The **procmail** setting allows **sendmail** to pass email along to the **procmail** MTA. On the other hand, the **smtp** setting tells **sendmail** to assume that it is using SMTP to pass mail data from one mail server to another. Some people like to include **MAILER(local)** as well, but this setting is assumed by default regardless. Adding it is just a formality. For a full set of the mailers available, see **www.sendmail.org/m4/mailers.html**.

The following is the final set of features:

```
FEATURE('access_db')
FEATURE('blacklist_recipients')
dnl We strongly recommend to comment this one out if you want to protect
dnl yourself from spam. However, the laptop and users on computers that do
dnl not have 24x7 DNS do need this.
FEATURE('accept_unresolvable_domains')
dnl FEATURE('relay_based_on_MX')
```

These features are explained in Table 12.6 along with those previously included in the file. Notice the warning before the last two. Both of these items expose you to the problem of spam, or large amounts of mass-generated email. Even worse, if you allow the relay_based_on_MX feature, someone can bounce email off your mail server to spam other people simply by pointing their MX record to your mail server. Little else will cause you to get as much angry email as when people think someone at your site is sending them junk email.

See the Immediate Solutions section "Protecting Yourself From Spam" for more information about how to keep this from happening.

Introduction To m4

When dealing with **sendmail** + IDA, you constantly hear about the **m4** program. This tool is the macro processor that converts the format you see in the MC file to what you see in the CF file (covered in the next section). Not only is **m4** used with **sendmail**, but it is also the brains behind the GNU Autoconf tool, which is used to create the "configure" scripts provided with many source code packages these days.

You use **m4** in the following format:

```
m4 options macrofile > cffile
```

See the Immediate Solutions section "Building sendmail.cf At The Command Line" for details on how to generate your **sendmail** server configuration file using **m4**.

The CF File

The **m4** tool is commonly used today to avoid directly editing the **sendmail** server configuration file, sendmail.cf. Even so, you should be able to look through the sendmail.cf file and make minor changes, which can save you some time by avoiding messing with macros for straightforward issues. The following discussion walks you through the relevant sections of the default Red Hat sendmail.cf and explains each section in turn.

A long section of copyright information and other background details begins the file. All of these lines begin with hash marks (#), which means everything is commented out. The section you are most likely to want to change is shown here:

```
##################
#   local info   #
##################
```

This is the information that applies to the mail server itself and the machine it is hosted on. Notice the format of this first item:

```
Cwlocalhost
```

Commands in sendmail.cf are grouped in single-letter categories, generally with another single letter after to specify exactly what you want to do. In this case, the category is **C**, which stands for *class*. A full list of sendmail.cf categories is given in Table 12.7. The **w** is the specific C-category command, which specifies that you are about to list what names this host is known by. In this case, only "localhost" is included.

NOTE: *The categories should look familiar now that you have learned how to read the macro file.*

Next in sendmail.cf is the following:

```
# file containing names of hosts for which we receive email
Fw/etc/sendmail.cw
```

The **F** category is a signal that you want to import information from a file. Command **w** with this category means pretty much the same thing that it does with **C**—you want to import the names of the machines that this host acts as. I use the phrase "pretty much" because the file /etc/sendmail.cw tends to contain a list of the machines on your network when you are configuring the mail server listed in an MX record.

Table 12.7 Command categories in /etc/sendmail.cf.

Category	Purpose
C	Creates a group
D	Creates a new macro
F	Imports a group's values from a file or FIFO
H	Defines mail-header information
K	Creates a keyed database
M	Defines a mailer or an interface to a mailer
O	Sets a global option
P	Creates a message precedence
R	Creates a rule in the rule set
S	Starts to build a rule set
V	Sets version information in the configuration file for your own benefit

Also, note that the /etc/sendmail.cf file is well commented. What follows after the code used to important data from the CW file is:

```
# my official domain name
# ... define this only if sendmail cannot
# automatically determine your domain
#Dj$w.Foo.COM
CP.
```


Two things need to be explained here. First is the commented-out code. Years ago, you had to fill in the **Dj** item—**D** for define a macro, and **j** for the official domain this mail host lives on. Second is another C-class item. The **P** command is not predefined. With it, this line creates a new class called P with the content of just a single dot.

TIP: *Uppercase commands in a macro are usually user-defined, not internal.*

After this, comes the following:

```
# "Smart" relay host (may be null)
DS
```

The **S** command for the D macro definition category does not exist. Once again, you are creating a new macro here. The DS macro is used only if you have machines that are not part of the main network and that otherwise would not know how to send mail to the outside. For example, these machines may be behind a firewall. A smart relay host knows where network traffic must pass through to get to the outside world.

Next is a set of three class definitions:

```
# operators that cannot be in local usernames (i.e., network indicators)
CO @ % !

# a class with just a dot (for identifying canonical names)
C..

# a class with just a left bracket (for identifying domain literals)
C[[
```

None of the three classes—CO, C., and C[—existed previously, so they are all brand-new macros. The first defines characters that are assumed not to be part of a login name. The second item is identical to class CP, insofar as all that it contains is a single dot. (See Chapter 11 for a discussion of CNAME entries to refresh your memory on what canonical names are.) The final class contains only a left bracket. A domain literal is a part of a mail header that contains an IP address in brackets. This IP address is not meant to be looked up through DNS. Instead, it is supposed to be used exactly as it is.

After this is a quartet of file definitions. These are all files that have to be created—or at least filled in—at some point during the **sendmail** setup process. The first three have a **K** category at the beginning, and so are keyed databases:

```
# Mailer table (overriding domains)
Kmailertable hash -o /etc/mailertable

# Virtual user table (maps incoming users)
Kvirtuser hash -o /etc/mail/virtusertable

# Access list database (for spam stomping)
Kaccess hash -o /etc/mail/access
```


The fourth entry, shown next, is different. F is a class category that loads its contents from the file listed. R is a user-defined class. Notice that the contents begin with **-o**. This is part of the **hash -o** command.

```
# Hosts that will permit relaying ($=R)
FR-o /etc/mail/relay-domains
```

Next is your policy regarding email addresses that are just a username, with no *@domain.extension* attached. The R macro is defined (**D**) to carry the instructions for this situation. Leaving it blank assumes that all mail addressed with only a username belongs within the local domain. This is a fair assumption.

```
# who I send unqualified names to (null means deliver locally)
DR
```

In a similar vein, after **sendmail** determines that the mail has a local destination, it has to know where to send that mail. The next entry determines this. The "who" reference refers to a host. If the main mail server is not the one that processes local mail, you need to fill in the hostname of the server that does.

```
# who gets all local email traffic ($R has precedence for unqualified names)
DH
```

After this, you have another keyed database. This time, it is a *dequoting* database. Dequoting refers to removing quotes that a previous application needed to add to process metacharacters and other special text. A dequoting database is used for protection against spam.

```
# dequoting map
Kdequote dequote
```

Next is a set of class options that determines how **sendmail** writes senders' names and locations into your mail headers. The options are CE, CL, and CM. CE and CL are described in the commented text in the following listing. However, the M class description refers to a variable **$M**, which contains data about what masquerading information you want to use. As you can see, by default, class E is used. This ensures that if each machine has a specific administrator—or the machines are grouped with a single administrator in charge of each group—mail meant for that machine's superuser goes directly there.

TIP: *Using class E allows you to set up an autoforward that sends email from each of the machines you administer to one central location of your choice. This enables you to keep the header information intact so there is no confusion over which machine the mail came from, but relieves you from having to log in daily as root on all of them.*

```
# class E: names that should be exposed as from this host,
#          even if we masquerade
# class L: names that should be delivered locally, even if we have a relay
# class M: domains that should be converted to $M
#CL root
CE root
```

Whereas CM lists which domains under your control should be converted to a single domain for mail purposes, DM specifies the actual domain used for masquerading. Typically, this term refers to your *domain.extension*, and the masquerading is done to make all of your mail look as if it comes from the domain itself, not from individual machines.

```
# who I masquerade as (null for no masquerading) (see also $=M)
DM
```

Lowercase macros typically are not user-defined. The **n** macro definition command refers to the daemon name to use when printing error messages:

```
# my name for error messages
DnMAILER-DAEMON
```

After this, the class P is created with the value **REDIRECT**. This term is typically used to create bounce messages for old user accounts that include pointers to their new email addresses.

```
CPREDIRECT
```

Finally, the last entry in the local information section of /etc/sendmail.cf is:

```
# Configuration version number
DZ8.9.3
```

This line simply creates a macro named Z with the contents 8.9.3.

Of course, /etc/sendmail.cf has much more to it. If you intend to make wide-sweeping changes, I recommend you go directly to the macro file and not edit this file. However, if you need to do something tiny, then consider the items in the Immediate Solutions section "Tweaking Your /etc/sendmail.cf."

TIP: *The* ***sendmail*** *documentation itself is located (in Red Hat) in /usr/doc/sendmail/doc/op/op.ps. This is a PostScript-formatted file. From within the GUI, type "gv /usr/doc/sendmail/doc/op/op.ps" to read this file in the GhostView PostScript viewer.*

Mailing Lists

One email service that comes in handy is the *mailing list*, an online discussion forum run completely through email—though it may have interfaces to other services, such as Web browsers. When someone posts a message to a mailing list, this post is redistributed to everyone on the list, typically showing in the From field that it came from the list itself.

It is important here to differentiate between mailing lists and spam. Spam generally is unwanted junk mail. Mailing lists are made up of people who chose to join it. Occasionally, others add people to a list either maliciously or as a joke, but as a general rule, the people on a list want to be on it. Or, at the very least, are required to be on it as part of a project team or other group.

Various mailing list programs are available to Linux users. Some popular ones are listed in Table 12.8.

NOTE: *The Ezmlm list server requires the* ***qmail*** *server, available at* ***www.qmail.org****. The Smartlist server requires* ***procmail****.*

Table 12.8 Popular Linux mailing list software.

Software	Home Page
Ezmlm	**www.ezmlm.org**
Listserv	**www.lsoft.com**
Majordomo	**www.greatcircle.com/majordomo**
Smartlist	**www.procmail.org**

Immediate Solutions

Installing All Of The Pieces

If you just installed your system, or have never seriously sat down to configure **sendmail**, do the following:

1. Log in as root on the machine you want to have as your mail server.
2. Place the Red Hat CD-ROM in your CD-ROM drive.
3. Type "mount /mnt/cdrom" to mount it onto your file system.
4. Type "cd /mnt/cdrom/RedHat/RPMS" to change into the packages directory.
5. Type "rpm -q sendmail" to see if you have the mail server installed.
6. If the mail server is not there, type "rpm -ivh sendmail-8" and press Tab to complete the file name, and then press Enter to install the package.
7. Type "rpm -ivh sendmail-cf" and press Tab to complete the file name, and then press Enter to install the package.

NOTE: *Other distributions have their own methods for handling the ancillary pieces that make up the full* ***sendmail*** *+ IDA tool. Hints are provided throughout this chapter to help you find the files you need to work with.*

Configuring Your **sendmail** Server At The Command Line

To configure a **sendmail** server from scratch at the command line, do the following:

1. Log in as root on the machine you want to have as your mail server.
2. Type "cd /usr/lib/sendmail-cf/cf" to change into the directory that contains the macro file you need to edit.

NOTE: *In some distributions, a file /etc/sendmail.mc is provided for you to start with. Look there, or try a search tool to find files that end in .mc. Also, look in your distribution documentation to see what your specific distribution has to say about setting up* ***sendmail****. The instructions in this section generally apply to most macro configuration files.*

---

3. Type "cp redhat.mc redhat-original.mc" to save a pristine copy of the default macro configuration file.

4. Type "vi redhat.mc" to open the default macro configuration file.
5. The following is the first line in this file:

```
divert(-1)
```

   However, it has no closing **divert** statement. Move the cursor to the minus.
6. Type "xx" to delete the -1.
7. Type "i" to enter Insert mode.
8. Type "0" to change the **divert** statement to the closing one, so that all the text in your file is not ignored.
9. Press the Esc key to return to Command mode.
10. Type "/REBUILD" and press Enter to jump down to the section of **define** macro statements you may want to edit.
11. Alter any of the items there you find necessary, using Table 12.6, provided earlier in the chapter, as a guide.
12. Alter any of the items in the FEATURE section beneath here, as well.
13. Press the Esc key to make sure you are in Command mode.
14. Type "G" to jump to the end of the file.
15. Move your cursor to the start of the line:

```
FEATURE('accept_unresolvable_domains')
```

16. Type "i" to enter Insert mode.
17. Type "dnl" to prevent this feature from being used. You should avoid it unless having it turned off causes problems for some of your users.
18. Press the Esc key, and then type "ZZ" to save and close the file.
19. If you chose a feature or macro that requires specific files to be created, go to the appropriate section. For example, "Building A CW File," "Building A Mailer Table," "Building A Virtual Addressing Table," and/or "Building An Access Database."
20. Repeat Step 19 until you have built all the necessary files.
21. Go to the section "Protecting Yourself From Spam" and then return to Step 22.
22. Go to the section "Building sendmail.cf At The Command Line."

Building sendmail.cf At The Command Line

To create your main **sendmail** configuration file, do the following:

1. Log in as root on the machine you want to have as your mail server.
2. Set up your MC file as instructed in the section "Configuring Your **sendmail** Server At The Command Line."
3. If you are using Red Hat or a Red Hat derivative distribution, type "cd /usr/lib/sendmail-cf/cf" to change into the directory that contains the macro file you need to edit. Otherwise, change into the directory that contains the MC file.
4. If you have been using a functional mail server for a while and are just making some changes, type "cp /etc/sendmail.cf /etc/sendmail-old.cf" to make a backup of the working configuration.
5. Type "m4 ./redhat.mc > /etc/sendmail.cf" to create the new **sendmail** server configuration file.
6. Type "/etc/rc.d/init.d/sendmail restart" to stop and start the mail server, loading the new configuration.

Tweaking Your /etc/sendmail.cf

Although a lot of people try to avoid working directly with the **sendmail** configuration file, sometimes it is worth doing so. For minor edits, it usually takes longer to work with the macro file and conversion process than to directly edit /etc/sendmail.cf.

Some of the items in this section may already have been done during other configuration phases, using the macro tools or Linuxconf. Take a moment to see whether this is the case before you start changing things.

Adding Additional Mail Server Hostnames

To add references for other hostnames used for the mail server machine, do the following:

1. Log in to the mail server as root.
2. Type "vi /etc/sendmail.cf" to open the **sendmail** configuration file.
3. Type "/Cw" and press Enter to jump down to the line that starts with:

```
Cwlocalhost
```

4. Type "$" to jump to the end of the line, or press the End key.

5. Add the missing hostnames. For example:

```
Cwlocalhost mail smtp pop
```

6. Press the Esc key, and then type "ZZ" to save and close the file.
7. Type "/etc/rc.d/init.d/sendmail restart" to load the new configuration file.

NOTE: *Although you could put this information in the /etc/sendmail.cw file, I like to keep names for this machine and other machines separate.*

Centralizing Your Outgoing Mail Addresses

If you want to make sure your email all looks centralized, rather than giving out host information in the From and Reply-To headers, do the following:

1. Log in to the mail server as root.
2. Type "vi /etc/sendmail.cf" to open the **sendmail** configuration file.
3. Type "/DM" and press Enter to jump down to see whether anything is assigned to the masquerading macro. If nothing is, you will see only the following:

```
DM
```

4. If nothing is there, add your *domain.extension*. For example:

```
DManimals.org
```

5. Press the Esc key, and then type "ZZ" to save and close the file.
6. Type "/etc/rc.d/init.d/sendmail restart" to load the new configuration file.

Adding Configuration File Version Information

It is a smart idea to keep track of when you last edited your **sendmail** configuration. To accomplish this, do the following:

1. Log in to the mail server as root.
2. Type "vi /etc/sendmail.cf" to open the **sendmail** configuration file, if you don't already have the file open.
3. Whenever you make a change, type "/DZ" and press Enter to jump down to the end of the local information section of /etc/sendmail.cf. It looks something like this:

```
DZ8.9.3
```

4. Increment the version number. You can also change the default version format to something that makes more sense to you and your needs, if you want to. Just make sure to not leave any blank spaces.
5. Press the Esc key, and then type "ZZ" to save and close the file.
6. Type "/etc/rc.d/init.d/sendmail restart" to load the new configuration file.

Setting Your Log Level

As with most services, you can set the amount of information that **sendmail** logs. To accomplish this, do the following:

1. Log in to the mail server as root.
2. Type "vi /etc/sendmail.cf" to open the **sendmail** configuration file, if you don't already have the file open.
3. Type "/LogLevel" and press Enter to jump down to where you can change this item. By default, the listing looks like this:

```
# log level
O LogLevel=9
```

The **O** means that you are specifying an option. LogLevel is one of the **sendmail** options. Table 12.9 lists the log levels available in **sendmail**.

NOTE: *Table 12.9 refers to two SMTP commands:* ***VRFY*** *and* ***EXPN****. The* ***VRFY*** *command is used to ensure that an account exists, and to get basic information about the email address.* ***EXPN*** *is used to expand mailing lists. Unfortunately, both of these commands are abused by spammers, so now they are implemented with workarounds to make them less useful for mass address gathering.*

Table 12.9 Logging levels available in sendmail.

Level	Logs
0	Nothing
1	System failures and security issues
2	Network and protocol problems
3	Malformed addresses, transient errors, and connection timeouts
4	Inaccurate alias databases and connection rejections
5	Statistics
6	Error message output and information regarding SMTP **VRFY** and **EXPN** commands
7	Mail delivery errors

(continued)

Table 12.9 Logging levels available in sendmail (continued).

Level	Logs
8	Mail delivery output and information about rebuilding internally used **sendmail** databases
9	Deferred messages (the default)
10	Expansion of the various **sendmail** database files
11	NIS errors and finished jobs
12	SMTP connections
13	Errors due to file permission problems or bad links
14	Refused connections
15	SMTP commands

4. Press the Esc key, and then type "ZZ" to save and close the file.
5. Type "/etc/rc.d/init.d/sendmail restart" to load the new configuration file.

Reducing Server Load

If your mail server continually has problems managing the traffic that passes through it, do the following:

1. Log in to the mail server as root.
2. Type "vi /etc/sendmail.cf" to open the **sendmail** configuration file, if you don't already have the file open.
3. Type "/load average" and press Enter to jump down to the text you want to look at. It should look similar to the following:

```
# load average at which we just queue messages
#O QueueLA=8

# load average at which we refuse connections
#O RefuseLA=12

# maximum number of children we allow at one time
#O MaxDaemonChildren=12

# maximum number of new connections per second
#O ConnectionRateThrottle=3
```

4. You can choose to try the defaults given for one or more options by deleting the hash mark in front of the appropriate **O**, so that it is no longer commented out.

5. Press the Esc key, and then type "ZZ" to save and close the file.
6. Type "/etc/rc.d/init.d/sendmail restart" to load the new configuration file.

Related solution:	Found on page:
Writing A Script To Monitor System Load	623

Configuring Your **sendmail** Server In Linuxconf

The Linuxconf tool provides several configuration tools that enable you to control your **sendmail** server's settings and functionality. Those who prefer to use GUI-based tools will like the fact that after you tweak your setup, Linuxconf generates your new sendmail.cf file for you.

Basic **sendmail** Configuration In Linuxconf

To set up basic **sendmail** functionality in Linuxconf, do the following:

1. Enter GNOME as root.
2. Click the footprint icon to open the main menu.
3. Click System|Linuxconf to open the Linuxconf configuration tool.
4. Expand Config|Networking|Server Tasks|Mail Delivery System (Sendmail) and then expand the Basic section.
5. Click Basic Information to open the Basic Sendmail Configuration dialog box, shown in Figure 12.1.
6. In the Present Your System As text box, type your *domain.extension*. For example, "animals.org". Doing this ensures that your outgoing email does not show up as coming from a specific host. Even more important, it makes sure that when someone replies to the email, it does not go just to that host—where you would not see it until you logged into that account on that specific machine—but instead to the main mail server.
7. If you are setting up your central mail server, click the Accept Email For *domain.extension* checkbox.
8. Type the hostname for the central server in the Mail Server text box, even if this machine is the central server.
9. If you are not setting up the central mail server, but instead are configuring mail service on a machine that does not have the direct ability to connect to the Internet—for example, suppose that you have a LAN, and a single

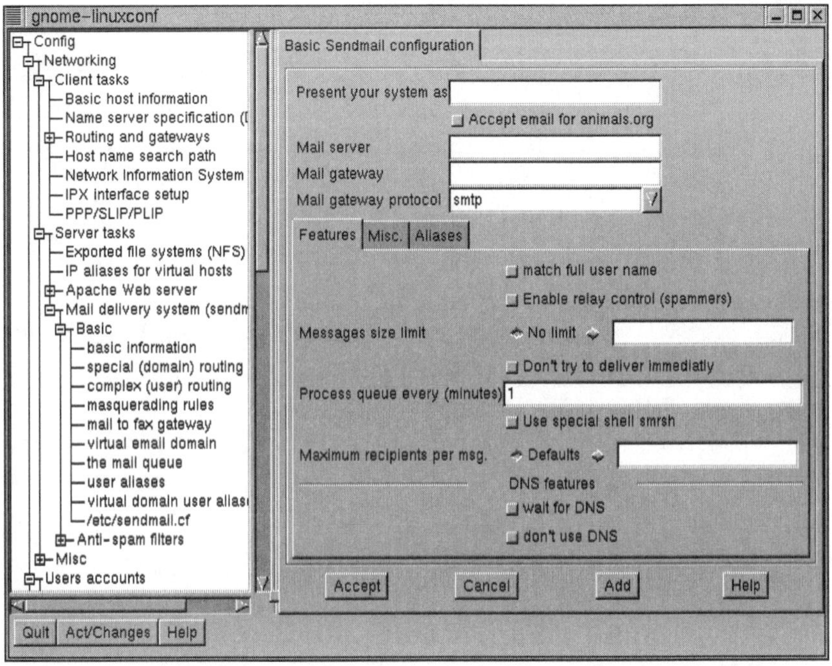

Figure 12.1 The Linuxconf Basic Sendmail Configuration dialog box, with the Features tab displayed.

machine is responsible for connecting the network at certain times—then enter the mail server's hostname in the Mail Gateway text box. See the discussion of the **DS** command in the In Depth section "The CF File" for a better understanding of gateways.

10. If you enter a Mail Gateway, choose the protocol this client machine needs to use to send mail to the gateway in the Mail Gateway Protocol drop-down list box. The options are explained in Table 12.10.
11. Move to the Features tab area.
12. Leave Match Full User Name unchecked unless you have a specific reason to check it.
13. As a general rule, you probably want to check the Enable Relay Control (Spammers) checkbox on the main mail server machine. If you check this box, take special care later when configuring antispam measures so that you do not accidentally block your own users from using email. When you set up any type of control measures such as this, you need to watch for any peculiarities that show up in the server's behavior, before you start to trust it to do its job properly.

Table 12.10 The protocols available for client machine mail transfer.

Protocol	Description
ESMTP	Extended SMTP. Supported by **sendmail** if you used the MAILER(smtp) macro. This is essentially SMTP with more modern extensions on top. If you are using **sendmail** otherwise on your system, you can select esmtp for the gateway.
ESMTPREM	Commonly referred to as "Expensive SMTP." If you have expensive telephone fees to deal with when your network dials in to send mail, you may want to choose this option. This protocol queues mail to go out in batch sends.
SMTP	Simple Mail Transfer Protocol. The protocol used to send email messages across TCP/IP networks and throughout the Internet.
UUCP	Unix-to-Unix Copy. Not as common as it used to be, when it was used regularly to send and receive mail and news batch jobs by machines not permanently connected to the outside world. It's still used in areas where telephone costs make permanent connections too expensive.
UUCP-DOM	A UUCP mailer that keeps addresses in Internet format. Not compatible with all UUCP MTAs.

14. If you want or need to limit the size of the email messages users can send, check the option next to No Limit and fill in the maximum message size you want to allow through. This size is expressed in kilobytes. For example, you might choose 500 if you do not want anything larger than .5MB to go through. Depending on what your user base does with email, however, this can be quite limiting. A more realistic value might be 2,000 (approximately 2MB) to prevent overly large items from entering.
15. If for any reason you want mail to wait to go out from this machine, check the Don't Try To Deliver Immediately checkbox. Typically, you would do this if the machine is not permanently connected to the rest of the network, or if it is the main server machine and is not permanently connected to the Internet.
16. If you checked the box in Step 15, then enter how often the mail that is queued should be sent out or to local machines in the Process Queue Every (Minutes) text box.
17. Check the Use Special Shell Smrsh box to have **sendmail** use its special shell. This is recommended on a mail server machine.
18. If you want to set your own Maximum Recipients Per Msg, then click the second checkbox and enter a number in the text box. Remember that sometimes legitimate reasons exist to have 10, 15, or more recipients. Furthermore, if you decide to host mailing lists, they can have user lists in the hundreds.

19. Choose the appropriate item under DNS Features:
    - Click Wait For DNS if the machine has constant access to a domain name server.
    - Click Don't Use DNS if the machine has intermittent or no direct access to a domain name server.
20. Click the Misc. tab to access its contents.
21. If you are using UUCP for some mail processing, do the following:
    - Uncheck the No Batching For UUCP Mail option if you want email sent out at timed dial-up intervals rather than immediately.
    - Change the number of bytes assigned to Max Size Of UUCP Messages if you want to make them larger or smaller. A single message exceeding this value will not be downloaded or uploaded. You can disable this by entering 0.
22. The Deliver Locally To Users text box contains a list of users that the mail server does not handle traffic for centrally. If you want anyone aside from the superuser handled this way—perhaps machine-specific administrative accounts are in use—add the usernames in this text box.
23. In addition to local delivery, you can choose to make it obvious to the recipient which host email came from for specific users. Once again, this is typically used for the superuser or particular administrative accounts. If you want this to work for more than root, add additional email addresses in the No Masquerade From Users text box.
24. Only add a username to the Trusted Users text box if you want this user to have access to your mail spools and queues.
25. If you want to apply special routing rules to your email delivery, check the Special Routing DB checkbox. This essentially activates the mailertable feature discussed previously in Table 12.6.
26. If you enable special routing, then you need to tell Linuxconf which database type you are using by selecting the proper entry in the Special Routing DB Format drop-down list box. The databases available are listed in Table 12.11.
27. Under Local Delivery Agent, choose procmail from the drop-down list box.
28. Unless you have a specific need to do so, do not check the Support Bogus Mail Clients option. This feature adds support for mail clients that send malformed greeting messages.
29. Click the Aliases tab to access its contents.
30. If you host any virtual domains, enter one *domain.extension* per text box. Clicking Add gives you additional text boxes.
31. Click the Accept button to save the changes. You are given the option of generating the new sendmail.cf file now or later.

Table 12.11 Database types available for special routing.

Type	Description
btree	Binary tree. Fast lookup times, but takes up more RAM. Does not scale well for large databases.
dbm	Data Base Manager. Older database format. Useful for backward-compatibility issues if you need to interface your routing database with another program.
hash	Default. Uses little RAM, but lookups can be slow. Scales well for large databases.
NIS	Use this format if you are using the NIS service on your system. See Chapter 16 for more information on the Network Information System (NIS).

32. Click Yes to generate the new **sendmail** configuration file now. If you want to wait until you finish configuring the server, then click No.

NOTE: *If this is the first time you have used Linuxconf to generate a new sendmail.cf file, you will be notified that your previous CF file was not generated by Linuxconf. It is safe to replace this with the Linuxconf version. A copy of the old configuration file is saved as specified in the dialog box, so you can revert to it if necessary.*

Configuring Mail Routing In Linuxconf

Two special cases for mail routing are available in Linuxconf that enable you to choose particular instances and have their mail delivered differently from how it is delivered to everyone else. One special case enables you to configure **sendmail** to deliver things differently to specific domains, whereas the other case focuses on individual users.

Configuring Special Domain Routing In Linuxconf

To set up mail routing for special cases in Linuxconf, do the following:

1. Enter GNOME as root.
2. Click the footprint icon to open the main menu.
3. Click System|Linuxconf to open the Linuxconf configuration tool.
4. Expand Config|Server Tasks|Mail Delivery System (Sendmail) and then expand the Basic section.
5. Click Special (Domain) Routing to open the Special Routings dialog box.
6. Click the Add button to create a new routing entry. This action opens the Special Routing dialog box, shown in Figure 12.2.
7. In the Destination text box, enter the *domain.extension* whose email you want to apply special routing to.
8. In the Forwarder text box, enter the hostname of the machine that you want to have handle the mail for the listed domain.

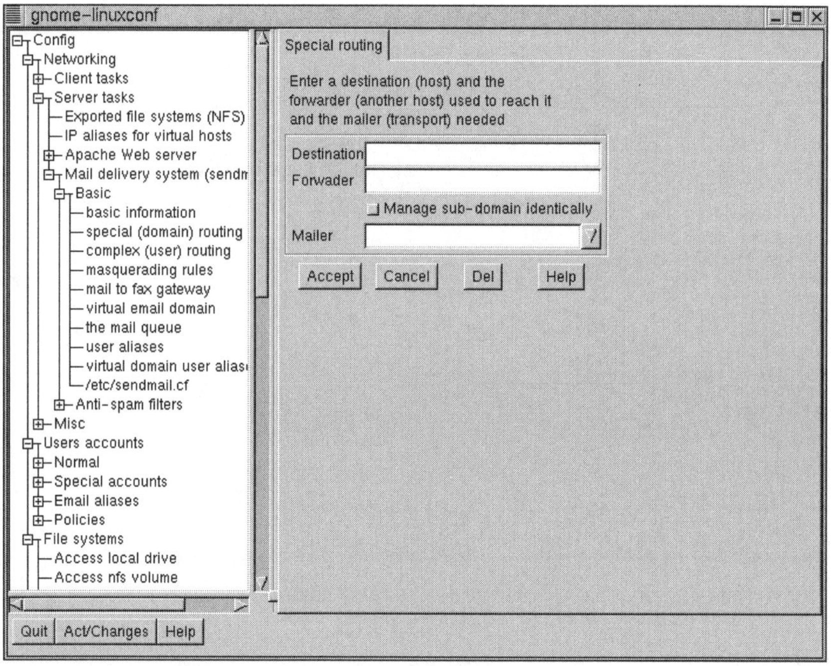

Figure 12.2 The Linuxconf Special Routing dialog box.

9. If you have this domain divided into subdomains, and want all mail for these parts treated the same as the parent domain, then check the Manage Sub-Domain Identically checkbox.
10. In the Mailer drop-down list box, choose the method with which this mail should get delivered to the forwarder. The methods are outlined earlier in Table 12.10.
11. Click Accept to return to the Special Routings dialog box.
12. Click Quit to close it.

Configuring Special User Routing In Linuxconf

If you need to isolate specific users and have their mail delivered differently from how it is delivered to others, do the following:

1. Enter GNOME as root.
2. Click the footprint icon to open the main menu.
3. Click System|Linuxconf to open the Linuxconf configuration tool.
4. Expand Config|Server Tasks|Mail Delivery System (Sendmail) and then expand the Basic section.
5. Click Complex (User) Routing to open the Complex Routings dialog box.

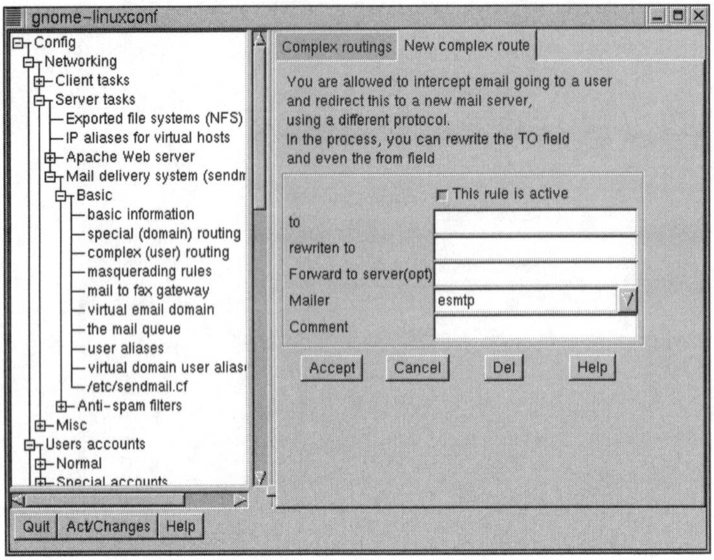

Figure 12.3 The Linuxconf New Complex Route dialog box.

6. Click Add to open the New Complex Route dialog box, shown in Figure 12.3.
7. Make sure the This Rule Is Active box is checked so that the new rule will get used. This checkbox gives you the handy ability to deactivate this rule later without deleting it.
8. Enter one of the following in the To text box:
   - The full email address of the person whose email you want to redirect. For example, calico@animals.org.
   - The domain, if you want to redirect the email for an entire domain to a single account. For example, @animals.org.
9. Enter the address you want to redirect the mail to in the Rewritten To text box. For example, to redirect calico@animals.org to cats@animals.org, you would enter the latter address.
10. If you want the redirected mail to go to a particular mail server, enter its *host.domain.extension* in the Forward To Server (Opt) text box. Then, choose the mail delivery method you want to use in the Mailer drop-down list box. Possible choices are explained earlier in Table 12.10.
11. If you want to include an explanation for your own use, enter it in the Comment field.
12. Click Accept to close the New Complex Route dialog box.
13. Click Quit to close the Complex Routings dialog box. You will be asked whether you want to generate a new sendmail.cf file. If so, click Yes, and

read any comments from Linuxconf carefully. Otherwise, click No, and remember to generate the new file later so that your changes are activated.

Configuring Email Masquerading In Linuxconf

To set up email on an IP masqueraded system under Linuxconf, do the following:

1. Enter GNOME as root.
2. Click the footprint icon to open the main menu.
3. Click System|Linuxconf to open the Linuxconf configuration tool.
4. Expand Config|Server Tasks|Mail Delivery System (Sendmail) and then expand the Basic section.
5. Click Masquerading Rules to open the Masquerading Rules dialog box.
6. Click Add to open the New Masquerading Rule dialog box, shown in Figure 12.4.
7. Make sure the This Rule Is Active box is checked so that the new rule will get used. This checkbox gives you the handy ability to deactivate this rule later without deleting it.
8. Enter one of the following in the From text box:
   - The full email address of the person whose email you want to masquerade as coming from somewhere else. For example, bonobo@animals.org.
   - The domain, if you want to masquerade all mail from a specific domain to look as if it is coming from somewhere else. For example, @animals.org.

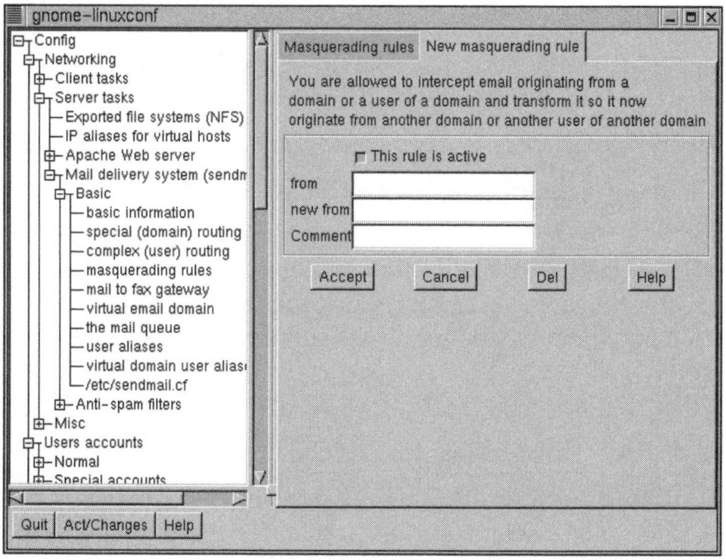

Figure 12.4 The Linuxconf New Masquerading Rule dialog box.

9. Enter one of the following in the New From text box:
   - The full email address you want people to see when they receive email from the From address. For example, monkey@animals.org.
   - The domain you want people to see when receiving email from any user from the From address. For example, @apes.org.
10. If you want to include an explanation for your own use, enter it in the Comment field.
11. Click the Accept button to return to the Masquerading Rules dialog box.
12. Click the Quit button to close this dialog box. You will be asked whether you want to generate a new sendmail.cf file. If so, click Yes, and read any comments from Linuxconf carefully. Otherwise, click No, and remember to generate the new file later so that your changes are activated.

Configuring Email-To-Fax Service In Linuxconf

If you want to allow your users to send faxes by sending email attachments that **sendmail** passes to a fax program, you can use Linuxconf to set it up as follows:

1. Enter GNOME as root.
2. Click the footprint icon to open the main menu.
3. Click System|Linuxconf to open the Linuxconf configuration tool.
4. Expand Config|Server Tasks|Mail Delivery System (Sendmail) and then expand the Basic section.
5. Click Mail To Fax Gateway to open the Mail To Fax Gateway Configuration dialog box, shown in Figure 12.5.
6. Click the Basic Information button to open the basic information portion of the Mail To Fax Gateway Configuration dialog box, shown in Figure 12.6.
7. Click the Mail To Fax Gateway Is Active checkbox to turn on this feature.
8. Enter the path to the script or program required to spool fax jobs in the Spool Command text box.
9. The other two features in this dialog box are not implemented in the Linuxconf that comes with Red Hat 6.1. Click the Help button to see current information about whether they are supported in the version you have. If so:
   - If you want to log all fax activity to a specific file, enter the path to the file that fax activity should be logged to in the Log File text box.
   - If you want to run a particular program to write log information somewhere each time a fax is sent, enter the path to the program in the Log Command text box.

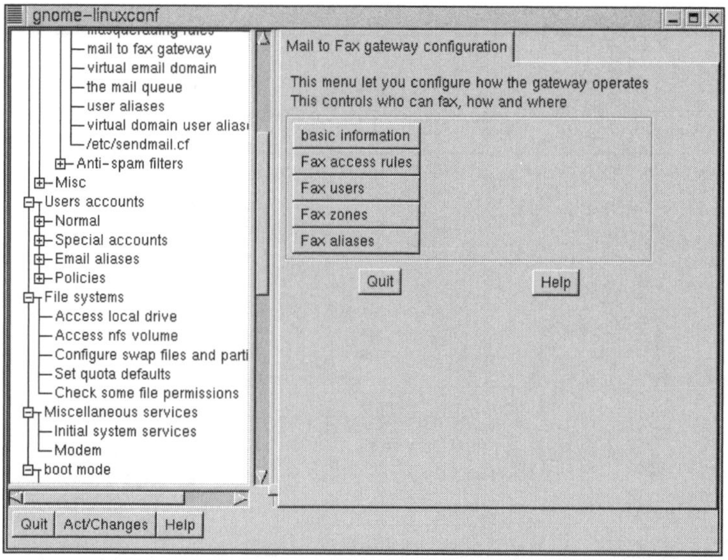

Figure 12.5 The Linuxconf Mail To Fax Gateway Configuration dialog box.

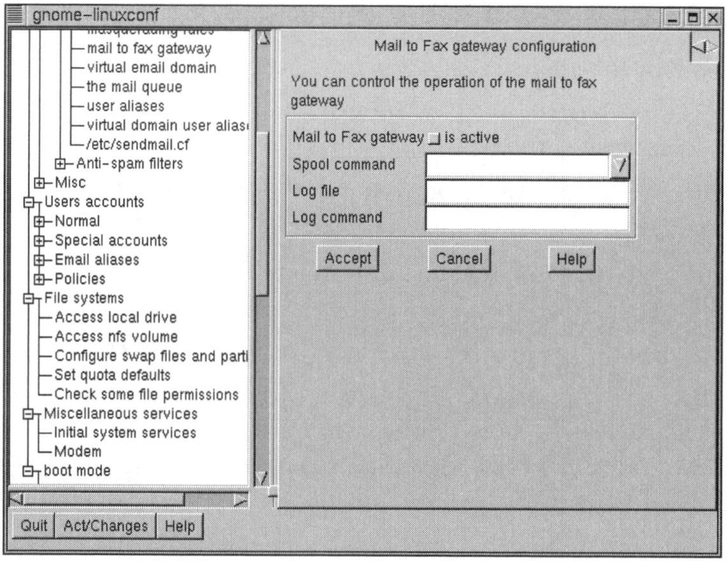

Figure 12.6 The basic information section of the Linuxconf Mail To Fax Gateway Configuration dialog box.

10. Click Accept to return to the main Mail To Fax Gateway Configuration dialog box.
11. Click the Fax Access Rules button to open the Fax Rules dialog box.
12. Click the Add button to open the One Access Rule dialog box, shown in Figure 12.7.

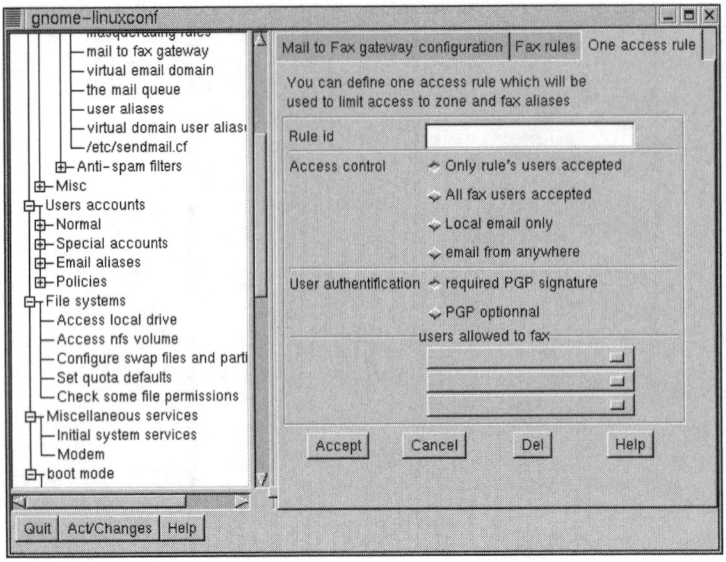

Figure 12.7 The Linuxconf One Access Rule dialog box.

13. Enter a short but descriptive label in the Rule ID text box.
14. Under Access Control, choose one of the following options:
    - *Only Rule's Users Accepted*—Allows only the users listed in this rule to send faxes using this method.
    - *All Fax Users Accepted*—Allows anyone listed as a fax user to send faxes using this method.
    - *Local Email Only*—Allows anyone on your domain to send faxes using this method.
    - *Email From Anywhere*—Allows anyone, anywhere, to send faxes using this method.
15. Under User Authentication, choose whether or not you require a PGP signature to be attached to the fax email. This signature is used to verify that the user in question really did send the fax.
16. Click Accept for now. You will return to add users later. You are now back in the Fax Rules dialog box.
17. Click Quit to return to the Mail To Fax Gateway Configuration dialog box.
18. Click the Fax Users button to open the List Of Fax Users dialog box.
19. Click Add to open the Fax User dialog box, shown in Figure 12.8.
20. In the User Email Address text box, enter the *user@domain.extension* of the person allowed to send faxes through this gateway.

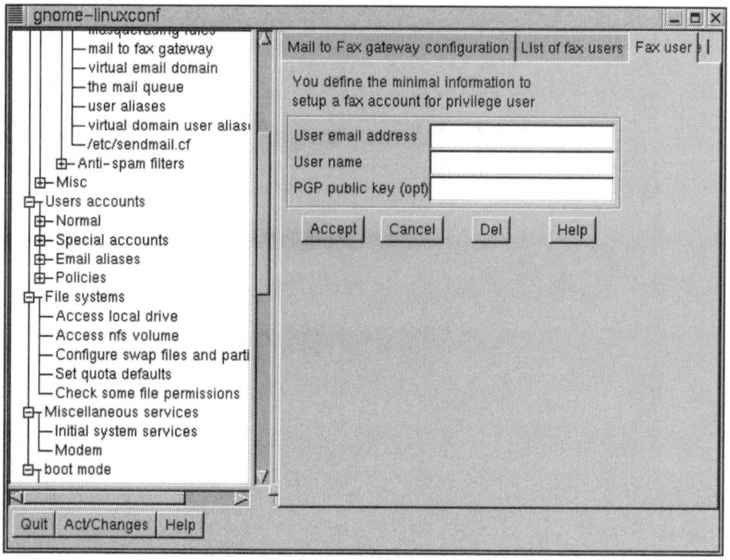

Figure 12.8 The Linuxconf Fax User dialog box.

21. If you want to, enter the user's name in the User Name text box.
22. If you want to utilize PGP authentication for sending faxes, copy or type the user's public key into the PGP Public Key (Opt) text box.
23. Click Accept to close the dialog box.
24. Return to Step 19 for each user you want to add.
25. Click Quit when you are finished adding users.

NOTE: *After you add the users, you can return to the One Access Rule dialog box at any time to choose the users the rule applies to from the drop-down list boxes.*

---

26. Click the Fax Zones button to open the Fax Zones dialog box.
27. Click the Add button to open the One Fax Zone dialog box, shown in Figure 12.9.
28. Enter a short, descriptive label in the Zone ID text box.
29. Enter the dialing prefix—often the area code—in the Phone Zone Prefix text box.
30. In the Phone Number Length text box, enter how long a phone number in this zone should be. For example, if the zone is for local calls, and your phone numbers tend to be in the format ###-####, enter 7 in the text box. If the zone is for long-distance calls, and the format is 1-###-###-####, enter 11.

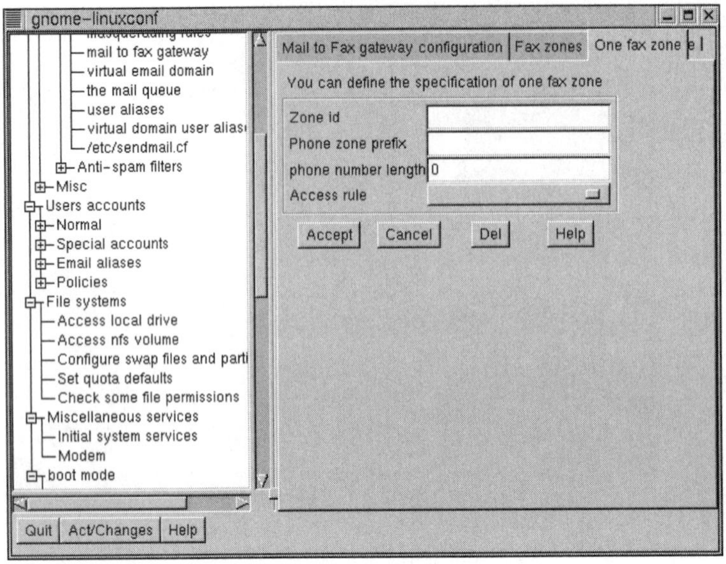

Figure 12.9 The Linuxconf One Fax Zone dialog box.

31. In the Access Rule drop-down list box, choose the rule that applies to this zone.
32. Click the Accept button to close the dialog box.
33. Click the Quit button to return to the Mail To Fax Gateway Configuration dialog box.
34. Click the Fax Aliases button to open the List Of Fax Aliases dialog box.
35. Click the Add button to open the Fax Alias dialog box, shown in Figure 12.10.
36. If you or your users intend to send faxes often to a certain person, then enter an alias email address for this person in the Alias text box. For example, if people often have to fax Jane Smith, then add jane.smith@fax.animals.org.
37. Enter this person's name in the Full Name text box. For example, Jane Smith. This name will be added to the To: field on the fax.
38. Enter the phone number to which faxes to this person should be sent to in the Phone Number text box.
39. Choose the appropriate access rule in the Access Rule drop-down list box.
40. Click the Accept button to close the dialog box.
41. Return to Step 35 for each commonly used recipient until you have all of your aliases in place.

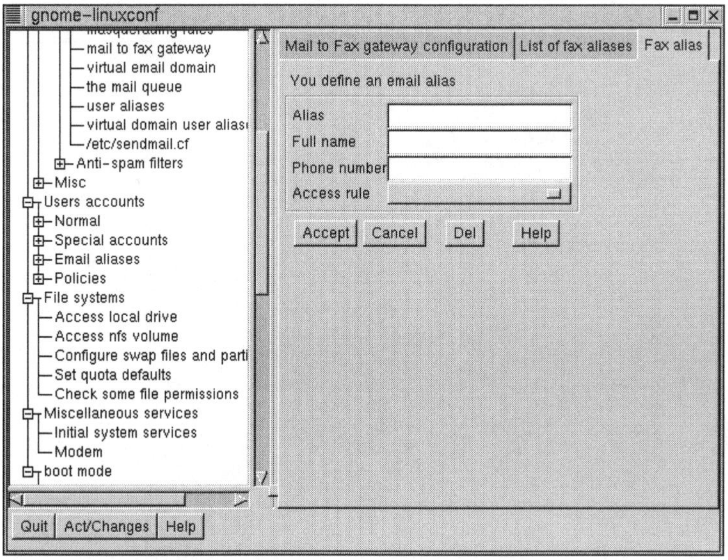

Figure 12.10 The Linuxconf Fax Alias dialog box.

42. Click the Quit button to return to the Mail To Fax Gateway Configuration dialog box.
43. Click the Quit button to close this dialog box. You will be asked whether you want to generate a new sendmail.cf file. If so, click Yes, and read any comments from Linuxconf carefully. Otherwise, click No, and remember to generate the new file later so that your changes are activated.

Configuring Virtual Email Service In Linuxconf

If you have virtual domains or services that you host on your site, you can use Linuxconf to set up email hosting for them by doing the following:

1. Enter GNOME as root.
2. Click the footprint icon to open the main menu.
3. Click System|Linuxconf to open the Linuxconf configuration tool.
4. Expand Config|Server Tasks|Mail Delivery System (Sendmail) and then expand the Basic section.
5. Click Virtual Email Domain to open the Virtual Email Domains dialog box.
6. Click the Add button to open the One Vdomain Definition dialog box, shown in Figure 12.11.
7. Enter the *domain.extension* for the virtual email domain you want to set up in the Virtual Domain (FQDN) text box.

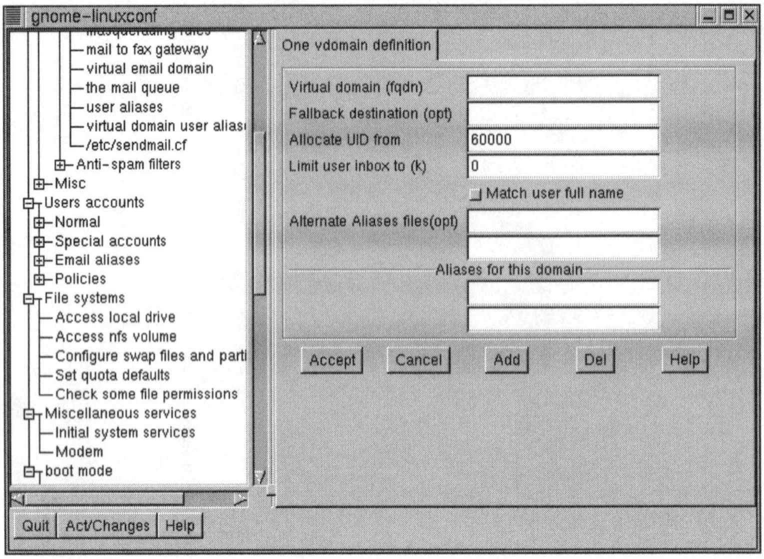

Figure 12.11 The Linuxconf One Vdomain Definition dialog box.

8. If you want to have a backup address for this domain or for specific people in it, then enter one of the following in the Fallback Destination (Opt) text box:
   - *Nothing*—If you leave the dialog box empty, mail sent to the virtual domain is rejected if the recipient does not exist.
   - *user@domain.extension*—You can direct all mail sent to an unknown recipient at this virtual domain to a specific user at a specific location.
   - *@domain.extension*—If all users on the virtual domain have identical login names to accounts on another domain, then you can point any mail arriving for the virtual domain with an unknown user to go to that user at the other domain.
   - *user*—You can direct all mail sent to an unknown recipient at the virtual domain to a specific user at the same domain.
9. In the Allocate UID From text box, enter the UID number you want to start with for this virtual domain. This number depends on how many users you anticipate to have in your other domains. If the UIDs end up mingling in the end because you run over budget, it will not matter. It just makes things more awkward to manage.
10. If you want to assign a limit to how much mail a user at the virtual domain can keep in their In mailbox, change the 0 in the Limit User Inbox To (K) text box. Enter the size, in bytes, that you want to limit it to. Leaving the value at 0 means there is no limit.

11. Linuxconf automatically creates the file /etc/vmail/aliases.*domain* to contain the alias information for this virtual domain. If you want to include pointers to one or two more alias files, you can do so in the two Alternate Aliases Files (Opt) text boxes.
12. If you want to point other domains to the same list of users you create for this virtual domain, then enter one or two more domains in the Aliases For This Domain text boxes.
13. Click Accept to close the One Vdomain Definition dialog box.
14. Click the Quit button to close this dialog box. You will be asked whether you want to generate a new sendmail.cf file. If so, click Yes, and read any comments from Linuxconf carefully. Otherwise, click No, and remember to generate the new file later so that your changes are activated.

Configuring Your Anti-Spam Settings Under Linuxconf

To set up your spam protection scheme in Linuxconf, do the following:

1. Enter GNOME as root.
2. Click the footprint icon to open the main menu.
3. Click System|Linuxconf to open the Linuxconf configuration tool.
4. Expand Config|Server Tasks|Mail Delivery System (Sendmail) and then expand the Anti-Spam Filters section.
5. Click Rejected Senders to open the Mail Rejected From dialog box.
6. Click the Add button to open the Rejected Message dialog box, shown in Figure 12.12.
7. Enter one of the following in the Email Origin text box:
   - *user@domain.extension*—The full offending email address. Spammers change these on a regular basis, so for general spam protection, this will not do you much good.
   - *domain.extension*—If you find that certain bogus domains out there seem to send only junk mail to your site, this is a good option. However, spammers can change these values as well.
   - *hostIP*—The full IP address for a machine that tends to be the origin of a lot of junk mail. This is reliable unless the spammer has a bank of IP addresses available.
   - *networkIP*—The full network address for a network that originates a lot of junk mail. It is much harder to obtain multiple network IPs. However, this is so wide-reaching that innocent senders may be screened out.
8. Enter the message that explains the bounce in the Error Message text box. For example, "Suspected spam."

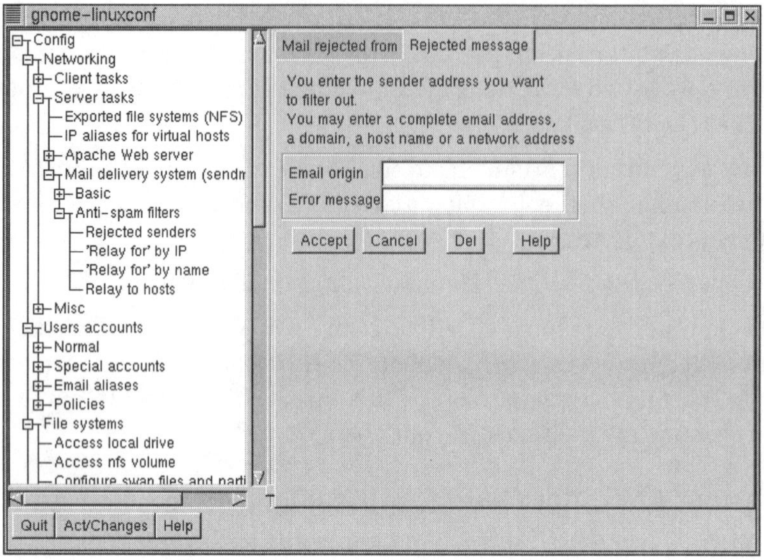

Figure 12.12 The Linuxconf Rejected Message dialog box.

9. Click Accept to close the Rejected Message dialog box.
10. If you need to add more rejection parameters, return to Step 6. Otherwise, click Quit to close the Mail Rejected From dialog box.
11. Click 'Relay For' By IP to open the May Relay Mail For dialog box.
12. Click Add to open the Allow This Host/Domain To Use Your Server (IP) dialog box.
13. In the Host IP Or Network text box, enter the IP address for the host or the network address for the machines that you want to allow to bounce mail off your mail server as though they were sending from their own site.
14. Click Accept to close the Allow This Host/Domain To Use Your Server (IP) dialog box.
15. Click Quit to close the May Relay Mail For dialog box.
16. Click 'Relay For' By Name to open the May Relay Mail For dialog box with the name focus.
17. Click Add to open the Allow This Host/Domain To Use Your Server dialog box.
18. In the Enter Host Or Domain Name text box, enter the *host.domain.extension* or the *domain.extension* of the machine you want to let bounce mail off your server.

19. Click Accept to close the Allow This Host/Domain To Use Your Server dialog box.
20. Click Quit to close the May Relay Mail For dialog box.
21. Click Relay To Hosts to open the May Relay Mail To dialog box.
22. Click the Add button to open the Relay To This Host/Network dialog box. The primary use for this option is to let your mail server know whom it is a gateway for.
23. Enter the hostname, IP address, or network address that this **sendmail** server acts as a gateway for.
24. Click Accept to close the Relay To This Host/Network dialog box.
25. Click Quit to close the May Relay Mail For dialog box.

Setting Up Mail Aliases By Hand

Mail aliases are a common tool for dealing with confusing email situations without having to create a number of different accounts. To create new mail aliases, do the following:

1. Log in as root on your mail server.
2. Type "vi /etc/aliases" to open the file you need to edit. A set of default entries is already there.
3. Type "G" to go to the end of the file.
4. Type "o" to open a new line for editing beneath the last line.
5. Press Enter to add a blank line.
6. Add a comment explaining what you are about to do. For example:

```
# Custom aliases added by superuser.
```

7. Add aliases in the following format:

```
original:      alias
```

For example:

```
john:    jon
alyce:   alice
rlt:     rich,rtl
```

__NOTE:__ A line may exist near or at the end of the main file, before you started adding, that is commented out and points all root mail somewhere. Uncomment the line and change the default location to where root's mail should go on your machine. This relieves you from needing to log in as the superuser more often than is absolutely necessary.

8. Continue adding until you are satisfied with the list. You can always come back and add more later.
9. Press the Esc key, and then type "ZZ" to save and close the file.
10. Type "newaliases" to load the changes into the alias database that **sendmail** creates from /etc/aliases.

Protecting Yourself From Spam

To set up spam protection for your mail server, do the following:

1. Log in as root on your mail server.
2. Locate your last macro file from the section "Configuring Your **sendmail** Server At The Command Line." If you used the macro file discussed in this chapter, it is /usr/lib/sendmail-cf/cf/redhat.mc.
3. Open the file in the **vi** editor.
4. Type "G" to go to the end of the file.
5. Type "o" to open a new line at the end of the file in Insert mode.
6. In many ways, protecting yourself from spam means learning how to open the doors to do what you need to do without letting people abuse your system in the meantime. Several features are available that you might consider adding, but it is imperative to understand the purpose and vulnerability of each. Table 12.12 outlines the ones you may want to implement or avoid. Some of these are already in the default MC file. Choose the features you want to implement.
7. Add the features you want to implement—if they are not already added by default—in the following format:

```
FEATURE('feature')
```

8. Press the Esc key to return to Command mode, and then type "ZZ" to save and close the file.
9. Go to "Building sendmail.cf At The Command Line" to build your new configuration file.

Table 12.12 Features that enable you to offer email services that may open you to spam.

Feature	Purpose	Problem	Reason To Consider
accept_unresolvable_domains	Tells **sendmail** to accept incoming email from domains that do not properly resolve when it does a DNS check.	If a spammer is using a fake domain, this feature lets them waltz right in and abuse your site.	You may be behind a firewall or have some other situation in which you do not have reliable access to DNS.
accept_unqualified_senders	Tells **sendmail** to accept incoming email from senders who have no *@domain.extension*, just a username.	If a spammer is using identity-spoofing software that tries to convince your system that the unqualified mail is from within, they will succeed with this option turned on.	You may have to turn this on if you are dealing with people on misconfigured systems and have no control over fixing them. However, rarely does a good reason exist to turn this feature on.
accessdb	Tells **sendmail** to check all incoming email against its access database to determine whether it comes from a person or location that is not allowed to send email to your site. If the email does come from a disallowed source, **sendmail** bounces the email.	You might reject email from innocents if you are not careful.	This enables you to prevent spammers from getting in the door, even if you have loosened your rules. Using the access database is recommended.
blacklist_recipients	Tells **sendmail** to check all incoming email against its access database to determine whether it is addressed to recipients that you do not allow to receive mail. If the email is so addressed, **sendmail** bounces the email.	Few concerns if you are careful about who you refuse to let have email.	You can block particular hosts and nonpeople from getting mail from spammers and cluttering mail spools.

(continued)

Table 12.12 Features that enable you to offer email services that may open you to *spam* (continued).

Feature	Purpose	Problem	Reason To Consider
rbl	Tells **sendmail** to go to **http://maps.vix.com** and access its blacklist database, and then add all of those entries to your **blacklist_recipients**.	Relies on an outside source to determine who is a spammer and who is not. You may block innocent people in the process, depending on how this service culls its database and how careful it is when building its rules.	If the service has a solid database, this method can save you a lot of spam hassles.
relay_based_on_MX	Tells **sendmail** to check MX records to determine whether it will relay mail. If **sendmail** finds its address listed in the incoming domain's MX records, it will relay.	Spammers can change their MX records at will.	Not recommended. Other, more reliable ways exist to allow relaying.
relay_entire_domain	Tells **sendmail** to allow relaying from any machine in your domain or in the domains you manage.	Spammers can spoof incoming mail addresses.	Makes email easier to manage for multiple domains.
relay_local_from	Tells **sendmail** to allow relaying for any mail with a return address pointing to a local machine.	Opens the doors wide for spammers. Anyone can set their return address to anything they please.	Too dangerous to activate.
relay_hosts_only	Tells **sendmail** to allow relaying for the main mail server at a domain but not for any of the hosts at that domain.	If the spammers figure it out, they may be able to spoof the right address.	Far more secure than **relay_local_from**.

Building A CW File

To build the proper contents for your /etc/sendmail.cw file, do the following:

1. Log in as root on your mail server.
2. Type "vi /etc/sendmail.cw" to open the file for editing.
3. Type "i" to enter Insert mode.
4. Enter the alternate names for your host, one name per line. For example, you might use the following for smtp.animals.org:

```
animals.org
mail.animals.org
pop.animals.org
stork.animals.org
```

5. Press the Esc key, and then type "ZZ" to save and close the file.
6. Type "/etc/rc.d/init.d/sendmail restart" to restart the mail daemon.

Building A Mailer Table

To build your mailer table database, do the following:

1. Log in as root on your mail server.
2. Type "vi /etc/mailertable" to open the file for editing. If you used a different file name, be sure to use the right one.
3. Type "i" to enter Insert mode.
4. Add your entries for the table in the following format:

```
procmail:domain
```

The domain value can be in one of the following formats:

```
domain.extension
.domain.extension
subdomain.domain.extension
```

5. When you are finished, press the Esc key, and then type "ZZ" to save and close the file.
6. Type "/etc/rc.d/init.d/sendmail restart" to restart the mail daemon.

Building A Virtual Addressing Table

To build your virtual addressing table, do the following:

1. Log in as root on your mail server.
2. Type "vi /etc/virtusertable" to open the file for editing.
3. Type "i" to enter Insert mode.
4. Add your entries to the table in this format:

   ```
   from:to
   ```

   The format for the ***from*** items must be an email address (*user@domain.extension*) or a wildcarded full domain (*@domain.extension*).
5. When you are finished, press the Esc key, and then type "ZZ" to save and close the file.
6. Type "/etc/rc.d/init.d/sendmail restart" to restart the mail daemon.

Building An Access Database

To build your access database, do the following:

1. Log in as root on your mail server.
2. Type "vi /etc/mail/access" to open the file for editing.
3. Type "i" to enter Insert mode.
4. Add your entries in this format:

   ```
   from     result
   ```

   The ***from*** portion has two different sets of formats:

   - For the **access_db** option, you might use *user@domain.extension*, *domain.extension*, or the network portion of an IP address—for example, 192.168.15.
   - For the **blacklist_recipients** option, you might use *user*, *host.domain.extension*, or *user@host.domain.extension*.

   The ***result*** portion can contain the items listed in Table 12.13.

Table 12.13 Results available in access.db.

Result	Purpose
### text	Rejects with an error response. The hash marks refer to a three-digit error code, and **text** is a response you include. The error code comes from RFC 821, which you can find at **www.faqs.org/rfcs/rfc821.html**. Search for the text "4.2.1. REPLY CODES BY FUNCTION GROUPS" to find the error code listing.
DISCARD	Tosses out any mail that matches this rule.
OK	Accepts this mail. Overrides any other rules that might reject it.
REJECT	Bounces the mail with a general error message.
RELAY	Allows relaying for mail matching these rules.

5. When you are finished, press the Esc key, and then type "ZZ" to save and close the file.
6. Type "/etc/rc.d/init.d/sendmail restart" to restart the mail daemon.

Removing Mail From The Queue Under Linuxconf

To alter your mail queue using Linuxconf, do the following:

1. Enter GNOME as root.
2. Click the footprint icon to open the main menu.
3. Click System|Linuxconf to open the Linuxconf configuration tool.
4. Expand Config|Server Tasks|Mail Delivery System (Sendmail) and then expand the Basic section.
5. Click The Mail Queue to open the Mail Queue dialog box, shown in Figure 12.13.
6. Click an entry in the dialog box to view its contents. You do not actually see the body of the email here. Instead, you see its size, its queue status, the sender, and the date it was sent. This is a good way to see if something got stuck in the queue.
7. To remove this entry from the queue, click the Del button in the entry's dialog box. Otherwise, click Cancel.
8. Click Quit to close the Mail Queue dialog box.

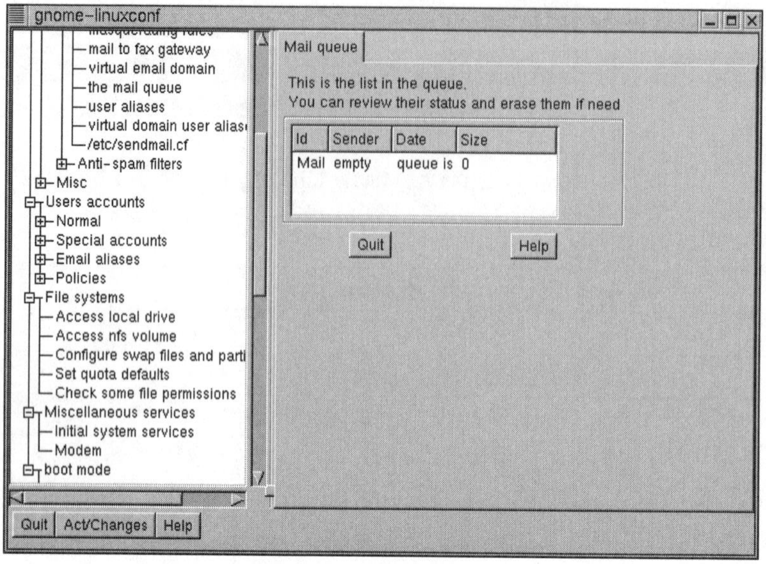

Figure 12.13 The Linuxconf Mail Queue dialog box.

Configuring **procmail**

To configure **procmail** as a local mailer, do the following on each machine for which you want to use **procmail** for local mail handling:

1. Log in as root.
2. Type "vi /etc/procmailrc" to create and open the **procmail** configuration file for editing.

NOTE: *This is the master **procmail** configuration file. Users can override its features for their own configuration in the ~/.procmailrc file.*

3. Type "i" to enter Insert mode.
4. Although you can mix and match all the pieces in a **procmailrc** file if you want to, this example uses a set order to keep things clear. Many environment variables are available that you can set to your requirements. Choose the mail-specific environment variables you want to change, listed in Table 12.14.

TIP: *To see what the values for any environment variables are set to, type "echo $VARIABLE".*

5. Choose the logging-related environment variables you want to change. These variables are listed in Table 12.15.

Table 12.14 The mail-specific environment variables available in /etc/procmailrc.

Variable	Definition	Default
DEFAULT	Identifies the default mailbox file for incoming mail.	**$ORGMAIL**
MAILDIR	Identifies the base directory from **procmail**'s point of view.	**$HOME/**
MSGPREFIX	Identifies an extension to add to the beginning of a file that is not being placed in a mail handler folder.	**msg**
NORESRETRY	Specifies the number of delivery retries to attempt every **$SUSPEND** seconds if the system is too overloaded to deliver a message. A negative number tells **procmail** to try indefinitely.	**4**
ORGMAIL	Identifies a mailbox to default to if **procmail** cannot properly deliver a piece of mail.	**/var/spool/mail/$LOGNAME**

Table 12.15 The logging-specific environment variables available in /etc/procmailrc.

Variable	Definition	Default
LOG	Stores a string of text that can be inserted into $LOGFILE when required.	Empty
LOGABSTRACT	Specifies whether to save basic, delivery-related information for every message **procmail** needs to process. Can be **no** or **all**.	**no**
LOGFILE	Indicates where to keep a copy of all diagnostic messages or error messages.	None kept

6. Choose the lockfile-related environment variables that you want to change. These variables are listed in Table 12.16.
7. Choose from the remaining environment variables that are not easily categorized. These are listed in Table 12.17.
8. Enter a line for each variable you want to change, in this format:

```
VARIABLE=value
```

TIP: *The values of some of these variables depend on others. Be sure that you enter them in an order that enables these values to propagate down through the list.*

Table 12.16 The lockfile-related variables available in /etc/procmailrc.

Variable	Definition	Default
LOCKEXT	Specifies the extension to use on local lock files.	**.lock**
LOCKFILE	Specifies a global file to use so that **procmail** cannot process more than one item at a time. Using local lock files instead is recommended.	None
LOCKSLEEP	Indicates how many seconds **procmail** waits before checking whether a lock file is gone, so that it can process the next item.	**8**
LOCKTIMEOUT	Indicates how many seconds **procmail** lets a lock file sit before deciding that it is stale and there in error. The lock file is removed at this point. A value of **0** shuts this feature off.	**1024**

Table 12.17 The remaining environment variables available in /etc/procmailrc.

Variable	Definition	Default
HOST	Specifies the hostname assigned to this machine. You can make nested /etc/procmailrc pointers if you have multiple names for the machine.	Current hostname
INCLUDERC	Specifies the RC file to load at this location in /etc/procmailrc.	Path to file relative to this RC file's directory
SHELLFLAGS	Specifies flags to use when invoking a shell.	**-c**
SHELLMETAS	Identifies metacharacters that signal that **procmail** needs to send the current line to $SHELL for processing.	**&|<>~;?*[**
SUSPEND	Indicates how many seconds to wait before trying again if **procmail** is waiting on something.	**16**
TIMEOUT	Indicates how many seconds to wait before terminating what may be a hung **procmail** child process. A value of **0** shuts this feature off.	**960**
UMASK	Specifies the **umask** to use when **procmail** creates files.	**077**
VERBOSE	Produces additional diagnostic data. Possible values are **yes** or **on** to use this feature, or **no** or **off** to not use it.	**no**

9. Now you need to build the delivery recipes you want to use. A recipe is in the following format:

```
:# flags
condition1
```

```
condition2
...
conditionN
action
```

To start your first recipe, type ":0 ".

10. Select the flags—if any—for this recipe from Table 12.18.
11. Add your flags to the format. For example, if you decide to use the **D** flag, then, so far, you might have the following:

```
:0 D
```

12. You do not have to have any conditions. This example assumes that you want to build on here, for the sake of teaching you how. A condition needs to start with one of the symbols listed in Table 12.19. Choose the starter that you want to use.

Table 12.18 Flags available for procmailrc recipes.

Flag	Purpose
a	Specifies to use this recipe only if it matches and if the last one above it without an **A** or **a** flag matched and was successfully executed.
A	Specifies to use this recipe only if it matches and if the last one above it without an **A** or **a** flag matched.
b	Feeds body information to the specified pipe, mail, or file. Default.
B	Runs the **egrep** command on the message body.
c	Makes a carbon copy of this mail. Used for delivery recipes.
D	Sets **egrep** to pay attention to case. It does not do this by default.
e	Specifies to use this recipe only if the previous recipe's action failed with an error.
E	Specifies to use this recipe only if the previous one did not match. Do not match any recipes right after this with an **E** flag.
f	Treats the pipe like a filter.
h	Feeds header information to the specified pipe, mail, or file. Default.
H	Runs the **egrep** command on the message header. Default.
i	Ignores write errors.
w	Makes sure the filter or program analyzing the information finishes without an error.
W	Makes sure the filter or program analyzing the information finishes without an error, but suppresses any error messages.

Table 12.19 Condition line starters in procmailrc recipes.

Starter	Purpose
*	Uses standard **egrep** regular expressions.
!	Inverts this condition.
$	Uses bash shell command-substitution rules to evaluate the rest of the condition.
?	Utilizes the exit code of the last program run.
<	Checks to see if the mail length matches its size delimiter.
>	Checks to see if the mail length matches its size delimiter.

13. Add the starter. To use the standard format, you would now have, in total, the following:

```
:0 D
*
```

14. Build the regular expression you want to deal with. Many metacharacters are available to you, as listed in Table 12.20.

Table 12.20 Metacharacters available for building procmailrc recipe regular expressions.

Metacharacter	Represents
^	Beginning of line. Also can match a newline.
$	End of line. Also can match a newline.
.	All characters except a newline.
*	When added after a character, any sequence of zero or more of that character. When added after a parenthetical phrase, any sequence of zero or more of that entire phrase.
+	When added after a character, any sequence of one or more of that character.
?	When added after a character, any sequence of zero or one of that character.
|	When placed between two sequences of characters, interpret as "either/or".
-	When placed between two characters, includes all characters between those listed, inclusive of those characters.
[ ]	Anything but the characters inside the brackets.
\	Escape the following metacharacter so it shows as a regular character.

For example, to search for any header that contains the domain "spammers.org" as your only condition statement, your entire phrase might be as follows:

```
:0 D
* spammers\.org
```

15. Add as many condition statements as you need.
16. Choose what starts your single action line. An action line can start with one of the items listed in Table 12.21.

    To deliver mail that matches this rule to a specific directory, you now have the following:

```
:0 D
* spammers\.org
!
```

17. Fill in the action itself. In the case of the example, I want the mail to go to /dev/null, which means it gets thrown out:

```
:0 D
* spammers\.org
! /dev/null
```

18. Finish adding any remaining recipes.
19. Press the Esc key, and type "ZZ" to save and close the file.

Table 12.21 Action line starters available in procmailrc recipes.

Starter	Purpose
!	Indicates to forward this mail to the following email addresses.
|	Indicates to start the specified program.
mailbox	Specifies the name of the mailbox to deliver this item to.

Chapter 13

The Apache Web Server

If you need an immediate solution to:	*See page:*
Installing Apache	439
Configuring Apache	439
Configuring Apache Access	440
Configuring **httpd**	443
Setting Up Virtual Web Service	446
Configuring What Web Browsers See	448
Customizing Your Logs	451
Setting Up .htaccess	452

In Depth

Web browsing is second only to email among popular uses of the Internet. Setting up a Web site may actually have been your first motivator for becoming a systems administrator. Many reasons exist to put up a Web site, but most of them are not very tolerant of downtime or servers that cannot support needed features. This is why the Apache Web server is so popular. Not only is it free—a major selling point—it is also robust and feature-rich. This chapter addresses setting up this server to suit your needs and the needs of any Web hosting clients you might have.

Introduction To Apache

The Apache Web server grew out of the National Center for Supercomputing Applications (NCSA) Web server, **httpd**. In the grand tradition of how open source programs evolve, some people decided that they wanted more features on top of the original **httpd**. These features began as a patch here, and a patch there, each applied to the original daemon for an individual's personal use. After a while, these patches were all combined together. The joke was that this was "a patchy" Web server. Hence, "Apache" was born in late 1995.

Apache Features

The Apache Web server has numerous features available. The features discussed here are those that come with the Apache version installed with Red Hat Linux 6.2. For a fully up-to-date version of Apache, see its Web site at **www.apache.org/httpd.html**. Features available at this time are the following:

- *Caching proxy server*—If you have part of your domain behind a firewall or a veil of IP masquerading, you often need to use a Web proxy server. Apache includes a module for this service.
- *CGI*—Almost all modern Web servers support CGI scripting. Apache is no exception.
- *Cookies*—Although some people still debate over whether cookies are an invasion of privacy, they seem to be here to stay. Regardless, this tool certainly has many ethical uses.
- *DSO*—Dynamic Shared Object support allows modules to be loaded and unloaded on the fly, in a similar manner to how the Linux kernel handles modules.

- *FastCGI*—The FastCGI module does not come with the Apache server. However, one is available at **www.fastcgi.com**.
- *Java*—If you have existing Java code, plan to include it in your sites, or have clients who want to be able to use it, you are in luck. Java users may be interested in Jakarta, which is an open source Java server solution project, at **http://jakarta.apache.org**. Also of interest is the Java Apache Project, at **http://java.apache.org**.
- *mSQL authentication*—If you want to database authentication information with mSQL, Apache can work with this.
- *PHP*—Apache supports the PHP server-side scripting language. See **www.php.net** for more information about this tool and its capabilities.
- *Password authentication*—If you need to require logins for any of your Web pages or sites, Apache supports this feature.
- *Perl*—The Perl programming language (covered in Chapter 21) is supported by the Apache Web server. For more on this issue, see **http://perl.apache.org**.
- *SSI*—Apache is capable of utilizing server-side includes as well as extended server-side includes (xSSI).
- *SSL*—Secure Sockets Layer implementations are encryption applications, and so the United States and some other governments consider them munitions. For this reason, SSL support is not included in the main Apache distribution. Go to **www.apache.org/related_projects.html** for a list of who provides Apache SSL support, and pointers to numerous other Apache-based projects.
- *URL rewriting*—If you need to be able to manipulate incoming URLs and reroute them, you can do this in Apache.
- *Virtual hosting*—You can use Apache to virtually host as many Web sites as your operating system can handle. Fortunately, Linux is robust enough to handle high Web loads. If you do run into trouble with slow Web service, consider adding more RAM to your server.
- *XML*—A special Apache project team is devoted to the Extensible Markup Language (XML). Go to **http://xml.apache.org** to learn more about Apache XML solutions.

Modules

Many Apache features are implemented with *modules*. This is a common feature of modern software applications. A modular program tends to have a central core that contains everything necessary to run the main program. The modules themselves each contain a specific feature or group of features. If you want to use a feature contained within this module, you add it to the core program.

A modular build strategy takes care of the problem of programs that can do anything but that also slow down your machines because the software itself takes up your entire RAM. This is referred to sometimes as *feature creep*. See the section "Configuring **httpd**" for information on how to insert a feature module into your server.

The Configuration File

At one time, three files were used to configure the Apache Web server: access.conf, httpd.conf, and srm.conf. Each of these files controlled a specific aspect of the server or its functionality. The file access.conf offered security control. You could use this file to turn on or off server capabilities, or specify who was allowed to access particular sections of your Web service. If you were running an Internet Web server and an intranet Web server on the same machine, you needed to spend some time properly configuring this file.

The httpd.conf file controlled **httpd** itself. Here was where you chose what modules—pieces of functionality—the server loaded, what it logged, and many other aspects of **httpd**. Finally, srm.conf kept track of where all the pieces needed by the server were. Everything from server components to Web page locations were set in there.

NOTE: *A standard Apache installation places these items in /usr/local/, but Red Hat's installation puts them in /etc/httpd/conf/.*

Beginning with Apache version 1.3—provided as an update RPM for Red Hat 6.1 and included by default with Red Hat 6.2—all of the configuration information is now in httpd.conf. The other two files still exist, but only contain pointers to the main file. Whenever you read documentation that refers to access.conf or srm.conf, you are looking at documentation for Apache versions 1.2 and earlier.

The Apache access file enables you to set various facets of your Web server's security. This file begins with a set of descriptive comments and then goes to the following:

```
ServerType standalone
```

NOTE: *I am deleting long sections of commentary from the code wherever they appear, because these descriptions are more useful in the file itself than displayed in this book.*

The **ServerType** declaration sets whether Apache runs its own **httpd** instance or lets **inetd** handle the incoming requests. Using **standalone** runs a separate daemon, whereas using **inetd** goes through the superdaemon instead. The next directive is also server-related; it tells **httpd** where to find its configuration, error, and sometimes log files:

```
ServerRoot /etc/httpd
```

Think of the **ServerRoot** directive as pointing to most of the information the server needs except for the Web pages themselves. After the server settings comes:

```
LockFile /var/lock/httpd.lock
```

The **LockFile** directive sets the default path to the lock file used to prevent child processes from trying to handle incoming requests that are already being dealt with by another process. After this is another file location setting:

```
PidFile /var/run/httpd.pid
```

Apache keeps track of its own Process ID in a special file set by the **PidFile** directive. In this case, a specific path is set to the file. You can also use a relative path that starts in the **ServerRoot** designation.

Another special file is set by **ScoreBoardFile**. The Linux operating system needs a file to pass information between the parent server and its child processes. In this case, **ScoreBoardFile** is set with a full path:

```
ScoreBoardFile /var/run/httpd.scoreboard
```

The next two statements relate back to the previous Apache version's method of configuration:

```
#ResourceConfig conf/srm.conf
#AccessConfig conf/access.conf
```

NOTE: *The hash marks at the beginning of each line are what cause Apache to ignore this code, hence commenting it out.*

The **ResourceConfig** statement points to Apache directives that are read after the server parses httpd.conf. The **AccessConfig** statement contains more directives that would be read after the **ResourceConfig** file. This used to be the way Apache operated. Now, you start getting into settings that do not involve files, such as:

```
Timeout 300
KeepAlive On
MaxKeepAliveRequests 100
KeepAliveTimeout 15
```

These timeout-related directives are outlined in Table 13.1.

Table 13.1 Timeout- and other time-related directives available in /etc/httpd.conf.

Directive	Purpose	Values
KeepAlive	Enables or disables full connections.	**On** or **Off**
KeepAliveTimeout	Specifies how many seconds Apache waits between requests before closing a connection.	Number of seconds
MaxKeepAliveRequests	Specifies the maximum number of requests a client can make while holding a connection open.	Number of requests; a value of 0 makes this infinite
Timeout	Specifies how many seconds Apache waits until a follow-up to a request arrives before closing a connection.	Number of seconds

After the time-related directives come the process-related directives:

```
MinSpareServers 8
MaxSpareServers 20
StartServers 10
MaxClients 150
MaxRequestsPerChild 100
```

The items listed here are discussed further in Table 13.2.

The next two directives tell Apache where to listen for incoming connections:

```
#Listen 3000
#Listen 12.34.56.78:80
```

Table 13.2 The process-related directives available in /etc/httpd.conf.

Directive	Result
MaxClients	Specifies the maximum number of simultaneous HTTP requests this server will accept
MaxRequestsPerChild	Specifies how many requests a child server should handle before closing down
MaxSpareServers	Specifies the maximum number of idle child servers you want to keep waiting for additional HTTP requests
MinSpareServers	Specifies the minimum number of idle child servers you want to keep available for additional HTTP requests
StartServers	Specifies the number of child servers created when the machine or Apache first starts up

A **Listen** directive can refer to a port (1000), an IP address (192.168.10.1), or a specific port at a specific IP address (192.168.10.1:1000). This directive refers to additional places to listen, on top of the defaults already set. It does not supercede the defaults.

The next item is important to anyone who intends to do virtual hosting:

```
#BindAddress *
```

The **BindAddress** directive tells Apache where to listen for connection requests. You can tell it to listen on any of the following:

- *—All IP addresses assigned to interfaces on this machine
- **IPaddress**—A single IP address
- **.domain.extension**—Your domain name

Only one **BindAddress** directive can be included in /etc/httpd.conf.

Next is a long section containing instructions for each module that Apache loads when it starts. The **LoadModule** directive is fairly self-descriptive. It loads the listed module from the listed library into the Web server. The first four lines of the module loading section of /etc/httpd.conf are listed here:

```
#LoadModule mmap_static_module modules/mod_mmap_static.so
LoadModule env_module         modules/mod_env.so
LoadModule config_log_module  modules/mod_log_config.so
LoadModule agent_log_module   modules/mod_log_agent.so
```

Some of the listed modules are commented out, such as the first line in the previous snippet. Many Web administrators simply leave the modules as they are unless they need to add more functionality to the Web server. If you are very security-conscious and do not have a lot of people creating their own Web pages on your server—which usually broadens the types of modules you need to have loaded—then you may want to trim down this list.

Loading a module does not actually mean that it is activated in the server. Some modules must be in a particular order, because some are dependent on others. For this reason, the loading and activating are done separately. Apache actually has a default list that it activates if you do not give it specific instructions. The following line clears that default list so that you can repopulate it on your own:

```
ClearModuleList
```

After this happens, every module that you intend to use has to be activated in the proper order. This activation is accomplished with the **AddModule** directive. The following are the first four of these directives:

```
#AddModule mod_mmap_static.c
AddModule mod_env.c
AddModule mod_log_config.c
AddModule mod_log_agent.c
```

Once you finish with the modules, you reach:

```
#ExtendedStatus On
```


The **ExtendedStatus** directive is either **On** or **Off**. If you have the **status** module activated, you can utilize this directive to create Web server status reports on the fly whenever people go to a certain URL. After this comes the network port that **httpd** listens on when Apache is set to **standalone**:

```
Port 80
```

Next, you tell **httpd** which login name and group to run under. I highly recommend that you do not change this information! The **nobody** user and group is important for system security, because **httpd** runs SUID. This section contains the following:

```
User nobody
Group nobody
```

After this is where you set the contact information for the Web server administrator:

```
ServerAdmin root@localhost
```

Once you have the Web administrator's email set, you get to:

```
#ServerName localhost
```

The **ServerName** directive sets the host name for your Web server. This is a useful statement for when you have more than one name assigned to the server machine. Now you move on to setting where the server looks for files:

```
DocumentRoot /home/httpd/html
```

The **DocumentRoot** directive tells Apache where to look for the Web files. This is the Web server's root directory. Anyone who goes to **http://www.*domain.extension***

is actually looking at the contents of DocumentRoot. Next, you get into setting parameters for parts of the file system:

```
<Directory />
Options None
AllowOverride None
</Directory>
```

The **<Directory *path*>** tag is used to block off a section of the access configuration file that refers to a specific segment of your file system. Items within the tag are referred to as *directives*. In this case, the directives refer to the entire file system, because the root directory is specified.

The first directive in this section of code is the **Options** directive. This feature accepts the arguments listed in Table 13.3.

The second unknown is **AllowOverride**. The options available with this statement are listed in Table 13.4.

NOTE: *As you can see, a lot of features are available with Apache. For a full listing with explanations, see* ***www.apache.org/docs/mod/core.html***.

Table 13.3 Features available with the Options directive.

Feature	Result
All	Specifies to include all features listed in this table except **None** and **MultiViews**. Default setting.
ExecCGI	Specifies that CGI scripts can be run from this location.
FollowSymLinks	Specifies that Apache can follow symbolic links here, unless in a **Location** setting.
Includes	Specifies to allow SSIs here.
IncludesNOEXEC	Specifies to allow SSIs here but disable the **#exec** and **#include** CGI directives.
Indexes	Specifies that when following a URL to a directory where no default page exists, Apache should give a list of the directory's contents.
MultiViews	Specifies to activate the **MultiViews** feature. See the module mod_negotiation for more on **MultiViews** (**www.apache.org/docs/content-negotiation.html**).
None	Specifies that no features are activated.
SymLinksIfOwnerMatch	Specifies that Apache should follow symbolic links if the target is owned by the UID who created the link, unless inside a **Location** directive.

Table 13.4 Features available with the AllowOverride directive.

Feature	Result
All	Includes all features except **None**.
AuthConfig	Allows the family of authorization directives listed in Table 13.5.
FileInfo	Allows the family of document type directives listed in Table 13.6.
Indexes	Allows the directory indexing family of directives listed in Table 13.7.
Limit	Allows host access directives: **allow**, **deny**, and **order**.
Options	Allows directory feature directives: **Options** and **XBitHack**.
None	Disallows all features listed.

Table 13.5 The authorization family of directives.

Directive	Purpose
AuthDBMGroupFile	Sets the name of a DBM file containing group authentication data.
AuthDBMUserFile	Sets the name of a DBM file containing user authentication data.
AuthGroupFile	Sets the name of a text file containing group authentication data.
AuthName	Sets a name for a directory's authorization requirements so the end user has context when asked to log in.
AuthType	Sets the type of user authentication required for this directory.
AuthUserFile	Sets the name of a text file containing user authentication data.
require	Sets which users, once authenticated, can access the directory.

Table 13.6 The document type family of directives.

Directive	Purpose
AddEncoding	Sets certain file name extensions to specific encoding types.
AddHandler	Maps file extensions to the internal routine that knows how to work with them.
AddLanguage	Sets certain file name extensions to represent specific languages.
AddType	Sets certain file name extensions to specific content types.
DefaultType	Specifies the file type to assume when there is no extension.
ErrorDocument	Specifies error responses.
LanguagePriority	Sets a list of priorities for which language to display information in if multiple languages are available and the end user does not make a specific request.

Table 13.7 The indexing family of directives.

Directive	Purpose
AddDescription	Specifies a text string to include with the file name in an index list.
AddIcon	Specifies an icon to represent file extensions in an index list.
AddIconByEncoding	Specifies an icon to represent MIME encoding.
AddIconByType	Specifies an icon to represent a specific MIME encoding type.
DefaultIcon	Specifies the icon to use when no specific one is set.
DirectoryIndex	Provides a list, in order of preference, of the files to look for when an end user browses to a directory instead of to a specific file.
HeaderName	Specifies the file to list first in a directory.
IndexIgnore	Specifies files to not list when giving a directory index.
IndexOptions	Specifies a command that allows you to define what types of indexing commands you accept for this directory.
ReadmeName	Specifies a file to append at the end of index lists.

It is important not to change this code. This section follows the solid security tenet that shuts off all access initially, and then one by one decides what is allowed in.

After the first **<Directory>** tag is:

```
<Directory /home/httpd/html>
Options Indexes Includes FollowSymLinks
AllowOverride None
order allow,deny
allow from all
</Directory>
```

NOTE: *A lot of comments are inside this* ***<Directory>*** *statement in the file. I have pulled it together here without the comments so that you can see the overall flow.*

This section's **<Directory>** tag is used to define the behavior of the section of your file system containing the Web files. By default, this is /home/httpd/html. The default **Options** for this section allows URLs pointing to other directories within the Web base to show the contents of that directory, allows SSIs, and allows the server to follow symbolic links within the Web base.

After you set the override information, you come to the **order** directive. This is part of the **<Limit>** class of directives described later in the chapter in Table 13.9. Its purpose is to state explicitly which hosts are allowed to access this set of directories. The values available with **order** are listed in Table 13.8.

Table 13.8 Values available with the order directive.

Value	Result
allow,deny	Looks at all the **allow** directives, and then at the **deny** directives.
deny,allow	Looks at all the **deny** directives, and then at the **allow** directives.
mutual-failure	Only lets in hosts that explicitly are set as **allow**, with no overriding **deny** statements.

Now that the order is set, the access statements start. The **allow** and **deny** statements both work in the following format:

```
statement from where
```

The ***statement*** portion is either **allow** or **deny**. The ***where*** portion takes more thought. It can be in one of the following formats:

- **all**—Anyone matches this statement
- **.domain.extension**—Anyone from this domain matches this statement
- **IPaddress**—Anyone from this specific IP address matches this statement
- **partialIP**—Anyone from this network or network segment matches this statement

Once you set the parameters for the main Web directory, you come to the **UserDir** directive:

```
UserDir public_html
```

If you have a Web server set up for your site, you likely offer Web page space for your users. On a Linux box—and for most Unix flavors—people access a user's Web space with the format **http://www.*domain.extension*/~*user***. The **UserDir** directive sets which directory inside each user's directory is the base for that user's own Web space. A request going to the URL mentioned earlier would actually go to /home/*user*/public_html with the default **UserDir** setting. This file system space is configured with the following **<Directory>** tag:

```
#<Directory /home/*/public_html>
#  AllowOverride FileInfo AuthConfig Limit
#  Options MultiViews Indexes SymLinksIfOwnerMatch IncludesNoExec
#  <Limit GET POST OPTIONS PROPFIND>
#    Order allow,deny
#    Allow from all
#  </Limit>
#  <Limit PUT DELETE PATCH PROPPATCH MKCOL COPY MOVE LOCK UNLOCK>
#    Order deny,allow
```

```
#    Deny from all
#  </Limit>
#</Directory>
```

The first unknown in this set of code is using **<Limit>** in context. As you can see, **<Limit>** is actual a blocked statement like **<Directory>**. You create a **<Limit>** statement in the general format:

```
<Limit method method ... method>
  rule1
  ...
  ruleN
</Limit>
```

Table 13.8 introduced you to what rules you can have within a **<Limit>** directive. The methods, however, refer to various types of data that HTTP sends to a Web server. These methods are listed in Table 13.9.

Table 13.9 Methods the <Limit> statement is aware of in HTTP.

Method	Purpose
CONNECT	Used to communicate with proxy servers.
COPY	Used to manipulate URLs so that a site and its contents can be presented as being from one place instead of another.
DELETE	Used to remove a URL's contents.
GET	Used to load the contents of a URL.
LOCK	Used to prevent HTTP modes that cause changes from being used on a URL until the lock is released.
MOVE	A cut-and-paste version of the **COPY** method. Used to remove the original URL's contents and place them in a new location.
MKCOL	Used to send a number of HTTP commands at once, rather than one at a time.
OPTIONS	Used to request a list of possible communication methods involving a particular URL.
PATCH	Used to send the information necessary to update an older version of a URL's contents to a newer one.
POST	Used to send information within a URL that should be added to a Web page or site.
PROPFIND	Used to request all properties of a particular URL.
PROPPATCH	Used to update a URL's properties.
PUT	Used to send information to be added to a Web page or site. The information is attached, not embedded in the URL.
TRACE	Used similar to a **ping**. Sends a request to a server that travels there and then back to the client, with all of its travel information stored. Used for diagnostic purposes.
UNLOCK	Used to remove a lock.

After this **<Directory>** definition is:

```
DirectoryIndex index.html index.shtml index.cgi
```

The **DirectoryIndex** directive sets a list of default directory home page types. When someone ends a URL in a directory instead of a file—for example, **http://www.*domain.extension***—Apache looks at the contents of **DirectoryIndex** and looks in this directory for each of the listed items in turn. If it finds one, it displays that page. Otherwise, it returns a "File Not Found" error.

Next is some security information:

```
AccessFileName .htaccess
```


The **AccessFileName** directive lets you specify which file contains information regarding who is allowed to view information from this directory. You can include more than one file name if you wish, if you find that people want to use a variety of file names and types. Apache will look for each in the order they are listed.

After this is another block-style statement:

```
<Files ~ "^\.ht">
  Order allow,deny
  Deny from all
</Files>
```

The **<Files>** directive is a method of access control. In the case of this specific code, the tilde (~) is used to tell Apache that you will be using a regular expression for the file name. The expression **^\.ht** breaks down to:

- The carat (^) refers to the beginning of the name.
- The period would refer to matching any character, but it is escaped with a slash, and so is taken literally as a period. So far the expression refers to a file name starting with a period.
- The **ht** is taken literally. Therefore, this expression looks for any file names beginning with ".ht".

The **<Files>** directive is used in the general format:

```
<Files name>
  rule1
  ...
  ruleN
</Files>
```

After the **<Files>** declaration is:

```
#CacheNegotiatedDocs
```

The **CacheNegotiatedDocs** directive allows a proxy server to cache documents that were chosen by the browser rather than the user. After this is:

```
UseCanonicalName on
```

The **UseCanonicalName** directive is used to determine what type of information the server uses to refer to itself. When Apache has to refer back to something else on its own site, you have to have this item turned on if you want it to use the value in the **ServerName** directive when constructing these references.

The next directive starts a section on data types:


```
TypesConfig /etc/mime.types
```

TypesConfig tells Apache where to find the master list of MIME types within the ServerRoot hierarchy. After this, you set which MIME type to assume a document is if no extensions are provided:

```
DefaultType text/plain
```

Next is a new statement type:

```
<IfModule mod_mime_magic.c>
  <MIMEMagicFile share/magic
</IfModule>
```

The <**IfModule>** directive checks to see if the specified module is compiled into Apache or not. In this case, it looks for the mod_mime_magic module, which is capable of examining a file's contents and determining what MIME type the file consists of. In the overall statement, if the mod_mime_magic module is compiled in, then the **MIMEMagicFile** directive is used to activate the module. This action is necessary because having a module loaded does not mean Apache is actually using it.

Next is another new directive:

```
HostNameLookups off
```

The **HostNameLookups** directive tells the Web server whether or not to look up name information about the hosts that client requests come from. Possible values for this directive are listed in Table 13.10.

Table 13.10 Values available for the ***HostNameLookups*** *directive.*

Value	Result
double	Looks up the name information associated with the IP address, and then looks up the IP address registered to that name. If these addresses do not match, access is denied.
off	Does not look up name information.
on	Looks up name information.

After this is the following line:

```
ErrorLog logs/error_log
```

The **ErrorLog** directive defines where **httpd** errors are stored. You can use either a full path or a relative path, as was done in the previous code snippet. A relative path begins in the ServerRoot-set location. Continuing the log-related directives is the following:

```
LogLevel warn
```

This directive sets how much information is logged, according to the standard syslog levels discussed in the section "What To Log" in the In Depth portion of Chapter 9.

We now come to more log settings. Whereas before the file set where data was logged to and what types of data were logged, this section utilizes the **LogFormat** directive to specify particular items to log and what format to use:

```
LogFormat "%h %l %u %t \"%r\" %>s %b \"%{Referer}i\" \"%{User-Agent}i\""
 combined
LogFormat "%h %l %u %t \"%r\" %>s %b" common
LogFormat "%{Referer}i -> %U" referer
LogFormat "%{User-agent}i" agent
```

To follow the preceding lines, you need to understand the format that **LogFormat** is used in:

```
LogFormat format name
```

The ***format*** portion of a **LogFormat** statement has many potential arguments, which are listed in Table 13.11.

The ***name*** item in the preceding **LogFormat** statement refers to the name of the custom log you want this data to go to. Anything that you set to log in custom

Table 13.11 Output statements available in the LogFormat directive.

Type	Result
%a	Identifies the IP address the request originated at.
%A	Identifies the IP address the request came to.
%B	Identifies the number of bytes sent, not including HTTP headers.
${*argument*}e	Identifies the contents of the listed environment variable.
%f	Identifies the name of the file.
%h	Identifies the name of the host the request came from.
%H	Identifies the protocol used in the request.
%{*argument*}i	Identifies the contents of the header line specified that was sent to the server.
%l	Identifies the remote login name if supplied by **identd**.
%m	Identifies the request method used.
%{*argument*}n	Identifies the contents of the specified note from another module.
%{*argument*}o	Identifies the contents of the specified header line that was sent in the reply from the server.
%p	Identifies the canonical port used by the server answering the request.
%P	Identifies the PID of the child process answering the request.
%r	Identifies the first line of the request.
%s	Identifies the status of the original request, after it is internally redirected.
%t	Specifies the time in **strftime** format.
%{*format*}t	Specifies the time in the listed ***format***. See the Immediate Solutions section "Customizing Your Logs" for more information.
%T	Specifies how many seconds it took to serve the request.
%u	Identifies the remote user.
%U	Identifies the URL requested.
%v	Identifies the canonical server name used for the server handling the request.
%V	Identifies the server name set by **UseCanonicalName**.

formats using the **LogFormat** directive is sent to a single log file if you leave the **CustomLog** directives in the following format:

```
CustomLog logs/access_log common
#CustomLog logs/referer_log referer
#CustomLog logs/agent_log agent
#CustomLog logs/access_log combined
```

NOTE: *Type "man strftime" to get the long list of time formatting options available to you.*

After the logging section is:

```
ServerSignature On
```

The **ServerSignature** directive tells Apache to place a footer at the bottom of all files it serves. Next is:

```
Alias /doc /usr/doc
```

The **Alias** command enables you to create an alias inside the Web hierarchy pointing to files that are not in that hierarchy. In this case, when the user tries to go to **http://www.*domain.extension*/doc**, they see the contents of /usr/doc.

NOTE: *An **Alias** directive location always has to begin with a slash, and any directory has to end in a slash.*

Now, Apache is told how to handle its base icon hierarchy:

```
<Directory "/home/httpd/icons">
  Options Indexes MultiViews
  AllowOverride None
  Order allow,deny
  Allow from all
</Directory>
```

Nothing new is introduced here. Next is the **ScriptAlias** directive:

```
ScriptAlias /cgi-bin/ /home/httpd/cgi-bin/
```

You use it in the same format as the **Alias** directive. These two directives differ in that **ScriptAlias** allows you to specify a location for where you store particular types of scripts. In this case, the directive tells Apache where to go for its CGI scripts.

The following is the next section of the default access file:

```
<Directory /home/httpd/cgi-bin>
AllowOverride None
Options ExecCGI
</Directory>
```

Most Web administrators want control over which CGIs are run on their systems. This **<Directory>** section defines the central CGI directory base and what is allowed within it. The two directives applied in this directory should already look familiar. More information on **AllowOverride** is available in Table 13.4, and more on **Options** is available in Table 13.3, both of which appear earlier in the chapter.

Although this next section is commented out as part of an explanation, it is important, so I have it included here:

```
# Format: Redirect fakename url
```

The **Redirect** command enables you to tell a client automatically that a page has moved, and have that client request the new URL. I find the commented statement confusing, so here is my own version of it:

```
Redirect original_url new_url
```

Now the file sets how Apache handles directory and file indexing:

```
IndexOptions FancyIndexing
```

There are a number of options available with the **IndexOptions** directive. These options are outlined in Table 13.12.

Table 13.12 Values available for the IndexOptions directive in httpd.conf.

Option	Purpose	Example
DescriptionWidth	Specifies how wide the file description column should be, in characters. To size this column automatically, use an asterisk.	**DescriptionWidth=***
FancyIndexing	Specifies to enable index processing.	**FancyIndexing**
FoldersFirst	Specifies to list directories at the top of an index listing, and then the files.	**FoldersFirst**
IconHeight	Specifies how many pixels high a file icon should be.	**IconHeight=90**
IconsAreLinks	Specifies that the user can click on the type icon as well as the file name to access a file. **FancyIndexing** must be activated.	**IconsAreLinks**
IconWidth	Specifies how many pixels wide a file icon should be.	**IconWidth=100**
NameWidth	Specifies how many bytes wide the file name column should be. To size this column automatically, use an asterisk.	**NameWidth=***

(continued)

Table 13.12 Values available for the IndexOptions directive in httpd.conf (continued).

Option	Purpose	Example
ScanHTMLTitles	Specifies to pull the contents of the **<TITLE>** tag from any HTML files listed and use them as a file descriptor. **FancyIndexing** must be activated.	**ScanHTMLTitles**
SuppressColumnSorting	Specifies to not make the column heads in index listings clickable. This results in not being able to click on a column head to sort the contents in the reverse form. **FancyIndexing** must be activated.	**SuppressColumnSorting**
SuppressDescription	Specifies to not display file descriptions. **FancyIndexing** must be activated.	**SuppressDescription**
SuppressHTMLPreamble	Specifies to only include the contents of the **HeaderName** file, if used, at the beginning of an index listing instead of the file's header information as well.	**SuppressHTMLPreamble**
SuppressLastModified	Specifies to not display the last time a file was changed in an index listing. **FancyIndexing** must be activated.	**SuppressLastModified**
SuppressSize	Specifies to not display the file size in an index listing.	**SuppressSize**

Now we proceed to more icon statements:

```
AddIconByEncoding (CMP,/icons/compressed.gif) x-compress x-gzip
```

The **AddIconByEncoding** statement is used in the general format:

```
AddIconByEncoding icon MIME-encoding
```

The ***icon*** portion of this directive can be included in two different formats. First is a path directly to the icon, such as /icons/compressed.gif. The second option is the one just demonstrated, which is typically in this format:

```
(ALT,/path/icon)
```

In both cases, the ***path*** is a URL path. This means that it is relative to DocumentRoot, but you actually have to write it as an absolute URL, so it has to start with a slash. The ***ALT*** portion of the format refers to the HTML **ALT** item, which is often used in an **<IMG>** tag as a clue for text browsers.

The ***MIME-encoding*** portion represents the method used to wrap encoding or encryption around a file. This method is used so that the file can be transmitted more quickly and yet come out whole and understandable by the machine on the other end. The two encodings listed by default are the only two typically used on the Web today.

The following is the next directive set:

```
AddIconByType (TXT,/icons/text.gif) text/*
AddIconByType (IMG,/icons/image2.gif) image/*
AddIconByType (SND,/icons/sound2.gif) audio/*
AddIconByType (VID,/icons/movie.gif) video/*
```

AddIconByType is used in exactly the same format that **AddIconByEncoding** is. In this case, however, many more types are available than are listed here. The current list of all available MIME media types is provided by the Internet Assigned Numbers Authority (IANA) at **www.isi.edu/in-notes/iana/assignments/media-types/media-types**.

When you add by type, you are telling Apache to make a guess about the file type. If you want to state explicitly which icon to use for which file type, use the **AddIcon** directive. The first four **AddIcon** lines are shown here:

```
AddIcon /icons/binary.gif .bin .exe
AddIcon /icons/binhex.gif .hqx
AddIcon /icons/tar.gif .tar
AddIcon /icons/world2.gif .wrl .wrl.gz .vrml .vrm .iv
```

An **AddIcon** directive is used in this format:

```
AddIcon icon ext
```

The ***icon*** portion of the directive is the path—written in an absolute format but really relative to DocumentRoot—to the icon you are assigning. To tell Apache to use this icon to show particular kinds of files, place a space-separated list of extensions in the ***ext*** portion.

Even the most experienced Web administrator cannot anticipate every file extension that users or clients may include on their Web sites. The **DefaultIcon** directive allows you to ensure that at least some kind of icon is used for unknowns:

```
DefaultIcon /icons/unknown.gif
```

Next is more icon indexing information:

```
#AddDescription "GZIP compressed document" .gz
#AddDescription "tar archive" .tar
#AddDescription "GZIP compressed tar archive"  .tgz
```

The **AddDescription** directive assigns text strings to describe the format a file is stored in. It is yet another of the **FancyIndexing** directive's suboptions. Now to a different pair of index listing details. You can use the **HeaderName** directive to tell Apache which file name—if it exists—to insert at the top of the list, and use **ReadmeName** to lay out which file name to have at the bottom. By default, these are set to the following:

```
ReadmeName README
HeaderName HEADER
```


Next is:

```
IndexIgnore .??* *~ *# HEADER* README* RCS
```

The **IndexIgnore** directive is used to tell Apache which items in your directories not to display in a file listing. An entry for this directive can be in one of the following formats:

- A file extension. For example, .bak.
- A partial file name with wildcards. For example, Index??.
- A full file name. For example, personal.txt.

Some Web browsers can actually uncompress information as they load it. Only some versions of Mosaic (**www.ncsa.uiuc.edu/SDG/Software/Mosaic/NCSAMosaicHome.html**) support this feature today, but hopefully more will in the future. The **AddEncoding** directive automatically compresses information sent to the browsers that are able to manipulate this. The default settings for **AddEncoding** are the following:

```
AddEncoding x-compress Z
AddEncoding x-gzip gz
```

The **AddLanguage** directive allows you to set what extensions are added to the end of documents in particular languages. This feature is of immense help for those who set up multilingual sites. You use this directive in the following format:

```
AddLanguage language_code .extension
```

The following are the Apache defaults:

```
AddLanguage en .en
AddLanguage fr .fr
AddLanguage de .de
AddLanguage da .da
AddLanguage el .el
AddLanguage it .it
```

You can also set which languages are more often requested than others—from most to least popular—with a line similar to this:

```
LanguagePriority en fr de
```

After this is:

```
<IfModule mod_php3.c>
  AddType application/x-httpd-php3 .php3
  AddType application/x-httpd-php3-source .phps
</IfModule>
```


You are already familiar with **<IfModule>** statements at this point. The **AddType** directive is briefly explained in Table 13.6. **AddType** assigns MIME file types to particular file extensions. So, in this statement, if the php3—a scripting language you can embed into HTML code, the Hypertext Preprocessor—module is loaded and active, MIME types are defined for both the .php3 extension and the .phps (PHP3 source) extension.

You use **AddType** in this format:

```
AddType MIME-encoding-type extension
```

The next PHP-related statement is:

```
<IfModule mod_php.c>
  AddType application/x-httpd-php .phtml
</IfModule>
```

This module is the older PHP implementation. If you have it loaded and active, then a new MIME type is assigned. Apache will recognize .phtml files as being PHP.

After this is a series of commented-out **AddType** and **AddHandler** directives, which were covered briefly earlier in Table 13.6. **AddHandler** enables you to tell Apache to run certain programs (handlers) when it encounters particular extensions. This directive is used in the following format:

```
AddHandler program extension
```

Another directive that allows you to specify what happens at specific times is **Action**. This directive is used in this format:

```
Action type script
```

The ***type*** is either a handler or a MIME content type; the ***script*** is the CGI script to run when you run across this type.

Now you come to the **Meta** class of directives. The two **Meta** directives commented out are these:

- **MetaDir**—The directory containing your collection of metafiles
- **MetaSuffix**—The suffix you use for your metafiles

Next is a section of commented-out items devoted to the **ErrorDocument** directive. You use this directive in this format:

```
ErrorDocument code message
```

The ***code*** is an error number you assign. For the ***message***, you have multiple options:

- A URL pointing to an external error page
- A URL pointing to an internal error page
- An error message with a double quote in front of it, but no end quote

The following is the final section:

```
BrowserMatch "Mozilla/2" nokeepalive
BrowserMatch "MSIE 4\.0b2;" nokeepalive downgrade-1.0 force-response-1.0
BrowserMatch "RealPlayer 4\.0" force-response-1.0
BrowserMatch "Java/1\.0" force-response-1.0
BrowserMatch "JDK/1\.0" force-response-1.0
```

The **BrowserMatch** directive is used in the following format:

```
BrowserMatch expression variable
```

The ***expression***—written typically as a regular expression, or regexp—tries to match a particular browser brand or version, depending on what you are looking for. It then activates certain HTTP environment variables for browser compatibility purposes. The other element, ***variable***, refers to the name of a variable you want to have manipulated if the expression matches the browser type. See Table 13.13 for the formats you have available for ***variable***.

Table 13.13 Formats to use for BrowserMatch variable.

Format	Description
variable	The name of an Apache variable to activate.
!*variable*	The name of an Apache variable to deactivate.
variable=value	The value to assign to the listed Apache variable.

Now to another module:

```
<IfModule mod_per.c>
  Alias /perl/ /home/httpd/perl/
  <Location /perl>
    SetHandler perl-script
    PerlHandler Apache::Registry
    Options +ExecCGI
  </Location>
</IfModule>
```

This **<IfModule>** statement looks for the Perl module. If it is there, first it tells Apache through an **Alias** directive that whenever someone requests the /perl directory, rather than looking in DocumentRoot/perl, it should look to /home/httpd/perl. Then, a **Location** directive is used to define acceptable behaviors for the perl directory and its contents. There are two new directives here. The first is **SetHandler**, which forces all files in perl to be passed to the listed handler. In this case, that handler is **perl-script**. This handler is part of the Perl module.

Now that Apache knows that requests for files in perl are really requests for /home/httpd/perl, and that the contents of this directory are to be treated as Perl scripts, Apache needs to know what to do with a Perl script. This is where the **PerlHandler** statement comes in. Whenever Apache needs to run a Perl script, it goes to the Apache::Registry module, which contains a general handler that interprets Perl CGI scripts.

Now it is time to bring some more modules on board:

```
#LoadModule put_module     modules/mod_put.so
#AddModule mod_put.c
```

These are two more new directives. **LoadModule** reaches out into the file system and adds a module to Apache into the list of active modules. This directive is used in the format:

```
LoadModule module file
```

AddModule, on the other hand, adds a module to Apache without making it active. You use this one differently:

```
AddModule module
```

So, you would not typically uncomment both of these items. Either you would load it, or you would add it. Not both. The module mod_put is available from **http://hpwww.ec-lyon.fr/~vincent/apache/mod_put.tar.gz**, and is used to implement the HTTP **PUT** and **DELETE** methods described in Table 13.9.

After these items is an HTTP upload area definition:

```
#Alias /upload /tmp
#<Location /upload>
#  EnablePut On
#  AuthType Basic
#  AuthName Temporary
#  AuthUserFile /etc/httpd/conf/passwd
#  EnableDelete Off
#  umask 007
#  <Limit PUT>
#    require valid-user
#  </Limit>
#</Location>
```


This commented-out section first tells Apache that whenever an HTTP client asks for anything in DocumentRoot/upload, the server should turn to the contents of the /tmp directory. Then, a **<Location>** statement outlines what is allowed for DocumentRoot/upload.

There are a few new directives defined here. The first is **EnablePut**. This directive, as you might have guessed, makes the **PUT** HTTP method described in Table 13.9 available for use. **AuthType**, although not new, was not defined in context earlier. The **AuthType** directive sets the level of user authentication required to access a directory. This ensures that this section of code does not let random people have access to the DocumentRoot/upload directory. There are two values available for **AuthType**, but only **Basic** is currently implemented. This value requires clients to log in to use this section of your Web space.

Three other directives in this section are needed to fully implement the authentication scheme. The next item in the code, **AuthName**, is one of these. It assigns a distinctive string to this particular authorization rule, so when the user tries to access the protected URL they are given information to put the password request in context. In this case, the text "Temporary" will appear in the authentication dialog box. **AuthUserFile**, another directive needed here, sets the path to the file that contains the user and password information for this file system segment.

The last necessary directive to put user authentication into effect is **require**, which appears near the end of this statement. You can use **require** in one of the following manners:

- Explicitly list the users who can log in to this portion of the Web site with the syntax:

```
require user user1 user2 ... userN
```

- Explicitly list the groups who can log in to this portion of the Web site with the syntax:

```
require group group1 group2 ... groupN
```

- Allow any valid user into the directory with the syntax:

```
require valid-user
```

All of the users referred to here must exist in the file specified by the **AuthUserFile** directive.

The next directive in this statement is **EnableDelete**. As you might guess, this directive activates the **DELETE** HTTP method described in Table 13.9. Then there is the **umask**, which sets the default mask for new files in this directory to ------rwx. Finally, all ability to use **PUT** to add a file to the upload directory is limited to those who log in properly.

WARNING!* *Allowing people to upload files in this manner is basically a method of allowing FTP access. Consider the security implications carefully!

The next commented-out section is:

```
#<Location /server-status>
#SetHandler server-status
#order deny,allow
#deny from all
#allow from .your_domain.com
#</Location>
```

Whereas the **<Directory>** directive controls access according to an item's location in the file system, the **<Location>** directive controls access with URLs. These are relative URLs, not full paths, and so **/server-status** on a default Red Hat setup would be in /home/httpd/html/server-status. The first item listed under this directive is **SetHandler**, which insists that the specified location refers to a particular Apache module for a service. Default handlers are listed in Table 13.14.

Basically, if activated, this section allows anyone from within the domain or network you specify to get a Web server status update. The next **<Location>** directive is:

```
#<Location /server-info>
#  SetHandler server-info
#  Order deny,allow
#  Deny from all
#  Allow from .your_domain.com
#</Location>
```


When configured properly, this code allows clients you choose go to DocumentRoot/server-info to find out how your Apache server is configured. The problem is that if someone spoofs an allowed address they can find out how you have things set up, and then use that information to cause some damage.

After this set of comments is:

```
Alias /doc /usr/doc
<Location /doc>
  order deny,allow
  deny from all
  allow from localhost
  Options Indexes FollowSymLinks
</Location>
```

Table 13.14 Default handlers for the SetHandler directive.

Handler	Purpose
cgi-script	Runs this item as a CGI script
imap-file	Consults the imap rule file for how to deal with this image
send-as-is	Treats this item as an .asis file, sending it with no HTTP headers
server-info	Displays server configuration information
server-parsed	Looks for SSIs in this document
server-status	Gets a server status report
type-map	Consults the type map for information on this file's encoding, language, length, and other values

This section sets DocumentRoot/doc to really point to /usr/doc, and allows people on the Web server to view the contents of /usr/doc through a Web browser. Then comes the section:

```
#<Location /cgi-bin/phf*>
#deny from all
#ErrorDocument 403 http://phf.apache.org/phf_abuse_log.cgi
#</Location>
```

This includes another **<Location>** directive. In this case, it refers to anyone trying to reach DocumentRoot/cgi-bin/phf*. This actually refers to a script that used to have a bug in it. This section is meant to catch anyone trying to take advantage of this old bug, and make a log of the instance.

Now we reach the proxy section:

```
#<IfModule mod_proxy.c>
#  ProxyRequests On
#  <Directory proxy:*>
#    Order deny,allow
#    Deny from all
#    Allow from .your_domain.com
#  </Directory>
```


If you do not want to go to the trouble of using the Squid caching proxy server discussed in Chapter 14, you can activate Apache's own proxy module here. The **ProxyRequests** directive refers to whether the Apache proxy functions go into effect. These functions are required if you are using a proxying firewall, as discussed in Chapter 9. Along with activating proxying, you can enable the Via: HTTP header to help control how information flows through the proxies with:

```
#  ProxyVia On
```

Next are the caching-related directives:

```
#  CacheRoot /var/cache/httpd
#  CacheSize 5
#  CacheGcInterval 4
#  CacheMaxExpire 24
#  CacheLastModifiedFactor 0.1
#  CacheDefaultExpire 1
#  NoCache a_domain.com another_domain.edu joes.garage_sale.com
#</IfModule>
```

These directives are further explained in Table 13.15.

Table 13.15 The caching-related /etc/httpd.conf directives.

Directive	Purpose	Value
CacheDefaultExpire	Sets the default amount of time an item remains in the Apache cache before expiring.	Number of hours
CacheGcInterval	Specifies how often to check the cache to ensure that its size is not over the specified limits.	Number of hours, including partial hours expressed in decimal format
CacheLastModifiedFactor	Implements a formula that calculates how often an item should remain cached as a factor of how long ago it was last changed.	The decimal factor to multiply the last changed time against
CacheMaxExpire	Specifies the maximum amount of time an item remains cached without checking the server it came from for a more recent version.	Number of hours
CacheRoot	Specifies where to store Apache's cache.	Path to cache
CacheSize	Specifies how large you are willing to let the cache get before it needs to be cleaned out.	Size in K
NoCache	Identifies specific items not to cache.	Space-separated list of hosts, domains, and terms in items that should not be included in the cache

Finally, we reach virtual hosting. First there is:

```
#NameVirtualHost 12.34.56.78:80
#NameVirtualHost 12.34.56.78
```

The **NameVirtualHost** directive is typically used in the following format:

```
NameVirtualHost IPaddress:port
```

This directive is used to specify what interfaces and ports contain virtual Web servers. Once you have this set, you continue to:

```
#<VirtualHost ip.address.of.host.some-domain.com>
#   ServerAdmin webmaster@host.some-domain.com
#   DocumentRoot /www/docs/host.some_domain.com
#   ServerName host.some_domain.com
#   ErrorLog logs/host.some_domain.com-error_log
#   CustomLog logs/host.some_domain.com-access_log common
#</VirtualHost>
```

A **<VirtualHost>** statement is used to define a host and its behavior more clearly. You can actually build a long set of directives within this statement if you need to. What you see here is instead a typical minimal setup. None of the elements used here are new. And, finally:

```
#<VirtualHost default:*>
#</VirtualHost>
```

It is recommended to uncomment this section if you do virtual hosting. It ensures that any HTTP request coming in to an address that is not a virtual host gets sent to the main server.

Other Linux Web Servers

Apache is certainly not the only Web server available under Linux. Several solutions are available. Some are open source, some are proprietary, and some have their own license that you should become familiar with before deciding on using it. Some of the alternatives are free, and some are commercial, or have commercial features to them. If you are not sure whether you want to use Apache, and want to investigate your options, or you need functionality that Apache cannot provide, then see Table 13.16 for a list of what is available and where you can get more information.

Table 13.16 Web servers available for Linux.

Name	Home
AOLserver	**www.aolserver.com**
EmWeb	**www.agranat.com/emweb/solutions/**
GoAhead Web Server	**www.goahead.com/webserver/webserver.htm**
Hawkeye	**http://hawkeye.net**
iServer	**www.servertec.com/products/iws/iws.html**
Java Web Server	**http://java.sun.com**
RapidControl For Web	**www.rapidlogic.com/products/rc_web.html**

(continued)

Table 13.16 Web servers available for Linux **(continued).**

Name	Home
RomPager	**www.allegrosoft.com/rpproduct.html**
Roxen	**www.roxen.com/products/**
SpyGlass MicroServer	**www.spyglass.com/solutions/technologies/microserver/**
vqServer	**www.vqsoft.com**
Xitami	**www.xitami.com**
Zeus Web Server	**www.zeustech.net/products/zeus3/**

There are also Web server solutions available with a "small footprint," meaning that they do not take up much RAM. These primarily are of interest to network device developers, but you may find that you have use for them for some purposes.

Immediate Solutions

Installing Apache

To install the Apache Web server under Red Hat Linux, do the following:

1. Log in as root on the machine you want to use for your Web server.
2. Put the Red Hat CD-ROM in the CD-ROM drive.
3. Type “mount /mnt/cdrom” to add the CD-ROM to your file system.
4. Type “cd /mnt/cdrom/RedHat/RPMS” to change to the packages directory.
5. Type “rpm -ivh apache-1” and press Tab to complete the file name, and then press Enter to install the package.

Configuring Apache

To configure your Apache Web server, do the following:

1. Log in as root on the machine you want to use for your Web server.
2. Set up server access information as described in the following section, “Configuring Apache Access.”
3. Set up the server itself as described in the section “Configuring **httpd**,” later in this chapter.
4. Set up what users can see when they look through your Web directories, as described in the section “Configuring What Web Browsers See,” later in this chapter.
5. Type “/etc/rc.d/init.d/httpd restart” to restart Apache.

NOTE: *You may have to use a different restart method in non-Red Hat distributions.*

Configuring Apache Access

To do your initial access configuration, do the following:

1. Log in as root on the machine you want to use for your Web server.
2. Type "vi /etc/httpd/conf/httpd.conf".

NOTE: *If you are using the original Red Hat 6.1 release or earlier, you may find that this information is instead in the file access.conf.*

3. Type "/Directory" and press Enter. You first jump down to this line:

```
<Directory />
```

4. Type "/" and press Enter again to repeat the search. This takes you down to the following line:

```
<Directory /home/httpd/html>
```


5. If you do not intend to store your Web pages in /home/httpd/html, type "i" to enter Insert mode, and then edit the directory to point to what you intend to use for your Web server's base directory.
6. Move the cursor down to the next line:

```
Options Indexes Includes FollowSymLinks
```

7. If you want to change these **Options** and are not currently in Insert mode, type "i". Table 13.3 outlines what each of these features does, and the alternatives available to you.
8. Move the cursor down to the next line:

```
AllowOverride None
```

9. If you want to change the allowable overrides and are not currently in Insert mode, type "i". Table 13.3 outlines the alternatives to the **None** feature. However, consider whether you really want to let these families of settings be overridden by anyone else for your entire Web hierarchy.
10. If you are setting up an intranet with this server, and your Internet Web server is on another machine, move the cursor down to the next line:

```
order allow,deny
```

Then, change it to **order deny,allow** or **order mutual-failure**.

11. If you are setting up an intranet with this server, and your Internet Web server is on another machine, move the cursor down to the next line:

```
allow from all
```

    Then, change it to reflect who should have access. For example, for the entire class C network 192.168.22.0, you might use:

```
allow from 192.168.22.
```

12. Move your cursor down to the following line:

```
<Directory /home/httpd/cgi-bin>
```

13. If you plan to keep the CGIs used by this server in another location, type “i” to enter Insert mode, and then change /home/httpd/cgi-bin to the new location.
14. If you do not plan to allow anyone to use CGIs, comment out this entire section, which means changing it to look like the following:

```
#<Directory /home/httpd/cgi-bin>
#AllowOverride None
#Options ExecCGI
#</Directory>
```

    I highly recommend leaving this **AllowOverride** statement alone. Do not give people freedom with your CGIs unless you have a particular reason to. Change the **Options** statement if you want to, but still be careful here. Table 13.3 lists the alternatives.
15. Move the cursor down to the following line:

```
#<Location /server-status>
```

16. If you want to allow people to see the status of your server at any given time, uncomment this section by removing the hash marks from in front of it so that it looks like this:

```
<Location /server-status>
SetHandler server-status
order deny,allow
deny from all
allow from .your_domain.com
</Location>
```

17. Move your cursor down to the line beginning with **allow**.
18. Type "i" if you are not already in Insert mode.
19. Change **.your_domain.com** to your own ***.domain.extension***. Leave the leading dot there.
20. Change any other part of the section if you want to. Be careful about letting outsiders get access to any information about your Web server. It could be used against you.
21. Move your cursor down to the next section, beginning with this line:

```
Alias /doc /usr/doc
```

22. If you have no need to provide access to your Linux documentation through a central Web server, then comment out this section so that it looks like the following:

```
#Alias /doc /usr/doc
#<Directory /usr/doc>
#order deny,allow
#deny from all
#allow from localhost
#Options Indexes FollowSymLinks
#</Directory>
```

23. If you want to keep this section, decide whether you want to make any changes to it and then implement them.
24. Now, move down to the section beginning with this line:

```
#<Location /cgi-bin/phf*>
```

25. If you think that people are trying to break in to your machine or Web server, or you are curious to see whether they are trying, then uncomment this section so that it looks like this:

```
<Location /cgi-bin/phf*>
deny from all
ErrorDocument 403 http://phf.apache.org/phf_abuse_log.cgi
</Location>
```

26. Add any additional sections you may need to add.
27. Press the Esc key, and then type "ZZ" to save and close the file.

Configuring httpd

To do your initial access configuration, do the following:

1. Log in as root on the machine you want to use for your Web server.
2. Type "vi /etc/httpd/conf/httpd.conf".
3. Type "/ServerType" and press Enter to jump down to the following line:

```
ServerType standalone
```

4. If you have a specific reason to run this Web server through the superdaemon, then type "i" to enter Insert mode, and then change the line to this:

```
ServerType inetd
```

5. Move the cursor down to the following:

```
Port 80
```

6. If you set your **ServerType** to **inetd**, comment this line out by putting a hash mark in front of it.
7. If you have reason to run this server on a nonstandard port, then carefully choose a new port number and change "80" to the new value. See /etc/services for a list of which processes use which ports.
8. Move the cursor down to the following line:

```
HostNameLookups off
```

9. If you want to log the name information for which hosts are accessing your machine, type "i" to enter Insert mode (if you are not already in it) and change the line to this:

```
HostNameLookups on
```

10. If you want to log the name information for which hosts are accessing your machine, and also be extra cautious about security, type "i" to enter Insert mode (if you are not already in it) and change the line to

```
HostNameLookups double
```

11. Cursor down to the following line:

```
ServerAdmin root@localhost
```

12. Type "i" if you are not already in Insert mode, and change **root@localhost** to the contact email address you want to use as the server administrator. People often create a mail alias to something such as webadmin.
13. Now, go down to this line:

```
ServerRoot /etc/httpd
```

Change this value only if you plan to move the entire contents of /etc/httpd elsewhere.

14. Use the cursor to move down to:

```
#BindAddress *
```

15. If you intend to have virtual hosts set up, consider uncommenting this line.
16. Cursor down to:

```
ErrorLog logs/error_log
```

17. If you do not want your error logs saved to $ServerRoot/logs/error_log, change this line to reflect where the log should go.
18. Move down to the following line:

```
LogLevel warn
```

19. If you want to use a different logging level, change **warn** to one of the levels described in Chapter 9.
20. Cursor down to the section where the **LoadModule** statements begin.
21. Look through the main list. If you want to remove things you do not intend to use, then see **www.apache.org/docs/mod/** for a starting point. You can also use this as a research area for deciding which of the commented-out modules to uncomment.
22. Make sure that all the Apache features you need are represented here. If not, find the module that you require and add a statement at the end of the **LoadModules** section in the following format:

```
#Additional modules I needed to add.
LoadModule module_name directory/library_file.so
```

23. Move down to the list of **AddModule** commands.
24. If you uncommented any modules in the **LoadModule** section, or commented any out, make sure you do the same to the module's corresponding **AddModule** item.
25. If you added modules at the end of the **LoadModule** list, investigate where in the hierarchy they need to be activated, and add lines for them in this format:

```
AddModule module_name.c
```

26. See the upcoming section "Customizing Your Logs" for information on how to adjust your log files. If you want to do a lot of statistical analyses on the accesses to your site, then this is a good idea.
27. Move down to:

```
#LockFile /var/lock/httpd.lock
```

28. If ServerRoot is on an NFS-mounted partition from another machine, uncomment this line. Your lock file has to be on the local file system.
29. Continue down to:

```
#ServerName new.host.name
```

30. If your Web server's hostname is not set to **www**, you probably want to uncomment this line and change it to the following:

```
ServerName www.domain.extension
```

NOTE: *You also need to set up name resolution for the name you set here.*

31. Analyze the time- and process-related items, as outlined in Tables 13.1 and 13.2, to ensure that they fit your own situation. If not, alter them appropriately.

TIP: *Both of these directive types have reasonable defaults. Typically, it is best not to tweak them unless you notice load problems or response-time problems in the future. If this happens, take a look at the process-related values.*

32. Cursor down to:

```
#ProxyRequests On
```

33. If you are using a proxying firewall, uncomment this line. Otherwise, you don't need to activate this service.
34. Determine whether you want to use *caching*—which keeps copies of Web pages requested from other servers—to speed load time for your users. If so, uncomment each of the following statements and alter their settings to suit your needs:

```
#CacheRoot /var/cache/httpd
#CacheSize 5
#CacheGcInterval 4
#CacheMaxExpire 24
#CacheLastModifiedFactor 0.1
#CacheDefaultExpire 1
#NoCache a_domain.com another_domain.edu joes.garage_sale.com
```

35. If you want to set up virtual Web hosting, go to the next section "Setting Up Virtual Web Service."
36. Press the Esc key, and then type "ZZ" to save and close the file.

Related solutions:	Found on page:
Analyzing Logs	281
Setting Up A Proxy Firewall	289

Setting Up Virtual Web Service

To set up virtual Web hosting on your Apache server, do the following:

1. Log in as root on the machine you want to use for your Web server (if necessary).
2. Type "vi /etc/httpd/conf/httpd.conf" to open the file (if necessary).
3. Type "/VirtualHost" to jump down to the virtual hosting section of the file.
4. Use the cursor to move down to the following section:

```
#<VirtualHost host.some_domain.com>
#ServerAdmin webmaster@host.some_domain.com
#DocumentRoot /www/docs/host.some_domain.com
#ServerName host.some_domain.com
#ErrorLog logs/host.some_domain.com-error_log
#TransferLog logs/host.some_domain.com-access_log
#</VirtualHost>
```

5. Move the cursor down below the last line in this section.
6. Type “o” to open a new line in Insert mode below the current position.
7. Make sure there is a blank line between the end of the commented section and where you are going to add yours.
8. The first thing you need to do is add an entry for localhost. This entry begins with the following:

```
<VirtualHost 127.0.0.1>
```

9. Next, set the email account people can write to if they need to contact the Web administrator, which might be similar to the following:

```
ServerAdmin you@animals.org
```

10. Each Web server should have its own root directory. Set this as follows:

```
DocumentRoot /home/httpd/html/animals.org
```

11. Now, you need to define what this virtual host refers to. In the case of localhost, point it to the default Web service you want to use. This might mean something similar to the following:

```
ServerName www.animals.org
```

12. Set the transfer and error logs to use for this virtual server, and close the statement. You might use:

```
#ErrorLog logs/animals.org-error_log
#TransferLog logs/animals.org-access_log
```

13. Now, on to the real work. Create a **<Directory>** directive for this virtual host. The following might be appropriate at a basic level:

```
<Directory /home/httpd/html/animals.org>
Options ExecCGI Indexes Includes
</Directory>
```

    Keep in mind that you can make a **<VirtualHost>** directive just as complicated as the main /etc/httpd.conf file if you need to.

14. Finally, close the statement with:

```
</VirtualHost>
```

15. Now, you need to create a similar statement for each of your own virtual hosts. Follow the same pattern as you did with the localhost statement. Make these **<VirtualHost>** directives as complex or as simple as you need them to be.
16. If you are finished configuring your /etc/httpd.conf file, press the Esc key, and type "ZZ" to save and close it.

Configuring What Web Browsers See

To set up what Web clients can see when looking through your Web information, do the following:

1. Log in as root on the machine you want to use for your Web server.
2. Type "vi /etc/httpd/conf/httpd.conf".

NOTE: *If you are using the original Red Hat 6.1 or later, you may find that this information is instead in smb.conf.*

3. Use the cursor to move down to the following statement:

```
DocumentRoot /home/httpd/html
```

4. If you want to keep your Web files elsewhere, type "i" to enter Insert mode, and edit /home/httpd/html to indicate your preferred document base.
5. Cursor down to:

```
UserDir public_html
```

6. If you want user Web space to go into a different directory inside a user's home directory, change this value.
7. Move the cursor down to this line:

```
DirectoryIndex index.html index.shtml index.cgi
```

8. If you want to add other default base page items to this list, add them in the order that they should be sought.
9. Move down to:

```
FancyIndexing on
```

10. If you have no intention of allowing anyone to look at the files in a Web directory, then change this to **off**. Doing this disables many of the indexing features.
11. Cursor down to the three **AddIcon** sections: **AddIconByEncoding**, **AddIconByType**, and **AddIcon**.
12. If you want to highly customize how your Web server graphically shows directory index listings, carefully go through these three segments and either change what is there or change the default icons that the statements point to.
13. Move down to:

```
DefaultIcon /icons/unknown.gif
```

14. If you want to use a different icon for the default, then move it into the DirectoryRoot/icons directory and reference it here. Or, you can replace the original unknown.gif with your new image.
15. Use the cursor to move down to:

```
ReadmeName README
```

16. If you want the trailing file in index listings to be something other than README—perhaps you use ReadMe by default instead—change the line appropriately.
17. The next line is:

```
HeaderName HEADER
```

18. If you want the leading file in index listings to be something other than HEADER—perhaps you use Index instead—change the line appropriately.
19. Proceed to:

```
IndexIgnore .??* *~ *# HEADER* README* RCS
```

20. You can have more than one **IndexIgnore** statement if you want. Be sure that all the files you want to keep hidden are covered. Because the **HeaderName** and **ReadmeName** items are going to be listed anyway, be sure to change those values in the preceding line if you changed them in the earlier statements.
21. Move down to the following line:

```
AccessFileName .htaccess
```

22. Change the authentication file name if you want to. If you choose to use the .htaccess file to require user authentication to see files in a directory, see the upcoming section "Setting Up .htaccess" for instructions on how to do this.
23. At this point, most of the options remaining are not items the average Webmaster would want to change. The rest of this section skips down just to the items that you may want to use.
24. Type "/Redirect" to jump down to the section ending in this line:

```
# Format: Redirect fakename url
```

25. If you need to re-point any old URLs to a new location, press the Esc key to return to Command mode, cursor down to the blank line beneath this comment, type "o" to open a new line for editing beneath the current position, and then enter your redirection statement. For example, if an administrator moved **http://www.animals.org/cats.html** to **http://www.animals.org/cats/index.html**, he or she might enter the following:

```
Redirect /cats.html /cats/index.html
```

NOTE: *If you do not use the entire URL, Apache assumes the files are relative to DocumentRoot.*

---

26. Now move down to:

```
Alias /icons/ /home/httpd/icons/
```

27. If you need to create more aliases, do so beneath here. For example, if I wanted to add an alias that allowed users to access the file /root/AdminNotes in the main DocumentRoot directory, I might use this:

```
Alias /AdminNotes /root/AdminNotes
```

28. Move down until you find:

```
#Alias /perl/ /home/httpd/perl/
#<Location /perl>
#SetHandler perl-script
#PerlHandler Apache::Registry
#Options +ExecCGI
#</Location>
```

29. If you intend to allow Perl programs, uncomment this group of code and make sure it is accurate for your setup.

30. Type "ErrorDoc" to jump down to the **ErrorDocument** section.
31. Uncomment any samples you may want to use.
32. Add your own customized error responses if you have some.
33. After you are finished with this file, press the Esc key, and then type "ZZ" to save and close it.

Customizing Your Logs

To customize your log file output, do the following:

1. Log in as root on the machine you want to use for your Web server (if necessary).
2. Type "vi /etc/httpd/conf/httpd.conf" to open the file (if necessary).
3. Type "/LogFormat" and press Enter to jump down to the section you want to work with.
4. Cursor down to the last **LogFormat** statement.
5. Type "o" to open a new line to edit beneath the current one.
6. Cursor down to it.
7. Build your own **LogFormat** statement in the following format:

   ```
   LogFormat format name
   ```

   Refer back to Table 13.11 for the various ***format*** options. For example, I might build the following to log the IP address and name of the recipient and the URL they requested to the name "mine":

   ```
   LogFormat "%a %h %U" mine
   ```

8. Now, you have to tell Apache where to put the items you told it to specially log. Use the **CustomLog** directive for this. Using the preceding example, I might write the following to save my custom information to my_log:

   ```
   CustomLog logs/my_log mine
   ```

9. Continue adding the **LogFormat** and **CustomLog** pairs until you have your custom logs built.
10. When you are finished, press the Esc key, and then type "ZZ" to save and close the file.

Setting Up .htaccess

To set up who is allowed to browse a particular Web directory, do the following:

1. Log in as root if this is a DocumentRoot portion of the Web hierarchy, or from your user account if you want to do this for a personal section.
2. Use the **cd** command to change to the directory that you want to limit access to.
3. Type "vi .htaccess" in this directory to open your new access regulation file for editing.

NOTE: *This file regulates this directory and everything below it. If you want different rules for files lower in the hierarchy, you need to set them in those subdirectories.*

---

4. Type "i" to enter Insert mode.
5. Using the directives listed earlier in Table 13.5, build the file. For example, you might use the following to set access controls for /home/bart/members/:

```
AuthUserFile /home/bart/members/.htpasswd
AuthGroupFile /dev/null
AuthName Bart's Members Only Area
AuthType Basic
```

   This section sets the user password file for /home/bart/members to /home/bart/members/.htpasswd, and tells Apache that no group authentication file is needed. It assigns the name "Bart's Members Only Area" to appear on the password prompt so that people know what they are accessing, and then sets the authorization type to Basic—the only other type is Digest.
6. Press the Esc key, and then type "ZZ" to save and close the file.
7. You do not create the .htpasswd file by hand. Instead, type "htpasswd -c *user*" to create your .htpasswd file with the **htpasswd** command. For example, **htpasswd -c mary**.
8. The program asks you to input the password for this user twice, just as it would for adding a login account.
9. For any subsequent new users, type "htpasswd *user*". The **-c** flag used earlier created the file. You only need to use it once for that particular file.

Chapter 14

The Squid Internet Object Cache

If you need an immediate solution to:	*See page:*
Installing The Squid	458
Configuring The Squid	458
Setting Up Parent And Sibling Caches	466
Setting Up Web Server Acceleration	469
Setting Up Multicasting	470
Configuring A Client To Utilize Caching	470

In Depth

Some people prefer large tools that integrate many functions under one banner. Others like smaller, specialized tools that have their own niche functionality. There is a time and a place for both approaches. The Squid tool is a highly specialized server whose function is to cache data from a limited number of services for fast reuse. If you are a fan of specialized tools, then this service is probably for you. Even if you are not, take the time to learn what it can do before you make your decision.

Introduction To Web Caching

You can have your users browse the Web in two different ways. The first method involves their using Web clients—typically Netscape when Linux is involved—to request pages directly from remote Web servers. This is the direct method and what you are probably already used to.

The other way involves Web *caching*. Whenever a user wants to look at a Web page, rather than having their client go directly to the remote server, the client asks the caching server for the page. The server then looks to see if this page has already been downloaded. If it has, the page is stored in the server's *cache*, or data repository. The server checks to see if there is a newer version of the page available—at least, this happens in a sophisticated caching server such as Squid—and if not, passes the version it has to the client directly.

Providing Web service in this fashion can immensely increase page download times. The pages that do not need to be downloaded only have to pass from your caching server to the client. Downloads of pages that are not already cached are not slowed by having to compete for bandwidth with Web page downloads that users on your site look at regularly. To set up your clients to look to a caching server, see the Immediate Solutions section "Configuring A Client To Utilize Caching."

An Introduction To The Squid

The Squid serves two basic purposes. One of these functions is to provide proxy service for machines that must pass Internet traffic through some form of masquerading firewall. The other function is caching. Squid can cache Web, FTP, Gopher, and DNS data. If your users frequently need to access the same base of information, then having a specialized caching server on hand can noticeably cut down on your bandwidth use. Squid is especially useful if you are charged for traffic to and from the Internet. Instead of downloading pages repetitively, Squid quickly checks whether the page on the remote server is newer than the one it has locally. If it's not, then Squid does not bother downloading it.

NOTE: *You do not have to use Squid in conjunction with a firewall.*

Concepts

You need to understand several concepts before you try to make sense of how Squid works. Some of these concepts involve the many ways you can fit caching servers together to share work. Other concepts revolve around the terminology used to describe the internal workings of Squid and other caching servers. Take a moment to read through this section before you proceed to any of the Immediate Solutions. It will save you a lot of confusion.

Server Configurations

Caching servers may be configured in several ways. The first is the simplest: Set up a single Squid caching server on your network and let all the machines—or just certain machines—use it. This server saves all the Web, FTP, and Gopher data, and even some of the DNS data, that you acquire. When anyone else whose system is configured to look to this server attempts to access the same information, Squid checks whether the information has been updated since it was cached. If it has not, Squid sends back the cached data, thereby saving the end user the download time.

Another method of setting up caching servers involves creating a hierarchy. The servers at the top of the hierarchy are *parent* servers; those lower in the hierarchy are *sibling* servers. A sibling machine will give you information if it has it, whereas a parent will actually grab the information if it does not have it. You can take this one step further and join a larger hierarchy of caching servers. See the Web site **www.ircache.net** if you are interested in following this course of action.

In discussions of caching hierarchies, you will also read about *neighbor*, or *peer*, machines. These terms simply refer to any machine you define as part of your cache network, regardless of where it stands in the overall hierarchy.

Protocols

Squid uses multiple protocols, because for each server that it can proxy or cache, it has to know the related protocol. Among the protocols Squid understands are the following:

- Hypertext Transfer Protocol (HTTP)—Used for Web data transfer.
- Internet Cache Protocol (ICP)—A UDP-based protocol that Squid and other cache servers use to talk to one another across the Internet. Although caching

servers could use another protocol to talk across the Internet, using a specialized, streamlined item, such as ICP, is more efficient.

- Hypertext Caching Protocol (HTCP)—Used behind the scenes to locate, manage, and monitor existing Web caches.

Other Vocabulary

Some terms defy simple categorization, such as the cache *digest*, which contains a compressed collection of all the URLs currently stored in Squid's cache. Another of these terms is *multicasting*. *Multicasting* is a concept that system administrators often encounter for the first time when they begin to work with caching servers. Other uses for multicasting typically involve multimedia broadcasts. An average site does not need to include multicast functionality with its caching server. If you want to investigate this option further, start at **www.squid-cache.org/Doc/FAQ/FAQ-13.html**.

In general, IP multicasting enables you to send a single IP packet to every server that is listening. This is as close in concept as the Internet comes to radio broadcasting in its current wave-born form. This type of TCP/IP network data transmission also gives rise to a whole host of other terms that need definitions.

You can have either an open or a closed multicast session. A *closed* session has little in common with modern radio. It consists of a private multicast setup, such as on a LAN, WAN, or VPN. *Open* sessions, however, also allow machines outside of your own network to jointly receive the packets. This happens over the *MBone*, or *multicast backbone*.

In the world of networking, a *backbone* is a high-bandwidth method of moving data from other, narrower-bandwidth network connections to a faster transport medium such as fiber optics. When people refer to the Internet's "Backbone," they mean a collection of thick trunks of cable between major phone companies. Data that needs to travel long physical distances over the Internet moves from the end user's machine to the Internet Service Provider (ISP) and then—if not destined for a network that the ISP is directly connected to—onto the Backbone.

The MBone is used specifically for multicast broadcasting purposes. It is divided into *channels*, each of which carries a specific programming item, just as television and radio stations have done for years. Each channel is composed of a class D network. All machines on the network listen for IP packets sent to any machine on the network. This method ensures that the multicasts are an opt-in broadcast, meaning they do not intrude where they are unwanted.

Many instances of MBone programming are available through RealNetworks at **www.real.com**. For a list of ISPs that are already on the MBone, look to **www.ipmulticast.com/isplist.htm**.

The squid.conf File

The Squid configuration file is squid.conf. In some distributions, you can find this file in /etc/squid.conf, but in Red Hat, it is located in /etc/squid/squid.conf. This file is heavily commented, so a detailed description here would be redundant. This file is laid out with long stretches of explanations and commented-out commands. Each command is set to the default listed in the example at the end of the explanation, unless you uncomment it and change its value.

Instead of a detailed description of the squid.conf file, the next part of this chapter discusses various ways to set up Squid to provide the services you require.

Immediate Solutions

Installing The Squid

To install the Squid server, do the following:

1. Log in as root to the machine you want to run Squid from.
2. Insert the Red Hat CD-ROM in the CD-ROM drive.
3. Type "mount /mnt/cdrom" to mount the CD-ROM onto the file system.
4. Type "cd /mnt/cdrom/RedHat/RPMS" to change to the directory containing the RPM packages on the CD-ROM.
5. Type "rpm -ivh squid" and press Tab to expand the file name, and then press Enter to install the RPM.

Configuring The Squid

To configure your Squid server, do the following after installing it:

1. Log in as root to the machine you installed Squid on.
2. Type "vi /etc/squid/squid.conf" to open the Squid configuration file for editing.
3. Move the cursor down to:

```
#http_port 3128
```

4. Do one of the following:
   - Leave the command commented out. If you do, Squid sticks with the default setting, which is to listen on port 3128.
   - Uncomment the command and add additional ports after the default.
   - Uncomment the command and change the port to another value completely.

TIP: *When you are adding port numbers to any server's configuration files, be sure to check /etc/services to ensure that these ports are not needed by another service. Also, watch that you do not choose ports below 1024, because these are typically reserved for use by other services. Even if you are not using those ports for their standard purposes, there may be queries from other machines on that port looking for those standard services.*

5. Cursor down to:

```
#icp_port 3130
```

6. If you want to change the default port that Squid listens for ICP requests on, uncomment this line and change the value.
7. Continue down to:

```
#htcp_port 4827
```

8. If you want to change the default port that Squid listens for HTCP queries on, uncomment this line and change the value.
9. Move down to:

```
#tcp_incoming_address 0.0.0.0
#tcp_outgoing_address 0.0.0.0
#udp_incoming_address 0.0.0.0
#udp_outgoing_address 0.0.0.0
```

10. Each of these items is used for a specific purpose. To change which IP address or *host.domain.extension* that Squid listens on for either HTTP or cache requests, uncomment the **tcp_incoming_address** line and edit it. For example:

```
tcp_incoming_address squid.animals.org
```

11. To change which IP address or *host.domain.extension* that Squid sends HTTP or cache requests through, uncomment the **tcp_outgoing_address** line and edit it. For example, to use squid.animals.org for outgoing TCP packets, the following could be used:

```
tcp_outgoing_address squid.animals.org
```

NOTE: *You can use the same address for all four of these items, a different one for each, or spread them around.*

12. To change which IP address or *host.domain.extension* that Squid listens for incoming ICP queries on, edit the **udp_incoming_address** line. For example, to use the address squid.animals.org for incoming UDP packets, the following could be used:

```
udp_incoming_address squid.animals.org
```

13. To change which IP address or *host.domain.extension* that Squid sends ICP packets through, edit the **udp_outgoing_address** line. For example, to use the same address for squid.animals.org for outgoing UDP packets, the following could be used:

```
udp_outgoing_address squid.animals.org
```

14. Type "/icp_query_timeout" and press Enter to jump down to the following:

```
#icp_query_timeout 0
```

15. If you want to manually set how long Squid waits before timing out an ICP query, uncomment this line and change 0 to the number of milliseconds it should wait. For example:

```
icp_query_timeout 4000
```


16. If you have items that you do not want to get cached, first type "/acl" to jump down to the following two lines:

```
#acl QUERY urlpath_regex cgi-bin \?
#no_cache deny QUERY
```

17. To create the Access Control List statement (**acl**) for items you do not want to have cached, build the statement in the following format:

```
acl name type item
```

which has the following components:

- ***name***—The name that corresponds to this ACL definition.
- ***type***—The kind of items contained in this definition, as explained in Table 14.1.
- ***item***—The argument appropriate to the ACL type. There can be more than one argument listed.

If you choose the **time** type, you need to know how to build a proper time argument. To set a day of the week to watch for, use one of the letters listed in Table 14.2.

If you want to set a time range to watch for, however, use this format:

```
hour1:minute1-hour2:minute2
```

Table 14.1 Squid ACL statement types.

Type	Purpose	Values
browser	Specifies the browser to look for	Regular expression that selects the proper browser(s)
dst	Specifies the remote machine IP address, network address, or address range to look for	IP address, network/netmask combination, or IP/netmask combination
dstdomain	Specifies the remote *host.domain.extension* or domain.extension to watch for	One or more names
ident	Specifies the user login to watch for	Username
method	Specifies the kind of request to watch for	One or more of the three HTTP actions: GET, HEAD, or POST
port	Specifies the port to watch for	Port number
proto	Specifies the protocol to watch for	The protocol itself, such as HTTP
src	Specifies the local IP address, network address, or address range to look for	IP address, network/netmask combination, or IP/netmask combination
srcdomain	Specifies the remote *host.domain.extension* or *domain.extension* to watch for	One or more names
time	Specifies time information to watch for	One or both of the following, in the order presented: *day specifictime* (see the text following this table for details on how to determine these two variables)
url_regex	Specifies a regular expression used to match a URL	Regular expression
urlpath_regex	Specifies a regular expression used to match a URL's path	Regular expression

Table 14.2 ACL day of the week settings in Squid.

Code	Day
S	Sunday
M	Monday
T	Tuesday
W	Wednesday
H	Thursday
F	Friday
A	Saturday

18. If you built an **acl** statement to tell Squid not to cache specific information on this machine, you need to create a **no_cache** statement beneath your **acl** statement. Use the format:

```
no_cache deny aclname
```

19. To define the amount of RAM you are willing to allocate for some of Squid's side functions, first proceed down to the following line:

```
#cache_mem  8 MB
```

20. If you want to change this value, because this machine is dedicated to caching or has a lot of RAM and few jobs, then uncomment it and change the number.
21. Proceed down to:

```
#cache_swap_low  90
#cache_swap_high 95
```


22. If you want to regulate when Squid begins clearing files out of the cache, uncomment these two lines. When the cache becomes **cache_swap_high** percent full, Squid starts removing the least-used items stored until it is down to **cache_swap_low** percent full. Uncomment these lines and edit these values if you want to change them.
23. If you want to set Squid not to cache files that are a certain size or larger, uncomment and then change the value assigned to:

```
#maximum_object_size 4096 KB
```

24. Continue down to:

```
#ipcache_size 1024
#ipcache_low  90
#ipcache_high 95
```

25. If you want to change how many IP address resolution values Squid stores, uncomment and change the value for **ipcache_size**.
26. If you want to change the cache-full percentage that causes Squid to start clearing out the least-used IP address resolution information, uncomment and change the value for **ipcache_high**.

27. If you want to change the cache-full percentage that causes Squid to stop clearing out the least-used IP address resolution information, uncomment and change the value for **ipcache_low**.
28. If you want to change how many domain names Squid stores information about, uncomment and change the value for the following:

```
#fqdncache_size 1024
```

29. Continue down to:

```
#cache_dir /var/spool/squid 100 16 256
```

30. This item enables you to define where your cache is stored. Keep in mind that the contents of this directory change frequently. This is a service whose data is worth putting on a separate partition, for a few reasons:
    - The cache could overrun the rest of the file system or partition it shares with other processes.
    - The more a file system changes, the greater the chances that it will be damaged. Keeping the cache to one partition limits which part of your total file system will get damaged.

    If you do not want to use the defaults listed, uncomment this line and change its values appropriately.
31. If you want to change where HTTP and ICP accesses are stored, uncomment and change the following line:

```
#cache_access_log /var/log/squid/access.log
```

32. If you want to change where general cache information—that which does not have a specific home in another file—goes, uncomment and change the following line:

```
#cache_log /var/log/squid/cache.log
```

33. If you want to change where the cache metadata logs are stored, uncomment and change the following line to point to the new path to use:

```
#cache_swap_log
```

34. Move down to:

```
#emulate_httpd_log off
```

35. If you have a specific reason for Squid to emulate the **httpd** logging format, change the **emulate_httpd_log** line to the following:

```
emulate_httpd_log on
```

36. Continue down to:

```
#log_mime_hdrs off
```

37. If you want to log all MIME headers used in HTTP transmissions, change the **log_mime_hdrs** line to:

```
log_mime_hdrs on
```

38. Jump down to:

```
#debug_options ALL,1
```


39. If you want to change the default log-level settings, first uncomment this line. **ALL** refers to all sections of the log file. Typically, you want to change the number portion following **ALL**. This number can be from 1 to 9. The higher the number, the more debugging information that is saved to your log file.
40. Go down to:

```
#log_fqdn off
```

41. If you want to log *host.domain.extension* information plus the relevant IP addresses, change this line to the following:

```
log_fqdn on
```

42. Use the cursor to move down to:

```
#dns_nameservers none
```

43. If you want to explicitly set which name servers Squid uses, uncomment this line and enter the servers' IP addresses. For example, you might have the following:

```
dns_nameservers 192.168.10.2 192.168.15.1
```

44. Jump down to:

```
# INSERT YOUR OWN RULE(S) HERE TO ALLOW ACCESS FROM YOUR CLIENTS
#
http_access allow localhost
http_access deny all
```

45. Move the cursor to the **allow localhost** line.
46. If you want to add rules specifically for your own clients, press the Esc key to ensure that you are in Command mode, and then type "o" to create a new line beneath the current position and enter Insert mode. Any lines you add should be in this format:

```
http_access allow aclname
```

Refer to Step 17 for help on how to build an **acl** statement to define the **aclname** you want to use.

47. Jump down to:

```
#cache_mgr root
```

48. If you want email to go to someone other than root@localhost when the cache dies, uncomment this line and change the email address listed.
49. Type "/append_domain" to jump down to:

```
#append_domain .yourdomain.com
```

50. To add the full name to any machines that are mentioned just as hosts, uncomment the line and change it to:

```
append_domain .domain.extension
```

51. Press the Esc key, and then type "ZZ" to save and close the file.

Related solutions:	Found on page:
Creating Linux File Systems	76
Adding Permanent Media	86

Setting Up Parent And Sibling Caches

To set up the Squid configuration for your cache hierarchy, do the following:

1. Log in to the machine you want to set up as a sibling.
2. Type "vi /etc/squid/squid.conf" to open the Squid configuration file for editing.
3. Type "/cache_peer" and press Enter to search down to the following line:

```
#cache_peer hostname type 3128 3130
```

4. Type "dd" to delete the line.
5. Type "o" to create a new line below the current location and enter Insert mode.
6. You need to take some time to build this statement and the subsequent ones. Each Squid caching server, regardless of where it is in the hierarchy, needs to have an entry in the Squid configuration file on all the other servers. Type the following to start the line:

```
cache_peer
```

7. After **cache_peer** comes the name of the machine that you are defining, in the *host.domain.extension* format. For example, so far you might have the following:

```
cache_peer squid.animals.org
```

8. Choose where in your hierarchy this machine belongs: parent or sibling. For example, if you are setting up a parent machine, you might have the following at this point:

```
cache_peer squid.animals.org parent
```

9. Specify on which port the machine being defined listens for incoming proxy requests. The default is 3128, so you might have the following:

```
cache_peer squid.animals.org 3128 parent
```

10. Specify which port the machine being defined uses to send and receive ICP traffic. The default here is 3130, so you might have the following:

```
cache_peer squid.animals.org 3128 3130 parent
```

11. If you want to add options, you can. The ones available are listed in Table 14.3.

    For example, to set this parent to a high priority, you might use the following:

```
cache_peer squid.animals.org 3128 3130 weight=10 parent
```

12. Build the lines for every other machine in your hierarchy.
13. If you want to have various parents specialize in information from specific domains, continue down to the next step. Otherwise, jump to Step 19.
14. Cursor down to the second of the following lines:

```
#          * There is also a 'cache_peer_access' tag in the ACL
#          section.
```

15. Type "o" to add a blank line beneath this position and enter Insert mode.
16. Start the line by typing the following:

```
cache_peer_domain
```

17. Enter the *host.domain.extension* for the Squid parent you want to have handle specific domains. For example:

```
cache_peer_domain squid.animals.org
```


Table 14.3 Hierarchy options available with the cache_peer Squid statement.

Option	Purpose	Value
closest-only	Specifies that if this parent does not have the requested URL in its cache, to resend the request to the parent with the fastest query response times	None
default	Specifies that the parent being defined should be used only if no other is available	None
login	Specifies that the parent providing proxy service requires login	*=login:password*
no-digest	Specifies not to request a digest from this machine	None
no-query	Specifies not to send ICP packets to this machine	None
proxy-only	Specifies not to store the data requested from the remote machine in its cache	None

(continued)

Table 14.3 Hierarchy options available with the cache_peer Squid statement (continued).

Option	Purpose	Value
round-robin	Specifies that this machine is a parent to be used in a sequence after the other round-robin parents for queries	None
weight	Specifies the priority of this parent compared to others	A positive integer; the higher the number, the higher the priority

18. Specify which domains you want this machine to query the defined parent about. You can use one of the following formats: *.extension*, *.domain.extension*, or either of the preceding with an exclamation point (!) directly in front to specify "not." For example, to turn to the specified parent for information about all .edu sites except for generic.edu, you might use this line:

```
cache_peer_domain squid.animals.org .edu !.generic.edu
```

19. You can set how long Squid waits to hear back from its peers before it determines that they are nonfunctional. To do this, first continue down to the following line:

```
#dead_peer_timeout 10 seconds
```

20. If you want to change the default value of 10 in Step 19, uncomment the line and change the 10 to the appropriate value. Squid still sends packets to this machine; it just does not expect to hear back until it finally receives a reply, so a dead machine can come back "alive" on its own.
21. You may not always want a machine to query other machines' caches for all data. To set up a machine to handle some items with its own cache, first go down to:

```
#hierarchy_stoplist cgi-bin ?
```

22. If you have particular URL portions that signal requests that have to be handled by this specific machine, rather than being forwarded to a caching server, uncomment this line and edit the items after the option.
23. Return to the section you came to this one from and continue setting up your Squid server.

Setting Up Web Server Acceleration

To set up Web server acceleration, do the following:

1. Log in as root to the machine you installed Squid on.
2. Type "vi /etc/squid/squid.conf" to open the Squid configuration file for editing.
3. Type "/http_port" to search down to the port setting line.
4. Type "i" to enter Insert mode.
5. Change the current port value so the line is:

```
http_port 80
```

6. Type "/httpd_accel" and press Enter to search down to the Web acceleration section of the Squid configuration file.
7. Using Squid for Web acceleration means having the cache server step in for any URL requests before the Web server gets involved. Continue down to:

```
#httpd_accel_host hostname
#httpd_accel_port port
```

8. Uncomment these two lines. For the first line, change **hostname** to the name of the machine that hosts the Web server, such as this:

```
httpd_accel_host www
```

9. Change **port** to the port number that the Web server listens on. For example:

```
httpd_accel_port 80
```

10. Turning on the acceleration feature actually turns off Web proxying. If you want to use Web proxying, first go to the following line:

```
#httpd_accel_with_proxy off
```

11. Change this line to the following to turn Web proxying back on:

```
httpd_accel_with_proxy on
```

12. Do one of the following:
    - Return to the section you came here from and continue through its instructions.
    - Press the Esc key to go to Command mode and then type "ZZ" to save and close the file.

Setting Up Multicasting

To set up Web cache multicasting, do the following:

1. Log in as root to the machine you installed Squid on.
2. Type "vi /etc/squid/squid.conf" to open the Squid configuration file for editing.
3. Type "/mcast_groups" and press Enter to jump down to:

```
#mcast_groups 239.128.16.128
```

4. If you want this machine to listen for offerings of multicast broadcasts, then uncomment this line and type "i" to enter Insert mode. Change the given IP address to the address for the group you are connected to.
5. Type "/mcast_icp" and press Enter to jump down to:

```
#mcast_icp_query_timeout 2000
```

6. If you want to set how long Squid waits to hear back from its ICP attempts to find out who is listening, uncomment this line and change the number of milliseconds listed.
7. Return to the section you came here from, or press the Esc key to enter Command mode, and then type "ZZ" to save and close the file.

Configuring A Client To Utilize Caching

To configure Netscape to look to the caching server instead of directly to Apache, do the following:

1. Log into the account you want to set up.

TIP: *If you take good notes, you can send each new user instructions on how to do this themselves.*

2. Enter the GUI.
3. Click the Netscape icon to open the Netscape browser. If this is the first time you have opened Netscape, you will get the Netscape License Agreement.
4. Read the License Agreement and click Accept. Netscape Navigator opens, as shown in Figure 14.1.

TIP: *A more recent version of Netscape, version 6, is available from* ***www.netscape.com****. However, 4.72 is what ships with Red Hat 6.2.*

---

5. Go to Edit|Preferences, to open the Netscape: Preferences dialog box, shown in Figure 14.2.
6. Click on the arrow next to the Advanced category to expand it.
7. Click on the Proxies category to open the Proxies information shown in Figure 14.3.

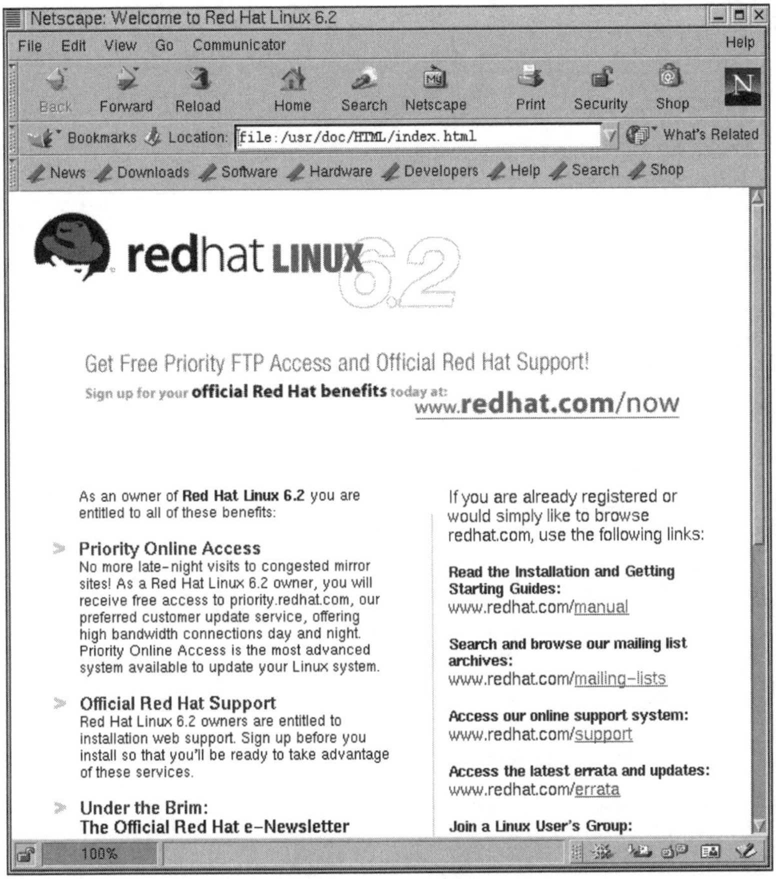

Figure 14.1 Netscape Navigator 4.72, opened to the default home page.

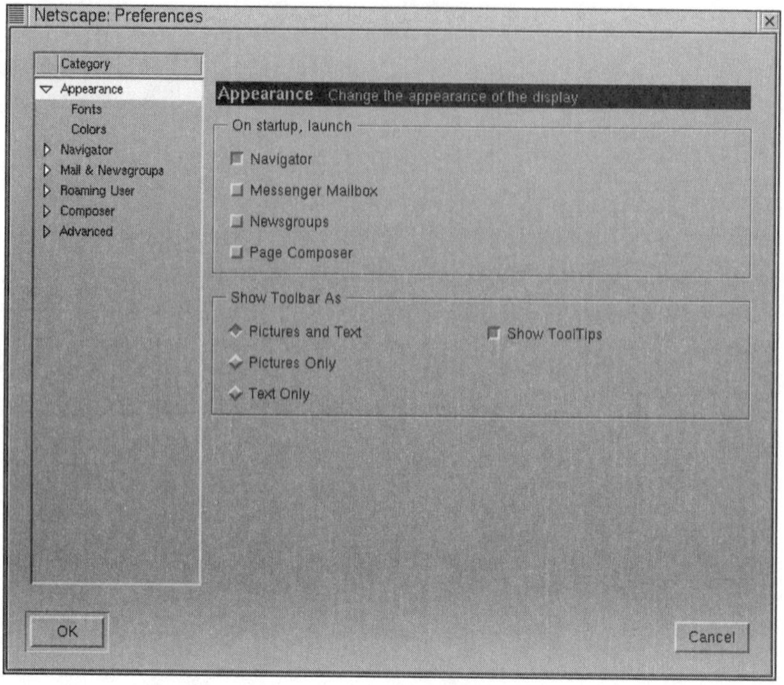

Figure 14.2 The Netscape: Preferences dialog box with the Appearance category displayed.

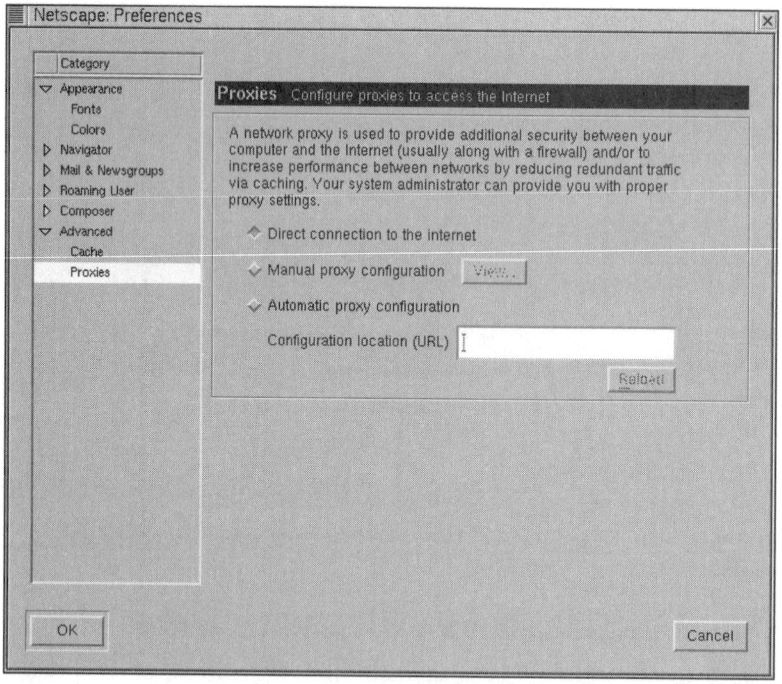

Figure 14.3 The Netscape: Preferences dialog box with the Proxies category displayed.

8. Click the Manual Proxy Configuration radio button.
9. Click the View button to open the Netscape: View Manual Proxy Configuration dialog box, shown in Figure 14.4.
10. In the HTTP Proxy text box, enter the IP address for the Squid proxy server you want this machine to use.
11. In the associated Port text box, enter the port number for the Squid proxy server if you do not have it on a standard port.
12. Click OK to close the Netscape: View Manual Proxy Configuration dialog box.
13. Click OK to close the Netscape: Preferences dialog box.

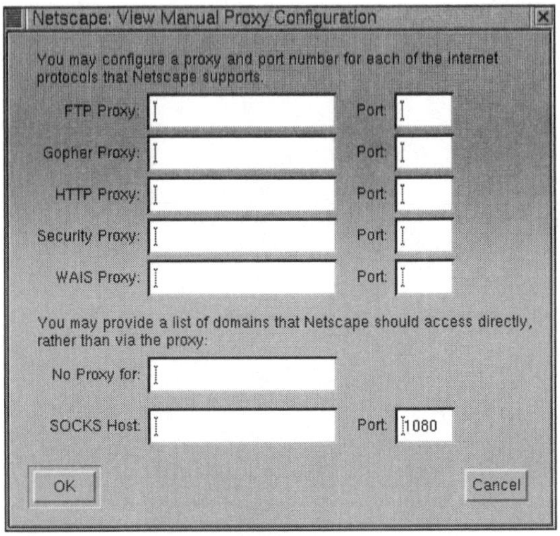

Figure 14.4 The Netscape: View Manual Proxy Configuration dialog box.

Chapter 15

FTP And Telnet

If you need an immediate solution to:	*See page:*
Securing FTP	483
Installing Anonymous FTP	487
Securing Telnet	488
Creating A **shutdown** Message	488

In Depth

Two simple but important services that most new system administrators only skim over when setting up a system are the File Transfer Protocol (FTP) and Telnet. Although certain aspects of these tools work by default with most Linux distributions, you need to know the security measures that are available and the risks that you are taking by allowing particular services to exist on your machines. This chapter discusses the issues involved with using FTP, anonymous FTP, and Telnet.

FTP Issues

The FTP service is used to upload and download files from a remote machine. Over time, many distributions (including Red Hat) have separated this service into two parts. The first part enables users who have shell accounts on the system to access their own file system space and upload or download information. This use of FTP is generally no more or less secure than a shell login prompt. It is the second common use of FTP that opens the door to a wealth of security concerns. This use is anonymous FTP, which allows anyone to connect to a section of your file system space and upload or download information.

The concerns for system administrators setting up anonymous FTP are numerous. If the file system space and FTP user information for public access are not carefully created with the right permissions and ownerships, unknown guest users can break out of the public space and go into restricted parts of the file system. Another issue concerns people using your FTP upload space to share illegal materials or other items prohibited by your policies with other users.

If you do not intend to allow anyone to use FTP to access a particular machine, be sure to disable this service in /etc/inetd.conf, as discussed in Chapter 9.

FTP Clients

The default FTP client under Linux—and most Unix flavors—is **ftp**. This is a relatively straightforward command-line tool. However, other FTP clients are available for those who have specific needs that are not met by **ftp**, or who simply like to experiment. These clients are listed in Table 15.1, and range from freely available clients designed to work under specific circumstances to complex clients with many features that you can test and purchase.

Many more FTP clients are available today, and more are certain to come. Table 15.1 represents a cross-section of some of the more interesting items. To find more

Table 15.1 FTP clients available for Linux users.

Name	Home
gFTP	**http://gftp.seul.org**
IglooFTP PRO	**www.littleigloo.org/iglooftp.php3**
NFTP	**www.ayukov.com/nftp/**
psftp	**http://nut.dhs.org/code/psftp/**
Yafc	**www.stacken.kth.se/~mhe/yafc/**

FTP clients, go to your favorite search engine and search for the following three words: "ftp", "linux", and "client".

FTP Servers

The default FTP server under Red Hat Linux is **wu-ftpd**. Many others are available, however. Some address particular security needs, whereas others provide a friendlier configuration interface to those who prefer not to use command-line tools. Table 15.2 gives an overview of some of the FTP servers available today.

Regardless of which FTP server you decide to use, be sure to take the time to secure who is allowed to access the server, how they may access it, and what parts of the file system the clients have access to. If you do not intend to offer anonymous FTP access, and the server you choose offers this automatically, be sure to disable it! Anonymous FTP is that big of a security risk. Do not have it enabled if you do not specifically intend to use it.

You may decide to deal with several files when it comes to securing **wu-ftpd**. Each of these files is covered separately in the following sections.

Regulating User Access

The file that you edit to tightly regulate how users are handled by the FTP server is /etc/ftpaccess. This section walks you through the default version of this file. It starts with the following line:

```
class   all   real,guest,anonymous   *
```

Table 15.2 FTP servers available for Linux administrators.

Name	Home
ftpd	**www.gnu.org/software/inetutils/inetutils.html**
glFtpD	**www.glftpd.org**
ProFTPD	**www.proftpd.net**
rsync	**http://rsync.samba.org**

A **class** statement enables you to define a group of users who should all be treated in the same manner. It is used in the following format:

```
class classname who
```

The arguments used in a **class** statement are listed here:

- ***classname***—The name for this class of users
- ***who***—One or a series of expressions that narrows down who belongs in the class

---

NOTE: *Although a **class** statement must be only one line long, if you need to extend your list of who portions, simply break them into multiple **class** statements using the same **classname** for each.*

Building an expression—also referred to as a *glob*—relies on the attributes listed in Table 15.3. These are the same for anything else that refers to "globbing."

After the initial **class** statement is:

```
email root@localhost
```

An **email** statement is much easier to follow. The argument is the email address of the person responsible for maintaining the FTP server and file space. Next is:

```
loginfails 5
```

The **loginfails** statement sets how many times a user can attempt to log in through FTP and enter a wrong username and password combination before the FTP server closes the connection to the FTP client. After this statement is a pair of **readme** statements:

```
readme  README*    login
readme  README*    cwd=*
```

Table 15.3 Wildcards used in glob expressions.

Character	Purpose	Example
?	Matches a single unspecified character	**c?t** matches cat and cut, but not cart
*****	Matches any sequence of unspecified characters	**c*t** matches cat, cut, cart, and can't, but not cute
[ ]	Matches any of the enclosed characters	**c[a-d]t** matches cat but not cut
{ }	Matches any of the comma-separated items in the list	**c{ar,our}t** matches cart and court, but not cut

You use this statement type to notify users in a specific ***classname*** that the file exists, and/or that changes were made since they last connected. A full **readme** statement might be as complex as the following:

```
readme  path  when  classname
```

The arguments used for **readme** are:

- ***path***—The path to the file you want to have monitored.
- ***when***—This item can be one of two different choices. The first text you can use here is **LOGIN**, which tells **wu-ftpd** to use this **readme** statement whenever someone meeting its rules logs in. The second option is **CWD=*path***. Using this choice tells **wu-ftpd** to process this **readme** statement whenever an FTP user uses the **cwd** (change working directory) command to the specified location.
- ***classname***—A previously defined ***classname*** from a **class** statement. Optional.

Next is the following pair of lines:

```
message /welcome.msg            login
message .message                cwd=*
```

A **message** statement enables you to specify text that is displayed the moment someone logs in or changes into a directory. You can use this statement in the following format:

```
message  path  when  classname
```

The arguments for **message** are the same as they are for **readme**. What follows is a collection of statements that all use a similar format:

```
compress        yes             all
tar             yes             all
chmod           no              guest,anonymous
delete          no              guest,anonymous
overwrite       no              guest,anonymous
rename          no              guest,anonymous
```

The first two lines involve file extensions. A **compress** statement refers to Z or GZ files, whereas **tar** refers to TAR files. In both cases, these commands are used in this format:

```
extensioncommand  active  who
```

The arguments here are as follows:

- ***extensioncommand***—Either **compress** or **tar**
- ***active***—Either **yes** or **no**; determines whether or not **wu-ftpd** knows how to convert this type of file
- ***who***—Either a ***classname***, or a globbed version that refers to multiple classes

After the file format statements are the **chmod**, **delete**, **overwrite**, and **rename** statements, which are used in the following format:

```
functioncommand  active  type
```

Arguments for these statements break down as follows:

- ***functioncommand***—One of **chmod**, **delete**, **overwrite**, or **rename**
- ***active***—Either **yes** or **no**; turns this feature on or off
- ***type***—One or more of the following, separated with commas and no spaces: **anonymous**, **class=*classname***, **guest**, or **real**

Next in the file is the following line:

```
log transfers anonymous,real inbound,outbound
```

The **log transfers** statement enables you to log file transfers. Its generic format is:

```
log transfers transfertype from
```

This statement's arguments are listed next:

- ***transfertype***—One or more of the following, separated with commas and no spaces: **anonymous**, **class=*classname***, **guest**, or **real**
- ***from***—One or both of **inbound** and **outbound**

A useful statement for ensuring that no one gets caught in midtransfer when you shut down the FTP server or the entire machine is:

```
shutdown /etc/shutmsg
```

See the Immediate Solutions section "Creating A **shutdown** Message" for information on how to make the most of this feature.

The following is the final line in the file:

```
passwd-check rfc822 warn
```

This statement determines the level of password enforcement used by **wu-ftpd**. Its generic format is:

```
passwd-check checktype level
```

The arguments for this statement are:

- ***checktype***—One of the following: **none** (do not bother with passwords), **trivial** (as long as an @ exists in the password, it is okay), or **rfc822** (use regular passwords)
- ***level***—One of the following: **warn** (tell users they entered a bad password, but allow them to stay) or **enforce** (tell users they entered a bad password, and disconnect them)

NOTE: *You can also regulate what users have access to your FTP service with the /etc/ftpusers file. Utilizing this file is covered in the Immediate Solutions section "Securing FTP."*

Keeping Hosts Out

You edit the /etc/ftphosts file to fine-tune what accounts people can FTP into from what hosts. Two types of statements are available here, **allow** and **deny**. Both are used in the same format:

```
allow_or_deny user where
```

This format breaks down into the following:

- ***allow_or_deny***—Either **allow** to specify a rule that lets people in, or **deny** to specify a rule that keeps them out.
- ***user***—The login name the rule applies to.
- ***where***—A host or hosts specified using the globbing format discussed in Table 15.3. In addition, you can use the format *network:netmask* or *network/bits*.

FTP Mirror Sites

One issue that comes up often in the world of FTP sites is *mirror sites*. Popular FTP sites quickly become overloaded. When this happens, it can be nearly impossible to log in to the site. Even when you can get into an overloaded site, watching your download trickle in can be like watching glaciers advance. When this happens, FTP administrators often encourage people to set up official mirror sites. These sites obtain an exact copy of the original FTP site and continually update whenever the original site changes. In this way, the load can be spread across a large number of sites, each of which is accessible and has decent download speeds.

For the latest version of the Linux FTP **mirror** program, go to **http://sunsite.org.uk/packages/mirror/**, where you can download the software as well as locate documentation.

Telnet Issues

The Telnet service is a handy tool for those who have accounts on multiple machines. Rather than moving files, Telnet enables you to actually log in to a machine remotely. After you are logged in through a Telnet session, you can work at the command line just as you would if you were directly at the machine's keyboard.

One of the main issues that new Linux users and administrators encounter is whether the superuser should be able to use Telnet to log in remotely. My answer—and the answer of many other experienced administrators—is an emphatic no. If you allow the root account to log in directly at a Telnet prompt, you offer potential intruders a one-step chance at breaking into the superuser's account. This action severely compromises any networked machine's security.

The alternative to allowing root to Telnet in directly is for the superuser to Telnet in to their user account, and then use the **su** command to enter superuser mode. Doing this ensures that any potential intruder has to follow two steps to become root instead of one. The more steps crackers have to take, the better the chance they will not figure out a password, or that you will catch them before they make it in.

If you do not intend to allow anyone to Telnet in to a machine, be sure to disable Telnet in /etc/inetd.conf, as discussed in Chapter 9.

Immediate Solutions

Securing FTP

To ensure that your FTP service with WU-FTP is as secure as possible, do the following:

1. Log in to the machine you want to secure as root.

NOTE: *See Steps 1 through 5 of the section "Installing Anonymous FTP" to ensure that you have the user FTP server installed.*

2. Type "vi /etc/ftpaccess" to open the file that regulates how **wu-ftpd** handles users.
3. Go to the following line:

```
class   all   real,guest,anonymous  *
```

4. This line creates a **class** of users named **all** that contains every type of FTP user possible. A **real** user is someone who has an account on your system. A **guest** logs in as "guest", and **anonymous** logs in as "anonymous". The difference between **guest** and **anonymous** is that a **guest** account is still an account. An /etc/passwd entry is involved, and a real password must be entered. Conversely, **anonymous** users log in as "anonymous" and typically use their email address as a password.

   If you want to add any additional classes, type "o" to open a new line below the current position and enter Insert mode, and add the new classes on the new blank line.
5. Continue down to the following line:

```
email root@localhost
```

6. If you are currently in Insert mode, press the Esc key. Move the cursor to **root@localhost** and press "x" one character at a time to delete it. Then, press "i" to enter Insert mode and add an email address that points to the FTP administrator. For example:

```
email ftpadmin@animals.org
```

7. Move down to:

```
loginfails 5
```

8. This statement declares that if someone connects to your FTP server, he or she has five chances to enter a username and password correctly before the server hangs up. If you find that people are trying to break into your system, then lowering this value to 2 or 3 is a good idea. I cannot think of many reasons to raise the value, because legitimate users really should be able to enter their username and password correctly within five tries.
9. Continue to:

```
readme  README*    login
readme  README*    cwd=*
```

10. The first line notifies all users when they log in that the file README with any text attached to the end is available. The second line then ensures that if you change with the **cwd** command within an **ftp** session into a directory containing any files that begin with README, you are notified that the file exists.

    If you want any other files to be handled in this manner, add the appropriate **readme** statements below the current ones. Also, if you use different names for the documents containing this kind of information, edit the existing statements.

TIP: *You can also comment out any line in this file by placing a hash mark (#) in front of it.*

11. Proceed to the following pair of lines:

```
message /welcome.msg          login
message .message              cwd=*
```

12. In this case, the first line specifies that every user sees the contents of the file welcome.msg—stored in the base directory of the FTP file system space—as part of the text that displays when they log in. The second states that when the user changes into any directory in your FTP file system space that contains a file named .message, the contents of the .message file are displayed immediately.

    If you want or need to do so, do one of the following:

    - Comment out existing **message** statement(s) by putting a hash mark at the beginning of the line.

- Edit the existing **message** statement(s) to suit your needs.
- Add new **message** statements to suit your needs.

13. Cursor down to the following section:

```
compress        yes         all
tar             yes         all
```

14. These two lines act in concert. If an **ftp** user requests a group of files or an entire directory, having these two capabilities turned on tells the server to use the **tar** tool to bunch the directory together, and then to use the **compress** tool to make the resulting bundle smaller.

    Many administrators today shut off these features and instead offer prepackaged file groupings for those who want them. The reason for doing this is that servers were getting overloaded constantly tarring and compressing data on the fly. If you want to do this, comment out the two lines with a hash mark, and then make sure to make tarballs of the various groups people might want.

15. Go down to the following set of lines:

```
chmod       no          guest,anonymous
delete      no          guest,anonymous
overwrite   no          guest,anonymous
rename      no          guest,anonymous
```

16. These lines set the FTP server such that anyone who is not a **real** FTP user cannot change file permissions, delete or rename a file, or replace it with another file. If you want to change one or more of these lines, or comment them out, do so.
17. Continue to this line:

```
log transfers anonymous,real inbound,outbound
```

18. This line states that **wu-ftpd** should log both incoming and outgoing file transfers for all **real** and **anonymous** users. You can change this statement in a number of ways if you want to. If your primary concern is what is coming into your site from anonymous users, and you are low on file system space, then you might want to change this to the following:

```
log transfers anonymous inbound
```

19. Cursor down to:

```
shutdown /etc/shutmsg
```

20. If you do not intend to use this feature, comment the line out. If you do intend to use it, see the upcoming section "Creating A **shutdown** Message" for details on how to implement it properly. You can also change the file the message should go into, if you want to.
21. Finally, go to:

```
passwd-check rfc822 warn
```

22. Leave this statement alone unless this machine only runs anonymous FTP service. If this is the case, change it to:

```
passwd-check trivial enforce
```

    This action ensures that **wu-ftpd** looks for email addresses—or at least the @ symbol—in the passwords it receives and will not connect a user without that information. You can better track who is coming through when you ensure that you get email addresses as the password.
23. Press the Esc key to enter Command mode, and then type "ZZ" to save and close the file.
24. Type "vi /etc/ftphosts" to open the next file.
25. Type "G" to go to the end of the file, and then type "o" to open a new line at the end and enter Insert mode.
26. Add **allow** statements if you want them. These enable you to specify who can access your FTP site through specific usernames.

WARNING! *If you add any **allow** statements, it is assumed that you only want hosts that you define as allowed to be able to access your FTP site. You must explicitly **allow** everything you want to let in.*

27. Add **deny** statements if you want them. These enable you to specify particular locations from which people cannot access certain login names through FTP.
28. Press the Esc key to enter Command mode, and then type "ZZ" to save and close the file.
29. Type "vi /etc/ftpusers" to open the final FTP security file.

30. This file consists of a list of login names, one per line. Type “G” to go to the end, and then type “o” to open a new line beneath the list and enter Insert mode.
31. Add any usernames, one per line, that should not be allowed to log in through FTP.
32. Press the Esc key to enter Command mode.
33. Move the cursor to any usernames you want to allow to log in that are currently disallowed, and type “dd” to erase the line they are on.

WARNING!* *Be very careful with this. The login names selected by default are there for security reasons.

34. Type “ZZ” to save and close the file.
35. Type “/etc/rc.d/init.d/inet restart” to restart the superdaemon, which handles FTP service.

Related solution:	Found on page:
Opening Or Creating Tarballs	110

Installing Anonymous FTP

To install anonymous FTP service with the Red Hat Linux distribution (or one based on Red Hat), do the following:

1. Log in to the machine you want to secure as root.
2. If you do not already have the Red Hat CD-ROM in the CD-ROM drive, insert it.
3. Type “mount /mnt/cdrom” to mount the CD-ROM onto the file system.
4. Type “cd /mnt/cdrom/RedHat/RPMS” to change to the packages directory.
5. Type “rpm -q wu-ftpd” to see if you have this package installed already. If you do not, type “rpm -ivh wu-ftpd” and press Tab to complete the file name, and then press Enter to install the package.
6. Type “rpm -q anon-ftp” to see if the anonymous FTP server is already installed. If it is, you are finished with this section.
7. If the anonymous FTP server isn’t installed, type “rpm -ivh anon-ftp” and press Tab to complete the file name, and then press Enter to install it.

Securing Telnet

To secure your Telnet service, do the following:

1. Log in to the machine you want to secure as root.
2. Type "vi /etc/issue.net".
3. Remove all information about the operating system and version from this file.
4. If you want to, replace the information you removed with a different welcome message.
5. Other than the preceding steps, little security is possible through Telnet itself. Consider using tcp_wrappers or ipchains to control Telnet access. Press the Esc key, and then type "ZZ" to save and close the file.
6. Type "/etc/rc.d/init.d/inet restart" to restart the superdaemon, which handles Telnet service.

NOTE: *For the best Telnet security, install the secure shell (ssh) and use its **stelnet** instead.*

Related solutions:	Found on page:
Obtaining And Installing ssh	267
Restricting Network Access With **tcp_wrappers**	269
Setting Up ssh On A Server	270
Setting Up ssh On A Client	276
Setting Up An IP Firewall	287

Creating A **shutdown** Message

To configure a **shutdown** message if you have scheduled maintenance time coming up, do the following:

1. Log in to the FTP server machine as root.
2. Type "vi /etc/shutmsg"—or the appropriate name and path if you used a different one—to open the file.
3. This file is empty by default. Type "i" to enter Insert mode.
4. You will enter your **shutdown** data in this format:

```
year month day hour minute whendeny whendisconnect message
```

For the ***year*** portion, enter the four-digit year. For example, if you plan to take the machine down for maintenance in 2001, you would start with

```
2001
```

5. The ***month*** item is not represented by 1 through 12, but instead by 0 through 11. Enter the month next. For example, to set the FTP server to know that it is going down in March 2001, you would have the following:

```
2001 2
```

6. The ***day*** item follows the same pattern. Enter a day from 0 through 30 that represents what day of the month you want. For example, to tell the FTP server it is going to shut down on March 5, 2001, you would have the following:

```
2001 2 4
```

7. Now, enter the precise ***hour*** and ***minute*** that the FTP server will be unavailable. As before, you start with 0, so the hours are 0 through 23 and the minutes are 0 through 59. To tell the FTP server it will shut down on March 5, 2001, at 20:00, you would now have the following:

```
2001 2 4 19 0
```

8. The ***whendeny*** item refers to the amount of time before the **shutdown** that the FTP server refuses to accept incoming **ftp** connections. Enter this time in the format ***hhmm***. If you want to tell your FTP server that it will shut down at 20:00 on March 5, 2001, and that you want it to refuse any incoming connections for three hours before this, because you have some large files on your site, then you would enter the following:

```
2001 2 4 19 0 0300
```

9. The ***whendisconnect*** item determines when the FTP server starts severing existing **ftp** connections, relative to the **shutdown** times. Enter this value in the same format you used for ***whendeny***. To tell your FTP server that it will shut down at 20:00 on March 5, 2001, that it should refuse new connections 3 hours before, and that it should sever current connections 30 minutes before, you would have the following:

```
2001 2 4 19 0 0300 0030
```

Table 15.4 Variables available when creating FTP shutdown text.

Variable	Purpose
%d	Specifies when all existing connections will be severed
%r	Specifies when all new connections will be refused
%s	Specifies when the system will shut down

10. Finally, enter the ***message***. This is the text that contains a brief informational message for the FTP server to send regarding the machine's **shutdown**. Table 15.4 lists three special variables you can use to include additional information in the text. To have the FTP server display the text "This server is going down on *time* for maintenance" at the end of the rest of the information you have already added, you would complete the statement with the following:

```
2001 2 4 19 0 0300 0030 This server is going down on %s for maintenance.
```

11. Press the Esc key, and then type "ZZ" to save and close the file.
12. Type "/etc/rc.d/init.d/inet restart" to restart the superdaemon.

Related solution:	Found on page:
Shutting Down And Rebooting	97

Chapter 16

NIS And NIS+

If you need an immediate solution to:	*See page:*
Installing The NIS Server	496
Installing The NIS Client	496
Setting Up An NIS Server	497
Setting Up An NIS Client	499

In Depth

The larger your network gets, the more difficult it is to manage individual user accounts on each and every machine. Fortunately, a service is available that enables you to centrally manage accounts you want to duplicate. This service is called the Network Information System (NIS). A newer and somewhat more advanced version is NIS+. It is important that you understand this service and whether it is right for you before implementing it. Otherwise, it will make your life more difficult rather than easier.

Introduction To NIS And NIS+

The Network Information System was originally developed by Sun to provide a centralized mechanism for managing a user base on a large network. Back then, it was called the Sun Yellow Pages—the name had to be changed because British Telecom in the U.K. trademarked the phrase "Yellow Pages." A newer and more security-savvy version of NIS is NIS+.

Unfortunately, each Linux distribution takes a different approach to whether to use NIS or NIS+. Because this book focuses on Red Hat Linux, its approach is discussed in depth. However, for those who are not using Red Hat, pointers are given to information on other distributions' implementations.

Differences Between NIS And NIS+

Several differences exist between NIS and NIS+. This applies only to the pure implementations, however, because various distributions actually mix NIS and NIS+ together. One of the primary differences between NIS and NIS+ is the ability of NIS+ to use shadow passwords. Classic implementations of NIS do not support shadow passwords. Removing the ability to hide your master password file is not something many system administrators are willing to do. This is actually one of the primary reasons many administrators moved to NIS+, which does support the shadow suite.

However, Red Hat's implementation of the NIS server—and those of some other distributions—does support shadow passwords. You do not have to disable them to run an NIS server under Red Hat, because Red Hat is one of the distributions that use a mix of NIS and NIS+.

One of the main differences between NIS and NIS+ is the ability to encrypt data between server and clients. Go to **www.suse.de/~kukuk/nisplus/download.html**

to grab the latest source code if you want to take a look at NIS+. Be sure to read the readme file in this directory. This book does not cover the Linux implementation of NIS+, because it is still experimental software and thus may change a lot between now and when you try it.

The Main Server Configuration File

The primary file used when configuring NIS under Red Hat is /etc/ypserv.conf, which sets up how **ypserv**—the NIS server—works. Two statement types are used in this file: option statements and access rules. Rather than walking you through the file itself, this section explains how to use the two types of statements.

Option statements guide **ypserv**'s overall behavior. Only three possible option statements are available in this file. These are listed in Table 16.1.

All option statements have a value of either **yes** or **no**. Use them in this format:

```
option: value
```

After you have the option statements in place, you can add any access control statements that you want, using this format:

```
host:map:security:mangle:field
```

The values in this statement break down as follows:

- ***host***—An IP address in one of the formats listed in Table 16.2.
- ***map***—The path to a database file containing specific information, such as passwords or hosts.
- ***security***—One of the values outlined in Table 16.3.
- ***mangle***—Hides the real value of one of the items in this statement by replacing it with an **x**. Possible values are **yes** and **no**. The default is to alter the **map** value.
- ***field***—Specifies which field to alter. Optional.

Table 16.1 Option statements in /etc/ypserv.conf.

Option	Description	Default
dns	Determines whether the NIS server contacts the name server for host information when it cannot find a host's name in its files	**no**
sunos_kludge	No longer used in this version (1.3.7) of **ypserv**	N/A
xfr_check_port	Determines whether the NIS server can run on ports 1024 or higher	**yes**

Table 16.2 IP address formats available for the host portion of an /etc/ypserv.conf access rule.

Format	Description	Example
###.###.###.###	Full, single host IP address	192.168.16.9
###.###.###.	The network address for an entire class C network	192.168.16.
###.###.	The network address for an entire class B network	192.168.
###.	The network address for an entire class A network	192.

Table 16.3 Security values available for /etc/ypserv.conf access rules.

Level	Description
deny	Refuses access to the listed map for incoming requests matching this rule.
none	Specifies to always allow access for hosts matching this rule.
port	Looks to see whether the NIS connection is coming in on a port less than number 1024. If it is, access is allowed. If not, access is allowed only if the ***mangle*** value is set to **yes**.

Using An NIS System

When you put NIS into use on your network, people logging in to and using centrally managed accounts need to be aware that they have a separate set of commands to take care of specific functions. These commands, which are outlined in Table 16.4, function almost identically to their local equivalents, which are also listed.

Table 16.4 Commands available to NIS client machine users.

Command	Purpose	Local Equivalent
ypchfn	Enables you to change your full name or other related information on the NIS server	**chfn**
ypchsh	Enables you to change your login shell on the NIS server	**chsh**
yppasswd	Enables you to change your password on the NIS server	**passwd**
ypwhich	Lists this machine's NIS server	None

The following two programs work together with the NIS server to provide the full range of NIS capabilities, including the ability to change passwords. They are bundled with the NIS server RPM in Red Hat. Under other distributions, you may need to install them separately:

- **yppasswdd**—The NIS password update server
- **ypserv**—The main NIS server

Immediate Solutions

Installing The NIS Server

To install your NIS server software under Red Hat Linux, do the following:

1. Log in as root to the machine you want to use as your NIS server.
2. Place the Red Hat CD-ROM into the CD-ROM drive, if it is not there already.

NOTE: *This section is Red Hat–specific. If you are not using Red Hat, then the materials you need to install might be found by searching your file system for one of the following terms: "yp", "nis", or "nys".*

3. Type "mount /mnt/cdrom" if this item is not already mounted onto the file system.
4. Type "cd /mnt/cdrom/RedHat/RPMS" to change to the packages directory.
5. Type "rpm -ivh ypserv" and press Tab to complete the file name, and then press Enter to install the server.
6. It is often a good idea to install the client as well on your server machine. This practice allows you to test the service without involving network issues, and so is good for debugging purposes. Follow the instructions in the following section if you want to accomplish this task.

Installing The NIS Client

To install your NIS client software under Red Hat Linux, do the following:

1. Log in as root to the client machine you want to set up.

NOTE: *This section is Red Hat–specific. If you are not using Red Hat, then the materials you need to install might be found by searching your file system for one of the following terms: "yp", "nis", or "nys".*

2. Place the Red Hat CD-ROM into the CD-ROM drive, if it is not there already.
3. Type "mount /mnt/cdrom" if this item is not already mounted onto the file system.
4. Type "cd /mnt/cdrom/RedHat/RPMS" to change to the packages directory.

5. Type "rpm -ivh ypbind" and press Tab to complete the file name; then, add a space, type "yp-tools", and press Tab again. You should have at this point something similar to the following:

```
rpm -ivh ypbind-3.3-28.i386.rpm yp-tools-2.4-1.i386.rpm
```

6. Press Enter to install the two client portions.

Setting Up An NIS Server

To set up your NIS server under Red Hat Linux, do the following:

1. Log in as root to the machine you want to use as your NIS server.
2. Type "vi /etc/ypserv.conf" to open the main NIS server configuration file.
3. Jump down to the following line:

```
dns: no
```

4. If you want to change this option or add any others, type "i" to enter Insert mode, and then make the changes you need to make.
5. Proceed to the following section:

```
# *                              : passwd.byname    : port        : yes
# *                              : passwd.byuid     : port        : yes
```

6. The first line tells **ypserv** to refer to the map file passwd.byname for all incoming NIS requests, and if the port the requests come in on is above 1023, the contents of the map file are mangled so that the client cannot see the file. The second line basically does the same thing, but instead mangles the contents of passwd.byuid. As the comments in /etc/ypserv.conf state, this method enables you to simulate shadow passwords. If you want to use this method, uncomment the code. You can also change the names of the maps.

NOTE: *If you want to regulate which hosts can access your NIS service itself, wait until Step 13. The definitions in this file regulate map access.*

7. Scroll down to the following:

```
*                          : shadow.byname    : port        : yes
*                          : passwd.adjunct.byname : port   : yes
```

8. This is the section that handles your actual shadow password functionality. If you choose to use the previous section instead, comment this one out. Otherwise, leave it alone.
9. Move down to the last entry in the default configuration file:

```
*                              : *                        : none
```

10. This item declares that no security checks are needed for anyone. If you plan to add any security checks, or decide to later, comment this line out by placing a hash mark (#) at the beginning.
11. Add any other lines that you require.
12. Press the Esc key to enter Command mode, and then type "ZZ" to save and close the file.
13. Type "vi /etc/yp/securenets" to open the file that regulates which hosts can use this server.

NOTE: *If you are using tcp_wrappers, skip this file and set access in the tcp_wrappers files.*

---

14. This file is initially empty. Type "i" to enter Insert mode.
15. Add the following line so that you can test the service from this machine:

```
host 127.0.0.1
```

16. The rest of the entries in the file need to be in the following format:

```
netmask networkIP
```

Use these two numbers to express the range of machines you want to allow to have access to the NIS server. For an entire network, such as 192.168.10.0, you would use:

```
255.255.255.0 192.168.10.0
```

17. After you finish entering the address combinations you need to use, press the Esc key to enter Command mode, and then type "ZZ" to save and close the file.
18. Type "ls /etc/netgroup". If this file does not exist, type "touch /etc/netgroup". Otherwise, the build process will fail.
19. Choose a name for your *NIS domain*. This term is quite misleading, because it does not refer to a "real" domain name, in the DNS sense. An NIS domain name exists only to machines in this NIS domain. It is a way of

making access to your user information even more difficult for outsiders. For example, I might choose animals.nis as my NIS domain, though this might be too easy for intruders to guess in a real-world situation.

20. Put the NIS domain into place by typing "/bin/domainname *nisdomain*". For example, "/bin/domainname animals.nis".
21. Type "/usr/lib/yp/ypinit -m" to start the program that builds your map files. This is an interactive program. This is the first text you see:

```
At this point, we have to construct a list of the hosts
which will run NIS servers. localhost.localdomain is in the
list of NIS server hosts. Please continue to add the names
for the other hosts, one per line. When you are done with
the list, type a <control D>.

    next host to add: localhost.localdomain
    next host to add:
```

22. Add the full *host.domain.extension* for each machine that needs access to the NIS server. Press Enter between each name, because the program adds one host at a time.
23. After you enter the last host, press the key combination Ctrl+D. This ends the host addition process and displays a list of the hosts that you entered, asking you whether the information was entered correctly. If yes, type "y" and proceed. If not, type "n" and reenter the hosts.
24. The **ypinit** program now creates all the map files and other items that the NIS server needs.

Related solution:	Found on page:
Restricting Network Access With **tcp_wrappers**	267

Setting Up An NIS Client

To set up an NIS client under Red Hat Linux, do the following:

1. Log in as root to the client machine you want to set up.
2. Ensure that you followed the instructions in the section "Installing The NIS Client," so that you have the client software already installed.
3. Type "vi /etc/yp.conf" to open the **ypbind**—the program that connects to the NIS server and manages communication with that server—configuration file.

4. This file initially consists of a few comments and nothing else. Type "O" at the beginning of the file to open a new line at the cursor position and enter Insert mode.
5. Use one of these three statement formats to tell **ypbind** how to behave:
   - If you have only one NIS server with one NIS domain name on your network, then use

     ```
     ypserver host
     ```

     where ***host*** is the name of the machine acting as the NIS server.
   - If you have more than one NIS server, each with its own domain name on your network, use a series of lines in this format

     ```
     domain NISdomainname server host
     ```

     where ***NISdomainname*** is the domain used by the NIS server you are defining and ***host*** is the machine this server resides on. Add one line for each domain.
   - If you do not want to state explicitly which machine hosts the NIS server, use the following format for each domain you are using:

     ```
     domain NISdomainname broadcast
     ```

     This tells **ypbind** to broadcast a message on your network to look for the machine that hosts the ***NISdomainname*** server.
6. After you finish adding your code, press the Esc key to return to Command mode, and then type "ZZ" to save and close the file.
7. Type "/etc/rc.d/init.d/ypbind restart" to stop **ypbind** and restart it with the new settings.

Chapter 17

NFS

If you need an immediate solution to:	*See page:*
Setting Up NFS Exports	505
Mounting Remote File Systems With NFS	505
Making And Mounting A Central /usr Directory	506
Creating The /usr Export	506
Mounting The /usr Export	508
Setting Up An NFS Installation Server	509

In Depth

The Network File System (NFS) is a boon to system administrators who need to make information accessible across a Linux network. It enables you to mount file system portions onto other machines on the network just as you would mount a floppy disk or CD-ROM. In this chapter you'll learn how to implement NFS to suit your needs and the concerns you need to keep in mind when you do it.

Introduction To NFS

NFS is a single-function service that enables you to mount Linux partitions from one machine onto another or onto many others. Although NFS is a client/server program, in this case, you are not dealing with a single server and many clients. Every machine that contains a file system segment that you want to share is an NFS server. Usually, all machines on the network tend to be NFS clients.

It is important to remember that any new network service comes with its own security risks. Creating an NFS export opens portions of your file system to outside access—how broad this access is depends on your configuration efforts. Any open door increases the risk that uninvited intruders will try to enter. This concern includes not only people trying to break in to the exports you offer but also those who have access to the exports trying to reach the rest of your file system from them.

If you need to enable NFS mounting of vital data for your business, I recommend doing this behind a firewall (Chapter 9) or IP masquerading (Chapter 7) setup so that outsiders cannot access it.

The NFS Configuration File

The file /etc/exports controls what portions of a machine's file system are made available as NFS exports and who can access them. This file consists of a series of one-line statements, each of which defines a particular item to offer and specifies to whom to offer it. All of these statements are in the following format:

```
path      rules
```

The ***path*** item is simply the path to the directory you want to export. The ***rules*** portion is the meat of the export definition. A rule generically breaks down into two parts: who can access the information, and what guidelines this user, host, or site needs to follow. So, an export statement looks like the following as it is broken down further:

```
path     who(how)
```

When designating ***who*** has access to the information, use one of the formats listed in Table 17.1.

A special item not included in Table 17.1 is **=public**. You have to use this ***who*** setting differently from the others. The following two lines have to be in a file if you want to declare a directory to be a publicly mountable NFS export:

```
path     =public
path     (how)
```

This example also illustrates how to set a rule that applies to everyone. If you have the ***how*** information displayed with no ***who*** information associated with it, it is assumed you mean that no limits exist on who can access this export.

When designating the ***how*** portion of an export rule, use the options listed in Table 17.2.

Putting all of these together results in interesting structures. The following revisits the general format for an export rule with all the pieces in place:

```
path     who1(how1) who2(how2) ... whoN(howN)
```

Any ***how*** item that consists of more than one option is used in this format:

```
(option1,option2,...,optionN)
```

Table 17.1 Formats available to designate who is allowed access in /etc/exports.

Format	Result	Example
****.domain.extension***	Specifies all hosts on the specific ***domain.extension*** listed	***.animals.org**
@netgroup	Specifies the NIS netgroup listed (for more on netgroups, see Chapter 16)	**@felines**
host	Specifies the hostname listed, as set in /etc/hosts	**cat**
host.domain.extension	Specifies the fully qualified domain name listed	**cat.animals.org**
hostIP	Specifies the IP address listed	**192.168.10.6**
network/netmask	Specifies the subnet or network listed	**192.168.10.0/255.255.255.0**

Table 17.2 Options available to designate how access is allowed in /etc/exports.

Format	Result	Example
all_squash	Maps all users accessing the specified export to be anonymous	**all_squash**
anongid	Sets to a specific value the GID used for anonymous access	**anongid=540**
anonuid	Sets to a specific value the UID used for anonymous access	**anonuid=570**
async	Tells the NFS server to write data to the disks when it chooses to	**async**
insecure	Allows incoming client requests to come in on any port	**insecure**
no_all_squash	Maps incoming client requests to users through one of the specified methods	**no_all_squash**
no_wdelay	Tells the NFS server to not anticipate other potential write requests; only available when **sync** is used	**no_wdelay**
no_root_squash	Allows root client requests to be mapped to root on the server machine	**no_root_squash**
ro	Sets the export to read-only status	**ro**
root_squash	Maps root client requests to an anonymous UID and GID	**root_squash**
rw	Sets the export to read-write status	**rw**
secure	Requires client requests to come from a port lower than 1024 on the client machine	**secure**
sync	Tells the NFS server to write data to the disks whenever it first comes available	**sync**
wdelay	Tells the NFS server to anticipate other potential write requests	**wdelay**

Immediate Solutions

Setting Up NFS Exports

To set up an NFS export on a machine, do the following:

1. Log in as root to the machine you want to export file system space from.
2. Type "rpm -q nfs-utils". If this package is already installed, skip to Step 7.
3. Place the Red Hat CD-ROM into the CD-ROM drive.
4. Type "mount /mnt/cdrom" to mount the CD-ROM onto the file system.
5. Type "cd /mnt/cdrom/RedHat/RPMS" to change to the RPMS directory.
6. Type "rpm -ivh nfs-utils" and press Tab to expand the file name, and then press Enter to install the RPM.
7. Type "vi /etc/exports" to open the NFS export configuration file.
8. This is an empty file. Type "i" to enter Insert mode.
9. One by one, build your export statements. For example, perhaps you want to export the /home directories for your users. You might use:

```
/home      *.animals.org(secure,rw,root_squash)
```

10. After you are finished, press the Esc key to enter Command mode, and then type "ZZ" to save and close the file.
11. Type "/etc/rc.d/init.d/nfs restart" to restart the NFS daemon, **nfsd**.

Mounting Remote File Systems With NFS

To mount an NFS export from another machine, do the following:

1. Log in as root to the machine you want to mount an NFS export onto.
2. Determine whether you want to mount this item permanently or temporarily.
3. If you want to mount the export temporarily, use the **mount** command in the following format, after which you are finished with this section:

```
mount host:/export /mountpoint
```

NOTE: *Proper technique requires* ***mount -t nfs****. However, the* ***mount*** *command recognizes the* ***host:/export*** *format as referring to an NFS export.*

---

4. If you want to mount the export permanently, type "vi /etc/fstab" to open the main file system management file.
5. Cursor to where within this file you want to add the new statement.
6. Type "O" to open a new line at your cursor position and enter Insert mode.
7. Add your line in the following format:

   ```
   host:export     mountpoint     nfs     options     dump  order
   ```

   For example, you might use:

   ```
   cat:/home     /mnt/nfshome     nfs     defaults  0  6
   ```

8. After adding all the exports you want to have permanently mounted, press the Esc key to enter Command mode, and then type "ZZ" to save and close the file. These changes will not go into effect until you reboot the system.

Related solutions:	Found on page:
Adding And Removing Media To The File System	84
Shutting Down And Rebooting	97

Making And Mounting A Central /usr Directory

A popular use of NFS is to create a single /usr directory that is mounted across all or most of your machines. This makes maintenance of the various programs used across your network easier, because you need to update them in only one place.

Creating The /usr Export

To set this up on the server, do the following:

1. Log in as root to the machine you want to set up to carry the centralized /usr directory.
2. Type "vi /etc/exports" to open the NFS exports file.
3. Type "G" to go to the end of the file.
4. Type "o" to open a new line below the current cursor location and enter Insert mode.
5. Open another virtual terminal.

```
[root@localhost /usr]# ls -la
total 144
drwxr-xr-x   21 root     root         4096 Apr  1 02:29 .
drwxr-xr-x   17 root     root         4096 Apr  1 02:11 ..
drwxr-xr-x    8 root     root         4096 Mar  6 08:20 X11R6
drwxr-xr-x    2 root     root        28672 Apr  1 02:45 bin
drwxr-xr-x    2 root     root         4096 Apr  1 02:43 dict
drwxr-xr-x  224 root     root         8192 Apr  1 02:45 doc
drwxr-xr-x    2 root     root         4096 Feb  6  1996 etc
drwxr-xr-x    2 root     root         4096 Apr  1 02:43 games
drwxr-xr-x    4 root     root         4096 Apr  1 02:16 i386-redhat-linux
drwxr-xr-x    3 root     root         4096 Apr  1 02:29 i486-linux-libc5
drwxr-xr-x   57 root     root         8192 Apr  1 02:45 include
drwxr-xr-x    2 root     root         8192 Apr  1 02:43 info
drwxr-xr-x    7 root     root         4096 Apr  1 02:29 kerberos
drwxr-xr-x   55 root     root        16384 Apr  1 02:45 lib
drwxr-xr-x    6 root     root         4096 Apr  1 02:37 libexec
drwxr-xr-x   11 root     root         4096 Apr  1 02:11 local
drwxr-xr-x    2 root     root        16384 Apr  1 02:09 lost+found
drwxr-xr-x   12 root     root         4096 Apr  2 04:02 man
drwxr-xr-x    2 root     root         4096 Apr  1 02:45 sbin
drwxr-xr-x   67 root     root         4096 Apr  1 02:43 share
drwxr-xr-x    4 root     root         4096 Apr  1 02:29 src
lrwxrwxrwx    1 root     root           10 Apr  1 02:11 tmp -> ../var/tmp
[root@localhost /usr]#
```

Figure 17.1 The contents of /usr in Red Hat Linux.

6. In this virtual terminal, type "ls -la /usr". You should get something similar to what is shown in Figure 17.1.
7. Change back to the exports file.
8. The goal here is to offer the entire /usr hierarchy for export except for /usr/local, because this directory is for use by individual machines. NFS allows you to export a directory either with all of its subdirectories or with none. No "except" functionality is available, unfortunately. So, you add a line for each of the subdirectories except for /usr/local. What you end up with might be similar to the following:

```
/usr/bin      *.animals.org(secure,ro)
/usr/dict     *.animals.org(secure,ro)
/usr/doc      *.animals.org(secure,ro)
/usr/etc      *.animals.org(secure,ro)
/usr/games    *.animals.org(secure,ro)
/usr/i386-redhat-linux    *.animals.org(secure,ro)
/usr/i486-linux-libc5     *.animals.org(secure,ro)
/usr/include *.animals.org(secure,ro)
```

```
/usr/info    *.animals.org(secure,ro)
/usr/kerberos    *.animals.org(secure,ro)
/usr/lib     *.animals.org(secure,ro)
/usr/libexec     *.animals.org(secure,ro)
/usr/lost+found  *.animals.org(secure,ro)
/usr/man     *.animals.org(secure,ro)
/usr/sbin    *.animals.org(secure,ro)
/usr/share   *.animals.org(secure,ro)
/usr/src     *.animals.org(secure,ro)
/usr/X11R6   *.animals.org(secure,ro)
```

NOTE: *I left out /usr/tmp because this is a link to a directory that you might choose to use locally rather than mount.*

9. Press the Esc key to enter Command mode, and then type “ZZ” to save and close the file.
10. Type “/etc/rc.d/init.d/nfs restart” to restart the NFS daemon, **nfsd**.

Mounting The /usr Export

To set up clients to mount an external /usr export, do the following on each client:

1. Log in as root on the client machine.
2. Type “cd /usr” to change to the /usr directory.
3. Type “vi /etc/fstab” to open the file system loading file.
4. Move the cursor to where you want to begin issuing mount instructions.
5. Type “O” to open a new line at the current cursor position and enter Insert mode.
6. You need to add a line for each of the directories you plan to mount. Use this format:

   ```
   host:/usr/dir     /usr/dir     nfs     options dump order
   ```

   Here are some example lines:

   ```
   cat:/usr/bin     /usr/bin     nfs     defaults  0  5
   cat:/usr/dict     /usr/dict     nfs     defaults  0  6
   cat:/usr/doc     /usr/doc     nfs     defaults  0  7
   ```

7. After you finish adding these lines, press the Esc key to enter Command mode, and then type “ZZ” to save and close the file.

8. Empty each of the directories you plan to mount. For example, to empty /usr/bin, type "cd bin" to change into the directory and then type "rm -rf *" to empty it. Repeat this step for each of the directories you are going to mount.

   You can choose to leave the files in these directories in place. However, you will not be able to access the local files while a remote NFS version is mounted over top of them. It is also hard to tell if the mount succeeded or not if you leave the old ones in place. The old files can waste file system space and cause confusion. Save leaving the local versions in place for machines that cannot afford any downtime—in case the NFS server goes down—or that you might want to use as a backup NFS /usr server. Just remember to update the programs on this machine as well as the main server.

WARNING!* *Always triple-check where you are in your directory structure before typing "rm -rf *", especially as root. Also, do not delete the directories themselves. You need them as mount points.

9. To put the changes into effect, you have three options:
   - Reboot the machine.
   - Type "mountall".
   - Type "mount -a".

Related solution:	Found on page:
Shutting Down And Rebooting	97

Setting Up An NFS Installation Server

If you need to install the same distribution on multiple machines across a network, it is useful to set up an NFS export on a server that contains the necessary installation data. To accomplish this for Red Hat Linux, do the following:

1. Log in as root to the machine you want to set up as your NFS install server.
2. Choose where you want to place the installation server. Because it needs to be mountable by all new machines, I recommend putting this data on its own partition. For an example, assume I have a partition on /dev/hdb1 mounted at /Install.
3. Place the CD-ROM in the CD-ROM drive.
4. Type "mount /mnt/cdrom" to mount the CD-ROM onto the file system.

5. Type “cd /mnt/cdrom” to change to the CD-ROM’s root directory.
6. Type “cp -rv * /Install” to recursively copy the entire contents of /mnt/cdrom to /Install in verbose mode. This causes a lot of information to scroll across your screen, but it at least gives you a sense of where in the process you are.
7. After the copy finishes, type “cd /” to leave the mounted segment of the file system.
8. Type “umount /mnt/cdrom” to remove the CD-ROM from the file system.
9. If you have additional items that you want to install, give them a home in the /Install equivalent of your file system. For additional RPMs, place them in the equivalent of /Install/RedHat/RPMS.
10. Type “vi /etc/exports” to open the master export management file.
11. Type “G” to go to the end of the file.
12. Type “o” to add a new line at the end of the file and enter Insert mode.
13. Create the export statement for this part of the file system. For example, because you do not actually need anyone to log in, you might use something similar to the following:

```
/Install    *.animals.org(all_squash,ro)
```

14. Press the Esc key to return to Command mode, and then type “ZZ” to save and close the file.
15. Type “/etc/rc.d/init.d/nfs restart” to restart the NFS daemon, **nfsd**.

Chapter 18

Samba

If you need an immediate solution to:	*See page:*
Installing Samba	527
Configuring Samba	527
Offering Linux Partitions	537
Building A File Share Statement	541
Mounting Windows Shares Under Linux	546
Offering Windows Shares	546
Offering Linux Printers	550
Building A Print Share Statement	551
Utilizing Windows Printers Under Linux	554
Implementing Encrypted Passwords Over Samba	555
Creating A User Map	556
Creating A Host Map	557
Creating Login Scripts	558

In Depth

Samba is a useful tool for anyone who needs to integrate machines running multiple operating systems. Although sharing bandwidth among operating systems is relatively simple when they are all utilizing TCP/IP as their networking protocol, getting these machines to actually read each others' files and share printers is not nearly so easy. That is, unless you use Samba!

Introduction To Samba

Samba is the Linux implementation of the Server Message Block (SMB) protocol. This protocol is used to allow file system and printer interaction across multiple-operating system networks. In plain English, using Samba enables you to do the following:

- Mount Microsoft Windows folders onto your Linux boxes
- Mount Linux file system segments onto your Windows boxes
- Mount file system segments between a Linux box and any other operating system that utilizes SMB—a Macintosh machine, other Unix flavors, or even another Linux box
- Print to a printer attached to a Windows machine from a Linux box
- Print to a printer attached to a Linux machine from a Windows box
- Utilize printers between operating systems that speak SMB

The Daemons And What They Do

Two different daemons provide SMB service on a Linux machine: **smbd** and **nmbd**. Each of these daemons has a specialized function that, together, provide everything you need to run Samba.

The **smbd** daemon is the service that handles file and print sharing. It receives requests from clients and reacts according to server configuration. When you are talking about something Samba does, you usually are referring to **smbd**. The exceptions are two specific functions handled by **nmbd** that help Linux's SMB implementation work well with other operating systems.

Primarily, **nmbd** handles Network Basic Input/Output System (NetBIOS) name translation. This is a machine naming system developed by IBM, but now used primarily by Microsoft, that enables applications to know machines by a NetBIOS name instead of needing to know what kind of network the machine is on.

NetBIOS requests are sent as Network Control Blocks (NCBs). This chunk of data includes the NetBIOS name of the machine it came from, and the NetBIOS name of the machine it needs to go to. The NCB is then handed off to the Transmission Control Protocol (TCP), which is TCP/IP's Transport layer (discussed in Chapter 7). **nmbd**'s job is to watch for NCBs and process them.

Another type of service available from **nmbd** is the Windows Internet Naming Service (WINS), which typically is run by a Microsoft Windows NT Server. WINS is an address mapping service. It is a supplement to Domain Name System (DNS), and even to the Dynamic Host Configuration Protocol (DHCP) service in many ways. If you are using DHCP to assign addresses to hosts, then you are probably running a WINS server on an NT machine if you have a collection of Windows machines. In this kind of situation, when a Windows machine boots, it gets its IP address from the DHCP server, although it likely has a static NetBIOS name already configured. Its WINS client then contacts the WINS server to inform it of the machine's current IP address. Thereafter, when any machine on the Windows side of the network needs to exchange packets with another machine, it asks the WINS server for the address assigned to the receiver's NetBIOS name, and data flows as usual.

The **nmbd** daemon enables Samba on a Linux box to make these same kind of WINS client queries to your NT WINS server.

Samba Concerns

You should not implement any network services without considering the risks inherent in making them available, and how you can minimize these risks. The major risk with Samba is that you are opening access to file system segments on specific machines. If people can find their way around your configured safety measures somehow, then they may be able to gain access to copy, change, or delete information.

One issue is *browsing*. Samba servers can respond to requests from authorized machines to give a list of the shares available. Giving out this list is like handing a potential intruder a sheet of targets. Take care in how you configure browsing access. Also, be sure to read up on all security features available. Be especially careful to allow access only to the people who really need it.

The Samba Configuration File

The configuration file used to configure Samba items offered under Linux is /etc/smb.conf. I will walk you through the default file and explain what is there, though a lot of commented-out text is removed for brevity's sake. Remember that a poorly configured network service provides open doors for intruders, so really take the time to understand what you are dealing with here.

Global Samba Settings

The /etc/smb.conf file is divided into three sections. The first is introduced as follows:

```
#======================= Global Settings =====================================
[global]
```

As usual, the lines beginning with hash marks (#) are commented out. Each of the sections begins with a marker line such as this, to help you keep things straight. The second line in the preceding listing is the actual share definition marker. It tells Samba that everything after it that is not a comment or a new share definition is a global setting, and so applies to all other shares. These global settings can be overridden for individual shared partitions or printers later in the file.

The following is the first statement in the global definitions section:

```
# workgroup = NT-Domain-Name or Workgroup-Name
  workgroup = MYGROUP
```

The **workgroup** setting enables you to assign a name to a group of machines. Using this item in the global area assigns a default name. After this line is the following:

```
# server string is the equivalent of the NT Description field
  server string = Samba Server
```

The **server string** setting assigns a text string to identify this Samba server. Now to a commented-out statement:

```
;   hosts allow = 192.168.1. 192.168.2. 127.
```

Two types of comments are available in /etc/smb.conf. You can use either a hash mark or a semicolon to tell the Samba server to ignore a line. Typically, hash marks are used to denote commentary in the configuration file, whereas semicolons are used to mark code that you can uncomment if you choose to.

The **hosts allow** setting provides a form of access control to the Samba server. Hosts can be specified in the formats listed in Table 18.1. Adding to the complexity of possible statements, you also have the **EXCEPT** operator available to you. When you specify a range of hosts that are allowed to access your Samba server, you can then use **EXCEPT** to single out hosts within that range that should not be included.

Table 18.1 Methods of specifying hosts in /etc/smb.conf.

Format	Description	Example
host	Specifies the name of the machine you are referring to	**blue**
hostIP	Specifies the IP address for the machine you are referring to	**192.168.160.5**
networkIP	Specifies an entire network of machines using a wildcard format	**192.168.160**
IPrange	Specifies a range of IP addresses	**192.168.160.0/ 255.255.255.110**

After setting what hosts are allowed, the file has the following statements:

```
printcap name = /etc/printcap
load printers = yes
```

The **printcap name** statement sets the file that Samba looks to when it needs to access printers. On the other hand, the **load printers** statement is more basic. If you answer **yes** here, then all printers in the file specified in the preceding line are loaded for use by Samba-connected machines. An answer of **no** refuses access to the printers over SMB.

After the basic printer issues are dealt with, you can ignore the following line:

```
;   printing = bsd
```

The **printing** statement determines how Samba tries to talk to the printers. Possible print system types—whether specific to a particular Unix flavor or independent of flavor—are listed in Table 18.2. Although the types defined in the table are uppercased because they are typically acronyms, they should be lowercased with the **printing** statement.

After the **printing** statement is more commented-out code:

```
;  guest account = pcguest
```

The **guest account** statement enables you to specify what username is assigned to guest logins, if they are activated for the service the user is trying to access. When this line is commented out, as you see now, guest accesses are assigned to the **nobody** account. After deciding on guest access, you reach the following:

```
log file = /var/log/samba/log.%m
```

Table 18.2 Print system types available in /etc/smb.conf.

Type	Operating System
AIX	A Unix flavor created and maintained by IBM
BSD	A Unix flavor created by Berkeley Software Distribution at the University of California at Berkeley and now maintained by Berkeley Software Design
HPUX	A Unix flavor created and maintained by Hewlett-Packard
LPRNG	A print spooling system based on that used by BSD; this is the collection of print tools used under many Linux distributions, including Red Hat
PLP	A print spooling system that also is used under some Linux distributions, such as SuSE
QNX	A Unix-flavor realtime operating system
SOFTQ	Another real-time Unix operating system
SYSV	A Unix flavor created and maintained by AT&T

As with most network services, several logging options are available with Samba. These statements are important because they enable you to keep data regarding connections, attempted connections, and more. The more data you have available, the better chance you have of catching potential intruders.

The **log file** statement sets the name and path of the file that Samba logs information to. Having **%m** at the end of the file name means that there will be a series of log files in the location specified by the path in this statement, each with the name log.*NetBIOS*. Other variables used in /etc/smb.conf are listed in Table 18.3.

After setting the log file's name and location, you reach this line:

```
max log size = 50
```

The **max log size** directive sets how large Samba should let its log files get. The associated value is in kilobytes, and using a 0 means the log file size is unlimited—a bad idea, unless you enjoy having your file system overrun by log files. When a file reaches the listed size, Samba renames the existing file with an .old extension and starts a new file using the original name. You can then have shell scripts—discussed in Chapter 20—back up and compress these files so that you can keep them for analysis, if you need them, without filling up the file system.

After you finish with the log information, it is time to move on to security:

```
security = user
```

The **security** statement determines how clients authenticate themselves with the server. There are four different security modes available in Samba 2, which is what you are using if you have Red Hat 6.2 or later. These modes are:

Table 18.3 Substitution variables used in /etc/smb.conf.

Variable	Value
%a	The remote machine's architecture, out of WfWg (Windows for Workgroups), Win95, WinNT, Samba, or UNKNOWN; not entirely reliable
%d	The Samba server PID
%g	The primary group assigned to the incoming user
%G	The primary group that the incoming user wanted access to
%h	The name of the host running the Samba server
%H	The home directory belonging to the incoming user
%I	The remote machine's IP address
%L	The server's NetBIOS name
%m	The remote machine's NetBIOS name
%M	The remote machine's hostname
%N	The name of the Network Information System (NIS) server
%p	The path to the NIS-served home directory
%P	The root of the accessed directory
%S	The name of the accessed Samba offering
%T	The current date and time
%u	The username assigned to the current Samba access
%U	The username the client requested
%v	The version number for the Samba server

- **security=domain**—Authenticates incoming connections through a Windows NT domain controller. Linux machines have to be added to the domain controller through the Linux **smbpasswd** command, and you must have the Samba **encrypt passwords** statement set to **yes**. For NT users to access the Linux box, they need to have an account on the Samba server with the same name as their NT account.
- **security=server**—Authenticates incoming connections with the help of another SMB-capable server. The server to use is specified by the **password server** statement.
- **security=share**—Does not require any form of authentication. It is primarily useful on print servers where you cannot count on incoming Samba requests coming from accounts that also exist on the server box.
- **security=user**—Ensures that Samba clients must authenticate at login time, just like any other user must. For this reason, this setting is useful when you are consistent in assigning login information regardless of the operating

system. If your Windows accounts are identical to your Linux accounts, then choose this security level. User security often is also necessary for connecting with Windows 95, 98, and NT machines. However, this setting does not work well with Windows for Workgroups—Windows 3.11—due to a bug in the share handling. This is the default setting.

After the security designation comes a line that you may need to configure, according to which option you chose:

```
;   password server = <NT-Server-Name>
```

This line is commented out. The **password server** statement—as hinted at earlier—enables you to point Samba to one or more SMB-capable servers. Often, this server is either another Linux or Unix Samba server, or a Windows NT server.

Moving on to more fine-tuned password issues, consider the following lines:

```
;  password level = 8
;  username level = 8
```

The **password level** statement is necessary in cases where not all of the machines you need to access with Samba handle upper- and lowercasing of passwords properly—such as Windows for Workgroups (Windows 3.11). The integer you set as the level represents how many characters in the password have the potential of being upper- or lowercase.

The **username level** statement functions the same as the **password level** statement.

Proceeding to yet more password-handling fine-tuning, you encounter the following lines:

```
;  encrypt passwords = yes
;  smb passwd file = /etc/smbpasswd
```

First among these two lines is the **encrypt passwords** statement, which has only two possible values: **yes** or **no**. When activated, this statement determines whether the Samba server requests encrypted passwords from the clients. The **smb passwd file** statement points to the file that contains the encrypted passwords that the Samba server may need to verify. More related statements follow:

```
;  unix password sync = Yes
;  passwd program = /usr/bin/passwd %u
;  passwd chat = *New*UNIX*password* %n\n *ReType*new*UNIX*password* %n\n
  *passwd:*all*authentication*tokens*updated*successfully*
```

The **unix password sync** statement, if uncommented along with **encrypt passwords**, ensures that the user's login password changes whenever the SMB-encrypted password changes. To accomplish this task, Samba calls the program specified by **passwd program**. The tool specified by the **passwd chat** statement regulates the discussion between the Samba server and the tool set in the **passwd program** statement. **passwd chat** contains the information necessary to answer the **passwd program**'s requests. In the preceding code, this exchange begins with the Samba server watching for ***New*UNIX*password***. The asterisks are wildcards that accept any text, the purpose of which is to ignore any formatting or additional language around these three keywords. When the Samba server receives this collection of words, it sends **%n**, which is the new password, and then finishes by sending the newline character, **\n**.

After the information is sent, the Samba server waits for ***ReType* new*UNIX*password***, once again using wildcards to assure that it is only watching for keywords. When it receives this text, it sends the new password and again sends a newline. The code continues on to the next line. When the server sees ***passwd:*all*authentication*tokens*updated*successfully***, it knows that all is well and considers the password changed.

The following line begins the code that handles usernames:

```
;  username map = /etc/smbusers
```

The **username map** statement points to a file containing data on how to convert usernames from remote machines to this machine. See the Immediate Solutions section "Creating A User Map" for instructions on how to set up one of these map files. The value for this statement is the path to the map file.

You can also set Samba to handle various machines differently, with the following:

```
;   include = /etc/smb.conf.%m
```

An **include** statement enables you to insert additional configuration files for particular machines. You can use any substitution method in this statement, except for **%u**, **%P**, or **%S**.

Next is the following line:

```
socket options = TCP_NODELAY SO_RCVBUF=8192 SO_SNDBUF=8192
```

The **socket options** statement sets what *network socket* the Samba server uses to talk to clients. A *socket* is the point through which network clients and servers send and receive data. After the sockets are set, you would have the following line if the IP addresses matched yours:

```
;    interfaces = 192.168.12.2/24 192.168.13.2/24
```

An **interfaces** statement enables you to explicitly tell Samba what interfaces—Ethernet cards, usually—to use when *broadcasting* information. Recall from Chapter 7 that the last address in a network or subnet address block is called the *broadcast address*, which is used to send information to every machine on the network. The kernel typically will tell Samba to use this address for its own broadcasts. However, you can override this function with the **interfaces** statement in one of the following formats:

- An interface name, typically eth0 or eth1
- A wildcarded interface name, typically eth*
- An *IPaddress/netmask* pair
- An *IPaddress/netbit* pair, such as shown in the previous example code

After the **interfaces** are configured or left commented out, the file continues with this line:

```
;    remote browse sync = 192.168.3.25 192.168.5.255
```

The **remote browse sync** statement is used to get the **nmbd** Samba daemon to update its NetBIOS list from a master **nmbd** daemon on another machine or machines. After this is the following:

```
;    remote announce = 192.168.1.255 192.168.2.44
```

This statement also deals with **nmbd**. The **remote announce** statement tells **nmbd** to broadcast its availability to a specific list of addresses, which might be individual IP addresses or network/subnet broadcast addresses.

The next section deals with SMB browsing. The following is the first line in this section:

```
;    local master = no
```

The **local master** statement is initially commented out because it is assumed that you want this **nmbd** daemon to offer its services to Samba clients wanting to see what shares you are offering. Next, you set this server's level of prominence in browser elections:

```
;    os level = 33
```

Browser elections involve each master browser offering its services to a client. The **os level** statement sets the **nmbd** server's likelihood to win in a browser election. After this is the following line:

```
;   domain master = yes
```

Each workgroup or subnet needs a master domain controller for browsing purposes. The **domain master** statement enables you to set a server to be that master domain controller. Another master-related statement is shown here:

```
;   preferred master = yes
```

This statement forces a browser election when the server comes online, and gives it an advantage in winning. The next statement handles Windows workgroup domain service:

```
;   domain logons = yes
```

The **domain logons** statement, when activated, tells this server to offer workgroup domain login service to Windows 95 and 98 machines. Next are two virtually identical lines provided for you to choose between the first line, which uses the client machine's NetBIOS name as the file name, and the second line, which uses the username that the client requested:

```
;   logon script = %m.bat
;   logon script = %U.bat
```

These two **logon script** statements enable you to tell a machine providing domain login service to download and run initialization scripts when they log in to the domain. Another Windows-related setting follows:

```
;   logon path = \\%L\Profiles\%U
```

The **logon path** statement enables Samba to hand out roaming profiles to Windows 95 and 98 machines. A *roaming profile* is a collection of data required to set up a user's desktop in the format they prefer. When roaming profiles are enabled, the Windows 95 and 98 machines will always get a copy of the profile when the user logs on, and then will save the current desktop information back to the Samba server as the user logs off.

Leaving the browsing options, you next see this line:

```
; name resolve order = wins lmhosts bcast
```

The **name resolve order** statement manually sets where the Samba server looks to map hostnames to IP addresses. This line is commented out because it is not needed unless you implement particular features, which are discussed in the Immediate Solutions section "Configuring Samba."

Now you come to a section that focuses on WINS. The first statement here is as follows:

```
;   wins support = yes
```

The **wins support** statement tells **nmbd** on this particular machine to offer WINS service. Next is this WINS configuration statement, which typically is not used with the previous one:

```
;   wins server = w.x.y.z
```

You use **wins server** to give the IP address for the WINS server that Samba should talk to when it needs WINS for address resolution. Next is another WINS-related setting:

```
dns proxy = no
```

When set to **yes**, the **dns proxy** statement is used for situations in which a WINS hostname is requested but no machine answers to that name. An active **dns proxy** statement tells **nmbd** in these situations to turn the NetBIOS name into a hostname, or a *host.domain.extension* if the NetBIOS name is formed in this fashion. Samba then tries to look up the address for the DNS version of the NetBIOS name.

The next set of statements controls how Samba handles upper- and lowercase characters in file names. The first is the **preserve case** statement:

```
;  preserve case = no
```

This statement is active by default. It sets whether the client has control over the case used in file names on Samba shares, or whether the server alters the case. Another data option is this statement:

```
;  short preserve case = no
```

The **short preserve case** statement is also active by default. It controls how file names in the format *ABCDEFGH.ZYX*—eight uppercase characters, followed by a three-uppercase-character extension—are treated. Next is the item that both of these previous statements need if they are set to **no**:

```
;  default case = lower
```

The **default case** statement sets how file names that need to be altered are changed. And, finally, the last item in the global section is the following:

```
;  case sensitive = no
```

This statement determines whether Samba requires its client users to enter file names exactly in the case they are represented with on the share, or if Samba checks whether a file exists regardless of the case used on the share.

Individual Share Settings

The second segment of the /etc/smb.conf file is where you set up each individual share that you want to offer from this machine. This section is clearly marked with this border:

```
#==================== Share Definitions ==================
```

Everything set from here on applies only to the particular share. In some cases, you will encounter global definitions that are being overridden. When setting up your own file, you may also realize that you tend to set the same values for each share, and thus may decide to make some of them global, as well, to save yourself some typing. If you decide you want to make these kinds of sweeping changes, be sure to look in the smb.conf man page to determine which statements are allowed in the global section, which are allowed in the shares section, and which are allowed in both.

Each share is named within brackets. For example, the first share definition is as follows:

```
[homes]
   comment = Home Directories
   browseable = no
   writable = yes
```

The **[homes]** share is reserved for Samba's use, so do not use it unless you intend to offer access to user home directories. In this definition statement, three share options are introduced. The **comment** option enables you to enter descriptive text that will be displayed when clients browse to see what your Samba server offers. Here, you walk a fine line between giving away too much information to potential intruders and providing enough information for users to find what they need to access.

The **browseable** option enables you to prevent or allow a particular share—in this case, user home directories—to be displayed when users browse the available shares on this Samba server. On the other hand, having the **writable** option set to **yes** configures the share as read-write.

This next share definition offers a Windows NT service:

```
; [netlogon]
;    comment = Network Logon Service
;    path = /home/netlogon
;    guest ok = yes
;    writable = no
;    share modes = no
```

NOTE: *The items **writeable** and **writable** are synonymous for the purpose of setting the ability to write to a share.*

The **[netlogon]** share is another reserved location. Instead of pointing to a section of the file system that you want to allow other Samba machines to have access to, **[netlogon]** activates a network logon authentication service. Many Windows system administrators use a system called Microsoft LAN Manager to handle logins to the local domain. LAN Manager not only handles user authentication but also keeps track of each machine's installed hardware and software, as well as each machine's current configuration.

One service offered by LAN Manager is Netlogon. This particular service keeps all the databases up to date so that when LAN Manager needs to hand out configuration information, it is not dealing with outdated data. The three new share options available here are the following:

- **path**—The portion of the file system you want to share
- **guest ok**—Enables accesses to the share from any account without asking for a password
- **share modes**—Simulates file mode capabilities used in Windows

The next definition also provides a Windows service:

```
;[Profiles]
;     path = /home/profiles
;     browseable = no
;     guest ok = yes
```

The **[Profiles]** share is used to store data for the Windows roaming-profile service, as discussed previously with regard to the **logon path** statement. After this is a statement dealing with print shares, not file shares:

```
[printers]
  comment = All Printers
  path = /var/spool/samba
  browseable = no
  guest ok = no
  writable = no
  printable = yes
```

Another reserved share name is **[printers]**. This share sets the defaults for all printers configured on this Samba server. The only new option here is **printable**, which sets whether or not the Samba server will allow clients to send print jobs.

The next statement returns you to file sharing:

```
;[tmp]
;   comment = Temporary file space
;   path = /tmp
;   read only = no
;   public = yes
```

The **[tmp]** share is not reserved, so if you want to define a whole new section with **[tmp]**, this is perfectly fine. Here, you learn two more share options. The first is **read only**, which enables you to control whether people can write to the share. Second, you have the **public** option. This is actually the same as using **guest ok**.

This next sample statement is more complex:

```
;[public]
;   comment = Public Stuff
;   path = /home/samba
;   public = yes
;   writable = yes
;   printable = no
;   write list = @staff
```

Once again, the **[public]** share is not reserved, so you can use the name for something else if you want. The tricky part in this statement is the **write list** option. This parameter enables you to set exactly who has access to the share. The two types of parameters you can use are usernames and group names. A username is simply typed as is; for example:

```
write list = sally
```

A group name, however, has an @ symbol at the front of it, as in the preceding **[public]** share definition.

After this section comes a series of example shares. Each of these shares demonstrates something you can do with Samba. Rather than covering these examples in detail in this chapter, you should look them over in the file on your own. Most of the elements should already be familiar, and explanations for any that you aren't familiar with are available in the man page for smb.conf.

Immediate Solutions

Installing Samba

To install Samba on a Red Hat Linux machine, do the following:

1. Log on as root to the machine you want to install one or more Samba components on.
2. Insert the Red Hat CD-ROM into the CD-ROM drive, if you have not already done so.
3. Type "mount /mnt/cdrom" if the CD-ROM is not already mounted onto your file system.
4. Before you install either the Samba client or server, you need to install program items needed by both. Type "rpm -ivh samba-common". Press Tab to expand the file name, and then press Enter to install the package.
5. If you want this machine to function as a Samba client, type "rpm -ivh samba-client". Press Tab to expand the file name, and then press Enter to install the package.
6. If you want this machine to function as a Samba server, type "rpm -ivh samba-2". Press Tab to expand the file name, and then press Enter to install the package.

Configuring Samba

You should look over some specific items before you proceed to set up particular Samba functions. To set up Samba for general use, do the following:

1. Log on as root to the machine on which you want to set up Samba services.
2. Type "vi /etc/smb.conf" to open the Samba configuration file.
3. Cursor down to the following line:

```
workgroup = MYGROUP
```

4. If you have a Windows workgroup that all of your machines need to be a member of, then change **MYGROUP** to the workgroup's name. Be sure to

keep the name in all uppercase letters. Otherwise, you can either comment this line out—by adding a semicolon at the beginning—or change the generic group name to something more interesting, such as COLORSGROUP for colors.org.

5. Continue down to:

```
server string = Samba Server
```

6. You can leave this value as is if you have only one Samba server on your system. Otherwise, you probably want to label this server uniquely. If you intend to offer any type of public server access, do not include the Samba server's software version or any identifying information about the type of machine it is running on. For example, colors.org might change its Samba server's designation to the following:

```
server string = Samba shares at colors.org
```

7. Use the cursor to move to:

```
;   hosts allow = 192.168.1. 192.168.2. 127.
```

8. If you want to globally set who has access to your Samba server—a good idea if you intend to let only people within your own network access this service—first uncomment the line by removing the semicolon, and then change the listed host identifiers. For example, if colors.org has the class C network 192.168.200.0 for its IP address assignment needs, but does not want to allow the machine 192.168.200.101 to use the Samba services because it is in a public location, you might use the following:

```
hosts allow = 192.168.200. EXCEPT 192.168.200.101
```

9. Continue to this statement:

```
printcap name = /etc/printcap
```

10. If you want to have a separate printer configuration file for print jobs coming in through SMB, then change this value. Otherwise, leave it alone. An example might be the following:

```
printcap name = /etc/smbprintcap
```

NOTE: *If you do point to a different printer configuration file, take care to set it up exactly the way you would set up /etc/printcap, including creating all the necessary files and directories.*

11. Move the cursor to the following line:

```
;  guest account = pcguest
```

12. If you want guest logins to come into an account other than **nobody**, uncomment this line by deleting the semicolon, and then change **pcguest** to the account name you want guests to use.

NOTE: *If the guest account does not exist yet, you need to create it before guest accesses will be able to occur.*

---

13. Continue to:

```
log file = /var/log/samba/log.%m
```

14. If you want the Samba log file to be stored by another name or in another location, edit the preceding statement. Depending on how you have your Samba shared items divided, you also may want to change the value used as the log file extension. For example, the following statement would keep separate logs for the root directory locations of each access:

```
log file = /var/log/samba/log.%P
```

15. Proceed to the following line:

```
max log size = 50
```

16. If you want to change how large Samba allows log files to get, change the value here. The following factors affect this decision:
    - How large your file system is, particularly the partition that contains /var/log or the new location you assigned log files to.
    - How you divided your log files with Samba variables. If you have a lot of individual log files, then you need to be more careful with sizing than if you have only one or two files.
    - Usage patterns. When you first set up Samba, it is worth spending some time watching the log files to see how many you have and how fast they grow. Then, adjust the **max log size** statement and the **log file** statement appropriately.
17. Cursor down to:

```
security = user
```

18. Choose which of the four options—share, user, domain, or server—you want to use. If you intend mostly to have guest connections, then change this line to:

```
security = share
```

19. The next item is:

```
;   password server = <NT-Server-Name>
```

20. If you want to assign a particular machine to handle authentications, give its NetBIOS name as the argument and uncomment the line. For example:

```
password server = DOMAINSERVER
```

Also review the **name resolve order** parameter to ensure that the Samba server knows how to resolve the NetBIOS name, unless this name is the same as its hostname. Special conditions for **password server** include:

- If you set the **security** parameter to **domain** earlier, then you must refer to domain controller(s) as the **password server** value(s).
- You can use variable substitutions in the **password server** value(s).
- You can list multiple servers if you separate them with commas.
- If you want Samba to try to find the password server itself, use an asterisk as the **password server** value. This tells the server to look in the file set by the **name resolution** parameter for the domain controller.
- If you set the **security** parameter to **server** earlier, then if you intend to use an NT domain controller, you need to set the users' ability to access that controller from the Samba server.

21. Continue to the following pair of lines:

```
;  password level = 8
;  username level = 8
```

22. If you tend to have mixed-case passwords or usernames, then uncomment the appropriate line. Count in how far case might be mixed—for example, the chance of capital letters may exist only in the first three characters—and change the number listed to reflect your needs.

23. Proceed to this pair of lines:

```
;  encrypt passwords = yes
;  smb passwd file = /etc/smbpasswd
```

24. If you have many machines running Windows NT 4, Service Pack 3 or later, or Windows 98, then uncomment the **encrypt passwords** statement. To use encrypted passwords with other Linux machines, see the section, "Implementing Encrypted Passwords Over Samba," later in the chapter.
25. If you do uncomment **encrypt passwords**, then uncomment **smb passwd file** as well.
26. Cursor down to:

```
;  unix password sync = Yes
;  passwd program = /usr/bin/passwd %u
;  passwd chat = *New*UNIX*password* %n\n *ReType*new*UNIX*password*
%n\n *passwd:*all*authentication*tokens*updated*successfully*
```

27. If you chose to encrypt your passwords and want to ensure that every time an SMB password is updated, the user's login password gets updated, uncomment the **unix password sync** statement.
28. If you chose to activate the **unix password sync** statement, you can also change the program the Samba server uses to actually change the passwords. This program is specified by the **passwd program** statement. The **%u** at the end of the value ensures that the username given by the client is passed to the program.
29. If you activated **unix password sync**, you also have the opportunity to customize the chat script used to update the passwords. You do this by changing the **passwd chat** value. Start by running the **passwd program** and making notes of what information you see and what you have to send. You have a few tools available to help you:
    - Two variables are allowed in a **passwd chat** value. You are already familiar with one, **%n**, which contains the new password you want to set. The other is **%o**, which contains the old password.
    - Four macros are available. The first is **\n**, which is the equivalent of pressing the old Linefeed key—this is typically the macro you use for a newline. Next is **\r**, which creates a carriage return instead. The other two macros are **\t**, which is used to send a Tab, and **\s**, which is used to include a blank space.
    - One wildcard is available. You can use an asterisk to refer to "any characters."
    - Double quotes are available to refer to strings that include spaces, so that Samba does not think they are separate entities.
30. Proceed to:

```
;  username map = /etc/smbusers
```

31. If you intend to build a user map, as discussed later in the section "Creating A User Map," uncomment this line and make sure the path matches where you plan to put your map file.
32. Continue to this line:

```
;    include = /etc/smb.conf.%m
```

33. If you want to have different types of configuration files available for each machine, then uncomment this line and adjust the value. The **include** statement is especially useful if you find that a particular group of machines needs special configuration options that you do not want to use for other boxes, or to set up how Samba handles machines running different operating systems.
34. Move the cursor to:

```
;    interfaces = 192.168.12.2/24 192.168.13.2/24
```

35. If you need to state explicitly what interfaces Samba should use, as a way of keeping it from using others, then uncomment this line of code and change the **interfaces** values to what is appropriate for your network.
36. Proceed to the following line:

```
;    remote browse sync = 192.168.3.25 192.168.5.255
```

37. If you have Samba servers on multiple Linux machines on your network, then uncomment this line of code and change the IP addresses given to point to your own master **nmbd** server machine.

NOTE: *You see two IP addresses in the example because you may have separate master* ***nmbd*** *daemons for separate workgroups.*

38. Continue down to:

```
;    remote announce = 192.168.1.255 192.168.2.44
```

39. If you need to have your Samba server periodically announce its presence to machines on a particular network or subnet, or even to an individual machine, uncomment the preceding code line. Then, enter the appropriate broadcast or IP addresses the announcements should be sent to in order to reach the particular machines or networks you want to receive the broadcast.

40. Cursor down to:

```
;   local master = no
```

41. If you do not want this machine to host one of the master **nmbd** browsing servers for your network, then uncomment this line.
42. Proceed to:

```
;   os level = 33
```

43. How this server fares in browser elections depends on its browser level—the higher the level, the higher the precedence in the election. A breakdown of critical levels is listed in Table 18.4. If you want this server's precedence to be non-zero, uncomment this line and change it to suit your needs.
44. Move the cursor to:

```
;   domain master = yes
```

45. If no Windows NT machine exists on a particular workgroup or subnet, you need to have another machine act as the domain master. If this machine is on that subnet or a member of that workgroup, and you want it to act as the master, then uncomment this line.
46. Continue to the following line:

```
;   preferred master = yes
```

47. If you set this machine to be the **domain master**, then uncomment this line as well. Be careful that you do not have any Windows NT or other **preferred master** machines on the same workgroup or subnet, because this can result in many unnecessary elections.

Table 18.4 Critical os level milestones for Samba browser elections.

Level	Distinction
0	Lowest allowed level. If any Windows machines are on the network, this server will lose browser elections to them. This is the default value.
2	Beats Windows 3.11 and Windows 95 machines in browser elections.
33	Beats Windows NT Advanced Server machines in browser elections.
255	Maximum level.

48. Move down to:

```
;   domain logons = yes
```

49. If you do not have any Windows NT machines on a particular subnet or workgroup, but want or need to provide workgroup domain login service, you can have a Samba server machine handle this for your Windows 95 and 98 machines. If you want this particular machine to provide this login service, then uncomment the **domain logons** code.
50. Cursor down to the following pair of lines:

```
;   logon script = %m.bat
;   logon script = %U.bat
```

51. If you enabled **domain logons**, you have the option of also creating scripts that download to the Windows client machines when they log in with the server and then execute. See the section "Creating Login Scripts," later in the chapter, for information on how to make the scripts used if you uncomment the **logon script** statements.

    When it comes to naming the script, you need to consider two items:

    - *The file extension*—For Windows machines that are not using NT, use the .bat extension for batch files. NT machines require the .cmb extension for a command file.
    - *Variables*—You can use any of the substitution values given earlier in Table 18.3 to point Samba toward files named with particular variables.
52. Proceed to this line:

```
;   logon path = \\%L\Profiles\%U
```

53. If you have Windows 95 and 98 machines in your domain, workgroup, or subnet with no Windows NT machine to serve roaming profiles, and you want to utilize this feature for your Windows users, then uncomment this line to allow Samba to handle these profiles for you. The value associated with the **logon path** statement is the path to where these files can be found. Once again, you have the variables listed in Table 18.3 available to you when setting this path.
54. Continue to the following statement:

```
; name resolve order = wins lmhosts bcast
```

55. If you want to specify how your server resolves hostnames, uncomment the **name resolve order** line and set it appropriately. Use the options listed in Table 18.5 in whatever order makes the most sense for your needs. You can use all of them, or just the ones that fit your setup.
56. Cursor down to:

```
;   wins support = yes
```

57. If you want Samba on this machine to act as a WINS server, uncomment this line.
58. Continue to:

```
;   wins server = w.x.y.z
```

59. If this machine is not a WINS server, but WINS service is available on your network, then uncomment this line and replace **w.x.y.z** with the IP address hosting the WINS server.
60. Proceed to:

```
dns proxy = no
```

61. If you are using WINS on your network and treat NetBIOS names as DNS hostnames, then change this line to the following, for times when WINS for some reason can't find a host properly:

```
dns proxy = yes
```

62. Cursor down to:

```
;  preserve case = no
```

Table 18.5 Options available for the name resolve order statement in /etc/smb.conf.

Option	Purpose
bcast	Specifies to send a broadcast out on all cards listed earlier in **interface**. This broadcast looks for the host needed, and, if successful, the host returns its IP address.
host	Specifies to look in the /etc/nsswitch.conf file to determine whether Samba should look in /etc/hosts, or should use NIS or DNS to get the host's IP address.
lmhosts	Specifies to look in the file /etc/lmhosts (see the section "Creating A Host Map," later in the chapter, for details on how to set this up) to get the host's IP address.
wins	Asks the WINS server at the IP address specified in the **wins server** statement for the host's IP address.

63. If you have reason to control the case of file names entered and added by Samba clients, then uncomment this line. It will treat file names according to the **default case** statement.
64. Jump to this line:

```
; short preserve case = no
```

65. If you want to have file names in *ABCDEFGH.ZYX* format sent by Samba clients converted to the **default case** setting, then uncomment this line.
66. Move down to:

```
; default case = lower
```

67. If you activated any case-changing statements, then uncomment this line. You have two choices for how to alter file name cases:
    - **lower**—Change all file names to lowercase
    - **upper**—Change all file names to uppercase
68. Continue to the following line:

```
; case sensitive = no
```

69. If you want Samba to require file names to be typed exactly as they are stored on its shares, uncomment this statement and change its value to **yes**.
70. Continue to the section "Offering Linux Partitions," and then return here when you're finished with it.
71. Continue to the section "Offering Linux Printers," and return here when you're finished with it.
72. Create any additional files that you need to make.
73. Type "/etc/rc.d/init.d/smb restart" to restart the Samba server with its new settings.

Related solutions:	Found on page:
Creating Shell Accounts	31
Setting Up A Local Printer In The Control Panel	225
Setting Up A Local Printer At The Command Line	228
Setting Up A Network Printer In The Control Panel	231
Setting Up A Network Printer At The Command Line	233
Setting Up Remote Printers To Print Over A Network	234

Offering Linux Partitions

To set up Linux partitions so that you can share them with other machines through the SMB protocol, do the following:

1. See the preceding section, "Configuring Samba," for details on the initial configuration setup.
2. If you have not already, log in as root to the machine whose partitions you want to offer.
3. If you are not already editing the file, type "vi /etc/smb.conf" to open the Samba configuration file.
4. Proceed down to the section starting with the following line:

```
#==================== Share Definitions ==================
```

5. Examine the following share definition:

```
[homes]
   comment = Home Directories
   browseable = no
   writable = yes
```

6. If you do not want to offer the user home directories in bulk for export, then comment out this entire statement by changing it to the following:

```
; [homes]
;    comment = Home Directories
;    browseable = no
;    writable = yes
```

7. If you want the description that people see for this share to be other than **Home Directories**, change the value assigned to the **comment** option.
8. If you want to allow all Samba clients to see the home directories listed when they browse this Samba server, change the **browseable** option to **yes**.
9. If you want to prevent anyone from writing to the home directories through Samba, then change the **writable** option to **no**. Although it often makes sense to allow Samba users to write to their home directories by mounting them as a share, some system administrators find it more comfortable, security-wise, to only allow these users to read their existing files.

10. Proceed to:

```
; [netlogon]
;   comment = Network Logon Service
;   path = /home/netlogon
;   guest ok = yes
;   writable = no
;   share modes = no
```

11. If you want this Samba server to provide Netlogon database management, then uncomment this definition so it looks like this:

```
[netlogon]
   comment = Network Logon Service
   path = /home/netlogon
   guest ok = yes
   writable = no
   share modes = no
```

    If you do not intend to use this feature, skip to Step 15.

12. If you want Netlogon data and the scripts specified in the **logon scripts** statement to be kept in another location, then change the **path** option's value.
13. If you want to force clients accessing the **[netlogon]** share to authenticate, then change the value of **guest ok** to **no**.
14. It is highly recommended that you do not change the **writable** option. If you allow clients to write to the **[netlogon]** share, the scripts there can be modified in destructive ways, especially if you still have guest access allowed. However, it is recommended that you change **share modes** to **yes** if you have Windows clients on your network—and you likely have them if you want the Netlogon service. Many Windows clients need access to file share modes.
15. Cursor down to:

```
;[Profiles]
;     path = /home/profiles
;     browseable = no
;     guest ok = yes
```

16. If you intend to utilize roaming profiles, then uncomment this section so that it looks like this:

```
[Profiles]
    path = /home/profiles
    browseable = no
    guest ok = yes
```

17. If you want to change where the roaming profiles are stored, alter the **path** option's value.
18. If you want to allow users to see this share when requesting a list of available shares, change the **browseable** value to **yes**.
19. If you want to ensure that people must be authenticated in order to access roaming profiles, then change the **guest ok** value to **no**.
20. Move down to the following block:

```
;[tmp]
;   comment = Temporary file space
;   path = /tmp
;   read only = no
;   public = yes
```

21. This statement essentially allows anyone to connect to a share called **[tmp]** hosted in the /tmp directory and upload files if they want to. In a way, using this statement is similar to offering anonymous FTP service. If you want to allow this type of access to anyone who browses this machine's Samba shares, then uncomment this section to look like this:

```
[tmp]
   comment = Temporary file space
   path = /tmp
   read only = no
   public = yes
```

22. If you want to change the share name, change the term **tmp** inside the brackets.
23. If you want to change the share label, change the **comment** value.
24. If you want to offer space to share files but do not want the space to be in the /tmp directory, change the **path** statement. For security reasons, it is a good idea to point the path for such a service to a segregated part of the file system.

25. If you want to only offer read-only access to this share, then change **read only** to **yes**. However, this defeats the whole purpose of having a public upload space.
26. If you want only authenticated users to have access to this space, then change **public** to **no**.
27. Proceed to:

```
;[public]
;   comment = Public Stuff
;   path = /home/samba
;   public = yes
;   writable = yes
;   printable = no
;   write list = @staff
```

28. If you want to utilize this definition to allow the public to view information on a share, but want to allow only particular users and/or groups to write to it, then uncomment it so that it looks like the following:

```
[public]
   comment = Public Stuff
   path = /home/samba
   public = yes
   writable = yes
   printable = no
   write list = @staff
```

29. If you want to rename this share, then change the name within the brackets.
30. If you want to change the identifier to be more descriptive, such as **Staff Policy Documents**, then change the value assigned to the **comment** option.
31. If you want to keep these documents in a different place, then change the **path** statement.
32. If you want no one to have write permissions through Samba mounting the export, then change the **writable** value to **no**. The **printable** option is actually unnecessary here, because you are not defining a print share.
33. Change the **write list** value to consist of a list of users and groups—in *@group* format—who are allowed to write to this share through SMB if you leave **writable** set to **yes**.
34. See the following section to build a share definition from scratch.

Building A File Share Statement

To build a file share statement from scratch, do the following:

1. If you have not already done so, log in as root to the machine whose partitions you want to offer.
2. If you are not already editing the file, type "vi /etc/smb.conf" to open the Samba configuration file.
3. Type "G" to go to the end of the file.
4. Type "o" to open a new line at the end of the file and then enter Insert mode.
5. Start with the share name. This name is formatted as follows: **[*sharename*]**. The name should have no spaces or punctuation. You can use any term except the reserved shares: **[global]**, **[homes]**, and **[printers]**.
6. Typically, the first option you set after the share name is **comment**. Indent this line under the share name so that it is obvious at a glance where this share definition starts and ends. The comment should be descriptive, but without giving too much information away to potential intruders. For example, so far, you might have the following:

   ```
   [ProjectP]
     comment = Documents needed by ProjectP staff
   ```

7. Next is often the **path** option. Here, you set the file system location of files that you want to share. Try to isolate this directory as much as possible so that people will not get access to files they should not be able to see or touch. For example, the definition might now be similar to the following:

   ```
   [ProjectP]
     comment = Documents needed by ProjectP staff
     path = /Projects/P/
   ```

8. This point is where a "typical" share definition stops being consistent. From here on, most shares are different from one another, so you can be a bit more freeform. A list of options you might want to utilize is given in Table 18.6. Examine this list thoroughly.

Table 18.6 Popular options used in individual Samba share definitions.

Option	Purpose	Value(s)	Example
admin users	Sets a list of users who access this share with superuser-like privileges. Strong security implications arise when you utilize this option, because not only do you allow the defined users to have the power to empty the share, change permissions, and more, but if an intruder gains access using one of these accounts, that intruder can alter the files as they see fit.	A space-separated list of users	**admin users = joe barb**
browseable	Specifies whether to allow Samba clients to see this share when requesting a list of shares available.	**yes** or **no**	**browseable = yes**
case sensitive	Specifies whether Samba handles file names as case-sensitive or ignores case entirely.	**yes** or **no**	**case sensitive = no**
copy	Tells Samba to copy all parameters from another share, and override those that are duplicated in this share.	Share name with no brackets	**copy = ProjectB**
default case	Sets the default case for file names created by clients.	**upper** or **lower**	**default case = lower**
dont descend	Explicitly refuses to allow Samba clients to access particular subdirectories.	A comma-separated list of subdirectories	**dont descend = /Projects/ProjectB/needs_approval**
follow symlinks	Tells Samba whether to follow symbolic links out of the share.	**yes** or **no**	**follow symlinks = no**
force group	Sets all users accessing this share to belong to the listed group.	Group name, or **+group** if you want only users who are already assigned to this group to create files under the group's name	**force group = project_staff**

(continued)

Table 18.6 Popular options used in individual Samba share definitions **(continued).**

Option	Purpose	Value(s)	Example
force user	Sets all users accessing this share to this particular username after the client properly authenticates.	Username	**force user = staff**
guest account	Sets the user account to use for guest logins.	Name of account; typically, this should be an account without normal shell access	**guest account = smbguest**
guest ok	Allows unauthenticated logins, and assigns all clients without a valid login to the **guest account**.	**yes** or **no**	**guest ok = yes**
guest only	Specifies that if **guest ok** is set to **yes**, all clients accessing this share will be logged on through the **guest account**.	**yes** or **no**	**guest only = yes**
hide files	Sets particular files to be accessible, but not show up in a file listing.	A slash-separated listing of files, with the wildcards ***** and **?** available, and also the substitution variables listed in Table 18.3	**hide files = master_data/ master*/temp???**
hosts allow	Provides access control that enables you to fine-tune who is allowed to mount this share. If a host is explicitly allowed, then it will not be denied even if listed in **hosts deny**.	Comma-, space-, or tab-separated list of host identifiers, as specified in the coverage of /etc/ hosts.allow in Chapter 9	**hosts allow = .colors.org**
hosts deny	Provides access control that enables you to fine-tune who is allowed to mount this share.	Comma-, space-, or tab-separated list of host identifiers, as specified in the coverage of /etc/ hosts.deny in Chapter 9	**hosts deny = ALL**

(continued)

***Table 18.6 Popular options used in individual Samba share definitions* (continued).**

Option	Purpose	Value(s)	Example
invalid users	Specifies users who cannot log in to this share.	Usernames: **@group** for both NIS netgroups and standard user groups, **+group** for standard user groups, and **&group** for NIS netgroups	**invalid users = root, wheel, @admin**
locking	Enables locks to be placed on files that a client has open for editing.	**yes** or **no**	**locking = yes**
mangle case	Sets whether to change file names that do not match the **default case**.	**yes** or **no**	**mangle case = no**
mangled map	Slightly alters file names requested and placed by SMB clients.	The item to change, with the asterisk wildcard allowed; the format is **(one other)**	**mangled map = (*.html *.htm)**
mangled names	Sets whether to convert non-DOS-formatted file names to DOS format.	**yes** or **no**	**mangled names = no**
max connections	Sets the maximum number of clients that can connect to this service.	Number of clients, or 0 for infinite	**max connections = 5**
oplocks	Enables use of opportunistic file locks to ensure that a file cannot be altered while someone else is altering it.	**True** or **False**	**oplocks = True**
postexec	Sets a command or script to run on the server when a client disconnects from this service.	Path to command, with standard substitutions listed in Table 18.3	**postexec = /root/bin/leave.scr**
preexec	Sets a command or script to run on the server when a client connects to this service.	Path to command, with standard substitutions listed in Table 18.3	**preexec = /bin/fortune**

(continued)

***Table 18.6 Popular options used in individual Samba share definitions* (continued).**

Option	Purpose	Value(s)	Example
preserve case	Sets whether to leave file name cases as is or convert them to the **default** case.	**yes** or **no**	**preserve case = no**
read list	Sets a list of users who have read-only access to this share, even if everyone else has write access.	Comma-separated list of users, or groups in the **@group** format	**read list = bob sue @temps**
short preserve case	Sets whether files in the *ABCDEFGH.ZYX* format stay in their original case or are altered to the **default case**.	**yes** or **no**	**short preserve case = yes**
valid users	Sets which users are allowed to access this share.	Comma-separated list of users, or groups in the **@group** format	**valid users = @project, supervisor, @staff**
write list	Sets a list of users who have write access to this share, even if everyone else has only read access.	Comma-separated list of users, or groups in the **@group** format	**write list = admin @project**
writable	Sets whether clients can write data to this share.	**yes** or **no**	**writeable = yes**

9. After you examine the list, complete your share definition. For example, perhaps you want only the ProjectP staff to be able to write to the share you are creating, but want other project staff to be able to read it. The final share definition might look like this:

```
[ProjectP]
  comment = Documents needed by ProjectP staff
  path = /Projects/P/
  writeable = no
  write list = @projectp
  valid users = @project
```

Related solution:	***Found on page:***
Restricting Network Access With **tcp_wrappers**	267

Mounting Windows Shares Under Linux

To mount a Windows partition through Samba on a Linux box, do the following:

1. Log in to the Linux box as root.
2. Make sure the mount point you want to use already exists. For example, type "mkdir /mnt/win" to make a generic mount point for Windows shares.
3. If you are unsure of the share you want to mount on a particular host you have two options:
   - If the share is set to be publicly browseable, use the following command to get a list of shares:

     ```
     smbclient -L host
     ```

   - If the share is not publicly browseable, you will have to look on the machine that hosts it in the /etc/smb.conf file to get the name.
4. Use the following format to mount the share:

   ```
   smbclient //NetBIOS_name/share_name
   ```

   This program is similar to an FTP client. Type "man smbclient" to get the full option list.

Related solution:	Found on page:
Adding And Removing Media To The File System	84

Offering Windows Shares

To make a Windows folder available to other machines through SMB, do the following:

1. Log in to the user account you want to configure shares for on the Windows 98 machine.
2. Click the Start button to open the Windows Start menu.
3. Go to Settings|Control Panel to open the Control Panel tool listing, shown in Figure 18.1.
4. Double-click the Network icon to open the Network dialog box, shown in Figure 18.2.

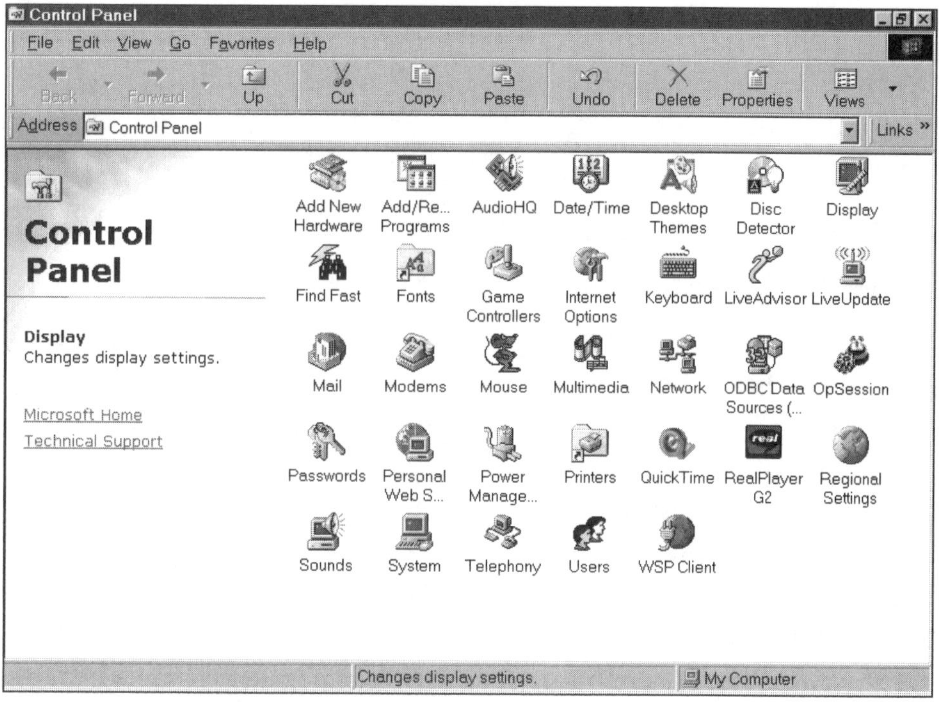

Figure 18.1 The Windows 98 Control Panel.

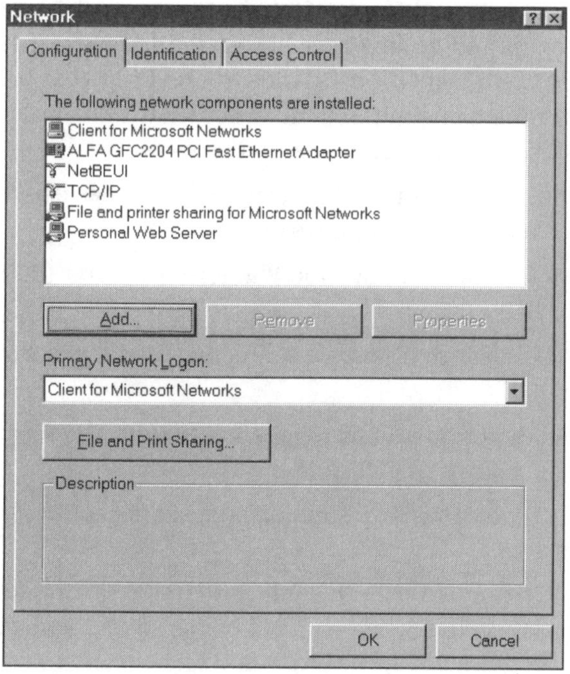

Figure 18.2 The Windows 98 Network Control Panel.

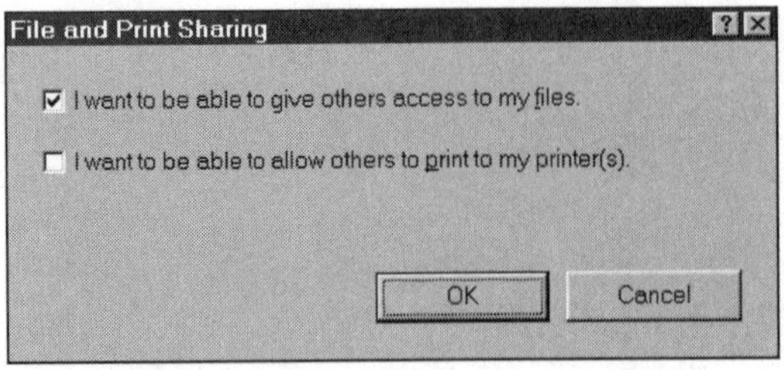

Figure 18.3 The Windows 98 File And Print Sharing dialog box.

5. Click the File And Print Sharing button to open the File And Print Sharing dialog box, shown in Figure 18.3.
6. Make sure a checkmark appears in the box next to I Want To Be Able To Give Others Access To My Files.
7. Click OK to close the File And Print Sharing dialog box.
8. Click the Access Control tab.
9. You have two options to choose from regarding how your share security is conducted:
   - *Share-Level Access Control*—Click this radio button if you want to use a single password for anyone accessing this share. If you do not want to require any passwords, then choose this level of access.
   - *User-Level Access Control*—Click this radio button if you want to determine which individual users and groups have access to this share. If you choose this option, the Obtain List Of Users And Groups From text box becomes available. Enter the name of the domain server Windows should look to in order to find this information in the text box.
10. Click OK to close the dialog box. If you changed any of the values listed, you will likely be asked to insert your Windows 98 CD-ROM.
11. Select Programs|Windows Explorer to open the Windows Explorer file browser, shown in Figure 18.4.
12. Browse to the directory you want to offer as a share, and then make sure you have it selected.
13. Right-click the highlighted directory you want to share to open the file-manipulation pop-up menu, shown in Figure 18.5.
14. Click Sharing to open the *Folder* Properties dialog box, similar to the example shown in Figure 18.6.
15. Click the Shared As radio button to make this folder sharable. Thereafter, much of the dialog box that previously was shaded opens so that you can fill it out.

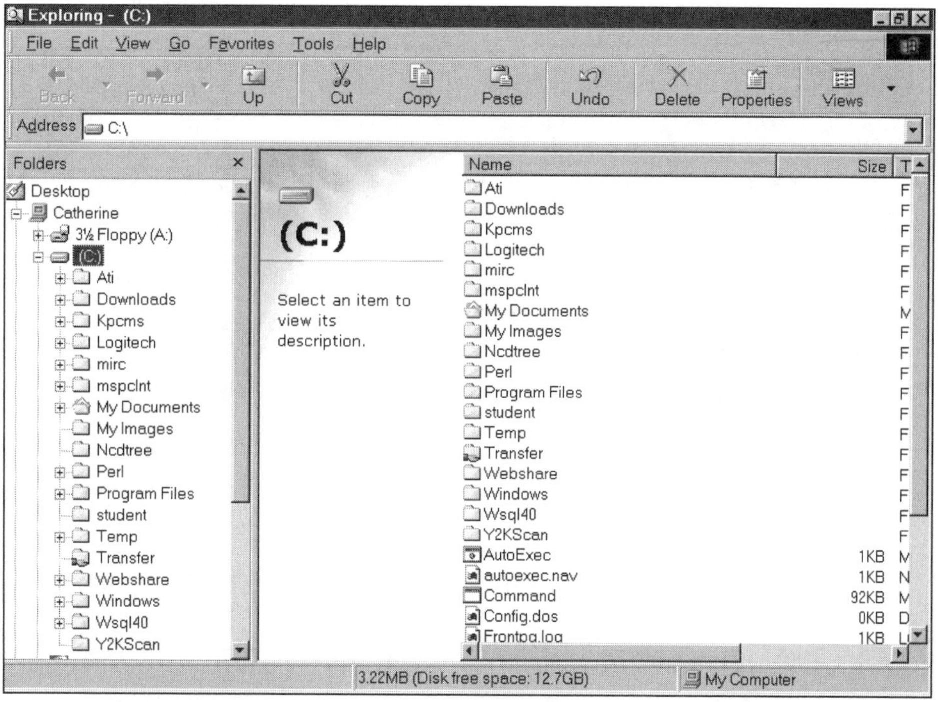

Figure 18.4 An example Windows Explorer window.

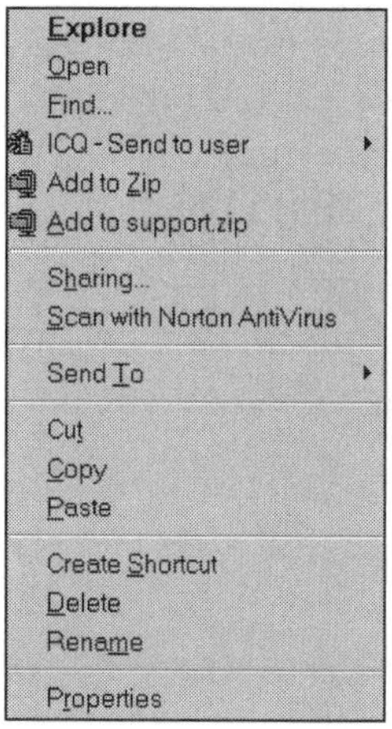

Figure 18.5 The file-manipulation pop-up menu available in Windows Explorer.

16. In the Share Name text box, change the name attached to this share if you do not want it to remain the name of the folder.
17. In the Comment text box, add descriptive information about what this folder contains.

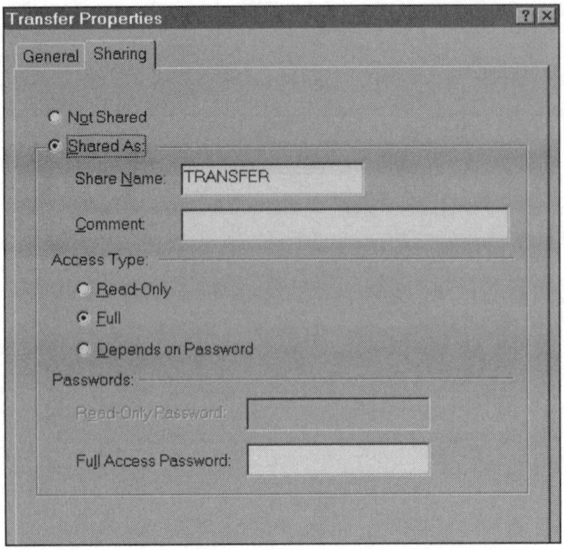

Figure 18.6 An example Windows 98 *Folder* Properties dialog box for the Sharing folder.

18. In the Access Type section, you have three options:
    - *Read-Only*—Prevents anyone from writing to the share. If you click this option, the Read-Only Password text box opens in the Passwords section. Fill in this text box if you want to password-protect the share.
    - *Full*—Offers the ability to both read and write to the share. If you click this option, the Full Access Password text box opens in the Passwords section. Fill in this text box if you want to password-protect the share.
    - *Depends On Password*—Offers you some flexibility, because you can give one password to people who you only want to allow to read the share, and another to those who you want to allow to read and write. Fill in both Password text boxes with different passwords if you choose this option.
19. Click OK to close the dialog box.

Offering Linux Printers

To set up Linux partitions so that you can share them with other machines through the SMB protocol, do the following:

1. See the section "Configuring Samba" for details on the initial configuration setup.
2. If you have not already done so, log in as root to the machine whose partitions you want to offer.

3. If you are not already editing the file, type "vi /etc/smb.conf" to open the Samba configuration file.
4. Type "/printers" and press Enter to jump down to the first statement mentioning printers, and then type "/" and press Enter again to jump down to the following section:

```
[printers]
   comment = All Printers
   path = /var/spool/samba
   browseable = no
   guest ok = no
   writable = no
   printable = yes
```

5. If you want to use a different text statement to define this print share, such as **All Printers On Antelope**, change the **comment** option's value.
6. If you want print jobs sent from Samba clients to be spooled elsewhere locally, then change the value for the **path** option.
7. If you want this share to show up in a client's browse listing, change the **browseable** value to **yes**.
8. If you want to allow nonauthenticated users to print to your printers, change the **guest ok** value to **yes**.
9. If you want clients to be able to send files directly to the printers via the **cat** command (for example), then change the **writable** value to **yes**.
10. If you do not want to allow people to print to any of the printers this machine has access to through SMB, then change the **printable** value to **no**.
11. See the following section for information on how to build a print share definition from scratch.

Building A Print Share Statement

To build a print share statement from scratch, do the following:

1. If you have not already done so, log in as root to the machine whose partitions you want to offer.
2. If you are not already editing the file, type "vi /etc/smb.conf" to open the Samba configuration file.
3. Type "G" to go to the end of the file.
4. Type "o" to open a new line at the end of the file and then enter Insert mode.

5. Start with the share name. This name is formatted as follows: **[*sharename*]**. The name should have no spaces or punctuation. You can use any term except the reserved shares: **[global]**, **[homes]**, and **[printers]**.
6. Typically, the first option you set after the print share name is **comment**. Indent this line under the share name so that it is obvious at a glance where this share definition starts and ends. For example, so far, you might have the following:

```
[laser]
  comment = Main laser printer
```

7. Next is often the **path** option. Here, you set where within the file system all print jobs sent from SMB clients should be spooled to. For example, the definition might now be similar to the following:

```
[laser]
  comment = Main laser printer
  path = /var/spool/samba/laser
```

8. Just as with file shares, this is the point at which print shares are no longer consistent. A different set of options from the ones used to configure file shares is of interest to those setting up print shares. Print share options are listed in Table 18.7. Examine this list carefully.

Table 18.7 Popular options used in individual Samba share definitions.

Option	Purpose	Value(s)	Example
lppause command	Sets the command used to either halt printing or halt spooling for a print job.	The path to the script or command to run, plus the substitution variables **%p** to refer to a specific printer and **%j** to refer to a specific job number	**lppause = /usr/bin/lp -l %p-%j -H hold**
lpq command	Sets the command used to display print queue information for a specific printer.	The path to the script or command to run, plus the **%p** substitution variable to refer to a specific printer	**lpq command = /usr/bin/lpq %p**

(continued)

Table 18.7 Popular options used in individual Samba share definitions **(continued).**

Option	Purpose	Value(s)	Example
lpresume command	Sets the command used to resume printing or spooling for a print job that was previously halted with **lppause command**.	The path to the script or command to run, plus the substitution variables **%p** to refer to a specific printer and **%j** to refer to a specific job number	**lpresume command = /usr/bin/lp -I %p-%j -H resume**
lprm command	Sets the command used to delete a print job.	The path to the script or command to run, plus the substitution variables **%p** to refer to a specific printer and **%j** to refer to a specific job number	**lprm command = /usr/bin/lprm -P%p %j**
max connections	Sets the maximum number of clients that can connect to this service.	Number of clients, or 0 for infinite	**max connections = 5**
max print space	Sets the maximum amount of free disk space necessary on the server, in kilobytes, before clients can spool print jobs to it.	Maximum space in kilobytes	**max print space = 1000**
print command	Sets the command or script used to process files in the print spool after they are spooled.	The path to the script or command to run, plus the substitution variables **%p** to refer to a specific printer, **%j** to refer to a specific job number, and **%s** to refer to a spool file	**print command = lpr -r -P%p %s**
printable	Sets whether print jobs can be sent to this printer over Samba.	**yes** or **no**	**printable = yes**
printer	Specifies the printer name associated with this definition.	Name of printer in /etc/printcap	**printer = laser**

(continued)

Table 18.7 Popular options used in individual Samba share definitions **(continued).**

Option	Purpose	Value(s)	Example
queuepause command	Sets the command or script used to pause the print queue on the server.	The path to the script or command to run, plus the substitution variable **%p** to refer to a specific printer	**queuepause command = lpc -P%p disable**
valid users	Sets which users are allowed to access this share.	Comma-separated list of users, or groups in the **@group** format	**valid users = @project, supervisor, @staff**

9. Now that you are aware of the options you have available, finish building your share. For example, perhaps this particular laser printer is located in an individual's office. Only that individual plus the people who typically need to produce documents for this person to examine and sign need to print to it. The final share definition might turn out as follows:

```
[laser]
  comment = Main laser printer
  path = /var/spool/samba/laser
  printable = yes
  valid users = sherry, @officemates
```

Utilizing Windows Printers Under Linux

To set up a Linux box so that it can use Samba to send print jobs to a printer installed on a Windows 98 machine, do the following:

1. Set up the printer as shared on the Windows 98 machine.
2. On each machine that needs to be able to print over Samba, you need to edit /etc/printcap. Type "vi /etc/printcap" to open the file.
3. Create a local print definition that passes the print job to the input filter /usr/bin/smbprint. For example:

```
ij|inkjet:\
  :sd=/var/spool/lpd/inkjet:\
  :sh:\
  :if=/usr/bin/smbprint:
```

4. Save and close the file.
5. Change to the spool directory.
6. Type "vi .config" to create a configuration file that tells **smbprint** what to do.
7. Type "i" to enter Insert mode.
8. The configuration needs to be in the following format:

```
server = NetBIOS_name
service = printer_service_name
password = "printerpassword"
```

   Typically, the password entry is empty because there is no password for the service. This would be entered as:

```
password = " "
```

9. Save and close the file.
10. Restart the Samba server by typing "/etc/rc.d/init.d/smb restart".

Related solutions:	Found on page:
Setting Up A Local Printer In The Control Panel	225
Setting Up A Local Printer At The Command Line	228

Implementing Encrypted Passwords Over Samba

If you want to use encrypted passwords with Samba instead of having clients send plain-text passwords, do the following:

1. Log in as root to the Samba server machine you want to set up with encrypted passwords.
2. Type "vi /etc/smb.conf" to open the Samba server's configuration file.
3. Type "/encrypt p" and press Enter to search down for the **encrypt passwords** statement. Unedited, this statement looks like this:

```
;  encrypt passwords = yes
```

4. Make sure that this line is uncommented—delete the semicolon—and that it is configured the way you want it, as covered in the section "Configuring Samba," earlier in the chapter.
5. Press the Esc key to return to Command mode, if necessary, and then type "ZZ" to save and close the file. If you made any changes, do not restart the Samba server yet.
6. Type one of the following to build the file smbpasswd, which will contain encrypted passwords in the format needed by Windows machines through Samba:
   - If you are not using NIS, type:

     ```
     cat /etc/passwd | /usr/bin/mksmbpasswd.sh >
     /usr/local/samba/private/smbpasswd
     ```

   - If you are using NIS, type:

     ```
     ypcat /etc/passwd | /usr/bin/mksmbpasswd.sh >
     /usr/local/samba/private/smbpasswd
     ```

NOTE: *In both cases, the command is typed all on one line.*

Creating A User Map

If you want to set up maps that help keep track of which users on different machines correspond to users on the server machine, do the following:

1. Log in as root to the Samba server machine you want to set up.
2. Type "vi /etc/smb.conf" to open the Samba server's configuration file.
3. Type "/username m" and press Enter to search down for the **username map** statement. Unedited, this statement looks like this:

   ```
   ;  username map = /etc/smbusers
   ```

4. Make sure that this line is uncommented—delete the semicolon—and that it is configured the way you want it, as covered in the section "Configuring Samba," earlier in the chapter.
5. Press the Esc key to return to Command mode, if necessary, and then type "ZZ" to save and close the file. If you made any changes, do not restart the Samba server yet.

6. Type "vi /etc/smbusers" or substitute the path and file you changed this to in Step 4. If you did change the file, copy /etc/smbusers to the new location, because a file is there already with the following contents:

```
# Unix_name = SMB_name1 SMB_name2 ...
root = administrator admin
nobody = guest pcguest smbguest
```

7. Each entry in this file is in the following format:

```
localuser = remote1 remote2 @localgroup ...
```

   The ***remote1*** and ***remote2*** entries represent the usernames that people are trying to log in to the Samba server with. You can, of course, use as many or as few of these as you need. When you use the format ***@localgroup***, you are referring to a group that already exists on the Samba server, all of whose members will log in to the service as ***localuser***. Edit the existing lines, if you want to, and then add more users to suit your needs. For example:

```
smbusers = @users
projects = @projectA @projectB @projectC
```

8. When you are finished, press the Esc key to return to Command mode, and then type "ZZ" to save and close the file.
9. Restart the Samba server by typing "/etc/rc.d/init.d/smb restart".

Creating A Host Map

If you want to set up a host map for your site, do the following:

1. Log in as root to the Samba server machine you want to set up.
2. Type "vi /etc/smb.conf" to open the Samba server's configuration file.
3. Type "/name resolve" and press Enter to search down for the **name resolve order** statement. Unedited, this statement looks like the following:

```
; name resolve order = wins lmhosts bcast
```

4. Make sure that this line is uncommented—delete the semicolon—and that it is configured the way you want it, as covered in the section "Configuring Samba," earlier in the chapter.

5. Press the Esc key to return to Command mode, if necessary, and then type "ZZ" to save and close the file. If you made any changes, do not restart the Samba server yet.
6. Type "vi /etc/lmhosts" to open the Samba host mapping file. By default, it contains only one line:

```
127.0.0.1 localhost
```

7. Type "o" to open a new line below this first line, and enter Insert mode.
8. Enter a line for each machine on your network in the following format:

```
IPaddress  NETBIOS_Name
```

   For example:

```
192.168.10.5   ADMIN1
192.168.10.6   ADMIN2
192.168.10.7   ADMIN3
192.168.10.19 PUBLIC6
```

9. When you are finished, press the Esc key to return to Command mode, and then type "ZZ" to save and close the file.
10. Restart the Samba server by typing "/etc/rc.d/init.d/smb restart".

Creating Login Scripts

If you want to set up login scripts for Samba clients, do the following:

1. Log in as root to the Samba server from which you want to provide logon scripts for Windows machines.
2. Type "vi /etc/smb.conf" to open the Samba server's configuration file.
3. Type "/netlogon" and press Enter to search down to the following code:

```
; [netlogon]
;    comment = Network Logon Service
;    path = /home/netlogon
;    guest ok = yes
;    writable = no
;    share modes = no
```

4. Uncomment this code by placing the cursor over each semicolon and then typing “x”. You should end up with the following:

```
[netlogon]
  comment = Network Logon Service
  path = /home/netlogon
  guest ok = yes
  writable = no
  share modes = no
```

5. Do not change the share’s name, because **[netlogon]** is a reserved share that tells Samba that you want to activate the Windows NT Netlogon service. It is safe, however, to change the other share definition options. If you want to do this, edit them now.
6. Press the Esc key to make sure you are in Command mode, and then type “1G” to jump to the beginning of the file.
7. Type “/logon script” and press Enter to search down to the following code:

```
#if you enable domain logons then you may want a per-machine or
#per user logon script
#run a specific logon batch file per workstation (machine)
;  logon script = %m.bat
#run a specific logon batch file per username
;  logon script = %U.bat
```

8. It is best to start with a generic **logon script** and use it for testing; then, when you are sure that it works in general, you can break it into more complex, specialized scripts. Start by adding the following line:

```
logon script = test.bat
```

NOTE: *The .bat extension is for scripts for Windows 95 and 98 machines, whereas .cmd is for Windows NT machines.*

9. Press the Esc key, and then type “ZZ” to save and close the file. Do not restart the Samba server yet, because the files are not in place.
10. Create your batch or command file(s) on a Windows machine, if you can. This avoids any discrepancies between how a Linux machine handles characters such as the Enter key and how a Windows machine handles them. Because batch and command file programming for Windows

machines is outside the scope of this book, the following are some suggestions on how to find resources to help you in your quest:

- Windows 95 and 98 users should go to their favorite Web search engine—for example, **www.altavista.com**—and enter a collection of search terms, such as these:

```
batch file programming
```

- Windows NT users should try **www.win32scripting.com**. Also, go to your favorite Web search engine and enter a collection of search terms, such as the following:

```
NT ".cmd"
```

11. Once you have the sample script finished, double-check the **path** option in your **[netlogon]** share definition. This is where Samba will look for the scripts.
12. Copy the script to the new location. Assuming that you used the defaults listed in earlier steps, the file should end up as /home/netlogon/test.bat.
13. Type "/etc/rc.d/init.d/smb restart" to restart the Samba server.
14. Go to the Windows machines that you want to use the script for, and configure a test machine to seek the startup script from the Netlogon server.
15. Reboot the machine. If the script works, then proceed to make increasingly more complex and specialized scripts, fine-tuning their names when appropriate with the substitutions in Table 18.3. Be sure to test at each point.

Chapter 19

Text Processing Tools

If you need an immediate solution to:	*See page:*
Maneuvering In **vi**	578
Filtering Text In **vi**	579
Copying And Pasting Text In **vi**	581
Indenting Text In **vi**	581
Using Regular Expressions	583
Running **sed** With Multiple Commands	584
Building A **sed** Script File	586
Running **sed** With External File Scripts	588
Using The **cut** Command	588
Using The **join** Command	589
Checking Spelling With **ispell**	590
Building **ispell** Dictionaries	592
Reducing **ispell** Dictionary Sizes	594
Using The **tr** Command	595

In Depth

You can't avoid the need to learn how to work with text documents under Linux. Even with the advent of GUI-based administration tools, you still have to spend time working with the text files underneath the fancy backgrounds and programs. This chapter covers two particular tools of the myriad that are available. One of these tools is the *Vi*sual editor—more popularly referred to as **vi**—which is the text editor utilized in the rest of this book. The other tool is **sed**, which enables you to search the contents of text files and then alter them. Both of these programs are intensely useful to a system administrator who knows how to put them through their paces.

The vi Editor

The **vi** editor is one of those tools that people seem to either love or hate. Most of its commands involve single characters, and some commands can be extended or refined with other single characters. The advantage of **vi**'s command structure is that it makes this editor incredibly fast. A drawback, of course, is having to remember the commands. They come fairly easily when you use **vi** on a regular basis. You'll quickly memorize some favorites that you use more frequently than the rest, and you'll sometimes have to look up the others.

What you find on Red Hat and other Linux distributions is often not the classic **vi**, but rather an alias pointing to **vim** (**vi** *Im*proved). Features added to the original **vi** editor include an unlimited capability to undo what you change, GUI (**gvim**) and command-line (**vi**) versions, mouse-based editing features for GUI mode, and color highlighting features for when you use the program for writing programs.

TIP: *If you are not sure which editor you have, type "man vi" and see what the man page says you are using.*

vi operates in three main modes, each of which has a specific purpose and a distinct method of interacting with the user. It is imperative that you understand what each of these modes is, what you can do within each mode, and how to switch from one mode to another.

NOTE: *Whenever I refer to **vi** in this book, I am actually referring to **vim**.*

Command Mode

The mode that **vi** opens in is Command mode, sometimes also referred to as Normal mode. This is a realm in which every keystroke has a special meaning. Because so many different possibilities exist, this chapter takes a two-tiered approach. This section contains a series of tables that group together types of commands. Then, in the Immediate Solutions section I walk you through some of the more common tasks that **vi** users encounter. You should be used to some of the commands by now from reading solutions in other chapters that require use of **vi**, so the examples in this chapter are more complex than what you have already seen.

See one of the following tables for a listing of many of the commands available in **vi**, broken into the following categories:

- *Table 19.1*—Moving through your document in **vi**
- *Table 19.2*—Editing content in **vi**
- *Table 19.3*—Miscellaneous **vi** commands
- *Table 19.4*—Searching through your document in **vi**

NOTE: *In many cases, you can add a number before a **vi** command to tell the editor to do something in multiples. The **Multiples?** column in each of the tables indicates whether multiples is available for a particular command.*

Table 19.1 Moving through a document in vi.

Keystroke	Result	Multiples?
Ctrl+B	Jumps backward one screen	Yes
Ctrl+D	Jumps forward half a screen	Yes
Ctrl+E	Jumps backward half a screen	Yes
$	Jumps forward to the end of the line	Yes
#%	Goes to the # percent point in the file	No
''	Jumps backward to the beginning of the last line you jumped somewhere from	No
'[	Jumps to the beginning of the first line in the section where you last edited material	No
']	Jumps to the beginning of the last line in the section where you last edited material	No
(	Jumps backward one sentence	Yes
)	Jumps forward one sentence	Yes

(continued)

Table 19.1 Moving through a document in vi (continued).

Keystroke	Result	Multiples?
+	Jumps forward to the beginning of the next line	Yes
-	Jumps backward to the beginning of the previous line	Yes
b	Jumps backward one word	Yes
J	Jumps cursor to end of screen	Yes
L	Jumps cursor to middle of screen	No
w	Jumps forward one word	Yes

Table 19.2 Editing a document in vi.

Keystroke	Result	Multiples?
Ctrl+6	If you have an alternate file open, changes the view to the alternate file	Yes
Ctrl+A	Jumps to the next number after the current cursor position, and increments it by 1; the number must be on the same line as the cursor	Yes
Ctrl+R	Redoes changes that you previously used the undo command to cancel	No
Ctrl+X	Jumps to the next number after the current cursor position, and decreases it by 1; the number must be on the same line as the cursor	Yes
1	Begins a filter operation	Yes
&	Repeats last substitution	Yes
<	Starts an operation that indents material to the left	Yes
>	Starts an operation that indents material to the right	Yes
a	Appends text after the cursor	Yes
A	Appends text at the end of the line	Yes
C	Cuts current line into the buffer	Yes
dd	Deletes current line	Yes
i	Enters Insert mode and enables you to input information	Yes
J	Brings beginning of next line up as part of the end of the current line	Yes
o	Inserts a new line beneath the cursor and enters Insert mode	Yes
O	Inserts a new line above the cursor's position and enters Insert mode	Yes

(continued)

Table 19.2 Editing a document in* vi *(continued).

Keystroke	Result	Multiples?
p	Pastes material from the buffer after the cursor's position	Yes
P	Pastes material from the buffer at the cursor's position	Yes
U	Undoes the last change made	Yes
x	Cuts the current character into the buffer	Yes
X	Cuts the character before the cursor into the buffer	Yes
Y	Copies (yanks) the current line into the buffer	Yes

Table 19.3 Difficult-to-categorize vi commands.

Keystroke	Result	Multiples?
Ctrl+G	Displays the file name, total number of lines, and current cursor position	No
Ctrl+L	Refreshes the screen	No
Ctrl+Z	As with many other Unix-based programs, places this **vi** instance in the background to free up the command line for other work	No
m	Sets a mark	No
R	Enters Replace mode, which enables you to type over existing text	Yes
ZQ	Quits the file without saving	No
ZZ	Saves the file, and then closes it	No

Table 19.4 Searching through a document in vi.

Keystroke	Result	Multiples?
#	Searches backward for the word the cursor currently rests on	Yes
*	Searches forward for the word the cursor currently rests on	Yes
/	Starts a search-forward operation	Yes
?	Starts a search-backward operation	Yes
?+Enter	Repeats a search-backward operation	No
n	Repeats a search operation	No
N	Repeats the last search operation in the opposite direction	Yes

Insert Mode

The mode in which you actually enter text is called Insert mode. A select group of commands takes you into this mode. Table 19.5 groups the commands that take you into this mode. To exit and return to Command mode at any time, press the Esc key.

Table 19.5 Commands that take you to Insert mode in vi.

Keystroke	Result	Multiples?
i	Enters Insert mode directly in front of the cursor	Yes
I	Jumps to the beginning of the line and enters Insert mode	Yes
o	Opens a new line below the cursor's current position and enters Insert mode	Yes
O	Opens a new line above the cursor's current position and enters Insert mode	Yes
S	Cuts the current line into the buffer and then enters Insert mode	Yes

The concept of multiples being allowed with an insert command may seem to make no sense initially. This feature functions as a repeater. For example, suppose you type the following on a blank line:

```
4I
```

This tells **vi** to go into Insert mode at the beginning of that line, and remembers the 4 for later. Suppose you next type this:

```
Happy Birthday!
```

So far, **vi** seems to ignore the 4. However, after you press the Esc key, this text changes to the following:

```
Happy Birthday! Happy Birthday! Happy Birthday! Happy Birthday!
```

So, now you have a total of four instances of the text you inserted.

TIP: *Insert mode actually has a cousin named Replace mode. If you type "R", you can then overtype material you already have entered.*

Line Mode

A mode that many **vi** users try to avoid these days is Line mode, sometimes called Colon mode. In Line mode, you have access to a series of commands formerly used in the **ex** editor—a precursor of **vi**—as well as access to additional search and filter commands. This mode's nickname comes from the fact that you type a colon (:) to enter the mode. Whenever you want to leave it, press the Esc key to go back to Command mode.

Many of the commands available in this mode are duplicated in Command mode. This mode is used today primarily for setting **vi** behavior options. Each of these options is set by using the following format:

```
:set option
```

If a value exists for the option, then use this format:

```
:set option=value
```

Some options that you may want to alter are listed in Table 19.6. Many of these items are toggles, which means that you activate them once to turn them on, and then again to turn them off—or vice versa.

NOTE: *Walking you through working with **vi** is difficult unless everyone is working on the same file. All the Immediate Solutions for **vi** deal with text files included on the CD-ROM or that you create during the steps. After you practice walking through these exercises, you should have a better understanding of how to accomplish the specified tasks.*

Table 19.6 Some behavior options available in vi's Line mode.

Option	Purpose	Value
autoindent	If the previous line is indented, causes the following lines to be indented equally	None
autowrite	Automatically saves file changes	None
backup	Keeps a backup of the previous version after saving changes	None
backupext	Sets the extension to be used for backup files	The extension
cindent	You are programming in C, so indents lines as they should be in this format	None
confirm	Does not save read-only or unsaved files without asking the user to confirm	None
history	Specifies the number of previous command-line commands to remember	None, or a positive integer
ignorecase	Disregards case when doing searches	None
insertmode	Immediately enters Insert mode when opening a file	None
smartcase	Ignores case except for uppercase letters in the regular expression	None

Pattern Matching

A critical skill for many applications is your ability to set up *regular expressions.* These statements are used to establish a pattern. The tool you are using then compares this pattern against the data it was told to examine. Some programs sometimes use slightly different pattern-matching characters than other programs use, but in general, many tools share the same pattern-matching habits.

The first thing you must know to build a pattern is what you are looking for. After you narrow down the common characteristics of what you want to find, you can then reach into your *metacharacter*—a character that represents information about other characters—toolbox and, as closely as possible, represent what it is you are looking for. The trick is that you also want to make sure that the things you are not looking for do not show up.

Characters

The most basic metacharacters available are those that refer to one or more individual characters. Two characters that are used for this function and that are available in almost all parsing tools are the period and the asterisk. You can use a period to specify that a single unknown item is missing from the pattern. For example, suppose you are looking for the permissions and ownerships on the series of files house1, house2, and house3. Typing the following in the directory containing those files would find it properly:

```
ls -la house.
```

The asterisk enables you to specify that one or more characters are unknown. Suppose that, along with the house files, you also had these files:

- car1, car2, and car3
- dog1, dog2, and dog3
- yard1, yard2, and yard3

For each set of 1's, 2's, and 3's, you want to assign the ownerships to the person they correspond to. You could do this either one by one, or by using something such as the following for the 3's (and also for the 1's and 2's later):

```
chown mary *3
```

TIP: *Sometimes, you may want to use a metacharacter literally. To accomplish this, put a backslash (\) in front of the metacharacter. Using a backslash in this context makes it an escape character.*

Locations

Other useful metacharacters enable you to look for items in a certain position among others. Once again, two metacharacters are available that serve this function. The first is the carat (^), which is used to specify that you are looking for something that is at the beginning of a line. Perhaps you have a document open in **vi** and are looking for a simple ASCII table you put together. It could be something as simple as this:

```
a b c
1 2 3
```

Maybe you discuss this data throughout the document, and so it would take quite some time to just search for the individual items. Rather than scrolling through the file, you can automate this search by typing "/" in Command mode to start a search, and then the pattern:

```
^a
```

If you want to look for something that is at the end of a line, use a dollar sign at the end of the search term. For example, if you want to find this same table, you could try the following search pattern:

```
c$
```

Groupings

Basic regular expressions can also let you include a set of characters to try to match. For example, suppose that you have the following search term:

```
.at
```

The problem with this search term is that you do not want all instances of three-letter words that end with "at"—you want only animal names to be returned, which includes bat, cat, and rat. This is a really small example. It is not difficult to skip regular expressions and just type three terms. But, what if you have 10 or 100 terms that need this kind of treatment?

Square brackets, [ ], enable you to group characters. In the preceding example, the following search term would give you exactly what you need:

```
[bcr]at
```

Notice the lack of commas or separators. If you instead want to look for a range of characters, you put a dash in the middle. Perhaps you have a series of data files named in the format data1, data2, and so on, but you want to examine only data files 3 through 9. Use the following term in this case:

```
data[3-9]
```

Finally, you can negate the items in the set by putting a carat in the beginning. To say "anything but 3 through 9", you would use:

```
data[^3-9]
```

Special Characters

Certain characters are either difficult or impossible to represent in a regular expression statement. For example, when was the last time you were able to press Enter and have the system not interpret the action as an instruction to run the command you just entered? Table 19.7 lists some of the special characters you may find useful when working with regular expressions.

The sed Editor

Two kinds of editors are discussed in this chapter. An editor such as **vi** is what most of us traditionally think about when we think of text editors. You use it to open a file, work on it, and save it to work on later. The **sed** (stream editor) tool is not one of those types of editors. You do not open files with **sed**. Because this editor is a complex program, this section walks you through the process of building a query, rather than trying to build a complex generic format.

You start a **sed** operation with the following command:

```
sed flag
```

The flags available with the **sed** command are outlined in Table 19.8. What you do next depends on how complex your statement is going to be.

Table 19.7 Special characters used in regular expressions.

Metacharacter	Represented Character
|	Or, in **sed**
\b	Backspace key
\n	Line feed; common end to a line in a Unix/Linux text file
\r	Carriage return, or Enter key; common end to a line in a Windows or MS-DOS text file
\t	Tab key

Table 19.8 Flags available for sed.

Flag	Purpose	Value
-	Uses STDIN as the input file	None
-e	After the flags are processed, executes the following commands as a **sed** script	Instructions on the command line
-f	After the flags are processed, utilizes the commands in the specified **sed** script file	Path to script file
-h	Prints a brief help message	None
-n	Does not print pattern information while editing	None
-V	Prints the program version	None

Knowing the flags is just the first step toward understanding **sed**, however. As you might have guessed from noting the phrase "**sed** script" in the table, this tool has a scripting language that goes along with it that consists of short commands that instruct **sed** on what to look for and what to change.

Simple **sed** statements might use the **-n** flag, but not **-e** (whose usage is covered in the Immediate Solutions section "Running **sed** With Multiple Commands") or **-f** (whose usage is covered in the Immediate Solutions section "Running **sed** With External File Scripts"). You then go straight into building your rules. These rules require **sed** commands. The more popular of these commands are outlined in Table 19.9.

Table 19.9 Commonly used sed commands.

Command	Purpose	Format
=	Prints to STDOUT the line number operated on	**=**
a	Appends text after line containing matching pattern	**#a\text**
c	Replaces contents of line containing matching pattern	**#c\text**
d	Deletes the matching text	**charsd**
D	Deletes through the next newline	**text/D**
g	Replaces selected pattern with given text	**text/g**
G	Adds the given text after the selected pattern	**text/G**
h	Copies the pattern to a temporary buffer	**h**
H	Adds the pattern to the end of the temporary buffer	**H**
i	Inserts text before line containing matching pattern	**#i\text**
l	Displays the stored pattern	**l**
l	Represents nonprintable characters as metacharacters	**l**

(continued)

***Table 19.9 Commonly used* sed *commands* (continued).**

Command	Purpose	Format
N	Includes next line as part of the pattern	**N**
p	Prints to STDOUT the matched patterns	**charsp**
P	Prints to STDOUT the first line of the matched multiline pattern	**P**
q	Quits after the pattern finds a match	**q**
r	Loads contents of the specified file as the pattern	**r file**
s	Searches for the specified text and replaces it as stated; see Table 19.10 for the flags available with this particular **sed** command	**s/original/replacement**
w	Adds the pattern to the end of the specified file	**w file**
x	Swaps the pattern with the contents of your temporary buffer	**x**

Table 19.10 Flags available for sed's s command.

Flag	Purpose	Value
g	Replaces all	None
I	Ignores case when matching terms	None
p	Prints to STDOUT the substitution results	None
w	Writes the substitution results to a file	Path to file

Grouping Commands

You can group **sed** commands by surrounding them with a pair of braces {}. Groupings can be performed within **sed** script files for formatting reasons or from the command line. If you build a script file, you cannot have any additional commands after the opening brace. For example, consider the following beginning for a **sed** statement:

```
sed '/Header/
```

So far, this just tells **sed** to look for the text "Header". Now, you want to apply multiple commands to this same text. You do this by adding the opening brace at the end of the line, as follows:

```
sed '/Header/{
```

To format this example nicely, place the command contents in a script, instead, starting with the following:

```
/Header/{
```

Now, every command you want to apply to this same term goes between the braces. First, you want to add an ASCII text break after the header. You have a file named ~/dashes that consists of a single line of dashes:

```
-----------------------------------------------
```

You can add this with a read command, as follows:

```
/Header/{
r ~/dashes
```

Now, perhaps you want to add an extra space after the text break. You can use the following, because the temporary buffer is empty:

```
/Header/{
r ~/dashes
H
}
```

Notice that the statement's closing brace is on a line by itself. This formatting is mandatory.

TIP: *To use braces at the command line, review your Linux or Unix knowledge for how to include multiple lines of code on the same line. You use a semicolon for this task. The preceding example would look as follows on the command line:* ***sed '/Header/{r ~/dashes;H;}'****.*

Expressing Locations

You will not get far with **sed** if you cannot properly tell it what patterns to look for. Several options are available to you for this. The first option is a single positive integer, which tells **sed** what line number to evaluate. Another simple option enables you to look at only the last line in the file. Use a dollar sign to do this.

You can also use a tilde (~) to work with line numbers, in the following format:

```
first~step
```

The ***first*** entry is the line to start on. The ***step*** item refers to how many lines to increment by. So, if you use 10~5, **sed** starts on line 10 and then goes to lines 15, 20, 25, and so on.

As you have already seen in some of the command demonstrations, you use a regular expression by surrounding it with forward slashes, such as ***/expression=***. Anything within the slashes is evaluated as part of the regular expression. If you need to use forward slashes in your expression, however, you can use the format ***\tregexpt***. This format actually has two variables. The ***t*** variable represents border characters that you use to mark the beginning and end of the expression. You can use anything you want there, but it has to start with the backslash. The other variable is the regular expression itself.

TIP: *If you want to ignore case in the regular expression in either of the two slash formats, add an **I** at the end of the statement. This makes the formats **/expression/I** and **\tregexptI**, which makes the search case insensitive.*

You can also express a range of addresses between which **sed** should examine. To do this, place a comma between the two items. Their format does not have to match. For example, you could use:

```
1,/finished/
```

Finally, adding an exclamation point at the end of any pattern expression tells **sed** to look for items that do not match the pattern.

Additional Tools

Many more simple but effective tools are available for text processing in Linux. Some of these tools are covered here to help round out your file-manipulation knowledge. Although many administrators have no desire to write the great American novel or other such large text files, you will have to work with many data and script files over time. The more tools you have in your tool belt, the better.

The cut File Splicer

The **cut** command enables you take text from a file and print it to STDOUT. You use this command in the following format:

```
cut flags file
```

The flags available for the **cut** command are listed in Table 19.11.

As you can see, many of the options listed take lists as input. Table 19.12 gives the formats that you have available to you when creating a list for a **cut** flag.

If you want to examine STDIN instead of a file, use a dash instead of a file name.

Table 19.11 Flags available for cut.

Flag	Purpose	Values
-b	Identifies the specific bytes to output	List of bytes
-c	Identifies the specific characters to output	List of characters
-d	Uses the specified character instead of Tab to mark a change in fields	Character
-f	Identifies the specific fields to output	List of fields
--help	Prints help information	None
-s	Does not output lines that contain neither a Tab nor the character specified with **-d**	None
--version	Prints version information	None

Table 19.12 Formats for lists in cut.

Format	Description	Example
#	Indicates a single value	**P**
#-	Indicates to start at the specified value and go to the end of the line	**3-**
#-#	Indicates to start at the first value and go to the second	**2-Y**
-#	Indicates to start at the beginning of the input and go until the value	**-f**

The join File Merger

The **join** command enables you to take text from two or more files and merge it, sending the results to STDOUT. You use this command in the following format:

```
join flags file1 file2
```

The flags available for the **join** command are listed in Table 19.13.

If you want to examine STDIN instead of a file, use a dash instead of a file name.

Table 19.13 Flags used with join.

Flag	Purpose	Values
-1	Implements the join on the specified field in the first file	Field
-2	Implements the join on the specified field in the second file	Field

(continued)

*Table 19.13 Flags used with **join** (continued).*

Flag	Purpose	Values
-a	Includes lines that cannot be joined from the specified file	Path to file
-e	When a field is empty but can be joined, enters the specified value in its place	Value
--help	Displays help information	None
-i	Ignores case when comparing fields	None
-l	Sorts data	None
-o	Builds output according to specified format	A comma- or space-separated list with one of two values: **file#.field** or **0**
-t	Uses the specified character as a field separator	Character
-v	Does not print matching lines from the specified file	Path to file
--version	Displays version information	None

The ispell Spelling Checker

Many people rely on spelling checkers to help catch their mistakes. In Linux, you do not have to use a word processor in order to access this handy tool. You can use the **ispell** program and its associated scripts to spellcheck any text document. How exactly you use this tool depends on the context. These issues are addressed in the Immediate Solutions sections "Checking Spelling With **ispell**," "Building **ispell** Dictionaries," and "Reducing **ispell** Dictionary Sizes."

The tr Text Transposer

Sometimes, you need to alter a file or data stream, but not in incredibly complex ways. A good tool to accomplish these jobs is **tr**. You use this command in the following format:

```
tr flags file(s)
```

The flags available with **tr** are listed in Table 19.14.

The values you use to determine a match come in more than one form. These forms can be mixed and matched where appropriate. One type of value available is a set of metacharacters in the format of a backslash and then a character. Each of these items represents a special function, such as the end of a line—a newline, or **\n**. Table 19.15 lists the metacharacters available with **tr**.

Table 19.14 Flags for the tr command.

Flag	Purpose
-c	If a number in binary format is negative, inverts all bits in the match, which is known mathematically as the "one's complement"; this is a method of making a negative number positive in a binary file
-d	Deletes matching characters
--help	Displays help information
-s	Reduces repeats of matching characters to a single instance
-t	Truncates length of matching characters down to the length of a second set of characters
--version	Displays version information

Table 19.15 Metacharacters for the tr command.

Metacharacter	Represents
\###	The octal value of the character you are referring to
****	A literal backslash
\a	Speaker bell
\b	Backspace
\f	Form feed
\n	Newline
\r	Carriage return
\t	Tab key
\v	Vertical tab

Table 19.16 Formats for representing individual characters with the tr command.

Format	Purpose	Example
char-char	Expresses a range of characters	**a-e**
[char*]	Adds the specified character repeatedly until the second file is the length of the first	**[+*]**
[char*times]	Adds the specified character the stated number of times	**[-*20]**

Another way of representing values with **tr** is directly with the characters. Table 19.16 lists the formats available for this feature.

You also have access to the reserved expressions described earlier for the **sed** command.

Immediate Solutions

Maneuvering In vi

To practice maneuvering in **vi**, do the following:

1. Place this book's companion CD-ROM into your CD-ROM drive.
2. Mount the CD-ROM.
3. Type "cp /mnt/cdrom/textfiles/aesops_fables.txt ~" to copy this file into the home directory for the account you are using.
4. Type "cd ~" to go to the directory where you placed the file.
5. Type "vi aesops_fables.txt" to open the file used in this example.
6. Type "/S FABLES" and press Enter to skip the introductory text—which is worth a read sometime—and jump forward to the beginning of the fables themselves. You now should be on the following line:

```
AESOP'S FABLES
```

7. First, because this file has 82 fables, you need to pick one particular fable to experiment with. Thus, for this example, cursor down to the following line:

```
The Wolf and the Lamb                        Androcles
```

8. Type "0" to jump to the beginning of this line.
9. Type "^" to jump to the first letter in the line, *T*.
10. Type "w" to jump to Wolf. Do so three more times, jumping first to "and", and then to "the", and then to "Lamb".
11. Type "+" to jump forward to the first letter, *T*, in the next line:

```
The Dog and the Shadow                      The Bat, the Birds, and the
Beasts
```

12. Press "$" (Shift+4) to jump to the last letter in the line, *s*.
13. Press Ctrl+D four times. Now you should be past all the listings and into the fables themselves.
14. If you are done for now, type "ZQ" to close the file without saving.

Filtering Text In vi

To practice filtering text—taking text as input, running a process on it, and then outputting it possibly in another format—in **vi**, do the following:

1. Log in to the account you want to practice with **vi** in.
2. Type "vi ~/filter_practice" to create and open the new file filter_practice in your home directory.
3. So far, you have a blank file. Type "i" to enter Insert mode.
4. Type the following:

```
The contents of /var/log are:

ls /var/log
```

5. Press the Esc key to return to Command mode.
6. Type "!!" to tell **vi** that you want to filter the entire line. At the bottom left of your screen, you should now see:

```
:.!
```

7. This prompt is waiting for you to input which filter **vi** should use to process the line. In the case of **ls**, you want to process a shell command. Type "sh"—for the bash shell—and press Enter. The entire contents of the /var/log directory are displayed, one item per line. The first six lines of this file are (possibly) now:

```
The contents of /var/log are:

boot.log
boot.log1
boot.log2
boot.log3
```

8. Use the arrow keys to move to the line that contains boot.log.
9. Type "4!!" to tell **vi** that you want to filter this line and the three after it. You get the filter prompt once again, but this time it looks like this:

```
:.,.+3!
```

10. Type "wc" and press Enter to get a word count of each of these files. In the example, this changes the first six lines of the file to the following:

```
The contents of /var/log are:

     4     4     42
cron
cron.1
cron.2
```

11. Type "1G" to go to the beginning of the file.

TIP: *Want to see which line is which? Type ":" to enter Line mode, and then type "set number". Press Enter, and now all of your lines are numbered.*

12. Type "20!!" to filter from lines 1 to 20.

NOTE: *You can only filter whole lines.*

13. At the prompt, type "sort -r" and press Enter. This rearranges the file in reverse alphabetical order. The first six lines are now as follows:

```
netconf.log
messages.3
messages.2
messages.1
messages
maillog.3
```

Other commands that act as filters are listed in Table 19.17.

Table 19.17 Some commands that act as filters.

Command	Use
awk	A simple programming language that allows manipulation of text patterns
grep	A tool for locating text patterns
sed	A text editor that does not require you to open a file
sh	The bash shell
sort	A tool for arranging data
tr	A tool for substituting or deleting characters
wc	A tool for obtaining word, character, and line counts

Copying And Pasting Text In vi

To practice copying and pasting text in **vi**, do the following:

1. If you have not already installed the "Aesop's Fables" practice file, place this book's companion CD-ROM into your CD-ROM drive. If you have already mounted it, skip to Step 4.
2. Mount the CD-ROM.
3. Type "cp /mnt/cdrom/textfiles/aesops_fables.txt ~" to copy this file into the home directory for the account you are using.
4. If the Aesop's Fables practice file is not already open, type "cd ~" to go to the directory where you placed the file. Otherwise, skip to Step 6.
5. Type "vi aesops_fables.txt" to open the file used in this example.
6. If you are not at the beginning of the file, type "1G" to jump there.
7. Type "/Wolf and the Kid" and press Enter to jump forward to the title in the title list.
8. Type "n" to jump forward to the story "The Wolf and the Kid."
9. Type "12Y" to copy the entire fable into the buffer. The text "12 lines yanked" appears at the bottom-left portion of your screen.
10. Often, either copy and paste or cut and paste is used to share or move data between different files. Type ":e WolfKid" to enter Line mode and open a second file.
11. Type "p" to paste the fable. Now you have two files open simultaneously.
12. Type ":w" to enter Line mode and save the contents of WolfKid. The following text appears at the bottom of the screen:

    ```
    "WolfKid" [New] 13L, 411C written
    ```

13. You still have two files open. Type ":rew" and press Enter. Now, you return to the original file.
14. Type "ZQ" to close the pair of files.

Indenting Text In vi

To practice indenting text in **vi**, do the following:

1. Log in to the account you want to practice with **vi** in.
2. Type "vi ~/indent_practice" to create and open a practice file.

3. Type "i" to enter Insert mode.
4. Type:

```
Left justified.
Indented.
```

5. Press the Esc key to return to Command mode. Be sure the cursor is on the second line of text still.
6. Type ">" and then press the right-arrow key. Now your text looks like this:

```
Left justified.
     Indented.
```

7. Type "o" to move to the next line and enter Insert mode.
8. Type:

```
The quick
brown fox
jumped over
the lazy
dog.
```

9. Notice that the text here is not indented at all. You do not have the autoindent option enabled. Press the Esc key to return to Command mode.
10. Type ":" to enter Line mode.
11. Type "set autoindent" and press Enter.
12. Make sure the cursor is on the last line of text.
13. Type "o" to start a new line at the end and enter Insert mode.
14. Type:

```
Start of automatic indent.
```

15. Press the Esc key to return to Command mode.
16. Type ">" and press the right arrow to indent the line.
17. Type "o" to start yet another new line and enter Insert mode. Notice that the cursor is directly under the start of the indented text. It should look like this:

```
     Start of automatic indent.
     _
```

18. Type:

```
The indents should follow
whatever is above them.
But I can change the indent level
```

19. Press the Esc key to return to Command mode.
20. Make sure the cursor is on the last line of text. Type ">" and press the right arrow to indent this line.
21. Type "o" to start yet another new line and enter Insert mode. Notice that the cursor is now under the indented B.
22. Type:

```
        whenever I want.
```

You should now have the following:

```
Left justified.
     Indented.
The quick
brown fox
jumped over
the lazy
dog.
     Start of automatic indent.
     The indents should follow
     whatever is above them.
          But I can change the indent level
          whenever I want.
```

TIP: *To shut off automatic indenting, go to Command mode and type ":set noautoindent".*

23. To close this file without saving it, type ":q!". The exclamation point overrides the warning you would otherwise get for trying to quit without saving.

Using Regular Expressions

To practice using regular expressions with **ls**, do the following:

1. Place this book's companion CD-ROM into your CD-ROM drive. If you already have it mounted, skip to Step 3.
2. Mount the CD-ROM.

3. Type "cd /mnt/cdrom/regexp" to change to the directory where you will do the following exercise.
4. Type "ls". This gives you a listing of all of the files in the directory by default.
5. Type "ls *". This gives you the same result. Every file in the directory is listed.
6. Type "ls .". This also gives you every file in the directory! The reason it does not only give files with one-letter names is that "." means "current directory" to file system commands.
7. Type "ls ?". You get files with only single-character names. Because the period cannot be used to denote a single letter for **ls**, you use the question mark instead.
8. Type "ls a?b". You get only three-letter file names that start with *a* and end with *b*.
9. Type "ls a[ac]b". You get only three-letter file names that start with *a*, end with *b*, and have as their middle letter an *a* or *c*.
10. Type "ls a[d-f]b". Now you get all three-letter file names that start with *a*, end with *b*, and have as their middle letter *d*, *e*, or *f*.

Running **sed** With Multiple Commands

To build command combinations for **sed**, do the following:

1. If you have not already mounted the CD-ROM, place this book's companion CD-ROM into your CD-ROM drive. If you have already mounted it, skip to Step 3.
2. Mount the CD-ROM.
3. Type "cd /mnt/cdrom/textfiles" to change to the directory you will use for these exercises.
4. The following are the two ways to include multiple commands on the same line with **sed**:
   - Separate the commands with a semicolon
   - Lead each command with the **-e** flag

   Typically, you use a semicolon for the end of brace groupings, or to try to shorten the command so that it fits onto one line. Table 19.18 lists special characters that can require you to break your **sed** command into multiple lines.

Table 19.18 Characters that require line breaks in sed.

Character	Purpose	Location	Example
:chars	Assigns a label of up to seven characters to the line matching the given pattern	Beginning of line	**:a;**
}	Closes a grouped command statement	Beginning of line	**;}**
b	Skips immediately to the label assigned earlier, or to the end if no label is given	End of line	**ba;**
r	Loads the contents of the specified file	End of line	**r file;**
t	If any substitutions were made in this line of code, skips to the label assigned earlier, or to the end if no label is given	End of line	**ta;**
w	Saves output to the specified file, appending to the end if the file already exists	End of line	**w file;**

The first order of business is to determine what it is that you need to do. For this example, you want to work with the file aesops_fables.txt again. You want to do three things here:

- Find every line with "wolf" or "Wolf" in it
- Replace each "wolf" with "canine" and replace each "Wolf" with "Canine"
- Save the altered document to the file canine.txt

5. After you know what you want to do, you need to break the task down into **sed** commands. You actually need two different command structures to accomplish this task. To convert "wolf" to "canine", you would build the following:

```
s/wolf/canine/g
```

TIP: *The **/g** at the end tells **sed** to replace all instances of the regular expression on the line, not just the first.*

To convert "Wolf" to "Canine", you need the following:

```
s/Wolf/Canine/g
```

In both cases, you want to save the information to the same file. To do this, you can just redirect the **sed** output from the screen to a file with the following:

```
> ~/canine.txt
```

6. Now that you have each of the commands that you need, determine the most efficient or logical way to combine them to accomplish the task. The example has more than one option. You could use:

```
sed -e s/wolf/canine/g -e s/Wolf/Canine/g aesops_fables.txt
> ~/canine.txt
```

Or, more correctly, you could use the following to avoid metacharacter problems:

```
sed -e 's/wolf/canine/g' -e 's/Wolf/Canine/g'
aesops_fables.txt > ~/canine.txt
```

You also could use:

```
sed 's/wolf/canine/g;s/Wolf/Canine/g' aesops_fables.txt
> ~/canine.txt
```

Building A **sed** Script File

To practice creating a script for **sed**, do the following:

1. Log in to the account you want to work with.
2. If you have not already mounted the CD-ROM, place this book's companion CD-ROM into your CD-ROM drive. If you have already mounted it, skip to Step 4.
3. Mount the CD-ROM.
4. Type "cd /mnt/cdrom/textfiles" to change to the directory you will use for these exercises.
5. Type "vi ~/sedscript" to create and open the file where you will create your practice script.
6. In a script file, it is a good idea to put each individual command on a separate line. Just as with any other situation in which you want to use **sed**, the first thing you need to do is break your task into components. For this practice script, you need to accomplish the following things:
   - Change all instances of "n." in the text file to "noun"
   - Change the first five instances of "v." to "verb"
   - Change the first instance of "adj." to "adjective"
   - Find the definition for MISFORTUNE and save it to the file ~/misfortune

7. Attend to each of your statements one at a time. For the first statement, you would use this command:

```
s/n\./noun/g
```

Notice the backslash (\) in front of the period. A period is a metacharacter, so you have to place an escape character (\) in front of it to tell **sed** to see it literally as a period.

8. For the second statement, you do not want to change all instances, just the first five. Although operators exist for choosing one line, all lines, or the last line, and for starting at a line and proceeding in numbered steps to the end, none exist for a range of lines. You might use the following instead:

```
s/v\./verb/1
s/v\./verb/2
s/v\./verb/3
s/v\./verb/4
s/v\./verb/5
```

9. For the third statement, you want to change only the first instance:

```
s/adj\./adjective/
```

10. Now, you want to find a definition and save it to a file. You know that the MISFORTUNE definition is only one line, so you might use the following:

```
/^MISFORTUNE/w /home/user/misfortune
```

NOTE: *The carat (^) is included to make sure the match is at the beginning of a line.*

11. All you have to do now is place each of these items in your script, as follows:

```
s/n\./noun/g
s/v\./verb/1
s/v\./verb/2
s/v\./verb/3
s/v\./verb/4
s/v\./verb/5
s/adj\./adjective/
/MISFORTUNE/w /home/user/misfortune
```

12. Be sure to save and close the file. Press the Esc key and then type “ZZ” to accomplish this.

Running **sed** With External File Scripts

To run **sed** with a script, do the following:

1. Log in to an account that has access to the **sed** script you want to use.
2. Type the following to run the script on a file:

```
sed -f script file
```

Or, type the following to run the script on input from STDIN:

```
process | sed -f script
```

To run the script that you wrote in the previous section, type:

```
sed -f ~/sedscript /mnt/cdrom/textfiles/dev_dict.txt
> /home/user/dev_dict_new.txt
```

Using The **cut** Command

To use the **cut** command, do the following:

1. Log in to the account you want to work with.
2. Determine the file or data you want to work with:
   - If you want to work with a file, start with the following:

   ```
   cut
   ```

   - If you want to work with data from another program, start with this format:

   ```
   generate_data | cut
   ```

3. Determine what you want to cut. For example, perhaps you want to alter a file listing in the format "ls -la" so that you get only the file's permissions. The "ls -la" command generates output in the following format:

```
permissions  links  owner  group  size  time_last_changed  name
```

Each of these items is a numbered field, beginning with 1. So, you want to keep field 1 only.

4. Determine what character is used to separate the fields. In this case, it is a space.
5. Build the command. For the example, you get the following:

```
ls -la | cut -d" " -f1
```

Using The **join** Command

To utilize the **join** command, do the following:

1. Log in to the account you want to work with.
2. Determine the first file or data item you want to work with:
   - If you want to work with a file, start with:

     ```
     join
     ```

   - If you want to work with data from another program, start with this format:

     ```
     generate_data | join
     ```

3. Choose from Table 19.13 earlier in the chapter what flags are appropriate for your **join** command.
4. Determine the second file or data item you want to work with:
   - If the first item is a file and the second is a file, then use this format:

     ```
     join flags file1 file2
     ```

   - If the first item is a file and the second is data, then use this format:

     ```
     generate_data | join file1 -
     ```

   - If the first item is data and the second is a file, then use this format:

     ```
     generate_data | join - file2
     ```

NOTE: *You cannot have both items as data—one must be a file.*

Checking Spelling With **ispell**

To utilize the **ispell** spelling checker, do the following:

1. Log in to the account you want to work with.
2. Locate the ASCII text file you want to check.
3. Begin by typing "ispell".
4. Choose the "common" flags—an **ispell** designation—you want to use from the list given in Table 19.19.

   For example, you might choose to make a backup file and to allow the character $ to be part of a word. So far, you would have the following:

```
ispell -b -w $
```

Table 19.19 Common ispell flags.

Flag	Purpose	Value
-b	Makes a backup of the original file, with the same name but .bak at the end	None
-B	Counts words joined together as errors—for example, thedog	None
-C	Does not count words joined together as errors	None
-d	Uses another standard dictionary file	Name of dictionary, typically the name of the language, such as **english** or **deutsch** (German)
-m	Offers root word and additive combinations that are not officially in the dictionary	None
-n	Expects the file to be in the nroff or troff layout formats	None
-p	Uses a personal dictionary file	Name of dictionary
-P	Does not offer root word and additive combinations that are not already in the dictionary	None
-S	Sorts alternative spellings by their likelihood to be right	None
-t	Expects the file to be in the TeX or LaTeX layout formats	None

(continued)

***Table 19.19 Common ispell flags* (continued).**

Flag	Purpose	Value
-T	Expects the file to be of the specified type, rather than getting it from the file name	A formatting type, such as nroff, troff, TeX, or LaTeX
-w	Lists characters that are not normally parts of words, but that you do not want **ispell** to complain about, such as $	The character(s) in question, with no separation
-W	Lists a word length that is always legal	Number of characters long this word should be
-x	Does not create a backup file	None

5. Choose whether you want **ispell**'s menu displayed at the bottom of the screen. If you do, then add the **-M** flag. If not, add **-N**. The menu contains the following, though the text is all on one line on the screen:

```
[SP] <number R)epl A)ccept I)nsert L)ookup U)ncap
          Q)uit e(X)it or ? for help
```

   In the example, perhaps you chose the menu. Now you have:

```
ispell -b -w $ -M
```

6. Determine whether you want additional lines of text to be displayed, to give context to the item **ispell** flags. If so, add the flag **-L** with the number of lines to include. To use four lines of context in the example, you would now have:

```
ispell -b -w $ -M -L4
```

7. Finally, add the file name at the end. In the example, you might now have:

```
ispell -b -w $ -M -L4 ~/sample.txt
```

8. The **ispell** program now steps through the file and displays all words that do not match its rules. Although the menu displays some of the commands you have available to you, the full list is given in Table 19.20.

Table 19.20 Full listing of ispell commands.

Command	Result
Space	Accepts this word just this time
Ctrl+L	Redraws the screen
Ctrl+Z	Moves this process to the background so you can use the command line for something else
#	Replaces with word # in the suggestion list
!	Runs the shell command prompted for after typing this character
?	Displays help information
A	Accepts the word for the rest of this document
I	Accepts the word exactly as it appears and adds it to your private dictionary
L	Looks up the word in the main dictionary
Q	Quits without saving
R	Replaces the incorrect word with the one **ispell** now prompts you for
U	Accepts the word and adds it to your private dictionary in all lowercase
X	Saves and quits immediately

Building **ispell** Dictionaries

To build a new **ispell** dictionary, do the following:

1. Log in to the account you want to work with.
2. You will use the program **buildhash** to create this dictionary. This portion of the **ispell** suite builds a compressed version of a word list that **ispell** can read. The first thing you must do, however, is provide the word list. This list should be a file full of word roots, one per line. The following capitalization rules apply:
    - Lowercase words will match any capitalization
    - An uppercase letter will only match other uppercase letters
    - If the word begins with an uppercase letter (or more than one), then the matches are only the exact case in which it is typed, and all capital
    - An all-uppercase word only matches uppercase

NOTE: *You can have more than one capitalization combination for a word in the dictionary.*

3. After you enter the base (root) words for this dictionary, you can specify which prefixes and suffixes apply. To do so, it is wise to work with two files simultaneously. Keep the word list open and also open a file to contain the prefixes and suffixes. You will make two tables. The prefix table is in this format:

```
prefixes : flag*
  [^beg][end] > -remove,add
  ...
  [^beg][end] > -remove,add
```

   These terms refer to the following:

   - ***beg***—The letter(s) to look for at the beginning of the word
   - ***end***—The letter(s) to look for at the end of the word
   - ***remove***—The letter(s) to remove from the beginning—led by a carat (^)—or end of a word
   - ***add***—The letter(s) to add to the beginning—led by a carat (^)—or end of a word

   For example, for a dictionary of chemical names, you might use the following:

```
prefixes : P*
  [^ABCDEFGHIJKLMNOPQRSTUVWXYZ] > BI
  [^ABCDEFGHIJKLMNOPQRSTUVWXYZ] > TRI
```

   Prefixes tend to have more free-flowing rules than suffixes.

4. Now, build your suffix table. This table works in the same format as the prefix table. To continue the example, you might have the following:

```
suffixes : S*
  IDE > -IDE,IC
  IDE > -IDE,ITE
```

5. Save and close the file. For example, press the Esc key and type "ZZ" to save and close it in **vi**.
6. Build the hashed dictionary file that **ispell** can use, by typing:

```
buildhash rootfile affixfile dictfile
```

Reducing **ispell** Dictionary Sizes

To reduce the size of your personal **ispell** dictionary, do the following:

1. Log in to the account you want to work with.
2. You have several tools available for making your personal dictionary smaller. If you have many root words in the file that appear multiple times with different prefixes and suffixes, use the **munchlist** tool in this format:

   ```
   munchlist flags files
   ```

   The available flags are listed in Table 19.21.
3. If you need to locate commonly used affixes to use in a new dictionary, use the **findaffix** tool in the following format:

   ```
   findaffix flags file
   ```

   Available flags are listed in Table 19.22.
4. If you want to test how effective a new prefix or suffix (otherwise known as an affix) will be in your dictionary, then use the **tryaffix** command in the format:

   ```
   tryaffix flags file affix
   ```

   Available flags are listed in Table 19.23.
5. Finally, you can get rid of redundant entries with the **icombine** command in this format:

   ```
   icombine affixfile
   ```

Table 19.21 Flags available for the munchlist command.

Flag	Purpose	Value
-c	Converts old dictionaries to the most current format	None
-D	Does not delete temporary files automatically unless debugging is required	None
-l	Chooses a specific prefix or suffix file	File name
-s	Removes words in the specified dictionary from the list you are operating on	Dictionary name
-v	Sends progress output to STDERR	None

Table 19.22 Flags available for the findaffix command.

Flag	Purpose	Value
-c	Presents the output in a human-readable format	None
-f	Sorts by number of times prefix or suffix appears instead of by how many bytes are saved with it	None
-l	Changes the limit of how many times a prefix or suffix has to appear to be listed; default is **10**	Positive integer
-m	Sets the smallest word that will be displayed when generated by the prefix or suffix; default is three characters	Positive integer
-M	Changes the maximum prefix or suffix length; default is **8**	Positive integer
-p	Examines existing prefixes	None
-s	Examines existing suffixes	None
-t	Uses the Tab key to separate fields	None

Table 19.23 Flags available for the tryaffix command.

Flag	Purpose	Value
-c	Instead of listing all roots that match the affix rule, gives a statistical summary	None
-e	Utilizes the expanded dictionary prepared with **ispell -e**	File name to use
-p	Sees the affix as a prefix	None
-s	Sees the affix as a suffix	None

Using The tr Command

To practice using the **tr** command to make simple text alterations, do the following:

1. Log in to the account you want to work with.
2. To demonstrate to you how useful **tr** is, this exercise uses it to build on the **cut** example introduced in the earlier section "Using The **cut** Command." Remember that the goal in this example is to pull data from the command **ls -la**. Because **cut** is limited, it could be used to get only the first part of the file listing, which is the permission set. Remember that the output of **ls -la** is in this format:

```
permissions  links  owner  group  size  time_last_changed  name
```

Each of these items is a numbered field, beginning with 1. This time, suppose you want to keep the fields 1, 3, 5, and 9—remember that every space is going to be counted as a field, and there are spaces in the ***time_last_changed*** field. So, start with:

```
ls -la |
```

3. The problem you'll run into with getting more than the first field in **cut** is that multiple spaces exist between each of the fields, and **cut** counts each of those as a field. You want to use **tr** to turn each group of spaces into a single space, which **cut** can work more easily with. You use the **tr** command in this format:

```
tr flags char(s)
```

4. Choose the flags you want to use. For this example, you want to squeeze multiple spaces down to one, which you can do with the **-s** flag. This now gives you the following:

```
ls -la | tr -s " "
```

If you just press Enter at this point, you see that only one space is between each field.

5. Now, to reduce the output to the fields specified earlier, use the **cut** command. Because you have already covered building **cut** commands in the section "Using The **cut** Command," the answer is given to you here:

```
ls -la | tr -s " " | cut -d" " -f1,3,5,9
```

Chapter 20

Shell Scripting

If you need an immediate solution to:	*See page:*
Changing The Active Shell	609
Installing The Public Domain Korn Shell	609
Changing Your Bash Login Prompt	610
Writing Your Own Package Update Script	611
Writing Your Own User Creation Script	615
Writing A Script To Find A File In Your RPMs	620
Writing A Script To Monitor System Load	623

In Depth

A valuable tool in a system administrator's toolbox is the ability to automate processes. Shell scripting enables you to build files that duplicate what you otherwise might do at the command line. This chapter introduces you to what shells are, the default Linux shell and the alternatives, and how to optimize both the shell and shell scripting. The logic used to create a script is also covered in some useful examples.

The Shell

A *shell* refers to the environment you are working in—not the graphical environment, but rather the collection of commands and variables you have access to at the command line. The default shell in Linux is the *bash* shell, otherwise known as the *Bourne Again shell*, which is patterned after the Unix sh shell (the Bourne shell). Some other shells that are available to Linux users are discussed next.

Available Shells

A wide variety of shells is available to Linux users. This chapter covers the shells that come with Red Hat Linux, because this list of shells represents a good cross-section of the more popular ones. The shells that come with Red Hat are outlined in Table 20.1.

Table 20.1 Shells available in Red Hat Linux.

Name	Claim To Fame
ash	Based on the System V default shell, a slight variation of sh. Smaller than many other shells.
bash	Default Linux shell. An updated version of the original Unix shell, the Bourne shell (sh). Aliased to sh under Linux. Contains features from both ksh (the original Korn shell) and csh.
bsh	Based on the AIX default shell, another variation of sh.
csh	The parent of the second Unix shell family tree. Its syntax is based on the C programming language.
pdksh	The public domain version of the Korn shell, which is based on the original sh. This shell has additional script debugging features that endear it to some scripting aficionados.
tcsh	An updated version of the original C shell, csh.

Environment Variables

The variables that each shell keeps track of to customize a user's experience are the *environment variables*. These variables tend to be written in all capital letters to distinguish them from *shell variables*, which are used to pass information within a program. The distinction between an environment variable and a shell variable is that an environment variable keeps its setting until you leave the shell, whereas a shell variable only lasts during the program it is set in. Table 20.2 lists some commonly used environment variables.

At any time, you can see the content of an environment variable in the bash shell by typing "echo $*VARIABLE*".

TIP: *To see all the environment variables currently set for your account, type "env".*

Two ways exist to set an environment variable's value. One way is covered in the following section, "Bash Shell Scripting." The other way is to set the value permanently by editing the file ~/.bash_profile. After doing so, this variable is activated whenever you log in to the account using a bash shell. Follow the process covered in the Immediate Solutions section "Changing Your Bash Login Prompt" to set other environment variables permanently.

Bash Shell Scripting

Because the bash shell is the default root shell and the most frequently used shell among Linux users, I cover bash shell scripting here. If you want to learn more about scripting in other shells, each has its own man page. Almost all bash shell scripts start with the following line:

```
#!/bin/bash
```

Table 20.2 Environment variables of interest.

Variable	Purpose
HOME	Stores your home directory
MAIL	Stores the path to your mail spool, which is the file that contains the mail in your inbox
PATH	Stores the list of directories that the system looks in when you run programs
PS1	Stores the login prompt
PWD	Stores the current directory you are in
SHELL	Stores the shell you are currently using
USER	Stores your login name

NOTE: *This line also might be **#!/bin/sh**, because bash and sh are just aliases to one another under Linux.*

This line tells the shell what command interpreter to use when running the script. Better yet, it enables you to run shell scripts written for one shell type from within another shell.

After this line, things get more complicated. This section of the chapter is subdivided into smaller sections that focus on different things you might want to do in a script. These sections are ordered in such a way that each section builds on skills you learned in previous sections. Thus, this is one area where it benefits you to read straight through, if you are trying to write a script.

Basic Shell Scripting

A shell script consists of commands that can be used directly on the command line. You run a command in a script by typing it just as you would on the command line, though it is wise to be more careful and include the path to the command as well. For example, you could run **ls -la** with just the following line in the script:

```
ls -la
```

No additional commands or special characters are required. You also may want to set environment or other variables. In the bash shell, you set both shell and environment variables in this format:

```
variable=value
```

There cannot be any space in between the variable and the equal sign. This helps the shell to know that you are referring to a variable and not a command. You actually use the values of these variables by putting a dollar sign in front of them, such as ***$variable***. For example, you might have the following pair of lines in different parts of the script:

```
count=10
nextcount=$count + 1
```

To assign a string, instead, you would use the following:

```
string="This is my string"
```

You can also set a variable to be the result of a command by placing the command in backward quotes:

```
variable=`command`
```

Often, you'll want to display the value of a variable. Just as you do at the command line, you can use the **echo** command for this purpose. However, you need to understand that what happens depends on the syntax you use. You might simply have the following:

```
echo $count
```

This command would just display "10" if you continue with the example. You might also have this line:

```
echo "The count is $count\."
```

Using double quotes tells the **echo** command to assess the value of variables and metacharacters that appear within the double quotes. If you want to have the statement print literally, you have to use single quotes, such as this:

```
echo 'The count is $count.'
```

Or, you could combine the two approaches and use:

```
echo 'The count is ' $count '.'
```

You can also add comments with a hash mark (#). Comments are useful for ensuring that later, when reexamining or trying to alter the code, you can understand what you were thinking when you created the code. You do not have to have the hash at the beginning of the line. If you want to add a comment on the same line as some code, you can do so in this format:

```
code  # Everything on the line after the hash is commented.
```

Input And Output

Some scripts need to interact with either the user or other programs. This requires that you understand the various options available to you for accepting incoming information. The first thing to realize is that you can include input directly on the command line when you call the script. If you simply type "*./script*", then there is no data to remember. However, if you type something like

```
./script jadams "John Adams" psmith Paulette Smith
```

then each of the data items is assigned to **$** variables. The first item on the command line after the script name is **$1**, so that is jadams. From there, "John Adams" is **$2**, psmith is **$3**, Paulette is **$4**, and Smith is **$5**. Other command line–related entries are listed in Table 20.3.

Table 20.3 Built-in shell variables referencing command-line arguments.

Variable	Contains
$@	A full list of all the command-line arguments, in quotes
$#	The number of command-line arguments
$*	A full list of all the command-line arguments

You can also use the **read** command to accept data from the user. This tool offers a prompt to the user and enables him or her to enter up to a line of material. To put all input into one variable, use this format:

```
read variable
```

It is also possible to have each individual item on the line—with spaces separating the values—placed into different variables, by using this format:

```
read variable1 variable2 variable3 ... variableN
```

Another valuable tool is **getopts**. You use this tool within loops in the following format:

```
getopts letters variable
```

The ***letters*** portion of the statement contains individual letters that correspond to input, with each letter representing a specific item. If the letter is just a command with no arguments with it, then just give the letter—such as "a". However, if it is a command with a corresponding argument, put a colon after it—such as "a:". The ***variable*** item is the name of the variable you want to use to step through the letters in a loop.

The following statement expects three different commands:

```
getopts a variable
```

However, this statement expects three commands and an argument:

```
getopts a: variable
```

The input for the first statement might be

```
more
```

whereas the input for the second might be

```
more /etc/profile
```

To access the argument, use the **OPTARG** variable.

---

*NOTE: The **getopts** command is not actually used to allow a user to input information. It is used as a method of parsing the information given at the command line.*

Not all input comes from the user. Some input comes from other programs. Essentially, two methods exist for sharing data between programs. The first is called *redirection*. You have likely seen this in countless examples, but as an administrator, you really should understand how to put it to use. Before you begin to learn how to use redirection, you need to understand some other basic shell concepts:

- *STDOUT (standard output)*—When you type a command—perhaps **ls**—that command often sends its output to STDOUT. Typically, STDOUT is your screen.
- *STDIN (standard input)*—Whenever you type information at the command line, you are using STDIN. Programs can use this interface, as well.
- *STDERR (standard error)*—Many programs send their error messages to STDERR.

When you deal with redirection, you are taking data that was meant for STDOUT, STDIN, or STDERR and altering its course to go where you want it to go. The operators used to do this are listed in Table 20.4.

NOTE: Linux tends to see everything as a file, including the STD trio. When you redirect something, you send it to or from a file.

The second method of controlling what happens to program output is the *pipe*. This feature is represented by a vertical line (|). Rather than dealing with files, using a pipe enables you to take the output of the command to its left as the input for the command to its right, as represented by the following:

Table 20.4 Symbols used for redirection in bash.

Symbol	Result	Example
>	Intercepts data going to STDOUT and sends it to the specified file	**ls -la > listing**
2>	Intercepts data going to STDERR and sends it to the specified file	**ls areyouthere 2> errors**
<	Opens the file specified and sends its contents to STDIN	**cat < listing**
>>	Intercepts data going to STDOUT and sends it to the specified file, appending the current information to what already exists if the file has text in it already	**ps aux >> processlist**

```
command1 | command2
```

You can have more than two commands when dealing with pipes; you could even have this structure:

```
command1 | command2 | command3 | command4 | command5
```

Conditionals And Loops

After you feel comfortable writing shell scripts at the basic level—and probably frustrated by not being able to do anything more complex—you're ready to start investigating some of the more interesting things you can do with a script. Now, you get into such things as the various types of *conditionals*—statements that work only if an item tests true—and *loops*—statements that repeat according to specified criteria—that are available in bash shell scripts. The conditional and loop types and their uses are listed in Table 20.5.

The **if** conditional statement is by far the most complex. In its most basic format, you use it as follows:

```
if condition
  then result
fi
```

This code results in the straightforward prospect that if the condition is true, all the lines of code—which can be just one, or many—from **then** to **fi** are executed. You can get more fancy with this format:

```
if condition
  then result
  else result
fi
```

Table 20.5 Loops and conditionals available in bash shell scripts.

Start	End	Intermediates	Purpose
for	**done**	**do**	Runs through the loop the prescribed number of times
if	**fi**	**then**, **else**, **elif**	Tests whether the given conditions are true or false; proceeds if true
until	**done**	**do**	Tests whether the given conditions are true or false; proceeds if false
while	**done**	None	Runs through the loop while the given condition is true

With this structure, your conditional now has options. It tests to see whether the condition is true and, if it is, proceeds to the line of code associated with the **then** clause. However, if the condition is false, instead of skipping the conditional completely, the code associated with the **else** clause runs.

Finally, the following is the most complex conditional:

```
if condition
  then result
  elif condition
    result
  fi
  else result
fi
```

The **elif** clause stands for "else if." Notice the placement in the statement. The initial **if** condition tests the values that you provide in the method you specify. A true result sends the script to the code associated with the **then** clause, and then continues past the entire conditional statement. If the condition tests as false, then a second condition is tested. A true result for the second condition runs the code associated with the **elif** clause. If both conditions are false, then the script jumps to the code associated with the **else** clause.

All three loop types—**for**, **until**, and **while**—use the same format:

```
looptype condition do
  results
done
```

The important task is determining which loop type you need to use—the purpose of each type was described previously, in Table 20.5. Sometimes, this choice is more of an art than a science. If you find yourself struggling to get a loop to work the way you started it, consider changing to one of the other types. Often, this will solve your problem.

Testing Conditions

Conditionals and loops both require that you test data for certain values or against other data types, so that they know how to proceed. These comparisons are done with the **test** command. Various ways exist to use **test**, depending on whether you are comparing items or looking for characteristics.

A file's type is one characteristic that you can test against. This information can be important when trying to ensure that your program has some finesse in handling any problems it may run into, such as needing to write to files that do not exist. Table 20.6 lists the operators available for using the **test** command in this fashion. All of these operators are used in this format:

```
test operator /path/file
```

Another type of test that you have available is to examine a file's permissions. This test is useful to ensure that files created by your script have their permissions set properly in the end even if you have changed the default permissions on your system since you wrote the script. Table 20.7 lists the permission testing operators that are available. These operators are used in this format:

```
test operator /path/file
```

You can also test additional information about files, mostly through comparisons. This is useful for ensuring that you are using the latest version of a file, or the

Table 20.6 File type operators for test.

Operator	Tests True When
-b	The *block special device*—meaning that it is storage media of some kind—exists.
-c	The *character special device*—meaning that it is an output device, such as a modem or monitor—exists.
-d	The directory exists.
-f	The file exists.
-L	The symbolic link exists.
-p	The FIFO—named pipe—exists.
-S	The socket exists.

Table 20.7 File permission operators for test.

Operator	Tests True When
-g	The file is SGID (set group ID).
-G	The file is owned by the GID (group ID) running the script.
-k	The file has its sticky bit set.
-O	The file is owned by the UID (user ID) running the script.
-r	The script has read permissions for this file.
-u	The file is SUID (set user ID).
-w	The script has write permissions for this file.
-x	The script has execution permissions for this file.

Table 20.8 Additional file operators for ***test****.*

Operator	Tests True When	Format
-e	The file exists.	**-e file**
-ef	The two files are hard links to one another.	**file1 -ef file2**
-nt	The first file was modified more recently than the second.	**file1 -nt file2**
-ot	The second file was modified more recently than the first.	**file1 -ot file2**
-s	The file exists and is larger than 0 bytes.	**-s file**

original instead of a link. Table 20.8 provides the full listing. In this case, the format in which you use the operators varies.

Not all testing operations are performed on files. You can also use **test** to examine strings. These operators are useful for checking user input, file contents, and more. Table 20.9 provides a list of string **test** operators.

You can compare numbers as well as letters and files. If you have done any programming in the past, this perhaps is the type of test that you are most familiar with. Table 20.10 lists the operators with which you can compare numerical values. All of these items are used in the following format:

```
test value1 operator value2
```

Table 20.9 String operators for ***test****.*

Operator	Tests True When	Format
=	The strings are the same.	**string1 = string2**
!=	The strings are not the same.	**string1 != string2**
-n	The string is not empty.	**-n string**
-z	The string is empty.	**-z string**

Table 20.10 Mathematical operators for ***test****.*

Operator	Tests True When
-eq	The two values are equal.
-ge	The first value is greater than or equal to the second.
-gt	The first value is greater than the second.
-le	The first value is less than or equal to the second.
-lt	The first value is less than the second.
-ne	The two values are not equal.

Finally, some operators work on **test** conditions overall. Placing an exclamation point in front of the condition tells **test** to reverse the true or false result. For example, the following results in false:

```
! 1 -eq 1
```


If you want to require that two different **test** conditions both must be true, then use this format:

```
condition1 -a condition2
```

Replace the **-a** (and) with an **-o** (or) if only one has to be true.

TIP: *You will start to notice after reading other people's shell scripts that they do not use the word* ***test****. Instead, they include the conditions in brackets ([ ]), which imply the* ***test*** *command.*

Text Menus

Sometimes, you may want to offer multiple options to a user without having to ask one by one what they want to do. Today's programmers might solve this issue with a fancy graphical menu. This obviously is not an option in a shell script. However, you can build text menus in bash shell scripts by using the **case** command in the following format:

```
case condition in
  value1) action1(s);;
  ...
  valueN) action(s);;
esac
```

This type of statement can get very complex because you must print all the instructions to the screen as well as offer the menu options. See the Immediate Solutions section "Writing Your Own User Creation Script" for a good example of implementing the **case** command.

Immediate Solutions

Changing The Active Shell

To change which shell is currently active for your account, do the following:

1. Log in to the account you want to set the shell in.
2. Type "chsh -l" to see what shells you have available to you, including their full pathname. With the default Red Hat installation, you should have the following available:

```
/bin/bash
/bin/sh
/bin/ash
/bin/bsh
/bin/tcsh
/bin/csh
```

3. Type "chsh -s */path/shell*" to change the default shell for your account.

TIP: *If you want to do this for someone else's account as root, you can either change the shell entry for their account in the /etc/passwd file or type "chsh -s /path/shell -u user".*

Installing The Public Domain Korn Shell

To install the public domain korn shell in Red Hat Linux, do the following:

1. Log in as root.
2. Insert the Red Hat CD-ROM into the CD-ROM drive, if necessary.
3. Type "mount /mnt/cdrom" to mount the CD-ROM onto the file system, if necessary.
4. Type "cd /mnt/cdrom/RedHat/RPMS" to change to the packages directory on the CD-ROM.
5. Type "rpm -ivh pdksh" and press Tab to complete the file name, and then press Enter to install the shell. It will now show up when you use the **chsh** command.

***TIP:** If you are using another distribution that does not come with **pdksh**, go to **www.cs.mun.ca/~michael/pdksh/** and download the shell from there.*

Changing Your Bash Login Prompt

To permanently change your login prompt in the bash shell, do the following:

1. Log in to the account you want to change.
2. Type "vi ~/.bash_profile" to open the file that contains your environment variables for a bash login session.
3. Look for the following line:

```
# User specific environment and startup programs
```

4. Move your cursor to the last line of definitions under the header.
5. Type "o" to create a new line below the current position and enter Insert mode.
6. Start the line with the following:

```
PS1="
```

7. Building the prompt requires that you know the characters available to you, which are outlined in Table 20.11.

Table 20.11 Bash prompt-building characters.

Character	Purpose
\!	Displays the upcoming *history* value—where it is stored in the history of typed commands—of the command executed at this prompt
\nnn	Displays the ASCII character matching the octal **nnn**
****	Displays a backslash
\d	Displays the date as "Day of Week Month Date" (e.g., Friday September 8 2000)
\h	Displays the machine's hostname
\n	Adds a newline to make a two-line prompt
\s	Displays the shell being used
\t	Displays the current time in "hh:mm:ss" format
\u	Displays the active username
\w	Displays the full path for the current directory
\W	Displays only the last portion of the current directory

Choose what information you want to include in your prompt. To use the username and the full path in your prompt, for example, include **\u** and **\w**.

8. Choose the format you want this information to be in. Any characters that do not have a backslash associated with them are included literally. For example, if you want your prompt to end with a dollar sign and a space, then just tack these items on the end. You would also want to separate the two entries with a space.
9. Complete the prompt statement. In the case of this example, you would have the following:

```
PS1="\u \w$ "
```

10. Press the Esc key to return to Command mode, and then type "ZZ" to save and close the file.
11. Log out from this shell instance and log back in. The new prompt should now be active.

TIP: *Set this file with executable permissions if you want to run it by typing "./script".*

Writing Your Own Package Update Script

To learn how to write your own package update script, do the following:

1. Log in as root, because this script is meant to update all packages.
2. Type "vi ~/bin/update.scr" to open the script file for editing.
3. Type "i" to enter Insert mode.
4. Type the following to ensure that Linux knows that this is a bash shell script:

```
#!/bin/bash
```

5. Determine the FTP or Web site you want your script to get its information and files from. A default might be **ftp.redhat.com**. You might have the following line included to establish this connection:

```
ftp ftp.redhat.com
```

6. The script cannot send any instructions to the server until it is properly connected, so you need to choose a loop that makes it wait for this to happen. An **until** loop would serve this function well, so start with:

```
until [
```

7. You have to be able to analyze the text resulting from the FTP connection to know when the connection is fully made. One way to start this process is to return to the line added in Step 5, and change it to the following:

```
ftp ftp.redhat.com >> /root/bin/data/ftpsession
```

8. Now, you can have the loop analyze the contents of this file until the appropriate characters indicate that the connection is finalized. The best way to know which characters to watch for is to actually make the connection by hand. The following is the final text that appears when connecting to **ftp.redhat.com**:

```
Data connection opened.
```

NOTE: *During busy periods,* ***ftp*** *connections can take many tries to go into effect. This script just tries once.*

---

9. Several ways exist to analyze the contents of the data file for the terms needed. One of these is by using the **grep** command—covered in Chapter 23—in this format:

```
grep -ic "Data connection" /root/bin/data/ftpsession
```

10. This command must be made a part of the **until** loop. You want the loop to continue until the **grep** command finds the data, which means that it will have a non-zero result. So, the **until** loop starter might be similar to the following:

```
conn=""
until [ $conn != ""] do
  grep -ic "Data connection" /root/bin/data/ftpsession
```

11. You simply want this loop to prevent the script from sending any **ftp** commands until the connection is made. So, just close it by typing "done".
12. Now you are connected to the FTP server. You need to build a list of the various update files available for your distribution version. The files for Red Hat 6.2, which you obtain manually, are located in the directory /pub/redhat/updates/6.2/i386. So, enter this command:

```
cwd /pub/redhat/updates/6.2/i386
```

13. Upon looking manually in this directory, you will see that a listing file is already provided. To grab the file ls-lR.gz, use the following command:

```
get ls-lR.gz /root/bin/data
```

14. That is all you need from the server at this point, so disconnect by typing "quit".
15. Change to the /root/bin/data directory, and **gunzip** the file:

```
cd /root/bin/data
gunzip ls-lR.gz
```

16. Now, your script needs to know exactly what packages are installed on your machine. You can use the **rpm** program to gather this information for the items you installed using this tool. A command similar to the following would get you the list you need—but do not put it in the script just yet, because you are still considering how to accomplish the goal, not laying out code:

```
rpm -qa
```

17. If you save this information to a file, you can take advantage of file comparison commands later. So, add a line similar to the following to your script:

```
rpm -qa > /root/bin/data/loadedrpms
```

18. You now need to make sure both files are in the same format. This requires breaking down the **ls-lR** listing into just the package names. Because this listing is in a file, you need to get it to STDIN before you can manipulate the data. Start the command with:

```
cat ls-lR |
```

19. Shrink all the spaces between fields to single spaces with **tr**:

```
cat ls-lR | tr -s " " |
```

20. Pull out only the file names with **cut**:

```
cat ls-lR | tr -s " " | cut -d" " -f9
```

21. You need this data saved to a file now:

```
cat ls-lR | tr -s " " | cut -d" " -f9 > lspkgs
```

22. You need to be able to compare the contents of the two files. They are not similar enough to use the **diff** command. Instead, you have to directly compare the terms to one another. Because you are interested in reducing the list of files available for download, a good approach is to load each term in the file, see whether it exists among your installed packages, and, if it does not, save it to a list of potential downloads.

    You might start this process with a clever use of code in a **for** loop:

```
package="empty"
for package in 'cat lspkgs' do
```

23. Within the loop, you now must test each package to see whether it is already installed. You can do this with a simple **grep** command in an **if** conditional, such as this:

```
loaded=""
loaded='grep -c $package loadedrpms'
 if [ $gloaded != "" ]
   then
   echo "$package" >> donthave
 fi
```

24. Close the loop by typing "done".
25. Automatically loading packages just because they are available isn't recommended. Even letting the script download is suspect, because it could be a huge waste of bandwidth if you have a metered Internet connection. Instead, have the script email you the list of RPMs available, which you can then review, choose from, and download by hand. Or, write a script to download the packages you choose. To handle the mailing, use something similar to the following:

```
cat donthave | mail -s "The RPM updates not already installed"  \
root@localhost
```

NOTE: *Change the email address to whatever makes sense for your needs.*

---

26. It is wise to clean up all the temporary files. You might want to do so in a separate script that runs about 30 minutes before this one.
27. Press the Esc key to enter Command mode, and then type "ZZ" to save and close the file.
28. Edit the file ~/.netrc to assign automatic login information for the FTP session. Use this format:

```
default login anonymous password email@address
```

TIP: *Set this file with executable permissions if you want to run it by typing "./script".*

Related solution:	Found on page:
Using **grep** To Find What You Need	685

Writing Your Own User Creation Script

To learn how to write your own user creation script, do the following:

1. Log in as root, because only root can add users.
2. Type "vi ~/bin/usercreate.scr" to open the script file for editing.
3. Type "i" to enter Insert mode.
4. Type the following to ensure that Linux knows that this is a bash shell script:

```
#!/bin/bash
```

5. Determine the basic steps that you tend to go through when creating a user account. In Red Hat, that might include running **useradd** and then running **passwd**.
6. Determine the more advanced steps you might want to add to your script. For example, perhaps you want to be able to set the real name field in /etc/passwd or set which shell the user wants to use. You might even want to set primary and additional groups.
7. Some people like to create shell scripts that can accept all terms from the command line. If you do not have a great memory, you may want your scripts to prompt you for the information they want. However, you do not

want the script to ask you a ridiculous number of questions. A menu will solve that problem. First, you do not want to exit the menu fully until you have selected every option you want to set. Placing it inside a **while** loop would help. If the variable that holds the menu choice is called **choice**, then you first need to initialize it:

```
choice="empty"
```

8. Now, you must build the menu. You might use the following code to print the options:

```
echo "Choose one or more of the following options to set
      for your new user account\n"
echo "[U]sername"
echo "[P]assword"
echo "[F]ull name"
echo "P[r]imary group"
echo "[A]dditional groups"
echo "[C]hange shell"
```

9. Because so many values are displayed, it would help to also provide a listing of what everything is currently set to. First, *zero* all the variables, which means to set them to a default value, as follows:

```
user="empty"
pass="empty"
name="empty"
group="empty"
moregroup="empty"
shell="empty"
```

10. Start the loop and tell it to exit only when you choose Quit in the menu:

```
while [$choice != "Q"] do
```

11. Print the current values:

```
echo "The current values are: user = $user, name = $name,
      group = $group, additional group = $moregroup, and
      shell = $shell\n"
```

12. Notice that you do not list the password here. You probably do not want to display this information. Instead, you might add a statement that tests to see whether the password is already set:

```
if [$pass = "empty"]
   then echo "Password is not yet set\n"
fi
```


13. Build the skeleton for the menu statement. Use the **echo** version as a template. In this case, it might be similar to the following:

```
case $choice in
  U|u) echo "Enter valid username: "

  P|p) echo "Enter secure password: "

  F|f) echo "Enter user's full name: "

  R|r) echo "Enter the group to assign this user to: "

  A|a) echo "Enter another group to add this user to: "

  C|c) echo "Enter the shell you want this user to work within: "

esac
```

NOTE: *The* ***C|c)*** *format enables the user to enter either the upper- or lowercase version, by recognizing both as valid entries. You do not have to use single letter choices, either.*

14. Now you need to display the menu. Use the skeleton for this with something like:

```
echo "Press U to add the username"
echo "Press P to add a password"
echo "Press F to add a user's full name"
echo "Press R to add this user's primary group"
echo "Press A to add an additional group for this user"
echo "Press C to change the user's default shell"
```

15. You have to read in the value for the menu to test against:

```
read choice
```

16. Now you can create how the menu responds to the choices. Each of the blank lines underneath the menu options corresponds to more code that must be filled in. They all need code in the same format:

```
read variable;;
```

After you fill it in, the **case** statement now looks like this:

```
case $choice in
  U|u) echo "Enter valid username: "
  read user;;
  P|p) echo "Enter secure password: "
  read pass;;
  F|f) echo "Enter user's full name: "
  read name;;
  R|r) echo "Enter the group to assign this user to if you do
            not want them in a group with the same name as
            their username: "
  read group;;
  A|a) echo "Enter another group to add this user to: "
  read moregroup;;
  C|c) echo "Enter the shell you want this user to work within: "
  read shell;; esac
```

17. You are still missing one choice, the **Q**. Add that before **esac** with

```
Q|q)echo "Quitting.";;
```

18. End the **while** loop now, with

```
done
```

19. All of this was necessary just to get your information! From here, you step through each of the tasks. The first task is to create the user account. You have multiple ways to do this. One option is to use the existing **useradd** program, simply by entering the following:

```
useradd $user
```

20. The next mandatory step in setting up a user account is to use **passwd** to assign the user's password. This is a three-step process. First, you start with:

```
passwd $user
```

21. The script now has to wait for the first **passwd** prompt. Adjust the previous line to:

```
passwd $user >> passwdoutput
```

22. Adding a password by hand gives you the following output:

```
Changing password for user pferd
New UNIX password:
Retype new UNIX password:
passwd: all authentication tokens updated successfully
```

So, the first thing you want to watch for is perhaps just **UNIX**. As with other examples in this chapter, you can create an **until** loop that waits for this word to appear, by entering the following:

```
until grep -c "UNIX" passwdoutput do
done
```

23. To answer the prompt, you need to send the password and then send a carriage return. You might use

```
echo "$pass\r"
```

24. You should do something similar for the second prompt:

```
until grep -c "Retype" passwdoutput do
done
echo "$pass\r"
```

25. The rest of the items are not necessary to set up a valid user account. Each of them should be handled with **if** statements. For the full name, you might start with:

```
if [$name != "empty"]
   then
   usermod -c $name $user
fi
```

26. To change from the default group, use:

```
if [$group != "empty"]
   then
```

```
   usermod -g $group $user
fi
```

27. To add the user to another group as well, use:

```
if [$moregroup != "empty"]
   then
   usermod -G $moregroup $user
fi
```

28. To change which shell the user enters at login time, use:

```
if [$shell != "empty"]
   then
   chsh -s $shell $user
fi
```

29. Now, just delete the temporary file you created (passwdoutput), and add some output to tell the superuser that the user was added, and you are done. You might use:

```
rm -f passwdoutput
echo "$user added."
```

TIP: *Set this file with executable permissions if you want to run it by typing "./script".*

Writing A Script To Find A File In Your RPMs

To write a script to dig through your RPM packages to find a specific file, do the following:

1. Log in as root if you only allow root to mount the CD-ROM, or under a user account if you will be doing these searches as a regular user.
2. Type "vi ~/bin/rpmsearch.scr" to open the script file for editing.
3. Type "i" to enter Insert mode.
4. Type the following to ensure that Linux knows that this is a bash shell script:

```
#!/bin/bash
```

5. You need to have your Red Hat CD-ROM mounted to use this script. Several ways exist to ensure this, ranging from lazy to sophisticated. Because other examples show lazy methods, this one is more sophisticated. You can tell what devices are mounted and where with the **df** command. This next line would start with:

```
df
```

6. Now, you want to analyze the actual output from the **df** command. To do this, you can use a pipe to pass the output to **grep**—covered in Chapter 23. If you have more than one mount point with "cdrom" in it, then you have to modify this item, but you should be able to just use the following:

```
df | grep "cdrom"
```

7. Your script needs to know whether the search term exists in the **df** listing. This requires analyzing the command's output. Because you want to add steps to the process only if the CD-ROM is not mounted, consider using the following **if** statement:

```
gcd='df | grep "cdrom"'
if [ $gcd = "" ]
   then
```

8. So, the script continues to the **then** only if the CD-ROM is not mounted. First, prompt the user:

```
echo "CD-ROM is not mounted. Please place the Red Hat" \
      CD-ROM into the CD-ROM drive.\n"
echo "When you have the CD-ROM in place, press Enter.\n"
```

9. The script must now wait until the user puts the CD-ROM into the drive and presses Enter. You will have to read this keystroke into a variable, so first initialize the variable:

```
keystroke="empty"
```

10. Create a loop that will wait until the user presses Enter. A simple **read** command works for this:

```
read keystroke
```

11. Now, you can have the script automatically mount the CD-ROM for the user:

```
mount /mnt/cdrom
```

12. Change to the RPM repository on the CD-ROM, and then close the **if** statement:

```
cd /mnt/cdrom/RedHat/RPMS
fi
```

13. Now, you have to build the command that gets a listing of the files in an RPM. The following is the base for this command:

```
rpm -ql package
```

However, you'll be using this script to query packages that are not installed so that you can decide which to add. Therefore, you need the following format:

```
rpm -qlp package
```

14. You need to search through every RPM on the CD-ROM. Although it might be tempting to just search all the packages at once, doing so will not give you any information about where the file was found. Instead, you need to have the script increment through the packages, which you can accomplish in one of several ways. This example shows you how to use a **for** loop in this situation. The **for** command can increment through a list of things, instead of just needing numbers. Use this to your advantage by starting the loop with:

```
for package in /mnt/cdrom/RedHat/RPMS/*
    do
```

15. Each time the script runs through this loop, the variable **package** contains the name of the RPM package being tested. This gives you the first part of the statement you need, which is:

```
rpm -qlp $package
```

16. You also need to have a regular expression for the file you are looking for. This expression can be gathered either from the command line or from a prompt before the **for** loop. In this case, you enter the file on the command

line, so that you can learn how to use this information in a script. You can pipe the list of packages to the **grep** command as follows:

```
rpm -qlp $package | grep $1
```

17. This is useless as is. If this command combination does find the file, you will not know what package the file was in. Although you could just have every package name echoed as the search continues, this would scroll a lot of information down your screen. Instead, try something such as this:

```
found='rpm -qlp $package | grep $1'
if [ $found != "" ]
   then
   echo "$1 found in $package\n"
fi
```

18. Close the **for** loop:

```
done
```

19. Press the Esc key to enter Command mode, and then type "ZZ" to save and close the file.

TIP: *Set this file with executable permissions if you want to run it by typing "./script".*

Related solution:	Found on page:
Using **grep** To Find What You Need	685

Writing A Script To Monitor System Load

To learn how to write a script that can monitor your system's load and notify you if any problems arise, do the following:

1. Log in as root.
2. Type "vi ~/bin/loadmon.scr" to open the script file for editing.
3. Type "i" to enter Insert mode.
4. Type the following to ensure that Linux knows that this is a bash shell script:

```
#!/bin/bash
```

5. The simplest form of output that includes system load figures comes from the command **uptime**, as in this example:

```
4:39am up 7 days, 22:19, 5 users, load average: 0.05, 0.01, 0.00
```

6. All that you want from this line are the three load average numbers. You could use any of a variety of tools to get these. The two that come to mind immediately are **cut** and **sed**. Before you can **cut**, you have to make sure that the same number of spaces exists between each item. The command starts with

```
uptime | tr -s " " |
```

7. Now, you can **cut** out the last three entries:

```
uptime | tr -s " " | cut -f11-13 |
```

8. Another pipe is included because you must do one more thing—get rid of the commas:

```
uptime | tr -s " " | cut -d" " -f11-13 | tr -d ","
```

9. You must determine what to do with this data. You can either save it in a file and store all load averages to watch trends, or simply examine what you have now. For the sake of this example, the script will examine the load averages and send you email whenever an average gets above 3. This means that you have to get the three numbers from the command in Step 8 into three separate variables. First, you can save the results of Step 8 into a variable as a string, with the following:

```
averages='uptime | tr -s " " | cut -d" " -f11-13 | tr -d ","'
```

10. Next, you can use the **cut** command three times to save all three numbers:

```
average1='echo $averages | cut -d" " -f1'
average2='echo $averages | cut -d" " -f2'
average3='echo $averages | cut -d" " -f3'
```

11. A set of **if** conditionals can now handle the warnings. First set the **warn** flag and then write the conditional:

```
warn=0
```

```
if [$average1 -gt 3] then
   warn=$warn + 1
fi
if [$average2 -gt 3] then
   warn=$warn + 1
fi
if [$average1 -gt 3] then
   warn=$warn + 1
fi
```


12. And, finally, add the conditional statement that decides whether to send email:

```
if [$warn -gt 0] then
   echo "Load averages are $average1 $average2 $average3." \
   | mail -s "Load average warning" root@localhost
```

NOTE: *Change the email address to whatever makes sense for your needs.*

13. Press the Esc key to enter Command mode, and then type "ZZ" to save and close the file.

TIP: *Set this file with executable permissions if you want to run it by typing "./script".*

Chapter 21

Perl Scripting

If you need an immediate solution to:	*See page:*
Installing Perl	636
Getting And Installing A Perl Library Module	636
Running A Perl Program	638
Writing A CGI Script With Perl	639
Processing A Web Form	639

In Depth

Sometimes, shell scripting just is not enough to meet your custom programming needs. You need a more powerful tool. Although many options are available for Linux today, Perl is still a popular choice for those who need to write small to midrange programs but do not want to resort to a language such as C or C++. One particularly common use for Perl is to write CGI scripts, which are programs used in conjunction with Web pages and sites. This chapter introduces you to the rudiments of programming with Perl.

Introduction To Perl

The Practical Extraction and Report Language (Perl) is an interpreted programming language that's based on C and several other languages. In the fine tradition of open-source software, Perl was developed by Larry Wall starting sometime in or before 1987—in the official Perl FAQ, the phrase is "Don't ask"—in conjunction with anyone else who was interested in participating on the project and had something useful to add. The current major version is 5, which is incremented with sub-version numbers such as 5.005.

You will often see Perl referred to as both a programming and a scripting language. Perl is modular, object-oriented, and otherwise similar to C and other high-level programming languages, but it is also a popular tool for creating CGI scripts for use on the Web. Part of the confusion stems from the fact that Perl programs can indeed be compiled but are traditionally interpreted. This chapter alternates between program and script.

One aspect that sets Perl apart from plain old shell scripting is that Perl is modular. Sets of specialized library modules are available for a wide variety of uses. Perl is also fairly portable, because Perl programs run on most modern operating systems. This doesn't mean that a program written for Perl under Linux will run with no alterations on a Macintosh, but Perl is certainly more portable than a shell script.

Perl Programming

The beginning of all Perl programs under Linux should be familiar to you. They must begin with something similar to the following:

```
#!/usr/bin/perl
```

TIP: *Type "which perl" to find the exact path on your machine. If nothing comes up, then you probably do not have Perl installed. See the Immediate Solutions section "Installing Perl" for directions on how to install it.*

From here, of course, things get far more complicated. The following sections detail how to use specific aspects of the Perl language and syntax.

In The Beginning

After the **#!** header, certain pieces of information typically belong at the beginning of a Perl script. Items that you also may want to have at the beginning of your Perl code are listed in Table 21.1.

NOTE: *The **require** statement expects files to have a .pm extension. If they do not, use the format **require 'file.extension';**.*

Perl Basics

When you start writing Perl and shell scripts, you may find yourself having to look back and forth between this chapter and the previous one to double-check syntax. For example, to assign a value to a variable in Perl, you use the following format:

```
$variable = value;
```

A variable in Perl always has a dollar sign in front of it. For a string, you might use instead:

```
$variable = "value";
```

Table 21.1 Starter pieces to a Perl script.

Code	Description	Example
#comments	It is good form to explain the purpose of the program at the beginning of the document. This can save you a lot of digging through code as you try to remember what a program is supposed to do.	**#This script calculates a customer's bill.**
require	Loads code from the specified file at runtime.	**require cgifunctions;**
use	Loads the specified module so that you have access to its functions and commands.	**use perl-cgi;**
variable declarations	Many people find it efficient to keep all of their variable initializations at the beginning of a script. This way, if you need to go back later and adjust your initial settings, you can find them all in one place.	**$cost = 1.24;**

NOTE: *Do not use an underscore (_) as the first character in a variable name. The notation* ***$_*** *is reserved in Perl.*

Notice that in both of these cases, a semicolon appears at the end of the line. This is true for the end of all Perl commands. Suppose that you want to display a line on the screen. You would use the **print** command in this format:

```
print "Message";
```


Just as in a shell script, if you include a variable in the format ***$variable*** in the quotes, the variable's contents will be displayed on the screen.

Arrays

One nice thing about having access to a "real" programming language—versus the limitations of shell scripting—is that you have access to some of the fancier features. One of these tools is the *array*, a single variable that holds multiple pieces of information. Each value in the array is keyed to a number, typically the order in which the item was added to the variable. Arrays in Perl are assigned in one of the following two formats:

```
@array = (value1, value2, ..., valueN);
@array = ("value1", "value2", ..., "valueN");
```

The values of these arrays are then expressed as follows:

```
$array[position - 1]
```

For example, ***value5*** in the preceding format listings would be ***$array*[4]** because array position counting begins at 0.

You actually can include one array inside another. For example, first you make the two arrays:

```
@colors = ("blue", "green", "orange");
@fruits = ("orange", "apple", "pear");
```

You can actually place the **@colors** array inside **@fruits** with:

```
@fruits = ("orange", "apple", "pear", @colors);
```

This phrase now expands to:

```
@fruits = ("orange", "apple", "pear", "blue", "green", "orange");
```

Or, more appropriately for this example, you can make a whole new array with this line:

```
@fruitsNcolors = (@fruits, @colors);
```

To then get the number of elements in an array, use this format:

```
$#array
```

This returns the *index*—the location of ***value*** within the array list—of the last value, so it gives you the number of elements minus one, because—once again—items in an array are counted starting from zero.

You can add and remove data from an array by using some new commands ("new" if you are not familiar with C and other similar programming languages). To add to the beginning of an array, use **push** in one of these formats:

```
push(@array, value);
push(@array, "value");
```

For example, consider the following code:

```
push(@fruits, "banana");
```

The **@fruits** array now contains **banana**, **orange**, **apple**, and **pear**. To remove an item from the end of the list, use **pop** in the following format:

```
$value = pop(@array);
```

Perl also supports another type of array. Rather than using an index number that refers to an item's position within the list, this array type—called a *hash* by programmers—groups terms according to assigned keys. You use a hash in this format:

```
$hash{key} = value;
```

For example, suppose you have the hash **toys**. This hash contains a variety of types of toys; specifically, **dolls**, **stuffed_animals**, and **vehicles**. These three terms are your keys, and you can have only one value for each key. If you want to add a value for each key here—the doll is **betty**, the stuffed animal is **phred**, and the vehicle is a **model truck**—then you might use the following:

```
$toy{doll, betty, stuffed_animal, phred, vehicle, 'model truck'};
```

Testing And Regular Expressions

You cannot use tools such as conditionals and loops without understanding how to test values. Perl enables you to test strings and numbers. These test characters are outlined in Table 21.2.

Perl also has its own way of handling regular expressions. It is somewhat **sed**-like insofar as you always enclose a regular expression between two slashes (***/regexp/***).

Conditionals And Loops

A programming language has no power without some kind of testing and looping mechanisms in place. Perl is no slouch in this regard. A conditional **if** statement, for example, is used in this format:

```
if ($variable operator value){
   commands;
}
```

In this case, no colons are used for the **if** statement itself. Colons are used only for the commands inside. Instead, the entire contents of the **if** statement are enclosed within braces ({ }). You also have access to **if-else** constructs, in the following form:

```
if ($variable operator value){
   commands;
}
else{
   commands;
}
```

Table 21.2 Perl's test operators.

Character	True If
!	Negates the test result, meaning a false (zero or empty) tests as true.
==	The two numerical values are equal.
!=	The two numerical values are not equal.
=~	The regular expression matches.
!~	The regular expression does not match.
&&	Both items are nonzero and nonempty.
||	One or the other is nonzero or nonempty.
eq	The two strings are equal.
ne	The two strings are not equal.

Also available is the "else if" term **elsif**, which you can use as many times as necessary—just make sure all instances are between the **if** and **else** clauses, such as in this example:

```
if ($variable operator value){
   commands;
}
elsif ($variable operator value){
   commands;
}
else{
   commands;
}
```

You also have access to the same set of looping mechanisms that you use in shell scripting, but with a bit of a twist. To start, there is the familiar **for** loop:

```
for (start; condition; increment by){
    commands;
}
```

Another type of **for** loop is available, too, which works much like the **for...in** combination in shell scripting. This type of loop is **foreach**. You use it as follows:

```
foreach $variable (items){
  commands;
}
```

Often, the ***items*** entry is an array: for example, **@fruits**. Another type of loop available in Perl is **while**:

```
while ($variable condition value){
  commands;
}
```

This operator has the same meaning that it does for shell scripting. It tells Perl to continue through the loop while the condition tests as true. The opposite, of course, is the **until** loop:

```
until ($variable condition value){
  commands;
}
```

An **until** loop continues through until the condition no longer tests as true. The twist on these two loop types is that you can run the test at the end of the loop instead of at the beginning. You do so using this format:

```
do {
  commands;
} looptype ($variable condition value)
```

Notice that the end of the loop statement still has no semicolon—just the end of each command within the loop has a semicolon.

TIP: *A special variable called* ***$_*** *in Perl is referred to as the default variable. Whenever you want to shorten a loop's requirements, you can assign the variable you want to test as* ***$_****. Then, all you need to put in the parentheses is the value to test against.*

File Manipulation

Whereas shell scripts enable you to work with files just as you would on the command line—using various Linux commands and redirection tools—you cannot do this in a programming language such as Perl. Instead, you need to learn how this language relates to files. To manipulate information within a file with Perl, you first need to **open** it in the following format:

```
open(NAME, "/path/file");
```

TIP: *Many Perl programmers prefer to first set a variable to the file name, such as* ***$file = '/path/file'****, and then refer to the variable in the* ***open*** *statement, resulting in* ***open(FILE, $file);****.*

One subtlety left out of the preceding code is the *file intent operator*, which tells Perl what you plan to do with this file. Table 21.3 lists the various operators available. For example, if you want to open the file in the preceding code to write data to it, you use the following:

```
open(NAME, ">/path/file");
```

Table 21.3 File intent operators in Perl.

Operator	Result
<	Reads data from file; default for the **open** command
>	Sends data to file
|	If at the beginning, pipes output to the specified command; if at the end, pipes in the input from the specified command
<-	Reads data from STDIN
>-	Sends data to STDOUT
>>	Appends data to the end of this file

You eventually must **close** a file after you have it open. To do this, use this format:

```
close(NAME);
```

While a file is open for input, consider it an array variable, except that you always refer to it as ***NAME***. So, if you have a file open to accept input from, you can write its contents to an array in the following format:

```
@contents = <NAME>;
```

When a file is open for output, use the following format to write to it:

```
print NAME "Message\n";
```

Immediate Solutions

Installing Perl

Because Perl is not automatically part of Linux, you need to install it before you can program with it. How you install Perl depends on what distribution you are using. These instructions are specific to Red Hat:

1. Log in as root.
2. Make sure the Red Hat CD-ROM is in the CD-ROM drive.
3. Type "mount /mnt/cdrom" to mount the CD-ROM.
4. Type "cd /mnt/cdrom/RedHat/RPMS" to change to the packages directory.
5. Type "rpm -ivh perl" and press the Tab key to expand the file name, and then press Enter to install the package.
6. Type "cd /" to exit the mount point.
7. Type "umount /mnt/cdrom" to remove the CD-ROM from your file system.

NOTE: *If your distribution does not come with Perl or if you want a newer version, try* ***www.perl.com****,* ***www.perl.org****, or* ***www.cpan.org****. You can get the official source code for the latest release at* ***www.perl.com/CPAN/latest.tar.gz****.*

Getting And Installing A Perl Library Module

To install a Perl library, do the following:

1. Log in as root.
2. Use a Web browser to go to **www.perl.com/CPAN-local/CPAN.html**. The Comprehensive Perl Archive Network (CPAN) is one of the definitive places to go for Perl source code and modules.
3. Scroll down to the section with the header "PERL MODULES."
4. This is where things get tough, because hundreds of modules are listed. CPAN uses two organizational tools to try to help you find what you need. First, the modules are arranged in alphabetical groups. The second tool is the handy one, however. The modules are arranged in subdirectories

corresponding to what tool or function they serve. Table 21.4 provides a list of what some of the module groups refer to (far too many module groups exist to include all of them here).

Table 21.4 Some module groups available for Perl.

Group	Purpose Of Modules
Apache	Interfacing with the Apache Web server
Audio	Manipulating sound files
Business	Clearing cash transactions
CGI	Enabling Perl to function as a CGI script
Chart	Graphing and plotting data
Convert	Formatting conversion
Crypt	Addressing some common forms of encryption
Data	Working with data structures
Date	Working with calendar dates
DBD	Interfacing with database formats
DBIx	Manipulating database contents
Devel	Providing Perl development tools
ExtUtils	Extending Perl so that it can work together with other code types
File	Manipulating files
Games	Using Perl to write games
Gimp	Writing extensions for the Gimp graphics program
HTML	Integrating Perl with HTML code
Image	Enabling Perl to manipulate images
Lingua	Enabling Perl to parse and manipulate documents of various languages
Log	Creating and manipulating log files
Mail	Enabling Perl to parse and interface with a variety of mail and mailing list formats
Math	Adding extensions that assist Perl in manipulating numbers in specific ways
Net	Interfacing with various networking tools
Statistics	Performing statistical analyses
String	Parsing and manipulating ASCII strings
Win32	Interacting with Windows 95 and later utilities
WWW	Interfacing with Web services
XML	Working with XML code

Click any module within the group you want to examine. This action opens a directory with all the modules within that group.

5. Each module is represented by two different files. The first is the .readme file that discusses what the module does and gives any instructions that you might need, including information about the modules that this one depends on. Be sure to read the .readme file and grab any modules this module depends on before you try to use it. Otherwise, you will have to come back and do it later. The second file is the module itself.
6. After you choose which modules you want to use, click their names to download them. You may find it useful to download the .readme file, too.
7. Each of the modules is stored as a tarball. Untar and **gunzip** it into your preferred download directory.
8. Typically, the next step is to type the following sequence of commands:

```
perl Makefile.PL
make
make install
```

9. To then include this module in your Perl programs, you need to use a line in the following format:

```
use modname;
```

Related solution:	Found on page:
Opening Or Creating Tarballs	110

Running A Perl Program

If you have a Perl program you want to run, do the following:

1. Either change to the directory containing the program or add it to your path.
2. You can run the program in either of two ways, depending on how you have it stored:
   - If the file is executable, type "*./filename*".
   - If the file is not executable, type "perl *filename*".

Writing A CGI Script With Perl

To write a CGI script in Perl, do the following:

1. Determine the file extension that your CGI script must have for the Web server to recognize it. For example, although Perl programs tend to have .pl at the end of their names, many Web servers will not recognize a Perl CGI program unless it ends in .cgi.
2. Determine the location in which your CGI script must be stored for the Web server to recognize it. Often, CGI scripts have to be contained within the central or individual user's cgi-bin directory. This allows for system administrators to easily locate the scripts used in Web sites for security control purposes.
3. Create the script with your favorite text editor either in a Web server CGI directory or in a separate test directory.
4. Make sure that you have the module CGI.pl installed.
5. Add the following line to the beginning of the script:

```
use CGI;
```

6. Write the script.
7. Save and exit the file.
8. Make the file executable, narrowing or loosening the permissions as needed.
9. Test the script.

Processing A Web Form

One of the most common uses of Perl CGI scripts is to process data coming in from a Web form. The following is an example of this use:

1. Type "vi ~/public_html/bin/info_form.cgi" to create and open the script file.
2. Tell the system you are writing a Perl script with the following line:

```
#!/usr/bin/perl
```

3. Tell the system to include the CGI module for this script, which this example already has installed, with the following line:

```
use CGI;
```

4. You need a form to work with for this example. Because this is not a book on HTML, I will just give you the form code here:

```
<FORM METHOD="POST" ACTION="http://www.domain.ext/~user/bin/
info_form.cgi">
  <P>Please fill in the following information.</P>
  <P>First Name: <INPUT TYPE="text" NAME="fname" SIZE="20"></P>
  <P>Last Name: <INPUT TYPE="text" NAME="lname" SIZE="20"></P>
  <P>Gender: <INPUT TYPE="radio" VALUE="female" CHECKED
NAME="gender">Female
     <INPUT TYPE="radio" NAME="gender" VALUE="male">Male</P>
  <P>Occupation: <SELECT SIZE="1" NAME="occupation">
    <OPTION>Consultant</OPTION>
    <OPTION>Programmer</OPTION>
    <OPTION>Student</OPTION>
    <OPTION>Writer</OPTION>
  </SELECT></P>
  <P><INPUT TYPE="submit" VALUE="Submit" NAME="B1">
     <INPUT TYPE="reset" VALUE="Reset" NAME="B2"></P>
</FORM>
```

   This form produces the page shown in Figure 21.1.

5. Read in the data that you collected from the Web page. You can use an array to do this along with the **&ReadForm** parameter, in the following format:

```
&ReadForm(*forminput);
```

6. The data from the Web page is now entirely contained within ***forminput**. You do not need to concern yourself with item order. Each of the variables is keyed to its name as assigned in the form. In the case of this example, the keys are **fname**, **lname**, **gender**, and **occupation**. So, you can access this information with **$forminput{fname}**, **$forminput{lname}**, **$forminput {gender}**, and **$forminput{occupation}**.

Figure 21.1 The form produced by the HTML code displayed in the info_form.cgi example.

The goal here is to write the collected data into a file and then send a simple thank-you page to the user. To write this data to the end of the file, you first need to open the file:

```
open(DATAFILE, ">>~/bindata/infodata");
```

7. Now, write the data to the file with a statement such as the following:

```
print DATAFILE $forminput{fname} " " $forminput{lname}
  " " $forminput{gender} " " $forminput{occupation} "\n";
```

8. You must close the file to ensure the data is saved properly:

```
close(DATAFILE);
```

9. Finally, you need to output a new Web page with some kind of thank you text. This example gives the simple text: "Thank you for filling in this information. We will only use it for internal purposes." To do this, tell the CGI module—which you added to this program in the beginning with the statement **use CGI;**—that you want to create a new CGI *object*:

```
$thankyou = new CGI;
```

NOTE: *If you are not familiar with object-oriented programming, then creating a new object may not seem to make a lot of sense. What you are doing here is naming an entity that represents the Web page you want to output. Think of it as opening a blank document, within which you will code the new page.*

10. You now use this object (**$thankyou**) to refer to data that needs to go to your Web page. Web pages need a header section. You assign this with a combination of the **header** function and the **start_html** operator. This example is not getting into anything fancy, so the **header** portion—which sends the client HTTP header information—is merely the following:

```
print $thankyou->header,
```

You send all the HTML information by using the **print** command. The "arrow" (**->**) operator calls a specific method within the CGI module. In this case, it is the **header** method. Notice that you have not yet closed the **print** statement with a semicolon.

11. The second portion of the **print** statement is the **start_html** function. This is where you create the HTML header for your document. It begins with:

```
$thankyou->start_html(
```

12. You have several items available that you can provide in a **start_html** statement. These items are outlined in Table 21.5. This example simply sets the title and the target with:

```
-title=>'Thank you for participating',
-target=>'_blank'),
```

NOTE: *The double arrow (**=>**) is actually a shortcut for creating a hash pair.*

13. Now you have an open Web document with its HTML **<HEAD>** tag properly in place. You can fill in the body, which is the following for this example:

```
$thankyou->"Thank you for filling in this information. We will only
 use it for internal purposes.",
$thankyou->p;
```


14. Your **print** statement is now closed. You simply need to close the Web document. Use the **end_html** method to do this, in the following format:

```
$thankyou->end_html;
```

15. Press the Esc key to return to Command mode, and then type "ZZ" to save and close the file.

Table 21.5 Components available in the CGI Perl module's start_html statement.

Component	Purpose
author	Describes who created this page; often this is an email address.
base	If **true**, tells the Web client to set this Web page's location as the base for calling up any pages within this current page that have no leading http://. Otherwise, this option explicitly sets the base to assume for this document.
BGCOLOR	Indicates the color to use for this Web page's background.
meta	Provides information about the contents of this Web page.
style	Identifies the style sheet to use for this Web page.
target	Specifies the HTML target tag.
title	Provides the title information for this Web page.

Chapter 22

Linux C Programming

If you need an immediate solution to:	*See page:*
Installing The C Compiler	647
Compiling C Code With **gcc**	647
Debugging Code With **gdb**	653
Finding Resource-Hogging Sections With **gprof**	656
Installing The Build Manager	658

In Depth

One of the most popular programming languages used today is C. Although many computer buffs never need to understand the language or how to work with it, Linux administrators need to have a basic knowledge of how Linux deals with packages written in C. The RPM format has reduced the number of programs people have to compile for their system, but sometimes you won't be able to avoid compiling in C. Knowing a bit about how Linux works with C code can help immensely when you need to fix a package that will not compile properly on your system.

Linux C Components

Several useful tools are available for C programmers under Linux. This chapter cannot possibly cover all of them, so only the most commonly available tools—mostly GNU tools—and most common tasks are presented here. Do not consider this chapter in any way to be a tutorial on C programming. If you are interested in learning more on this subject, try a book, such as *A Book On C, Second Edition*, by Al Kelley and Ira Pohl (The Benjamin/Cummings Publishing Company, Inc., 1990).

The Compiler And Helpers

C is a *compiled language*, which means that you do not just run C code by itself. Instead, you run it through a processing program that converts your C program into *machine language*—raw bits and bytes. Compiled software typically runs faster than interpreted software, because the computer does not have to spend time converting the code into its own language.

The C—and C++—compiler used in Linux is often **gcc** (GNU C Compiler). When you utilize this program to build your code into a machine-executable format, it follows a particular progression of tasks, unless you tell it to do otherwise. This progression breaks down as follows:

1. *Preprocess the code.* This task involves locating the macros contained within the code and expanding them. These macros are typically declared with the **#define** command.
2. *Compile the code.* The actual job of converting the code to machine language.
3. *Assemble the code.* C code tends to be spread among a collection of files. This task merges the combined compiled code into one file.

4. *Link the code.* When you have external *object files*—a type of library containing code for external routines—called within your C code, pointers are added to these files at this stage.

Several helper programs also are available for Linux C programmers. One of these helpers is the GNU Debugger, **gdb**. If you are having trouble getting your C program (or one that you downloaded) to work properly, use this tool to step through the code and try to find the problem.

If you have a large program that is becoming a problem because it hogs up RAM and CPU time, then consider using the **gprof** tool. (See the Immediate Solutions section "Finding Resource-Hogging Sections With **gprof**" for more information about this tool.)

The Libraries

When you are dealing with C programming, you often hear the term *library*. A library is a collection of precompiled subroutines that you or the users on your system can point to, rather than having to reinvent the wheel for common applications. You can find your overall libraries in the /usr/lib hierarchy. The ones that specifically come with **egcs**—the latest version of the GNU C Compiler—are in /usr/lib/gcc-lib/i386-redhat-linux/egcs-*version*/include/. This directory is full of .h (header) files. If you dig through these files, you will see a series of comments for what each routine in them does.

The Build Manager

The tool that you are most likely to have to deal with is the build manager: **make**. Whenever you download source code, it almost always comes with a Makefile. This file automates the compilation process so you and other users do not have to figure out all the flags and other items necessary to get the program compiled with **gcc**. A Makefile is especially helpful for the many people who are Linux aficionados but not professional programmers.

A Makefile has a specific structure to it that can be represented as follows:

```
maintarget : requirements
            instructions
target1 : requirements1
        instructions1
...
targetN : requirementsN
        instructionsN
```

As you can see, each of the line pairs—though there can be more than one set of instructions—follows the same format. It starts with the *target*, which is one of the following:

- A C object file (*file*.o).
- A **make** argument called a *make target.* This type of target enables you to type some of the standard installation instructions, such as **make install**, automating the entire process.
- The executable program itself.

The *requirements* refer to object files that have to be built before this particular target's instructions can be run. This is simply a space-separated list of object files. Finally, the *instructions* are typically simple **gcc** commands. A brief Makefile might be similar to the following:

```
main : main.o sub1.o sub2.o
      gcc -o all main.o sub1.o sub2.o
main.o : main.c
      gcc -c main.c
sub1.o : sub1.c
      gcc -c sub1.c
sub2.o : sub2.c
      gcc -c sub2.c
```

NOTE: *Manuals for all the GNU tools discussed here are available at* ***www.gnu.org/manual/manual.html****.*

Immediate Solutions

Installing The C Compiler

To install the C compiler, do the following:

1. Log in as root.
2. See whether you already have the C compiler in place by typing "rpm -q egcs". If this package is located, you do not need to proceed.
3. Place the Red Hat CD-ROM into your CD-ROM drive.
4. Mount the CD-ROM by typing "mount /mnt/cdrom".
5. Change to the packages directory by typing "cd /mnt/cdrom/RedHat/RPMS".
6. Install the C compiler by typing "rpm -ivh egcs-1" and then pressing Tab to expand the file name. Press Enter.

NOTE: *You may be wondering why I said the compiler is **gcc** earlier in the chapter but you are installing the package egcs. The GNU C Compiler is officially maintained by EGCS as a way of merging two separate development projects. The latest information about this venture is available at **http://gcc.gnu.org**.*

Compiling C Code With gcc

To compile C code with **gcc**, do the following:

1. Log in to the account that owns the code you want to work with.
2. Change to the directory containing the code by using the **cd** command.
3. Start by typing "gcc" at the command line. Do not press Enter yet.
4. Each of the four steps used by **gcc** has its own set of available command options. Choose the preprocessing options you want to use from Table 22.1. For this example, you want to go past the preprocessing point, so you will avoid the **-E** option. You also want to specify that your header files are in ~/bin/ccode/headers, and save out information that can help in building a Makefile. At this point, then, you have the following:

```
gcc -idirafter ~/bin/ccode/headers -MD
```

Table 22.1 Commonly used preprocessor options available for gcc.

Option	Purpose	Value	Example
-D	Depending on usage, defines a macro that has a result of the string or defines a macro with a specific result **1**	Macro name or macro name and result	**-Done** or **-Dtwo='2'**
-dD	Outputs all macro definitions in their proper places	None	**-dD**
-dN	Outputs all macros as their **#define** statements	None	**-dN**
-E	Does the code preprocessing and then stops; see Table 22.2 for additional options for use with this option	None	**-E**
-H	Prints header file names	None	**-H**
-idirafter	Specifies the directory in which to look for header files if they are not found where they are expected	Path to look in	**-idirafter ~/ccode/headers**
-imacros	Processes the specified file before preprocessing the code, but discards its output	Path to file	**-imacros addthis**
-include	Processes the specified file before preprocessing the code	Path to file	**-include additions**
-iprefix	Specifies the prefix argument for the **-iwithprefix** option	Top directory	**-iprefix ~**
-isystem	Specifies an additional system header directory	Path	**-isystem ~/bin/sys**
-iwithprefix	Specifies a directory in which to look for header files if they are not found where they are expected, where this directory's path hangs off of the specified **-iprefix** directory	Remaining path	**-iwithprefix ccode/headers**
-iwithprefixbefore	Specifies a directory in which to look for header files initially, where this directory's path hangs off of the specified **-iprefix** directory	Remaining path	**-iwithprefixbefore ccode/headers**

(continued)

Table 22.1 Commonly used preprocessor options available for gcc (continued).

Option	Purpose	Value	Example
-MD	Outputs statements that can be used for building a Makefile for this program, but saves the dependency information to a file with a .d extension so as to not interfere with the remaining compilation steps	None	**-MD**
-MMD	Outputs statements that can be used for building a Makefile for this program, but saves the dependency information to a file with a .d extension so as to not interfere with the remaining compilation steps; ignores system header files	None	**-MMD**
-nostdinc	Ignores system header directories	None	**-nostdinc**
-trigraphs	Ensures that standard C code is outputted, though this is often undesirable because of its strict nature	None	**-trigraphs**
-U	Undefines the specified macro	Macro name	**-Uthree**
-undef	Specifies that no macros should be defined unless specifically done so in the code	None	**-undef**
-Wp,	Passes a specific option—or more than one—to the preprocessor	Option(s), comma-separated if more than one	**-Wp,-MG**

Table 22.2 Options for use when only preprocessing with gcc.

Option	Purpose
-C	Leaves comments intact
-dM	Outputs only the macro definitions that have been set when preprocessing is finished
-M	Outputs statements that can be used for building a Makefile for this program
-MG	Outputs statements that can be used for building a Makefile for this program, assuming that the header files are in the same location as the source files

(continued)

Table 22.2 Options for use when only preprocessing with gcc (continued).

Option	Purpose
-MM	Outputs statements that can be used for building a Makefile for this program, but leaves out **#include** commands
-P	Leaves **#line** commands intact rather than expanding them

5. After the preprocessor finishes, the compilation itself begins. Many options are available for compiling C code. Anyone who is used to compiling C programs knows that you sometimes end up with a lot of warning messages, some of which are meant to be ignored, whereas others are important. See Table 22.3 to choose from the warning options available to you. For this example, it is useful to make sure that items are defined before they are used. You now should have the following:

```
gcc -idirafter ~/bin/ccode/headers -MD -Wimplicit
```

NOTE: *The option **-Wall** activates many of the warnings listed in Table 22.3.*

Table 22.3 Commonly used warning options available for gcc during the compilation phase.

Option	Purpose
-fsyntax-only	Ignores everything but syntax errors
-pedantic	Gives warnings for everything that is not standard C; often not desirable, because standard C is very strict
-pedantic-errors	Produces error messages rather than warnings for anything that is not standard C
-w	Shuts off all warnings
-Wchar-subscripts	Produces a warning when an array subscript is assigned to the **char** type
-Wcomment	Warns regarding nested comments—two **/*** items without closing the comment—or if **//** appears in a comment
-Werror	Changes all warnings to error messages; not typically recommended if you use a lot of warnings
-Werror-implicit-function-declaration	Gives an error when a function is used before it is defined
-Wformat	Ensures that commands that require formatting arguments are being used properly
-Wimplicit	Uses both the **-Wimplicit-int** and **-Wimplicit-function-declaration** options

(continued)

***Table 22.3 Commonly used warning options available for gcc during the compilation phase* (continued).**

Option	Purpose
-Wimplicit-function-declaration	Warns when a function is used before it is defined
-Wimplicit-int	Warns when a variable declaration does not include a type declaration
-Wmain	Gives a warning if the main function has been given a bad type
-Wmultichar	Warns if any multicharacter constants were assigned
-Wno-import	Shuts off all warnings dealing with **#import** statements
-Wparentheses	Warns about potential parentheses omissions
-Wunused	Combines several options that warn about variables, functions, and more that are created but not used anywhere in the code

6. Several useful debugging switches also are available. See Table 22.4 for a list of the debugging switches that are available, and choose those that are appropriate. The important issue here is to make sure your code is **gprof**-readable. So, you now have the following:

```
gcc -idirafter ~/bin/ccode/headers -MD -Wimplicit -pg
```

Table 22.4 Commonly used debugging options available for gcc during the compilation phase.

Option	Purpose	Value	Example
-a	Generates additional code grouping information for **gprof**	None	**-a**
-ggdb	Outputs debugging information in a format useful for GDB	None	**-ggdb**
-pg	Generates code in the format needed by **gprof**; you commonly need this item	None	**-pg**
-print-file-name=	Prints the full path to the library that would be used during the linking stage, and then stops	Library name	**-print-file-name= /usr/lib/printlib**
-print-prog-name=	Prints the full path to the program that would be used during the linking stage, and then stops	Program name	**-print-prog-name=cpp**

(continued)

***Table 22.4 Commonly used debugging options available for gcc during the compilation phase* (continued).**

Option	Purpose	Value	Example
-print-search-dirs	Prints the names of the directories that **gcc** will search during the compilation	None	**-print-search-dirs**
-Q	Prints progress information, such as statistics and a list of the functions as they are compiled	None	**-Q**
-save-temps	Saves all temporary intermediate files so that you can examine them	None	**-save-temps**

7. If the code you are compiling is going to produce a large program, you probably want to utilize some of the optimization parameters available for the compiler phase. See Table 22.5 for a brief list of the optimization parameters to choose from. The program you are setting up to compile in this example is not going to be huge. Use the lowest level of optimization, giving you the following:

```
gcc -idirafter ~/bin/ccode/headers -MD -Wimplicit -pg -O
```

8. You may find that you need to tell **gcc** explicitly where to find various types of files. Table 22.6 outlines the choices you have available. For this example, you do not need any of these options.
9. You are finally finished with compiler options. I assume that you are not trying to insert assembly code in with the C code, so now we move directly to the linking phase. Choose the options you want to use from Table 22.7. For the example, you do not need any of these options.

Table 22.5 Commonly used optimization parameters available for gcc during the compilation phase.

Option	Purpose	Value	Example
-O	Takes the extra time and compilation resources to optimize the code	None	**-O**
-O0	Does not take the extra time and compilation resources to optimize the code	None	**-O0**
-O2	Optimizes the code more than would be done with just **-O**	None	**-O2**
-O3	Uses the highest level of optimization	None	**-O3**
-Os	Optimizes for size instead of speed	None	**-Os**

*Table 22.6 File location parameters available for **gcc**.*

Option	Purpose	Value	Example
-B	Specifies the starting point where **gcc** should look for compiler components	Path to starting point	**-B/usr/local/gcc**
-I	Specifies the first directory to look in for header files	Path to directory	**-I~/bin/ccode/headers**
-I-	Does not treat the current directory as the first source for header files	None	**-I-**
-L	Specifies the first directory to look in for library files	Path to directory	**-L~/personal_libs**

*Table 22.7 Linking parameters available for **gcc**.*

Option	Purpose
-c	Only compiles and assembles the source, does not link it
-nodefaultlibs	Does not use the standard system libraries when linking
-S	Only compiles the source, does not assemble it
-static	Does not use shared libraries

10. Now you just add the .c or .cpp file name extension:

```
gcc -idirafter ~/bin/ccode/headers -MD -Wimplicit
-pg -O ~/bin/ccode/myprog.c
```

11. Press Enter to start the compile. The compile can take seconds, minutes, or hours, depending on how long the program is, how much optimization you want, how fast your CPU is, how fast your RAM is, and what else you are doing at the time.

Debugging Code With **gdb**

To debug your code using **gdb**, do the following:

1. Log in to the account that owns the code you want to work with.
2. Change to the directory containing the code by using the **cd** command.

3. First you need to compile a special version of your code for debugging. You can do this by using **gcc** with the **-ggdb** option. For example, you might have the following:

```
gcc -ggdb ~/bin/ccode/myprog.c
```

4. After the compilation finishes you have an executable file. Type "gdb" but do not press Enter yet.
5. Several options are available for **gdb** at the command line. See Table 22.8 for a listing and choose those that are appropriate for your needs. In the example, you do not need any of these options, except perhaps for quiet mode:

```
gdb -q
```

6. Now, type in the program name and press Enter to start your debugging session. For example:

```
gdb -q ~/bin/myprog.exe
```

7. You are now within the **gdb** session. Nothing really has happened yet. From here, you direct the debugger with a series of commands—one at a time. A commonly used set of commands is listed in Table 22.9. If you want information about everything available, see the online documentation or type "help" for assistance.

Table 22.8 Options available when debugging code with gdb.

Option	Purpose	Value	Example
-c	Examines the specified core dump	Path to file	**-c ~/bin/ccode/core**
-cd	Uses the specified directory as the base for seeking files	Path to directory	**-cd ~/bin/ccode**
-d	Searches in the specified directory for needed files	Path to directory	**-d ~/bin/ccode**
-e	Uses the specified file as executable data	Path to file	**-s ~/bin/ccode/exec**
-q	Suppresses copyright and introductory information	None	**-q**
-s	Reads a symbol table from the specified file	Path to file	**-s ~/bin/ccode/symbols**
-se	Uses options **-e** and **-s**, applying them to the same file	Path to file	**-se ~/bin/ccode/ symbolexec**

*Table 22.9 Commands often used in a **gdb** session.*

Command	Result	Value	Example
break	Specifies a place to stop the program during debugging	See Table 22.10 for a list of possibilities	**break +10**
clear	Removes a breakpoint	The argument displayed when you list the breakpoints already set	**clear 265**
continue	Keeps running the program until it exits	None	**continue**
finish	Runs until the current function is completed	None	**finish**
info breakpoints	Lists the breakpoints you currently have set	None	**info breakpoints**
info program	Displays current status information about the program	None	**info program**
next	Runs the next command in the source code	None	**next**
path	Specifies the location to look in first for code by adding it to the front of the PATH environment variable	Path to directory	**path ~/bin/ccode**
pwd	Prints the current directory **gdb** is using to find code in	None	**pwd**
quit	Exits **gdb**	None	**quit**
run	Starts stepping through the program	None	**run**
set args	Assigns the command-line arguments to use when you **run** the program	Arguments	**set args one two three**
set env	Specifies the value for the given environment variable	Variable and value	**set env USER = tom**
show args	Displays the command-line arguments used when testing the program	Arguments	**show args**
show env	Lists all environment variables in use or a specific variable	Nothing or a specific variable	**show env USER**

(continued)

Table 22.9 Commands often used in a gdb session (continued).

Command	Result	Value	Example
show paths	Lists the contents of the PATH environment variable	None	**show paths**
step	Continues running the program until it reaches the next command or through a specified number of commands	Nothing or number of commands	**step 15**
unset env	Removes the value of the specified environment variable	Variable and value	**unset env USER**
until	Runs until the specified breakpoint	Breakpoint, as listed among the **info breakpoint** output	**until 26**

Table 22.10 Values available for the break command in gdb.

Value	Purpose
#	Sets a breakpoint at the line number specified
+#	Looks where you currently are in the execution and sets a breakpoint **#** of lines down from it
-#	Looks where you currently are in the execution and sets a breakpoint **#** of lines up from it
file: #	Sets a breakpoint in the specified file, at the specified line number
file: function	Sets a breakpoint in the specified file, at the specified function
function	Stops when the debugger reaches the specified function

8. Now, press Enter to start the command. Depending on what **gdb** options you use, a variety of things will happen.

Finding Resource-Hogging Sections With gprof

If you want to cut down on the resources a program is using and you have the source code, do the following:

1. Log in to the account that owns the code you want to work with.
2. Change to the directory containing the code by using the **cd** command.

3. First you need to compile a special version of your code for profiling. You do this with the **-pg** and **-a** options for **gcc**. For example, you might use something like the following:

```
gcc -pg -a ~/bin/ccode/myprog.c
```

4. Now you can run **gprof** on the data file. Start by typing "gprof", but do not press Enter.
5. Choose the options appropriate for your situation. Table 22.11 identifies several of the flags available for **gprof**. To leave the comments in and skip the long explanations, you would start with:

```
gprof -A -b
```


Table 22.11 Options used in the gprof code-profiling tool.

Option	Purpose	Values	Example
-A	Specifies to leave the comments in the source code	None	**-A**
-b	Specifies not to print out long explanations of the data that appears in the output tables	None	**-b**
-c	Specifies to output a graph with the functions that were called and information regarding them	None	**-c**
-C	Prints a tally of functions and how often they were called	None	**-C**
-i	Specifies to display summary information about the code in question	None	**-i**
-I	Specifies directories to look in for source code	Paths to examine	**-I ~/bin/ccode**
-J	Specifies not to include comments	None	**-J**
-l	Specifies to use bar graphs to give line-by-line data on how many resources are being used	None	**-l**
-L	Specifies to include the path with the source file names	None	**-L**
-s	Creates a summary file (gmon.sum) of the file analysis	None	**-s**

(continued)

***Table 22.11 Options used in the gprof code-profiling tool* (continued).**

Option	Purpose	Values	Example
-v	Specifies to display **gprof** version information	None	**-v**
-w	Specifies how wide to make the output	How many characters wide the output should be	**-w 60**
-Z	Specifies not to print a tally of functions and how often they were called	None	**-Z**

6. Add the executable to the command statement and press Enter. For example:

```
gprof -A -b ~/bin/myprog.exe
```


Installing The Build Manager

To install the **make** build manager, do the following:

1. Log in as root.
2. See whether you already have the build manager in place by typing "rpm -q make". If this package is located, you do not need to proceed.
3. Place the Red Hat CD-ROM into your CD-ROM drive.
4. Mount the CD-ROM by typing "mount /mnt/cdrom".
5. Change to the packages directory by typing "cd /mnt/cdrom/RedHat/RPMS".
6. Install the C compiler by typing "rpm -ivh make" and then pressing Tab to expand the file name. Press Enter.

Chapter 23

Additional System Administration Tools

If you need an immediate solution to:	*See page:*
Installing The **automount** Daemon's Controller	666
Configuring The Automounter	666
Configuring A Base Mount Point	667
Configuring Who Can Use **at**	668
Creating An **at** Job	669
Listing Existing **at** Jobs	671
Deleting Existing **at** Jobs	672
Changing The **batch** Load Average	672
Altering System **cron** Jobs	672
Manipulating User **cron** Jobs	674
Using **find**	676
Changing The **locate** Database Update Time	684
Using **locate** To Find Files	684
Using **which** To Find Programs	685
Using **grep** To Find What You Need	685

In Depth

Although *Linux System Administration Black Book* is more of a systems administration guide than a general reference for using Linux, every administrator should be familiar with a specific set of tools. Thus, this chapter covers setting up automatic file system mounting, timed processes, and search tools. These programs will round out the basics of your system administration skills, as well as make your job a lot easier.

The Automounter

Many Linux users often complain about the complexity of dealing with file system media, until they get used to the **mount** command. These complaints lead system administrators to jump through all sorts of hoops to set up command aliases and try to make their users' lives easier. Even if this is not done out of kindness, it cuts down on technical support issues. Fortunately, you now have the automounter to help in some cases. This chapter explains what this relatively new tool does and how to configure it to suit your needs.

Linux distributions running kernel 2.2.0 and later have automounting capability built right into the kernel. Using this tool, you can set certain partitions to mount on the fly when you need them. You might wonder at first why you would not just permanently mount the item in /etc/fstab. In some cases, this is indeed a better practice. However, this does not work for all situations. The best-known examples involve temporary media or directories on other systems that do not really need to always be mounted onto this machine. This issue is best shown through shared network drives. Keeping these drives mounted on a continual basis if they contain software that is only needed 1 percent of the time is a monumental waste of network resources. Instead, you can have this drive mounted only when it is needed automatically.

A few components work together to provide this service. The central piece is the **automount** daemon. One daemon exists for each definition in the /etc/auto.master configuration file (covered in the Immediate Solutions section). When a user tries to change to a directory configured through this service, the **automount** daemon mounts the device or partition on the fly. It then checks in regular intervals to see if the device is no longer in use. Once it finds the device not in use, the daemon unmounts it.

Another piece of the **automount** puzzle is the daemon controller script, **autofs**. This item is not necessarily installed by default, so see the section "Installing The **automount** Daemon's Controller" if you want to use this service. The **autofs** script resides in /etc/rc.d/init.d and accepts the commands listed in Table 23.1.

Timed Processes

Throughout this book, you likely have thought many times that you need a way to set up a script or program to run regularly at specific intervals, or could really use a way to run some intensive tool in the wee hours of the night without having to be awake to do it. Unix and Linux fortunately provide the tools necessary to accomplish both of these tasks. Two different automation tools are available: **at** and **cron**.

The **at** program allows you to use the command line to set an individual event. Both the system administrator and the users have access to this tool, though it is not used as often as its cousin, **cron**. One essential item to understand about dealing with **at** is that it has a hierarchy of queues. Each of these queues refers to a **nice** level, or how much of the machine's processing time this job is allowed to take up. The levels are named with a single character, which can be from **a** through **z**, or **A** through **Z**. The further the lowercase queue designation gets from the beginning of the alphabet, the less processor time the job is allowed to take up. If you use the uppercase queue designation, the same rules apply, plus the **at** job is treated as a **batch** job. A **batch** job is never run until the CPU load average gets below 0.8.

The **cron** program, on the other hand, typically is used to handle jobs that need to run more than once. This is a far more complex tool than **at**. How you use **cron** depends on who you are. When setting up **cron** jobs for the system itself as the superuser, you set it up through file editing, as discussed in the Immediate Solutions section "Altering System **cron** Jobs." Users, on the other hand—including root—use a command to do the same thing. See the Immediate Solutions section "Manipulating User **cron** Jobs" for details.

Table 23.1 Commands accepted by autofs.

Command	Description
reload	Stops all **automount** daemons and restarts them with the most current settings
start	Starts all **automount** daemons
status	Displays configuration information, and lists the **automount** daemons currently running
stop	Stops all **automount** daemons

Utilizing **cron** involves understanding how to represent time for a **cron** job, which is significantly different from how you do so with an **at** job. A **cron** time statement breaks down into the following parts:

```
A H D M W
```

Each one of these items is represented numerically, so **cron** needs placeholders even if you are not going to use the item. The entries for a **cron** time statement are listed in Table 23.2.

The possibilities get more complex from here. You have a choice of operators that you can use to express ranges and other items that allow you to express multiple time values for your **cron** job. These operators are explained in Table 23.3.

NOTE: *You can actually mix and match the dash and the comma operators; for example,* ***1,3,5-10,11,13***.

Search Tools

Few would argue that modern Linux is a large operating system. A standard workstation installation might span 850MB, and a server installation might need 1.7GB! The space needed by Linux and its associated tools, games, and more

Table 23.2 Entries used in a cron time statement.

Entry	Purpose	Value Range
A	Specifies the number of minutes after the hour	0 through 59
H	Specifies the hour, in 24-hour time	0 through 23
D	Specifies the date, or day of the month	1 through 31
M	Specifies the month of the year	1 through 12, or the first three letters of the month name
W	Specifies the day of the week	0 (Sunday) through 6 (Saturday), or the first three letters of the day name

Table 23.3 Operators available in a cron time statement.

Operator	Purpose	Example
*	Specifies all possible values	*
-	Specifies the range of values between and including those on either side of the dash	**Mon-Fri**
,	Specifies the individual values listed	**1,3,5**
/	Specifies steps a group of values should follow instead of incrementing by 1	***/4**

spans thousands of files over a large tree of directories. Finding any one item within this mess can be maddening. Fortunately, several search tools are available to you in the Unix/Linux world.

The most flexible—and hence, the most difficult to figure out—file system search tool in the Unix world is **find**. Many people use this command as a last resort. Those who know it well, however, keep it tucked in with their most regularly utilized system administration tools.

The **find** command searches through a selected portion of the live file system. An alternative to this tool is **locate**, which works in conjunction with a database that it keeps of your entire file system. The database is built on a daily basis—exactly when this happens is determined by the system **cron** job /etc/cron.daily/slocate.cron. So, when you do a file system search with **locate**, you are not actually looking through the live file system. Instead, you are looking at a snapshot of what you had the last time the database was built. This makes the tool faster than **find**.

An even more specialized search tool is the **which** command, which looks through only the directories you have in your PATH environment variable. If the target is not within the PATH, **which** cannot find it. The **which** tool is used almost exclusively to find out what runs if you type a certain command. This is helpful if you find out that you have two programs named identically and want to know which one runs when you type its name.

The final tool, **grep**, is not a straightforward file system search tool like the others. Instead, this program searches text. It is quite handy in conjunction with many other tools. Three different versions of this program exist:

- **grep**—The standard version of this command.
- **egrep**—Extended **grep**. Allows for the use of extended regular expressions. Equivalent to **grep -E**.
- **fgrep**—Fixed-string **grep**. Tells **grep** to look for one of the specified strings. Equivalent to **grep -F**.

The Many Faces Of grep

A quick bulleted list is not nearly enough information to get across the differences between the three **grep** programs. Many people only ever use the main version. It is certainly flexible enough for most purposes, and accepts the regular expression formats discussed in Chapter 19. The Immediate Solutions section focuses on the main **grep** program, so to make sure that you come away from this chapter with a good feeling for the other two versions of **grep** as well, they are explained next.

Extended grep

The difference between the **grep** and **egrep** programs is that you can use extended regular expressions with **egrep**. An extended regular expression is expressed in this format:

```
[expression]
```

Anything between the brackets is a possible match. For example, if you want to match the first five lowercase letters in the alphabet, then you would use the following:

```
[abcde]
```

The most useful aspect of this command is the set of reserved extended expressions listed in Table 23.4. Note that all reserved expressions are written in the following format:

```
[[:expression:]]
```


TIP: *You can say "not the specified group of characters" by placing a caret between the first two brackets:* ***[^[****.*

Also available are some characters in extended regular expressions that allow you to specify repetitions. These characters are outlined in Table 23.5. You add them at the end of an expression. For example, the following code would match anything that was a single number, or had no number:

```
[[:digit:]]?
```

Table 23.4 Reserved extended regular expressions in egrep.

Expression	Matches
[[:alnum:]]	All numbers and all lower- and uppercase letters
[[:alpha:]]	All lower- and uppercase letters
[[:cntrl:]]	Control characters
[[:digit:]]	Numbers
[[:graph:]]	All viewable characters except for the space and control characters
[[:lower:]]	All lowercase letters
[[:print:]]	All printable characters; no control characters
[[:punct:]]	All characters used to denote punctuation
[[:space:]]	All characters that produce empty space
[[:upper:]]	All uppercase letters
[[:xdigit:]]	All characters used in hexadecimal values

Table 23.5 Extended regular expression repeaters in egrep.

Expression	Matches
?	Any or no single instance of the preceding item
*****	Any number of or no instance of the preceding item
+	Any number of instances of the preceding item
{#}	Exactly # of the preceding item
{#,}	# or more of the preceding item
{#,#}	The range of # to #, inclusive

NOTE: *Instead of* ***[[:alnum:]]****, you can use* ***\w****, and instead of* ***[^[:alnum:]]****—which stands for "not any number, lowercase letter, or uppercase letter"—you can use* ***\W****.*

Fixed-String grep

The difference between **grep** and **fgrep** is how the program takes in its search parameters. You can build a file containing one search parameter per line. The **fgrep** program looks in this file and treats it as a long "or" statement. It will try to match each one of the parameters and is satisfied with a single match. This is an excellent method to use when trying to find a list of different errors in a log file.

NOTE: *The* ***fgrep*** *program does not include* ***egrep****'s extended expressions.*

Immediate Solutions

Installing The **automount** Daemon's Controller

To install **autofs**, do the following:

1. Log in as root to the machine you want to install the **automount** controller on.
2. Place the Red Hat CD-ROM in the CD-ROM drive.
3. Type "mount /mnt/cdrom" to add the CD-ROM onto the file system.
4. Type "cd /mnt/cdrom/RedHat/RPMS" to change to the packages directory.
5. Type "rpm -ivh autofs", press Tab, and then press Enter to install the package.

Configuring The Automounter

To set up how and where the automounter does its job, do the following:

1. Log in as root to the machine you want to set up.
2. Type "vi /etc/auto.master" to open the main configuration file, in which you see the following text:

```
# $Id: auto.master,v 1.2 1997/10/06 21:52:03 hpa Exp $
# Sample auto.master file
# Format of this file:
# mountpoint map options
# For details of the format look at autofs(8).
/misc   /etc/auto.misc   --timeout 60
```

3. The existing entry is just an example. Go down to the line beginning with /misc, type "i" to enter Insert mode, and then add a hash mark at the beginning of the line so that it looks like the following:

```
#/misc   /etc/auto.misc   --timeout 60
```

4. Press the Esc key to enter Command mode, and then type "o" to open a new line beneath the current location and enter Insert mode.

5. You now start building your own entries. In this file, you use the following format:

```
mountbase  configfile   --timeout time
```

These values correspond to the following:

- ***mountbase***—You do not define every single mount point in /etc/auto.master. Instead, you define a base point on which a number of different mount points might exist.
- ***configfile***—Each mount base has its own configuration file. Typically, these files are named /etc/auto.*base*, so you do not have to guess later which file goes to which group.
- ***time***—Specifies how many seconds the **automount** daemon should wait between checks to see whether the file system is busy. If the device is not in use, the daemon unmounts it. A common time for this value is 60 seconds, because if you make this time slot too short, the daemon will end up jumping the gun and unmounting items that people are not finished with.

So, for example, if you wanted a different **automount** daemon for each physical device, you might add the lines:

```
/mnt/cdrom  /auto.cdrom  --timeout 60
/mnt/floppy /auto.floppy --timeout 60
```

Then, you might include other entries, such as this:

```
/usr  /auto.usr  --timeout 60
```

6. After you finish adding these entries, press the Esc key to go to Command mode, and then type "ZZ" to save and close the file.
7. Proceed to the following section.

Configuring A Base Mount Point

To set up a base mount point after you have created it (as discussed in the preceding section), do the following:

1. Log in as root to the machine you want to set up.

2. Follow the rest of this process for each of the base mount points you configured in /etc/auto.master. Type "vi /etc/auto.*base*" to create the file for the base mount point.
3. Type "i" to enter Insert mode.
4. Each entry in the base mount point configuration file uses the following format:

   ```
   mountpoint  options  :device
   ```

   The values listed are as follows:

   - ***mountpoint***—The end directory name that the automounter watches for, to help it see which rule it wants to use.
   - ***options***—The mount options to use for this location.
   - ***device***—The device driver to use to mount this object.

   For example, if you want the **automount** daemon to add a floppy to the file system every time you type "cd /mnt/floppy"—rather than you having to type the **mount** process yourself—you might enter:

   ```
   floppy  -fstype:ext2  :/dev/fd0
   floppy  -fstype:vfat  :/dev/fd0
   ```

   As you can see, you can have definitions for the same item twice. First, the automounter will try the Linux file system format, and then Windows 98.
5. After you finish adding the items for this /etc/auto.*base*, press the Esc key to enter Command mode and then type "ZZ" to save and close the file.
6. Return to Step 2 if you have more /etc/auto.*base* files to configure.
7. Type "/etc/rc.d/init.d/autofs reload" to have the **automount** daemon(s) load the new settings.

Configuring Who Can Use **at**

To configure who can use the **at** tool, do the following:

1. Log in as root to the machine you want to configure.
2. If you want to allow only specific users to access the **at** command, type "vi /etc/at.allow" to open the allowed access configuration file. If you want to allow everyone to use **at**, proceed to Step 5.

3. Add to the file every user who you want to let use this command, one username per line.

NOTE: *If the /etc/at.allow file exists, users who are not explicitly allowed in will not be let in at all.*

4. Press the Esc key to return to Command mode, and then type "ZZ" to save and close the file.
5. If you want to specifically deny particular users access to the system, type "vi /etc/at.deny" to open the denied access configuration file. If you do not want to deny particular users, then you are finished with this section.
6. Add to the file every user who you want to prevent from using this command, one username per line. For example, you might add the following:

```
guest
nobody
```

7. Press the Esc key to return to Command mode, and then type "ZZ" to save and close the file.

Creating An **at** Job

To add a new **at** job as either the system administrator or a user, do the following:

1. Log in to the machine and account you want to have the **at** job set for.
2. Decide which options you want to use with the **at** command. Available options are listed in Table 23.6.

Table 23.6 Options available with at.

Option	Purpose
-c	Concatenates (**cat**) the output from the commands to STDOUT
-d	Alias for the **atrm** command (see "Deleting Existing **at** Jobs," later in the chapter)
-f	Takes input from the specified file, rather than expecting it from the command line
-l	Alias for the **atq** command (see "Listing Existing **at** Jobs," later in the chapter)
-m	Sends email to the originating user when the job is complete
-q	Assigns job output to a specific queue; the queue **=** refers to the jobs currently running
-V	Gives the **at** version number

3. Choose the supporting data needed with the options, where appropriate. For example, perhaps you want to create an **at** job that is not allowed to take up as much CPU time as it wants to. You would start with

```
at -q c
```

4. After you know the options and their values, you have to determine when this job should run. The **at** tool has a complex series of time formats available. See Table 23.7 for a list.

   So, perhaps you want to run your job two minutes from now, just to test out this **at** tool. You might use the following:

```
at -q c now + 2 minutes
```

Table 23.7 Time formats available with at.

Generic	Description	Example
***h* X M**	Runs the job at the hour specified—in 12-hour time; use **AM** for morning, and **PM** for night	**9 PM**
hh:mm	Runs the job when the hour—in 24-hour time—and minute are reached	**22:30**
month day year	Runs the job on the specific day of the year, spelling out the month and using the full four-digit year; the ***year*** portion is optional, because **at** assumes you want the job to run the next time the month and day come around	**October 11**
mmddyy	Runs the job on the given date	**051106**
mm/dd/yy	Runs the job on the given date	**04/15/02**
mm.dd.yy	Runs the job on the given date	**07.26.01**
time date	Runs the job at the specified time and date, using any of the time and date formats described in this table	**5 AM March 10**
***time* today**	Runs the job today, at the given time	**01:55 today**
***time* tomorrow**	Runs the job tomorrow, at the given time	**noon tomorrow**
midnight	Runs the job at midnight	**midnight**
noon	Runs the job at 12:00 P.M.	**noon**
teatime	Runs the job at 16:00	**teatime**
now + *# units*	Counts from right now, using the given number of units—minutes, hours, days, or weeks	**now + 5 days**

5. Press Enter. This action brings you to the **at** command line:

```
at>
```

6. Everything you type until you close the **at** command line is considered part of the job. For the test job, you might enter the following:

```
at> cat /dee/heythere.txt | mail -s "Hey there!" dee@localhost
at> echo "Mail sent."
```

7. After you finish typing the commands you want to execute, type Ctrl+D to queue the job.

Listing Existing at Jobs

To see what **at** jobs are already in the queue, do the following:

1. Log in to the account and machine you want to check.
2. You use the **atq** command to view **at** jobs. Decide which options you want to use from Table 23.8.
3. Choose the supporting data, if any, you want to use. For example, to check on the job you added in the preceding section, "Creating An **at** Job," you would type:

```
atq -q c
```

4. Press Enter to view the information.

Table 23.8 Options available with the atq command.

Option	Purpose
-q	Specifies the letter corresponding to the queue you want to check, or **=** if you want to look at jobs currently running
-v	Includes jobs in the listing that have started but not finished, along with those scheduled and when they will run
-V	Prints version information

Deleting Existing **at** Jobs

To remove existing **at** jobs from the queue, do the following:

1. Log in to the account and machine whose **at** jobs you want to modify.
2. Locate the job ID(s) by following the instructions in the preceding section.
3. Use the **atrm** command to remove the job(s), in the following format:

```
atrm jobID1 jobID2 ... jobIDn
```

Changing The **batch** Load Average

To change the **batch** load average so that **at** jobs placed into uppercase queues will run at a load average other than 0.8, do the following:

1. Log in as root to the machine whose setup you want to modify.
2. Determine the load average that you want **batch** jobs to be held until.
3. Run the **at** daemon, **atd**, in the following format:

```
atd -l ldavg
```


Altering System **cron** Jobs

To create a **cron** job for the Linux box itself—not for a specific user—do the following:

1. Log in as root to the machine you want to set up the **cron** jobs for.
2. Type "vi /etc/crontab" to open the system's **cron** hierarchy file. By default, this file has the following as its contents:

```
SHELL=/bin/bash
PATH=/sbin:/bin:/usr/sbin:/usr/bin
MAILTO=root
HOME=/

# run-parts
01 * * * * root run-parts /etc/cron.hourly
02 4 * * * * root run-parts /etc/cron.daily
```

```
22 4 * * 0 root run-parts /etc/cron.weekly
42 4 1 * * root run-parts /etc/cron.monthly
```

3. Type "i" to enter Insert mode.
4. If any of the jobs called in one of the individual **cron** files is not within the **PATH** specified, then add the necessary path information onto the end, in this format:

```
:/path
```

5. Change the **MAILTO** address, unless you have root's mail automatically forwarding elsewhere. Try to avoid using the root account for anything unnecessary, such as reading email.
6. The hourly **cron** jobs run at one minute past each hour. If you want to use a different time, change the 01 in the /etc/cron.hourly line.
7. The daily **cron** jobs run at 4:02 A.M. If you want to use a different time, change the 02 for the minutes or the 04 for the hour in the /etc/cron.daily line.
8. The weekly **cron** jobs run at 4:22 A.M. on Sunday. If you want to use a different time, change the 22 for the minutes, the 04 for the hour, or the 0 for the day of the week in the /etc/cron.weekly line.
9. The monthly **cron** jobs run at 4:42 A.M. on the first of the month. If you want to use a different time, change the 42 for the minutes, the 04 for the hour, or the 1 for the day of the month in the /etc/cron.monthly line.
10. If you have system **cron** jobs that you want to have run on a schedule that is not the standard hourly, daily, weekly, or monthly groups, you can create another grouping to contain these jobs. Use this format:

```
time root run-parts /etc/cron.label
```

TIP: *If you do create a new grouping, you need to also create the directory to house this grouping. At the command line, type "mkdir /etc/cron.label". Then, you need to make sure the file has the proper permissions and ownership. Type "chmod 755 /etc/cron.label" to change the permissions, and type "chown root.root /etc/cron.label" to change the ownership.*

---

11. Press the Esc key to return to Command mode, and then type "ZZ" to save and close the file.

12. If you want to edit one of the system **cron** jobs, change to the directory that corresponds to its runtime by typing "cd /etc/cron.*label*". For example, type "cd /etc/cron.daily" to change to the directory that controls the **cron** jobs that run every day. If you do not want to edit any of the system **cron** job files, skip to Step 14. The following are the default contents of the /etc/cron.daily directory under Red Hat Linux 6.2:

```
total 28
drwxr-xr-x    2 root      root          4096 Apr 15 04:49 .
drwxr-xr-x   30 root      root          4096 Apr 29 07:07 ..
-rwxr-xr-x    1 root      root           276 Mar  3 08:41 0anacron
-rwxr-xr-x    1 root      root            51 Feb 24 10:15 logrotate
-rwxr-xr-x    1 root      root           402 Feb 29 16:03 makewhatis.cron
-rwxr-xr-x    1 root      root           102 Feb  3 10:29 slocate.cron
-rwxr-xr-x    1 root      root           104 Feb 14 11:57 tmpwatch
```

13. Adding, removing, or changing system **cron** jobs involves manipulating the files in the appropriate directory. Each of these files contains a short shell script that either calls the particular program in question or actually performs the routine itself. Do one of the following:
    - To remove a job, delete the script
    - To alter a job, edit the script
    - To add a job, create a script
14. When you are finished, either return to Step 12 to make changes in another **cron** job group or restart the **cron** daemon by typing "/etc/rc.d/init.d/crond restart".

Manipulating User **cron** Jobs

To create a **cron** job as a user—even for the superuser when the job is not for the system itself—do the following:

1. Log in to the account you want to create the **cron** job for, or log in as root if you want to create a job for one of your users, on the machine you want the job on.

2. Type one of the following:
   - To add a **cron** job as the user, type "crontab -e"
   - To add a **cron** job for a user as root, type "crontab -u *user* -e"

   In both cases, the current **crontab** data file opens. All users start with a blank file.
3. To delete a **cron** job, go to the line containing the job and type "dd" to remove it.
4. To edit a **cron** job, go to the line containing the job, type "i" to enter Insert mode, and then modify the entry.
5. Adding a **cron** job is, of course, the most complicated issue. Such jobs are entered in this format:

   ```
   time command
   ```

   Begin by assigning the time, as explained in the In Depth section "Timed Processes." For example, if you want this command to run at noon on the third day of each month, you would type "o" to open a new line and enter Insert mode, and then start this line with the following:

   ```
   0 12 3 * *
   ```

6. The command should be whatever you would type to accomplish what needs to be done. This command can be only one line long. Fortunately, it can point to a shell script. For example, suppose you want to have **cron** remind you to put new fertilizer on your flowers:

   ```
   0 12 3 * *  mail -s "Fertilize those flowers!"
   ```

   Because this is for your personal **crontab**, you do not need to assign who this mail goes to. It will go to the **crontab** owner.
7. Continue to manipulate the file until you are finished.
8. Press the Esc key, and then type "ZZ" to save and close the file. The new values are loaded for the **cron** daemon.

Using **find**

To locate a file with **find**, do the following:

1. Log in to an account that has the access you think is necessary to see the file you are looking for, on the machine where you want to locate the file.
2. You use the **find** command in this general format:

```
find where what
```

Start with the ***where***. If you have no idea of where this file is within the file system, use the root directory. Otherwise, enter the top of the path tree that **find** should begin looking in. For the sake of an example, I will start in root:

```
find /
```

NOTE: *You can give multiple paths. Just use the format "find path1 path2 ... pathN".*

3. The ***what*** portion is where things can get complicated. Let's start with the regular expression you want to search for. For example:

```
find / *bob*
```

4. If you want to, add test flags to narrow down the search parameters. Available test flags are listed in Table 23.9.

For example, perhaps you want to look at all files with the text **bob** anywhere in the name that are owned by the user **webadmin**. You would have the following, so far:

```
find / -user webadmin *bob*
```


Table 23.9 Test flags available for the find command.

Flag	Purpose	Values	Example
+#	Looks for anything greater than the listed number; used with flags and options that include a numeric value	A positive integer	**+5**
-#	Looks for anything less than the listed number; used with flags and options that include a numeric value	A positive integer	**-2**

(continued)

Table 23.9 Test flags available for the* find *command **(continued).**

Flag	Purpose	Values	Example
#	Looks for exactly the number listed; used with flags and options that include a numeric value	A positive integer	**9**
-amin	Looks for a file accessed the listed number of minutes ago	One of the three **#** possibilities	**-amin 40**
-anewer	Looks for a file that was accessed since the listed file was changed	File name of changed file	**-anewer /etc/smb.conf**
-atime	Looks for a file that was accessed in the last factor of 24 hours	The number to multiply by 24	**-atime 3**
-cmin	Looks for a file whose status changed **#** minutes ago	Number of minutes	**-cmin 30**
-cnewer	Looks for a file whose status has changed since the listed file was changed	File name of changed file	**-cnewer /var/log/messages**
-ctime	Looks for a file whose status has changed in the last factor of 24 hours	The number to multiply by 24	**-ctime 6**
-empty	Looks for an empty file or directory	None	**-empty**
-fstype	Looks for a file stored on the specified file system type	File system types currently supported under Linux are **adfs**, **affs**, **autofs**, **coda**, **devpts**, **efs**, **ext2**, **hfs**, **hpfs**, **iso9660**, **minix**, **msdos**, **ncpfs**, **nfs**, **ntfs**, **proc**, **qnx4**, **romfs**, **smbfs**, **sysv**, **udf**, **ufs**, **umsdos**, and **vfat**	**-fstype nfs**
-gid	Looks for a file owned by the specified GID	An existing GID from /etc/group	**-gid 300**
-group	Looks for a file owned by the specified group or GID	An existing group name or GID from /etc/group	**-gid projectB**

(continued)

Table 23.9 Test flags available for the find command (continued).

Flag	Purpose	Values	Example
-ilname	Looks for a symbolic link pointing to a file whose main name matches the given expression	A regular expression, not case-sensitive	**-ilname *docs***
-iname	Looks for a file whose name matches the given expression	A regular expression, case-sensitive	**-iname *phil***
-inum	Looks for the file matching the given inode number	The inode pointing to the file you are looking for	**-inum 16463**
-ipath	Looks for the entity that matches the regular expression, including the entire path as the regular expression	A regular expression, not case-sensitive	**-ipath /home/*/ public_html**
-iregex	Looks for the file that matches the regular expression, including the entire path as the regular expression	A regular expression, not case-sensitive	**-iregex / home*_html/ index2.html**
-links	Looks for a file that has the listed number of links	A positive integer	**-links 2**
-lname	Looks for the symbolic link whose name matches the given expression	A regular expression, case-sensitive	**-lname *[D,d]ocs***
-mmin	Looks for a file whose data was last modified the specified number of minutes earlier	Number of minutes	**-mmin 30**
-mtime	Looks for a file whose data was modified in the last factor of 24 hours	The number to multiply by 24	**-mtime 2**
-name	Looks for a file whose name matches the given regular expression	The regular expression to look for	**-name 00????txt**
-newer	Looks for a file that was modified after the specified file	Path to file to use as base time	**-newer /etc/ hosts**
-nogroup	Looks for a file whose group ownership aspect belongs to a nonexistent group	None	**-nogroup**

(continued)

***Table 23.9 Test flags available for the find command* (continued).**

Flag	Purpose	Values	Example
-nouser	Looks for a file whose user ownership aspect belongs to a nonexistent account	None	**-nouser**
-path	Looks for the entity that matches the regular expression, including the entire path as the regular expression	A regular expression, case-sensitive	**-path /etc/rc.d/ rc?.d**
-perm	Looks for a file whose permission bits are a particular octal value, where all the specified permission bits are on, or where any of them are on	Octal permission set; precede with nothing for an exact match, a minus for all, or a plus for any	**-perm +755**
-regex	Looks for the file that matches the regular expression, including the entire path as the regular expression	A regular expression, case-sensitive	**-regex / var*Printers/**
-size	Looks for the file whose size equals the given amount	Number for size, with one of the following units after: **b** (blocks), **c** (bytes), **k** (kilo-bytes), or **w** (2-byte words)	**-size 50k**
-type	Looks for a file of the specified type	Available types are **b** (block special), **c** (character special), **d** (directory), **p** (named pipe), **f** (regular file), **l** (symbolic link), and **s** (socket)	**-type f**
-uid	Looks for a file owned by the UID listed	The UID to look for	**-uid 50**
-used	Looks for a file that was accessed the listed number of days since its status last changed	Positive integer	-**used 5**
-user	Looks for a file owned by the user or UID listed	The username or UID	**-user frank**

Table 23.10 Option flags available for the find command.

Flag	Purpose	Values	Example
-daystart	Measures times for the test flags **-amin**, **-atime**, **-cmin**, **-ctime**, **-mmin**, and **-mtime** from midnight instead of from 24 hours ago	None	**-daystart -atime 7**
-depth	Rather than looking at the directory and drilling down through its contents, looks at the contents first and the directory last	None	**-depth**
-follow	When encountering symbolic links, looks at the original file the link points to, not at the link itself	None	**-follow**
-help	Displays help information	None	**-help**
-maxdepth	Does not go beyond the listed number of subdirectory levels when searching the specified path	Positive integer	**-maxdepth 3**
-mindepth	Skips the subdirectory levels specified, and then starts searching	Positive integer	**-mindepth 2**
-mount	Does not proceed into other file systems during the search; ignores the mounted items	None	**-mount**
-noleaf	Searches non-ext2-formatted file systems	None	**-noleaf**
-version	Displays **find**'s version information	None	**-version**

5. If you want to, add option flags to narrow down the search parameters. Option flags are listed in Table 23.10.

   For example, perhaps you tend to have your Red Hat CD-ROM in the drive and do not want **find** to waste time searching on the CD-ROM. You could add the **-mount** flag to now have the following:

```
find / -user webadmin -mount *bob*
```

6. By default, **find** displays what matches the search criteria to STDOUT—the screen. If you want **find** to do something else with its output, specify the appropriate action flags. The action flags available are listed in Table 23.11.

   For example, perhaps you want to send what you find in this search to a file, but without any fancy formatting. You now might have the following:

```
find / -user webadmin -mount *bob* -fprint ~/boblist
```

Table 23.11 Action flags available for the find command.

Flag	Purpose	Values	Example
-exec	Runs the specified command on any files that match the search criterion	Command to run	**-exec more**
-fls	After the files matching the search criterion are located, saves the match listing to a file in the format "ls -dils"	Name of file	**-fls ~/listing**
-fprint	Saves the full paths of all matching items to the specified file	Name of file	**-fprint ~/filelist**
-fprintf	After the files matching the search criterion are located, saves the match listing to a file in the specified format	File name and listing format; see Table 23.12 for a list of the formatting codes available	**-fprintf ~/files %p %s**
-ls	After the files matching the search criterion are located, displays the match listing on STDOUT in the format "ls -dils"	None	**-ls**
-ok	Asks the user if the specified command should be run on each file that matches the search criterion	Command to run	**-ok less**
-print	Prints the names of the files matching the search criterion to STDOUT	None	**-print**
-printf	Prints information about the files matching the search criterion in the specified format to STDOUT	Formatting codes; see the list in Table 23.12	**-printf %p %a \n**
-prune	Looks only in the top directory level listed, unless the **-depth** flag is used	None	**-prune**

Table 23.12 Formatting codes available in find's -printf and -fprintf flags.

Code	Represents
\a	Sounds a beep
\b	Backspaces one character
\f	Form feeds to next page
\n	Proceeds to next line
\r	Enters key
\t	Tabs horizontally
\v	Tabs vertically
****	Prints a backslash (\)
%%	Prints a percent sign
%a	Prints file's last access time
%A	Prints the file's last access time in the specified format; see Table 23.13 for a list of the formats available
%b	Prints file's size in 512-byte blocks
%c	Prints the time the file's status last changed
%C	Prints the time the file's status last changed, in the specified format; see Table 23.13 for a list
%d	Prints how deep the file is in the directory tree
%f	Prints only the file name, no path
%F	Prints the type of file system this file is on
%g	Prints the group name or GID owning this file
%G	Prints the GID owning this file
%h	Prints only the path associated with the file
%H	Prints the immediate directory the file is located in, not the whole path
%i	Prints the file's inode number
%k	Prints the file's size in 1K blocks
%l	Prints the main file the symbolic link points to
%m	Prints the numeric permission set for the file
%n	Prints the number of hard links associated with this file
%p	Prints the file's name
%P	Prints the file's name and immediate directory
%s	Prints the file's size in bytes
%t	Prints the last time this file was modified

(continued)

Table 23.12 Formatting codes available in *find's -printf* and *-fprintf* flags (continued).

Code	Represents
%T	Prints the last time this file was modified in the specified format; see Table 23.13 for a list of the formats available
%u	Prints the user who owns this file, or their UID
%U	Prints the UID for the file's owner

Table 23.13 Time formats available for *find's -printf* and *-fprintf* flags.

Code	Represents	Example	Example Output
@	Number of seconds since January 1, 1970, 00:00 GMT	**%A@**	**946080000**
a	First three letters of day	**%Ca**	**Wed**
A	Full name of day	**%TA**	**Monday**
b	First three letters of month	**%Cb**	**Dec**
B	Full name of month	**%AB**	**January**
c	Full date and time	**%Tc**	**Wed Oct 18 16:47:50 PST 2000**
d	Numeric day of the month	**%Ad**	**5**
D	Date	**%CD**	**09/13/01**
H	Hour in 24-hour time	**%AH**	**03**
I	Hour in 12-hour time	**%TI**	**11**
k	Hour in 24-hour time, not using leading zeros to preserve two digits	**%Ck**	**2**
j	Numeric day of year	**%Aj**	**203**
l	Hour in 12-hour time, not using leading zeros to preserve two digits	**%Al**	**5**
m	Numeric month	**%Cm**	**7**
M	Minute	**%TM**	**30**
p	A.M. or P.M.	**%Ap**	**AM**
r	Time in 12-hour format	**%Ar**	**05:20 PM**
T	Time in 24-hour format	**%CT**	**16:14**
U	Which Sunday this is in the year	**%AU**	**10**
w	Day of week, starting with 0 as Sunday	**%Tw**	**4**

(continued)

Table 23.13 Time formats available for find's -printf and -fprintf flags (continued).

Code	Represents	Example	Example Output
W	Which Monday this is in the year	**%CW**	**15**
x	Full date	**%Ax**	**05/15/03**
X	Full time	**%TX**	**2:45:4**
y	Last two digits of year	**%Ty**	**01**
Y	Full year	**%AY**	**2001**
Z	Time zone	**%CZ**	**PST**

Related solution:	See page:
Using Regular Expressions	583

Changing The **locate** Database Update Time

To change the time that your **locate** database updates, do the following:

1. Log in as root on the machine that you want to change the time for.
2. Type "vi /etc/crontab" to open the system **cron** configuration file.
3. Cursor down to the following line:

```
02 4 * * * * root run-parts /etc/cron.daily
```

4. Change the time portion of the daily **cron** job line, because the database update is a daily task.
5. Press the Esc key, and then type "ZZ" to save and close the file.
6. Type "/etc/rc.d/init.d/crond restart" to load the new settings.

***NOTE:** If you want to change the database update time to run hourly, weekly, or monthly, then move the file /etc/cron.daily/slocate.cron to the appropriate directory. Keep in mind, however, that this database build is process-intensive. Hourly builds are not recommended.*

Using **locate** To Find Files

To search the file system with the **locate** tool, do the following:

1. Log in to the account you want to search from and the machine you want to search on. Be sure that this account has the privileges to search where you need to go.

2. Build the regular expression needed to find what you need.
3. Type "locate *regexp*" to run your search.

Related solution:	See page:
Using Regular Expressions	583

Using **which** To Find Programs

To utilize the **which** program to search through your PATH, do the following:

1. Log in to the account you want to search from and the machine you want to search on.
2. Determine the name of the program you want to look for.
3. Type "which *program*" to run your search.

Using **grep** To Find What You Need

To utilize **grep** to examine data going to STDOUT or data within a file, do the following:

1. Log in to the account you want to search from and the machine you want to search on.
2. Determine whether you want to use **grep**, **egrep**, or **fgrep**—covered in the section "The Many Faces Of **grep**." This example uses **grep**.
3. Choose the options you want to use for your search, as listed in Table 23.14. These options work for all **grep** versions.
4. Build the search term, using regular expressions if you need to. For the example search, assume you cannot remember which document contains the data you need to reference. Suppose you know that the file resides in the doc directory, but don't know whether it is in the main directory or one of the subdirectories. Also, you want some context, in case a match exists in multiple places, and you want to be given the line number where the match occurred. The following is the command you would end up with when running **grep** from the doc directory:

```
grep -B3 -H -i -n -r "Pricing Breakdown"
```

Table 23.14 Options available for grep, egrep, and fgrep.

Option	Purpose	Value
-a	Treats binary files as text files	None
-A	Prints the specified number of lines after the matched line when a match is found	A positive integer
-b	Prints how many bytes into the file the matched data lies	None
-B	Prints the specified number of lines before the matched line when a match is found	A positive integer
-c	Prints only the count of matching lines from the file, not the matched lines	None
-C	Prints the specified number of lines of output context, on either end of the match	A positive integer
-d	Performs the specified action if told to look at a directory instead of a file	**read** (treat the directory as a file), **skip** (ignore the directory), or **recurse** (drill the search down through the directory)
-h	Does not print file names when a match occurs	None
-H	Prints file names when a match occurs	None
-i	Ignores case	None
-l	Prints the file names containing matches	None
-L	Prints the file names containing no matches	None
-n	Prints the line number that the match was found on, as well as the match	None
-q	Does not print anything until it finds the first match, and then exits the search	None
-r	Drills down through all the subdirectories, as well as searching in the main directory	None
-s	Does not print error messages	None
-U	Assumes that the file is binary	None
-v	Reverses the search and prints only lines that do not match	None
-V	Prints the **grep** version	None
-w	Prints only matches that are full words	None
-x	Prints only matches that are the entire line	None

Appendix

GNU General Public License

We have included the GNU General Public License (GPL) for your reference as it applies to the software this book was about. However, the GPL does not apply to the text of this book.

Version 2, June 1991
Copyright (C) 1989, 1991 Free Software Foundation, Inc.
59 Temple Place, Suite 330, Boston, MA 02111-1307 USA

Everyone is permitted to copy and distribute verbatim copies of this license document, but changing it is not allowed.

Preamble

The licenses for most software are designed to take away your freedom to share and change it. By contrast, the GNU General Public License is intended to guarantee your freedom to share and change free software—to make sure the software is free for all its users. This General Public License applies to most of the Free Software Foundation's software, and to any other program whose authors commit to using it. (Some other Free Software Foundation software is covered by the GNU Library General Public License instead.) You can apply it to your programs, too.

When we speak of free software, we are referring to freedom, not price. Our General Public Licenses are designed to make sure that you have the freedom to distribute copies of free software (and charge for this service if you wish), that you receive source code or can get it if you want it, that you can change the software or use pieces of it in new free programs; and that you know you can do these things.

To protect your rights, we need to make restrictions that forbid anyone to deny you these rights or to ask you to surrender the rights. These restrictions translate to certain responsibilities for you if you distribute copies of the software, or if you modify it.

For example, if you distribute copies of such a program, whether gratis or for a fee, you must give the recipients all the rights that you have. You must make sure that they, too, receive or can get the source code. And you must show them these terms so they know their rights.

We protect your rights with two steps: (1) copyright the software, and (2) offer you this license which gives you legal permission to copy, distribute and/or modify the software.

Also, for each author's protection and ours, we want to make certain that everyone understands that there is no warranty for this free software. If the software is modified by someone else and passed on, we want its recipients to know that what they have is not the original, so that any problems introduced by others will not reflect on the original authors' reputations.

Finally, any free program is threatened constantly by software patents. We wish to avoid the danger that redistributors of a free program will individually obtain patent licenses, in effect making the program proprietary. To prevent this, we have made it clear that any patent must be licensed for everyone's free use or not licensed at all.

The precise terms and conditions for copying, distribution and modification follow.

Terms And Conditions For Copying, Distribution, And Modification

This License applies to any program or other work, which contains a notice placed by the copyright holder saying it may be distributed under the terms of this General Public License. The "Program," below, refers to any such program or work, and a "work based on the Program" means either the Program or any derivative work under copyright law: that is to say, a work containing the Program or a portion of it, either verbatim or with modifications and/or translated into another language. (Hereinafter, translation is included without limitation in the term "modification".) Each licensee is addressed as "you."

Activities other than copying, distribution and modification are not covered by this License; they are outside its scope. The act of running the Program is not restricted, and the output from the Program is covered only if its contents constitute a work based on the Program (independent of having been made by running the Program). Whether that is true depends on what the Program does.

1. You may copy and distribute verbatim copies of the Program's source code as you receive it, in any medium, provided that you conspicuously and appropriately publish on each copy an appropriate copyright notice and

disclaimer of warranty; keep intact all the notices that refer to this License and to the absence of any warranty; and give any other recipients of the Program a copy of this License along with the Program.

You may charge a fee for the physical act of transferring a copy, and you may at your option offer warranty protection in exchange for a fee.

2. You may modify your copy or copies of the Program or any portion of it, thus forming a work based on the Program, and copy and distribute such modifications or work under the terms of Section 1 above, provided that you also meet all of these conditions:

   (a) You must cause the modified files to carry prominent notices stating that you changed the files and the date of any change.

   (b) You must cause any work that you distribute or publish, that in whole or in part contains or is derived from the Program or any part thereof, to be licensed as a whole at no charge to all third parties under the terms of this License.

   (c) If the modified program normally reads commands interactively when run, you must cause it, when started running for such interactive use in the most ordinary way, to print or display an announcement including an appropriate copyright notice and a notice that there is no warranty (or else, saying that you provide a warranty) and that users may redistribute the program under these conditions, and telling the user how to view a copy of this License. (Exception: if the Program itself is interactive but does not normally print such an announcement, your work based on the Program is not required to print an announcement.)

   These requirements apply to the modified work as a whole. If identifiable sections of that work are not derived from the Program, and can be reasonably considered independent and separate works in themselves, then this License, and its terms, do not apply to those sections when you distribute them as separate works. But when you distribute the same sections as part of a whole which is a work based on the Program, the distribution of the whole must be on the terms of this License, whose permissions for other licensees extend to the entire whole, and thus to each and every part regardless of who wrote it.

   Thus, it is not the intent of this section to claim rights or contest your rights to work written entirely by you; rather, the intent is to exercise the right to control the distribution of derivative or collective works based on the Program.

   In addition, mere aggregation of another work not based on the Program with the Program (or with a work based on the Program) on a volume of a storage or distribution medium does not bring the other work under the scope of this License.

3. You may copy and distribute the Program (or a work based on it, under Section 2) in object code or executable form under the terms of Sections 1 and 2 above provided that you also do one of the following:

   (a) Accompany it with the complete corresponding machine-readable source code, which must be distributed under the terms of Sections 1 and 2 above on a medium customarily used for software interchange; or,

   (b) Accompany it with a written offer, valid for at least three years, to give any third party, for a charge no more than your cost of physically performing source distribution, a complete machine-readable copy of the corresponding source code, to be distributed under the terms of Sections 1 and 2 above on a medium customarily used for software interchange; or,

   (c) Accompany it with the information you received as to the offer to distribute corresponding source code. (This alternative is allowed only for noncommercial distribution and only if you received the program in object code or executable form with such an offer, in accord with Subsection b above.)

   The source code for a work means the preferred form of the work for making modifications to it. For an executable work, complete source code means all the source code for all modules it contains, plus any associated interface definition files, plus the scripts used to control compilation and installation of the executable. However, as a special exception, the source code distributed need not include anything that is normally distributed (in either source or binary form) with the major components (compiler, kernel, and so on) of the operating system on which the executable runs, unless that component itself accompanies the executable.

   If distribution of executable or object code is made by offering access to copy from a designated place, then offering equivalent access to copy the source code from the same place counts as distribution of the source code, even though third parties are not compelled to copy the source along with the object code.

4. You may not copy, modify, sublicense, or distribute the Program except as expressly provided under this License. Any attempt otherwise to copy, modify, sublicense or distribute the Program is void, and will automatically terminate your rights under this License. However, parties who have received copies, or rights, from you under this License will not have their licenses terminated so long as such parties remain in full compliance.

5. You are not required to accept this License, since you have not signed it. However, nothing else grants you permission to modify or distribute the Program or its derivative works. These actions are prohibited by law if you do not accept this License. Therefore, by modifying or distributing the Program (or any work based on the Program), you indicate your acceptance of this License to do so, and all its terms and conditions for copying, distributing or modifying the Program or works based on it.
6. Each time you redistribute the Program (or any work based on the Program), the recipient automatically receives a license from the original licensor to copy, distribute or modify the Program subject to these terms and conditions. You may not impose any further restrictions on the recipients' exercise of the rights granted herein. You are not responsible for enforcing compliance by third parties to this License.
7. If, as a consequence of a court judgment or allegation of patent infringement or for any other reason (not limited to patent issues), conditions are imposed on you (whether by court order, agreement or otherwise) that contradict the conditions of this License, they do not excuse you from the conditions of this License. If you cannot distribute so as to satisfy simultaneously your obligations under this License and any other pertinent obligations, then as a consequence you may not distribute the Program at all. For example, if a patent license would not permit royalty-free redistribution of the Program by all those who receive copies directly or indirectly through you, then the only way you could satisfy both it and this License would be to refrain entirely from distribution of the Program.

   If any portion of this section is held invalid or unenforceable under any particular circumstance, the balance of the section is intended to apply and the section as a whole is intended to apply in other circumstances.

   It is not the purpose of this section to induce you to infringe any patents or other property right claims or to contest validity of any such claims; this section has the sole purpose of protecting the integrity of the free software distribution system, which is implemented by public license practices. Many people have made generous contributions to the wide range of software distributed through that system in reliance on consistent application of that system; it is up to the author/donor to decide if he or she is willing to distribute software through any other system and a licensee cannot impose that choice.

   This section is intended to make thoroughly clear what is believed to be a consequence of the rest of this License.
8. If the distribution and/or use of the Program is restricted in certain countries either by patents or by copyrighted interfaces, the original copyright holder who places the Program under this License may add an explicit

geographical distribution limitation excluding those countries, so that distribution is permitted only in or among countries not thus excluded. In such case, this License incorporates the limitation as if written in the body of this License.

9. The Free Software Foundation may publish revised and/or new versions of the General Public License from time to time. Such new versions will be similar in spirit to the present version, but may differ in detail to address new problems or concerns.

   Each version is given a distinguishing version number. If the Program specifies a version number of this License which applies to it and "any later version", you have the option of following the terms and conditions either of that version or of any later version published by the Free Software Foundation. If the Program does not specify a version number of this License, you may choose any version ever published by the Free Software Foundation.

10. If you wish to incorporate parts of the Program into other free programs whose distribution conditions are different, write to the author to ask for permission. For software, which is copyrighted by the Free Software Foundation, write to the Free Software Foundation; we sometimes make exceptions for this. Our decision will be guided by the two goals of preserving the free status of all derivatives of our free software and of promoting the sharing and reuse of software generally.

No Warranty

11. BECAUSE THE PROGRAM IS LICENSED FREE OF CHARGE, THERE IS NO WARRANTY FOR THE PROGRAM, TO THE EXTENT PERMITTED BY APPLICABLE LAW. EXCEPT WHEN OTHERWISE STATED IN WRITING THE COPYRIGHT HOLDERS AND/OR OTHER PARTIES PROVIDE THE PROGRAM "AS IS" WITHOUT WARRANTY OF ANY KIND, EITHER EXPRESSED OR IMPLIED, INCLUDING, BUT NOT LIMITED TO, THE IMPLIED WARRANTIES OF MERCHANTABILITY AND FITNESS FOR A PARTICULAR PURPOSE. THE ENTIRE RISK AS TO THE QUALITY AND PERFORMANCE OF THE PROGRAM IS WITH YOU. SHOULD THE PROGRAM PROVE DEFECTIVE, YOU ASSUME THE COST OF ALL NECESSARY SERVICING, REPAIR OR CORRECTION.

12. IN NO EVENT UNLESS REQUIRED BY APPLICABLE LAW OR AGREED TO IN WRITING WILL ANY COPYRIGHT HOLDER, OR ANY OTHER PARTY WHO MAY MODIFY AND/OR REDISTRIBUTE THE PROGRAM AS PERMITTED ABOVE, BE LIABLE TO YOU FOR DAMAGES, INCLUDING ANY GENERAL, SPECIAL, INCIDENTAL OR CONSEQUENTIAL DAMAGES

ARISING OUT OF THE USE OR INABILITY TO USE THE PROGRAM (INCLUDING BUT NOT LIMITED TO LOSS OF DATA OR DATA BEING RENDERED INACCURATE OR LOSSES SUSTAINED BY YOU OR THIRD PARTIES OR A FAILURE OF THE PROGRAM TO OPERATE WITH ANY OTHER PROGRAMS), EVEN IF SUCH HOLDER OR OTHER PARTY HAS BEEN ADVISED OF THE POSSIBILITY OF SUCH DAMAGES.

How To Apply These Terms To Your New Programs

If you develop a new program, and you want it to be of the greatest possible use to the public, the best way to achieve this is to make it free software which everyone can redistribute and change under these terms.

To do so, attach the following notices to the program. It is safest to attach them to the start of each source file to most effectively convey the exclusion of warranty; and each file should have at least the "copyright" line and a pointer to where the full notice is found.

```
<one line to give the program's name and
 a brief idea of what it does.>
Copyright (C) 19yy  <name of author>

This program is free software; you can
redistribute it and/or modify it under the
terms of the GNU General Public License as
published by the Free Software Foundation;
either version 2 of the License, or
(at your option) any later version.

This program is distributed in the hope that
it will be useful, but WITHOUT ANY WARRANTY;
without even the implied warranty of
MERCHANTABILITY or FITNESS FOR A PARTICULAR
PURPOSE. See the GNU General Public License
for more details.

You should have received a copy of the GNU
General Public License along with this
program; if not, write to the Free Software
Foundation, Inc., 59 Temple Place, Suite 330,
Boston, MA  02111-1307  USA
```

Also add information on how to contact you by electronic and paper mail.

If the program is interactive, make it output a short notice like this when it starts in an interactive mode:

```
Gnomovision version 69, Copyright (C) 19yy
name of author Gnomovision comes with
ABSOLUTELY NO WARRANTY; for details type
'show w'. This is free software, and you are
welcome to redistribute it under certain
conditions; type 'show c' for details.
```

The hypothetical commands 'show w' and 'show c' should show the appropriate parts of the General Public License. Of course, the commands you use may be called something other than 'show w' and 'show c'; they could even be mouse-clicks or menu items—whatever suits your program.

You should also get your employer (if you work as a programmer) or your school, if any, to sign a "copyright disclaimer" for the program, if necessary. Here is a sample; alter the names:

```
Yoyodyne, Inc., hereby disclaims all copyright
interest in the program 'Gnomovision'
(which makes passes at compilers) written
by James Hacker.

<signature of Ty Coon>, 1 April 1989
Ty Coon, President of Vice
```


This General Public License does not permit incorporating your program into proprietary programs. If your program is a subroutine library, you may consider it more useful to permit linking proprietary applications with the library. If this is what you want to do, use the GNU Library General Public License instead of this License.

Index

A

A record, 330-331
accept_unqualified_senders, 395
accept_unresolvable_domains, 395
access.conf, 410
access.db, 399
AccessConfig, 411
accessdb, 395
AccessFileName, 420
Account attacks, 256
Account creation defaults, 42-45
acl, 323
Action, 430
AddDescription, 428
AddEncoding, 428
AddHandler, 429
AddIcon, 427
AddIconByEncoding, 426-427
AddIconByType, 427
Adding permanent media, 86-88
Adding temporary media, 84-85
AddLanguage, 428-429
AddModule, 414, 432
Address Resolution Protocol (ARP), 179
AddType, 429
AfterStep, 153
Alias, 424, 431
Aliases, 148
allow, 418
AllowOveride, 416
Anonymous FTP, 487
AOL server, 437
Apache Web server, 407-452
  configuration file, 410-437. *See also* /etc/httpd/conf.
  configuring Apache, 439
  configuring **httpd**, 443-446
  customizing log file output, 451
  features, 408-409
  initial access configuration, 440-442
  installing Apache, 439
  modules, 409-410
  reference Web sites, 408, 415
  setting up .htaccess, 452
  setting up what Web clients can see, 448-451
  virtual Web service, 446-448
Application layer, 176-177
apsfilter, 235-236
Architecture-specific files, 131
ARP, 179
Arrays, 630-631
ash, 598
at, 661, 668-672
atq, 671
atrm, 672
Attacks and intrusions, 254-256. *See also* System security.
AuthName, 432
AuthType, 432
AuthUserFile, 433
autofs, 661, 666
Automounter, 660-661, 666-668

B

Backup, 69-74, 81-83. *See also* Restore.
  creating a routine, 81-83
  file system structure, 80-81
  frequency, 69
  hardware, 72-74, 82
  incremental, 70-72
  portion of file system, 69
  redundancy, 69-71
Base mount joint, 667-668
bash, 598
Bash shell, 598. *See also* Shell scripting.

batch load average, 672
Berkeley Internet Name Domain (BIND), 317
Binary files, 111
BIND, 317
BindAddress, 413
Blackbox, 153
blacklist_recipients, 395
bogus, 327-328
Book on C, Second Edition, A (Kelley/Pohl), 644
Boot disk, 98, 308
Bourne Again shell, 598
Braces (command line), 573
Broadcast address, 178, 520
BrowserMatch, 430-431
bsh, 598
Buggy program, 24

C

C programming, 643-658
  Build Manager, 645-646, 658
  compiler, 644-645
  compiler code (**gcc**), 647-653
  debugging code (**gdb**), 653-656
  installing the compiler, 647
  libraries, 645
  resource management (**gprof**), 656-658
cache_peer Squid statement, 466-468
CacheNegotiatedDocs, 421
Caching. *See* Squid internet object cache.
Caching-only name servers, 317
case, 608
case sensitive, 523
category, 327
cd, 84, 95, 111, 112, 145
CD rewriter, 73, 82
CD writer, 72, 82
CGI script, 639-642
Changing desktops, 167
Changing ownerships, 79
channel, 325
Channels, 456
chgrp, 79
chmod, 77-78
chown, 79
Class C network, 189-191
Classless routing, 180
Cloning machines. *See* KickStart.
Closed multicast session, 456
CNAME record, 331
Command line (braces), 573
Command prompt
  GNOME, 14-15
  KDE, 19
Comprehensive Perl Archive Network (CPAN), 636
compress, 102, 108-109
Compression tools, 102, 108-109
Conditional statements
  Perl, 632-634
  shell scripting, 604-605
config kernel configuration tool, 137-141
Configuration files, 157
controls, 324
core domain, 188-189
cp, 84
CPAN, 636
Crack, 283-284
cron, 661-662, 672-675
crontab, 675
csh, 598
Custom boot disk, 98
Custom installation class, 5
CustomLog, 423
cut, 574-575, 588

D

Daemons, 24, 42
Datagrams, 175-176
.deb extension, 103
Debian, 103
default case, 522-523
Default run level, 168-169
Defragmenting tools, 68
Denial of service, 255, 285
deny, 418
Dequoting, 367
Desktop environments, 154, 167. *See also* GNOME; KDE.
df, 89, 621

Dial-out connections, 206-213
diff, 112
dig, 333-334
Digest, 456
<Directory>, 415, 417, 418, 424
DirectoryIndex, 420
Disk fragmentation, 68
Disk quotas, 75, 95-97
Display managers, 153
DNS, 315-349
  configuration file (/etc/named.conf), 319-328. *See also* /etc/named.conf.
  configuring
    forwarding-only server, 340-342
    master name server, 336-338
    slave name server, 338-340
  debugging your setup (**dnswalk**), 334, 348-349
  domain extensions, 188-189
  domain registration, 187-188
  domain zone file, 344-346
  encrypted keys, 347-348
  getting information from hosts (**host**), 334-335
  getting information from name servers (**dig**), 333
  initial cache file, 342
  installing name server, 336
  name server control program (**ndc**), 335
  name service, 317-319
  programs, 333-335
  reverse domain zone file, 346-347
  reverse local zone file, 343
  root servers, 316-317
  zone files, 328-333, 343-347
dns proxy, 522
dnskeygen, 347-348
dnswalk, 334, 348-349
Documentation files, 130-134
DocumentRoot, 414
Domain extensions, 188-189
domain logons, 521
domain master, 521
Domain Name System. *See* DNS.
Domain names, 187-189
Domain registration, 187-188
Domain zone file, 344-346
Downloading, 104-105
dpkg, 103
DSA/DSS, 325
dumpe2fs, 64, 77
DVD rewriter, 73, 82
DVD writer, 73, 82

E

echo, 601
egcs, 645
egrep, 664-665, 686
Email. *See* **sendmail** + IDA.
Emergency fix kit, 282
EmWeb, 437
EnableDelete, 433
EnablePut, 432
Encrypt passwords, 518
Encrypted keys, 347-348
Enlightenment, 153
Environmental variables, 599
ErrorDocument, 430
ErrorLog, 422
ESMTP, 378
ESMTPREM, 378
/etc/conf.modules, 148
/etc/cron.daily/slocate.cron, 663,
/etc/dhcpd.conf, 181-184
/etc/exports, 502-504
/etc/fstab, 86-88
/etc/ftpaccess, 477
/etc/ftphosts, 481
/etc/group, 26-27
/etc/httpd.conf, 410-437
  AccessConfig, 411
  AccessFileName, 420
  Action, 430
  AddDescription, 428
  AddEncoding, 428
  AddHandler, 429
  AddIcon, 427
  AddIconByEncoding, 426-427
  AddIconByType, 427
  AddLanguage, 428-429
  AddModule, 414, 432
  AddType, 429

Alias, 424, 431
allow, 418
AllowOveride, 416
AuthName, 432
authorization family of directives, 416
AuthType, 432
AuthUserFile, 433
BindAddress, 413
BrowserMatch, 430-431
CacheNegotiatedDocs, 421
caching-related directives, 435-436
CustomLog, 423
deny, 418
<Directory>, 415, 417, 418, 424
DirectoryIndex, 420
document type family of directives, 416
DocumentRoot, 414
EnableDelete, 433
EnablePut, 432
ErrorDocument, 430
ErrorLog, 422
ExtendedStatus, 414
<Files>, 420
HeaderName, 428
HostNameLookups, 421-422
HTTP upload area definition, 432
icon statements, 426-427
<IfModule>, 421, 429, 431, 435
IndexIgnore, 428
indexing family of directives, 417
IndexOptions, 425-426
<Limit>, 419
Listen, 412-413
LoadModule, 413, 431
Location, 431
<Location>, 433-435
LockFile, 411
LogFormat, 422-423
LogLevel, 422
MetaDir, 430
MetaSuffix, 430
NameVirtualHost, 436-437
Options, 415
order, 417-418
PerlHandler, 431
PidFile, 411
process-related directives, 412
ProxyRequests, 435
ReadmeName, 428
Redirect, 425
require, 433
ResourceConfig, 411
ScoreBoardFile, 411
ScriptAlias, 424
ServerName, 414
ServerRoot, 411
ServerSignature, 424
ServerType, 410
SetHandler, 431, 434
timeout-related directives, 411-412
TypeConfig, 421
UseCanonicalName, 421
UserDir, 418
<VirtualHost>, 437
/etc/hosts.allow, 258
/etc/hosts.deny, 258
/etc/issue.net, 244
/etc/named.conf, 319-328
  acl, 323
  categories, 326-327
  controls, 324
  include, 324
  key, 324-325
  logging, 325-327
  options, 319-321
  server, 327-328
  statement types, 323
  zones, 321-323
/etc/passwd, 25
/etc/printcap, 218
/etc/procmailrc, 401-405
/etc/pump.conf file, 214-215
/etc/sendmail.cf, 364-369, 372-376
/etc/sendmail.cw, 397
/etc/sendmail.mc, 357-364
/etc/skel, 27
/etc/squid/squid.conf, 457
/etc/ssh_config, 277-278
/etc/smb.conf, 513-526
  case sensitive, 523
  comments, 514
  default case, 522-523
  dns proxy, 522
  domain logons, 521

domain master, 521
encrypt passwords, 518
example shares, 526
global settings, 514-523
guest account, 515
[homes], 523-524
hosts allow, 514-515
include, 519
individual share settings, 523-526
interfaces, 520
local master, 520
logfile, 516-516
logon path, 521
logon script, 521
max log size, 516
name resolve order, 521-522, 535
[netlogon], 524
os level, 520-521, 533
password chat, 518-519
password level, 518
password program, 518-519
password server, 518
preferred master, 521
preserve case, 522
print system types, 516
printcap name, 515
[printers], 525
printing, 515
[Profiles], 524
[public], 525-526
remote announce, 520
remote browse sync, 520
security, 516-518
serverstring, 514
share definitions, 523-526
short preserve case, 522
smbpassword file, 518
socket options, 519
substitution variables, 517
[tmp], 525
unix password sync, 518-519
username level, 518
username map, 519
wins server, 522
wins support, 522
workgroup, 514
/etc/swatchrc, 254
/etc/syslog.conf, 249-250
/etc/ypserv.conf, 493-494
Experimental kernel, 127-128
EXPN, 374
ext2 file system, 61-64
ExtendedStatus, 414
Ezmlm, 369

F

Fax service, 384-389
fdisk, 83
Feature creep, 410
fgrep, 665, 686
FHS, 65-66
file, 325
File compression tools, 102, 108-109
File intent operators, 634
File merger (**join**), 575-576, 589
File share statement, 541-545
File splicer (**cut**), 574-575, 588
File System Hierarchy Standard (FHS), 65-66
File system management, 59-99
adding permanent media, 86-88
adding temporary media, 84-85
backup, 69-74, 81-83. *See also* Backup.
boot disk, 98
changing groups, 79
changing ownerships, 79
creating file systems, 76-77
disk quotas, 75, 95-97
errors, 79-80
ext2 file system, 61-64
FHS, 65
GNOME (GNU Midnight Commander), 89-93
KDE (KFM), 94-95
limiting user storage space (quotas), 75, 95-97
listing settings, 77
mounting/unmounting, 84-89
moving file system portions onto partitions, 83-84
partitions, 67-68
permissions, 66-67, 77-79
rebooting, 97-98

removing permanent media, 88-89
removing temporary media, 85-86
rescue disk, 98-99
shutting down, 97-98
umask, 79
File System Standard (FSSTND), 64-65
File Transfer Protocol. *See* FTP.
<Files>, 420
Filtering firewalls, 258-262, 287-289
find, 663, 676-684
FirePlug EDGE Project, 263
Firewall Tool Kit (FWTK), 262
Firewalls, 256-263
filtering, 258-262, 287-289
proxying, 262-263, 289-290
pseudo-firewall (**tcp_wrappers**), 257-258, 267-269
standalone, 263
Floppy disks, 72, 82
for loop
Perl, 633
shell scripting, 604-605
foreach loop, 633
Forward zone, 322
Fragments, 176
fsck, 79-80
FSSTND, 64-65
FTP, 475-490
anonymous, 487
clients, 476-477
keeping hosts out, 481
mirror sites, 481-482
regulating user access, 477-481
securing, 483-487
servers, 477
shutdown message, 488-490
ftp, 476
ftpd, 477
Full user account, 23
FWTK, 262

G

Gateway, 179
Gateway address, 178
gcc, 647-653
gdb, 653-656
gdm, 153
General kernel files, 130
getopts, 602-603
GhostScript, 223-224
ghostview, 224
GID, 25-26
glFtpD, 477
Globbing, 478
GNOME, 6, 9-15
changing to KDE, 167
command prompt, 14-15
configuring the GUI, 10-11
disabling users, 49
files, 157
forwarding user mail, 57-58
groups, 53-56
help, 13-14
installation, 160-161
KDE, compared, 6, 154
Linuxconf, 12-13. *See also* Linuxconf.
Midnight Commander, 89-93
opening programs, 11-12
packages, 161
removing users, 50-52
renaming users, 46-48
restricted access accounts, 38-40
RPM, 116-119
shell accounts, 31-34
user defaults, 44
window managers, 162-163
GNOME Control Center, 10
GNOME Help Browser, 14
GNOME Linuxconf system configuration tool, 13
GNOME main menu, 12
GNOME RPM, 116-119
GNOME System menu, 13
GNU Midnight Commander, 89-93
GNU Network Object Model Environment. *See* GNOME.
GoAhead Web Server, 437
gprof, 656-658
grep, 663, 685-686
Group access, 29
Group isolation, 29-30
Group storage, 29

Groups, 29-30, 53-56, 79
grpconv, 264
grpunconv, 264
gs, 223
guest account, 515
GUI management, 151-169. *See also* GNOME; KDE.
  changing desktops, 167
  choosing between GNOME/KDE, 6, 154
  default run level, 168-169
  desktop environments, 154, 167
  display managers, 153
  finding components online, 162
  GNOME files, 157
  KDE files, 157
  restarting X server, 167-168
  system performance, 154-155
  themes, 164-167
  window managers, 153, 162-164
  X files, 155-156
  X server, 152, 158-159, 167-168
gunzip, 108-109, 613
gv, 224
gvim, 562
gzip, 102, 108

H

halt, 97
Hard drive, 61
Hardware-specific files, 131-133
Hawkeye, 437
HeaderName, 428
Help
  GNOME, 13-14
  KDE, 19
HINFO record, 331
HMAC, 325
HOME, 599
Home directory, 27
[homes], 523-524
Host map, 557-558
host, 334-335
HostNameLookups, 421-422
hosts allow, 514-515
HTML, 640
httpd, 408. *See also* Apache Web server.
httpd.conf, 410. *See also* /etc/httpd.conf.

I

IceWM, 153
if statement
  Perl, 632-633
  shell scripting, 604-605
<IfModule>, 421, 429, 431, 435
IglooFTP PRO, 477
include, 324, 519
Incremental backup, 70-72
IndexIgnore, 428
IndexOptions, 425-426
inetd, 244
init 0, 97
init 6, 97
Inode, 62-63
Installation, 2-6
  anonymous FTP, 487
  Apache, 439
  autofs, 666
  binary files, 111
  C compiler, 647
  classes, 4-5
  Crack password checker, 283-284
  GNOME, 160
  KDE, 160-161
  kernel, 136-137
  NIS client, 496
  NIS server, 496
  partitions, 2-3
  Perl, 636
  public domain korn shell, 609
  repeat installations (KickStart), 293-314
  RPM, 114-115, 117-119, 120-121
  Samba, 527
  sendmail, 370
  software, of, 53
  Squid server, 458
  swatch, 281
  upgrade option, 6
  X server, 158-159
Installation classes, 4-5
interfaces, 520

Internet email. *See* **sendmail** + IDA.
Internet layer, 175
Intrusions, 254-256. *See also* System security.
IP address, 173
IP address classes, 174
IP aliasing, 197
IP datagram, 175-176
IP filtering, 258-262, 287-289
IP Fundamentals (Maufer), 180
IP masquerading, 179, 205-206
ipchains, 259-262
iServer, 437
ispell, 576, 590-595

J

Java Web Server, 437
join, 575-576, 589

K

K Desktop Environment. *See* KDE.
KDE, 6, 15-19
  changing to GNOME, 167
  command prompt, 19
  configuring the GUI, 15-16
  disabling users, 50
  files, 157
  forwarding user mail, 58
  GNOME, compared, 6, 154
  groups, 54-56
  help, 19
  installation, 160
  KFM, 94-95
  Kpackage, 120-123
  opening programs, 17
  packages, 161
  removing users, 52
  renaming users, 48
  restricted access accounts, 40-41
  RPM, 120-123
  shell accounts, 35-36
  user defaults, 44-45
  window managers, 163-164
KDE Control Center, 17
KDE File Manager (KFM), 94-95
KDE Help browser, 20
KDE main menu, 18
kdm, 153
Kerberos authentication, 249
Kernel development stream, 129
Kernel documentation, 130-134
Kernel management, 125-150
  aliases, 148
  architecture-specific files, 131
  choosing a new kernel, 127-128
  configuration
    config, 137-141
    menuconfig, 141-143
    xconfig, 143-145
  customization, 126-127
  development paths, 127-129
  documentation files, 130-134
  extra-useful files, 133-134
  general kernel files, 130
  hardware-specific files, 131-133
  inserting modules manually, 145-146
  installing new kernel, 136-137
  kernel components, 126
  kernel source, 135
  kernel name, 128
  kernel version, 135
  kernel, defined, 126
  /lib/modules/version subdirectory, 146
  LILO, 149-150
  listing loaded modules, 145
  miscellaneous files, 134
  options, 148-149
  reference web site, 130
  removing modules manually, 146-147
  setting module parameters, 148-149
  system information, 147-148
  upgrading, 127
  version of kernel, 135
key, 324-325
keys, 328
KFM, 94-95
KickStart, 293-314
  action type, 298-299
  adding KickStart data to DHCP server, 311
  boot disk, 308
  booting directly to, 309

building initial KickStart file, 307
cloning machine configurations, 313-314
device probing, 297
devices present, 296-297
identical hardware setups, 295
install method, 296
installing, 311-312
installing first machine, 306
keyboard type, 297
language settings, 295-296
mouse types, 299-300
network settings, 296
packages, 300
partition settings, 297-298
post-installation instructions, 303-304
scripting, 308
setting up NFS installation export, 310
system configuration, 299-303
system information, 295-303
test-edit cycle, 304-305
time zone, 300
upgrading, 312-313
uses, 294
Kpackage, 120-123
kppp, configuring, to connect, 210-213

L

LILO, 149-150
<Limit>, 419
Linux C programming. *See* C programming.
Linux distributions, 6-7
Linux Loader (LILO), 149-150
Linux Software Map (LSM), 104
Linuxconf
assigning multiple IP addresses to same interface, 197
basic routing, 201
dial-out PPP connection, 206-208
IP aliasing, 197
networking for LAN, 193-196
opening, 12-13
PPP connection, 206-208
routing among networks, 202
routing daemon, 204
routing for concurrent networks, 203-204
routing to remote hosts, 203
second network interface, 199-200
sendmail, 376-393. *See also* Linuxconf--**sendmail**.
Linuxconf—**sendmail**, 376-393
basic configuration, 376-380
email-to-fax service, 384-389
IP masquerading, 383-384
mail queue, 399-400
mail routing, 380-383
spam protection, 391-393
special domain routing, 380-381
special user routing, 381-383
virtual email service, 389-391
Listen, 412-413
Listserv, 369
Load average, 154-155
LoadModule, 413, 431
local master, 520
Local Networking layer, 174
Localhost, 174
locate, 663, 684-685
locate database update time, 684
Location, 431
<Location>, 433-435
LockFile, 411
Log monitoring (**swatch**), 252-254, 281-282
logfile, 515-516
LogFormat, 422-423
Logging, 249-254, 280-282
logging, 325-327
Logging in, 240-243, 290-291
LogLevel, 422
logon path, 521
logon script, 521
Loopback address, 174
Looping mechanisms
Perl, 632-634
shell scripting, 604-605
lpc, 220-221
lpd, 221
lpq, 221, 237
lpr, 237
lprm, 221-222, 237
ls, 145, 583-584
LS-120 floppies, 72, 82
LSM, 104

.lsm extension, 104
lsmod, 145

M

m4, 364
MAC, 179
Machine attacks, 255-256
magicfilter, 235-236
MAIL, 599
Mail aliases, 393-394
Mail queue, 399-400
Mailer table, 397
Mailing list, 369
Majordomo, 369
Make a file system, 76-77
Make target, 646
make Build Manager, 645, 658
Makefile, 645-646
Man, 264
Mask, 67
Mass installations. *See* KickStart.
Master name server, 317
max log size, 516
Maximum Transmission Unit (MTU), 176
MBone, 456
Media Access Control (MAC), 179
menuconfig kernel configuration tool, 141-143
Message Identification And Referral header fields, 355
MetaDir, 430
MetaSuffix, 430
Midnight Commander, 89-93
Minicom, configuring, to connect, 209
mkdir, 84
mke2fs, 76-77
mkfifo, 280
mkinitrd, 137
Mounting devices, 84-89. *See also* Automounter.
Mounting remote file systems, 505-506
MTU, 176
Multicast backbone, 456
Multicasting, 456, 470
Multiple lines of code on same line (command line), 573
mv, 83, 137
MX record, 331-332

N

name resolve order, 521-522, 535
Name servers, 317
Name service, 317-319. *See also* DNS.
named, 317
Named pipe, 252, 280, 324
NameVirtualHost, 436-437
NCB, 513
ndc, 324, 335
Neighbor machines, 455
NETBIOS, 512-513
[netlogon], 524
Netmasks, 177-178, 190
Network address, 178
Network attacks, 255, 285
Network Control Block (NCB), 513
Network File System. *See* NFS.
Network Information System. *See* NIS.
Network Solutions, 188
Networking, 171-216
  administering machines remotely, 216
  assigning multiple IP addresses to same interface, 197
  centrally managed management, 185
  centrally managed network, 180-184
  checking whether domain name is taken, 189
  classless routing, 180
  configuring, 186
  configuring second network interface at command line, 198
  DHCP, 180-184, 213-214
  dial-out connections, 206-213
  expressing address ranges, 192
  get set of IP addresses, 187
  IP aliasing, 197
  IP masquerading, 179, 205-206
  kppp, configuring, to connect, 210-213
  Linuxconf. *See* Linuxconf.
  minicom, configuring, to connect, 209
  network address components, 177-178
  partial address class, 180

pump client, 214-215
registering domain name, 187-188
routers/routing, 179, 200-204
setting up basic TCP/IP networking, 192-193
subnetting, 178-179, 189-191
TCP/IP, 173-177
virtual sites, 178, 196
NFS, 501-510
configuration file, 502-504
KickStart, 310
mounting remote file systems, 505-506
setting up NFS exports, 505
setting up NFS installation server, 509-510
/usr directory, 506-509
NFTP, 477
NIS, 491-500
commands, 494-495
configuration file, 493-494
installing the client, 496-497
installing the server, 496
NIS+, compared, 492
setting up the client, 499-500
setting up the server, 497-499
NIS+, 492
nmbd, 512-513
NS record, 332

O

Open multicast session, 456
Opening programs
GNOME, 11-12
KDE, 17
Options, 148-149
Options, 415
order, 417-418
os level, 520-521, 533

P

pac, 222
Package management, 101-123
binary files, 111
compress, 108-109
compression tools, 102, 108-109
dependencies, 106-107
downloading, 104-105
general principles, 105-107
gzip, 108
location, 106
LSM, 104
naming, 106
packaging tools, 102-103
RPM. *See* RPM.
tar, 109-110
tarballs, 110
Package update script, 611-615
Packaging tools, 102-103
PAMs, 247
Parent caches/servers, 455, 466-468
Partitions, 2-3, 61, 67-68
password chat, 518-519
Password level, 518
password program, 518-519
Password server, 518
Passwords
choosing, 240-241
Crack, 283-284
entry into /etc/group, 27
entry into /etc/password, 25
Samba (encrypted passwords), 555-556
shadow, 241-242, 264
testing viability, 283-284
PATH, 599
Pattern matching, 568-570
pdksh, 598
Peer machines, 455
Perl scripting, 627-642
$_, 634
arrays, 630-631
CGI script, 639-642
conditionals/loops, 632-634
end-of-line character, 630
file intent operators, 634
file manipulation, 634-635
installing Perl, 636
installing Perl library, 636-638
module groups, 637
regular expressions, 632
running a Perl program, 638
starter pieces, 630

test operators, 632
variables, 629-630
Web form, 639-642
PerlHandler, 431
Permanent media, 86-89
Permissions, 66-67, 77-79
PGP, 285-287
PGP-signed RPM, 116
Phoenix Adaptive Firewall, 263
PidFile, 411
Pipe, 603
Pluggable Authentication Modules (PAMs), 247
PPP connection, 206-208
preferred master, 521
preserve case, 522
Pretty Good Privacy (PGP), 285-287
Print fitters, 235-236
Print share statement, 551-554
printcap name, 515
[printers], 525
printing, 515
Printing, 217-237
canceling a job, 237
commands, 220-222
configuration file (/etc/printcap), 218-219
configuration options, 219
filters, 235-236
GhostScript, 223-224
how the process works, 222-223
life of simple print job, 222-223
printing a file, 236-237
setting up local printer
at the command line, 228-231
at the control panel, 225-228
setting up network printer
at the command line, 233-235
at the control panel, 231-233
stair stepping, 228, 232
testing the printer, 236
things to remember, 223
troubleshooting, 224
viewing contents of print queue, 237
/proc subdirectory, 147-148
procmail, 400-405
Production kernel, 127-128
[Profiles], 524
ProFTPD, 477
Programming. *See* C programming; Perl scripting; Shell scripting.
Programs, 24, 42
Proxying firewalls, 262-263, 289-290
ProxyRequests, 435
PS1, 599
psftp, 477
PTR record, 332
[public], 525-526
Public domain korn shell, 609
pump, 180
pump client, 214-215
pwconv, 264
PWD, 599
pwunconv, 264

Q

qFTPs, 477
Quotas, 75, 95-97

R

RAID backup, 73-74, 82
RAID types, 74
RapidControl For Web, 437
rbl, 396
read, 602
ReadmeName, 428
reboot, 97
Rebooting, 97-98
Red Hat Announce mailing list, 8
Red Hat Linux, 8
Red Hat Package Manager. *See* RPM.
Red Hat Update Agent, 245, 247
Red Hat updates, 8
Red Hat Watch list, 246
redhat.mc, 361-363
Redirect, 425
Redirection, 603
Registering domain name, 187-188
Registration, 245
Regular expressions, 568-570, 583-584, 632
relay_based_on_MX, 396

relay_entire_domain, 396
relay_hosts_only, 396
relay_local_from, 396
remote announce, 520
remote browse sync, 520
Removable rack hard drives, 73, 82
Removing permanent media, 88-89
Removing temporary media, 85-86
Repeat installations. *See* KickStart.
require, 433
Rescue disk, 98-99
Resolver, 318
Resource records, 328-333
ResourceConfig, 411
Restarting X server, 167-168
Restore
  file system structure, 80-81
  file systems, 83
Restricted access accounts, 24, 37-41
Reverse domain zone file, 346-347
Reverse local zone file, 343
Reverse zone, 322-323
Rewritable CD/DVD, 73, 82
rlogin, 242-243
rm, 84, 112
Roaming profile, 521
RomPager, 438
Routers/routing, 179, 200-204
Roxen, 438
rpm, 114-116, 279, 613
RPM, 103
  creating, 111-114
  GNOME, 116-119
  installing, 114-115, 117-119, 120-121
  KDE, 120-123
  list of those installed, 115
  PGP, and, 116
  removing, 115
  removing unnecessary packages, 279
  verifying, 115-116
  viewing contents, 115
RSA, 325
rsync, 477
Run levels, 168-169, 264-265
Run the program as root, 67

S

Samba, 511-560
  browsing, 513
  configuration file, 513-526. *See also* /etc/smb.conf.
  configuring, 527-536
  encrypted passwords, 555-556
  file share statement, 541-545
  host map, 557-558
  installing, 527
  login scripts, 558-560
  mounting Windows shares, 546
  NETBIOS, 512-513
  nmbd, 512-513
  offering Linux partitions, 537-540
  offering Linux printers, 550-551
  offering Windows shares, 546-550
  print share statement, 551-554
  risks, 513
  smbd, 512
  user map, 556-557
  utilizing Windows' printers, 554-555
  WINS, 513
Sawmill, 153
ScoreBoardFile, 411
ScriptAlias, 424
Scripting. *See* Perl scripting; Shell scripting.
Search tools, 662-665
  egrep, 664-665, 686
  fgrep, 665, 686
  find, 663, 676-684
  grep, 663, 685-686
  locate, 663, 684-685
  which, 663, 685
Second extended (ext2) file system, 61-64
Secure shell (ssh), 248, 269-279
Security. *See* System security.
Security fixes, 245
Security Web sites, 246
security, 516-518
sed editor, 570-574, 584-588
  characters requiring line breaks, 585
  command combinations, 584-586
  commonly used commands, 571-572
  expressing locations, 573-574

flags, 571
grouping commands, 572-573
running **sed** with external file scripts, 588
script, 586-588
Sender and Recipient Indication header fields, 355
sendmail + IDA, 351-405
access database, 398-399
adding additional mail server hostnames, 372
adding configuration file version information, 373
centralizing outgoing mail addresses, 373
CF file, 364-369, 372-376
configuring server at command line, 370-371
configuring server in Linuxconf, 376-393. *See also* Linuxconf—**sendmail**.
CW file, 397
documentation, 369
fax service, 384-389
how email travels, 352
installation, 370
IP masquerading, 383-384
logging levels, 374-375
m4, 364
mail aliases, 393-394
mail leaders, 353-357
mail queue, 357, 399-400
mailer table, 397
mailing lists, 369
MC file, 357-364
procmail, 400-405
server load, 375-376
spam protection, 391-396
virtual addressing table, 398
virtual email service, 389-391
server, 327-328
Server installation class, 4-5
Server load, 375-376
Server Message Block (SMB) protocol. *See* Samba.
ServerName, 414
ServerRoot, 411
ServerSignature, 424
serverstring, 514
ServerType, 410
SetHandler, 431, 434
SGID, 67, 78-79
Shadow groups, 264
Shadow passwords, 241-242, 264
Shadow suite, 264
SHELL, 599
Shell, 598
Shell accounts, 23, 31-36
Shell scripting, 597-625
available shells, 598
changing the active shell, 609
changing the login prompt, 610
conditionals/loops, 604-605
environment variables, 599
finding a file in RPM packages, 620-623
input/output, 601-604
monitoring system load, 623-625
package update script, 611-615
pipe, 603
prompt-build characters, 610
public domain korn shell, 609
redirection, 603
shell variables, 599
testing conditions, 605-608
text menus, 608
user creation script, 615-620
Shell variables, 599
short preserve case, 522
shutdown, 97-98
Sibling caches/servers, 455, 466-468
Sinus Firewall, 263
Skeleton directory, 27, 43
Slave name server, 317
slp, 103
.slp extension, 103
Smartlist, 369
SMB protocol. *See* Samba.
smbd, 512
smbpassword file, 518
SMTP, 378
SOA record, 328-330
Socket, 519-520
socket options, 519
SOCKS, 262
Software accounts, 42
Source RPM (SRPM), 111
Spam protection, 391-396

Spelling checker (**ispell**), 576, 590-595
SpyGlass MicroServer, 438
Squid internet object cache, 453-473
  ACL day of week settings, 461
  ACL statement types, 461
  configuring client to utilize caching, 470-473
  configuring the Squid, 458-465
  installing the Squid, 458
  multicasting, 456, 470
  parent/sibling caches, 455, 466-468
  protocols, 455
  purposes, 454
  server configurations, 455
  squid.conf file, 457
  Web caching, 454
  Web server acceleration, 469
srm.conf, 410
SRPM, 111
ssh, 248, 269-279
ssh2, 248
Stair stepping, 228, 232
Stampede, 103
Standalone firewalls, 263
start_html statement, 642
Start of Authority (SOA) record, 328-330
startx, 155
STDERR, 603
STDIN, 603
STDOUT, 603
Sticky bit, 67, 78-79
Stream editor tool. *See* **sed** editor.
su, 166, 216, 283, 482
Subnetting, 178-179, 189-191
SUID, 67, 78-79, 244
Superblock, 64
Superuser, 283
swatch, 252-254, 281-282
syslogd, 249-251, 325
System information, 147-148
System load, 154-155, 375, 623-625
System performance, 154-155
System security, 239-291
  account attacks, 256
  denial of service, 255, 285
  distribution fixes, 245
  emergency fix kit, 282
  firewalls. *See* Firewalls.
  Kerberos authentication, 249
  log monitoring (**swatch**), 252-254, 281-282
  logging, 249-254, 280-282
  logging in, 240-243
  machine attacks, 255-256
  mailing lists, 245-246
  named pipe, 252, 280
  network attacks, 255, 285
  notification lists, 245-246
  online resource, 245-246
  PAMs, 247
  passwords. *See* Passwords.
  permissions, 66-67, 77-79
  PGP, 285-287
  recovering from a breach, 282
  refusing login access to nonroot users, 290-291
  secure shell (ssh), 248, 269-279
  shutting off unnecessary processes, 243-244, 264-267, 279
  SUID, 244
  superuser, 283
  Update Agent, 245, 247
  Web sites, 246

T

Tape backup, 73, 82
tar, 72, 83, 103, 109-111
Tarballs, 110
TCP/IP, 173-177
tcp_wrappers, 257-258, 267-269
tcsh, 598
Telnet, 482, 488
telnet, 216
Temporary media, 84-86
test, 605-608
Text editor. *See* **vi** editor.
Text processing, 561-596
  file merger (**join**), 575-576, 589
  file splicer (**cut**), 574-575, 588
  pattern matching, 568-570
  regular expressions, 568-570, 583-584
  sed editor. *See* **sed** editor.
  spelling checker (**ispell**), 576, 590-595

text transposer (**tr**), 576-577, 595-596
vi editor. *See* **vi** editor.
Text transposer (**tr**), 576-577, 595-596
Themes, 162, 164-167
Timed processes
at, 661, 668-672
cron, 661-662, 672-675
[tmp], 525
Torvalds, Linus, 128
touch, 95
tr, 576-577, 595-596
Trace Information header types, 354
Transmission Control Protocol/Internet Protocol (TCP/IP), 173-177
Transport layer, 176
TypesConfig, 421

U

UDP, 176
UID, 25-27
uname, 135
unix password sync, 518-519
Unmask, 67, 79
unmask, 79
Unmounting, 84-89
until loop
Perl, 633-634
shell scripting, 604-605
Update Agent, 245, 247
Updates, 8
Upgrading, 6, 127, 312
Usage quotas, 75, 95-97
UseCanonicalName, 421
USER, 599
User creation script, 615-620
User Datagram Protocol (UDP), 176
User defaults, 27, 42-45
User management, 21-58
account creation defaults, 42-45
disabling users, 49-50
forwarding user mail, 57-58
groups, 29-30, 53-56
home directory, 27
installing software for users, 53
programs/daemons, 24, 42
removing users, 50-52
renaming users, 46-48
restricted access accounts, 24, 37-41
shell accounts, 23, 31-36
software accounts, 42
user defaults, 27, 42-45
useradd, 25-27
userdel, 28
User map, 556-557
useradd, 25-27, 285
userdel, 28
UserDir, 418
usermod, 285
username level, 518
username map, 519
/usr directory, 506-509
/usr/local/etc/netperm-table, 262
UUCP, 378
UUCP-DOM, 378

V

vi editor, 561-567, 579-583
command mode (normal mode), 563-565
copy/paste, 581
edit commands, 564-565
filtering text, 579-580
indenting text, 581-583
insert mode, 565-566
line mode, 566-567
moving through the document, 563-564, 578
searching, 565
vim, 562
vim, 562. *See also* **vi** editor.
Virtual addressing table, 398
Virtual email service, 389-391
Virtual sites, 178, 196
Virtual Web service, 446-448
<VirtualHost>, 437
Visual editor. *See* **vi** editor.
vnc, 216
vqServer, 438
VRFY, 374

W

Wall, Larry, 628
Web caching, 454. *See also* Squid internet object cache.
Web form, 639-642
Web servers, 437-438. *See also* Apache Web server.
which, 663, 685
while loop
  Perl, 633
  shell scripting, 604-605
Window Maker, 153
Window managers, 153, 162-164
Windows Internet Naming Service (WINS), 513
WINS, 513
wins server, 522
wins support, 522
WKS record, 332-333
workgroup, 514
Workstation installation class, 5
wu-ftpd, 477

X

X files, 155-156
X server, 152, 158-159, 167-168
X Window System, 152
xconfig kernel configuration tool, 143-145
xdm, 153
XFree86, 152
Xitami, 438

Y

Yafc, 477
ypchfn, 494
ypchsh, 494
yppasswd, 494
yppasswdd, 495
ypserv, 495
ypwhich, 494

Z

Z **compress**ed files, 108-109
zcat, 109
Zeus Web Server, 438
Zip disk, 72, 82
Zone files, 328-333, 343-347
Zones, 316, 321-323

Other CORIOLISOPEN™ PRESS Titles

Setting Up a Linux Internet Server Visual Black Book

ISBN: 1-57610-569-5
$29.99 U.S. • $44.99 Canada

Uses illustrations to visually guide you through specific tasks in a step-by-step manner. Covers IP addresses, security issues, setting up a network router, creating mail servers, sending and receiving mail in Windows, and customizing Web servers, FTP servers, and proxy servers.

Open Source Development with CVS

ISBN: 1-57610-490-7
$39.99 U.S. • $58.99 Canada

Learn the best practices of open source software development with CVS—a tool that allows several individuals to work simultaneously on the same document. CVS is covered in detail, as is the GNU license, software design and development, coding styles, documentation procedures, testing, release of software, and troubleshooting.

Apache Server Commentary

ISBN: 1-57610-468-0
$39.99 U.S.
$58.99 Canada

The authors conduct a line-by-line examination of the core code, as well as the standard Apache modules that control logging, directory indexing, access control, CGI, and many other aspects of running a full-featured Web site. Flow charts illustrate how to extend the server's capabilities and optimize performance.

Linux Graphics Programming with SVGAlib

ISBN: 1-57610-524-5
$49.99 U.S. • $74.99 Canada

Teaches programming techniques and covers 3D animation, rotating images, and effects such as creating fire, landscapes, and skies. Shows how to apply graphics to game development and how to write a paint program that enables an image to be drawn on screen with a mouse.

Perl Core Language Little Black Book

ISBN: 1-57610-426-5
$24.99 U.S. • $36.99 Canada

Master the full Perl 5 syntax and write professional, real-world Perl applications. You will learn how to create Web-based guest books, create Perl classes and objects, connect Perl to the Tk Toolkit, and more. Nearly 400 working examples in 500 individual Perl topics are included.

Apache Server for Windows Little Black Book

ISBN: 1-57610-391-9
$29.99 U.S. • $43.99 Canada

Set up and configure Apache, establish user accounts, construct a virtual Web site, work with log files, tune the server to optimize performance, and implement Apache's extensive security capabilities. You will also learn how to run CGI scripts that access databases and produce dynamic HTML Web pages.

The Coriolis Group, LLC Telephone: 800.410.0192 • www.coriolis.com
Coriolis books are also available at bookstores and computer stores nationwide.

Other CORIOLISOPEN™ PRESS Titles

Linux Programming White Papers

ISBN: 1-57610-473-7
$24.99 U.S. • $36.99 Canada

Linux community leaders present in-depth discussions on the major subsystems of Linux. Kernel architecture details, including file systems, system and subsystem structure, network dependencies, and network interface are shared. Diagrams and flow charts clarify complex relationships among the components of the architecture. Foreword by **Eric Raymond**.

Samba Black Book

ISBN: 1-57610-455-9
$49.99 U.S. • $74.99 Canada

Details the smooth operation of a heterogeneous network, involving Linux and Windows. Examines Samba 2.0 and includes information on installation, network management, file sharing, firewall and network security, network Internet connectivity, FTP servers, and network file and print servers. Troubleshooting tips are also provided.

Linux IP Stacks Commentary

ISBN 1-57610-470-2
$39.99 U.S.
$58.99 Canada

Contains over 42,000 lines of code with accompanying explanations. Covers Linux network stack and code, including the General Network Layer, the Core Services Layer, the Network Protocols Layer, and the Device Drivers Layer. Includes extensive cross-referencing and architectural flow charts.

Linux Core Kernel Commentary

ISBN: 1-57610-469-9
$39.99 U.S.
$58.99 Canada

Line-by-line, the Linux core code is examined and explained. Covers the folowing main subsystems of the Linux kernel: Memory Manager, Process Scheduler, and Interprocess Communication. Extensive cross-referencing enhances understanding of the structure of the code.

Linux Install and Configuration Little Black Book

ISBN: 1-57610-489-3
$24.99 U.S. • $36.99 Canada

Provides detailed solutions to installing and configuring Red Hat and Caldera versions of Linux. Details the how-tos of partitioning hard drives, creating user accounts, working with file systems, networking, ISP connectivity, Xwindows, and more. Also covers hot new technologies like Gnome and Samba and how they relate to configuring Linux.

Under the Radar

How Red Hat Changed the Software Business—and Took Microsoft by Surprise

ISBN: 1-57610-506-7
$27.50 U.S. • $37.50 Canada

Under the Radar is an adventure story about the rise and development of the Open Source software movement. Learn about the insider deal-making, the controversies, and how Fortune 500 companies have taken notice and responded to it.

The Coriolis Group, LLC Telephone: 800.410.0192 • www.coriolis.com
Coriolis books are available at bookstores and computer stores nationwide.

What's On The CD-ROM

Linux System Administration Black Book's companion CD-ROM contains elements specifically selected to enhance the usefulness of this book, including:

- The alien package format conversion utility that allows you to convert DEB files to RPMs and vice versa.
- The Filesystem Hierarchy Standard so you can refer to it when you want to remind yourself of where files on a standard Unix flavor machine should go.
- The wvdial package, which is a boon to everyone who needs to use a modem to connect to the Internet.
- The HTML-formatted text to the Linux Documentation Project publication "The Linux Kernel."
- The text to the Red Hat book *Maximum RPM.*
- Text files used for projects in the book.
- The scripts covered in Chapter 20, "Shell Scripting."
- A collection of Request for Comments (RFC) documents, which are the definitive guides to how many Internet applications work behind the scenes.

System Requirements

Software

- Your operating system must be Red Hat Linux or another Linux distribution. This is really the only requirement!

Hardware

- An Intel (or equivalent) 386 processor is the minimum platform required.
- 16MB of RAM is the minimum requirement.
- Hard drive space varies, though a minimum of 900MB is recommended.